Political Psychol

Political Psychology

Edited by

KRISTEN RENWICK MONROE

University of California, Irvine

LEA   LAWRENCE ERLBAUM ASSOCIATES, PUBLISHERS

2002   Mahwah, New Jersey   London

Lawrence Erlbaum Associates, Inc., Publishers
10 Industrial Avenue
Mahwah, NJ 07430

Cover design by Kathryn Houghtaling Lacey

Library of Congress Cataloging-in-Publication Data

Political psychology / edited by Kristen Renwick Monroe.
    p.   cm.
    Includes bibliographical references and index.
    ISBN 0–8058–3886–4 (cloth) — ISBN 0–8058–3887–2 (pbk.)
    1. Political psychology. I. Monroe, Kristen R., 1946–
JA74.5 .P634 2001
320'.01'9—dc21
                                            2001033185

Books published by Lawrence Erlbaum Associates are printed on acid-free paper,
and their bindings are chosen for strength and durability.

Printed in the United States of America
10   9   8   7   6   5   4   3   2   1

Contents

PART II. POLITICAL PSYCHOLOGY IN RELATION TO OTHER FIELDS

PART III. SPECIAL AREAS OF APPLICATION

PART IV. FOCUS ON THE FUTURE

Political Psychology: An Overview

KRISTEN R. MONROE
University of California, Irvine

What is political psychology? How does it differ from political science and from other branches of psychology? What are its key concepts, methodologies, and texts? What are the main research topics, fields, and controversies that enliven political psychology, giving it both passion and value in our immediate lives, as well as in our scholarship? These were the questions posed to the contributors to a volume that I hope will both inform the newcomer and chart the direction for future scholarly research in this exciting field.

I must count myself a newcomer and confess that part of my interest in this project emanated from my own desire for answers to the questions posed above. In this, I have been amply rewarded by the contributors, who include some of the most distinguished scholars in the field. Moreover, their intellectual diversity means they have provided a richly diverse portrait of a common enterprise.[1]

Overview of the Book

Part 1 of the volume presents six contrasting views on political psychology as a field. The book opens with an updated and revised version of a classic article on the nature of political psychology, an article that helped define political psychology at a critical point in its inception. Deutsch and Kinnvall note the long philosophical heritage of political psychology and then

---

[1] In describing the chapters in this book, I relied heavily on the abstracts sent me by the authors themselves and tried to repeat their own characterizations of their work as much as possible. I apologize for those instances when I deviated from their own words and hope my rephrasings have not done undue harm to the specifics of the content. It has been a joy to work with these authors and a pleasure to be able to acknowledge publicly my great personal and intellectual debt.

describe how political psychology became a separate field in the mid-20th century in response to dissatisfactions with the behavioral movement. The piece provides a valuable overview suggesting the richness of political psychology and the key areas of concentration within the discipline. It finds that research clusters into 12 areas: the individual as political actor; political movements; political leadership; political alignments and structures; intergroup relations; political processes; case studies; human development and the political economy; voting and decision making; foreign policy and group think; government and self-esteem; and identity and group conflict. The Deutsch–Kinnvall chapter ends by reassessing the field of political psychology utilizing the five tenets proposed in the first *Handbook of Political Psychology*. As originally outlined by Hermann, the *Handbook of Political Psychology* suggested that when constructing work in political psychology, we need to focus attention on the interaction of political and psychological phenomena, to ask how responsive and relevant is political psychology to societal problems, and whether context makes a difference for the problem being analyzed. We also need to emphasize the process as well as the outcome and to be tolerant of multiple methods for gathering and analyzing data.

These concerns are further developed by Margaret Hermann in her chapter, which asks if political psychology is a fad, a fantasy, or a new field. Hermann concludes that political psychology might be appropriately considered an approach or perspective on politics, and that it is "a way of understanding politics no matter the issue, topics, or problem under consideration." Hermann then outlines the set of assumptions that serve as the consensual premises and scope conditions. She argues that individuals matter in politics but that process matters, too. Hermann argues that determining preference orderings helps us understand political behavior and that emotion and motivation are as relevant as cognition to understanding politics. Hermann concludes by arguing that political psychology has underlined the importance of context and that how researchers define time, situation, political system, and culture has great implications for what is then perceived as a political problem. Her piece ends with a plea for both increased interdisciplinary work and for methodological diversity, for utilizing a wide variety of methods when we construct our research.

An early student in the important and too briefly lived political psychology program at Yale, Dana Ward traces the origins of political psychology and outlines the discipline's development. Ward's chapter includes a summary of the first works in political psychology, the publication of the first handbooks and texts, the establishment of the first training programs, and the founding of the International Society of Political Psychology. As Executive Director of the International Society of Political Psychology, Ward brings a particularly encompassing view of the field, paying special attention to the social context in which the discipline developed in both Europe and the United States. His chapter provides a marvelous assessment of the current status of an important discipline in flux and as it reaches out to political psychologists throughout the world.

Jon A. Krosnick and Kathleen M. McGraw also speak from a unique perspective, that of heads of the Summer Institute in Political Psychology run jointly by the International Society of Political Psychology and Ohio State University. Krosnick and McGraw address the question, "What is political psychology?" by describing two sorts of political psychology, defined not by substantive, conceptual, or methodological cleavages but rather by the fundamental priorities of the research enterprise. They argue that *psychological political science* is an apt description of most research in the field, which can be viewed as a subset of political science in which psychological theories are applied to political phenomena. What they identify as *political psychology "true to its name,"* on the other hand, places a high priority on contributing to the development of psychological theory. Krosnick and McGraw provide examples from their own research programs on both types of political psychology. Their conclusion suggests why an increase in *political psychology true to its name* is important for the continued legitimacy and influence of the field.

The chapter by George Marcus illustrates how the personal becomes the political and the intellectual. Marcus traces his own personal route to political psychology, suggesting how his experience as a child of Holocaust survivors provided his life's research program: How does a nation secure tolerance for all its diverse individuals? Marcus relates work in political psychology to work in classical political theory that inquires about the conditions in which democracy can be a just society. Marcus suggests how political psychology differs from other branches of psychology and turns to political philosophy for a discussion of the central texts, concepts, and debates that animate political psychology.

The last chapter in Part 1, by Janice Gross Stein, provides a rich conceptualization of political psychology as a field and links the field to other branches of social science through an analysis of political learning and choice. Stein's chapter is particularly helpful in anticipating many later arguments by other authors, and forms a natural bridge to later works in this volume. Stein defines political psychology broadly by focusing on "patterns of political thinking, feeling, and identity, the interaction of these patterns, and their impact on political choice and other forms of political behavior." The central core for political psychology resides, for Stein, in a concern with how cognition and emotion intervene between the environment and political behavior. Essentially, Stein conceptualizes a political psychology with three goals: to uncover the psychological and the political origins of political thoughts, feelings, and identities; to understand how the choice and behavior of one actor affect the thoughts, feelings, and acts of others; and to discern the feedback loops connecting political choice and behavior to thinking and feeling about politics and to self-perception.

The rich aptness of Stein's conceptualization is demonstrated by the remarkable degree to which her chapter anticipates concerns expressed by other contributors, from Jervis's interest in the international to Crenshaw's interest in decision making and the emphasis on perception found throughout Jervis's work and articulated in terms of an explicit paradigm for political psychology in the last chapter by Monroe. Stein's interest in the normative aspect of political psychology is echoed in the chapters by Marcus, Simon and Jackman, and Suedfeld. As Stein outlines the challenges for political psychology in the future, she illustrates and buttresses her arguments by contrasting political psychology's important contribution to the analysis of political decision making with its more limited contribution to the analysis of political learning.

Political Psychology in Relation to Other Fields

Works in Part 2 suggest the unique value of political psychology for particular research fields and topics. Stanley Renshon's chapter forms a natural connection from discussions in Part 1. Indeed, it is the distinction between political psychology's origins and its current applications that Renshon considers a major concern for political psychology as a field, and Renshon cautions that political psychology risks losing its connection to its early foundations, especially those from cultural anthropology. Like Stein, Renshon notes that although political psychology as a field has traditionally drawn on cultural anthropology—in addition to psychology and political science—this influence has diminished in recent years. Indeed, Renshon suggests that little contemporary research in political psychology makes explicit use of culture in its explanations. This, Renshon argues, leaves political psychology as a field woefully unprepared, both conceptually and theoretically, to explain the unprecedented levels of conflict that have a heavy cultural nature. Renshon documents political psychology's early debt to cultural analysis and assesses the contemporary questions that would benefit from a more sophisticated cultural analysis.

Renshon's concern with culture and conflict is echoed by Martha Crenshaw, who argues that the utility of political psychology lies primarily in its applicability to pressing political problems, such as ethnonationalist conflict, terrorism, and the proliferation of weapons of mass destruction. For Crenshaw, political psychology as a field is valuable because it is both interdisciplinary and oriented toward policy issues. As a conceptual framework for analysis, then, it combines theoretical rigor and practical relevance. Yet Crenshaw's analysis reveals that the political psychological approach is not simple; the wide variety of psychological concepts that can be applied to political questions can be confusing. Thus researchers in the field need to be knowledgeable about both psychology and politics. Furthermore, it is also essential that political psychology be cross-cultural and avoid parochialism, especially if it is to play a constructive role in developing American foreign policy for the 21st century.

Willem Doise and Christian Staerklé focus on the links between the social and the political, arguing that because social and political psychology share many research topics, it is not easy to draw clear boundaries between them. Instead, Doise and Staerklé suggest that it is societal psychology— aimed at articulating individual and societal factors in explaining political behavior, attitudes, and judgments—that provides the link between the two research traditions. In their chapter, Doise and Staerklé demonstrate how analyses of societal dimensions may fruitfully complete more individualistic approaches of political processes. In particular, they argue that social representations theory provides the theoretical framework for analyzing the links between individual cognitive functioning and more general societal factors that orient the way people think, act, and interact in society. Evidencing common lay knowledge about socially relevant issues and analyzing organizing principles that structure individual positionings in this realm are the main features of a social representational approach to political psychology. Doise and Staerklé illustrate the societal approach to political psychology by discussing and reinterpreting politically relevant research on individual positionings in terms of locus of control, on political socialization, on social representations of human rights and democracy, and on normative stereotypes and their justification function.

Daniel Bar-Tal expands on themes found in the chapter by Doise and Staerklé. More particularly, Bar-Tal focuses on the extent to which political psychology, as a discipline that combines psychology and political science, is concerned with those political issues that involve the political functioning of both individuals and groups. What makes political psychologists unique, Bar-Tal argues, is their use of psychological terms, conceptions, theories, and/or empirically accumulated psychological knowledge in order to analyze political issues. Bar-Tal demonstrates political psychology's close ties to social psychology through a classification of the articles published in the 19-plus volumes of *Political Psychology* through 1998.[2] These classifications suggest political psychology is greatly influenced by the dominant social cognitive orientation of social psychology. The accumulated knowledge of the study of social perception and cognition suggests several derivations

---

[2]This analysis indicates that 80% of the articles derive from the discipline of social psychology and personality psychology. Another classification shows that about 40% of the articles are based on cognitive theory.

about the nature of political behavior. Bar-Tal's chapter discusses three derivations and points out their implications for the study of political psychology: subjectivism, which suggests that reality, as perceived and cognized by the individual, is subjective; commonalism, which suggests that individuals share cognitions; and distinction between universalism and particularism, which refers to the difference between what can be universally generalized and what is particular.

Fred Alford also emphasizes the importance of groups in his analysis of political psychology, although his tack differs significantly from that of Bar-Tal or of Doise and Staerklé. Alford argues that men and women are group animals, more bound to the group than our Western culture of individualism allows us to appreciate. For Alford, one of the most important contributions of political psychology is to make us aware of this reality, a reality that accounts for so many of the horrors of the 20th century. Alford argues that an awareness of our "groupishness" can mitigate its unconscious power over us, allowing a more realistic and tempered individualism to emerge. Like Marcus and Ward, Alford links work in political psychology to work in classical political theory, arguing that the classical political theorists understood the importance and nature of our group identity better than do most contemporaries.

Special Substantive Areas of Application

Chapters in Part 3 suggest how political psychological analysis can be utilized to inform us more fully about specific political topics. Providing a slightly different take on the importance of group versus individual analyses, Simon Jackman and Paul Sniderman focus on the importance of political psychology for understanding public opinion and political behavior. They turn to the vast body of works that can be described as concentrating on "internalist" accounts of political choice, explaining why citizens think as they do on the basis of their desires and patterns of judgment. Jackman and Sniderman, however, make the argument that an externalist account must come first. Their analysis suggests accounts of public opinion and political behavior should proceed from features of the institutional context and elite strategy, that is, analysis should move *from* politics and *to* the reasoning of citizens about political choices. For most citizens of most democracies most of the time, a rich universe of possibilities is not an offer; instead, citizens almost always are presented with a reasonably simple choice space, the result of elite competition that is tightly structured by constitutional arrangements, electoral procedures, and the logic of party competition. Several empirical regularities in public opinion and political behavior can be shown to flow in this "top-down" manner. Sniderman and Jackman argue that we should emphasize political parties and the role of party identification in structuring elite strategy and mass opinion, respectively. Heuristics—a key concept in contemporary political psychology—are effective only to the extent that the choice space is simplified by political institutions and elite strategy in the first place. Jackman and Sniderman do not seek to write off "internalist" accounts of political choice, but they do insist that any explanation of citizen choice must first recognize how political institutions coordinate the number and arrangement of alternatives available for consideration.

Howard Lavine addresses the importance of political psychology for public opinion through a review and a critique of process models of political opinion formation. One class of models highlights a reliance on memory and the probabilistic and constructive nature of the attitude response process. Such "memory-based" models emphasize the notion that most citizens do not have preformed opinions about most political issues, but instead must retrieve and integrate accessible considerations on the spot. In contrast, "on-line" models emphasize a more goal-directed and efficient political information processor. On-line models assume that citizens have spontaneous affective responses to political actors and issues and that they maintain and update effective summaries as new information becomes available in the political environment. Lavine provides a conceptual framework for understanding the circumstances that mediate the occurrence of on-line versus memory-based information processing; furthermore, he suggests contexts within which hybrid processes (i.e., those that combine elements of each of the pure models) occur. Lavine's analysis focuses on the determinants of citizens' ability and motivation to engage in on-line processing, the nature of their processing goals, and the inherent qualities or "affordances" of issue versus candidate political objects in evoking on-line versus memory-based processing.

A nice complement to the preceding three chapters is provided by David Sears, who notes that a recurrent issue in political psychology has been whether the workings of popular democracy are best described by elite-driven, top-down models, or by citizenry-driven, bottom-up models. One central arena in which this question has been debated concerns the effects of political events on public opinion. The standard literature on political behavior offers three simple models for predicting the effects of political events on public opinion: rational change, demagogic manipulation, and predisposition-based polarization. Early research on political socialization emphasized the central role of psychological processes and left relatively little room for the impact of such exogenous events. Sears presents data illustrating the crucial role of events on political socialization, levels of attitude constraint, and framing and agenda setting. He then presents several case studies of longer term effects of political events that seem to require more complex psychological models: racial and government spending policy issues that prime the same predispositions irrespective of how the issue is framed; collective memories that may depend on the symbolic nature of the event itself; gender differences in the bases on which people responded to the political events of the 1960s; children's responses to the assassination of President Kennedy, with consequences for later protest and political disengagement; and the generational lag in responses to the incarceration of Japanese Americans in World War II. These cases illustrate both the importance of ordinary citizens' predispositions in governing their responses to events and the role of events in political socialization.

Leonie Huddy performs a similar kind of analysis, drawing on the diverse methodologies utilized by psychologists and political scientists and focusing on recent research on attitudes and persuasion. Huddy picks up on Hermann's call for tolerance of a variety of methodologies by highlighting the benefits of methodological pluralism. She does this by suggesting the ways in which methods influence research findings in a diverse assortment of fields. Huddy contrasts the use of experiments with content analysis and focus groups, as well as the kind of interpretive analysis of case studies that constituted the core of Freudian psychoanalysis and that now are evident in leadership studies. Her in-depth analysis of work in political tolerance utilizing both the experimental and the survey approaches, her overview of work on attitude change and persuasion, and her work on the fluidity and change in identity utilizing these different approaches is a masterful overview of several substantive fields that ably proves her central point: Methods differ, and the kind of tool we use to analyze a problem does much to determine our substantive findings.

The chapter by Robert Jervis moves discussion from the domestic to the international and echoes Crenshaw's concerns with issues of world peace. Jervis builds on his substantial work on signaling and perception to show how analysts have generally treated the subjects separately. Jervis argues that signaling and perception need to be joined, creating a lynchpin of game theory and political psychology. He shows how the meanings imputed to and inferred from behavior by perceivers are crucial, since these interpretations will determine the impact of signals. Psychological theory and research show that the interpretation of signals often varies from one observer to another and differs from that intended by the sender. Perception depends on the observer's implicit or explicit theories, which are subject to variation and dispute. Both cognitive and motivated biases also play a large role in this process. Jervis's chapter on the importance of perception anticipates my concluding chapter about an underlying paradigm in political science, focused on perceptions of self in relation to others.

Focus on the Future

The book concludes with five chapters designed to focus the research agenda for political psychologists in the years to come. It begins with a chapter by Peter Suedfeld, a chapter that addresses the nature of doing objective and scientifically or empirically verifiable research on topics that contain a heavy component of subjective perception. His chapter relates to those by Bar-Tal, Alford, and Doise and Staerklé in its concern with groups and to the concerns with methodology evident in the chapters by Hermann, Huddy, and Rosenberg. Essentially, Suedfeld addresses social science's recent experiences with postmodernism. He suggests that the humanities and social science have been influenced by the constructivist component of postmodernism, the concept that there may be no objective truths in these fields or, if objective truths do exist, that they are undiscoverable because all enquiry and understanding is biased by the background, motives, and personality of the scholar. Suedfeld argues that identity politics often has carried this epistemological argument one step further, to imply that there are different truths for groups according to their sex, ethnicity, religion, etc. The implication of this is that all research, teaching, and learning must take such different truths into account and, some postmoderns have argued, should be directed toward the benefit of "disadvantaged" groups. Suedfeld's chapter is a provocative examination of how these views, and the political positions related to them, have influenced research in four major areas of political psychology: authoritarianism, traditional versus modern racism and sexism, voting behavior, and leader assessment at a distance. He concludes with some suggestions on how best to deal with the issues that arise from conflicting philosophies of science and from political disagreement. His chapter is the clearest articulation I have seen of political psychology's unique value in being able to address many of these difficult political issues in a careful and scientific way.

Shawn Rosenberg addresses some of these same issues but does so by taking a quite different tack. Rosenberg's focus is the challenge to the foundational assumptions on which political psychology is based, in particular the notion of objective reality. He takes seriously the postmodernist claims that what is true and real is less a result of some direct or even mediated experience of the world and more a matter of culture, and the postmodern view that truth is a social construction that is consistent with the aims and structure of particular groups or societies. The implication of this for research methodologies, of course, is that these methods themselves are no longer considered neutral. Rosenberg does not address the merits of the postmodern claims directly but instead asks why such claims have enjoyed such popularity during the last 15 years. He refuses to retreat to a "cultural chauvinism," but he also refuses to be left with the alternative "amorphous, postmodern world where all value and knowledge is relative." For Rosenberg, the challenge for political psychology is to provide understanding and normative direction that moves us beyond either of these unacceptable positions. His essay is an ingenious attempt to meet this challenge by generating a new analytical foundation to guide future research as we meet the criticisms of postmodernism and provide cultural and political direction for an increasingly multicultural world. This third route presented in Rosenberg's chapter will incite much excitement and controversy but may provide a major, new approach to political psychology in the new century.

The concern with normative issues is evident in the next chapter, by Robert Lane. One of the founders of political psychology as a field, Lane underscores the link between political psychology and normative concerns by arguing that we need to turn political psychology upside down. Whereas political psychology has successfully employed psychological theory and research to explain political behavior and outcomes, Lane suggests we ought now to reverse this order and study how politics influences the thoughts, feelings, and behavior of bureaucrats, politicians and, above all, citizens themselves. This "upside down" version of political psychology has the advantage that political psychologists then try to explain matters closer to ultimate ends, such as subjective well-being and human development, as contrasted to the focus on such means as freedom and equality now to represent the ultimate explicanda of political science. If we make subjective well-being the sole end of politics, Lane argues, we would recapitulate the faults of utilitarians and actually violate the logic of the pursuit of happiness. By adding human development, our agenda would embrace most of the ends mentioned in the philosophies of the right and the good. If we can advise governments on how to promote subjective well-being—mostly by substituting companionship for money, at least in the West—there will be only modest resistance. But government influence on human development seems intrusive and more dangerous. Employing research in cognition and affect, a focus on how governments can influence cognitive development and emotional maturity, would have great benefits. Lane's research agenda reminds us of the origins of political psychology in classical philosophy and links nicely into the remaining works in this section, in which analysts effectively set a research agenda for the future.

David Winter's chapter expands on his 1999 Presidential Address to the International Society of Political Psychology. This address outlined an intellectual agenda for political psychology in order to understand the interlocking complex of power, sex, and violence that has characterized much of society and political life during the 20th century. In his chapter, Winter focuses on several important questions: How can "compensatory" and "offensive" power strivings be distinguished? How can all power strivings be tempered, or even renounced? How can the forces of empathy, curiosity, and cosmopolitan identity be mobilized to overcome the human tendency—exacerbated by threat—to construct and magnify "differences?" Winter shows how political psychology, as an inherently broad and interdisciplinary field, can draw on the complementary strengths of its component disciplines—as well as those of its cognate fields—to be uniquely and advantageously situated to develop answers to these questions.

In my concluding chapter, I try to address what surely will be a central concern for political psychology in the future: Is there one basic theory associated with political psychology? An underlying paradigm that gives unity and coherence to political psychology as a field? In assessing the field as a whole, I would argue that it is not the lack of theory but rather a surfeit of insightful theories that blinds us to an underlying paradigm in political psychology. Such a paradigm does exist, however, and can be discerned if we review the major theories in political psychology with an eye for the common element. I argue that political psychology rests on an underlying theoretical framework that I call *perspective*. Indeed, the importance of perspective is evident in much political psychology, including the preceding chapters by Deutsch and Kinnvall, Crenshaw, Jervis, Bar-Tal, Doise and Staerklé, Sears, and Alford among others. My chapter begins by describing perspective and its basic, core assumptions. I next suggest how perspective draws on several bodies of literature in political psychology, from framing theory to social cognition theory. I conclude by noting possible tests and applications that might be constructed to help flesh out the paradigm of perspective in years to come, providing a common framework around which political psychology as a discipline can build.

PART I

Political Psychology:
An Overview of the Field

1

What Is Political Psychology?

MORTON DEUTSCH
Columbia University

CATARINA KINNVALL
Lund University

Although its ancestry in social philosophy can be traced back to ancient times, modern political psychology as an academic discipline was born in the decades between the First and Second World Wars. It is a child of political science and psychology, having been conceived in the ambivalent mood of optimism and despair that has characterized the scientific age. Rapidly expanding knowledge, the increasing confidence in scientific methods, and the ever quickening technological developments stimulated the awareness that scientific methods might be applied to the understanding of political behavior. The increasing political turmoil, the irrationality and destructiveness of the First World War, the development of modern totalitarian regimes with their barbarities, the emergence of the mass media and their systematic use by propagandists, suggested an urgent need for more systematic knowledge about the relationship between political and psychological processes.

The first notable link between psychology and political science in the United States developed at the University of Chicago under the encouragement of the political scientist Charles Merriam (Davies, 1973). Merriam (1925, 1934) explicitly called for a scientific political science that would draw on psychology. It was one of Merriam's students, Harold D. Lasswell, who responded to that call and, through his writings and his teachings, became the American founding father of political psychology as a new academic discipline.

Although Lasswell's prolific writings touched on almost every topic of interest to political psychologists, his special emphasis on psychological processes as they affect political processes has been influential in shaping the approach of most American social scientists to the field of political psychology. His early books—*Psychopathology and Politics* (1930), *World Politics and Personal Insecurity* (1935), *Politics: Who Gets What, When, and How* (1936), *Power and Personality* (1948)—helped to establish a distinctive psychological perspective for understanding political behavior, politics, and politicians. This perspective leads to a political psychology largely centering on individual and social psychological processes—such as motivation, conflict, perception, cognition, learning, socialization, attitude formation, and group dynamics—and on individual personality and psychopathology as the causal factors influencing political behavior.

The strong emphasis on psychological processes as determinants of political processes in American political psychology has led to a relative neglect of the study of the influence of political processes on psychological processes. European political psychology, although much influenced by American political psychology, has been less one-sided. The greater impact of the Marxist perspective in Europe has evoked more awareness of the role of political processes in shaping psychological processes and personality. Thus, Max Horkheimer, in his 1931 inaugural address as Director of the Institute for Social Research at the University of Frankfurt, insisted that institute members should explore the interconnection between the economic life of society, the psychic development of the individual, and transformations in the realm of culture (Held, 1980). Various members of the Frankfurt school and those associated with the development of "critical theory"—Horkheimer, Adorno, Marcuse, Fromm, and Habermas—have made important contributions to the integration of the political–economic orientations of Marxist theory with the psychological perspectives of Freudian theory.

How political, economic, and social processes are affecting individuals has also been the concern of a number of more recent European sociologists such as Anthony Giddens and Ulrich Beck. Giddens, in the development of his structuration theory (Giddens, 1979, 1984, 1990), depicts the view that agency and structure, or the individual and society, are mutually constituted and cannot be understood as separate entities. Similar to earlier sociologists such as Bourdieu (1977), Bauman (1973), and Berger and Luckmann (1966), Giddens is especially interested in those aspects of human agency that express the power of individuals to transform their social and political circumstances. The influence of sociology on political psychology has taken a number of expressions. Theorists concerned with political culture (Almond & Verba, 1963; Pye, 1986; Inglehart, 1990, 1996), political socialization (Renshon, 1977, 1989, 2000; Merelman, 1986;

Wilson, 1988), and learning (Gudykunst & Ting-Toomey, 1988; Sigel, 1989; Bermeo, 1992; Levy, 1994), have all contributed to the understanding of how structures and cultures inform individual action and behavior.

In our view, the field of political psychology is the study of the interaction of political and psychological processes; this is a bidirectional interaction. Just as cognitive capabilities limit and affect the nature of the political and social world of political agents so, also, the structures and processes of politics affect cognitive capabilities. Thus, 5-year-olds and mature adults, partly as a result of their differences in cognitive capabilities, develop rather different sorts of political structures and processes; similarly, certain sorts of political structures and processes foster the development of the intelligent, autonomous, reflective, active characteristics of mature adults, whereas others encourage the development of immature, passive, dependent, uncritical cognitive capabilities resembling those of a submissive child.

The field of political psychology is defined not only by its subject-matter, the interrelationship between political and psychological processes, but also by its approach to its subject-matter. This approach has historically been in the scientific tradition. As Nagel (1961) pointed out: "It is the desire for explanations which are at once systematic and controllable by factual evidence that generates science" (p. 4). The scientifically oriented political psychologist seeks to develop explanatory hypotheses for the phenomena of interest that have logical consequences precise enough to be genuinely testable. The explanatory hypotheses, in other words, must be subject to the possibility of rejection through empirically verifiable and scientifically competent evidence that has been obtained by procedures employed with the intent of eliminating known sources of error. As Nagel (1961) indicated:

> The practice of scientific method is the persistent critique of arguments, in the light of tried canons for judging the reliability of the procedures by which evidential data are obtained, and for assessing the probative force of the evidence on which conclusions are based. (p. 13)

A scientifically oriented political psychology must, by necessity, be concerned with "methodology": It must be concerned with developing the "tried canons" for judging the reliability of procedures for collecting data and for assessing the validity of the evidence for testing explanatory hypotheses. It must also be concerned with developing the data collection procedures that will produce reliable and valid data.

The practice of scientific method in a field such as political psychology is difficult to achieve and to sustain. The inherent nature of its subject-matter makes it largely inappropriate to transfer uncritically the methodological canons of the well-established physical and biological sciences to political psychology. Yet there is the common temptation to use the natural sciences as a model and also the opposite temptation to reject the possibility of a scientific approach because the appropriateness of the model is rejected. The scientific approach of the natural sciences has mainly reflected a technical cognitive interest (Habermas, 1971) that has been oriented toward developing knowledge for instrumental action toward defined goals under given conditions. To the extent that the social sciences, including political psychology, have uncritically imitated the methodologies appropriate to a technical cognitive interest, they have tended to neglect the fact that human action has to be understood with reference to the meanings that the action has for the actors and for its audience: Human action is rooted in intersubjective contexts of communication, in intersubjective practices and forms of life that have distinctive historical origins (Bernstein, 1976; Giddens, 1984, 1991). The uncritical imitation of the technical orientation of the natural sciences has also led many social scientists to ignore how their theoretical and empirical work—that is, their scientific activities—are influenced by the implicit assumptions, the value positions, ideological orientations, and political–economic viewpoints in the communities in which they participate.

Common as such imitation of an exalted, older idol is, it has had some ill-effects on the development of a scientific political psychology. It has led some to confuse "scientism" and science: namely, to consider techniques labeled "objective," "behavioristic," "value free," and "quantitative" as scientific even when critical reflection would have revealed how inappropriate the techniques (as well as the labels) were, and also how thoroughly value-laden they were. Others have reacted against the pseudo-objectivism of scientism by a retreat to an unbridled subjectivism, a subjectivism which, in effect, denies the possibility or value of an intersubjective methodology for the scientific study of political psychology. Present academic discourse tends to describe these in the juxtaposed terminology of rationalism versus postmodernism, where the former reflects a belief in active, rational, goal-oriented individuals with strong selves, whereas the latter sees individual subjectivity as a historical discursive construction lacking any such thing as a core-self. Both are, of course, simplified accounts of complex processes. Not only do they disregard the intersubjective nature of individuals, but they also fail to acknowledge the bidirectional interplay between psychological and political processes.

Fortunately, neither scientism nor subjectivism is the dominant trend in political psychology. Most political psychologists are practitioners of the well-tried art of "methodological opportunism." They employ research designs and established procedures—for example, content analysis, systematic interviewing, questionnaire methods, analysis of nonverbal behavior, small-group experiments, projective techniques, controlled observations, polling, analysis of recorded data—borrowed from any of the various behavioral and social science disciplines and adapted so as to be appropriate to the problem they are investigating. If the research design or procedures are poorly implemented by the researcher or inappropriate to the research problem, one can normally expect that the "persistent critique of arguments, in the light of tried canons" will reveal the deficiencies in the research (if the research is considered significant enough to warrant attention). Sometimes, of course, error goes unrecognized because everyone in a field of study is subject to the same incorrect assumption.

Much of the work being done in political psychology is exploratory and formulative, meant to stimulate insight and to develop hypotheses rather than to test them. There is considerable latitude in doing such research but inasmuch as there are no good rules for being creative, a good deal of exploratory research turns out to be unproductive. The latitudes for acceptable descriptive and hypothesis-testing kinds of studies are much smaller. The rules and procedures for conducting such studies are fairly well articulated. Nevertheless, many such studies, even when done well technically, are often of little value because not enough critical thought has preceded the formulation of the research problem. A common critique of small-group experiments and controlled observations, for instance, has to do with their sometimes irrelevant conclusions for understanding and predicting an outside world affected by cultural and structural constraints under whose influence individuals act. Another and more recent critique has to do with the methodological differences between political science and psychology which, according to Hermann (1989), may threaten to make the promise of a field of political psychology a mere fantasy. This divide is particularly evident in case study research (Tetlock, 1983), where political scientists and psychologists simply lack a common language for their investigations (Kaarbo & Beasley, 1999).

Although much political psychology is in the scientific tradition, it is also concerned with being socially useful and with applying its knowledge and insights to improvement of political processes and to human betterment. Many of the "applications" are speculative in the sense that there are numerous important gaps in our relevant theoretical and empirical knowledge and we must take a speculative leap to make specific recommendations from the shaky foundations of currently existing knowledge. However, the major social value of intellectual work in political psychology resides not in its specific recommendations but rather in its providing organizing frameworks, clarifying ideas and systematic concepts for helping those who are engaged in practical political work to think about their activities in a more comprehensive way, more analytically, and with more concern for the empirical soundness of their working assumptions.

THE CONTENT OF POLITICAL PSYCHOLOGY

Political psychologists have investigated a wide range of topics. To get some personal feeling for the variety of topics that have fallen under the rubric of *political psychology*, we reviewed the contents of the programs of the annual scientific meetings of the International Society of Political Psychology (ISPP). ISPP was founded in January 1978 as an international and interdisciplinary scholarly society. Its international membership includes psychologists, political scientists, psychiatrists, sociologists, historians, anthropologists, and people in government or public life who have a scholarly interest in political psychology. It can be considered the focal point of scholarly activity in the field of political psychology. We have reviewed the contents of the ISPP's journal, *Political Psychology*, since its first year of publication and have also examined the contents of a number of books devoted to political psychology (Knutson, 1973; Di Renzo, 1974; Renshon, 1974; Elms, 1976; Dawson, Prewitt, & Dawson, 1977; Barner-Barry & Rosenwein 1985; Hermann, 1986; Lau & Sears, 1986; Stone & Schaffner, 1988; Iyengar & McGuire, 1993; and Le Doux, 1996, among others).

At first sight, a listing of the titles of articles, chapters, papers, and symposia produced a bewildering diversity of topics, giving a sense of chaos in political psychology. Fortunately, after reflecting on the diversity, a reasonably clear structure emerged from the surface chaos. Not only did it become relatively clear how political psychology as a field has developed, but it also gave some indication of where political psychology may be heading. Next we identify a number of key areas that have preoccupied political psychologists for the last 30 years or so. In most cases we have indicated one or more references that provide the reader with a guide to important work that has been done in the relevant area. This is followed by a brief summary of some illustrative studies of the field.

The Individual as Political Actor

This area is at the center of a cluster of studies concerned with the determinants and consequences of the individual's political behavior. Studies of political socialization, the formation of political attitudes, political participation, political alienation, voting behavior, the social backgrounds of political terrorists, the relationship between personality and political attitudes, group membership and political attitudes/behavior, situational factors influencing political behavior, the influence of the mass media, etc., are some of the many studies in political psychology that could be identified under this heading. This is by far the largest area of research in political psychology as it constitutes the basis for most other research within the field.

The individual as a political actor is at the heart of the debate on how political psychology differs from rational choice models as it seeks to explain behavior that is outside the Hobbesian world of individuals as instrumentalist rational creatures. Instead, political psychology insists that individuals may reason differently in different circumstances and that emotional aspects guide interaction and action in the social world. How we define the individual as a political actor also has implications for how we understand collective identity formation and collective action. Instrumentalist explanations have difficulties in explaining circumstances when people identify themselves with the group for reasons other than those that are purely instrumental. Emotional aspects of belonging, or other needs for identification and bonding, are often overlooked and so is the desire for mutual recognition and community building. As noted by Marcus (this volume), works on the psychology of emotion and on emotion in politics are starting to have a serious impact on the field of political psychology. Collective identity, whether based on ethnicity, class, gender, race, religion, nation, or the state must, in other words, be understood within the framework of how individuals constitute political actors. The focus, and problem, of aggregating from the individual level to the group level is thus at the forefront of political psychology.

Political Movements

Studies of political movements make up the nexus of investigations of such social formations, groups, organizations, and communities in which the political actor is not an individual but rather a social unit composed of interacting individuals and groups. Both social identity theory and its derivative, self-categorization theory, have been attempts to create a nonreductionist cognitive social psychological model of group processes (Monroe, Hankin, & Bukovchik VanVechten, 1999). Proceeding from and developing Tajfel's (1982) "minimal group paradigm," a number of political psychologists have applied social identity theory to understand political movements and other social formations (Abrams, 1994; Hogg & Abrams, 1988; Oakes, Haslam, & Turner, 1994). As early as 1982, Helmut Moser for instance, in a review of political psychology in the Federal Republic of Germany, identified studies of the "youth movement" and studies of action groups of citizens as two of the major topics that had been studied extensively by political psychologists in that country. Similarly, there have been studies of the women's movement (Carroll, 1989; Clayton & Crosby, 1992), of terrorist groups (Crenshaw, 1986, 1990 and this volume; Reich, 1990), of religious sects (Robins & Post, 1997), of the development of ethnic and/or national movements (Staub, 1989; Druckman, 1994; Volkan, 1997), and of intergroup relations and group conflict more generally (Duckitt, 1992; Sniderman, Brody, & Tetlock, 1993). However, as noted by Crenshaw, Bar-Tal, and Stein (this volume), among others, political psychology is not only concerned with explaining group conflict and violence but also with conflict resolution and concrete policy prescriptions. See, for example, Deutsch and Coleman (2000), where the implications for the practice of negotiation and mediation in various social contexts are drawn from specific social psychological theories having relevance to the process involved in conflict resolution.

The Politician or Political Leader

This area is closely related to the first one except that the research here deals with a special category of political actors, those who are identifiable as playing or having played a particularly significant role in the political process. Studies of political leaders and political leadership, the personalities of politicians, psychobiography, and psychohistory fall under this heading. Analyses of political leaders have been concerned with a number of issues, such as decision making in general and foreign policy making in particular, crisis behavior, national and international negotiation behavior, group dynamics, and charismatic leadership. Political psychologists have analyzed how attribution and inference guide interpretation of political events and how signaling, misperceptions, groupthink, self-images, and images of the other have consequences for negotiation tactics and the escalation of violence and war (Janis, 1982; Jervis, Lebow, & Stein, 1985; Larson, 1985; Tetlock, 1993; Jervis, 1997).

Many studies of political leaders have been done because of the inherent interest in personalities that have loomed large in history. Recent attempts to explain differences in leadership style, from Roosevelt via Nixon to Clinton, using a psychobiographic approach are evidence of this trend (Farnham, 1997; Volkan, Itzkowitz, & Dod, 1997; George & George, 1998; Greenstein, 2000). Most leadership analyses include the personality component of leadership, although a minority of scholars study the interrelation between personality and environment. Personality trait analyses are at the heart of those interested in the relationship between images of the political leader and voting behavior. Studies have shown that judgments about the personality traits of political leaders affect both overall evaluations of those leaders and individual vote decisions (Stewart & Clarke, 1992; Jones & Hudson, 1996; Pancer, Brown, & Widdis Barr, 1999).

Political Alignments and Structures

This area is similar to "political movements" except that the research here is concerned with the social formations, groupings, and organizations that develop among politicians. The focus is on such questions as how coalitions are formed, what leads to splintering of groups, what gives rise to particular leader-follower relations, and what initiates cooperative rather than competitive relations. More generally, here the interest is in the "sociometric" structures and interactions that occur among the politicians in a given political unit, what has given rise to them, and what are their consequences. As demonstrated by Jackman and Sniderman (this volume), recent studies have focused on the role of political parties in large-scale representative democracies, the extent to which partisan elites maintain and organize coalitions along ideological lines, and the way in which party ideologies constrain the opportunities for candidates to raise questions (Poole & Rosenthal, 1993; Aldrich, 1995; Sniderman, 2000).

Political Intergroup Relations

This area is similar to the preceding one but is centered on investigations dealing with the structures and interactions existing among political units and not on those among individual politicians. The political units may be local governments, nations, alliances, international organizations, and so on. The study of hostile interrelations such as are involved in threat, war, deterrence, etc., as well as the study of cooperative interrelations such as mutual aid, scientific and cultural exchanges, and trade are included under this rubric (Jervis, 1989; Woshinsky, 1994; Axelrod, 1997; Reich, 1990). Under this and the preceding heading, as well as the one following, the distinctive orientation of political psychology is concerned with the role of individual and group psychological processes in affecting, as well as being affected by, the natural development of political structures, political interactions, and political processes. Here, so to speak, political psychology contributes a distinctive emphasis to the understanding of the subject matters of political science and international relations; it does not provide a substitute for these disciplines.

Political Processes

Perhaps the most central area in political psychology concerns the various individual and group processes that are involved in, and affect as well as are affected by, the behavior of political entities. The study of political processes is at the heart of all previously mentioned areas, but a number of these processes have been studied fairly extensively and warrant distinctive and major subareas. These include: perception and cognition (Jervis, 1976, 1997; Lebow, 1981; Hopf, 1994), decision-making (Janis & Mann, 1977; George, 1969, 1980; Stein, 1989; Moscovici & Doise, 1994), persuasion (Doob, 1948; Nimmo, 1970; Petty & Cacioppo, 1996; Pratkanis &

Aronson, 1991; Taylor, 1998), learning (Dawson et al., 1977; Levy, 1994; Stein, 1994), conflict (Deutsch, 1973; Deutsch, 1983; Deutsch & Coleman, 2000; Snyder & Diesing, 1977; Walter & Snyder, 1999), and mobilization (Etzioni, 1968; Alford, 1994; Bar-Tal & Staub, 1997).

Case Studies

Cross-cutting the structure of political psychology organized around relatively abstract areas is an organization around particular "cases"—for example, understanding the voting or nonvoting behavior of individuals in particular localities; studying particular political leaders such as Churchill, Roosevelt, Hitler, Gorbachev, or Saddam Hussein; investigating conflict in the Middle East, Afghanistan, or Rwanda; studying the images and perceptions of opposing parties in conflict; investigating decision making in specific situations such as the Cuban missile crisis, the Gulf War, or Indian nuclear testing. Such case studies are primarily meant to describe in a meaningful way a historically significant person or episode. However, a well conceptualized case study will not only have relevance to the particular individual or episode being characterized, it will also have relevance for general, theoretical ideas; it should not only provide understanding of the case that was studied but also help us to understand other cases. The literature of political psychology and other social science disciplines is dotted with many case studies: Some of them have considerable general import but many, by themselves, go no further than providing interesting descriptions of the object of study.

Human Development and the Political Economy

The first area of interest focused on the individual as someone whose actions have political consequences; the present area centers on the consequences for the individual (for his or her personal development, self-esteem, cognitive development, and so forth) of living in a society that has a political economy with given characteristics. Here, the focus is on how politico–economic structures and processes affect sociopsychological processes and structures rather than the reverse. Marxist theorists (Venable, 1945; Bowles & Gintis, 1976; Giddens & Held, 1982; Giddens, 1990, 1991) have written extensively on these matters. So have such theorists as Weber (1930), Merton (1957), Berger and Luckmann (1966), Lane (1982, 1991, 2000), Baumeister (1986), Kristeva (1991), and Cash (1996). There is much of relevance to this area in a good deal of the research in psychological anthropology (Le Vine, 1974; Casson, 1981; Bock, 1988; Renshon, 2000); in the research on the effects of class, caste, race and sex on personal development (Deutsch, Katz, & Jensen, 1968; Unger, 1979; Scarr, 1981;

Flax, 1990; Sowell, 1994; Sainsbury, 1996); in the research on the psychological effects of unemployment, inflation, an expanding economy (Brenner, 1973; Hayes & Nutman, 1981; Whelan, Hannan, & Creighton, 1991; Gallie, Marsch, & Vogler, 1994); in the studies of the effects of democratic versus authoritarian groups (e.g., Lewin, Lippitt, & White, 1939; Altemeyer, 1996; Milburn & Conrad, 1996); and in the investigations of the social psychological consequences of different systems of distributive justice (e.g., Deutsch, 1985; Lane, 1982, 1991).

ILLUSTRATIVE STUDIES OF POLITICAL PSYCHOLOGY

In this section, we summarize briefly some studies in the field of political psychology, which provide a more specific picture of work being done in this field.

How Voters Decide

Empirical works on how voters decide generally take one of two theoretical approaches. Either the belief is that people choose the party that will improve their overall economic benefits (Downs, 1957; Erikson, 1990; Page & Shapiro, 1992; Miller & Shanks, 1996), or it is argued that people prefer parties that take an ideological, economic, and political stand on certain issues, such as social welfare, foreign policy, or employment issues (Furnham, 1982; Heaven, 1990). The former belief is grounded in self-interest theory, which suggests that individuals choose alternatives that maximize expected utilities, whereas the latter is founded on the belief that people are socialized into a particular ideological system that molds their values and attitudes. Some of the earliest research in political psychology supported the ideological approach by pointing to certain predispositions of the voter, such as party identification, affecting the electoral choice (Lazarsfeld, Berelson, & Gaudet, 1948; Campbell, Converse, Miller, & Stokes, 1960). However, these studies also found that income and socioeconomic status were associated with voting preference and thus concluded that self-interested motivation may play a role in forming political party preference.

Empirical studies of how voters decide provide a mixed pattern. Himmelweit, Humphreys, Jaeger, and Katz (1981), whose work in the field of political psychology greatly strengthened the understanding of human decision making by voters, conducted a longitudinal study of voting behavior in the United Kingdom over a period of six elections, extending from 1959 to 1974. They used a consumer model of voting that is an application of multiple-attribute utility theory (MAUT; Von Winterfeld & Fischer, 1975; Humphreys, 1977). MAUT assumes that a person chooses the alternative with the highest total subjective or expected utility among the possible objects of choice. Based on their MAUT analysis, Himmelweit et al. predicted the vote of 80% of their sample correctly for the 1974 elections, whereas predictions based on the voter's prior voting history were correct only for 67% of the sample. These results are clearly consistent with the thesis that British voters mostly make their voting decisions so as to increase their perceived chances that the policy issues they favor will be implemented: that is, voting behavior is rational. They also reported that the voters they studied had clearly structured, interrelated attitudes or "ideologies" which persisted over time and which were closely related to their voting. This finding runs counter to Bell's claim (1962) about the demise of ideology in advanced Western societies and to Converse's (1964) early conclusion that, apart from a small elite, the mass public had no coherent set of political beliefs that could be construed as a political ideology.

The importance of ideology and/or symbolic dispositions has also been the concern of Sears and his colleagues in a number of studies. Sears and Funk (1991) argued, for instance, that in cases when proximal measures of self-interest are used and the effects of ideology or symbolic predispositions on party references are statistically controlled, self-interest rarely has a significant effect. In later research, using the Terman longitudinal study following a number of individuals for approximately 40 years, the same authors concluded that basic political predispositions tend to be stable over time and that significant political events are likely to polarize attitudes around predispositions (Sears & Funk, 1999; Sears, this volume). Sears and Funk (1991) did suggest, however, that there may be times when a large and unambiguous stake in a certain outcome can increase the role of self-interest in forming political party preference. Recent studies of voting behavior in New Zealand confirm this mixed pattern by suggesting that voters who have the most to gain or lose from the parties' proposed economic policies make their choices more on economic interests, whereas the remainder form party preference from ideological compatibility (Wilson, 1998; Allen & Ng, 2000).

The continuous emphasis on ideological and symbolic predispositions points to the fact that political issues have a life history. As Berelson, Lazarsfeld, & McPhee suggested as early as 1954, an issue goes through certain stages which have bearing on its relevance to the vote from initial rejection to hesitant acceptance to being taken as a given in the society. The salience and importance of an issue to voting or to an individual's ideology depends on where the issue is in its life history.

Foreign Policy Analyses

Since the mid-1950s, the psychological aspects of international relations have become an increasingly important area of research, and a number of significant empirical studies have been published. Among the more influential are Janis' (1972, 1982, 1983) studies of group dynamics, or so-called *groupthink;* Larson's (1985) application of ideas taken from cognitive psychology to the origins of American Cold War policies; George's (1969, 1980) development of operational codes and other cognitive limits on rational decision making; Jervis' (1976, 1997) systematic analyses of signaling and perception in international politics; and Hermann's (1977, 1980) work on the psychological dimensions of leadership and foreign policy. Although most of these works belong to what Hudson (1995) named the first generation of foreign policy analysis, they still play a vital role and have been revisited in various empirical and theoretical works. A few of these are outlined next, followed by a discussion of their impact on more current research.

Janis' (1972, 1982) work on groupthink launched a new research tradition. Drawing on social psychology, Janis explored the unique dynamics of small group decision making in foreign policy settings. He did six case studies of historic fiascoes to identify the sources of defective decision making in governmental policy-making groups concerned with foreign policy decisions. The case studies included: (a) Neville Chamberlain's inner circle, (b) Admiral Kimmel's ingroup of naval commanders in the autumn of 1941; (c) President Truman's advisory group on the Korean War; (d) President Kennedy's advisory group concerning the Bay of Pigs invasion of Cuba; (e) President Johnson's "Tuesday Luncheon Group" regarding the war in Vietnam; and (f) President Nixon's inner circle and the way they handled the Watergate cover-up. One major source of defective decision making running through these diverse fiascoes was a concurrence-seeking tendency (referred to as *groupthink*). Janis showed how the incentive to maintain group consensus and personal acceptance by the group impacted negatively on the quality of the decisions.

Janis' work was extended in the empirical research of Tetlock (1979), Semmel (1982), and others using experimental data as well as case studies, and groupthink became an important psychological dimension of later works on foreign policy decision making (Hudson, 1995). Janis' concept of groupthink has been revisited, refined, and critiqued in a number of recent studies (Herek, Janis, & Huth, 1987; t'Hart, 1990; Purkitt, 1992). Purkitt (1992) showed, for instance, how the closure of options is a much more tentative and fluid process than was previously understood. In this he points to the Cuban Missile Crisis, where options that had previously been ruled out resurfaced time and again throughout the crisis (Hudson, 1995).

Larson's (1985) study of how Harriman, Truman, Byrnes, and Acheson contributed to the development of cold war policies also constituted a novel approach. She was among the first to explore in some detail the extent to which attitude change was likely to occur among political leaders.

Using historical documents such as policy memoranda, diaries, and letters, Larson tried to establish what information policy makers were exposed to, how they interpreted it, and its effects on their beliefs. By comparing different theoretical interpretations of individual cognitive processes, such as the Hovland approach, cognitive dissonance theory, and self-perception theory, Larson was able to detail the shifts in attitudes at the end of the Second World War. This use of different explanatory frameworks for understanding the same leader has been utilized in a number of recent studies (Jones & Hudson, 1996), and has allowed for the inspection of each framework's relative strengths and weaknesses (Hudson, 1995). Larson herself has continued to study how different cognitive frameworks offer several explanations to a common phenomenon, such as the persistence of negative images (1988), or how mistrust may cause partisans to exaggerate the extent to which their interests are in conflict (1997).

The study of perceptions and images, especially as they are related to war and deterrence, thus continues to be an important area of research. The works of Jervis (1976) deserve special mention in this respect. In his studies of superpower behavior, he unraveled the severe consequences of preconceived images and misperceptions in foreign policy situations by exploring the roots of such conceptions. In these and later works (Jervis, 1997), he also provided evidence of how leaders may learn from previous encounters and how sometimes such lessons are overextended. Jervis supplied not only warnings, however, but also advice and suggestions for improved policy making. The influence of Jervis and others (Jervis, Lebow, & Stein, 1985; Lebow & Stein, 1990; Hermann, 1993), resulted in a number of more recent studies of how perceptions become linked to the formation of images and to the development of various types of image theory. One such type has been concerned with national role conceptions which serve to bridge the conceptual gap between the general beliefs held in a society and the beliefs of foreign policy decision makers (Le Prestre, 1997). National role conceptions are viewed as social phenomena that can be shared among most of the individuals within a state (Mercer, 1995; Wendt, 1992, 1994), and even in cases when such role conceptions are not shared, the individuals who make foreign policy in the name of the states do so on the basis of their ideas about the role of their states in the world and which roles will be acceptable to their constituents (Putnam, 1988; Chafetz, Abramson, & Grillot, 1996). As a result, there has been a renewed interest in empirical studies of the relationship between culture and foreign policy (Wilkening, 1999; Hudson, 1997) as well as in the topic of comparative political socialization and political learning (Voss & Dorsey, 1992; Duckitt, 1992; Renshon & Duckitt, 2000). However, as noted by both Stein and Renshon (this volume), political psychology as a field is still in need of more empirical research on these issues.

Government and Self-Esteem

In a number of studies, Lane made significant contributions to the study of government and self-esteem (1982) and to how the market affects social well-being and human development (1991, 2000, this volume). In a very evocative theoretical paper (1982), Lane drew on his deep knowledge of political science, moral philosophy, and psychology to present an analysis of the effect of government on individual self-esteem. He rejected the view advanced by Rawls (1971) that political equity is central to self-esteem. Instead Lane (1982) asserted that "political life is simply not important enough to bear this burden" (p. 7). Public opinion surveys indicate that the national government or political organizations are rarely mentioned as sources of life satisfaction, and people spend relatively few minutes a week engaging in political activities. There also appears to be little correlation between rankings of satisfactions with one's own life and national life. Work, family life, leisure-time activities, and standard of living are, in Lane's view, much more likely to be the "dimensions" along which people measure themselves and their worth. Lane (1982) pointed out that:

> People who value themselves are more likely to value others; low self-esteem makes people deeply unhappy, and high self-esteem offers the condition for life happiness or life satisfaction; and high self-esteem serves as the psychological basis for learning, and hence, for growth. This generative power of self-esteem makes it of crucial importance to government. (p. 26)

All governments engage in the distribution and redistribution of the conditions that facilitate self-esteem. Government actions give significance, power, honor, opportunities, and wealth to some, but not to others. These actions also indicate that certain dimensions for self-evaluation (money, education, ethnicity, experience, sex) are better than others. Thus, there is no point in saying that esteem is not the business of government; the government is inevitably engaged in that business. Based on philosophical as well as psychological considerations, Lane (1982) set forth a set of rules for governmental promotion of self-esteem. In his elaboration of these rules, Lane suggested that since achievement is so central to self-esteem, "The first right is the right to work" (p. 27). He also stressed the importance of participation in self-direction at work: "The second basic right, therefore, is the right to participate in decisions affecting one's work." Compared with many other theorists, he placed much less emphasis on the importance of the political rights of participation in the political sphere than on the rights of participation in the sphere of work as an influence on self-esteem.

Lane developed this line of reasoning in his later works. Discussing the relationship between democracy and happiness, he proceeded from Veenhoven's (1993) recent analysis of 23 countries which argued that across nations it is the level of income, not democracy, that has increased subjective well-being (SWB; Lane, this volume). However, it is not money itself that buys happiness. Instead social well-being has to do with the less easily defined issues of work satisfaction and good family relations (Lane, 2000). To promote social well-being and facilitate the pursuit of happiness, the most emancipating idea for a government is an understanding of the *economistic fallacy,* which says that beyond the poverty level in advanced economies, increased income is irrelevant. In concrete terms, Lane argued (1991, this volume), that governments can do more to promote SWB by relieving poverty, which has a demonstrable effect on SWB, than by promoting equality, which does not. Also, to promote work satisfaction and good family relations in advanced economies, governments can subsidize firms to give maternity and paternity leave for employees with new family responsibilities even at the cost of some loss of productivity.

Identity and Group Conflict

Empirical studies that fall under this heading can be found at both the national and the international level. Identity, as a more general term, has commonly been used to signify broad social categories based on such factors as ethnicity, culture, class, race, gender, or nationality, among others. The emphasis has been on identity formation in the form of collective identities, and the attempt has been to show (in various ways) how different categories of people come to share a sense of collective identity that can serve to explain collective action. Examples range from Marxist theory to political culture theories, to contemporary feminism, to Foucault's discourse theories, as well as to present-day rational choice theories. This approach, which is common in political science and macro-sociology, differs from the way identity is conceptualized in psychology and micro-sociology, where a more subjective version of some kind of unique self is put into focus (Lemert, 1994; Mennell, 1994). Here the construction of self is commonly viewed as a social process that most human beings pass through, and self-identity is predominantly seen as a universal human property. Central here are the writings of George Herbert Mead as developed through the tradition of symbolic interactionism and psychoanalytic theories of identification.

Psychological explanations of identity construction and identity conflicts have seen an upsurge in contemporary literature in combination with a renewed (albeit limited) focus on culture and learning. In a recent publication, Monroe et al. (1999) outlined a number of social psychological explanations to issues of prejudice, racism, genocide, and ethnic violence. Apart from social identity theory and self-categorization theory mentioned earlier, some of these include: psychodynamic approaches; works on symbolic racism; social dominance theory; and realist group conflict theory. Works taking a psychodynamic approach (Adorno, Frenkel-Brunswik, Levinson, & Sanford, 1950; Fromm, 1965; Cash, 1989) attribute discriminatory and racist behavior to the psychological structures of the unconscious. Ross's (1995) work on ethnic conflict, for instance, privileged object relations theory in favor of the older drive-based theories of psychodynamic functioning. Works on symbolic racism, in contrast, draws on attitudinal research to explain prejudice. Kinder and Sears (1981; see also Sears, 1988, 1993) argued, for example, that White racism against African-Americans is based on symbolic dispositions learned early in life. In comparison, social dominance theory views symbolic predispositions not as the cause but rather as the legitimizing myths that mediate more basic individual and group motivations into individual or institutional acts of discrimination (Sidanius, 1993). Another attempt to explain these phenomena can be found in realist (instrumentalist) group conflict theory, where identification with the in-group and prejudice against the out-group is based on group members' perceptions of group competition for resources (Sherif, 1966; Monroe et al., 1999). Empirical studies taking social identity theory and social categorization as their point of departure have, however, consistently shown that individuals will identify with the in-group, support group norms and, in a competitive social context, derogate outgroup members along stereotypical lines, even when there is no individual gain at stake (Gagnon & Bourhis, 1996; cf. Monroe et al., 1999).

Both social-psychological and psychoanalytical approaches offer means to understand the relationship between "self" and "other" as it affects intergroup conflict. At an international level, issues of self, other, and identity conflict have been studied by, among others, Volkan (1988, 1997) and Kristeva (1982, 1991). Volkan conducted a number of studies of group conflict in the post–Cold War world of former Yugoslavia, Cyprus, Latvia, Estonia, and elsewhere. As a psychological phenomenon, the essentialization of self and others within these processes has been explained by Volkan (1988), using object relations theory, as the externalization and projection of our unwanted elements onto enemies. He argued, for instance, that the closer the resemblance between self and other, the more likely the other is to become a suitable target for projection. However, by viewing the other as an object, he also implied that the enemy-other *already* exists and *is* different from the self, which comes close to an essentialist view of identity construction. Kristeva's treatment of these phenomena differs in that she sees the creation of self as an internal psychological process. The other, she says, can exist in individuals' minds even when they are not physically present, such as the Jews in Poland despite the fact that there are few Jews actually living there (Kristeva, 1982; Murer, 1999). This phenomenon is what Kristeva (1991) referred to as the "strangers within ourselves." The important point here is that the enemy-other is not only created by the self, but has previously been part of the self. It becomes the *abject* (Kristeva, 1982), which differs from Volkan's object. What causes abjection is that which disturbs identity, system, or order, such as traumatic changes. Abject becomes a major ingredient of collective identity formation when the familiar "stranger" is suddenly recognized as a threat.

Within this process, hate and dehumanization construct a link between the present, the future, and a recreated past and may serve as a social chain for successive generations as a particular event or trauma is mythologized and intertwined with a group's sense of self (Murer, 1999). This is what Volkan (1997) referred to as a "Chosen Trauma." A chosen trauma is often used to interpret new traumas. Thus it relies on previously experienced (real or imagined) rage and humiliation associated with victimization in the case of the Chosen Trauma, which is validated in a new context. A recent comparative study (Kinnvall, 2001) of the Hindu–Muslim conflict in northern India and the Sikh–Hindu conflict in Punjab seem to confirm such tendencies. Although a subjective perception of discrimination existed among the Sikhs of Punjab in the 1980s, there was no clear Chosen Trauma to rely on for generating and sustaining xenophobic hostility toward the Hindus. Partition could not, as has been the case for Hindu–Muslim antagonism, work as a source of reference (a Chosen Trauma) for the Sikhs of Punjab experiencing the traumatic effects of modernization and party polarization.

What Kristeva and Volkan show in their different interpretations is how feelings of "ancient hatred" are constructed and maintained. These are not, as today's mass media often make them out to be, primordial feelings of hatred or entrenched animosities waiting to break out in a largely chaotic world. Instead, as Volkan's and Kristeva's texts show, they are structural and psychological make-ups that manifest themselves in Chosen Traumas. By emphasizing the other as a mental image, an intra-psychic abject-other, onto which the self projects its (or the group's) unwanted (constructed) traits, we may escape the tendency to describe conflicts in essentialized terms. The emphasis on traumatic events, shared anxiety, regression, stressful conditions, and/or disturbances also brings attention to the emotional aspects of human relatedness. As such, it points to the need for ontological and existential security, which is an important topic for current and future research in political psychology.

IN CONCLUSION

In the edited volume of *Political Psychology* (1986), Margaret Hermann suggested five tenets of political psychology that had helped to define the field in the years that had elapsed since *Handbook of Political Psychology* was published in 1973. By using the same tenets 15 years later, we hope to continue

Hermann's discussion of how the field of political psychology has evolved to date.

Focus Is on the Interaction of Political and Psychological Phenomena

The bidirectional interaction of politics and psychology is still at the heart of political psychology. Perceptions, beliefs, motives, and values influence political behavior at the same time as cultural and structural factors have an impact on who we are. However, as noted in a number of contributions to this volume, works focusing on how the political system influences individual behavior remain a clear minority, and those examining interactions are even fewer (Dana Ward). And Stanley Renshon argues that there has been a gradual, but steady erosion of the connection between the field's early foundations and its subsequent development where the undertheorization of culture has been particularly evident. In a similar vein, Janice Gross Stein emphasizes how political psychologists have made a major contribution to the analyses of political socialization and mass attitude formation and change, whereas they have paid less attention to how individuals and groups learn from their historical and personal experience. These chapters show that a more even theoretical and empirical balance needs to be reached if we are to more fully understand the bidirectional interaction of political and psychological phenomena. This is particularly important in a world where individuals experience increasing demands and pressures from a rapidly changing environment. Martha Crenshaw's (this volume) argument that the development of cross-cultural psychology will be critical in a world of globalization and interdependence should thus be taken seriously.

Research Is Responsive and Relevant to Societal Problems

As Hermann (1986) noted, a number of people become interested in political psychology because they believe they can make a difference in response to issues they feel strongly about, such as the environment, inequality, violence and war, dissatisfaction with the government, populism and political leadership, etc. The "political" side of political psychology is very much manifest in this current volume and is perhaps especially evident among those interested in conflict, identity, and power politics. David Winter argues, for instance, that political psychology is uniquely poised to understand how power, sex, and violence are related and maintains that it is important to explore ways for people and societies to live "beyond" power and difference. Fred Alford's discussion of moral psychology and the need for more empirical research within the field also underlines how attachment and empathy towards "others" can have real political consequences. Kristen Monroe's call for a paradigm shift in which political action is understood in intersubjective terms, as a product of how we see ourselves in relation to others, is yet another reflection of how conflict and identity can be explained, understood, and (in the case of conflict) hopefully prevented.

In this, it is important to reemphasize the claim by Crenshaw, Bar-Tal, and Stein that political psychology is not only concerned with explaining group conflict and violence but also with conflict resolution and concrete policy prescriptions. An example of actual policy description is Robert Lane's suggestion that governments may benefit from policy changes which increase individuals' subjective well-being, such as expanded parental benefits. Thus it is clear that a number of researchers within this field remain political in their responses to current social and political problems and in relation to concrete policy prescriptions and solutions.

Context Can Make a Difference

This tenet is concerned with how a researcher defines time, situation, political system, and culture as such definitions have implications for both what he or she perceives is an important societal problem and how psychological and political phenomena are viewed as interacting (Hermann, 1986). The case studies previously described show how some empirical work is very context-specific where a specific problem is located at a given point in time, such as the analysis by Himmelweit et al. of the 1974 British election, whereas others work from a more general empirical perspective, such as Jervis' studies of signaling and images or Volkan's discussion of Chosen Traumas. That both are relevant for the field of political psychology as such becomes clear when reading Daniel Bar-Tal's (this volume) discussion of the particular versus the universal. The discovery of universal processes is important for explaining and predicting political behavior, whereas content-bound research aims to describe the political behavior of specific individuals or groups functioning in a specific time and place (Bar-Tal).

Emphasis Is on Process as Well as Outcome

Political psychologists continue to be interested in how political behavior evolves (process) as well as in the actual behavior itself (product). The extent to which decisions are affected by groupthink, how stereotypes and images of the other are created, the way voters decide, the fashion in which policy decisions affect social well-being, and the means by which we can better understand the construction of identity and group conflict, are all examples of how a particular outcome is related to process. David Sears' chapter (this volume) on long-term psychological consequences of political events provides a convincing example of how different processes may produce novel and more complex outcomes than are commonly assumed in much public opinion research. Comparative works of how political and psychological processes interrelate in various ways dependent on contexts are essential both for gaining particular understandings about a certain outcome and for increasing the possibility of generalizing across contexts. As argued by Hermann (1986), "Once delineated in one political setting, descriptions of processes offer the possibility of generalization to other political contexts with somewhat similar characteristics" (p. 3).

There Is a Tolerance of Multiple Methods for Gathering Data

As noted earlier, there is still little dogmatism in preferred method in political psychology. Instead, research design and methodology demonstrate a variety of established procedures taking their respective cues from a number of disciplines. The fact that political psychology at its outset was interdisciplinary in character has, of course, influenced the openness and tolerance for various methods. However, as noted in a number of chapters of this current volume, there has been a propensity to neglect previously important fields in political psychology, such as anthropology, microsociology, and cultural studies. To provide a more dynamic and complex picture of political action, it is important that this omission is rectified, that we balance the scales between the individual and society.

As this brief outline shows, Hermann's five tenets still remain important for understanding how the field of political psychology has developed and in which direction it may be heading. Here it is yet to be explored how the bidirectional study of politics and psychology can become more even. As argued earlier, human action can only be understood with reference to the meanings that the action has for the actors and for its audience as it is rooted in intersubjective contexts of communication and in intersubjective practices and forms of life that have distinctive historical origins. The call for a paradigm shift, for cross-cultural research, for multidisciplinary work and method, and for studies that take emotions and human relatedness seriously, can hopefully provide more insightful and satisfactory accounts of human action, thought, and understanding and may even lay the foundation for new political theory.

ACKNOWLEDGMENT

This chapter is a revised and updated version of a paper by Morton Deutsch, "What is political psychology?" which appeared in the *International Social*

Science Journal, XXXV #2, 1983, pp. 221–236. The revision was prepared by Catarina Kinnvall. Blackwell Publishers has granted permission for this usage.

REFERENCES

Abrams, D. (1994). Political distinctiveness—An identity optimizing approach. *European Journal of Social Psychology, 24,* 357–365.

Adorno, T., Frenkel-Brunswik, E., Levinson, D. J., & Sanford, R. N. (1950). *The authoritarian personality.* New York: Harper and Row.

Aldrich, J. H. (1995). *Why parties? The origin and transformation of party politics in America.* Chicago: University of Chicago Press.

Alford, F. (1994). *Group psychology and political theory.* New Haven, CT: Yale University Press.

Allen, M. W., & Ng, S. H. 2000. "Self interest, economic beliefs, and political party preference in New Zealand. *Political Psychology, 21,* 323–345.

Almond, G., & Verba, S. (1963). *The civic culture.* Newbury Park, CA: Sage Publications.

Altemeyer, B. (1996). *The authoritarian specter.* Boston: Harvard University Press.

Axelrod, R. M. (1997). *The complexity of cooperation.* Princeton, NJ: Princeton University Press.

Bauman, Z. (1973). *Culture as praxis.* London: Routledge.

Baumeister, R. F. (1986). *Identity: Cultural change and the struggle for self.* New York: Oxford University Press.

Barner-Barry, C., & Rosenwein, R. (1985). *Psychological perspectives on politics.* Englewood Cliffs, NJ: Prentice-Hall.

Bar-Tal, D., & Staub, E. (Eds.). (1997). *Patriotism: In the lives of individuals and nations.* New York: Burnham.

Bell, D. (1962). *The end of ideology.* New York: Collier.

Berger, P., & Luckmann, T. (1966). *The social construction of reality.* New York: Doubleday.

Bernstein, R. J. (1976). *The restructuring of social and political theory.* Philadelphia: University of Pennsylvania Press.

Bermeo, N. (1992). Democracy and the lessons of dictatorship. *Comparative Politics, 24,* 273–292.

Berelson, B., Lazarsfeld, P. F., & McPhee, W. P. (1954). *Voting: A study of opinion formation in a presidential campaign.* Chicago: University of Chicago Press.

Bock, P. K. (1988). *Rethinking psychological anthropology.* New York: Basic.

Bourdieu, P. (1977). *Outline of a theory of practice.* Cambridge: Cambridge University Press.

Bowles, S., & Gintis, H. (1976). *Schooling in capitalist America.* New York: Basic.

Brenner, M. (1973). *Mental illness and the economy.* Cambridge, MA: Harvard University Press.

Campbell, A., Converse, W., Miller, W., & Stokes, D. (1960). *The American voter.* New York: Wiley.

Carroll, S. J. (1989). Gender politics and the socializing impact of the women's movement. In R. Sigel (Ed.), *Political learning in adulthood* (pp. 306–339). Chicago: The University of Chicago Press.

Cash, J. (1989). Ideology and affect—The case of Northern Ireland. *Political Psychology, 10,* 703–724.

Cash, J. (1996). *Identity, ideology and conflict.* New York: Cambridge University Press.

Casson, R. W. (1981). *Language, culture, and cognition: Anthropological perspectives.* New York: Macmillan.

Chafetz, G., Abramson, H., & Grillon, S. (1996). Role theory and foreign policy: Belarussian and Ukrainian compliance with the nuclear nonproliferation regime. *Political Psychology, 17,* 727–758.

Clayton, S. D., & Crosby, F. (1992). *Justice, gender and affirmative action.* Ann Arbor: University of Michigan Press.

Converse, P. E. (1964). The nature of belief systems in mass publics. In D. E. Apter (Ed.), *Ideology and discontent* (pp. 206–261). New York: Free Press.

Crenshaw, M. (1986). The psychology of political terrorism. In M. Hermann (Ed.), *Political psychology* (pp. 247–260). San Francisco: Jossey-Bass.

Crenshaw, M. (1990). The logic of terrorism: Terorism as the product of strategic choice. In W. Reich (Ed.), *Origins of terrorism: Psychologies, ideologies, theologies, states of mind.* Cambridge: Cambridge University Press.

Davies, J. C. (1973). Where from and where to? In J. N. Knutson (Ed.), *Handbook of political psychology* (pp. 1–27). San Francisco: Jossey-Bass.

Dawson, R. E., Prewitt, K., & Dawson, K. S. (1977). *Political socialization* (2nd ed.). Boston: Little, Brown & Co.

Deutsch, M. (1973). *The resolution of conflict: Constructive and destructive processes.* New Haven, CT: Yale University Press.

Deutsch, M. (1983). Preventing World War III: A psychological perspective. *Political Psychology, 4,* 3–31.

Deutsch, M. (1985). *Distributive justice: A social-psychological perspective.* New Haven, CT: Yale University Press.

Deutsch, M., & Coleman, P. T. (Eds.). (2000). *The handbook of conflict resolution: Theory and practice.* San Francisco: Jossey-Bass.

Deutsch, M., Katz, L., & Jensen, A. R. (Eds.). (1968). *Social class, race, and psychological development.* New York: Holt, Rinehart & Winston.

Di Renzo, O. J. (1974). *Personality and politics.* Garden City, NY: Anchor Press.

Doob, L. W. (1948). *Public opinion and propaganda.* New York: Henry Holt.

Downs, A. (1957). *An economic theory of democracy.* New York: Harper-Row.

Druckman, D. (1994). Nationalism, patriotism, and group loyalty: A social psychological perspective. *Mershon International Studies Review, 38,* 43–68.

Duckitt, J. (1992). *The social psychology of prejudice.* New York: Praeger.

Elms, A. C. (1976). *Personality in politics.* New York: Harcourt, Brace Jovanovich.

Erikson, R. S. (1990). Economic conditions and the congressional vote: A review of the macrolevel evidence. *American Journal of Political Science, 34,* 373–399.

Etzioni, A. (1968). *The active society.* New York: Free Press.

Farnham, B. R. (1997). *Roosevelt and the Munich crisis: A study of political decision-making.* Princeton, NJ: Princeton University Press.

Flax, J. (1990). *Thinking fragments: Psychoanalysis, feminism & postmodernism in contemporary west.* Berkeley: University of California Press.

Fromm, E. (1965). *Escape from freedom.* New York: Avon.

Furnham, A. (1982). Why are the poor always with us? Explanations of poverty in Britain. *British Journal of Political Psychology, 24,* 19–27.

Gagnon, A., & Bourhis, R. Y. (1996). Discrimination in the minimal group paradigm—Social identity of self-interest. *Personality and Social Psychology Bulletin,* Vol. 22, No. 12, 1289–1301.

Gallie, D., Marsch, C., & Vogler, C. (Eds.). (1994). *Social change and the experience of unemployment.* Oxford: Oxford University Press.

George, A. (1969). The operational code: A neglected approach to the study of political leaders and decision-making. *International Studies Quarterly, 13,* 190–122.

George, A. (1980). *Presidential decision-making in foreign policy: The effective use of information and advice.* Boulder, CO: Westview Press.

George, A., & George, J. L. (1998). *Presidential personality & performance.* Boulder, CO: Westview Press.

Giddens, A. (1979). *Central problems in social theory: Action, structure, and contradiction in social analysis*. Berkeley: University of California Press.

Giddens, A. (1984). *The constitution of society*. Berkeley: University of California Press.

Giddens, A. (1990). *The consequences of modernity*. Stanford, CA: Stanford University Press.

Giddens, A. (1991). *Modernity and self-identity: Self and society in the late modern age*. Cambridge, UK: Polity Press.

Giddens, A., & Held, D. (1982). *Classes, power and conflict*. Berkeley, CA: University of California Press.

Greenstein, F. (2000). *The presidential difference: Leadership style from Roosevelt to Clinton*. New York: Free Press.

Gudykunst, W. B., & Ting-Toomey, S. (1988). *Culture and interpersonal communication*. Berkeley, CA: Sage.

Habermas, J. (1971). *Knowledge and human interests*. London: Heinemann.

Hayes, J., & Nutman, P. (1981). *Understanding the unemployed: The psychological effects of unemployment*. London: Tavestock.

Heaven, P. (1990). Suggestions for reducing unemployment: A study of Protestant work ethic and economic locus of control beliefs. *British Journal of Social Psychology, 29*, 55–65.

Held, D. (1980). *Introduction to critical theory: Horkheimer to Habermas*. Berkeley, CA: University of California Press.

Herek, G. M., Janis, I. L., & Huth, P. (1987). Decision making during international crises: Is quality of process related to outcome? *Journal of Conflict Resolution, 4*, 203–226.

Hermann, M. (1977). *A psychological examination of political leaders*. New York: Free Press.

Hermann, M. (1980). Explaining foreign policy behavior using personal characteristics of political leaders. *International Studies Quarterly, 24*, 7–46.

Hermann, M. (Ed.). (1986). *Political psychology*. San Francisco: Jossey-Bass Publishers.

Hermann, M. (1989, August). *Political psychology: Fad, fantasy or field*. Paper presented at the annual meeting of the American Psychological Association, New Orleans.

Hermann, M. (1993). Leaders and foreign policy decision making. In D. Caldwell & T. McKeown (Eds.), *Diplomacy, force, and leadership: Essays in honor of Alexander George*. Boulder, CO: Westview Press.

Himmelweit, H. T., Humphreys, P., Jaeger, M., & Katz, M. (1981). *How voters decide*. London: Academic Press.

Hogg, M., & Abrams, D. (1988). *Social identifications: A social psychology of intergroup relationships and group processes*. New York: Routledge.

Hopf, T. (1994). *Peripheral visions: Deterrence theory and American foreign policy in the Third World, 1965–1990*. Ann Arbor: University of Michigan Press.

Hudson, V., with Vore, C. S. (1995). Foreign policy analysis yesterday, today, and tomorrow. *Mershon International Studies Review, 39*, 209–238.

Hudson, V. (Ed.). (1997). *Culture and foreign policy*. Boulder, CO: Lynne-Rienner.

Humphreys, P. C. (1977). Applications of multiattribute utility theory. In H. Jungermann & G. de Zecuro (Eds.), *Decision-making and change in human affairs* (pp. 165–208). Amsterdam: Reidel.

Inglehart, R. (1990). *Cultural shift in advanced industrial society*. Princeton, NJ: Princeton University Press.

Inglehart, R. (1996). *Modernization and postmodernization: Cultural, economic and political change in 43 countries*. Princeton, NJ: Princeton University Press.

Iyengar, S., & McGuire, W. (1993). *Explorations in political psychology*. Durham, NC: Duke University Press.

Janis, I. L. (1972). *Groupthink*. Boston: Houghton Mifflin.

Janis, I. L. (1982). *Groupthink: Psychological studies of policy decisions and fiascos.* Boston: Houghton Mifflin.
Janis, I. L. (1983). Groupthink. In H. H. Blumberg, A. P. Hare, V. Kent, & M. Davies (Eds.), *Small group and social interaction* (Vol. 2). New York: John Wiley.
Janis, I. L., & Mann, L. (1977). *Decision making.* New York: The Free Press.
Jervis, R. (1976). *Perception and misperception in international politics.* Princeton, NJ: Princeton University Press.
Jervis, R. (1989). *The logic of images in international relations.* Princeton, NJ: Princeton University Press.
Jervis, R. (1997). *System effects: Complexity in political and social life.* Princeton, NJ: Princeton University Press.
Jervis, R., Lebow, N., & Stein, J. G. (1985). *Psychology and deterrence.* Baltimore, MD: Johns Hopkins University Press.
Jones, P., & Hudson, J. (1996). The quality of leadership: A case study of John Major. *British Journal of Political Science, 26,* 229–244.
Kaarbo, J., & Beasley, R. K. (1999). A practical guide to the comparative case study method in political psychology. *Political Psychology, 20,* 369–403.
Kinder, D. R., & Sears, D. O. (1981). Prejudice and politics: Symbolic racism versus racial threats to the good life. *Journal of Personality and Social Psychology, 40,* 414–431.
Kinnvall, C. (2001). *Globalization and the construction of identity: Democracy, diversity and nationhood in India.* London and New Delhi: Sage.
Knutson, J. (1973). *Handbook of political psychology.* San Francisco, CA: Jossey-Bass.
Kristeva, J. (1982). *Powers of horror: An essay of abjection.* New York: Columbia University Press.
Kristeva, J. (1991). *Strangers to ourselves.* New York: Columbia University Press.
Lane, R. E. (1978). Markets and the satisfaction of human wants. *Journal of Economic Issues, XII,* 799–827.
Lane, R. E. (1982). Government and self-esteem. *Political Theory, 10,* 5–31.
Lane, R. E. (1991). *The market experience.* New York: Cambridge University Press.
Lane, R. E. (2000). *Loss of happiness in market democracies.* New Haven, CT: Yale University Press.
Larson, D. (1985). *Origins of containment: A psychological explanation.* Princeton, NJ: Princeton University Press.
Larson, D. (1988). Problems of content analysis in foreign policy research: Notes from the study of the origin of cold war belief system. *International Studies Quarterly, 32,* 241–255.
Larson, D. (1997). Trust and missed opportunities in international relations. *Political Psychology, 18,* 701–734.
Lasswell, H. D. (1930). *Psychopathology and politics.* New York: Viking.
Lasswell, H. D. (1935). *World politics and personal insecurity.* New York: McGraw-Hill.
Lasswell, H. D. (1936). *Politics: Who gets what, when and how.* New York: Peter Smith.
Lasswell, H. D. (1948). *Power and personality.* Westport, CT: Greenwood.
Lau, R., & Sears, D. (1986). *Political cognition.* Hillsdale, NJ: Lawrence Erlbaum Associates.
Lazarsfeld, P. F., Berelson, B. R., & Gaudet, H. (1948). *The people's choice.* New York: Columbia University Press.
Lebow, N. (1981). *Between peace and war: The nature of international crises.* Baltimore, MD: Johns Hopkins University Press.
Lebow, N., & Stein, J. G. (1990). Deterrence: The elusive dependent variable. *World Politics, 42,* 336–339.
LeDoux, J. (1996). *The emotional brain: The mysterious underpinnings of emotional life.* New York: Simon & Schuster.
Lemert, C. (1994). Dark thoughts about the self. In C. Calhoun (Ed.), *Social theory and the politics of identity.* Oxford: Blackwell.

Le Prestre, P. (Ed.). (1997). *Role quests in the post-cold war era: Foreign policies in transition.* Montreal: McGill–Queen's University Press.

Le Vine, R. A. (Ed.). (1974). *Culture and personality: Contemporary readings.* Chicago, IL: Aldine.

Lewin, K., Lippitt, R., & White, R. K. (1939). Patterns of aggressive behavior in experimentally created "social climates." *Journal of Social Psychology, 10,* 271–99.

Levy, J. (1994). Learning and foreign policy: Sweeping a conceptual minefield. *International Organization, 48,* 279–312.

Mennell, S. (1994). The formation of we-images: A process theory. In C. Calhoun (Ed.), *Social theory and the politics of identity* (pp. 175–197). Oxford: Blackwell.

Mercer, J. (1995). Anarchy and identity. *International Organization, 49,* 229–252.

Merelman, R. (1986). Revitalizing political socialization. In M. Hermann (Ed.), *Political Psychology* (pp. 279–319). San Francisco: Jossey-Bass.

Merriam, C. E. (1925). *New aspects of politics.* Chicago, IL: University of Chicago Press.

Merriam, C. E. (1934). *Political power.* New York: Collier.

Merton, R. K. (1957). *Social theory and social structure* (Rev. ed.). Glencoe, IL: Free Press.

Milburn, M. A., & Conrad, S. D. (1996). *The politics of denial.* Cambridge, MA: MIT Press.

Miller, W. E., & Shanks, M. J. (1996). *The new American voter.* Cambridge, MA: Harvard University Press.

Monroe, K., Hankin, J., & Bukovchik VanVechten, R. (1999). *The psychological foundations of identity politics: A review of the literature.* Manuscript accepted for publication.

Moscovici, S., & Doise, W. (1994). *Conflict and consensus: A general theory of collective decisions.* London: Sage.

Murer, J. S. (1999). *New approach to understanding nationalism and ethnic conflict.* Paper presented at the 22nd annual conference of the ISPP, Amsterdam, the Netherlands.

Nagel, E. (1961). *The structure of science.* New York: Harcourt, Brace & World.

Nimmo, D. (1970). *The political persuaders.* Englewood Cliffs, NJ: Prentice-Hall.

Oakes, P., Haslam, A., & Turner, J. (1994). *Stereotyping and social reality.* Cambridge, MA: Blackwell.

Page, B. I., & Shapiro, Y. (1992). *The rational public: Fifty years of trends in Americans' policy preferences.* Chicago: University of Chicago Press.

Pancer, S. M., Brown, A. D., & Widdis Barr, C. (1999). Forming impressions of political leaders: A cross-national comparison. *Political Psychology, 20,* 345–368.

Petty, R., & Cacioppo, J. (1996). *Attitudes and persuasion: Classic and contemporary approaches.* Boulder, CO: Westview Press.

Poole, K. T., & Rosenthal, H. (1993). Spatial realignment and the mapping of issues in American history. In W. Riker (Ed.), *Agenda formation.* Ann Arbor: University of Michigan Press.

Pratkanis, A. R., & Aronson, E. (1991). *Age of propaganda: The everyday use and abuse of persuasion.* New York: W. H. Freeman & Co.

Purkitt, H. (1992). Political decision making in small groups: The Cuban missile crisis revisited—One more time. In E. Singer & V. M. Hudson (Eds.), *Political psychology and foreign policy* (pp. 219–245). Boulder, CO: Westview Press.

Putnam, R. (1988). Diplomacy and domestic politics: The logic of two-level games. *International Organization, 42,* 427–460.

Pye, L. (1986). Political psychology in Asia. In M. Hermann (Ed.), *Political psychology* (pp. 467–486). San Francisco: Jossey-Bass.

Rawls, J. (1971). *A theory of justice.* Cambridge, MA: Harvard University Press.

Reich, W. (Ed.). (1990). *Origins of terrorism: Psychologies, ideologies, theologies, states of mind.* Cambridge: Cambridge University Press.

Renshon, S. (1974). *Psychological needs and political behavior.* New York: Free Press.

Renshon, S. (1977). *Handbook of political socialization: Theory and research.* New York: Free Press.

Renshon, S. (1989). Psychological perspectives on theories of adult development and the political socialization of leaders. In R. Sigel (Ed.), *Political learning in adulthood* (pp. 235–270. Chicago: The University of Chicago Press.

Renshon, S., & Duckitt, J. (Eds.). (2000). *Political psychology: Cultural and cross-cultural foundations.* London: Macmillan.

Robins, R. S., & Post, J. M. (1997). *Political paranoia: The psychopolitics of hatred.* New Haven, CT: Yale University Press.

Ross, M. (1995). Psycho-cultural interpretation theory and peacemaking in ethnic conflict. *Political Psychology, 16,* 523–544.

Sainsbury, D. (1996). *Gender, equality and welfare states.* Cambridge: Cambridge University Press.

Scarr, S. (1981). *Race, social class and individual differences in I.Q.* Hillsdale, NJ: Lawrence Erlbaum Associates.

Sears, D. O. (1988). Symbolic racism. In P. A. Katz & D. A. Taylor, (Eds.), *Eliminating racism: Profiles in controversy.* New York: Plenum.

Sears, D. O. (1993). Symbolic politics. In A. Iyengar & W. J. McGuire (Eds.), *Explorations in political psychology.* Durham, NC: Duke University Press.

Sears, D. O., & Funk, C. L. (1991). The role of self-interest in social and political attitudes. *Advances in Experimental Political Psychology, 24,* 1–91.

Sears, D. O., & Funk, C. L. (1999). Evidence of the long-term persistence of adults' political predispositions. In press, *Journal of Politics.*

Semmel, A. K. (1982). Small group dynamics in foreign policy-making. In G. W. Hopple (Ed.), *Biopolitics, political psychology and international politics* (pp. 94–113). New York: St. Martin's Press.

Sherif, M. (1966). *In common predicament: Social psychology of intergroup conflict and cooperation.* Boston: Houghton Mifflin.

Sidanius, J. (1993). The psychology of group conflict and the dynamics of oppression: A social dominance perspective. In S. Iyengar & W. J. McGuire (Eds.), *Explorations in political psychology* (pp. 183–219). Durham, NC: Duke University Press.

Sigel, R. (Ed.). (1989). *Political learning in adulthood.* Chicago: The University of Chicago Press.

Sniderman, P. M., Brody, R. A., & Tetlock, P. (Eds.). (1993). *Reasoning and choice: Explorations in political psychology.* New York: Cambridge University Press.

Sniderman, P. (2000). Taking sides: A fixed choice theory of political reasoning. In A. Lupia, M. McCubbins, & S. Popkins (Eds.), *Elements of political reason: Understanding and expanding the limits of rationality.* New York: Cambridge University Press.

Snyder, G. H., & Diesing, P. (1977). *Conflict among nations.* Princeton, NJ: Princeton University Press.

Sowell, T. (1994). *Race and culture.* New York: Basic Books.

Staub, E. (1989). *The roots of evil: The origins of genocide and other group violence.* Cambridge: Cambridge University Press.

Stein, J. G. (1989). *Getting to the table: The processes of international prenegotiation.* Baltimore, MD: Johns Hopkins University Press.

Stein, J. G. (1994). Political learning by doing: Gorbachev as an uncommitted thinker and motivated learner. *International Organization, 48,* 155–83.

Stewart, M. C., & Clarke, H. D. (1992). The (un)importance of party leaders: Leader images and party choice in the 1987 British election. *Journal of Politics, 54,* 447–470.

Stone, W., & Schaffner, P. (1988). *The psychology of politics.* New York: Springer-Verlag.

Tajfel, H. (1982). *Social identity and intergroup relations.* New York: Cambridge University Press.

Taylor, P. M. (1998). *War and the media: Propaganda and persuasion in the Gulf War.* Manchester: Manchester University Press.

Tetlock, P. E. (1979). Identifying victims of groupthink from public statements of decision-makers. *Journal of Personality and Social Psychology, 37,* 1314–1324.

Tetlock, P. E. (1983). Psychological research on foreign policy: A methodological review. *Review of Personality and Social Psychology, 4,* 45–78.

t'Hart, P. (1990). *Groupthink in government.* Amsterdam: Swetz & Zeitlinger.

Unger, R. K. (1979). *Female and male: Psychological perspectives.* New York: Harper & Row.

Venable, V. (1945). *Human nature: The Marxian view.* New York: Alfred A. Knopf.

Volkan, V. D. (1988). *The need to have enemies and allies: From clinical practice to international relationships.* Northvale, NJ: Jason Aronson.

Volkan, V. D. (1997). *Bloodlines: From ethnic pride to ethnic terrorism.* Boulder, CO: Westview Press.

Volkan, V. D., Itzkowitz, N., & Dod, A. W. (1997). *Richard Nixon: A psychobiography.* New York: Columbia University Press.

Von Winterfeld, D., & Fischer, G. W. (1975). Multiattribute utility theory: Models and assessment procedures. In D. Wendt & C. Bieck (Eds.), *Utility, probability and human decision-making.* Amsterdam: Reidel.

Voss, J., & Dorsey, E. (1992). Perception and international relations: An overview. In E. Singer & V. Hudson (Eds.), *Political psychology and foreign policy* (pp. 3–30). Boulder, CO: Westview Press.

Walter, B., & Snyder, J. (Eds.). (1999). *Civil wars, insecurity, and intervention.* New York: Columbia University Press.

Weber, M. (1930). *The Protestant ethic and the spirit of capitalism.* New York: Scribner.

Veenhoven, R. (1993). *Happiness in nations.* Erasmus University, Center for Socio-Cultural Transformation, RISBO Rotterdam, 50.

Wendt, A. (1992). Anarchy is what states make of it: The social construction of power politics. *International Organization, 42,* 391–425.

Wendt, A. (1994). Collective identity formation and the international state. *American Political Science Review, 88,* 384–398.

Whelan, C. T., Hannan, D., & Creighton, S. (1991). *Unemployment, poverty and psychological distress.* Washington DC: Economic & Social Research Institute.

Wilkening, K. E. (1999). Culture and Japanese citizen influence on the transboundary air pollution issue in Northeast Asia. *Political Psychology, 20,* 701–724.

Wilson, M. (1998). *Social psychology and political interaction in pre/post MMP New Zealand.* Unpublished doctoral thesis, School of Psychology, Victoria University of Wellington.

Woshinsky, O. H. (1994). *Culture and politics: An introduction to mass and elite political behavior.* New York: Prentice-Hall.

2

Political Psychology as a Perspective in the Study of Politics

MARGARET G. HERMANN
Maxwell School, Syracuse University

In the past two decades, political psychology has become of increasing interest to scholars engaged in the study of politics. As a result, we now have an International Society of Political Psychology, a section in the American Political Science Association devoted to political psychology, and numerous smaller formal and informal organizations both within the United States and abroad that bring scholars together to talk about how political and psychological phenomena interrelate. The journal *Political Psychology* is now recognized as an important outlet for research and leading American and European journals in political science across the spectrum of specializations contain a growing number of articles using a political psychological perspective. Indeed, there are currently numerous articles in mainstream psychology journals that focus on political issues. And, each year new political psychology courses are added at the undergraduate and graduate levels in colleges and universities around the United States and elsewhere in the world.

However, because political psychology draws researchers and practitioners from a variety of disciplines and covers topics ranging, for example, from voting behavior to ethnic conflict to norm creation to leaders' decisions to use force, it has been difficult to arrive at a consensus about the nature of the field and how to train its future professionals. Those in leadership positions have preferred to "let 100 flowers bloom" rather than to seek closure too quickly, although recent meetings of both international and domestic political psychology associations have included sessions focused on defining the field and exploring issues related to what should be involved in educating a political psychologist. The purpose of this chapter is to synthesize the ideas that have been presented in these discussions across the last decade and to propose a set of tenets around which there is growing agreement.

FAD, FANTASY, OR FIELD?

A little over a decade ago, this author made a presentation at the American Psychological Association (Hermann, 1989) raising the question of whether political psychology was a fad, fantasy, or field. An examination of the literature in political psychology at that time indicated the presence of all three.

As Fad

There was an inherent interest in current problems—in what might be deemed *fads*. As Sears (1989) observed, the topics in political psychology tended to reflect the headlines. In fact, those interested in political psychology were often drawn into this arena because they were responding to current problems that had become politicized. There was a sense of urgency about these problems—something needed to be done to avoid disaster. Among such concerns were AIDS, terrorism, ethnic conflict, race relations, the decline in social capital, and the faultlines of democracy. All are issues that "crucially affect the quality and the quantity of human life today" (Knutson, 1973, p. vii), and their solutions seem open to insights about the relationship between people and politics.

As a consequence of this focus on societal problems, there has been a temporal and applied quality to political psychology. Thus, topics have come and gone as the salience of issues, institutions, and peoples has changed; handbooks and textbooks written 5 to 10 years apart bear little relationship to one another. There has also been a tension between wanting to make a difference and maintaining an analytic perspective. Some scholars and practitioners (e.g., Fisher & Ury, 1981; Kelman, 1979b; Quandt, 1988; Saunders, 1987; Volkan, 1985) have become committed and energized to have an impact on what is happening and have chosen to engage in interventions, share knowledge with policymakers and the public, or become participant observers in the process; others (e.g., special symposium in *Political Psychology,* see Tetlock, 1994) have raised questions regarding the nature of the ethical imperatives and social responsibilities that should guide political psychology.

As Fantasy

Because those engaged in political psychology have come from a variety of disciplines (e.g., anthropology, communications, history, political science, psychiatry, psychology, and sociology), they examine how political and psychological phenomena interrelate in different ways. In a similar fashion to Martin Luther King, Jr., scholars who call themselves political psychologists have a dream. That dream assumes that by sharing points of view, expertise, and methodologies around important topics of concern across disciplines, we can arrive at a more comprehensive understanding of a problem. At issue is whether or not this dream is merely a fantasy or can be transformed into reality.

Being multidisciplinary has forced political psychologists to deal with a set of roadblocks that surround the interaction of diverse scholars from across the disciplinary spectrum. For one thing, there is the need to create a common language and set of definitions as well as shared knowledge about the concepts from each discipline that are relevant to understanding the issue of concern. A major hurdle to arriving at such a shared core of knowledge is the willingness of those involved to generalize across situations, individuals, groups, and institutions, or, put conversely, the demand for contextualization. Anthropologists, historians, political scientists, and those in communications caution about the importance of the context to understanding political phenomena, whereas psychologists, psychiatrists, and sociologists are interested in more law-like generalizations. In fact, both of these approaches can contribute to the examination of people and politics, but cooperation among those with each approach demands a degree of tolerance that is often difficult to achieve.

Another obstacle to cross-disciplinary collaboration centers around what methods are deemed "best" for the study of a particular problem and what is considered data. Scholars who are used to collecting quantitative data and employing the experimental method have difficulty tolerating those whose data are qualitative and not representative of any particular population, and those who are committed to intensive case analysis wonder if the scholars with so-called hard data are living in the real world or a world of their own creation. Both these roadblocks raise problems for the training of future political psychologists. What should be included in the curriculum?

As Field

Such a question thrusts us into consideration of whether or not political psychology is a field. Political psychology certainly has the accouterments of a field, as we observed in the beginning of this chapter—professional organizations, journals, handbooks, undergraduate and graduate courses

—but there seems to be little consensus regarding its subject matter. For some, the focus of attention is on understanding mass politics: how people's political views are developed and maintained and the effect of such views on political behavior. For others, concern is centered around elites and how public policy is made as well as who has the authority to make public policy and with what effects. For still others, interest revolves around intergroup conflict and how such conflicts can be managed and resolved. And so on and so forth. Many psychologists, for example, see politics as merely a domain in which to apply their theories and concepts just like they do in the arenas of health, law, education, industry, and consumer products. Political scientists perceive psychology as a good place from which to borrow ideas about people to explore their relevance to politics. Neither views political psychology as a field nor would they claim to be practicing political psychology; they are merely borrowing a context or orientation, not engaging in building a field.

A PERSPECTIVE?

Across the past decade, the writer has come to believe that there is merit in the critics' contentions. Political psychology may be more appropriately considered an approach or perspective on politics than either a fad, fantasy, or field. Like several alternative perspectives—political economy and political culture, to name two—political psychology is a way of understanding politics no matter the issue, topic, or problem under consideration. As a perspective, political psychology is built on a set of assumptions that serve as consensual premises and scope conditions, indicating the important concepts and ideas that must be covered in any curriculum or training intended to help students and scholars discover political psychology. In effect, political psychology is a way of describing the role that people play in politics and, as such, represents one construction of political reality. Consider the following propositions.

Individuals Matter in Politics

Political psychologists focus on the individual person as the unit of analysis —not the group, not the institution, not the government, not the international system. Of critical importance is how individuals (voters, protesters, opinion makers, leaders) interpret, define, and represent their political environments. The assumption is made that people play an active role in constructing their views of politics; their experiences may lead them to challenge as well as to respect the constraints that the other potential levels of analysis impose on them. They are not merely responsive to their political environments nor are they passive receptacles easily shaped by the milieu in which they are located. In effect, it is individuals who engage in politics—in voting; in exhibiting discrimination; in bargaining and negotiation; in resolving disagreements; in engaging in trade-offs and log-rolls; in mobilizing others to espouse their ideology; in proposing and authoring constitutions, laws, and treatises; and in dying for a cause. Moreover, it is individuals who seek to give structure to unstructured events and an interpretation to ambiguous and uncertain situations. Although reference groups, institutions, and political systems may influence the kinds of experiences individuals can have, unless all reinforce one another in lockstep, people are presented with some choice.

True, in much of politics, people are embedded in groups, institutions, cultures, and governments, and it is the decisions of these entities that we seek to understand. However, it is individuals who identify and frame the problems that face such entities, who have disagreements and jockey for position, who generate compromises and build consensus, and who originate and implement change. Leaders are chosen by individuals either through election, selection, or the use of coercion; ideologies and causes are delineated and promulgated by individuals; ideas and norms become shared through the efforts of individuals. Consider what we have discovered about the effects on the risk-taking behavior of political entities when the persons involved in identifying the problem interpret the situation as involving a political loss as opposed to a political gain (e.g., Kahneman & Tversky, 1979; Levy, 1992; Stein, 1992). Or what might have happened differently in the history of the Cold War if those men who were members of the Ex Com during the Cuban Missile Crisis had decided that the Soviet missiles were defensive rather than offensive (e.g., May & Zelikow, 1997; Sylvan & Thorson, 1992) or had resolved the disagreement in the State Department immediately after World War II by believing that future Soviet behavior would be defensive rather than aggressive (for a discussion of this debate, see Weldes, 1998)? Or, observe how the differences in leadership style between two autocratic leaders in the Middle East—Saddam Hussein and Hafez al-Assad—led one to precipitate interstate war when he attacked and occupied Iraq and the other to elicit almost no response when at the same point in time he facilitated his country's consolidation of power over Lebanon (e.g., Hermann, 1988, 1999). Moreover, consider the various social constructions of reality that often clash in the political arena; indeed, the media classify such individuals into groups and give them names such as the "greens," "soccer moms," "angry White males," the "religious right," "new Democrats," etc.

In describing the relevance of human nature to politics, Simon (1985) argued that to understand how individuals are going to act politically the analyst must take into account what they want, how they process information, the ways in which they represent various aspects of their world, what they pay attention to, and their beliefs—in other words, what he said "bounded" their rationality. To decipher a person's goals in a particular situation demands information about the individual's motives, beliefs, and capacities as a decision maker. How people define what is in their self-interest, what is salient to them, what they feel compelled to act on can differ depending on the lenses through which they view the world. In Abelson's (1986) terms, these lenses become their "possessions" and descriptive of who they are politically and what they value. The political analyst can make a mistake by assuming that individuals experiencing the same political event have similar goals and will choose similar responses without information suggesting that their definitions of the situation and beliefs are somewhat equivalent. Thus, the conservative voter may select one candidate in a presidential primary on the basis of information that would lead a more moderate voter to choose the other candidate. Often leaders in one government believe the leadership of another country is pursuing the same goals as they are in a specific situation, without considering that the other set of leaders may have different beliefs and practices and be facing a different domestic political scene. There are many instances in the recent discussions among American and Vietnamese policymakers involved in decision making during the Vietnam War that evidence the consequences of this lack of understanding—what the American policymakers perceived were behaviors that would push the Vietnamese to surrender were interpreted by the Vietnamese leadership as ammunition to increase the nationalism of the population and the resolution to stay the course (see McNamara, Blight, & Brigham, 1999).

Determining Preference Orderings Facilitates Understanding Political Behavior

If political rationality is bounded, determining how individuals develop their preferences and the manner in which they order such preferences becomes relevant to understanding what will motivate action and frame interpretation as well as choice. The political psychology perspective can be viewed as complementing that of political economy. Instead of assuming certain preference orderings and making preference formation exogenous to modeling political behavior, however, as the political economy perspective does, the political psychology perspective has as a major focus ascertaining where preferences come from and the ways in which individuals resolve the conflicts among values that determine preference orderings. What political psychologists seek to understand becomes the input for the behavior political economists wish to model.

A large portion of the literature described under the heading *political psychology* focuses on the issue of preference formation. From studies of identity formation to research on framing to examinations of generational experiences, interest centers around how preferences are shaped in the mass public, among opinion makers, and within the leadership. Concern has also been targeted on the issue of how preferences can be modified or changed, for example, in protracted social conflicts or in multicultural settings. Three decades ago, this research bore the label *political socialization*. Today such studies can be found in the literatures on voting, the mass media, social movements, terrorism, nationalism, transnational politics, and discussions of the development and sustainability of norms. The research centers around particular types of preferences and political entities; it has become contextualized.

At issue is understanding whose preferences, aspirations, and prejudices are necessary to understanding the workings of a specific political system. In other words, we are interested in ascertaining whose positions count and, thus, whose preferences need to be taken into account. Whose preferences are representative of a particular political constituency or who is involved in making a particular decision or framing an issue? By answering this question, we limit the number of individuals on whom we need to gather information while still collecting data on what their preferences are. Campaign consultants regularly engage in this process as they define the various types of constituencies that comprise the political arena for a particular candidate. These constituencies are surveyed to ascertain what is important to them and their views on the candidate. The candidate then weighs this evidence in choosing issues and framing any program to be proposed. Policy analysts perform similar functions in determining whom in a leadership to consider and follow. Is there one person who appears in control or is it a group, a coalition? Frameworks have been developed to aid in identifying whose positions count in such policy analysis (for reviews, see Hermann & Hagan, 1998; Hermann & Hermann, 1989; Stern & Verbeek, 1998). Those in comparative politics who are studying democratic transitions and European integration (e.g., Aguero, 1998; Nagle, 1999; Slomcyznski & Shabad, 1998) are also involved in ascertaining whose preferences must be taken into account in understanding what will happen next. There are debates in this literature on just who and how many of the constituencies in a polity need to be included in such considerations. Some argue we need information on the constituency that is most dominant at the particular point in time; others propose that we need to compare and contrast the political preferences of the different generations represented in the society to know what preferences to use; and still others suggest focusing on what the agents of socialization are promulgating currently to understand the views that will soon be in evidence.

Regardless of the debates and different approaches taken, this research and these practices indicate that whose preferences are assessed has implications for what views are considered representative of a particular political entity. Based on one's research question, careful thought needs to be given to who constitutes the political entity under study and their internal dynamics in deciding where to focus attention. It may be misleading to assume a mass public, institution, bureaucracy, government, international regime, or nongovernmental organization has a specified set of preferences without taking into account whose positions count in setting policy within these settings and the nature of their preferences.

Political Process Matters

Those engaged in political psychology are as interested in understanding how a particular political behavior came about as in the behavior itself; that is, they are intent on studying political process as well as the political output and outcome. In other words, political psychology as a perspective involves the examination of politics as process. How do members of the electorate decide for whom to cast their vote and, indeed, whether or not to vote? How can political conflict be avoided, managed, and resolved? What are the influences on the ways in which policymakers process information? How do leaders mobilize followers? How do young people become politically socialized? How do political ideas become shared and evolve into norms or social constructions of reality? Answers to these questions focus on what is happening in the political process. There is an assumption here that the political process, in turn, helps to shape what happens politically— the total vote, the negotiated agreement or lack thereof, the options considered, whether a leader is effective in exercising leadership, the distribution of political views among those 18 to 35, and the nature of the norm or socially constructed reality. In effect, political psychology is focused on understanding what goes on among those involved in politics—on just how the interactions among people affect what happens politically.

As a result of the focus on process, scholars and practitioners with this perspective are interested in exploring a number of political processes such as consensus building, log-rolling, value trade-offs, bargaining and negotiation, coalition formation, the effects of different decision rules, how compromises are achieved, and the nature of framing. In so doing, they become interested in the rules by which preferences are aggregated in constituencies, groups, organizations, institutions, and governments. If we know whose positions count, what are the processes by which their preferences become conjoined in determining an output? An important reason leading many to focus attention on what institutions, bureaucracies, and governments do as a unit instead of the individuals who comprise these entities is the difficulty involved in determining how the preferences of such people become aggregated into a single output. In some cases there are rules: a majority vote, a two-thirds vote, a unit veto. However, much of politics occurs prior to or as a consequence of the implementation of these formal procedures. Is status in the group the determining factor? What about expertise, a prevailing value, a consistent position, loyalty, offering a different perspective, sharing a particular interest, coercive resources? To illustrate this discussion, consider the literature that suggests that political groups where the loyalty of members is to that group engage in different processes than do political groups where members' loyalty is to organizations and institutions outside the group. The former is ripe for "groupthink," the latter for "bureaucratic politics." As a result, the former often evidence extreme and risky behaviors; the latter compromise or deadlock. (For reviews of this literature, see Hermann, 1993; 't Hart, Stern, & Sundelius, 1997; Stern & Verbeek, 1998.) Where one's loyalty lies becomes relevant to explaining how the group members' preferences are going to be aggregated. What it is about loyalty that helps to set these two processes in motion becomes an interesting subject for political psychological study.

Consider also the critical experiences that can happen to different parts of a population that help to shape the way they view politics and the nature of their political participation. Research has suggested that those young Americans who fought in the Vietnam War and those who protested against this war developed political views on a number of issues that are polar opposites and that have stayed with them through their adulthood. These differences in views were not found in the two groups before the Vietnam War experiences, nor were they reflected in parents' positions (see Jennings, 1987). Moreover, observe how the media deal with issues around which political leaders have achieved some consensus and those over which there is disagreement and conflict. The American media are much more likely to report on the instances of disagreement than those where there is concurrence; these cases are viewed as more newsworthy and as relevant for the public to become involved. And political leaders are interested in framing the issue to gain support and facilitate their positions prevailing. (For a review of relevant literature, see Powlick & Katz, 1998.) One can wonder how much influence emphasizing only policymakers' dissensus has on the American public's view of the polarization within government and their distrust of politicians; the picture being broadcast is distorted and the people are not necessarily aware of the nature of the bias.

Emotion and Motivation Are as Relevant as Cognition to Understanding Politics

Among the victims of the rush to embrace the so-called "cognitive revolution" have been the contributions that emotion (affect) and motivation can make to an understanding of politics, particularly when individuals are the center of attention. Ideas, beliefs, stereotypes, heuristics, schemas, images, cognitive maps, constructions of reality, methods for processing information, rationality have taken center stage and influenced the way scholars have studied the relevance of people to politics. Feelings, passions, needs, drives have been neglected even though they have been found to turn ideas, beliefs, and schemas into ideologies and crusades, stereotypes into prejudice and discrimination, heuristics into biases, constructions of reality into objects of persecution, and rationality to irrationality. Emotion and motivation can make a heretofore ignored topic highly salient, lead apparently rational individuals to dehumanize others, generate mob rule, keep people isolated and apart, and lead to misunderstandings and misrepresentations. Inasmuch as the emphasis here is on the negative, a better metaphor might be that emotion and motivation transform cold cognition (analytical reasons) into hot cognition (passions) because these two can have positive effects, too. Leaders can become Pied Pipers of Hamelin, infecting people with their cause, movement, or charisma; individuals can choose to engage in nonviolent activities; persons can help others even at risk of their own lives; and people can become mobilized to vote or to participate in order to see that something happens.

In the last decade there has been a growing interest in putting emotion and motivation back into politics—in understanding how they may influence or interact with cognition in shaping what people do politically. Thus, we have learned that people become a lot more involved politically around issues that are particularly salient to them; the more important the topic or problem to them, the more actively they will search for information on the issue and join others in organizations dedicated to the topic—they participate in politics around that concern (see, e.g., Krosnick, 1990; Marcus & MacKuen, 1993). We also have discovered that voters process information on candidates in an election "on-line," remembering how they feel about the candidates rather than the information on which the feeling is based (Lodge, Steenbergen, & Brau, 1995). Moreover, we know that elites (opinion makers, legislators, political appointees, and politicians) under stress can become more rigid and inflexible in their views, quickly and easily believe that the so-called adversary is in charge and is "pulling the strings," narrow the options under consideration, and focus only on the present (see, e.g., Heifetz, 1994; Hermann & Hermann, 1990). Furthermore, we have learned how easy it is to generate "ingroup bias." Individuals will favor their own group even if they have not met any of its members and the group is formed around something as apparently absurd as the placement of dots on a page. Consider how much more intense such ingroup bias might be were the individual to have had to go through an initiation rite to belong to the group and be highly motivated and committed to its cause (for reviews of this literature, see Brewer, 1991; Brewer & Kramer, 1985).

More attention to date in political psychology has been paid to how to reduce the effects of emotion and motivation on political behavior than in demonstrating how they influence politics. Acknowledging how important these two factors are to prolonging protracted social conflicts, scholars like Kelman (1979b), Saunders (2000), and Volkan (1985), to name but a few, have developed mediation techniques to work on helping those engaged in such conflicts recategorize their enemies or, at the least, become aware of the fact that there are members among the enemy with whom they may share more in common than they do with members of their own group. Called *track two diplomacy*, these techniques use contact, discussion, debate, and argument as ways of breaking down emotional barriers. Participants have ranged from citizens to midlevel members of governments to leaders and have been drawn from such conflicts as those in Northern Ireland, the Middle East, and Cyprus. As a member of one of these workshops observed, tears streaming down his face, "I had never met one of them before and did not know how they felt or what they perceived we had done to them—are we really that bad?" It is important to note that the persons who are willing to participate in the track two interactions are those with more moderate attitudes and not those who are hardliners and committed to the cause. Thus, a long-term investment is needed to change cognition in such groups. Indeed, some research suggests that only by being brought up in a diverse ethnic/religious/cultural setting can one avoid such biases and prejudices (e.g., see Pettigrew, 1998). Such an observation indicates how important studying emotion and motivation are if we are to understand some of the critical political issues of our time.

Context Can Make a Difference

Lane (1983) observed that political psychology is the study of the person in a particular time and situation. One could add to this as well "in a particular political system and culture." How researchers define time, situation, political system, and culture has implications for what is perceived as a political problem as well as the relevance of individuals as an object of study. As Kelman (1979a) cautioned, "If we define the problem as the psychological problem of a certain group of people, we [are] more likely to develop policies that involve changing these people, rather than policies that involve changing the structures that help to sustain their powerlessness" (p. 102). Political psychology offers a contingent or conditional approach to the study of politics. There is a recognition that contextual factors help to determine the influence that individuals can have politically. Thus people appear to be constrained differently in turbulent times than in stable times, in ambiguous situations as opposed to well-defined situations, in autocratic regimes versus democratic regimes, and in cultures that are more interdependent than those where independence is fostered. In studying political leaders, for instance, the writer (Hermann, 1986; Hermann & Hagan, 1998; Hermann & Kegley, 1995) has found that what heads of government are like has a greater effect on their country's foreign policy behavior in more authoritarian regimes, in crisis situations, when their advisory structures are formal and hierarchical, following a dramatic success, and in cultures that value strong and forceful leadership.

Given that scholars and practitioners espousing political psychology as a perspective come from a variety of disciplinary backgrounds, there is often a debate, as we noted earlier, between those who search for law-like generalizations that cut across time, situation, political system, and culture and those who work within a specific context. There is a natural tension regarding the uniqueness of any context. Much like the adage "We are at the same time like no other person, like some other people, and like all other people," historians, anthropologists, and political scientists caution about the context-specific nature of their research in political psychology whereas psychologists, psychiatrists, and sociologists seek the more general. As Greenstein (1973) observed about discussions of the American presidency, political scientists tend to focus on "aspects of the political psychology of presidents that are presidency-specific," whereas psychologists are more likely "to deal with the psychology of leadership as a general phenomenon" (p. 457).

Such dialogue enables us to explore how various contexts amplify or diminish the effects that are expected from our more general theories of behavior. Indeed, these considerations facilitate the development of theoretical frameworks that include both some law-like generalizations and how those generalizations may need to be modified under certain circumstances. Examples of such undertakings are found in a volume focused on elaborating the concept of problem representation (Sylvan & Voss, 1999) and the bank of cases amassed as part of the Crisis Management Europe research program (Stern, 1999; Sundelius, Stern, & Bynander, 1997). In the former, psychologists and political scientists wrestled with delineating the relevance of how the problem is defined and represented to the nature of the decision-making process, tempering their overarching framework as they explored the concept in a variety of different political settings around the world. In the latter, political scientists and practitioners applied a framework derived from the more general crisis management literature to explore how individuals handle crises around Europe and in a variety of types of situations ranging from floods to taking hostages to events like Chernobyl, contextualizing the theory as the number of cases builds. As Thomas Ostrom, a social psychologist, noted to the author (personal communication, July 11, 1990), by being urged by colleagues with a political psychology perspective to explore if context mattered in his theory of person perception, he had discovered a number of important factors that he had not considered relevant previously, and he had learned under what conditions they became important as well as why he had missed them.

The Use of Multiple Methods Is Encouraged

An examination of the research reported in *Political Psychology* and attendance at annual meetings of the International Society of Political Psychology lend credence to the perception that political psychology as a perspective is not wedded to any one type of methodology. The reader and observer find researchers using experiments, surveys, focused groups, elite interviews, content analysis, ethnography, historical narratives, discourse analysis, and case studies, to name a few. Among the younger scholars with a political psychology perspective, it is no longer novel to see a psychologist exploring political phenomena combining an experiment with an interview or survey study in the field, or a political scientist doing an archival content analysis study complemented by an experiment. There is an assumption that by adopting a political psychology approach, one both has an understanding, however rudimentary, of an array of potential tools for studying individuals and is tolerant of those using these different methodologies.

Instead of pressure to adopt and use one technique or tool, there is encouragement to consider multiple strategies because of the variety of information that is thus garnered about a topic. Much as the clinician or physician does in arriving at a diagnosis, the scholar engaged in political psychology is interested in examining a wealth of different kinds of data—in being presented with both quantitative and qualitative data as well as subjective reactions and the historical record in determining what is happening in the political arena. There is an interest in the triangulation of methods and data. Consider how much more we learn about a particular constituency's political views by not only doing a phone survey, but by also intensively interviewing a random sample or by putting such a group into a simulated or experimental environment like that involved in the deliberative polling technique. We gain a sense of not only how they would respond to a standard set of political questions, but also how they interpret the queries being asked and if their views can be changed with more or different types of information.

Where arguments arise, they occur over the criteria for assessing how well the information gleaned from the various techniques matches or overlaps as well as over issues related to internal and external validity. There is an increasing trend among those adopting a political psychology perspective to choose as subjects of study individuals that are representative of the population that is the target of the research. For instance, instead of bringing college sophomores into the laboratory for an experiment focused on the effects of television frames on political views, an attempt is made to involve a sample of the voting public that ranges in age. Moreover, researchers are being more innovative in recognizing natural experiments occurring in the public policy arena that they can use to gain more control over the factors of interest to them. Indeed, a number of scholars have proposed that case studies can be made more experiment-like by engaging in what is called "structured, focused comparison" (see, e.g., George, 1979; Kaarbo & Beasley, 1999). In a similar manner, those generally predisposed to experiments or the use of survey and aggregate data have begun to let more of the response material be open-ended and to do case studies of outliers or what might be considered critical cases. On all sides, there appears to be a movement toward arriving at a set of standards to guide research and an interest in building equivalences across techniques.

Political Psychology Is Intentionally Multidisciplinary

Perhaps not unexpectedly, the largest number of scholars who have adopted political psychology as a point of view are political scientists. That having been said, the perspective has benefitted greatly from the scholars and practitioners from other disciplines that are engaged in exploring the role of people in politics. Psychologists from a variety of areas within that discipline—for example, social, personality, industrial/organizational, decision theory—have become interested in how individuals shape and are shaped by the political context. Some have been hired into political science departments to ensure that students are taught this perspective by those with training in the concepts, theories, and methods of the psychologist. Sociologists who take this point of view ask why individuals become part of political groups and organizations, seek to understand the bases of intergroup conflict, and study individuals as agents of institutional change. Historians examine how people have influenced and been influenced by political events at certain points in time. Those with this perspective from the communications arena are interested in framing as well as who shapes public opinion and how. Psychiatrists with this approach explore how intrapsychic phenomena and life experiences affect people's political behavior, and anthropologists want to know how the political aspects of culture impact members of the culture and vice versa. All contribute to broadening our knowledge about how individuals matter in politics; each brings different questions, methodologies, and theories to bear in the development of the perspective.

Given the multidisciplinary makeup of its proponents, an important question, and one debated regularly, concerns what constitutes adequate training in political psychology. Do students need to be trained in more than one discipline and, if so, which ones? Is training in this perspective more appropriate at the postdoctoral than the predoctoral level? Does such training demand a multidisciplinary team of teachers who, themselves, represent different disciplinary backgrounds? Or is learning this perspective best done by joining a multidisciplinary team of researchers or a network of scholars examining a particular topic of interest to the student? Currently all these questions are being answered "yes." We have an increasing number of graduate courses and programs with a political psychology focus around the world; indeed, as was already observed, many are taught in political science departments by scholars with doctoral degrees in some area of psychology. The Summer Institute in Political Psychology (Krosnick & Hermann, 1993; Wituski, Clawson, Oxley, Green, & Barr, 1998) has been in existence for over a decade now, training graduate students, junior faculty, and policy analysts in this perspective from across the globe. It brings together as teachers during a month-long period those engaged in research at the frontiers of our knowledge in political psychology from various disciplinary homes. A second, and similar, institute will soon be in place in Europe. Networks of scholars from multiple disciplines have been formed around specific issues, and teams of such scholars are beginning to publish research from a political psychology perspective that is intended to have an impact in several disciplines (e.g., Druckman & Mitchell, 1995; Renshon & Duckitt, 2000; Sylvan & Voss, 1999; 't Hart et al., 1997; Young & Schafer, 1998). What has become evident in these various endeavors is that both students and faculty leave the experiences having been challenged and with their ideas about the perspective broadened; they learn who are the experts in a variety of disciplines that one should consult or include in a team in studying a particular topic; and they generally become convinced of the relevance of the perspective to all aspects of politics, however well-defined their specific interests in the beginning.

IN SUM

Although there have been calls for political psychology to become a discipline in its own right or, if not that, a defined field within political science, the argument presented here focuses on political psychology as a perspective, approach, or point of view revolving around the role of individuals in politics writ broadly. In a fashion similar to the manner in which a large number of political scientists have embraced political economy as a way of understanding a wide array of political phenomena, we are observing a push by others to view political psychology as a perspective with the characteristics delimited here. Political psychology is viewed as "value added" to the disciplinary training received in a particular field in political science, be it American politics, public policy, comparative politics, international relations, political philosophy, etc.

Political psychology is a dynamic perspective and still evolving. In 1979, Merelman compared political psychology to Humpty Dumpty, wondering if those espousing this perspective were so fragmented and fad-oriented that there would be no way to create a coherent whole. In the past two decades, a consensus has begun to develop around the broad outlines of this approach to politics. In this chapter, the author has attempted to synthesize the set of parameters that appear to guide the research of those espousing this perspective. The purpose has been to provide us with some ground rules around which to build a common identity.

ACKNOWLEDGMENTS

This chapter has benefitted from discussions with participants in nine Summer Institutes in Political Psychology as well as with the members of the interdisciplinary Mershon Center Research Training Group on the Role of Cognition in Collective Political Decision Making sponsored by the National Science Foundation (DIR-9113599), faculty at two conferences focused on teaching political psychology, attendees at the International Political Psychology Seminar Series in the Global Affairs Institute at the Maxwell School, and a series of roundtables intended to define political psychology held at various meetings of the International Society of Political Psychology across the past decade.

REFERENCES

Abelson, R. P. (1986). Beliefs are like possessions. *Journal for the Theory of Social Behavior, 16,* 224–256.

Aguero, F. (1998). Legacies of transitions: Institutionalism, the military, and democracy in South America. *Mershon International Studies Review, 42,* 383–404.

Brewer, M. B. (1991). The social self: On being the same and different at the same time. *Personality and Social Psychology Bulletin, 17,* 475–482.

Brewer, M. B., & Kramer, R. M. (1985). The psychology of intergroup attitudes and behavior. *Annual Review of Psychology, 36,* 219–243.

Druckman, D., & Mitchell, C. (Eds.). (1995, November). Flexibility in international negotiation and mediation. Special Issue of *The Annals of the American Academy of Political and Social Science, 542.*

Fisher, R., & Ury, W. (1981). *Getting to yes: Negotiating agreement without giving in.* Boston: Houghton Mifflin.

George, A. L. (1979). Case studies and theory development: The method of structured, focused comparison. In P. G. Lauren (Ed.), *Diplomacy: New approaches to history, theory, and policy.* New York: Free Press.

Greenstein, F. I. (1973). Political psychology: A pluralistic universe. In J. N. Knutson (Ed.), *Handbook of Political Psychology* (pp. 450–472). San Francisco: Jossey-Bass.

Heifetz, R. A. (1994). *Leadership without easy answers*. Cambridge, MA: Harvard University Press.

Hermann, C. F. (1993). Avoiding pathologies in foreign policy decision groups. In D. Caldwell & T. J. McKeown (Eds.), *Diplomacy, force, and leadership: Essays in honor of Alexander George* (pp. 179–207). Boulder, CO: Westview.

Hermann, M. G. (1986). The ingredients of leadership. In M. G. Hermann (Ed.), *Political psychology: Contemporary problems and issues* (pp. 167–192). San Francisco: Jossey-Bass.

Hermann, M. G. (1988). Hafez al-Assad, President of Syria: A leadership profile. In B. Kellerman & J. Rubin (Eds.), *Leadership and negotiation: A new look at the Middle East* (pp. 70–95). New York: Praeger.

Hermann, M. G. (1989, August 12). *Political psychology: Fad, fantasy, or field*. Invited address presented at the annual meeting of the American Psychological Association, New Orleans, LA.

Hermann, M. G. (1999). *The leadership styles of Saddam Hussein and Bill Clinton: Two case studies*. Hilliard, OH: Social Science Automation.

Hermann, M. G., & Hagan, J. D. (1998, Spring). International decision making: Leadership matters. *Foreign Policy, 100,* 124–137.

Hermann, M. G., & Hermann, C. F. (1989). Who makes foreign policy decisions and how: An empirical inquiry. *International Studies Quarterly, 33,* 361–387.

Hermann, M. G., & Hermann, C. F. (1990). Hostage taking, the presidency, and stress. In W. Reich (Ed.), *Origins of terrorism: Psychologies, ideologies, theologies, states of mind* (pp. 211–229). Cambridge: Cambridge University Press.

Hermann, M. G., & Kegley, C. W., Jr. (1995). Rethinking democracy and international peace: Perspectives from political psychology. *International Studies Quarterly, 39,* 511–533.

Jennings, M. K. (1987). Residues of a movement: The aging of the American protest generation. *American Political Science Review, 81,* 367–382.

Kaarbo, J., & Beasley, R. K. (1999). A practical guide to the comparative case study method in political psychology. *Political Psychology, 20,* 369–391.

Kahneman, D., & Tversky, A. (1979). Prospect theory: An analysis of decision under risk. *Econometrica, 47,* 263–291.

Kelman, H. C. (1979a). Ethical imperatives and social responsibility in the practice of political psychology. *Political Psychology, 1,* 100–102.

Kelman, H. C. (1979b). An interactional approach to conflict resolution and its application to Israeli-Palestinian relations. *International Interactions, 6,* 99–122.

Knutson, J. N. (1973). Preface. In J. N. Knutson (Ed.), *Handbook of political psychology* (pp. i–xii). San Francisco: Jossey-Bass.

Krosnick, J. A. (1990). Government policy and citizen passion: A study of issue publics in contemporary America. *Political Behavior, 12,* 59–92.

Krosnick, J. A., & Hermann, M. G. (1993). The Summer Institute in Political Psychology: Report on a training innovation. *Political Psychology, 14,* 363–373.

Lane, R. E. (1983, July 19–22). What is political psychology? Remarks made during a roundtable at the annual meeting of the International Society of Political Psychology, St. Catherine's College, Oxford University.

Levy, J. S. (1992). Prospect theory and international relations: Theoretical applications and analytical problems. *Political Psychology, 13,* 283–310.

Lodge, M., Steenbergen, M., & Brau, S. (1995). The responsive voter: Campaign information and the dynamics of candidate evaluation. *American Political Science Review, 89,* 309–326.

Marcus, G. E., & MacKuen, M. B. (1993). Anxiety, enthusiasm, and the vote: The emotional underpinnings of learning and involvement during presidential campaigns. *American Political Science Review, 87,* 672–685.

May, E. R., & Zelikow, P. D. (Eds.). (1997). *The Kennedy tapes: Inside the White House during the Cuban missile crisis*. Cambridge, MA: Harvard University Press.

McNamara, R. S., Blight, J. G., & Brigham, R. K. (Eds.). (1999). *Argument without end: In search of answers to the Vietnam tragedy.* New York: Public Affairs.

Merelman, R. M. (1979). On the asking of relevant questions: Discussion notes towards understanding the training of political psychologists. *Political Psychology, 1,* 101–109.

Nagle, J. (1999). *Democracy and democratization: Post-Communist Europe in comparative perspective.* London: Sage Publications.

Pettigrew, T. F. (1998). Intergroup contact theory. *Annual Review of Psychology, 49,* 65–85.

Powlick, P. J., & Katz, A. Z. (1998). Defining the American public opinion/foreign policy nexus. *Mershon International Studies Review, 42,* 29–61.

Quandt, W. B. (Ed.). (1988). *The Middle East ten years after Camp David.* Washington, DC: The Brookings Institution.

Renshon, S. A., & Duckitt, J. (Eds.). (2000). *Political psychology: Cultural and crosscultural foundations.* New York: New York University Press.

Saunders, H. H. (1987, July). International relationships: To go beyond "we" and "they." *Negotiation Journal,* 245–274.

Saunders, H. H. (2000, July 1–4). Two challenges for the new century: Transforming relationships in whole bodies politic. Invited address at the annual meeting of the International Society of Political Psychology, Seattle, WA.

Sears, D. O. (1989). The ecological niche of political psychology. *Political Psychology, 10,* 501–506.

Simon, H. (1985). Human nature in politics: The dialogue of psychology with political science. *American Political Science Review, 79,* 293–304.

Slomcyznski, K. M., & Shabad, G. (1998). Can support for democracy and the market be learned in school? A natural experiment in post-Communist Poland. *Political Psychology, 19,* 749–779.

Stein, J. G. (1992). International cooperation and loss avoidance: Framing the problem. In J. G. Stein & L. Pauly (Eds.), *Choosing to cooperate: How states avoid loss.* Baltimore: Johns Hopkins University Press.

Stern, E. K., & Verbeek, B. (Eds.). (1998). Whither the study of governmental politics in foreign policymaking? A symposium. *Mershon International Studies Review, 42,* 205–255.

Stern, E. K. (1999). *Crisis decisionmaking: A cognitive institutional approach.* Stockholm: University of Stockholm Studies in Politics 66.

Sylvan, D. A., & Thorson, S. (1992). Ontologies, problem representation, and the Cuban missile crisis. *Journal of Conflict Resolution, 36,* 709–732.

Sylvan, D. A., & Voss, J. F. (Eds.). (1999). *Problem representation in foreign policy decision making.* Cambridge: Cambridge University Press.

Sundelius, B., Stern, E. K., & Bynander, F. (1997). *Crisis management the Swedish way—In theory and practice.* Stockholm: The Swedish Agency for Civil Emergency Planning.

Tetlock, P. E. (1994). Political psychology or politicized psychology: Is the road to scientific hell paved with good moral intentions. *Political Psychology, 15,* 509–529.

't Hart, P., Stern, E. K., & Sundelius, B. (1997). *Beyond groupthink: Political group dynamics and foreign policy-making.* Ann Arbor: University of Michigan Press.

Volkan, V. D. (1985). The need to have enemies and allies: A developmental approach. *Political Psychology, 6,* 219–247.

Weldes, J. (1998). Bureaucratic politics: A critical constructivist assessment. *Mershon International Studies Review, 42,* 216–225.

Wituski, D. M., Clawson, R. A., Oxley, Z. M., Green, M. C., & Barr, M. K. (1998). Bridging a disciplinary divide: The Summer Institute in Political Psychology. *PS: Political Science and Politics, 31,* 221–226.

Young, M. D., & Schafer, M. (1998). Is there method in our madness? Ways of assessing cognition in international relations. *Mershon International Studies Review, 42,* 63–96.

3

Political Psychology:
Origins and Development

DANA WARD
Pitzer College

One obvious first step toward answering the question, "What is political psychology?" is to trace the discipline's origins and development. Whether one's inclination is to adopt an etiological or an etymological stance, either approach will eventually reach natural limits. As helpful as it may be to establish the germinal conditions that gave rise to the discipline and to understand how political psychology's terms, tools, and institutions have evolved, the discipline is sufficiently mature to render patrimony and early socialization less determinative than perhaps they were even 10 years ago. At the turn of this new century, political psychology has found its legs. Where it will take us is very much open to speculation. For that reason, in addition to paying attention to origins and development, we also must ask, "Of what use is political psychology?" Eventually this question is addressed, but first I turn to the issue of origins.

ORIGINS

Since political philosophy's first stirrings, theorists have puzzled over Psyche's interaction with the polity. As Stone (1981) noted, the nature of citizenship, Plato's "myth of the metals" (1945, pp. 106–107), and the effects of participating in the polis are ancient topics finding modern echoes in discussions of biopolitics, community psychology, and political efficacy.

61

Machiavelli (1532) still speaks to political psychologists studying leadership, political motivation, negotiation, and diplomacy, and the early modern political philosophers did not shrink from musing over the political mind. Indeed, modern political philosophy begins with a concerted effort by the likes of Hobbes (1651), Locke (1690), Hume (1739, 1748), Rousseau (1762), Godwin (1793), and others to account for the fact that most political actions are not physical exchanges, but mental transactions. Although these thinkers are revered for their treatment of political institutions, they all were equally concerned with the qualities of mind that sustain or threaten liberal institutional arrangements, an issue that much occupied early debates in political psychology (Merelman, 1979). Similarly, human nature, however defined, always crept into philosophers' understanding of how individuals affect and are affected by political structures, a theme continued by modern political psychologists (e.g., Davies, 1963; Knutson, 1972; Renshon, 1974). In a sense, then, the ancient and the early modern political philosophers conducted inquiries into political psychology alongside their inquiries into political philosophy and political economy.

During the two centuries after Hobbes and Locke, the once all-encompassing political philosophy they articulated divided into the various branches of inquiry known today as the social sciences. Economics, philosophy, political science, sociology, anthropology, and psychology gradually developed distinct disciplinary boundaries that all too often were jealously guarded against interlopers. By the turn of the twentieth century, the various social sciences had developed sufficiently robust identities that it became possible to contemplate an occasional remarriage, or at least a flirtation across the disciplinary divides. Wallas (1908), inspired by James (1890), was among the first to begin a formal attempt to account for psychology's role in political life. However, his was not a full interdisciplinary embrace. Indeed, Wallas (1908) cautioned his audience to avoid academic works in what he called "applied political psychology" in favor of cultivating one's own psychological sophistication that could then be applied to political problems encountered in everyday political life:

> I believe that at the present stage of the science, a politician will gain more from reading, in light of his own experience, those treatises on psychology which have been written *without special reference* to politics, than by beginning with the literature of applied political psychology. (p. v, emphasis added)

Significantly, Wallas did not tell his readers to steep themselves in political science in order to apply the lessons learned to psychological life. The first forays into political psychology were very much psychological raids into political territory.

The raid that proved most definitive for the new discipline was conducted by Wallas's contemporary, Sigmund Freud, who turned the tools of his newly minted trade toward understanding individual and collective political behavior. Freud's analysis of the origins of society (1913), war (1915/ 1963, 1932/1963), leadership (1921/1922), and culture (1930), as well as his attention to individual actors (e.g., his "collaboration" with Bullitt on Woodrow Wilson, 1966), were among the first works in "applied political psychology." The impact of psychoanalysis proved formative for the nascent discipline, eclipsing all the earlier tentative explorations into political psychology. It would be a generation before political psychology came to be seen as something other than a subfield of psychoanalysis.

Although political psychology would not become an independent field of inquiry until after World War II, the first steps toward independence were taken during the interwar period. It appears that the first chair in political psychology was created in 1924 at the Maxwell School of Syracuse University, when the social psychologist Floyd Allport suggested that the chair created in his honor be in "Social and Political Psychology" (Katz, 1979). Adding another first, Floyd Allport taught the first course entitled *political psychology* (Katz, 1979). A decade later, the first journal employing the term *political psychology* in its title appeared in 1934–1935. This German language periodical, whose English translation is the *Journal of Political Psychology and Sexual Economy*, was edited by Wilhelm Reich, one of Freud's more notorious followers (Van Ginneken, 1988, p. 11). In terms of the field's later evolution, however, perhaps the most significant development occurred when University of Chicago political scientist Merriam (1925) explicitly called for a union of psychology and political science. One of Merriam's students, Harold D. Lasswell, took Merriam's message to heart, with the result that Lasswell is broadly recognized today as the founding father of modern political psychology.

Lasswell's approach was very much informed by psychoanalytic theory and followed a unidirectional trajectory: from psychology to politics. His most famous formulation, $p \} d \} r = P$, reflects both Freud's impact on his thinking and the primacy of psychology in the marriage of psyche and polity. Lasswell (1930/1960) defined the terms of his formula as follows: "p equals private motives, d equals displacement onto a public object; r equals rationalization in terms of public interest; P equals the political man; and $\}$ equals transformed into" (pp. 75–76). Lasswell went on to write a number of other books in political psychology, and would have written more had not his interview notes and other materials burned in a highway accident while moving from the University of Chicago to Washington, DC, in the 1940s.[1]

During the period between the publication of *Psychopathology and Politics* and the formal establishment in 1978 of the discipline's professional

---

[1]According to Lucian Pye, lecture on the origins of political psychology, March 3, 1999, seminar marking the founding of the Southern California Section of ISPP held at USC.

association, the International Society of Political Psychology (ISPP), political psychology struggled to establish its identity. To a large degree, that
identity could be characterized as a patchwork of political subtopics sown
together over a base of somewhat tattered psychological theory, theory that
for the most part was influenced by psychoanalysis. Political scientists dealing with issues of political socialization, public opinion, voting behavior,
leadership, political culture, and personality and political behavior turned
to psychology for help in understanding these issues. Several psychologists
also turned the tools of their trade to the subject of politics, but like their
counterparts in political science, psychologists relied on psychological theories to inform their analysis of political behavior. The problem, of course,
was that political science programs in virtually every graduate school did not
provide students with training in psychology, nor did psychology programs
encourage students to pursue training in political science. Consequently,
work by political scientists could easily be characterized as psychologically
unsophisticated, and work by psychologists could be too easily dismissed as
politically uninformed. Under such conditions, only the bravest (or perhaps the most foolhardy) graduate students could afford to pursue a career
in political psychology, for indeed there were no such career paths to be
followed.[2] Until the last two decades, the discipline, by and large, was populated by relatively well-established scholars who could risk moving into
uncharted territory.

This identity stage in the discipline's life cycle saw the publication of
seminal works that continue to inform the field. Merely listing these works
gives some idea of how much the patchwork quilt covered, but more importantly, such a list identifies what might be considered the critical mass that
was necessary in order for the discipline to take on a life of its own without
its umbilical connection to the parent disciplines. Leaving aside journal
articles and edited volumes,[3] a partial listing[4] of the works emerging during
political psychology's identity stage includes:

Lasswell's *Psychopathology and Politics* (1930), *World Politics and Personal
Insecurity* (1935), and *Power and Personality* (1948)

Fromm's *Escape from Freedom* (1941)

Kardiner's *Psychological Frontiers of Society* (1949)

---

[2]For example, when I went on the job market in the early 1980s, the only institution specifically seeking to hire political psychologists was the CIA.

[3]Naturally, listing only books will leave out important articles and contributors to the field.
Two journals that published a number of important articles in political psychology that the
interested reader may wish to consult are *The Journal of Abnormal and Social Psychology*, which
began publishing in 1921, and *The Journal of Social Issues*, which began publishing in 1945.

[4]The list ends with works published in 1973, the year Knutson's *Handbook of Political Psychology* was published, thus marking a new phase in the history of the discipline.

Adorno, Frenkel-Brunswick, Levinson, and Sanford's *The Authoritarian Personality* (1950)

Reisman's *The Lonely Crowd* (1950)

Erikson's *Childhood and Society* (1950), *Young Man Luther* (1958), and *Ghandi's Truth* (1969)

Leites's *The Operational Code of the Politburo* (1951)

Eysenck's *The Psychology of Politics* (1954)

Marcuse's *Eros and Civilization* (1955)

George and George's *Woodrow Wilson and Colonel House* (1956)

Smith, Bruner, and White's *Opinions and Personality* (1956)

Bay's *Structure of Freedom* (1958)

Lee's *Freedom and Culture* (1959)

Hyman's *Political Socialization* (1959)

Brown's *Life Against Death* (1960)

Rokeach's *Open and Closed Mind* (1960)

Campbell, Converse, Miller, and Stokes' *The American Voter* (1960)

Verba's *Small Groups and Political Behavior* (1961)

Lane's *Political Ideology* (1962)

Pye's *Personality, Politics and Nation Building* (1962)

Lifton's *Thought Reform and the Psychology of Totalism* (1963)

Davies's *Human Nature in Politics* (1963)

Almond and Verba's *The Civic Culture* (1963)

Edelman's *The Symbolic Uses of Politics* (1964)

Greenstein's *Children and Politics* (1965) and *Personality and Politics* (1969)

Barber's *The Lawmakers* (1965) and *Presidential Character* (1972)

Wolfenstein's *The Revolutionary Personality* (1967)

De Rivera's *Psychological Dimensions of Foreign Policy* (1968)

Milgram's *Obedience to Authority* (1969)

Easton and Dennis's *Children in the Political System* (1969)

Christie and Geis' *Studies in Machiavelianism* (1970)

Kovel's *White Racism* (1970)

Janis's *Victims of Groupthink* (1972)

Wilson's *The Psychology of Conservatism* (1973)

Winter's *The Power Motive* (1973).

Surely there are other important works that could be added to this list, but none could be omitted from any list purporting to describe the discipline's "critical mass."[5] This critical mass eventually led to the consolidation of a disciplinary identity independent from, but closely allied with, the parental disciplines.

By 1969 the critical mass had sufficiently cohered to warrant establishment of the first graduate program in political psychology. With support from the National Science Foundation, Yale created a program leading to a double PhD in psychology and politics. The program was housed in the political science department and required an extra year of coursework in order to obtain the degree. Students took the full course load required to earn a PhD in political science and the full course load required of students working toward their doctorates in the psychology department, but wrote a single dissertation on a topic in political psychology. The program's structure derived from the belief that only a thorough grounding in both disciplines would permit a truly interdisciplinary political psychology. As is often noted, those who engage in interdisciplinary work are generally not trained in the crossover discipline. They are "professionals" in their home discipline, but very much "amateurs" in the crossover discipline. Reviewers may even take this into account, allowing work to be published that would never pass muster within the crossover discipline's journals. More frequently, however, interdisciplinary work is not published because the author's grounding in the crossover discipline is regarded as inadequate. By providing thorough training in both disciplines, Yale's program helped avoid these pitfalls. So far as I know, subsequent programs have not followed suit.

Ten years after Yale started the ball rolling, a program at SUNY–Stony Brook followed in 1979, and the next decade saw programs established at the University of Wisconsin in 1982, CUNY in 1988, UCLA and UC Irvine in 1989, and Ohio State University in 1990. In the 1990s, the program at Yale died after Robert Lane's retirement, but other programs emerged at the University of Minnesota, George Washington University, and elsewhere. In all the post-Yale programs, political psychology is treated very much like a subfield, usually of political science and occasionally of psychology, rather than requiring full training in both political science and psychology. Outside the United States, only a handful of graduate level degrees are offered, including programs at the University of Melbourne, Berlin Free University, Copenhagen, Hebrew University, and London School of Economics (Sears & Funk, 1990). I can also report that in 1986 while on a Fulbright Teaching

---

[5]For a rather comprehensive bibliography of books, edited volumes, and journal articles dealing with political psychology up to 1973, the reference section of Knutson (1973) is invaluable. Also useful is Michael Lerner's "Bibliographical Note" in Greenstein (1969/1975, pp. 154–184).

Fellowship at Ankara University in Turkey, I learned that all undergraduates were required to take a course on political psychology (a major focus of the course was the political psychology of terrorism). As Merelman (1979) noted, most of the trickle of traffic into political psychology originated in political science, despite the fact that many of the seminal works in this identity-forming period were penned by psychologists. Perhaps for this reason, programs have tended to be housed more often in political science departments than psychology departments.

Once programs began admitting students, it was but a short period of time before political psychology texts began to appear. By far the most important step toward disciplinary legitimacy was the publication of Knutson's *Handbook of Political Psychology* (1973). Containing articles by more than a dozen leading political psychologists, the *Handbook* did for the discipline in 1973 what this volume hopes to do a quarter century later. It not only summarized the history and status of the discipline, but "made a greatly needed intellectual contribution by creatively analyzing and critically assessing the issues, the models, and the methods of inquiry employed in . . . political psychology" (Knutson, 1973, p. viii). The *Handbook* began with a look at personality, attitudes, and beliefs; moved on to socialization, authoritarianism, and anomie-alienation as areas of concern; next turned to an assessment of leadership, international politics, aggression, violence, revolution, and war; ending with an examination of methods and an overview. These chapters were not watered-down summaries. Each moved the research examined forward, and targeted practicing political psychologists as the intended audience. Consequently, the field still required introductory level texts.

There is widespread agreement that the early texts, although useful, failed to adequately represent the discipline's diversity and did not capture the sense of excitement and utility that motivated the early political psychologists (an assessment that remains true today). Greenstein and Lerner (1971), although providing important resources, was by no means a comprehensive text in political psychology. Elms (1976) unfortunately focused too narrowly on American politics and only lightly touched on international relations. Stone (1976) did provide far more comprehensive coverage at a level accessible to undergraduates and first year graduate students than Elms, but suffered from the same light coverage of international relations (no entry in the index for either "international" or "foreign"). Van Ginneken's (1988) introductory chapter in the second edition of Stone's text did include valuable consideration of the non–North American origins of political psychology, but the theme was essentially dropped for the remainder of the book. The same criticisms apply to DiRenzo's anthology (1974), which contains articles still assigned today in political psychology courses. All these texts tended to place emphasis on the individual level of analysis and gave far too little consideration to collective political behavior, group psychology, and international relations. Furthermore, it could be argued that an underlying assumption in some of these texts is that psychology's impact on politics is largely negative. That is, the traits and behaviors examined tend to be negative or deficiency traits: the individual with diminished self-esteem seeks power as a compensatory value; the authoritarian personality seeks to control others' behavior as a function of projecting his or her own problems with impulse control onto others; the machiavellian dehumanizes the other in order to manipulate processes for self-aggrandizement; Elms' text includes a picture of Hitler with the caption "The paranoid as politician;" and so forth. Certainly the texts deal with voting behavior and other "normal" political behaviors, but the sustained treatments tend to be reserved for the deficiency traits.

The situation in the 1980s and 1990s did not substantially change. Stone and Schaffner (1988) came out with a new edition of Stone's text, and Barner-Barry and Rosenwein (1985) published a text with a similar organization to Elms' book but with more coverage of collective behavior and international conflict (reissued in 1991). Perhaps the most important development on the text front during the 1980s was Hermann's *Political Psychology* (1986a), an update of Knutson's *Handbook*. The volume is structured like the original handbook and had the same goal, that is, to bring the informed reader up-to-date on research in the field and to expand our understanding of the psychological roots of political behavior. Like the original, Hermann's *Political Psychology* is targeted at the advanced graduate student and practicing political psychologists. The only other development on the text front worthy of mention is Iyengar and McGuire's *Explorations in Political Psychology* (1993), which collected cutting edge articles and fulfilled a function similar to Knutson (1973) and Hermann (1986), but with no claim to being a comprehensive overview of the field. Having followed the tracks laid down by textbooks in political psychology, it is necessary to return to the exploration of political psychology's disciplinary origins and identify the final cornerstone in political psychology's professional identity.

With a critical mass of works in political psychology, the establishment of training programs, and the publication of texts, the next step in the consolidation of the discipline's identity was the establishment of a professional organization. In 1978, Knutson's enormous energy and dedication resulted in the founding of the International Society of Political Psychology (ISPP). Knutson traveled widely to generate interest in her vision of a professional association of political psychologists. In the beginning, her models were the American Political Science Association and the American Psychological Association. However, at a meeting in Boston to promote the new association, several senior scholars argued that such an organization would be overshadowed by those two giant professional organizations. During an open discussion, Ithiel de Sola Pool suggested that the new organization should be an international society, and from that simple suggestion the new organization took on a completely different character. It was to be the International Society of Political Psychology, and the hope was that it would remain a relatively close-knit international society in which members knew each other well, thus providing ample opportunities for collaboration and communication of research results. Knutson took up the post of executive director, serving until her untimely death in late 1981 (Davies & Montville, 1981, p. 270). The first annual meeting took place in New York in 1978 with Robert Lane as the founding president. Originally, Lasswell was the general chairman for the first annual meeting, but one week after accepting the post, a massive stroke left him incapacitated. Stanley Renshon served as the program chair and more than 170 people participated on panels at the meeting. Finally, the following Spring the first edition of the Society's new journal, *Political Psychology*, reached libraries and ISPP members' mailboxes. With these steps, political psychology achieved its adult identity, even if it had not yet reached maturity.

Over the next 20 years, ISPP evolved into an organization with over 800 members in any one year and more than 1,300 individual members over any 3-year period, including members from more than 55 countries. Graduate students constitute roughly one fifth of ISPP membership and North Americans make up roughly half the membership. The 22nd Annual Scientific Meeting in Amsterdam (July, 1999) listed more that 500 people participating on panels. Despite its growth, the Society remains a relatively intimate organization much like the founders originally envisioned. Contributing to that intimacy has been the attention paid to socializing and training young scholars. Since 1990, ISPP has sponsored the Summer Institute in Political Psychology (SIPP) with the collaboration of Ohio State University. More than 500 graduate students have gone through the month-long training program with instruction by leading political psychologists. The intellectual friendships and mentoring fostered by SIPP have helped sustain ISPP and contributed to a collegial atmosphere that sets ISPP apart from most other professional organizations.

DEVELOPMENT

Thus far attention has been paid to the institutions, individuals, and works that form the foundation of modern political psychology, but little has been said about the milieu in which those works and institutions were created, or about the concepts and techniques that have become part of the political psychology tool kit. As Van Ginneken (1988) noted:

One should not content oneself with painting a succession of "great men" making "great discoveries," leaving out the wider context and all the false leads. Nor should one limit oneself to the other extreme of merely examining their own ideologies and interests and those of their clients and employers, thereby denying any real progress in conceptualization and technique. It is better to deal with these heterogeneous contributions within their own historical contexts: that is, to show how preferred themes often corresponded to the spirit of the time, place, and social category. (p. 4)

Behavior, and the developmental processes preceding behavior, are always the product of interactions between the organism and the environment, whether we are dealing with mollusks or political psychologists (Piaget, 1978). An interactional analysis is essential not only because individuals and institutions cannot be divorced from their surrounding environments, but because such an analysis helps to address the question with which this essay will end: Of what use is political psychology? What, then, can we say about the environment whence political psychology arose?

Deutsch (1983) argued that political psychology was "conceived in the ambivalent mood of optimism and despair which has characterized the scientific age" (p. 221). The despair derived from the increasing "political turmoil, the irrationality and destructiveness of the First World War, the development of modern totalitarian regimes with their barbarities, [and] the emergence of the mass media and their systematic use by propagandists" (p. 221). The optimism came from the belief that scientific methods applied to the relationship between psychology and politics might produce an understanding of these horrors that might ultimately lead to preventing such problems from recurring. The subsequent living nightmares experienced during World War II only heightened the need for solutions to our intraspecies violence.

Van Ginneken disputed anglophone slants, such as in the previous section, on political psychology's history, arguing that political psychology originated with conservative French and Italian authors, augmented by German and Austrian intellectuals. Beginning with Taine's study of French national character, Van Ginneken followed the trail from Taine's colleague Boutmy's *The English People: A Study of Their Political Psychology* (1901) and *The American People: Elements of Their Political Psychology* (1902), on to Le Bon's work on crowds and group psychology, including *Political Psychology and Social Defense* (1910), and ending with the classic elite theorists Pareto, Mosca, and Michels. Indeed, these may well be the works that Wallas had in mind when he dismissed applied political psychology as being of little utility, at least judging by Wallas's comments on Le Bon and his withering critique of Boutmy's student, Ostrogorski (Wallas, 1908, pp. 124–126). In any event, Van Ginneken argued that the impetus that led to the application of psychology to politics came not from the doom and gloom of the interwar period, but in response to the revolutionary impulses that gave rise to the Paris Commune (1871) and radical working class movements in Europe. Van Ginneken noted that:

> The fourfold capitalist, industrial, urban, and democratic revolution was gradually shattering the bonds of traditional society, holding out the image of a free man making his own choices as a consumer and as a citizen. This made it imperative to analyze his natural inclinations and predict his behavior in more accurate ways than before. (cited in Stone & Schaffner, 1988, p. 4)

Much like de Tocqueville responding to the upheavals stimulated by the great French Revolution, late nineteenth century conservative intellectuals sought to understand the fourfold revolution taking place around them so that they might better accommodate themselves and their political institutions to these changes. They did indeed employ quasipsychological constructs in their analyses, but by and large these constructs were profoundly primitive and unsystematic.

In Mosca's 1896 masterpiece, *Elementi di Scienza Politica,* translated into English as *The Ruling Class* (1939), there is not even an entry in the index for "psychology" or "mental." When Mosca did employ these terms, the impact of interior mental life on exterior political behavior is reduced to a radical environmentalism: "Save for rare and rarely complete exceptions, a person thinks, judges and believes the way the society in which he lives thinks, judges and believes" (Mosca, 1939, p. 26). He went on to describe a variety of environments, concluding that environments create a "sort of psychological mold that shapes to its own contour any individual who happens to be cast into it" (p. 26). Mosca did try to identify different types of people, but the psychological applications bore a much closer resemblance to Plato's constructs than to the systematic psychological theories of the psychoanalytic and post-Freudian era. Similarly, Pareto (1966) argued in his manual on political economy that "Clearly psychology is the basis of political economy and, in general, the social sciences" (p. 25). But Pareto did little more than pay lip service to the importance of psychology, and in *Trattato di Sociologia Generale,* he wrote: "It is for psychology to study [these] psychic state[s]; in this inquiry we accept it as a fact without seeking to go any further than that" (Pareto, 1966, p. 36). As Finer commented in the introduction to Pareto's selected works, psychology in Pareto's system is a "paradoxical psychologism without the psychology" (Pareto, 1966, p. 36). Neither Mosca nor Pareto employed any sort of systematic psychology, opting instead for *ad hoc* constructs devoid of any attempt at testing or even systematic observation, be it of an individual on a couch, individuals in labs, or citizens responding to inquiries.

Robert Michels, in contrast, can stake a much more legitimate claim to being part of the taproot of modern political psychology insofar as the iron law of oligarchy is activated by psychological tendencies on the part of both the leader and the led. Two major sections of *Political Parties* (Michels, 1915/1962) address the psychological foundations of the iron law of oligarchy: Part One, Section B is titled *Psychological Causes of Leadership* and Part Three is devoted to *The Exercise of Power and Its Psychological Reaction Upon the Leaders.* But Michels's use of psychological theory or constructs is on precisely the same level as de Tocqueville, who is one of Michels's sources, as are the philosopher Hume, the anthropologist Frazer, and the individualist anarchist Stirner. Nevertheless, Michels did base his study on systematic observation rather than armchair cogitation as in the case of his two important influences, Pareto and Mosca. Although prior to the interwar period, surely there was interest in psychology's role in political life, to argue that there is much of a direct line from Mosca, Pareto, and Michels to modern political psychology is strained. These elite theorists (with the partial exception of Michels) share much more in common with de Tocqueville, Locke, and other early theorists than they do with Lasswell, Leites, Lane, Fromm, Sanford, and other early pioneers of modern political psychology. What distinguishes the founding generation's approach from the early explorations into the link between psychology and politics is the use of systematic psychological theory, theory based on at least some form of direct, controlled observation of human behavior.

Both Deutsch and Van Ginneken linked the emergence of political psychology to fundamental social change. In both interpretations, political psychology is developed as a means of coping with political upheaval, and this may be the key to answering the question concerning the discipline's utility, but to be useful that key must unlock both sides of the door between psychology and political science. Political psychologists can not be content to focus on individual or psychological explanations of political behavior, nor can we limit our attention to the systemic roots of individual psychology. Individuals and systems interact and that interaction transforms both the individual and the system, sometimes almost imperceptibly and on occasion radically.

Perhaps because of Lasswell's influence, during the discipline's first decades the arrow of analysis pointed primarily from psychology to politics, but in the past two decades far more attention has been paid to the polity's impact on psyche. By the 1980s, the bidirectional nature of political psychology was explicitly acknowledged by both Deutsch (1983) and Hermann (1986). Hermann wrote that the interaction between psychology and politics

is viewed as bidirectional. . . . That is, the perceptions, beliefs, motives, opinions, values, interests styles, defenses, and experiences of individuals—be they citizens, leaders, group members, bureaucrats, terrorists, or revolutionaries—are seen as influencing what they do politically; and, in turn, the political culture, political system, mechanisms of political socialization, political movements and parties, and the international system are perceived as having an impact on what people are like. (p. 2)

Although the bidirectional nature of political psychology is now well established, works focusing on how the political system influences individual behavior remain a clear minority, and those that examine interactions are rarer still. Studies of political culture, such as Almond and Verba's *Civic Culture* (1963), led the way from politics to psychology, and political culture, including political socialization, remains the most dominant area of study among those who assess the polity's impact on personality. Chilton (1988a, 1988b, 1991), for example, looked at how the implicit "moral structures" within cultural systems inform individual behavior. In particular, Chilton argued that institutions are subject to developmental dynamics that both mirror and shape individual moral development. According to Chilton:

> One especially important link between the individual and cultural systems is the normative evaluations of a culture. On one hand, the evaluations are part of the individual system: one person's evaluation does not depend of necessity upon another person's. On the other hand, shared evaluations that are known to be shared are part of the cultural system. (1988a, p. 137)

In short, cultures create evaluative systems that prefigure individual judgments. Most individuals within a particular culture come to perceive and judge the world in ways common in their society, a point Mosca took to the extreme. However, there is always slippage. Not all individuals absorb the cultural messages equally and some individuals find the cultural judgments inadequate. Thus, there is enough variation—some individuals function in sync with the culture, some function at a more primitive level than is commonly found in the culture, and some develop beyond their culture's capacity to render adequate judgments—to produce at least the potential for disequilibrium, which in turn is the engine for progress or disintegration. These points of friction between the individual and the culture are perhaps the most important areas political psychologists can study. Here is where we can discover the links between individual, social, and cultural change.

When the implicit moral structure found in a culture's significant political institutions is in advance of the culture's modal personality, these institutions can serve to enrich and advance citizens' mental functioning and moral judgments, much like the Greeks believed the polis functioned to produce more fully realized human beings. When, however, institutional development lags behind individual development, significant segments of the polity may find institutional arrangements to be wanting, thus generating movement for institutional reform. A good example of this process is provided by Radding (1985) in *A World Made by Men: Cognition and Society, 400–1200*, a book that should be much more widely known among political psychologists. Radding applied a Piagetian analysis to the development of law in the Middle Ages and found very close parallels between individual cognitive development and institutional development. Early legal systems focused on the effect of an action, excluding any consideration of motivation, and simply tried to find the appropriate legal category for a particular transgression, rather than arriving at an independent judgment about the transgression. The result was that "debaters quoted authority as a substitute for argument" (Radding, 1985, p. 131). Radding went on to argue:

> In the early Middle Ages the habit of looking to superiors had been reinforced by the ready availability of authority. By the eleventh century, however, the power of rulers was disintegrating in much of Europe. Unable any longer to count on their superiors to settle their disputes, disputants found it useless to cite rules and authorities in support of their position; the other side simply answered with citations of their own. Instead, people had to learn ways of persuading their peers by showing their interpretation of texts was correct, by answering the arguments of their opponents, and in general by appealing to the good sense of their audience. The effort to adapt to this necessity stimulated the development of cognitive skills that had rarely been required since the time of Cicero. (p. 155)

A similar attempt to evaluate macro level influences on the individual can be found in Lane's work over the past two decades. In a series of papers and articles, many of which are incorporated in his book, *The Market Experience* (1991), Lane focused on the psychological consequences of participating in various markets, be it for goods, friends, mates, or leaders. Lane found that political and economic markets structure experience differently, placing different cognitive and affective demands on individuals. For example, economic markets are based more on reward, political markets more on punishment (Lane, 1983). The rules of political life encourage simplistic thinking insofar as obedience is expected, but economic markets require calculation, economizing, and a more active, purposive posture on the part of the individual. Another difference is that political participation is voluntary, market participation is not (Lane, 1983, p. 457). On the other hand, political markets expect a much different level of understanding on the part of voters compared to the level of understanding markets expect of consumers. "Market thinking is more concrete than political thinking, partly because it deals with things, partly because it involves more first-hand knowledge" (p. 473). From his analysis of the different roles and tasks found in economic markets compared to political markets, Lane (1983) identified the systematic effects each market has on individual affective and cognitive life:

> Market tasks develop cognition characterized by frequent, personality significant, cybernetically informed, socially discussed, direct experiences more

often regarded as rewarding than punishing. In contrast, political tasks often demand, but cannot effectively teach, abstract, personally remote, cybernetically less-informed cognitions required for effective citizenship. Market cognition tends to dominate political cognition because of its vividness and personal consequences, but the cognition taught by the market is often inappropriate for political tasks. (p. 455)

What these all too brief examples demonstrate is that political psychology has developed well beyond its initial focus on how individual psychology contributes to political behavior. Political psychology is no longer unidirectional, but bidirectional. Psyche influences political behavior, and the polity impacts psyche. We can even perceive the beginnings of an interactional analysis in which there are relationships more complex than can be revealed by a focus on one direction or the other. The personality system and the political system may be systems in mutual equilibrium such that changes in one not only produce changes in the other, but produce fundamentally different re-equilibrations.

OF WHAT USE IS POLITICAL PSYCHOLOGY?

Deutsch (1983) answered this question by saying:

... the major social value of intellectual work in political psychology resides not in its specific recommendations but rather in its providing organizing frameworks, clarifying ideas and systematic concepts for helping those who are engaged in practical political work to think about what they do more comprehensively, more analytically, and with more concern for the empirical soundness of their working assumptions. (p. 224)

Such a response, however, could be used to address the same question for any of the social sciences. Certainly political psychology has provided specific recommendations that have contributed to the resolution of particular political problems, conflicts, or processes, and the overarching frameworks provided by political psychology do offer useful tools for acquiring deeper understanding of the political dilemmas we face. Indeed, were Wallas reviewing the literature today, surely he would no longer recommend that the practicing politician avoid works in applied political psychology. There is much in our toolkit that is of use to the practicing politician. We could point to decision-making models that political leaders would find informative, or paths to conflict resolution that might bring bitter enemies to the bargaining table, or theories of how voters' choose candidates that any campaign manager would be foolish to ignore. Personally, however, I find such answers wanting. These kinds of "mechanical" answers are not what I was looking for when I first became interested in political psychology.

After almost three decades, I continue to look to political psychology for ways in which it can help pave the way for all of us to become autonomous actors, liberated from the dictates of authority and the disabilities produced by constricted psyches. Of course, political psychology, like everything else, can be a double-edged sword. It can be used for manipulative, authoritarian purposes as easily as it can be used for more benign purposes. In the end, we each have our own answer to what political psychology is good for. For me, political psychology is where I can find the resources for personal liberation, the road map for living a just life, and the key to unlocking my share of human potential. In a word, what I find political psychology good for is freedom.

REFERENCES

Adorno, T., Frenkel-Brunswik, E., Levinson, D., & Sanford, N. (1950). *The authoritarian personality*. New York: Harper and Row.

Almond, G. A., & Verba, S. (1963). *The civic culture: Political attitudes and democracy in five nations*. Princeton, NJ: Princeton University Press.

Barber, J. D. (1965). *The lawmakers: Recruitment and adaptation to legislative life*. New Haven: Yale University Press.

Barber, J. D. (1972). *Presidential character*. Englewood Cliffs, NJ: Prentice-Hall.

Barner-Barry, C., & Rosenwein, R. (1985). *Psychological perspectives on politics*. Englewood Cliffs, NJ: Prentice-Hall.

Bay, C. (1958). *Structure of freedom*. Stanford, CA: Stanford University Press.

Brown, N. O. (1960). *Life against death: The psychoanalytic meaning of history*. New York: Vintage.

Campbell, A., Converse, P., Miller, W., & Stokes, D. (1960). *The American voter*. New York: Wiley.

Chilton, S. (1988a). A Piagetian developmental theory of political insitutions. In S. Rosenberg, D. Ward, & S. Chilton (Eds.), *Political reasoning and cognition: A Piagetian view* (pp. 127–160). Durham, NC, and London: Duke University Press.

Chilton, S. (1988b). *Defining political development*. Boulder, CO: L. Rienner.

Chilton, S. (1991). *Grounding political development*. Boulder, CO, and London: Rienner.

Christie, R., & Geis, R. (1970). *Studies in Machiavelianism*. New York: Academic Press.

Davies, J. C. (1963). *Human nature in politics*. New York: Wiley.

Davies, J. C., & Montville, J. (1981). Requiem for Jeanne Nickell Knutson. *Political Psychology, 3*, pp. 269–270.

De Rivera, J. (1968). *The psychological dimension of foreign policy*. Columbus, OH: Merrill.

Deutsch, M. (1983). What is Political Psychology? *International Social Science Journal, 35*, pp. 221–236.

DiRenzo, G. J. (1974). *Personality and politics*. New York: Anchor Books.

Easton, D., & Dennis, J. (1969). *Children in the political system*. New York: McGraw-Hill.

Edelman, M. (1964). *The symbolic uses of politics*. Chicago: University of Illinois Press.

Elms, A. C. (1976). *Personality in politics*. New York: Harcourt Brace Jovanovich.

Erikson, E. (1950). *Childhood and society*. New York: W. W. Norton.

Erikson, E. (1958). *Young man Luther*. New York: W. W. Norton.

Erikson, E. (1969). *Ghandi's truth*. New York: W. W. Norton.

Eysenck, H. (1954). *The psychology of politics*. London: Routledge & Kegan Paul.

Freud, S. (1913). Totem and taboo. In J. Strachey (Ed. and Trans.), *The standard edition of the complete psychological works of Sigmund Freud* (Vol. 13, pp. 1–161). London: Hogarth Press.

Freud, S. (1963). Reflections on war and death. *Imago.* Reprinted in *Character and Culture,* Collier Books edition of *The Collected Papers of Sigmund Freud.* New York: Collier Books. (Original work published 1915)

Freud, S. (1922). *Group psychology and the analysis of the ego.* London and Vienna: International Psycho-Analytical Press. (Original work published 1921)

Freud, S. (1930). *Civilization and its discontents.* London: Hogarth Press.

Freud, S. (1963). Why war? Reprinted in *Character and Culture,* Collier Books edition of *The Collected Papers of Sigmund Freud.* New York: Collier Books. (Original work published 1932)

Freud, S., & Bullitt, W. G. (1966). *Thomas Woodrow Wilson: A psychological study.* Cambridge, MA: Houghton Mifflin Company.

Fromm, E. (1941). *Escape from freedom.* New York: Holt, Rinehart and Winston.

George, A., & George, J. (1956). *Woodrow Wilson and Colonel House: A personality study.* New York: John Day Company.

Godwin, W. (1976). *Enquiry concerning political justice.* London: Pelican Books. (Original work published 1793)

Greenstein, F. I. (1965). *Children and politics.* New Haven: Yale University Press.

Greenstein, F. I. (1969). *Personality and politics: Problems of evidence, inference and conceptualization.* Chicago: Markham.

Greenstein, F. I. (1973). Political psychology: A pluralistic universe. In J. N. Knutson (Ed.), *Handbook of political psychology.* San Francisco: Jossey-Bass.

Greenstein, F. I. (1975). *Personality and politics: Problems of evidence, inference, and conceptualization.* New York: W. W. Norton. (Original work published 1969, Markham Publishing Co., Chicago)

Greenstein, F. I., & Lerner, M. (1971). *A source book for the study of personality and politics.* Chicago: Markham.

Hermann, M. G. (Ed.). (1986). *Political psychology.* San Francisco: Jossey-Bass.

Hobbes, T. (1948). *Leviathan.* Oxford: Clarendon. (Original work published 1651)

Hume, D. (1992). *Treatise of human nature.* Buffalo, NY: Prometheus Books. (Original work published 1739)

Hume, D. (1956). *An enquiry concerning human understanding.* Chicago: Gateway Editions; distributed by H. Regnery Co. (Original work published 1748)

Hyman, H. H. (1959). *Political socialization: A study in the psychology of political behavior.* Glencoe, IL: Free Press.

Iyengar, S., & McGuire, W. (1993). *Explorations in political psychology.* Durham, NC: Duke University Press.

James, W. (1890). *The principles of psychology.* New York: Henry Holt.

Janis, I. L. (1972). *Victims of groupthink.* Boston: Houghton Mifflin.

Kardiner, A. (1949). *Psychological frontiers of society.* New York: Columbia University Press.

Katz, D. (1979) Obituary: Floyd H. Allport (1890–1978). *American Psychologist, 34,* 351–353.

Kovel, J. (1970). *White racism: A psychohistory.* New York: Columbia University Press.

Knutson, J. (1972). *The human basis of the polity.* Chicago: Aldine-Atherton.

Knutson, J. (1973). *Handbook of political psychology.* San Francisco: Jossey-Bass.

Lane, R. E. (1962). *Political ideology: Why the American common man believes what he does.* New York: Free Press.

Lane, R. E. (1983). Political observers and market participants: The effects on cognition. *Political Psychology, 4,* 455–482.

Lane, R. E. (1991). *The market experience.* Cambridge and New York: Cambridge University Press.

Lasswell, H. D. (1960). *Psychopathology and politics.* New York: Viking Press. (Original work published 1930)

Lasswell, H. D. (1935). *World politics and personal insecurity.* New York: McGraw-Hill.

Lasswell, H. D. (1948). *Power and personality.* Westport, CT: Greenwood.

Lee, D. (1959). *Freedom and culture.* Englewood Cliffs, NJ: Prentice-Hall.

Leites, N. (1951). *The operational code of the Politburo.* New York: McGraw-Hill.

Lifton, R. J. (1963). *Thought reform and the psychology of totalism.* New York: W. W. Norton.

Locke, J. (1894). *Essay concerning human understanding.* Oxford: Clarendon Press. (Original work published 1690)

Machiavelli, N. (1532). *The prince. The discourses.* New York: Modern Library, 1940.

Marcuse, H. (1955). *Eros and civilization.* Boston: Beacon Press.

Merelman, R. (1979). On the asking of relevant questions: Discussion notes towards understanding the training of political psychologists. *Political Psychology, 1,* 104–109.

Merriam, C. E. (1925). *New aspects of politics.* Chicago: University of Chicago Press.

Michels, R. (1962). *Political parties.* New York: Collier Books. (Original work published 1915)

Milgram, S. (1969). *Obedience to authority.* New York: Harper & Row.

Mosca, G. (1939). *The ruling class [Elementi di scienza politica].* (A. Livingston, Ed., & H. D. Kahn, Trans.). New York: McGraw-Hill. (Original work published 1896)

Pareto, V. (1966). *Sociological writings.* (S. E Finer, Ed., & D. Mirfin, Trans.). London: Pall Mall Press.

Piaget, J. (1978). *Behavior and evolution.* New York: Pantheon.

Plato. (1945). *The republic of Plato.* (Francis Macdonald Cornford, Trans.). London: Oxford University Press.

Pye, L. (1962). *Personality, politics and nation building.* New Haven, CT: Yale University Press.

Radding, C. M. (1985). *A world made by men: Cognition and society, 400–1200.* Chapel Hill, NC, and London: University of North Carolina Press.

Reisman, D. (1950). *The lonely crowd.* New Haven, CT: Yale University Press.

Renshon, S. A. (1974). *Psychological needs and political behavior: A theory of personality and political efficacy.* New York: Free Press.

Rokeach, M. (1960). *Open and closed mind.* New York: Basic Books.

Rousseau, J. J. (1911). *Émile.* (B. Foxley, Trans.). London: Dutton. (Original work published 1762)

Sears, D. O., & Funk, C. L. (1990, July 11–14). *Graduate education in political psychology in the United States.* Paper presented at the annual meeting of the International Society of Political Psychology, Washington, DC.

Smith, M. B., Bruner, J. S., & White, R. W. (1956). *Opinions and personality.* New York: Wiley.

Stone, W. F. (1976). *The psychology of politics.* New York: Free Press.

Stone, W. F. (1981). Political psychology: A Whig history. In S. Long (Ed.), *The handbook of political behavior* (pp. 1–67). New York: Plenum Press.

Stone, W. F., & Schaffner, P. (Eds.). (1988). *The psychology of politics.* New York: Springer-Verlag.

Van Ginneken, J. (1988). Outline of a cultural history of political psychology. In W. F. Stone & P. Schaffner (Eds.), *The psychology of politics* (pp. 3–22). New York: Springer-Verlag.

Verba, S. (1961). *Small groups and political behavior: A study of leadership.* Princeton: Princeton University Press.

Wallas, G. (1929). *Human nature in politics.* London: Constable and Company. (Original work published 1908)

Wilson, G. D. (1973). *The psychology of conservatism.* London: Academic Press.

Winter, D. (1973). *The power motive.* New York: Free Press.

Wolfenstein, E. V. (1967). *The revolutionary personality.* Princeton, NJ: Princeton University Press.

4

Psychological Political Science Versus Political Psychology True to Its Name: A Plea for Balance

Jon A. Krosnick
Kathleen M. McGraw
The Ohio State University

"What is political psychology?" the editor asks. There are as many different answers to this question as there are chapters in the volume. Everyone with a nodding scholarly acquaintance with "political psychology" understands that it is the intellectual and scientific activity that takes place at the intersection of political science and psychology. Some prominent commentators on the "state of political psychology," perhaps wisely, avoid more precise definitions beyond this Venn diagrammatic designation (e.g., Iyengar & McGuire, 1993; Sears, 1987).

In our view, answering the question "What is political psychology?" requires acknowledging that there are really two very different sorts of political psychology. These two types are defined not by substantive, conceptual, or methodological cleavages that exist in the discipline, but rather by the fundamental priorities of the research enterprise. Our goals in this chapter are threefold: (a) to clarify the distinction between the two types of political psychology; (b) to assess the prevalence of each type; and (c) to evaluate the current state of political psychology and its future potential within the framework.

POLITICAL PSYCHOLOGY AND
PSYCHOLOGICAL POLITICAL SCIENCE [1]

A brief linguistic analysis of the label *political psychology,* certainly the dominant label for our interdisciplinary exercise, is quite illuminating. The two constituent disciplines are represented, but *political* is a modifier or qualifier of the noun *psychology.* Absent any understanding of the actual practice of political psychology, this ordering suggests that the goals of psychology are central to the enterprise. From this perspective, political psychology could be viewed as a subtype of the larger discipline of psychology, comparable to the core subdisciplines of cognitive, social, developmental, and clinical psychology. The discipline of psychology has enormous range, and its territory borders on the biological sciences on the one end and social sciences such as anthropology and sociology on the other. According to Zimbardo (1988), the fundamental concern of psychology writ large is "the scientific study of behavioral and mental processes . . . [with an interest] in discovering general laws" (p. 5). Because the goal of psychology is *generalizations* about human nature, scholars engaged in political psychology "true to its name" (Krosnick, in press) would *not* be primarily interested in identifying and explaining relationships that hold *only* in the political context, but rather would make use of the political context to generate more general principles that are pancontextual.

Why should scholars interested in psychological questions engage in political psychology true to its name? That is, why should one stray from the usual approaches to psychological research in order to explicitly pay attention to the political context? At least one answer to this question begins with the recognition that research by cognitive and social psychologists during the last century has often been done with a relatively restricted subpopulation of people (i.e., college students) and in laboratory settings that are intentionally constructed to be barren, simple, and streamlined, focusing participants' attention on the stimuli on which they are intended to focus, minimizing their attention to other stimuli, and minimizing the baggage they bring to the situation from prior experiences. All this makes perfect sense if we wish to understand how people respond to such unusual situations. And all this makes sense if we want to minimize between-person variance in participants' thinking and behavior in order to maximize the statistical power of the study to detect the effects of manipulations that are implemented.

However, there is a cost paid when taking this approach, in terms of theoretical richness. When researchers design laboratory experimental paradigms to test psychological theories, they typically choose stimuli relatively

---

[1] This section is drawn heavily from Krosnick (in press).

arbitrarily, because their theories should, in principle, apply to all stimuli. So a study of attitude change could be done equally well regardless of whether a persuasive message is about vegetables or about vacationing in Alaska or about tooth brushing. In building a laboratory experiment, researchers typically want to strip away the unique complexities that may come along with any particular attitude object. This allows for a clean test of the hypothesis the researcher brings, based on abstract theory, to the testing situation.

Yet careful attention to the idiosyncrasies of a particular target and situation can have wonderful payoffs for the development of basic, pancontextual theory. In particular, this can lead to new insights about moderators and mediators of effects (Baron & Kenny, 1986), as well as new effects that researchers might not previously have considered. Imagine, for example, a researcher who is interested in the organization of social information in memory, and in particular the question of how individuals represent the various (human) alternatives in a choice task (e.g., which secretary to hire, which suitor to marry). This is, interestingly enough, an issue that the social cognition literature has largely overlooked, a central question being the extent to which such choices are represented as person-centered or attribute-centered structures. A researcher approaching this question from the perspective of political psychology true to its name might turn to the political domain for insights, because this representational problem is intrinsic to voting decisions. From his or her understanding of the political context, the researcher might design studies aimed at specifying the moderators, or "conditions under which," different representational outcomes occur. For example, he or she might determine the impact of different information presentation formats (e.g., "holistic" candidate-centered formats such as campaign brochures versus attribute-centered formats such as point-by-point newspaper summaries of candidates' differences), or investigate how participant characteristics, such as membership in or identification with relevant social groups, or the subjective importance of the decision, influence the representation of the alternatives. The researcher might also specify the critical psychological mediating processes, such as affective responses to the alternatives taken individually and relative to each other, that shape the content and structure of the representation. Moreover, she or he might then examine how the representation of the alternatives influences the decision-making process. Eventually, the researcher might turn to other social contexts (e.g., organizations, interpersonal relations) to verify and extend these principles.

The key point of this hypothetical example[2] is that the goal of the research process is to develop psychological theory that is intended to be

---

[2]In fact, the example is not fully hypothetical; see Rahn (1995; Rahn, Aldrich, & Borgida, 1994) for evidence relevant to the choice representation problem.

applicable across contexts. More generally, in doing political psychology true to its name, the conclusions are relevant not only to politics but rather are more general and pancontextual. The research may be done in the context of politics, but describing political events and the processes underlying them is not the central goal.

Of course, in practice, the enterprise of political psychology rarely looks like this. To more accurately capture what most political psychologists actually do, the modifier and noun should be reversed in the label, yielding *psychological political science* as a more apt descriptor of most scholarship in the field. That is, political psychologists usually have a primary interest in serving the core goals of political science. In general, the scientific study of politics is regarded as the attempt to understand how and why the processes of politics unfold as they do, with no interest in generalizing beyond the political context to other domains of human behavior. From this perspective, political psychology is a subtype of political science, and its distinguishing feature is theoretical explanations of political phenomena that are rooted in psychological theory and concepts (as opposed to, for example, economics or sociology). Definitions of political psychology that emphasize the application of psychological theory to understanding political processes have this perspective in mind. In contrast to *political psychology true to its name,* the label *psychological political science* emphasizes that the enterprise is a subtype of political science, not psychology.

One especially prominent example of *psychological political science* is Lodge, McGraw, and Stroh's (1989) research on processes of candidate evaluation (see Rahn & Sullivan, in press, for a similar analysis of Lodge et al., 1989). In 1986, Hastie and Park, social psychologists, published a paper in the prestigious *Psychological Review,* drawing a distinction between memory-based and on-line decision making. Memory-based judgment occurs when a person is prompted to express an opinion or choice, and at the time the judgment is expressed, the person canvasses his or her memory to retrieve whatever information is available and deemed relevant. That information is then integrated to form an opinion, so that the judgment is constructed on the spot. In contrast, on-line processing occurs when the person is motivated to form an opinion about some entity (person, policy, group) on his or her own and updates a "running tally" of that opinion as new relevant information about the object is encountered in the course of daily life. When asked to express an opinion about the object, the person simply retrieves the existing on-line tally from memory, not the specific pieces of information about the object that are available in memory.

Lodge et al. (1989) devised and conducted an experiment that extended Hastie and Park's general assertions about human decision making to the political domain of candidate evaluations. The study provided compelling evidence that at least under some conditions, citizens evaluate political candidates in an on-line fashion. Those familiar with the social psychological literature at this time may have very likely reacted to this political demonstration by saying, "How could it be otherwise?" As such, the Lodge et al. (1989) study represents a very common form of psychological political science: taking an existing political theory and applying it to understand a political phenomenon.

This study could have been designated as "merely applied," accompanied by a sneer, implying it was a second-rate undertaking, because it did not involve the development and testing of new and original theoretical ideas. Applied work is often regarded as mechanical application of others' theoretical ingenuity. The Lodge et al. (1989) study was not accorded this second-rate status, and it seems to us there are two main reasons for its acceptance and influence. The first is that the study challenged reigning presumptions in political science that citizens evaluate candidates in a memory-based fashion (Kelley, 1983; Kelley & Mirer, 1974) and so forced a reconsideration of the processes by which candidate evaluations and vote choices emerge. The second is that it motivated subsequent work, extending and modifying the on-line view of voters (e.g., Lodge & Steenbergen, 1995; Lodge & Taber, 2000; McGraw, Lodge, & Stroh, 1990; Rahn, Aldrich, & Borgida, 1994; Rahn, Krosnick, & Breuning, 1994) as well as ongoing controversies about the on-line model's validity (e.g., Redlawsk, 2001; Zaller, 1992), and so generated a continuing stream of productive intellectual discourse.[3]

THE DOMINANCE OF PSYCHOLOGICAL POLITICAL SCIENCE

A number of indicators underscore our suspicion that *psychological political science* dominates *political psychology true to its name*. One set of indicators appears to reveal the value placed on the enterprise by the disciplines of psychology and political science. If the enterprise of political psychology is often "true to its name," then we would expect to see more value placed on it by psychologists, because the goals of psychology are fundamental. On the other hand, if the enterprise of political psychology usually has the characteristics of psychological political science, it is likely to be valued more by political scientists, because the concerns of political science are central. And in fact, these indicators suggest that psychological political science dominates its cousin.

For example, one prominent indicator of disciplinary value is hiring practices at major research universities. Political science departments have

---

[3]For an extended discussion of other research that might be classified as psychological political science, see Krosnick (in press) and Rahn and Sullivan (in press).

hired faculty members with Ph.D.s in psychology (in particular, social psychology; e.g., Leonie Huddy, Don Kinder, Rick Lau, and Tom Nelson), but to our knowledge, there are no scholars with Ph.D.s in political science who hold primary appointments in psychology departments at major research universities.

Publication trends in scholarly journals reflect the same asymmetry. Psychology Ph.D.s on occasion publish articles in major political science journals (even when their primary affiliation is in psychology; e.g., David Sears, Jim Sidanius, and Philip Tetlock). In contrast, it is more difficult to identify publications in major psychology journals and book series written by political science Ph.D.s (John Zaller, Shanto Iyengar, John Sullivan, and Richard Herrmann are notable recent exceptions).

A third indicator of the asymmetry is revealed by the enrollment rates at the Summer Institute of Political Psychology, run at Ohio State University for the past 10 years. The Summer Institute is a 1-month intensive training program in political psychology. Each year, an imbalance between psychologists and political scientists has been evident, with the proportion of participants from psychology generally hovering around 25%; most of the remainder have been from political science. Taken together, these indicators demonstrate that the practice of political psychology has been more valued by the discipline of political science than by the discipline of psychology.

A PLEA FOR MORE POLITICAL PSYCHOLOGY TRUE TO ITS NAME

We make a plea for a more balanced political psychology, one in which a genuine *political psychology true to its name* complements *psychological political science*. This requires a very real shift in the practice of political psychology, through a self-conscious attempt to contribute to psychological theory by paying careful attention to the political context. Our recommendation here is not for research that borrows from political science to inform psychological theory (applied political science) because we find it difficult to imagine what such an enterprise would look like. Rather, the more modest version of *political psychology true to its name* that we have in mind is a research enterprise that contributes regularly (if not equally) to both psychology and political science, and it is a research enterprise in which we hope more psychologists will become engaged.

The primary means by which this balance can be accomplished is by recognizing that careful attention to the key parameters of the *political context* often inspires modifications, elaborations, and extensions of psychological theory developed in context-free work. The presumption underlying much psychological research (particularly laboratory research in social psychology) is that psychological processes that are simple, basic, and generalizable across social contexts can be identified and explained, but this is rarely a tenable assumption. In fact, we believe that one of the challenges in studying the psychology of political thought and action lies in grappling with the parameters of the political context and the nature of the differences between types of actors that often complicate the straightforward application of psychological theory.

Next, we illustrate what we mean with examples from our own separate research programs. We want to apologize in advance for confining this discussion to our own work—this is not meant to suggest that our work is unique or even especially good for illustrating the principles of interest here. Instead, this is simply a choice of convenience, one driven by the fact that we know our own work and its genesis best. So we settle for a few of the many possible examples that could be used for this purpose, ones we hope can help motivate further consideration of political psychology true to its name.

Each research program we describe next began with an interest in understanding a political phenomenon and looked first for relevant insights in the psychology literature. Thus, we set out doing psychological political science. Then, after thinking about the real-world history, context, and implications of the political phenomena of interest, we developed and tested hypotheses that ultimately led to insights that went beyond the psychological theories we initially consulted. In some cases, we found effects of variables that the psychological theories had not anticipated. In other cases, we found that psychological theories we thought would explain a phenomenon did not, in fact, do so and that instead a different psychological account was required. Thus, we were able to identify limiting conditions of the applicability of the original theory. Stated generally, the examples we review next illustrate instances in which careful attention to politics uncovered mediators and moderators of effects that had not yet been incorporated in psychological theory.

To be clear, these are not examples of researchers setting out to do political psychology true to its name, and we do not want to suggest that researchers must begin their work with the goal of evolving psychological theory in mind in order to achieve that goal. Quite the contrary, in fact. We set out first and foremost to understand a political phenomenon, and the payoffs for psychological theory were unintended and incidental. What is not unintended and incidental, though, are our efforts to *highlight* the payoffs for psychological theory after the fact. So looking again at much of the psychological political science already completed may lead people to see findings that can help to advance psychological theory. We hope to encourage researchers to take such looks at the work they have done and that they do in the future and to make efforts to spotlight those payoffs in what they write.

Illustrations of Political Psychology "True to its Name"

News Media Priming.   The notion of *priming* in psychology refers to the impact of recently activated cognitive constructs on subsequent judgments. Iyengar, Kinder, Peters, and Krosnick reasoned that this psychological process offered the promise of identifying a new type of effect the news media might have on public opinion: By focusing on some issues and not others, the news media might shape the "ingredients" contributing to the public's approval and disapproval of the president. Laboratory experiments and survey data all lent support to this notion (Iyengar & Kinder, 1987; Iyengar, Kinder, Peters, & Krosnick, 1984; Krosnick & Brannon, 1993; Krosnick & Kinder, 1990), and these studies are elements of the reinvigorated literature on media effects. These studies were clearly psychological political science because they applied the notion of accessibility to media effects, and the findings seemed to lend support to the psychological theories employed.

Contributions to psychological theory occurred as a byproduct of this work when Krosnick and his associates explored contingency effects, focusing in particular on the impact of political expertise on priming effects. The research began with a relatively straightforward demonstration that priming effects are strongest among people who knew relatively little about politics (Krosnick & Kinder, 1990). This suggested that perhaps accessibility effects are minimal when a person is expert in a domain, a possibility not yet recognized in the psychology literature. These investigators realized, however, that knowledge about politics is positively correlated with two other variables that might have different moderating impacts on priming: interest in political news and exposure to political news. Indeed, when controlling for these latter two variables, it appeared that political knowledge facilitated priming rather than impeding it (Krosnick & Brannon, 1993). This is consistent with the notion that "those who have, get," in the sense that knowledge breeds the accumulation of more knowledge. This raised for the first time the idea that news media priming might not be mediated by cognitive priming (i.e., increases in the accessibility of constructs in memory) at all but rather might be the result of learning.

Miller and Krosnick (2000) investigated this latter issue directly, by exploring whether news media priming is, in fact, mediated by changes in accessibility and found that it is not. This surprise further encouraged consideration of the possibility that news media priming is the result of learning. Another finding of Miller and Krosnick's (2000) supported that notion even more: Media priming was only apparent among people who knew a lot about politics *and* were highly trusting of the media to provide accurate and unbiased information. Furthermore, Miller and Krosnick (2000) found that among these people, priming was mediated by judgments of the national importance of issues: Media coverage of an issue led these people to infer that it was a more important issue for the country than they had thought, which led them to weigh that problem more heavily in evaluating the president's job performance.

Thus, the search for moderators of an effect led these investigators to explore the mediators of the effect, which in turn yielded a challenge to the most significant and fundamental assumption underlying the literature on this and other effects of the news media: that these effects result from changes in construct accessibility. In doing so, this work yielded an important lesson for psychology: Despite the highly plausible applicability of a psychological theory to a real-world phenomenon, this leap must be made cautiously. What appeared to be cognitive priming turned out not to be.

Indeed, this finding raises an even more intriguing possibility. Many psychological studies thought to have demonstrated cognitive priming did not, in fact, measure accessibility and demonstrate through mediational analyses that accessibility shifts were, in fact, responsible for the effects documented. Therefore, it is conceivable that these effects occurred as the result of rather different processes, a possibility definitely worth testing. Doing such testing may lead to further refinement of psychological theory. More generally, this line of thinking reminds all researchers that we should always try to measure presumed mediators and document their roles statistically, rather than taking those roles for granted.

Attitude Importance and Policy Issues. Throughout the 20th century, psychologists regularly acknowledged the idea that some attitudes are stronger than others, presumably meaning that some attitudes are more crystallized and consequential. However, that literature was foggy in two particularly important regards: what exactly *is* attitude strength and where does it come from.

Krosnick's work on attitude importance had its impetus in Converse's (1964) seminal chapter on belief systems in mass publics. In the conclusion of that piece, Converse proposed that rather than attending to the entire array of policy issues facing the nation and forming crystallized and consequential attitudes on each one, the ordinary citizen focuses on just a handful of issues. Attitudes on those issues, he thought, become anchored within cognitive structures and have powerful consequences for political thought and action. However, Converse himself provided very little by way of data to test this proposition.

Krosnick (1988, 1990) set out to explore the viability of this idea and quickly confronted the problem of how to identify the few issues people focus on. Drawing on work from psychology exploring attitude strength, he chose to use an empirical handle available in a number of national survey data sets at the time: people's reports of the personal importance of issues to them. Krosnick (1990) demonstrated that attitudes on policy issues that are more subjectively important exhibit greater stability, greater ideological constraint, and have greater impact on candidate preferences and voting. All this reinforced Converse's notion of issue publics and helped to clarify how issue preferences are formed and influence political behavior.

Because studying the world of politics always requires consideration of normative implications, Krosnick and his colleagues were pushed to think about whether the existence of issue publics was good or bad for a democratic society. To fully understand the normative implications of his evidence on issue publics, Krosnick and his colleagues set out to understand *why* personally important attitudes are more resistant to change and more impactful, and what the causes of personal importance are. The result of their work was an elaborate causal model of the causes and consequences of attitude importance (Boninger, Krosnick, Berent, & Fabrigar, 1995) that is still the subject of empirical research today, highlighting the origins and consequences of attitude strength. The work was valuable to psychology in two principal ways.

With regards to the origins of attitude importance, Krosnick and colleagues' work has pointed to three principal causes: self-interest, social identification with individual and reference groups, and core values. This finding helped to build a bridge between the long-established literature on attitude functions (which was quite cognizant of the roles these three classes of factors play in justifying the existence of attitudes but not specific at all about any other consequences they might have) and the quite separate literature on the cognitive and behavioral effects of attitudes.

Krosnick and colleagues' thinking about *how* importance has its effects led them to develop the notion that importance is first and foremost a choice by an individual to attach significance to an attitude, and this choice has an array of controlled consequences (e.g., gathering relevant information, thinking carefully about it, placing weight on an issue when evaluating a political candidate). However, Krosnick et al. also realized that these processes will have automatic effects eventually, in terms of increased attitude accessibility, the building of links between nodes in memory, and more. All this represented an advance in basic understanding of attitude strength processes.

This led to serious consideration of the relations between importance and various other attitude features thought to be related to their strength, including accessibility, knowledge, certainty, extremity, and more (see Petty & Krosnick, 1995). Some observers have asserted that multiple features actually reflect single underlying constructs (Bassili, 1996; Pomerantz, Chaiken, & Tordesillas, 1995). Others have argued that the dimensions are actually all independent constructs and deserve theoretical status as such (e.g., Krosnick, Boninger, Chuang, Berent, & Carnot, 1993; Lavine, Huff,

Wagner, & Sweeney, 1998). This debate is currently quite active in psychology and far from resolved, and its payoffs are likely to be quite valuable for the study of attitudes.

Managing Blame. McGraw's program of research on political blame management was rooted in her social psychological research in the area of attribution theory. She became interested in applying that perspective toward understanding attributions of responsibility for political predicaments, and so set about designing a study that was a rather straightforward adaptation of key principles from social psychological attribution theory (e.g., manipulating outcome severity and target similarity). The resulting design was frustratingly inadequate because it failed to capture what anyone familiar with the political context would take to be self-evident: namely, that when politicians find themselves in some predicament, they provide an explanation or account to contain the political damage. Recognizing that public officials are not passive bystanders but rather take an active role in trying to shape citizens' reactions to political events led McGraw to refocus the research project on the impact of accounts on attributions of responsibility.

There is a psychological and sociological literature on accounts, but it did not provide much in the way of theoretical guidelines as to the psychological process mechanisms and conditions under which accounts might have an impact on public opinion, nor was there a link between the psychological literatures on attribution of responsibility and accounts. To remedy these omissions, McGraw created a 2 × 2 typology of four different types of accounts (excuses, justifications, concessions, and denials), and developed a theoretical framework that specified the unique impact of the different types of accounts on specific political judgments, such as attributions of responsibility, trait inferences, and opinions about controversial policies (McGraw, 1991, in press). The key lesson here is that different types of accounts have an impact on subsequent global evaluations through different mediational routes, such as changing attributions of responsibility, or by shaping perceptions of character traits, or by changing opinions about the severity of the problem. Later work considered the impact of critical political individual difference variables (in particular, sophistication and trust in government) and situational parameters that moderate the impact of political accounts (McGraw, Best, & Timpone, 1995; McGraw & Hubbard, 1996), and extended the model to consider the impact of political accounts on opinions about the political institutions and organizations where wrongdoing occurs (McGraw, 1999).

Specifying the impact of political explanations on public opinion is critical to political scientists' understanding of the delicate and negotiated relationship between citizens and their elected representatives, but this research also enriches, in several ways, more general psychological theory about attributions of responsibility and accountability. First and foremost, it suggests that the static and impoverished laboratory paradigm used to study attributions of responsibility overlooks a critical aspect of most real-world wrongdoing, namely that alleged transgressors make excuses, offer justifications, and in general are quite adept at trying to manipulate the perceiver's reactions to the event. Second, the theoretical model developed by McGraw and her colleagues, and the subsequent empirical validations, identified a set of mediating and moderating principles that spell out why and when accounts have an impact on opinions about others in our social world in greater detail than previous social psychological theorizing had considered.

Suspicion. McGraw and her colleagues (McGraw, Lodge, & Jones, 2000) also investigated the antecedents and consequences of political suspicion for public opinion. There is an emerging literature on suspicion in social psychology (e.g., Hilton, Fein, & Miller, 1993), and in thinking about the implications of suspicion for understanding public opinion, McGraw et al. were struck by a paradox. The dramatic decline in political trust that has been documented over the past several decades has arguably made contemporary politicians particularly vulnerable to suspicion about the sincerity of their stated policy positions. However, the psychological literature indicates that suspicion produces an active state of cognitive appraisal and scrutiny. Although it may well be that citizens are predisposed to be suspicious of the positions taken by public officials, the heightened state of cognitive activity that is the defining characteristic of suspicion is anathema to most citizens (Kinder, 1998). In other words, although a generalized cynicism toward politics is widespread, suspicion directed toward specific political actors seems unlikely because of the amount of cognitive work that is required in sustaining suspicion.

Thinking about this paradox led McGraw and her colleagues to think carefully about the strategies politicians use when setting forth their policy stands, and in particular about how strategically rational politicians are skillful at crafting political communications that are congruent with their audience's preferences (*pandering* is the pejorative term for this practice). This in turn led to a consideration of the evaluative reactions that citizens can have to potentially suspect communications, and the theoretical prediction (supported empirically) that citizens' reactions to political policy statements regulate the experience of suspicion: policy agreement derails suspicion and its attendant negative consequences, whereas policy disagreement magnifies the experience of suspicion.

The systematic social psychological study of suspicion is in its infancy, and the McGraw et al. (2000) study points to important considerations that might shape future developments. Whereas current formulations empha-size the cognitive processing mechanisms involved in suspicion (Hilton, Fein, and Miller, 1993), the work of McGraw and her colleagues points to the critical role that evaluative reactions play in regulating the experience of suspicion: simply, perceivers are less likely to be suspicious of communi-cations that they agree with or that make them happy. In addition, as with the McGraw work on accounts and blame management, consideration of the political context underscores the importance of understanding the influence of strategic interactions among social actors in the dynamics of suspicion: Skilled communicators have tools at their disposal to minimize the arousal of suspicion.

Implications

All four of these examples are cases where we set out to do psychological political science—to apply established psychological theories to under-stand a political phenomenon. However, the political context forced us to think more deeply and carefully about the limits of those existing theories and to generate new extensions and modifications that could better cap-ture the complexity of political reality; the results are findings and insights that psychologists may find of use. But recognizing these uses is the result of a constant interplay between psychological and political theory when fac-ing real-world phenomena. So beyond pursuing the goal of understanding political phenomena, we have found ourselves contributing to psychologi-cal theories of human thought and behavior.

The proposition that theories developed in a context-specific environ-ment can illuminate cross-contextual generalizations may seem counter-intuitive, but it is an insight harkening back to the explanatory framework proposed by Lewin in 1936, when he stated, "Every psychological event depends upon the state of the person and at the same time the state of the environment, although their relative importance is different in different cases" (p. 216). More precise is Lewin's classic formulation:

$$\text{Behavior} = f (\text{Person, Environment}).$$

From this perspective, theory develops as new "conditions under which" principles are identified and empirically supported. These conditions are both the situations in which certain outcomes are more or less likely to occur and the classes of people among which outcomes are more or less likely to be observed. It seems to us to be no coincidence that some of the most prominent elaborations of Lewin's notion of the interplay between personal and situational factors have been proposed by scholars working at the intersection of political science and psychology: Smith's (1968) "intel-lectual strategy" for the study of political personality; McGuire's (1969) matrix of persuasibility and his (1983) "contextualist theory of knowledge;" and Sniderman and his colleagues' contributions to our understanding of the dynamics of public opinion (1993; Sniderman, Brody, & Tetlock, 1991).

In sum, we are convinced that taking the political context seriously results in scholarship that contributes to both political science and psychology (see Rahn and Sullivan, in press, for additional examples). In our experience, practicing political psychology true to its name yields lots of intellectual satisfaction, just as does the successful application of psychological theory required by "psychological political science." If political scientists and psychologists alike focus their efforts, at least on occasion, to highlight the payoffs of their work for psychological theory, this may enhance the apparent value of political psychology in the eyes of all psychologists. The most important payoffs of such perceptions may be a greater flow of students into the field of political psychology within psychology, more faculty hiring in the area in psychology departments, and greater financial support for our efforts by psychological funding agencies, all of which would contribute to the vitality of the field.

CONCLUSION

Our hope in raising the distinction between *psychological political science* and *political psychology true to its name* is that scholars will be more self-conscious in thinking about the findings their research generates, always on the lookout for ways that their evidence can help to advance basic psychological theory. We recognize that contributing to both political science and psychology is not an easy task, but we believe the payoffs—for both individuals and the disciplines—can be substantial.

ACKNOWLEDGMENTS

Our sincere thanks to Wendy Rahn for her helpful comments.

REFERENCES

Baron, R. M., & Kenny, D. A. (1986). The moderator–mediator variable distinction in social psychological research: Conceptual, strategic, and statistical considerations. *Journal of Personality and Social Psychology, 51,* 1173–1182.

Bassili, J. N. (1996). Meta-judgmental versus operative indexes of psychological attributes: The case of measures of attitude strength. *Journal of Personality and Social Psychology, 71,* 637–653.

Boninger, D. S., Krosnick, J. A., Berent, M. K., & Fabrigar, L. R. (1995). The causes and consequences of attitude importance. In R. E. Petty & J. A. Krosnick (Eds.), *Attitude strength: Antecedents and consequences* (pp. 159–190). Hillsdale, NJ: Lawrence Erlbaum Associates.

Converse, P. E. (1964). The nature of belief systems in mass publics. In D. E. Apter (Ed.), *Ideology and discontent* (pp. 206–261). New York: Free Press.

Hastie, R., & Park, B. (1986). The relationship between memory and judgment depends on whether the task is memory-based or on-line. *Psychological Review, 93,* 258–268.

Hilton, J. L., Fein, S., & Miller, D. T. (1993). Suspicion and dispositional inference. *Personality and Social Psychology Bulletin, 19,* 501–512.

Iyengar, S., & Kinder, D. R. (1987). *News that matters.* Chicago: University of Chicago Press.

Iyengar, S., Kinder, D. R., Peters, M. D., & Krosnick, J. A. (1984). The evening news and presidential evaluations. *Journal of Personality and Social Psychology, 46,* 778–787.

Iyengar, S., & McGuire, W. J. (1993). *Explorations in political psychology.* Durham, NC: Duke University Press.

Kelley, S. (1983). *Interpreting elections.* Princeton, NJ: Princeton University Press.

Kelley, S., & Mirer, T. (1974). The simple act of voting. *American Political Science Review, 68,* 572–591.

Kinder, D. R. (1998). Opinion and action in the realm of politics. In D. T. Gilbert, S. T. Fiske, & G. Lindzey (Eds.), *The handbook of social psychology* (4th ed., pp. 778–867). New York: Oxford University Press.

Krosnick, J. A. (1988). The role of attitude importance in social evaluation: A study of policy preferences, presidential candidate evaluations, and voting behavior. *Journal of Personality and Social Psychology, 55,* 196–210.

Krosnick, J. A. (1990). Government policy and citizen passion: A study of issue publics in contemporary America. *Political Behavior, 12,* 59–92.

Krosnick, J. A. (in press). Is political psychology sufficiently psychological? Distinguishing political psychology from psychological political science. In J. Kuklinski (Ed.), *Citizens and politics: Perspectives from political psychology.* New York: Cambridge University Press.

Krosnick, J. A., Boninger, D. S., Chuang, Y. C., Berent, M. K., & Carnot, C. G. (1993). Attitude strength: One construct or many related constructs? *Journal of Personality and Social Psychology, 65,* 1132–1149.

Krosnick, J. A., & Brannon, L. A. (1993). The impact of the Gulf War on the ingredients of Presidential evaluations: Multidimensional effects of political involvement. *American Political Science Review, 87,* 953–975.

Krosnick, J. A., & Kinder, D. R. (1990). Altering the foundations of support for the President through priming. *American Political Science Review, 84,* 497–512.

Lavine, H., Huff, J. W., Wagner, S. H., & Sweeney, D. (1998). The moderating influence of attitude strength on the susceptibility to context effects in attitude surveys. *Journal of Personality and Social Psychology, 75,* 359–373.

Lewin, K. (1936). *Principles of topological psychology.* New York: McGraw-Hill.

Lodge, M., McGraw, K. M., & Stroh, P. (1989). An impression driven model of candidate evaluation. *American Political Science Review, 83,* 399–420.

Lodge, M., & Steenbergen, M. (1995). The responsive voter: Campaign information and the dynamics of candidate evaluation. *American Political Science Review, 89,* 309–326.

Lodge, M., & Taber, C. (2000). Three steps toward a theory of motivated political reasoning. In A. Lupia, M. D. McCubbins, & S. L. Popkin (Eds.), *Elements of reason: Cognition, choice, and the bounds of rationality* (pp. 183–213). New York: Cambridge University Press.

McGraw, K. M. (1991). Managing blame: An experimental test of the effects of political accounts. *American Political Science Review, 85,* 1133–1158.

McGraw, K. M. (1999). *Institutional responsibility and reputations in times of crisis: An investigation of the Navy Tailhook scandal.* Manuscript under review.

McGraw, K. M. (in press). Political accounts and attribution processes. In J. Kuklinski (Ed.), *Citizens and politics: Perspectives from political psychology.* New York: Cambridge University Press.

McGraw, K. M., Best, S., & Timpone, R. (1995). "What they say or what they do?" The impact of elite explanation and policy outcomes on public opinion. *American Journal of Political Science, 39,* 53–74.

McGraw, K. M., & Hubbard, C. (1996). Some of the people some of the time: Individual differences in acceptance of political accounts. In D. C. Mutz, P. Sniderman, & R. Brody (Eds.), *Political persuasion and attitude change* (pp. 145–170). Ann Arbor: University of Michigan Press.

McGraw, K. M., Lodge, M., & Jones, J. (2000). *The pandering politicians of suspicious minds.* Manuscript under review.

McGraw, K. M., Lodge, M., & Stroh, P. (1990). Online processing in candidate evaluation: The effects of issue order, issue salience and sophistication. *Political Behavior, 12,* 41–58.

McGuire, W. J. (1969). The nature of attitudes and attitude change. In G. Lindzey & E. Anderson (Eds.), *Handbook of social psychology* (2nd ed., pp. 136–314). Reading, MA: Addison-Wesley.

McGuire, W. J. (1983). A contextualist theory of knowledge: Its implications for innovation and reform in psychological research. In L. Berkowitz (Ed.), *Advances in Experimental Social Psychology* (Vol. 16, pp. 1–48). New York: Academic Press.

Miller, J. M., & Krosnick, J. A. (2000). News media impact on the ingredients of Presidential evaluations: Politically knowledgeable citizens are guided by a trusted source. *American Journal of Political Science, 44,* 295–309.

Petty, R. E., & Krosnick, J. A. (Eds.). (1995). *Attitude strength: Antecedents and consequences.* Hillsdale, NJ: Lawrence Erlbaum Associates.

Pomerantz, E. M., Chaiken, S., & Tordesillas, R. S. (1995). Attitude strength and resistance processes. *Journal of Personality and Social Psychology, 69,* 408–419.

Rahn, W. M. (1995). Candidate evaluation in complex information environments: Cognitive organization and comparison process. In M. Lodge & K. M. McGraw (Eds.), *Political judgment: Structure and process* (pp. 43–64). Ann Arbor: University of Michigan Press.

Rahn, W. M., Aldrich, J. H., & Borgida, E. (1994). Individual and contextual variations in political candidate appraisal. *American Political Science Review, 88,* 193–199.

Rahn, W. M., Krosnick, J. A., & Breuning, M. (1994). Rationalization and derivation processes in survey studies of political candidate evaluation. *American Journal of Political Science, 38,* 582–600.

Rahn, W. M., & Sullivan, J. L. (in press). Political psychology and political science. In J. Kuklinski (Ed.), *Citizens and politics: Perspectives from political psychology.* New York: Cambridge University Press.

Redlawsk, D. (2001). You must remember this: A test of the on-line model of voting. *Journal of Politics, 63,* 29–58.

Sears, D. O. (1987). Political psychology. *Annual Review of Psychology, 38,* 229–255.

Smith, M. B. (1968). A map for the analysis of personality and politics. *Journal of Social Issues, 24,* 15–28.

Sniderman, P. M. (1993). The new look in public opinion research. In A. W. Finifter (Ed.), *Political science: The state of the discipline II* (pp. 219–245). Washington, DC: American Political Science Association.

Sniderman, P. M., Brody, R. A., & Tetlock, P. E. (1991). *Reasoning and choice: Explorations in political psychology.* Cambridge: Cambridge University Press.

Zaller, J. R. (1992). *The nature and origins of mass opinion.* New York: Cambridge University Press.

Zimbardo, P. G. (1988). *Psychology and life.* Glenview, IL: Scott, Foresman and Co.

5

Political Psychology: A Personal View

GEORGE E. MARCUS
Williams College

WHAT IS POLITICAL PSYCHOLOGY?

There are a number of ways to approach defining political psychology. For a very long time, humans have inquired about their nature, seeking to reconcile their political beliefs and aspirations with what they took to be their underlying essence. It has been a common presumption that whatever this essence is, and however it might be stretched by growth or stunted by deprivation, we must begin with a sound understanding of human psychology. Aristotle, Plato, Montesquieu, Rousseau, Descartes, Hume, Hobbes, Locke, and Madison are just some of the most obvious who began in this fashion.[1] Speculations about the "state of nature," wherein the true, uncontaminated nature of humans would be revealed, abound in Western political philosophy.[2] Additionally, "human nature" is taken to be at the heart of explaining how people, as organized in nations or communities, interact. When Herodotus and Thucydides wrote the earliest histories of the Greeks and of the wars that engaged them among the various city-states and between the

---

[1] For Aristotle, both *The Politics* (1983) and *Rhetoric* (1954); for Plato, *The Republic* is a good place to begin (1974); for Monstequieu, *The Spirit of the Laws* (1955); for Rousseau, *On the Social Contract* (1983); for Descartes, *Discourse on Method and Meditations* (1637/1960); for Hume, *A Treatise on Human Nature* (1739/1984); for Hobbes, *Leviathan* (1968); for Locke, *The Second Treatise on Government* (1689); and for Madison, all of the Federalist Papers he wrote, but especially, no. 10 (Madison, Hamilton, & Jay, 1961).

[2] Though of course, it was always an effective rejoinder, that given by Aristotle, that our nature could only be fully revealed not in a state of nature but in the *polis*.

Greeks and Persians, human nature—the psyche, as they understood it—
was at the very center of their accounts.

So from the very outset, political thinkers and historians have drawn on
insights from what we now think of as psychology, although as a discipline
psychology would not achieve its current status as a scientific field within
the university structure until centuries later. Political psychologists seek to
answer political questions, to gain an understanding of how people go
about politics, in part from inquiring about their psychology. That said,
there are numerous sources that speak to the enterprise of political psychology. Although some are dated, there are a number of handbooks and a
variety of published collections of research reports. More recently, compi-
lations of new work can be found in the annual series, *Research in Micropolitics*[3] and the journal of the International Society of Political Psychology,
Political Psychology.[4] Even the briefest exploration shows the field of political
psychology to be vast and expanding. Given its expanse, then, trying to provide a suitable definition of political psychology and its current applications
is a daunting task. Let me approach it from my own intellectual history.

I came to political psychology for personal reasons. Those reasons
explain both why political psychology has become my devotion and why
particular areas of political psychology have dominated my own research
agenda. I was born to a couple, a German father and an Austrian mother,
who met and married in Vienna. They left Vienna, Germany, in March of
1939. I trust most of you will have caught the national designation. My parents lived in hiding for about one year after the Anschluss until they could
secure the necessary permissions to enter another country and escape from
the Nazis. They left because, as Jews, had they stayed they would have experienced the same fate as did most of their families along with the six millions Jews who perished. Very few members of my family (my maternal
grandparents, but not my paternal grandmother, a few cousins scattered
around the world) managed to escape deportation to the camps. I was born
in 1943, therefore, the events of World War II shaped me in various ways.
A number of questions were then and now pervasive and enduring for me:
Why did my parents not talk much about their family or their experiences
in Europe? Why did they not teach me German, their mother tongue?
More pressing, what did they expect of me? And, had I been born a bit
earlier, while in Germany (for Vienna was then a part of Germany), what
would have become of me?

Apart from shaping my youth, the events of my family's history informed
what have become the principal questions that motivate my life's research
program: How does a nation secure tolerance for all its diverse individuals?

---

[3]Published by JAI Press and edited by M. Delli Carpini, L. Huddy, and R. Y. Shapiro.
[4]There is also an excellent website maintained by the Society. It can be found at ISPP.ORG.

Are there conditions in which democracy can be a just society? If so, what are they? This century has provided ample evidence that people will actually choose to go down a path of hatred and destruction. For me, then, political psychology has been defined by my search for answers to the questions surrounding political tolerance (Marcus, Sullivan, Theiss-Morese, & Wood, 1995; Sullivan, Piereson, & Marcus, 1982) and questions that explore the nature of democratic citizenship (Marcus, 1988a, 1988b; Marcus & Hanson, 1993; Marcus & MacKuen, 1993). My personal agenda thus is not very different from that which has dominated the study of human nature for the past millennia: how to construct just societies that are capable of self-rule.

The answers to these questions can be found in conventional wisdom and in various ideologies—liberal, conservative, democratic, or elitist. However, I have always been deeply suspicious of contemporary accounts. For if the Enlightenment was supposed to bring progress and justice, why did some of the most advanced nations embrace the greatest evil? And, if Marxism saw revolution as the inevitable result of increasingly industrial societies, why did Communist revolutions occur in the backwaters and in agrarian societies (e.g., Russia, China, and Cuba)? I thus was drawn to the rigor and skepticism of science and of its attendant premise that the strength of beliefs held by people throughout history teaches us less about their inherent truth than about the dynamics of popular enthusiasms. It is more than merely a footnote to suggest that some of the most important findings in political psychology demonstrate the enduring power of convictions to overwhelm reality testing (Sears, Hensler, & Speer, 1979; Sears, Lau, Tyler, & Allen, 1980).

Because of this, my hope for my students is that they, too, are similarly drawn to political psychology as a science. I hope they have the good fortune to discover those political and moral questions that most engage them, for these can animate a career and give personal meaning to a professional life.

HOW DOES POLITICAL PSYCHOLOGY DIFFER FROM OTHER FORMS OF PSYCHOLOGY?

This question posits that there is a discipline called psychology. Gazzaniga (1998) recently suggested there is no longer a discipline of psychology. Certainly, psychology has gone through a process of increasing balkanization such that there is little unifying theorizing going on. Gazzaniga invited us to pick and choose among the fields that seek to replace psychology. From among a variety of fields, some new, some old, we have cognitive science, neuroscience, social psychology, clinical psychology, and so on. These, among others, are effectively divided into independent fiefdoms. So an important issue is not how political psychology differs from other forms of psychology, but which of the various extant fields offer some promise for political psychology.

The other implication of this question derives from its presumption that political psychology is essentially an applied field, in which it is the job of the researcher to gather knowledge to better understand politics. In that sense, political psychology is more firmly a part of political science than it is a part of psychology. Political scientists have placed political psychology at the heart of the political enterprise of constructing political communities for centuries, whereas psychologists tend to treat political psychology as just one field among many.

There is, however, a danger in the inclination of political psychologists to rely solely on psychology for theoretical illumination. That danger is evident to anyone who has read, for example, Emile Durkheim's *Suicide* (1951). Durkheim showed that although it may appear evident that psychological effects (in this instance, ending one's life) are due to psychological causes, this is not always the case. Yet political psychologists too rarely embed psychological effects and their proximate causes within a broader theoretical sweep that encompasses sociological factors. Political psychology cannot, by itself, provide a complete theoretical account of politics. However, in conjunction with other disciplines, it can contribute an essential element in a fuller explanation. That political psychology cannot by itself provide a complete account does not undermine its central position in contributing to such an account.

WHAT ARE THE CENTRAL TEXTS, CONCEPTS, AND DEBATES?

So, where to begin if one is going to inquire about human nature? I began with the Greeks: everything available by Homer, Aeschylus, Sophocles, Euripedes, Aristophones, and of course, much, if not all, of Plato and his student and arch critic, Aristotle. For issues writ large, one cannot do better than Herodotus and Thucydides. To get a firm grip on the emergence of the nation state, of course Hobbes, but we tend to read Hobbes from our contemporary vantage, encased in our modernity and little affected by his description of the state of nature. When teaching Hobbes, I like begin by having my class read *Njal's Saga,* the magnificent Icelandic saga, to provide a vivid and compelling account of life in the absence of the Leviathan. Oakeshott (1975) is also helpful on the complex process that leads to the modern national state. Of course, much of the corpus of political philosophy remains a valuable source of concepts and insights, as well as theoretical and empirical assertions.

Fiction constitutes another rich realm of texts worth reading. It is fair to say that most political psychologists live in the privileged, secure, and tranquil settings of the academy. Individually, we can directly observe and experience only a very restricted and biased sample of the full range of historical human experience. Fiction offers one way of extending the reach of our imagination if only vicariously. I personally love Joseph Conrad (especially *The Heart of Darkness, Nostromo,* and *The Secret Agent*), Trollope, Dostoevsky, Robertson Davies. For commentary, it's hard to ignore George Orwell (especially on the Spanish Civil War). Taken together as well as singly, these provide insight not only into human nature but also into conventional taxonomies readily available to us all to impose order and sense on the rich variety of human experience.

I mentioned earlier my disinclination to take an overly rhapsodic view of democracy. Tocqueville is indispensible, not only *Democracy in America* (1835/1974), but also *The Ancien Régime and the French Revolution* (1856/1978), and his recently found (1835/1977) minor work on pauperism.[5] I further recommend not only the Federalist Papers (Madison, Hamilton, & Jay, 1961), but also Hofstadter's important work, especially his essay on the paranoid style (Hofstadter, 1965). It was the first to uncover an important consequence of a diverse and extended republic—if the public is "in charge" yet bad things happen, then the only sound explanation is that there must be some unseen conspiracy to explain why.[6] Fromm (1941/1965), as well as many others, also touches on the dark underside of popular rule. Merely asserting that the public ought to rule should not be taken to mean that, automatically, material well-being and justice will necessarily follow.[7]

So what are the crucial issues that political psychology should engage? For me, the following have proved of enduring interest: Although not true in the 17th and 18th centuries, and not fully realized until the 20th century, citizenship is now defined as the individual expression of preferences and judgments, expected to be expressed without the oppressive imposition of partisan and other tribal obligations.[8] Moreover, citizens are expected to make decisions based on their conceptions of the public good and of justice. Equally demanding, they are expected to take on the stance of impartiality (the Kantian categorical imperative lives on in the liberal tradition

---

[5]These can be found in Tocqueville (1835/1974, 1978, 1835/1997).

[6]This is a rather dangerous example of the attribution bias (i.e., good things are attributed to our own efforts, failures are attributed elsewhere to deflect blame and guilt).

[7]Too often participatory democratic theorists (Barber, 1984; Pateman, 1970), pushing for more democracy, blithely ignore evidence that more democracy will not inevitably produce the untrammeled utopia they envision.

[8]A nice review of the changing definition of citizenship, in the American context, is presented in Schudson (1998).

[Rawls, 1971]). That raises the recurring issue of how well citizens meet that demanding set of obligations (Marcus & Hanson, 1993; Thompson, 1970). It raises the issue of what we mean by rationality, by judgment and justice. It also raises the question of how best to secure the values that liberal, plural, representative democracies require for stability as well as for justice and freedom.

The standard tradition in social science has been to ask people to construct their reasons, attitudes, beliefs, and values. Given such information as these provide, we then draw theoretical and empirical models to depict the prized beliefs (e.g., support for democratic principles) and assess causal factors believed to strengthen, or undermine. More recently, I, as well as others in political psychology, have been engaged in exploring the role of emotions in this mix of issues. Recent reviews on the psychology of emotion (Cacioppo & Gardner, 1999; Zajonc, 1998) and on emotion in politics (Glaser & Salovey, 1998; Marcus, 2000) have been published suggesting that interest in emotion is burgeoning. Emotion may be of interest not only as a potentially interesting set of causal factors, but also as a factor that may encourage or—more conventionally—discourage proper citizen judgment and belief.[9]

Recently, after a long period of being engaged by social psychology, I have relied increasingly on current work in neuroscience (Marcus, 1988b; Marcus & MacKuen, 1993; Marcus, Neuman, & MacKuen, 2000; Marcus et al., 1995). The remarkable work now ongoing in neuroscience ends the long period of speculation of how the brain works.[10] From at least Descartes (1637/1960, 1649/1989) through Freud, how the brain generates emotion, reason, consciousness, memory, and so forth has been driven by the unreliable and often misleading devices of external observation, introspection, and self-report. Prior to the development of the measurement technologies developed by neuroscience, the many suggestions, such as Locke's view of the mind as an empty vessel, or the many who speculate about passion— Hume (1739/1984), Adam Smith, James Madison, or even William James (1883, 1894, 1890/1981)—were each developed from interpretations that had little in the way of direct evidence. Inasmuch as the human senses are directed at external observation, to provide some sense of the world as it presents itself and impacts on us, we have little access to those mysterious sensations expressed as feelings (as when we feel depressed either from dis-

---

[9]That emotion is most often thought of as a force that should be at least controlled if democracies are to be safe is a long-standing view, shared by James Madison and John Rawls, among many others. Thus, it often proves to be a surprise, even to political psychologists, when emotion seems to initiate and sustain the most generous of Samaritan behavior even in the absence of belief or conviction (Monroe, 1996).

[10]A number of excellent sources exist to begin to get familiar with this work, including Damasio (1994), Gray (1987), LeDoux (1996), Rolls (1999), and Zuckerman (1991).

position, current fatigue, or external circumstances). Feelings are notoriously difficult to interpret both as to what they are and as to the underlying cause.[11] Also, however flawed our senses are for external observation, they provide little in the way of accurate insight into how the senses function or how the brain itself performs its many tasks. Yet neuroscience is now providing the tools to dramatically change how the brain functions, and, more to this point, how to change our conception of emotion as the dangerous and hidden force beyond the reach of serious scientific work.

Putting emotion in the center of the study of human judgment may seem a long delayed yet obvious move. It is in part made possible by the work of neuroscientists (Armony & LeDoux, 1997; Damasio, 1994; Davis, 1992; Gray, 1987, 1990; LeDoux, 1987, 1995). Extending that work to politics is now the effort of an increasing number of political psychologists, myself among them. Perhaps most important is this central finding: The brain collects far more information than is represented in conscious awareness. Indeed, the current best estimate is that the brain processes about a million bits of information, received from the various senses, for every bit available in consciousness (Nørretranders, 1998). The recent interest in "information processing" in political psychology unfortunately has been restricted to the "information" that is available for semantic representation and recall (Ferejohn & Kuklinski, 1990). Thus, for the most part, political psychologists have been studying a much reduced, and biased, sample of the information available to the human brain, that which is available in conscious awareness. This would be not unreasonable if that were the only information that influenced political affairs, but if that presumption is false, then the results obtained thereby are suspect.

We have learned that the brain does not collect excess sensory information for no purpose. The emotional systems of the brain, along with other systems that do not present in consciousness, play essential functions in interpreting the sensory flow in the human brain. Not only do these systems attend to *more* of that information than appears in consciousness, they do so *before* some little part of that information appears in consciousness, but these systems also initiate behavior and direct how and on what consciousness dwells (Marcus et al., 2000). For the first time in human history, political psychologists have the tools to study these and other effects on politics. We need entirely new theories, new concepts, and new data. That process is well underway. We can expect a stream of new work that has the possibil-

---

[11] Even more so than to discern the underlying sources of our beliefs, values, or other mental constructs presumed to be embedded in "schemas" (Hastie, 1986; Lau, 1986; Lodge & Hamill, 1986; Miller, Wattenburg, & Malanchuk, 1986). For a critique of the current enthusiasm for placing schemas as the principal metaphor for mental representations, see Kuklinski, Luskin, and Bolland (1991).

ity of reshaping not only political psychology but also what we know about politics.

THE METHODS, APPROACHES AND SUBSTANTIVE DISCUSSIONS MOST FRUITFUL

As with all social sciences, political psychology suffers from the problem that we are studying ourselves. We are limited by the very senses we bring to bear on our investigations. What we see and hear is limited by the structure of our senses (e.g., we cannot see light above and below the visible range, we cannot hear sounds that many other species readily detect). Moreover, the manner by which humans preserve what they have learned, at least that which is encoded semantically into beliefs, attitudes, and values, is suspect for a variety of reasons. Festinger's (1956, 1957) pioneering work evidenced compelling support for the inclination of humans to preserve what they believe to be true even in the face of explicit counterfactual experience. But perhaps the most compelling account of the dilemmas associated with the study of ourselves is that given by James Madison in the less noted Federalist Paper, no. 37. In Federalist no. 37, Madison (Madison et al., 1961) argued that human knowledge is always difficult for three reasons. First, he cited the problem of taxonomy: Knowledge depends on finding suitable categories but categories are often confronted with instances that do not comfortably fit within their definitional bounds. Second, we have to rely on "organs of perception" that are themselves fallible. Finally, whatever we perceive must be described by words so that "however accurately the discrimination may be considered, the definition of them may be rendered inaccurate by the inaccuracy of the terms in which it is delivered. And this unavoidable inaccuracy of the terms in which it is delivered" (Madison et al., 1961). Summing up, there are three natural barriers that obscure our otherwise clear understanding of things: "indistinctness of the object, imperfection of the organ of conception, [and] inadequateness of the vehicle of ideas" (Madison et al., 1961). So even before we get the complicating problem of passion, interest, and politics, there are serious and unavoidable barriers to certain knowledge.

How do we meet this difficult challenge? Of course, double blind studies, experiments in which neither the person contacting the subjects, nor the subjects themselves, know the intent of the study or the particulars bearing on the subject, are an essential tool. Requiring data to be public and requiring evidence to be continually subject to replication and reinvestigations are also vital.

There are a number of recurring patterns of analysis that should give us cause for concern. Too often we contribute research reports in which a series of variables, possible "causes," are dumped into the conventional ordinary least squares regression model (or correlation matrix). Although this approach *might* offer modest evidence that the particular factors of interest have something to do with the behavior, belief, emotion, or attitude at hand, in point of fact such findings offer less than meets the eye. The primary problem is that this approach assumes that causal factors can be influential only through their direct effects. Because effects may occur through mediating variables, or by modulating (i.e., interaction effects) the effects of other factors, effects that are not revealed by OLS (ordinary least squares), testing for statistical significance in such models may actually exclude important effects from further consideration.

This becomes especially important when we theorize that humans have dynamic abilities—to act or not, to confirm or set aside convictions, to rely on habit, or to strike for new ideas or new solutions. This capacity of humans, to be adaptive and imaginative at least in certain circumstances, requires that our theoretical and methodological models provide for such dynamic contingencies. Happily, the increased popularity of experiments in political science generally, and political psychology in particular, offers some hope that we will see theoretical formulations that provide the richer accounts of the range of human experience that studies of political behavior demand (Kinder & Palfrey, 1993). For example, the effects of mood on judgment is a topic that has begun to receive a lot of attention recently.[12] A full examination of such effects will almost certainly require theoretical models that provide for direct, mediating, and moderating relationships (Rusting, 1998). And, some important findings of such effects are now being reported (Feldman & Stenner, 1997).

CONCLUSION

Conventional wisdom, whether as to substantive conclusions, methodologies, or typologies, is, by definition, well entrenched. As such, the "state of the field" often becomes resistant to self-examination due to our comfort with prevailing accounts. After all, political psychologists are no less a part of our field of study than is everyone else and subject to the curiosities we see all around us.

Some 30 years ago, Thompson (1970) wrote a fine book on the relationship between empirical work on citizenship and democratic theory. He laid out a useful typology to organize the ways in which social science empirical findings can be useful. First, by offering careful description, we can assay

---

[12]The most useful citations are Clore, Schwarz, and Conway (1994), Forgas (1994, 1995), Marcus et al. (1995), and Marcus et al. (2000).

the current state of things. Second, by identifying causal patterns, we can identify trends that will, given continuity of circumstances, likely lead to predictable changes. For example, if we know the effects of greater education on a public, then as the proportion of the public completing high school or college increases, we can make confident, if contingent, predictions about these consequence effects. Thirdly, and more speculatively, if the effects we hope for are dependent on radical modification of the "background conditions," we will have a harder time being confident that the anticipated results will be delivered consistent with expectations. The disastrous consequences of social engineering, on the left and right, in this century, give more than sufficient confirmation for the appropriate trepidation for such social engineering. Still, however circumspect we must be in advancing our current understandings, we should not shy away from the obligation to do an ever better job of self-examination, for how else can political psychology become that scientific enterprise?

REFERENCES

Aristotle. (1954). *Rhetoric* (W. R. Roberts, Trans.). New York: Modern Library.

Aristotle. (1983). *The politics* (T. A. Sinclair, Trans.) (Rev. ed.). New York: Penguin Books.

Armony, J. L., & LeDoux, J. E. (1997). How the brain processes emotional information. *Annals of the New York Academy of Sciences, 821,* 259–270.

Barber, B. (1984). *Strong democracy: Participatory politics for a new age.* Berkeley and Los Angeles, CA: University of California Press.

Cacioppo, J. T., & Gardner, W. L. (1999). Emotion. *Annual Review of Psychology, 50,* 191–214.

Clore, G. L., Schwarz, N., & Conway, M. (1994). Affective causes and consequences of social information processing. In R. S. Wyer, Jr. & T. K. Srull (Eds.), *Handbook of social cognition* (2nd ed., Vol. 1, pp. 323–417). Hillsdale, NJ: Lawrence Erlbaum Associates.

Damasio, A. R. (1994). *Descartes' error: Emotion, reason and the human brain.* New York: G. P. Putnam's Sons.

Davis, M. (1992). The role of the amygdala in conditioned fear. In J. P. Aggleton (Ed.), *The amygdala: Neurobiological aspects of emotion, memory, and mental dysfunction* (pp. 255–305). New York: Wiley-Liss, Inc.

Descartes, R. (1960). *Discourse on method and meditations.* Indianapolis, IN: Bobbs-Merrill. (Original work published 1637)

Descartes, R. (1989). *The passions of the soul* (S. H. Voss, Trans.). Indianapolis, IN: Hackett. (Original work published 1649)

Durkheim, E. (1951). *Suicide.* Glencoe, IL: Free Press.

Feldman, S., & Stenner, K. (1997). Perceived threat and authoritarianism. *Political Psychology, 18*(4), 741–770.

Ferejohn, J. A., & Kuklinski, J. H. (Eds.). (1990). *Information and democratic processes.* Urbana: University of Illinois Press.

Festinger, L. (1956). *When prophecy fails.* Minneapolis: University of Minnesota Press.

Festinger, L. (1957). *A theory of cognitive dissonance.* Stanford, CA: Stanford University Press.

Forgas, J. P. (1994). The role of emotion in social judgments. *European Journal of Social Psychology, 24*(1), 1–24.

Forgas, J. P. (1995). Mood and judgment: The affect infusion model (AIM). *Psychological Bulletin, 117*(1), 39–66.

Fromm, E. (1965). *Escape from freedom.* New York: Avon Publishers. (Original work published 1941)

Gazzaniga, M. S. (1998). *The mind's past.* Berkeley: University of California Press.

Glaser, J., & Salovey, P. (1998). Affect in electoral politics. *Personality and Social Psychology Review, 2*(3), 156–172.

Gray, J. A. (1987). *The psychology of fear and stress* (2nd ed.). Cambridge: Cambridge University Press.

Gray, J. A. (1990). Brain systems that mediate both emotion and cognition. *Cognition and Emotion, 4*(3), 269–288.

Hastie, R. (1986). A primer of information-processing theory for the political scientist. In R. Lau & D. Sears (Eds.), *Political cognition* (pp. 11–39). Hillsdale, NJ: Lawrence Erlbaum Associates.

Hobbes, T. (1968). *Leviathan.* London: Penguin Books.

Hofstadter, R. (1965). *The paranoid style in American politics, and other essays* (1st ed.). New York: Knopf.

Hume, D. (1984). *A treatise of human nature.* London: Penguin Books. (Original work published 1739)

James, W. (1883). What is emotion? *Mind, 9,* 188–204.

James, W. (1894). The physical basis of emotion. *Psychological Review, 1,* 516–529.

James, W. (1981). *The principles of psychology.* Cambridge, MA: Harvard University Press. (Original work published 1890)

Kinder, D. R., & Palfrey, T. R. (Eds.). (1993). *Experimental foundations of political science.* Ann Arbor: University of Michigan Press.

Kuklinski, J. H., Luskin, R. C., & Bolland, J. (1991). Where is the schema? Going beyond the "S" word in political psychology. *American Political Science Review, 85*(4), 1341–1356.

Lau, R. R. (1986). Political schemata, candidate evaluations, and voting behavior. In R. R. Lau & D. O. Sears (Eds.), *Political cognition* (pp. 95–126). Hillsdale, NJ: Lawrence Erlbaum Associates.

LeDoux, J. (1996). *The emotional brain: The mysterious underpinnings of emotional life.* New York: Simon & Schuster.

LeDoux, J. E. (1987). Emotion. In F. Plum (Ed.), *Handbook of physiology. Section 1: The nervous system, Vol. 5 Higher functions of the brain, Part 1* (Vol. 5, pp. 419–459). Bethesda, MD: American Physiological Society.

LeDoux, J. E. (1995). Emotion: Clues from the brain. *Annual Review of Psychology, 46,* 209–235.

Locke, J. (1689). *The second treatise on government.* London: Awnsham Churchill.

Lodge, M., & Hamill, R. (1986). A partisan schema for political information processing. *American Political Science Review, 80,* 505–520.

Madison, J., Hamilton, A., & Jay, J. (1961). *The Federalist papers.* Cleveland: World Publishing.

Marcus, G. E. (1988a). Democratic theories and the study of public opinion. *Polity, 21*(1), 25–44.

Marcus, G. E. (1988b). The structure of emotional response: 1984 presidential candidates. *American Political Science Review, 82*(3), 735–761.

Marcus, G. E. (2000). Emotions in politics. In N. W. Polsby (Ed.), *Annual review in political science* (Vol. 3, pp. 221–250). Palo Alto, CA: Annual Reviews.

Marcus, G. E., & Hanson, R. L. (Eds.). (1993). *Reconsidering the democratic public.* University Park, PA: Pennsylvania State University Press.

Marcus, G. E., & MacKuen, M. (1993). Anxiety, enthusiasm and the vote: The emotional underpinnings of learning and involvement during presidential campaigns. *American Political Science Review, 87*(3), 688–701.

Marcus, G. E., Neuman, W. R., & MacKuen, M. (2000). *Affective intelligence and political judgment.* Chicago: University of Chicago Press.

Marcus, G. E., Sullivan, J. L., Theiss-Morse, E., & Wood, S. (1995). *With malice toward some: How people make civil liberties judgments*. New York: Cambridge University Press.

Miller, A., Wattenburg, M., & Malanchuk, O. (1986). Schematic assessments of candidates. *American Political Science Review, 80*, 521–540.

Monroe, K. R. (1996). *The heart of altruism: Perceptions of a common humanity*. Princeton, NJ: Princeton University Press.

Montesquieu, C. d. S. (1955). *The spirit of laws*. Cambridge, UK: Cambridge University Press.

Nørretranders, T. (1998). *The user illusion* (J. Sydenham, Trans.). New York: Viking.

Oakeshott, M. (1975). *On human conduct*. Oxford: Oxford University Press.

Pateman, C. (1970). *Participation and democratic theory*. Cambridge: Cambridge University Press.

Plato. (1974). *The republic* (2nd ed.). New York: Penguin.

Rawls, J. (1971). *A theory of justice*. Cambridge, MA: Harvard University Press.

Rolls, E. T. (1999). *The brain and emotion*. New York: Oxford University Press.

Rousseau, J.-J. (1983). *On the social contract*. Indianapolis: Hackett.

Rusting, C. L. (1998). Personality, mood, and cognitive processing of emotional information: Three conceptual frameworks. *Psychological Bulletin, 124*(2), 165–196.

Schudson, M. (1998). *The good citizen: A history of civil life*. New York: The Free Press.

Sears, D. O., Hensler, C., & Speer, L. (1979). Whites' opposition to "busing": Self-interest or symbolic politics? *American Political Science Review, 73*, 369–385.

Sears, D. O., Lau, R. R., Tyler, T. R., & Allen, H. M., Jr. (1980). Self-interest vs. symbolic politics in policy attitudes and presidential voting. *American Political Science Review, 74*(3), 670–684.

Sullivan, J. L., Piereson, J., & Marcus, G. E. (1982). *Political tolerance and American democracy*. Chicago: University of Chicago Press.

Tocqueville, A. de (1974). *Democracy in America*. New York: Schocken. (Original work published 1835)

Tocqueville, A. de (1978). *The old regime and the French revolution* (S. Gilbert, Trans.). Gloucester, MA: Peter Smith. (Original work published 1856)

Tocqueville, A. de (1997). *Memoir on pauperism*. Chicago: Ivan R. Dee. (Original work published 1835)

Thompson, D. (1970). *The democratic citizen: Social science and democratic theory in the twentieth century*. New York: Cambridge University Press.

Zajonc, R. B. (1998). Emotions. In D. Gilbert, S. Fiske, & G. Lindzey (Eds.), *Handbook of social psychology* (4th ed., Vol. I, pp. 591–632). New York: McGraw Hill.

Zuckerman, M. (1991). *Psychobiology of personality*. Cambridge, England: Cambridge University Press.

6

Political Learning and Political Psychology: A Question of Norms

JANICE GROSS STEIN
University of Toronto

Learning from political experience is widely regarded as an important driver of change and as a source of progress in international politics (Haas, 1990, 1997; Levy, 1994). One of the principal contributions of political psychology to the analysis of international politics has been its discovery of the systematic biases toward the status quo in patterns of thinking. Without learning, embedded patterns of political thought and behavior are likely to persist as long as environments remain relatively constant. If political psychologists are not fully satisfied with the status quo, analysis of political learning should be a central focus of analysis.

Surprisingly, it has not been. It is deeply puzzling that political psychology, as a field of inquiry, has paid relatively little attention to learning. Although learning traditionally has been a central concern in educational and developmental psychology, very few political psychologists have made a direct contribution to the analysis of "political learning." That they have not done so speaks to some of the ways in which the field of political psychology has yet to mature and some of the challenges it has yet to meet.

To illustrate these challenges, I contrast the important contribution of political psychology to the analysis of political decision making with its limited contribution to the analysis of political learning. Political psychology has challenged successfully some of the normative standards current in models of choice, but it has yet to engage with some of the normative issues that are central in psychological research on learning. I contrast these two

107

bodies of scholarship to argue that political psychology must build its capacity to deal with some of the normative issues that are at the core of politics.

POLITICAL PSYCHOLOGY AS A FIELD OF INQUIRY

Political psychology, conceived broadly as a field of inquiry, analyzes patterns of political thinking, feeling, and identity, the interaction of these patterns, and their impact on political choice and other forms of political behavior. All political psychologists, whatever their specialized interest, share the assumption that human cognition and emotion mediate the impact of the environment on political action. As a field, political psychology has reasoned backward in an attempt to uncover the political and psychological sources of "political" thoughts, feelings, and identities. It has reasoned forward to examine the impact of political choice and behavior of one actor on the thoughts, feelings, and actions of others in processes of strategic interaction. Finally, it has studied the feedback loops that connect political choice and behavior back to thinking and feeling about politics and, more generally, to self-perception.

Two comments are in order about this skeletal definition of political psychology. I choose the term *field of inquiry* rather than *discipline* deliberately, because political psychologists may well agree about the scope of their inquiry, but do not necessarily share overarching theoretical perspectives, agreement on central terms, or on methodologies. From this perspective, political psychology is not very different from many of the other so-called disciplines in social science.

Nor do political psychologists agree on the relevant bodies of literature that speak to their concerns. Within psychology, some draw on cognitive psychology, some on psychoanalytic theories, some on artificial intelligence and neuroscience, others on social psychology, and still others on human needs' theories and motivational psychology. Indeed, the scope of psychology itself is now so broad, and the terrain so contested, that it is misleading to think of psychology as a tightly structured discipline with accepted "rules of the game."

Political psychologists, with their explicit focus on the "political," often roam well beyond the confines of psychology to explain political identities, thoughts, and feelings. Cultural anthropology has been a rich source of inspiration in the past; unfortunately, it is less so now. Sociology has helped political psychologists to contextualize their work and move beyond the individual as the unit of analysis to examine the collective thoughts and identities—or cultures—of societies and their impact on individual and collective political action. In short, what defines political psychology as a field of inquiry is a rich multidisciplinarity, which informs a very broad domain. It is this multidisciplinarity and breadth that is political psychology's greatest asset and greatest challenge.

One final introductory comment: The founders of modern political psychology in this century—those who wrote its seminal texts—all shared an explicitly normative agenda. Like their colleagues in other social sciences, they were shocked by the brutality of World War I and by the ruthless totalitarianism that grew up in its wake. Their interest in political psychology was instrumental as well as inherent: They hoped that systematic study would improve the capacity to prevent unnecessary wars, to defeat aggression, and to build peaceful, democratic societies. The normative was intimately linked to the scientific agenda. I return to this normative agenda in my discussion of future directions for the field.

My work is in one small corner of political psychology: the analysis of political decision making on international issues, often, although not always, in the context of conflict and conflict resolution. In the last several decades, research by political psychologists has cumulated to challenge the foundations of the prevailing paradigm in the field. I contrast the significant contributions made by political psychologists to the analysis of political choice with the failure to engage seriously on the question of political learning.

EXPLANATIONS OF CHOICE

At the individual level, political psychologists, drawing on cognitive and motivational psychology and behavioral decision theory, have explained individual political preferences and choices (George, 1980; Jervis, 1976, 1980, 1986; Lebow, 1981; Vertzberger, 1990). Explanations include the formation of preferences, the processing of information, the construction of meaning, the selection of memories, and processes of decision. These explanations are far broader, richer, and more diverse, and, consequently, far less parsimonious than their counterpart models of rational choice that treat preferences as given and use a single decision rule.

Political psychologists have demonstrated repeatedly that people do not conform to the normative standards of instrumental rationality and optimization that are implicit in much of current theorizing in political science, economics, and organizational development. The contributions of behavioral decision theorists, for example, have widely informed analyses of foreign policy decision making (Kahneman, Slovic, & Tversky, 1982; Kahneman & Tversky, 1979; Nisbett & Ross, 1980; Ross, 1977; Tversky, 1972). There is no one model of decision making that has achieved wide acceptance; rather, political psychologists have identified a large variety of heuristics and "biases" that inform decision making. Thus far, however, they have been generally unable to establish with confidence the contextual political conditions that promote one rather than another kind of process. This has not been a concern of psychologists, but should be a central concern of political psychologists. From this perspective, there are insufficient politics in the political psychology of choice.

Political psychologists have also analyzed the interaction among leaders that create unexpected and anomalous patterns (Druckman, 1977; Janis & Mann, 1977; Jervis, 1970, 1976; Jervis, Lebow, & Stein, 1985; Levy, 1983). Analyses of spirals of misperception, systematic errors of attribution and inference, and the difficulties of signaling and reading intentions accurately now inform the literature on escalation, war, and bargaining. This literature is generally more explicitly attentive to the political context that contributes to interactive cycles of misperception.

At the elite level, political psychologists have made a significant contribution by examining group processes of decision making about international issues. Models of rational choice cannot aggregate individual preferences: They model individual choice or, for convenience, treat the state or the group as isomorphic to the individual. Political processes of preference formation are assumed, rather than analyzed, and processes of aggregation become unnecessary complications.

Political psychologists, drawing on work in social psychology, examine both these processes explicitly. Analyses of group dynamics trace the impact of group membership on individual preference and explain the aggregation of individual preferences into a collective outcome (Dion, Baron, & Miller, 1978; Janis, 1982, 1989; Taylor & Moghaddam, 1987; t'Hart, 1990). Here too, however, the political conditions that promote one rather than another process remain largely unspecified. It is not clear, for example, that the group dynamics characteristic of decision making by a small group of policy makers in an international crisis are significantly different from those of senior management in a large corporation facing a difficult decision or leaders of a university facing unexpected enrollment challenges. In the analysis of group choice, there are also insufficient politics in political psychology. Context, so widely appreciated in earlier cultural anthropological analyses, and in social psychology, is disappearing quickly from the research agenda of political psychology.

Finally, political psychologists have explored the connections between the dynamics of mass political behavior and violence and war. They have examined the creation of collective political identities that shape and constrain the choices political leaders can make (Mercer, 1995; Tajfel, 1981, 1982). They have also analyzed the interactions between leaders and publics that allow leaders to inflame and exploit nationalist sentiment to justify escalation to conflict and violence with other groups and states (Druckman, 1994; Messick & Mackie, 1989; Sherif, 1966; Stern, 1995).

The work of political psychologists has changed the understanding of patterns of decision making in foreign policy, of interactive sequences of escalation, of the causes of war, and of sequences of bargaining and negotiation. Underlying the choice of subject matter is an implicit normative agenda that seeks to prevent unintended escalation, improve the pattern of decision making, and help the parties in international negotiations to pick up most of the available surplus on the table.

No such cumulation exists in the analysis of the learning. I turn now to an examination of the reasons for the neglect of a core concept in psychology, which is clearly central to politics.

POLITICAL LEARNING UNEXPLORED

The analysis of political learning is central to the empirical and normative concerns of political psychology.[1] Political psychologists have made major contributions to the analysis of political socialization and mass attitude formation and change (Bandura, 1969, Beck & Jennings, 1982; Dawson, Prewitt, & Dawson, 1977). They have paid relatively less attention to how leaders and groups "learn lessons," draw inferences from their historical and personal experience, and apply these lessons to current and future dilemmas. Through observation and experience, political leaders acquire new knowledge and new skills, increase their confidence in their knowledge, and enhance their capacity to achieve their goals (Levy, 1994). Evidence is strong that leaders "learn" too much from history, that they overextend the lessons of the past. Only a handful of political psychologists, however, has systematically examined when, how, and what leaders learn (Breslauer & Tetlock, 1991; Etheridge, 1985; Jervis, 1976; Khong, 1992; Nye, 1987; Stein, 1994). Even fewer have engaged the explicitly normative component inherent in any concept of learning (Adler & Barnett, 1998; Adler & Crawford, 1991; Haas, 1990, 1997; Stein, 1994).

If political psychologists who study learning by individuals and groups are to be consistent with the conventional meaning of the concept, they must come to grips with the issue of evaluation and judgment. In educational and developmental psychology, analysts of learning measure performance against a set of agreed-upon criteria. Generally, these criteria are "accuracy" and "efficiency," or an improved capacity to match means to ends. Often, the consensus around these criteria is so wide and so deep that

---

[1]Learning is a central concept not only in psychology but also in sociology, history, and applied game theory. Hall (1993) applied concepts drawn from social learning theory, primarily behavioral rather than cognitive in its focus, to the analysis of the state and of policy making. May (1973) examined learning from the historical past, and Wagner (1989) modeled rational learning in the context of strategic interaction.

they are considered "objective." There is very little room for disagreement, for example, on "accuracy" in elementary mathematics. Even when accuracy is unambiguous, educational psychologists nevertheless debate appropriate conceptual skills that support and enhance performance.

Psychological studies of learning do not travel easily when they are exported to politics. Assessment of the accuracy of learning requires some standard; without a standard, evaluation of accuracy or efficiency is impossible. In politics, however, widely agreed-upon standards of accuracy rarely exceed the trivial.[2] Almost all the important issues and, at times, even the "facts" are contested and subject to multiple interpretations. In this sense, politics is an ill-structured environment, very different from the well-structured environment of elementary mathematics or chemistry. In ill-structured environments, assessment is generally less rigorous, more subjective, more variable, and frequently shaped by the analytical and normative biases of the analyst. We need only think of the variation in peer review of articles submitted to journals in political psychology to intuit the variation and the subjectivity.

Yet, to refrain from assessment because of the subjectivity of the standards is to eviscerate the concept of learning. Some political psychologists have abandoned assessment entirely—because of the inherent subjectivity —and describe political learning as equivalent to change in political beliefs or change in the confidence in these beliefs (Levy, 1994). If learning becomes equivalent to any change, the concept is devoid of content and disappears as a theoretically relevant term.

The crux of the problem is apparent. If political psychologists are to analyze political "learning" by leaders and groups, they must engage with standards. These standards cannot be as "objective" as those in elementary education, yet even in the absence of objective standards, political psychologists will have to make qualitative judgments. They will have to become more comfortable with the inherent complexity of political discourse and action, and be prepared to make assessments using some set of normative criteria.

This is not a comfortable position for political psychologists who, as a collectivity, are overwhelmingly committed to "scientific" processes of knowledge generation. This commitment to scientific processes, often incorrectly equated with "objectivity," has, at times, inappropriately narrowed the scope of the research agenda of political psychology. It is no surprise that political psychology has contributed significantly to the critique of normative models of rational choice through controlled experi-

---

[2]Tetlock (1991) argued that assessment of learning is straightforward only when there are well-defined evidential standards for determining success and failure, when controlled experiments can eliminate alternative causal hypotheses, and when instruments of measurement are derived from well-established laws. These conditions are never met in a political context.

mental studies, but has been far more reluctant to use standards to make judgments about political learning in the absence of "objective" measures.

Assessment is difficult but not impossible in an ill-structured environment.[3] Political psychologists can draw on work in sociology, international politics, and organizational theory to devise a range of criteria that may be appropriate when science does not—and cannot—provide clear answers.

One set of criteria may be best estimates of accuracy in a contested environment. The seminal work on learning in political psychology by Jervis (1976) used these kinds of criteria implicitly. When he concluded, for example, that leaders "overlearned" lessons from history, he suggested implicitly a knowable, if not known, zone of accuracy, which sets the parameters for the judgments he makes.

Judgments of this kind are made all the time in medicine, for example, when knowledge is uncertain and practitioners are required to make diagnostic decisions. These decisions are often evaluated both at the time and after the fact, recognizing the element of uncertainty that inheres. After the fact evaluation is problematic in medicine as well as in politics: Diagnoses can be right for the wrong reasons, right for the right reasons, wrong for the right reasons, and wrong for the wrong reasons. The outcome is not fully determinative of accuracy.

A second set of criteria attempts to measure accuracy indirectly by assessing changes in the pattern of thinking rather than in its content. When arguments become more complex, the logic more elaborate and sophisticated, some analysts conclude that leaders have "learned" (Tetlock, 1991, pp. 22, 32–35). An increase in the capacity to differentiate arguments, to recognize inconsistencies among arguments, to discriminate between evidence that supports and contradicts prevailing arguments, and an increased sensitivity to the obvious uncertainties are all indicators of learning.

A related argument expands the logical chain by linking learning explicitly to progress through improved reasoning. Haas maintained that progress occurs when collectivities think about what they do and consider doing things differently in the future. Progress occurs when conceptions of political problems and their solutions are informed by "scientific" reasoning. This process he termed *learning* (1990, 1997; Adler & Crawford, 1991).

These "structural" measures are attractive to political psychologists for several reasons. First and foremost, they eliminate the uncomfortable reliance on either "subjective" measures or explicitly normative measures to make judgments. Second, they mirror the scientific method of reasoning that is consistent with what political psychologists themselves do. Third, these criteria eliminate the problem of the classification of all change as

---

[3]For a related argument on strategies to solve ill-structured problems, see Voss and Post (1988).

learning: The simplistic changes that are often characteristic of stereotypical, or even paranoid thinking would be excluded (Stein, 1994). No political psychologists would be comfortable designating these kinds of changes as learning.

These measures do not fully solve the difficult problem of assessing cognitive change to determine whether or not it is learning. The implicit assumption is that as thinking becomes more complex and sophisticated, understanding of the environment improves, and the capacity to match means to ends—realism—grows as well. As Levy (1994) argued, these criteria sneak accuracy in the back door. But, it is possible to be complex and inaccurate, and simple and accurate. Compounding the problem, more complex cognitive structures are more resistant to change because they are better able to accommodate discrepant evidence along one of the many branches of an argument. Indeed, as cognitive psychologists have demonstrated, people develop elaborate arguments both to rationalize and to bolster existing beliefs. An increase in complexity does not necessarily equate to learning.

A third approach is to identify consensual knowledge, or emergent consensual knowledge, and then assess whether changes in leaders' beliefs are moving them closer toward or further from this consensus. This approach is consistent with work on "social learning," which examines changes in collective beliefs. Political psychologists have relied on consensual knowledge produced by "epistemic" communities or shared constructions as the benchmark to assess learning. Indeed, scholars working within the tradition of social constructivism put the strong argument that it is less important that new knowledge be "true" than that it be collectively shared (Adler, 1991, 1997; Adler & Barnett, 1998).

Social constructivism does not escape the normative dilemma inherent in the analysis of learning. Movement toward shared constructions that stereotype or stigmatize others, or intolerant nationalisms and racism, for example, would be difficult to classify as learning. Their poor fit with existing scientific research, as well as with evolving norms of tolerance and respect for diversity, would currently exclude such patterns of thinking from qualification as learning. I have chosen an easy case, however, for the weight of scientific evidence and evolving norms reinforce one another in rejection of racist thought. The hard case occurs when there is no body of supporting scientific evidence.

There is no escape from the inherent normative dimension to analysis of learning when learning is linked to progress. In politics, there will rarely be the scientific evidence Haas looked for as the basis of knowledge, and even "scientific reasoning" frequently lends itself to contested conclusions (Bernstein, Lebow, Stein, & Weber, 2000). Yet, the linkage Haas traced between progress and learning is deeply embedded in several important traditions of political thinking about international politics, as well as more generally in much of enlightenment thinking of the last three centuries. If we reject the linkage between progress and learning, then learning becomes of trivial theoretical interest; analysis of change suffices. If we accept this linkage, then the analysis of what constitutes political learning is both important and inescapably normative, precisely because the political world is so deeply contested.

Traditionally, political psychologists have used the most powerful analytic tools available to study problems and issues that were of both theoretical and normative consequence. The challenge remains: to deal explicitly with normative issues, even when norms are disputed and reality is contested. As we move deeper and deeper into knowledge-based societies, where knowledge replaces capital and labor as the most valuable resource and input to growth in an increasingly connected world, it will be more important than ever for political psychologists to contribute significantly to the analysis of political learning. To do so, we will have to return to the traditions of the founders of political psychology and use explicit normative as well as evidentiary standards in uncharted waters.

REFERENCES

Adler, E. (1991). Cognitive evolution: A dynamic approach for the study of international relations and their progress. In Adler and Crawford, *Progress in postwar international relations* (pp. 43–88). New York: Columbia University Press.

Adler, E. (1997). Seizing the middle ground: Constructivism in world politics. *European Journal of International Relations, 3,* 319–363.

Adler, E. & Barnett, M. (Eds.). (1998). *Security communities.* New York: Cambridge University Press.

Adler, E. & Crawford B. (Eds.) (1991). *Progress in postwar international relations.* New York: Columbia University Press.

Bandura, A. (1969). Social learning theory of identificatory processes. In D. A. Goslin (Ed.), *Handbook of socialization theory and research* (pp. 213–262). Chicago: Rand McNally.

Beck, P. & Jennings, M. K. (1982). Pathways to participation. *American Political Science Review, 76,* 94–108.

Bernstein, S., Lebow, R. N., Stein, J. G., & Weber, S. (2000). God gave physics all the easy problems. *European Journal of International Relations.*

Breslauer, G. W., & Tetlock, P. E. (Eds.) (1991). *Learning in U.S. and Soviet foreign policy.* Boulder, CO: Westview Press.

Dawson, R. E., Prewitt, K., & Dawson, K. S. (1977). *Political socialization.* New York: Little, Brown.

Dion, K. L., Baron, R. S., & Miller, N. (1978). Why do groups make riskier decisions than individuals? In L. Berkowitz (Ed.), *Group processes* (pp. 227–299). New York: Academic Press.

Druckman, D. (1994). Nationalism, patriotism, and group loyalty: A social psychological perspective. *Mershon International Studies Review, 38,* 43–68.

Druckman, D. (1977). *Negotiations: Social psychological perspectives.* Beverly Hills, CA: Sage Publications.

Etheridge, L. S. (1985). *Can governments learn? American foreign policy and Central American revolutions.* New York: Pergamon Press.

George, A. L. (1980). *Presidential decisionmaking in foreign policy: The effective use of information and advice.* Boulder, CO: Westview Press.

Haas, E. B. (1990). *When knowledge is power: Three models of change in international organizations.* Berkeley: University of California Press.

Haas, E. B. (1997). *Nationalism, liberalism, and progress: The rise and decline of nationalism.* Ithaca, NY: Cornell University Press.

Hall, P. A. (1993). Policy paradigms, social learning, and the state. *Comparative Politics, 25*(3), 275–296.

Janis, I. L. (1982). *Groupthink: Psychological studies of policy decisions and fiascoes.* Boston: Houghton Mifflin.

Janis, I. L. (1989). *Crucial decisions: Leadership in policymaking and crisis management.* New York: Free Press.

Janis, I. L., & Mann, L. (1977). *Decision making: A psychological analysis of conflict, choice, and commitment.* New York: Free Press.

Jervis, R. (1970). *The logic of images in international relations.* Princeton, NJ: Princeton University Press.

Jervis, R. (1976). *Perception and misperception in international politics.* Princeton, NJ: Princeton University Press.

Jervis, R. (1980). Political decision making: Recent contributions. *Political Psychology, 2,* 86–101.

Jervis, R. (1986). Representativeness in foreign policy judgments. *Political Psychology, 7,* 483–505.

Jervis, R., Lebow, R. N., & Stein, J. G. (1985). *Psychology and deterrence.* Baltimore, MD: Johns Hopkins University Press.

Kahneman, D., Slovic, P., & Tversky, A. (Eds.). (1982). *Judgment under uncertainty: Heuristics and biases.* Cambridge, UK: Cambridge University Press.

Kahneman, D., & Tversky, A. (1979). Prospect theory: An analysis of decision under risk. *Econometrica, 47,* 263–291.

Khong, Y. F. (1992). *Analogies at war: Korea, Munich, Dien Bien Phu, and the Vietnam decisions of 1965.* Princeton, NJ: Princeton University Press.

Lebow, R. N. (1981). *Between peace and war: The nature of international crisis.* Baltimore, MD: Johns Hopkins University Press.

Levy, J. S. (1983). Misperception and the causes of war: Theoretical linkages and analytical problems. *World Politics, 36,* 76–99.

Levy, J. S. (1994). Learning and foreign policy: Sweeping a conceptual minefield. *International Organization, 48,* 279–312.

May, E. R. (1973). *"Lessons" of the past: The use and misuse of history in American politics.* New York: Oxford University Press.

Mercer, J. (1995). Anarchy and identity. *International Organization, 49,* 229–252.

Messick, D., & Mackie, D. (1989). Intergroup relations. *Annual Review of Psychology, 40,* 45–81.

Nisbett, R. E., & Ross, L. (1980). *Human inference: Strategies and shortcomings of social judgment.* Englewood Cliffs, NJ: Prentice Hall.

Nye, J. S., Jr. (1987). Nuclear learning and U.S.–Soviet security regimes. *International Organization, 41,* 371–402.

Ross, L. (1977). The intuitive psychologist and his shortcomings: Distortion in the attribution process. In L. Berkowitz (Ed.), *Advances in experimental social psychology* (Vol. 10, pp. 173–220). New York: Academic Press.

Sherif, M. (1966). *In common predicament: Social psychology of intergroup conflict and cooperation.* Boston: Houghton Mifflin.

Stein, J. G. (1994). Political learning by doing: Gorbachev as an uncommitted thinker and motivated learner. *International Organization, 48,* 155–183.

Stern, P. (1995). Why do people sacrifice for their nations? *Political Psychology, 16,* 217–235.

Tajfel, H. (1981). *Human groups and social categories.* Cambridge, UK: Cambridge University Press.

Tajfel, H. (1982). *Social identity and intergroup relations.* New York: Cambridge University Press.

Taylor, D. M., & Moghaddam, F. M. (1987). *Theories of intergroup relations: International and social psychological perspectives.* New York: Praeger.

t'Hart, P. (1990). *Groupthink in government: A study of small groups and policy failure.* Baltimore, MD: Johns Hopkins University Press.

Tetlock, P. E. (1991). Learning in U.S. and Soviet foreign policy: In search of an elusive concept. In G. W. Breslauer & P. E. Tetlock (Eds.), *Learning in U.S. and Soviet foreign policy* (pp. 20–61). Boulder, CO: Westview Press.

Tversky, A. (1972). Elimination by aspects: A theory of choice. *Psychological Review, 79,* 281–299.

Vertzberger, Y. (1990). *The world in their minds: Information processing, cognition, and perception in foreign policy decisionmaking.* Stanford, CA: Stanford University Press.

Voss, J. F., & Post, T. A. (1988). On the solving of ill-structured problems. In M. H. Chi, R. Glaser, & M. J. Farr (Eds.), *The nature of expertise* (pp. 261–285). Hillsdale, NJ: Lawrence Erlbaum Associates.

Wagner, H. (1989). Uncertainty, rational learning, and bargaining in the Cuban Missile Crisis. In P. C. Ordeshook (Ed.), *Models of strategic choice in politics* (pp. 177–205). Ann Arbor: University of Michigan Press.

PART II

Political Psychology
in Relation to Other Fields

7

Lost in Plain Sight: The Cultural Foundations of Political Psychology

STANLEY A. RENSHON
The City University of New York

In the beginning there was no field, only disparate disciplinary interests. Lasswell's (1930) pioneering work established the field's twin centers of gravity, with one theoretical and substantive pillar firmly anchored in psychology and the other firmly anchored in politics. Since then, political psychology's success has become self-evident.[1]

However, successfully establishing an interdisciplinary field does not guarantee either its legitimacy or its consolidation and development. Consider the fate of psychohistory, whose early successes (Erikson, Mazlish, Low-

---

[1]Political psychology is a growth stock. There are now at least eight doctoral programs in which it is a primary specialization and many others in which it is a well-established and substantial concentration (Sears & Funk, 1991). It is, as well, an established and growing presence at the undergraduate level (Funk & Sears, 1991). Institutionally, the field has its own journal, now two decades old, an international summer institute modeled on the University of Michigan's summer consortium research methods, its own international professional society, and a new fast growing section in the American Political Science Association. Moreover, a great many disciplinary conferences in the fields of psychology and political science routinely include political psychology presentations.

The field's public visibility and importance have also reached unprecedented levels. Political psychologists are routinely asked to explain and help clarify public debates on issues ranging from abortion to war. Political psychologists have testified before Congress on the psychology of the Gulf War, and have been tapped as commentators for such important events as the Oklahoma bombing. Indeed, in such areas as presidential campaigns, and politics more generally, it is now fairly routine to have political psychologists as commentators.

enberg) did not keep it from ending in an interdisciplinary cul de sac, if not a disciplinary dead end. Paradoxically, success may sometimes prove more an epilogue than a prologue. Who would have thought—certainly not its founder, Herbert Hyman—that the basic insights developed by political socialization research would become so generally accepted as "conventional wisdom"[2] that the field ceased to attract much scholarly interest or produce much new research.

Certainly, there seems little risk that contemporary political psychology will repeat psychohistory's experience. Nor does there seem much danger, given the predominance of rational choice theory in political science or cognitive theory in psychology, of the field becoming "conventional wisdom" in either discipline. No, what threat exists comes from an entirely different direction. In the years since the field's founding, there has been a gradual, but steady erosion of the connection between the field's early foundations and its subsequent development.

Is this not only a logical, but a desirable development? Some think so. Their evidence, and it is not inconsiderable, is found in the increasing sophistication of the field's models, its increasing ability to specify and measure the variables it uses and, as a result, its increased disciplinary legitimacy.

Yet, something very important has been lost in all these gains. Our models may be more elaborate and refined, but their explanatory power has not kept pace. Our theoretical sophistication and real-world understanding seem to run on increasingly divergent tracks. Paradoxically, while keeping our gaze firmly fixed on what our models might predict of the future, we have lost sight of what it takes to understand the present. As a result, we are ill prepared to contribute our understanding to a set of the most important contemporary political issues of our age.

THE LOST LEGACY OF POLITICAL PSYCHOLOGY

We can define our field either by what it is or what it does. A focus on the latter asks what practitioners study and defines the field accordingly. A more theoretically based definition tries to reflect the field's essential purposes and aspirations. From this perspective, political psychology is "simply" the study of the interrelationships of psychological and political process (Renshon, 1996).

Traditionally, the field has drawn on three major disciplines—cultural anthropology, psychology, and political science. In the 1950s and 1960s, sociology replaced anthropology as a conceptual and theoretical source for

---

[2]The evidence to support this view is found elsewhere (Renshon, 1992).

the field, only to eventually fade. At present, only political science and psychology remain as primary resources for our field. Although rich in their own viewpoints, both lack grounding in the larger perspective that frames the major issues with which they are concerned.

Psychology permeates political life. Yet each alone, and both collectively, are embedded in numerous cultural contexts. We can simply, and provisionally, define culture as the shared range of acquired conscious and unconscious understandings, and their associated feelings, that are embedded in the individuals' interior psychology, the cultural group's societal (social, economic, and political) institutions, and its public practices and products.[3] Thus defined, its relevance for the concerns of political psychology would seem to be reasonably self-evident.

Yet, paradoxically, although political psychology has made substantial substantive and institutional progress in the past seven decades, little of the field's theory and less of its research has examined culture explicitly. As a result, it is woefully unprepared, both conceptually and theoretically, for the unprecedented levels of intercultural contact and conflict that now permeate almost every modern multiethnic state. This was not always the case.

THE MIXED LEGACY OF CULTURAL ANTHROPOLOGY

Early studies exploring the intersection of psychology, culture and politics were strongly influenced by cultural anthropology (cf., Linton, 1930, 1945; see also Kardiner, with Linton, 1939) and more specifically by the "culture and personality" work associated with Benedict (1934), Mead (1939), Kluckhohn and Murray (1953), and others.[4] Those pioneers studied relatively small, homogeneous, and slowly evolving societies to chart the links among culture, socialization, and personality on one hand, and the continuity of societal conventions (embedded in political, economic, religious, and social institutions) on the other. Perhaps not surprisingly, given the kinds of societies they studied, the links appeared solid. However, those who studied large, heterogeneous, and rapidly changing societies

---

[3]Compare this with Linton's (1945) definition of culture as "the configuration of learned behavior and results of behavior whose component elements are shared and transmitted by the members of a particular society" (p. 22). Also relevant is Eckstein's (1997) more recent definition of culture as "the variable and cumulatively learned patterns of orientations to action in societies" (p. 26).

[4]Bock (1988; see also Barnouw, 1963) divided the "culture and personality" school into four related, but distinguishable approaches: configurationalist, basic and modal personality, national character, and cross-cultural. He associated these approaches respectively with the work of Benedict (1934), DuBois (1944), Kluckhohn (1957), and Whiting and Child (1953). One can gain a more detailed perspective on the development of the field by examining Inkeles and Levinson (1954, 1968–1969), and more recently, Inkeles (1990–1991).

were certainly justified in asking what useful implications this genre held for them.

Moreover, members of the early cultural-and-personality school often wrote as if personality were culture writ large,[5] and viewed the former through the powerful, but scarcely refined, lens of early psychoanalytic theory. Those uncomfortable with a view of internal psychology as little more than a barely contained caldron of urges set for life in instinctual concrete, and culture as a defense against them, had legitimate questions to ask. As a result, the culture-and-personality paradigm seemed ill-suited for answering the questions growing out of the intersection of culture, psychology, and politics in the societies studied by most political psychologists, and in important ways it was.

Still, that early paradigm contained an important set of understandings about culture and its influences on social practices. It is worthwhile to recall these because they provide a basis for exploring culture's impact on the psychology and political practices of larger, culturally heterogeneous societies.

Understanding Culture

A primary legacy of that early work is that culture is, first and foremost, human made, and its practices highly diverse. Culture is a constant across human groupings, but its content in any particular group is variable. Therefore, culture in any group must be learned and its impact on that group's practices will be related to its content. Documenting and comparing cultural organization and understandings in an attempt to trace their impact on the psychology of group members and their interpersonal and social practices was *the* fundamental rationale for the field. That basic set of questions, however, soon led to more specific ones.

On what basis did cultures develop? Benedict (1934) believed that cultures developed around one dominant, or a few central concerns. Linton (see Kardiner, with Linton, 1939) criticized that view arguing that "cultures are not dominated by an *idée fixe*" (p. viii). Yet, early cultural anthropologists were united in their view that culture arose as a response to environmental circumstances. In other words, culture was a solution to the problem of how groups might live in the physical and psychological circumstances in which they found themselves.[6]

---

[5]Spiro (1961) argued that because of its very success, "culture and personality" anthropology can, and should, reorient its focus more toward sociocultural systems.

[6]Benedict (1934) argued, however, that even cultures organized around the same general themes, like the aggressive cultural stance of the Dobu Islanders in Melanesia and the Kwakiutl Indians of British Columbia, might develop different cultural configurations. The particular ways in which culture was organized was always an empirical, not an a priori theoretical, matter.

Early cultural anthropologists were also united in their view that cultural practices served adaptive functions. A culture's practices might seem odd, even bizarre, to an outsider. Yet, from the point of view of those inside it, culture could be seen to serve some purposes.

An underappreciated corollary to this perspective is that the early cultural anthropologists were remarkably open and nonjudgmental about a wide array of cultural practices. Mead's (1935) classic study of sex and temperament in several New Guinea societies documented the cultural variability associated with their expression and relationship. Benedict (1934) matter-of-factly noted the range of reactions, including acceptance and in some cases special acclaim, given to homosexuals in some societies at the same time that hers branded them psychiatrically.

Certainly, governmental, religious, and economic organizations motivated to justify their exploitation or cultural intervention emphasized the difference between "civilized" and "primitive" cultures. However, they received no support from major figures in the field either substantively[7] or politically.[8] For the culture and personality anthropologists, unlike some modern multiculturalists, cultural always trumped race as an explanation of cognitive and behavioral practices.[9]

Culture's Consequences: Psychology

Although "functionalist" anthropologists insisted that specific, discrete cultural traits behavior always served some purpose, the culture and personality anthropologists went further. They argued that cultures were best understood as integrated patterns of thought and behavior (Benedict, 1934) and that cultural institutions both reflected and reinforced them. The reason for this, according to Kardiner and Linton (1939) was that individuals growing up in them had common experiences resulting in similar understandings and even common psychological tendencies.

Building on early psychoanalytic theory, culture and personality anthropologists sought to document culture's role in producing basic personality

---

[7] As early as 1911 in his book, *The Mind of Primitive Man,* Boas (1911/1939) stated categorically, "there is no fundamental difference in the ways of thinking between primitive and civilized man" (p. v). He further added that the view that different races of man stand on distinct stages of the evolutionary stage "cannot be maintained" (p. 130).

[8] When Canadian officials outlawed the Kwakiutl potlatch in British Columbia, Franz Boas was at the forefront of those trying get the authorities to reconsider their ban.

[9] For example, in the first chapter of his classic book, *Patterns of Culture,* Benedict (1934) pointed out that on the basis of field research, cultural theories of group differences have a much stronger evidentiary basis than racial ones. For a survey of some contemporary views that begin with, and reach, opposite assumptions, see Pangle (1998).

structures, modal personality structures, and national characters.[10] In retrospect, it is easy to see the limits of these frameworks. Relying on the unconscious to anchor these frameworks made them methodologically vulnerable and risked slighting the importance of purposeful adaptation.

Moreover, identical socialization experiences could not be assumed even in small, contained cultural groups. Even if it could, variations in family dynamics and individual temperament would make the process unlikely to produce uniform results. And, even if they did, the similar results they might produce were more likely to manifest themselves in a range than a mode. Finally, it was not clear how representative any individual could be of the range of national character traits associated with large nation states, especially as many become more culturally diverse.

Culture's Consequences: Understandings and Practices

Early cultural anthropologists were united in the view that culture had very practical consequences. Its effects are found in the most common and ordinary social practices and, as well, in the larger basic understandings that shape community life. These "cultural truths" are "self-evident," often not fully explicit or articulated understandings that shape individual and cultural life. Thus Kardiner (with Linton, 1939) argued that for members of the Tanala in Madagascar, "the pattern of love and security in return for obedience is the most prominent pattern of adaption for the greatest number of people in the society" (p. 361). A more contemporary illustration of cultural truth can be found in the beliefs associated with the work ethic in Westernized societies, essentially the "Protestant ethic" minus the religious element.

Culture's consequences could be seen as well in the regulation of expression. Some cultures prize excess in personal expression, others moderation (cf. Benedict's "Apollonian" and "Dionysian" cultures, 1934). In some cultures, laughter covers embarrassment; in others, it reflects a sense of humor. In some cultures, looking at someone directly is a sign of respect; in others not looking at them directly is respectful.

Finally, cultural's consequences can be seen in the ways in which elements of interior and interpersonal psychology are combined. For example, the Japanese term *giri* is ordinarily translated as "repayment," as for a social obligation. However, it also covers gratitude and revenge. As Benedict (1934) noted:

---

[10]The first were conceptualized as the common denominators of the personalities passing through a uniform set of child-rearing experiences. The second did not require psychological uniformity as a consequence of a culture's socialization practices, but concentrated instead on uncovering their most common (modal) outcomes. The third, national character studies, applied the assumptions of the first and the second to larger, national culture units in the search for essential characteristics of a country's general population.

A good man feels as strongly about insults as he does about the benefits he receives. Either way it is virtuous to repay. He does not separate the two, as we do, and call one aggression and one non-aggression, because so long as one is maintaining giri and clearing one's name of slurs, one is not guilty of aggression. (p. 146)

It is worth noting that the actual feelings remain constant across cultures in this example. Yet, because the feelings are put into different categories of understanding, they carry with them different prescriptions for action. Different moral calculations follow as well.

Culture's Consequences: Continuity and Change

Early cultural anthropologists were not blind to the fact that change occurred naturally *within* cultural traditions. But they were particularly interested in cultural change brought about by forced contact with disparate cultures. This had the effect of focusing attention away from cultural evolution and toward cultural conflict.

Understandings of modern intercultural exchange represent a hybrid of these two sources of cultural change. Certainly, in an increasingly interconnected world, the avoidance of cultural contact is not a realistic option. Therefore, attention to change resulting from cultural intrusion is worth continued attention. However, concerns about cultural "imperialism" and its postmodern successor, hegemonic design, give less credit to the staying power of the traditional cultures in whose name they say they speak. The ability of strong cultural traditions to repress, restrict, or even to moderate, modify, revise, and transform other's traditions to their own uses is a second important focus of this book. It is also another key element of a modern cultural and cross-cultural political psychology.

Culture's Consequences: Policy

The early theoretical development of culture and personality anthropology preceded the onset of World War II by only a few years. As early as 1939, the Committee for National Morale drew on psychologists and anthropologists to study the maintenance of morale during wartime. After Pearl Harbor, developing and applying psychological cultural anthropology became a matter of military urgency as well as of academic theory. Ruth Benedict, Clyde Kluckhohn, and others moved to Washington to help in war-related research and planning. Japanese, German, and Nazi (and later, Soviet) cultures were scoured by the Allies for understanding and advantage.

Ultimately, of course, military power, not the political uses of cultural psychology, proved decisive. But it is worth noting that whereas the former won the war, the peace could not have been secured without the latter.

Allied occupational authorities were not simply content to administer the defeated countries, but to change them. To accomplish this, they attempted to transform two culturally distinct societies from totalitarian to democratic. That seminal historic event remains to be fully explored, but its enormous consequences underscore the critical role that culture plays in the intersection between psychology and politics.

However, there is another, equally if not more critical, set of culturally framed policy questions unfolding. Inglehart (1997) demonstrated there are empirically distinct cultural regions in the world, and Huntington (1996) argued that the reassuring view that modernization and the Western values with which it became associated would trump other cultures' core values is, in his view, "false, immoral, and dangerous" (p. 310). Rather, he argued (1996), "culture and cultural identities, which at the broadest level are civilization identities, are shaping the patterns of cohesion, disintegration, and conflict in the post-Cold War world" (p. 20). The high-rise buildings of New York and Beijing may look the same, but the core cultural values and views of those who inhabilt them are not necessarily parallel.

The fact that culture and psychology intersect so directly with political and social practices helps make this field inherently controversial to some. Drawing little distinction between analysis and judgment, "deconstructionists" and "postmodernists" ask whether scholarship can ever trump personal values, and answer that it cannot. However, as Pye (2000) pointed out, these "critical" theorists are more than willing to use the concept of culture for their own decidedly political purposes, itself a blatant manifestation of the criticisms they level at others. The same inconsistency may be seen among some multiculturalists who insist on the psychological importance and political primacy of racial or ethnic identities, while disavowing any less desirable group tendencies that derive from these same powerful currents.

In the United States, "culture of poverty" analyses elicited loud protests that such theories blamed, vilified, and further marginalized the victims. As a result, ameliorative social policy was hobbled. Now, several decades later, research by a distinguished African American sociologist (Wilson, 1996; see also Sowell, 1994) has demonstrated that the poor underclass are indeed different in terms of their experiences and outlooks, and equally importantly, on those practices concerned with the work ethic. That work ethic and associated cultural beliefs are, to some (cf. Landes, 1996), central to explaining larger macro political and economic developments in and between nations.

Clearly, an appreciation of culture and psychology has an important role to play in designing policy, especially in multicultural countries. However, those who wish to utilize its insights must be prepared to defend their substantive insights, not only intellectually, but politically.

A SPORADIC LEGACY:
CULTURE AND MODERN POLITICAL PSYCHOLOGY

As Pye (2000) suggested, the concept of culture is "elusive, but indispensable" in the social sciences and political psychology. Its persistence, in spite of its elusiveness, supports his point. In the late 1940s, Leites (1948) was already reformulating the psychoanalytic approach to examining culture's impact on the psychology of political practices. The culmination of his efforts was his now-classic work on operational codes (Leites, 1951), a concept explicated by George (1969).[11]

In Leites's classic revision, the foundation of political practices was not to be found in the cultural expression of universal unconscious principles. Rather, it was to be found in the internalization and operation of core beliefs, which infused experience with meaning. The intersection of culture, psychology, and politics was no longer primarily a matter of affective conflicts, but as well of assumptions and the strategies of life and work that followed from them.

Nor were the origins of political practices necessarily found in childhood. Rather, culture's impact on political psychology was to be found at the intersection of the cultural group's actual historical and psychological experience. Members of the Soviet Politburo did not act as they did solely, and perhaps even primarily, as a result of harsh fathers or distant mothers. Rather, it was that their childhoods had prepared them all too well to view the political world through the powerful prism of their own ruthless and conspiratorial political histories.

The next logical step, the development of culture as belief in relation to political practice, was Almond and Verba's (1963) landmark five-nation study of political culture. It is arguably one of the most influential political science books of that decade. They relied on national surveys and focused on culture as embedded in the beliefs and attitudes that support different political practices. Building on the culture and personality school, they viewed political culture as the result of a set of interrelated personal, institutional, and historical experiences. "Subject" and "participant" political cultures differed because in each family, school, social, and later political experience shaped, then reinforced a particular view of one's self in the

---

[11] George's reformulation of Leites's work led to a rich and continuing literature in international politics, bargaining, and conflict theory (Mandell, 1986). Not the least of the contributions growing out of Leites's revised culture-as-belief-system approach to culture and crosscultural political analysis was the literature on misperception and conflict (Jervis, 1976). Avoidable wars, according to White (1970), could be traced to differences of perception and understanding rooted in distinctive cultural frames and historical experiences.

world. In short, congruence and coherence were still the foundations of culture's impact on psychology and the political practices they shaped.

Inglehart's (1989, 1997) influential studies approached political culture and its implications from another perspective. He viewed culture as embedded in values, which are, in turn, a reflection of the level of need satisfaction that a society has achieved. Building on Maslow's (1954) need theory of personality and psychological development, Inglehart argued that the satisfaction of more basic human needs (physiological, safety, esteem, and belonging needs) frees up individuals and societies to be concerned with other, postmaterial, concerns.

One of Inglehart's contributions is his use of a wholistic, but not psychoanalytic, theory of personality as the basis of understanding culture's impact on psychology and political practices and concerns. However, he made another contribution as well—his insight that different historical generations, within the same culture, can have vastly different psychological experiences. In his work, cultural's impact on the psychology of political views and practices is no longer a function solely of family, institutional, or political experience, but of historical circumstances during which it unfolds. Thus does the modern sometimes reaffirm the traditional, albeit in new ways, as Ingelhart's use of generational analysis recaptured and updated Benedict's (1934) insistence on the importance of history to cultural psychology analysis.

AMERICA'S NEW CULTURAL POLITICAL PSYCHOLOGY

Paralleling and dwarfing the lonely contemporary political psychology scholarship that takes culture seriously are political trends that threaten to overwhelm not only our cultureless theories, but our culture itself. The problem is well captured by two quotes from President Clinton:

> It is really potentially a great thing for America that we are becoming so multiethnic. . . . But it's also potentially a powder keg of problems and heart break and division and loss. And how we handle it will determine, really,—that single question may be the biggest determination of what we look like fifty years from now . . . and what the children of that age will have to look forward to. (Clinton, 1997a)

> Can we define what it means to be an American, not just in terms of the hyphen showing our ethnic origins, but in terms of the primary allegiance to the values that America stands for and values we really live by? (Clinton, 1997b)

These are not trivial questions. Fueled in part by enormous, and in this century, unprecedented numbers of new immigrants, the United States is becoming dramatically more diverse—racially, ethnically, and culturally. Figures show that the number of immigrants living in the United States has almost tripled since 1970, rising from 9.6 million to 26.3 million today and far outpacing the growth of the native-born population (Escobar, 1999).

At the same time, the stability of American political and normative culture has been challenged in recent decades by an assertive expansion of individual and group rights, acerbic debates regarding the legitimacy and limits of these claims, and a preference on the part of national political leaders to finesse rather than engage these controversies. Freed by the end of the cold war from a need to focus on external enemies, the country appears at a crossroad.

Race relations have in many ways improved, yet paradoxically worsened. Immigrants are idealized by some, even as high levels of immigration are greeted with suspicion and apprehension by many others. Definitions of the family and relations between men and women, at home and in the work place, have dramatically changed, but a question remains as to whether they have improved. In short, while America is undeniably more diverse than at any time in its history, Americans appear more fragmented, alienated, and polarized.

Advocates of diversity have given more attention to pressing and expanding their claims than to the psychological requirements necessary to build a consensus that would support and sustain them. Critics of diversity have yet to explain how to satisfactorily accommodate the reality of diversity and its opportunities, without recourse to traditional hegemony.

Moderating and working through the increasingly pointed demands of both groups is perhaps the fundamental domestic issue facing American society. Success is by no means assured. Divisive issues such as affirmative action, abortion rights, English as the primary language, homosexual marriage, the apparent conflict between merit and equality, and many more matters of heated contemporary debate raise important questions, political and psychological. They also raise profound questions of national psychology and identity. Is it inevitable that cultural, psychological, and political diversity lead to a fragmented and thus dysfunctional national identity? Can it be avoided, and if so, how?

Some (Isbister, 1996, 1998; Maharidge, 1996), applaud these developments. They view the decline of key American cultural traditions, and especially its "dominant elites," as a necessary step in developing a less hegemonic, more democratic society. Others (Miller, 1998; Schlesinger, 1992) are much less certain. They see an America whose central traditions, many of which in their view are critical to supporting a free democratic society, are in danger of being lost, perhaps past the point of recovery.

These two views frame a debate with the most profound consequences for the country. What does it mean to be an American? Given enormous diversity, what if anything, binds us together as a country? What will happen to the psychological elements that have been essential to our country's history and development—a commitment to pragmatic excellence, achievement, mobility, and the ambition that underlies them?

Consider the concept of assimilation. Some wonder whether it has been damaged as an ideal and practice with a corresponding loss in the sense of a national American identity (Glazer, 1993). That question is doubtless a matter of concern. Yet, in spite of its importance, it may be peripheral to an even more fundamental question: Just what is the nature of the culture to which we want immigrants to assimilate? Salins (1997) argued that the matter would be resolved if immigrants would just continue to learn English, abide by the work ethic, and take pride in American identity, believing in America's liberal democratic and egalitarian principles .

Would that it were so simple! Rumbaut (1997) reported the results of a large multiyear survey of 80,000 students in the San Diego Unified School district. He reported that on a number of measures, "there is a negative association between length of time of residence in the U.S. and second generation [immigrant] status with both GPA and educational aspirations" (pp. 937–938). Some insight into how this happens is made clearer by looking at number of hours viewing TV. In multivariate analysis, it is the single best predictor of GPA (less TV correlates with higher GPA). No doubt, more television watching is not what advocates of assimilation have in mind, but it is an aspect of what is happening. Portes and Zhou (1994) reported that among Haitians in Florida and Hispanics in a California community, physical proximity to cultural and political "adversarial groups" often resulted in immigrant children dropping their educational aspirations in order not to appear to be "acting White."

Nor is "pride in American identity," even if it includes beliefs in democracy and equality, of much use as a criterion unless one knows just what that means. True, Lipset (1963) was right when he called attention to the historical persistence of these ideals. However, Riesman (with Glazer, 1951) and Lasch (1979) were also correct in pointing out that the old ideals have changed. How can both be right?

A basic flaw of the values/ideals approach to American national identity is not that values do not carry much actual behavioral or psychological weight. They do. Most advocates of this approach have never really addressed the issue of how the highly abstract ideals they find embedded in American history and culture actually serve as a framework for psychological development and behavior at the level of the actual lives that people lead.

Some theorists of American values discuss them as if they were independent and unitary—the ideal of democracy, the ideal of equality, and so on. Others have focused on conflict between values, a commitment to achievement, for example, being at odds with a commitment to equality.

However, it seems more useful to focus on *clusters* of national ideals, if as in the United States, this focus can be substantively supported. Viewed not as discrete, isolated entities, but as integrated cultural packages, it might then be easier to distinguish one national cultural cluster "package" from another. It would also be easier to understand how such packages can both remain constant and change. And finally, it would be possible to more easily discern how a particular national psychology or "character" might develop in relation to a particular "package" of national ideals.

What are these cultural pacakages and how do they operate? That, regrettably, is not a question of much concern to the field—yet. However, these and other questions are central to our ability to understand some of the most important contemporary political and psychological issues. What is culture and its role in psychological and identity development? What is identity, and what, exactly, is the relationship between individual and national identity? Is there any relationship between national identity and national character? Is one more central to contemporary issues of diversity in America, or do both play important roles?

OLD ANSWERS, NEWER QUESTIONS

The core elements of cultural's consequences were worth noting not because they produced ideal societies,[12] but rather because they produced coherent and integrated ones. How then did cultural anthropologists understand culture's consequences. First, culture's influence was to be found within the boundaries of shared experience. The smaller cultural units that early anthropologists studied were united, psychologically and culturally, by the accumulated weight of the common experience. Second, culture's impact was to be found in the shared perception of that experience. Common frames of reference and understanding, whether in the form of cultural narratives or practices, helped to insure that accumulated cultural history was not only broadly experienced, but widely shared. Third, the integrating effects of common experience and understanding were instrumental in forging an individual identity linked to common group identity. No group members searched for their identity, or constructed it, they simply assumed it.

Few, if any, of the features that aided early cultural anthropologists to develop their theories characterize the societies of interest to modern political psychology. The societies of most contemporary interest are large and

---

[12]Such societies were not necessarily harmonious or peaceful. Intertribal warfare was frequent, and detailed social rankings coupled with the dominant power of chiefs limited mobility and opportunity for many group members.

diverse. Populated by disparate cultural groups, it is increasingly difficult to assume common socialization practices, a common psychology, or even common understandings.

The results are evident worldwide. An essential question, therefore, is how diverse cultural traditions can be integrated into political units that transcend them. This is the fundamental dilemma of the modern multi-ethnic, multicultural states, and should be a key concern of political psychology. But there are other and related important questions as well.

Early cultural anthropologists viewed cultures as integrated units whose parts made adaptive and functional sense. It is highly questionable whether this conceptualization remains wholly useful. The problem is not only one of strong, diverse cultural traditions leading in different directions, although that is certainly true. The problem, as Bell (1954) pointed out in his seminal book, *The Cultural Contradictions of Capitalism,* is that some deeply rooted cultural practices can, in the absence of a binding, limiting cultural or political framework, undermine their own foundations.

Early cultural anthropologists also viewed cultural change as evolutionary, not revolutionary. Cultural contacts in the societies they studied were sporadic, limited, and even when forced, were filtered through a solid and widely shared foundation of cultural experience. One reason was that the culture and its people largely stayed in place, retaining ties to their historical cultural experience. Modern "cultural contact" appears, in important respects, quite different. The reasons are not solely a function of the world as global village and the cultural interpenetration facilitated by modern communications.

An unprecedented amount of modern intercultural contact is brought about by migration and immigration. This in turn has resulted in some wholly new questions, or at least questions needing to be addressed on a wholly different, larger scale than previously.

What happens to a group's cultural foundation when it gets transplanted to a new, substantially different cultural setting? What happens to predominant cultural traditions when they try to integrate diverse, and perhaps incompatible, foreign cultural traditions? Is there a difference between shallow and deep cultural integration?[13] What is the process of cultural and intercultural change in circumstances where two or more major cultural traditions share the same physical and political space? What conceptual

---

[13]Hermans and Kempen (1998) argued that "modern," "hybrid" cultures make the assumption of cultural coherence problematic. Yet, it remains to be seen whether hybrid cultures that go against the basic cultural traditions of a community will become integrated, as opposed to a more surface level of accommodation. Or, in other words, just because Muslims in Iraq wear Levis and listen to rock, should we assume that they share the major cultural values of the countries from which these items are imported?

models help us to understand the processes of cultural assimilation, interdependence, or autonomy?

The major figures in early cultural anthropology, seeing the unity of the cultures they studied, drew no conclusions about the relative merit of cultural practices. There is an echo of this laissez faire tradition in the modern insistence that all cultural practices be accorded equal respect and honor, even when they violate deep cultural understandings and traditions (Pangle, 1998). How cultures can honor, even embrace, traditions wholly at variance with their own cultural foundations is a question of no small import in modern multicultural democracies. Fish's complaint (1998) that American culture professes tolerance, "but resists the force of the appreciated culture at precisely the point at which it matters most to its strongly committed members" (p. 60) is precisely right. However, the question is whether it can be otherwise. Can a democracy embrace and honor an antidemocratic cultural tradition and remain democratic?

Are all cultural traditions equally deserving of respect and accommodation? As Sowell (1994) pointed out, even the dominant Roman imperium culture adapted Arabic numerals over their own more clumsy counterparts because they were functionally superior. In our own culture, the devastating consequences of divorce on children have been well documented, as has the generally positive experience of growing up in a warm, supportive, intact family. Must we really conclude that the former is preferable for raising children, if we respect the need for choice in making and keeping marital commitments?

Finally, there are the questions of identity with which modern cultural and cross-cultural political psychology must grapple. Erikson's defining insight was that identity must be twice fitted. It must fit the individual's interior psychology—ambitions, skills, ideals, and relations with others—but it must also find a comfortable fit in the array of places that every culture makes available to its members.

For obvious reasons, the development of a psychologically robust and socially supported identity, whether it is called that or not, is an aspect of socialization in every viable culture. Identity provides a strategic, reciprocal relationship for the individual and culture. A fitting identity provides the individual with a sense of place and purpose. It also serves larger cultural and social functions. Individuals with identities that fit, buttress their culture—its understandings, institutions, and practices, as well as themselves.

The early cultural anthropologists studied cultures in which the understanding of who individuals were, and how they fit in, were not matters of debate or wide personal choice. The exact opposite is true in contemporary societies. The array and mix of biological, psychological, racial, ethnic, religious, political, national, and professional identities present in increasingly heterogeneous societies provides unprecedented opportunities for choice, conflict, and confusion.

Identity has made more progress as a political slogan than as a substantive term. The political uses (Norton, 1998) and abuses (Schlesinger, 1996) of identity politics have become clearer n the past two decades. However, the development of comparative psychology theories of identity formation and consolidation have lagged far behind.

Is it possible, for example, to forge a new New Zealand national identity at the same time that its major non-English group, the Maoris, are in the midst of a cultural revival and in the process of consolidating a transition from tribal to Maori identity (Durie, 1998)? What are the consequences for national identities when various ethnic groups insist on their cultural and political autonomy? Can a homosexual man, whose identity is primarily defined by his sexual orientation, be patriotic in a country that continues to deny him the opportunity to a legally sanctioned marriage, or even the ability to serve in its armed forces if he publicly expresses his identity preferences? Must identities primarily defined by race be nationally divisive? Are such identities necessarily "racist?" When individuals define their identities primarily in racial (or ethnic, gender, or other noninclusive) frames, how are other possible identifications organized psychologically?

These are not idle questions. Their answers have substantial implications for individuals and the societies of which they are a part. However, as yet, we have little substantive basis on which to resolve them. Sixty years ago, Lasswell (1930) observed, "Political science without biography is a form of taxidermy" (p. 1). Modern political developments have brought us to the point where we might add the following to Lasswell's observation: political psychology analysis detached from its cultural foundations is like designing a *grand prix* race car without wheels. It can be done, but it is unlikely to result in much theoretical or substantive mileage.

ACKNOWLEDGMENT

This paper draws on, and builds on, two of the author's papers, one in which he is the senior author (Renshon & Duckitt, 2000), the other of which he is the sole author (Renshon, 2000).

REFERENCES

Almond, G., & Verba, C. (1963). *The civic culture.* Princeton, NJ: Princeton University Press.
Barnouw, V. (1963). *Culture and personality.* Homewood, IL: Dorsey Press.
Bell, D. (1954). *The cultural contradictions of capitalism.* New York: Basic Books.

Benedict, R. (1934). *Patterns of culture.* New York: Mentor.

Boas, F. (1939). *The mind of primitive man.* New York: Macmillan. (Original work published 1911)

Bock, P. K. (1988). *Rethinking psychological anthropology.* Prospect Heights, IL: Waveland Press.

Clinton, W. J. (1997a, April 11). Remarks and question and answer session with the American Society of Newspaper Editors. *Weekly Compilation of Presidential Documents, 14,* April, *33*(15), 509.

Clinton, W. J. (1997b, June 14). Remarks at the University of California at San Diego commencement ceremony. *Weekly Compilation of Presidential Documents, 23,* June, *33*(25), 877.

DuBois, C. (1944). *The people of Alor* (Vol. 1 & 2). New York: Harper and Row.

Durie, M. (1998). *Te mana, te Kawanatanga: The politics of Maori self-determination.* New York: Oxford.

Eckstein, H. (1997). Social science as cultural science, rational choice as methaphysics. In R. J. Ellis & M. Thompson (Eds.), *Culture matters: Essays in honor of Aaron Wildavsky* (pp. 21–44). Boulder, CO: Westview.

Escobar, G. (1999, January 9). Immigrants' ranks tripled in 29 years. *The Washington Post,* p. A01.

Fish, S. (1998). Boutique multiculturalism. In A. M. Melzer (Ed.), *Multiculturalism and American democracy* (pp. 69–88). Lawrence: University of Kansas.

Funk, C. L., & Sears, D. O. (1991). "Are we reaching undergraduates: A survey of course offerings in political psychology." *Political Psychology, 12,* 559–572.

George, A. (1969). The "operational code": A neglected approach to the study of political leaders and decision makers. *International Studies Quarterly, 13,* 190–222.

Glazer, N. (1993). Is assimilation dead? *The Annals of the American Academy of Political Science, 530,* 122–136.

Hermans, H. J. M., & Kempen, H. J. G. (1998). Moving cultures: The perilous problems of cultural dichotomies in a globalizing society. *American Psychologist, 53*(10), 1111–1120.

Huntington, S. P. (1996). *The clash of civilization and the remaking of world order.* New York: Simon & Shuster.

Isbister, J. (1996). *The immigration debate: Remaking America.* New York: Kurnarian Press.

Isbister, J. (1998). Is America too white? In E. Sandman (Compiler) *What, then is the American, this new man?* (pp. 25–32). Washington, DC: Center of Immigration Studies.

Inglehart, R. (1989). *Cultural shift in advanced industrial society.* Princeton, NJ: Princeton University Press.

Inglehart, R. (1997). *Modernization and postmodernization: Cultural, economic and political change in 43 countries.* Princeton, NJ: Princeton University Press.

Inkeles, A. (1990–1991). National character revisited. *The Tocqueville Review, 12,* 83–117.

Inkeles, A., & Levinson, D. J. (1954). National character: The study of modal personality and sociocultural systems. In G. Lindzey (Ed.), *The handbook of social psychology* (pp. 977–1020). Reading, MA.: Addison-Wesley.

Inkeles, A., & Levinson, D. J. (1968–1969). National character: The study of modal personality and sociocultural systems. In G. Lindzey & E. Aronson (Eds.), *Handbook of social psychology* (Vol. 4, pp. 418–506). New York: McGraw-Hill.

Jervis, R. (1976). *Perception and misperception in international relations.* Princeton, NJ: Princeton University Press.

Kardiner, A., with Linton, R. (1939). *The individual and his society.* New York: Columbia University Press.

Kluckhohn, C. (1957). *Mirror for man.* New York: Premier.

Kluckhohn, C., & Murray, H. A. (Eds.) (1953). *Personality in nature, society, and culture* (2nd ed.). New York: Knopf.

Landes, D. S. (1996). *The wealth and poverty of nations: Why some are so rich, and others so poor.* New York: Norton.

Lasch, C. (1979). *The culture of narcissism: American life in an age of diminishing expectations.* New York: Basic Books.

Lasswell, H. D. (1930). *Psychopathology and politics.* Chicago: University of Chicago Press.

Leites, N. (1948). Psychocultural hypotheses about political acts. *World Politics, 1,* 102–119.

Leites, N. (1951). *The operational code of the politburo.* New York: McGraw-Hill.

Linton, R. (1930). *The study of man.* New York: Appleton-Century-Crofts.

Linton, R. (1945). *The cultural background of personality.* New York: Appleton-Century-Crofts.

Lipset, S. M. (1963). *The first new nation.* New York: Basic Books.

Maharidge, D. (1996). *The coming white minority: California's eruptions and America's future.* New York: Times Books.

Mandell, R. (1986). Psychological approaches to international politics. In M. Hermann (Ed.), *Political psychology,* (pp. 251–278). San Francisco: Jossey Bass.

Maslow, A. (1954). *Motivation and personality.* New York: Harper and Row.

Mead, M. (1935). *Sex and temperament in three primitive societies.* New York: Apollo.

Mead, M. (1939). *From the South Seas.* New York: Morrow.

Miller, J. J. (1998). *The unmaking of Americans: How multiculturalism has undermined America's assimilation ethic.* New York: Free Press.

Norton, A. (1998). The virtues of multiculturalism. In A. M. Melzer, J. Weinberger, & M. R. Zinman (Eds.), *Multiculturalism and American democracy* (pp. 130–138). Lawrence: University of Kansas.

Pangle, L. (1998). Multiculturalism and civic education. In A. M. Melzer, J. Weinberger, & M. R. Zinman (Eds.), *Multiculturalism and American democracy* (pp. 173–196). Lawrence: University of Kansas.

Portes, A., & Zhou, M. (1994). Should immigrants assimilate? *The Public Interest, 11*(6), 18–33.

Pye, L. (2000). The elusive concept of culture and the vivid reality of personality. In S. A. Renshon & J. Duckitt (Eds.), *Political psychology: Cultural and cross cultural foundations* (pp. 18–32). London: Macmillan.

Renshon, S. A. (1992). Political socialization: The development of an interdisciplinary field. In M. Hawkesworth & M. Kogan (Eds.), *Routledge Encyclopedia of Government and Politics* (Vol. 1, pp. 443–447). London: Routledge.

Renshon, S. A. (1996). Political psychology. In A. Kuper & J. Kuper (Eds.), *The social science encyclopedia* (2nd ed., pp. 443–470). London: Routledge.

Renshon, S. A. (2000). American character and national identity: The dilemmas of cultural diversity. In S. A. Renshon & J. Duckitt (Eds.), *Political psychology: Cultural and cross cultural foundations* (pp. 285–310). London: Macmillan.

Renshon, S. A., & Duckitt, J. (in press). Cultural and cross-cultural political psychology: Revitalizing a founding tradition for a new subfield. In S. A. Renshon & J. Duckitt (Eds.), *Political psychology: Cultural and cross cultural foundations.* London: Macmillan.

Riesman, D., with Glazer, N. (1951). *Faces in the crowd: Individual studies in character and politics.* New Haven, CT: Yale University Press.

Rumbaut, R. (1997). Assimilation and its discontents: Between rhetoric and reality. *International Migration Review, 31*(4), 923–960.

Salins, P. (1997). *Assimilation, American style.* New York: Basic Books.

Schlesinger, A., Jr. (1992). *The disuniting of America: Reflections on a multicultural society.* New York: Norton.

Sears, D. O., & Funk, C. L. (1991). Graduate education in political psychology. *Political Psychology, 12,* 345–362.

Sowell, T. (1994). *Race and culture.* New York: Basic Books.

Spiro, M. E. (1961). An overview and suggested reorientation. In F. L. K. Hsu (Ed.), *Psychological anthropology: Appoaches to culture and personality* (pp. 459–492). Homewood, IL: Dorsey.

Whiting, J. W. M., & Child, I. L. (1953). *Child training and personality. A cross-cultural study.* New Haven: Yale University Press.

White, R. K. (1970). *Nobody wanted war: Misperception in Vietnam and other wars.* New York: Doubleday.

Wilson, J. (1996). *When work disappears.* New York: Knopf.

8

The Utility of Political Psychology

M ARTHA C RENSHAW
Wesleyan University

THE DISTINCTIVENESS OF POLITICAL PSYCHOLOGY

What makes political psychology distinctive and valuable? First, it is broadly interdisciplinary. Although its core lies in the application of psychological theories and concepts to political issues, its scope extends well beyond the intersection of psychology and political science. Political psychology incorporates approaches and applications in sociology, education, criminology, history, women's studies, communication, and anthropology. This range is expanded further when research links different areas of psychology—for example, personality theory and social psychology.

Second, many critical problems in politics require explanations based on psychological insights. Their utility is not only theoretical, in that explanations based on political psychology can be more convincing than narrower models, but also practical because political psychology lends itself not just to explanation but to prescription. Thus, policy makers and scholars benefit.

One major intellectual contribution of political psychology is explaining how preferences or interests are formed, how they are ranked, the intensity with which they are held, and how they are implemented. Furthermore, political psychology deals with these questions at both individual and group levels.

Rational choice theory assumes that behavior is directed toward maximizing a utility or value. However, defining that utility lies beyond the scope of the theory, however sophisticated the subsequent modelling of behavior may be. Political psychology, in contrast, disaggregates the decision. The establishment of a preference is viewed as the outcome of a process rather than the starting point for analysis. Political psychology thus explains what rational choice or econometric theory assumes.

Furthermore, political psychology explains behavior that is not obviously instrumental or self-interested. This does not mean that political psychology focuses only on apparently irrational action, although it does explore consistent biases in reasoning due to cognitive processes, as well as less predictable emotional effects on behavior. It does mean that political psychology addresses questions that rational choice theory leaves unanswered. A political psychological approach does not assume that an actor cannot have a preference or perform an action that does not accord with material self-interest. Moreover, political psychology accounts for the subjectivity of conceptions of self-interest.

Consider, for example, the free rider problem. Why would individuals engage in the pursuit of public goods that they could enjoy without effort or risk? In particular, why would they engage in rebellious collective action? Here the classic dilemma for a rational choice model is that behavior that is "rational" for the individual is "irrational" for the collectivity. The rational individual would not participate in revolution or protest, or indeed any behavior requiring the mobilization of large numbers in order to be successful. The dilemma is that people obviously do.

Rather than solving this problem by positing the existence of selective incentives or stretching the concept of "utility" or self-interest so far that it loses analytical precision, political psychology points directly to highly specific and differentiated motivations for participation in violent opposition movements or legal protest demonstrations.[1] It identifies a variety of both individual and social predispositions as well as triggering factors.

Rational choice theory must assume that everyone has the same conception of the common "good," rather than different understandings, levels of commitment, and perceptions of the value of the goal to be attained. Political psychology insists that people have different emotional stakes in political outcomes and that they may reason differently. It also suggests that individuals may participate (a) in political activities that they do not expect to succeed and (b) when they do not necessarily feel personally efficacious. Their "expected utility" may actually be low. Moreover, political psychology asks why certain behaviors (such as belonging to a group, performing acts of cruelty and violence, avenging a perceived wrong, even suffering and

---

[1]For example, Muller and Opp (1986) suggested a "private interest" theory of selective incentives that included "psychic" or "entertainment" rewards as well as social rewards such as affiliation, solidarity, image, status, and the expectations of others. They also added that people might realize the danger of free riding as a result of social learning. Their explanation thus departed considerably from rational choice theory, although they considered themselves merely to have modified the framework.

sacrifice) provide "psychic rewards" rather than simply stating that they may do so.

Another related problem for rational choice theory is the escalation of violence beyond the levels required to achieve a goal, whether that goal is rebellion or the suppression of dissent. The destructiveness of ethnonationalist conflicts almost always exceeds the levels of harm that would be necessary to "win" and is frequently counterproductive. Hardin (1995), who rightly discounted the "primordial hatreds" thesis, attempted to explain such reputedly "irrational phenomena" with the premise that what is rational depends on the knowledge or information one possesses. Familiarity with and corresponding knowledge of one's own group produce ethnonationalist identification and thus, inevitably, conflict with others. As Hardin (1995) put it, "There may be foolishness, craziness, morality, and extra-rational group identification at work for many participants in violent ethnic conflict. But they are given their field of play by the individually rational tendencies to group identification" (p. 180). Yet Hardin also admitted that "Violence is a tipping phenomenon because, once it begins or reaches a high enough level, it is often self-reinforcing" (p. 155). He continued, "The general stability of expectations of reasonable behavior can collapse . . ." (p. 155). He also cited the importance of opportunistic and unscrupulous leaders who manipulate ethnic hatreds for personal advantage. However, neither of these phenomena—escalation of group violence beyond what is "reasonable" and exploitative leader–follower relations—is explicable without psychological concepts. Why, for example, did violence become so brutal and indiscriminate, involving large numbers of civilian casualties and ghastly atrocities, in so many diverse cultures and locations— Algeria, Bosnia, Rwanda, Sierra Leone, Kosovo, or East Timor? Why do ambitious and unscrupulous leaders who appeal to group prejudices attract followers? Why is it beneficial for politicians to play the ethnic card to get support? Why do individuals choose one identity over another? Does every group require an enemy in order to maintain identity and internal cohesion?

Both psychoanalytical and social–psychological approaches offer different answers.[2] Volkan's (1997) explanation for ethnic violence stressed the effects of fear, stress, and anxiety. Perceived threats to identity trigger processes such as dehumanization of the enemy and the reactivation of historical myths, which Volkan calls *chosen wounds and chosen glories*, in order to justify violence against the other. Ross (1993), on the other hand, linked conflict to culture. He focused on the culturally shared images and perceptions of the outside world that form the basis of an interpretive framework that influences individual and group reactions to others. He referred to these as *psychocultural dispositions* that are learned in early life. He noted,

---

[2]My examples here are selective but they are representative of the literature.

as Volkan did, that stress and anxiety intensify predispositions. As Ross (1993a) emphasized, such a theory can both address the issue of the intensity of conflict, which goes well beyond the objective interests at stake between combatants, and link individual behavior to collective action.

Explaining terrorism as a particular subset of political violence or rebellious action also requires an approach that integrates the interests of those who engage in violence as well as their interpretations or perceptions of adversaries, supporters, and the future. Terrorism can be analyzed as logical behavior for groups who have few alternatives and for whom terrorism serves explicit instrumental purposes (Crenshaw, 1978, 1990). This argument can be a useful corrective to the "irrational fanaticism" stereotype. Terrorism can be instrumental; it is not a simple result of primitive emotions or "tribal" loyalties. It is often part of a calculated and reasonable strategy of mobilizing support, polarizing society, increasing the costs of engagement for a colonial power, and gaining international attention. However, a general theory of motivations for terrorism must incorporate social psychological explanations, particularly desire for vengeance, resentment of perceived injustice, solidarity with the group, peer pressure, and competition with rivals (Crenshaw, 1981, 1985). Because terrorism is a form of violence that involves small numbers of participants, psychological interpretation is a critical component of any explanation. Furthermore, a variety of general psychological theories and concepts can usefully be applied to terrorism (Crenshaw, 1986, 1988, 1992).

Political psychology is concerned not only with the causes and processes of violence but also with conflict resolution and concrete policy prescriptions. Volkan (1997), for example, described attempts to help countries in the process of change (e.g., components of the former Soviet Union) shape new identities less prone to antagonistic relationships with former enemies. Ross (1993b) extended his approach explicitly to argue for processes of constructive conflict management based on reconciling interests and interpretations. He warned policy makers that issues that may seem objectively trivial to the outside observer may be emotionally compelling to the participants in a conflict; the success of any conflict resolution process depends on recognizing such emotional investments. Thus political psychological approaches to negotiation and mediation deal with the psychological bases of establishing trust as much as the tasks of creating compromises based on interest and guaranteeing commitments through institutions.[3]

---

[3]Another example of an analysis that does not employ a political psychology approach but that nevertheless relies on psychological factors is Walter's (1999) argument that third party security guarantees are essential to civil war settlement. She concluded, for example, that combatants must "believe" that peacekeepers will do their job and that their fearfulness and insecurity make them reluctant to disarm, no matter what institutional guarantees are provided for their protection.

In addition to ethnonationalist violence and terrorism, a critical problem for contemporary world politics is the proliferation of nuclear, chemical, and biological weapons.[4] Why would or do states or nonstates wish to acquire weapons of mass destruction? What utility is gained by the possession of such capabilities? It is difficult to explain such ambitions exclusively in terms of material interest. Consider, for example, India's decision to proceed with underground nuclear tests in 1998, thus moving from the status of *opaque proliferant* to *full transparency* (to use the jargon of security studies). Two factors have to be considered, in this case as well as in others. The first is the issue of national identity in a framework of perceived power relationships. The efforts of Western states to establish a nonproliferation regime, however well intentioned, generated resentment in a nationalist government already sensitive to slights from abroad and challenges to authority at home. Nuclear weapons appeared essential to international recognition as a "great power," a status that Indian elites and masses expected and felt the nation deserved. A second factor in explaining proliferation is perceptions of threat.[5] In objective terms, opponents of proliferation argue that India has nothing to fear from either Pakistan or China. In fact, the risk of fueling a costly and crisis-prone arms race should outweigh any gain from the acquisition of a vulnerable nuclear delivery system. However, Indian perceptions of threat and conceptions of its own security are subjective. Western policy makers trying to influence Indian decision making must recognize that Indian elites can sincerely believe that the possession of nuclear weapons constitutes an effective deterrent against aggression rather than dismissing such explanations as superficial and self-serving rationales for irresponsible behavior.

These are only two examples of the contribution of political psychology to contemporary world problems. Both demonstrate the elementary proposition, central to political science, that the concept of power must be based not just on material capabilities but on subjective considerations.

PROBLEMS IN APPLIED POLITICAL PSYCHOLOGY

The chief drawback to the political psychology approach, especially as compared to a rational choice or interest-based theory of political action, is that it requires detailed information about how individuals and groups reach

---

[4]Political psychology has made significant contributions to the study of foreign policy decision making in general, which is not reviewed here, but see the chapters by Janice Stein and Robert Jervis in this volume.

[5]An early work recognizing the importance of psychological constructions of threat is Cohen (1979).

decisions, carry them out, and react to the behavior of others. Such knowledge is often difficult to acquire, especially during active conflicts. Decision makers may be inaccessible; their recollections of the past may be flawed. It is difficult to capture motivation.

A related problem is that the psychological theories adopted by political scientists are often based on empirical data derived from laboratory rather than "real world" settings. It is difficult, for example, to compare the risk of losing a small amount of money or a coffee mug, as is common practice in social psychology experiments, often with undergraduate students, to losing thousands of lives or even losing an election. The consequential nature of outcomes in politics makes a difference to the stakes. Thus practical constraints on research may create conceptual barriers to using psychological theories.[6]

If the political scientists who use psychological ideas do not fully understand them, the applicability of their findings may be further diminished. Borrowing can be selective and out of context; it can mix together hypotheses and concepts that are based on incompatible theoretical assumptions. It can also lead to vague generalizations and faulty certainties.

On the other hand, psychological research or political psychological research should avoid being ahistorical. Psychological explanations of individual or group behavior must be rooted in an understanding of the historical context. As Ross (1993b) noted, prevailing ideologies, values, norms, beliefs, images, and/or myths constitute the cultural background for individual interpretations. Researchers also need to look at the role of political and social institutions and the dynamics of the relationships between governments and oppositions. All these factors affect learning and the availability of action repertoires.

CENTRAL CONCEPTS AND DEBATES

The central concepts behind political psychology are rich and diverse. This comprehensiveness is valuable, but it creates a sometimes bewildering complexity, even confusion. Furthermore, addressing almost any question about political attitudes or action (e.g., what contributes to moral or ethical reasoning or to tolerance) requires the integration of several different foundational theories and concepts. There is no simple one-to-one relationship between political or social problem and psychological explanation.

Starting at the level of the individual, the central concepts of political psychology include personality, cognition, affect and motivation, and atti-

---

[6]It it not, however, impossible to gain psychological insights through interviews. See, for example, the work of Della Porta (1995) based on life histories of participants in violence. See also Juergensmeyer (2000).

tudes or beliefs and how they change. However, thinking about attitudes or beliefs necessitates moving from the level of the individual to that of the group or society inasmuch as attitudes are not formed and certainly are not altered in isolation from the attitudes (or perceived attitudes) of others. Ideologies and social expectations come into play. Personality, too, is shaped by the individual's early interactions with others in the family. Cognitive processes are driven by the need to deal with information and stimuli coming from the political and social environment. The purpose of cognitive reasoning is to simplify dealing with the world, find useful mental shortcuts, and interact with others by both understanding them and persuading them to accept one's own "framing" of an issue. Hence there is a need to study the development of heuristics and biases, as well as the attribution of motives to others and perceptions of their expectations. Critical components of the study of attitudes and beliefs include stereotypes, prejudice, and discrimination against others perceived as different. Emotions and cognitive processes contribute to hatred and intolerance.

Social identity theory is necessary to understand why individuals acquire, construct, or choose one group identity rather than another. Individuals can often select among available identities based on different affiliations, according to religion, ethnicity, gender, or social class, for example. Identity is a flexible and malleable concept rather than something permanently fixed and unchanging. Identities may be not only multiple but conflicting. The individual may be thrust into an unchosen or even unwanted identity by society or by an opposing out-group. These processes are essential to understanding ethnic conflict, for example. The perception of threat from a different group can force individuals into identities that had previously seemed unimportant and even undesirable. Stereotyping can lead to identification (even negative identification). The perception of a threat to identity causes reactive or preventive violence and thus activates the security dilemma.

Socialization shapes identity and attitudes generally, and political socialization is appropriately an established field in political science. For example, threats would not produce solidarity unless there were shared norms and experiences and a common body of knowledge. (However, the extent to which cohesion requires prior familiarity is a question to be studied.) The relationship between the individual and society and the roles of the social institutions that shape identity and beliefs—family, religion, education, news media, and government—are critical. If policy makers are to be successful at conflict resolution, for example, they cannot wait until violence erupts to try to change hostile attitudes toward out-groups.

The study of group dynamics and collective decision making is also central to political psychology. How do individuals try to persuade others to agree with them and join in a collective endeavor? What is the nature of social influence? What is the nature of leadership? The political psychologist must examine narratives, scripts, metaphors, and other methods by which reality is "constructed" to give it meaning. How are problems or issues framed or defined? How does framing or the establishment of a reference point determine political outcomes? Are specific historical lessons or analogies powerful for emotional or cognitive reasons? What determines creativity and innovation in problem solving?

These questions link elite and mass politics because they are central to agenda setting and the engagement of public opinion on political issues. Problem representation is part of small-group decision making, but it is also part of the communication process between leaders and publics. A central concern of politics is putting the right "spin" on issues. Agenda setting involves competition among actors over framing issues. For example, the definition of an issue often determines which government agency gets institutional responsibility (or blame). If, for example, terrorism is war, and especially if it is linked to the proliferation of weapons of mass destruction, then it is the province of national security agencies, including the Department of Defense. If, however, it is crime, it is a problem for police and law enforcement.

A central debate in the field of political psychology focuses on the division between elite and mass politics. In the United States, this is often manifested as a divide between scholars interested in American political behavior (e.g., public opinion or voting) and those concerned with foreign policy decision making. This distinction, however, may be artificial. Why should the two focuses not be complementary? For example, foreign policy decision makers, especially the president, are acutely concerned with the legitimacy of policy and consequently with public opinion. The expectation of the domestic reaction is an important determinant of decisions. With the growing interest among international relations theorists in the domestic sources of foreign policy, and with the increased integration of domestic and foreign issues, perhaps the intellectual gap between the study of elite decision making and the study of mass politics will be bridged.

Another issue is how problem-oriented or "applied" political psychology should be. At one extreme is abstract theory building and methodology without empirical grounding; at the other extreme is a reckless and simplistic application of complicated and carefully delimited theories to "hot" topics. Political psychology should find a cautious middle ground.

FUTURE ISSUES

The development of cross-cultural psychology will be essential in a world of globalization and interdependence. It is difficult to think of a contemporary issue that does not require such broad understanding. This need is not only compelling for international relations, but for politics within countries that are becoming increasingly diverse, interconnected, and cosmopolitan. Consider, for example, the issues of immigration and refugees or domestic ethnic and racial tensions. The study of political psychology, therefore, must be genuinely international. It cannot be a purely Western enterprise. Parochialism will be too costly.

Such a cosmopolitan understanding will be essential for an effective American foreign policy. If U.S. preponderance has created a unipolar world, then how will the rest of the world react? If the democratic peace hypothesis is accepted as a universal law of international relations, how can democracy be promoted it if others perceive it as a form of Western domination? Resistance to Western or American interests will take new forms. So-called religious or fundamentalist terrorism, for example, may be a reaction not only to American material power but to the threat conveyed by Western culture and values. Moreover, how can American leaders persuade the public to support policies of engagement, especially when those policies are costly in terms of both treasure and human lives? Is consistent and regular involvement in international affairs possible without adversaries, or will American leaders be tempted to construct mythical enemies in order to forge domestic consensus? Political psychology can address these problems.

REFERENCES

Cohen, R. (1979). *Threat perception in international crisis.* Madison: University of Wisconsin Press.

Crenshaw, M. (1978). *Revolutionary terrorism: The FLN in Algeria, 1954–1962.* Stanford: Hoover Institution Press.

Crenshaw, M. (1981). The causes of terrorism. *Comparative Politics, 13,* 379–399.

Crenshaw, M. (1985). An organizational approach to the analysis of political terrorism. *Orbis, 29,* 465–489.

Crenshaw, M. (1986). The Psychology of political terrorism. In M. G. Hermann (Ed.), *Political psychology: Contemporary problems and issues* (pp. 379–413). San Francisco: Jossey-Bass.

Crenshaw, M. (1988). The subjective reality of the terrorist. In R. O. Slater & M. Stohl (Eds.), *Current perspectives on international terrorism* (pp. 12–46). London: Macmillan, and New York: St. Martin's.

Crenshaw, M. (1990). The logic of terrorism: Terrorism as the product of strategic choice. In W. Reich (Ed.), *Origins of terrorism: Psychologies, ideologies, theologies, states of mind* (pp. 7–24). Cambridge, UK: Cambridge University Press.

Crenshaw, M. (1992). Decisions to use terrorism: Psychological constraints on instrumental reasoning. In D. della Porta (Ed.), *Social movements and violence: Participation in underground organizations. International Social Movement Research, 4,* 29–42. Greenwich, CT: JAI Press Inc.

Della Porta, D. (1995). *Social movements, political violence, and the state: A comparative analysis of Italy and Germany.* Cambridge, UK: Cambridge University Press.

Hardin, R. (1995). *One for all: The logic of group conflict.* Princeton, NJ: Princeton University Press.

Juergensmeyer, M. (2000). *Terror in the mind of God: The global rise of religious violence*. Berkeley: University of California Press.

Muller, E. N., & Opp, K.-D. (1986). Rational choice and rebellious collective action. *American Political Science Review, 80,* 2, 471–488.

Ross, M. H. (1993a). *The culture of conflict: Interpretations and interests in comparative perspective.* New Haven: Yale University Press.

Ross, M. H. (1993b). *The management of conflict.* New Haven: Yale University Press.

Volkan, V. (1997). *Bloodlines: From ethnic pride to ethnic terrorism.* New York: Farrar, Straus and Giroux.

Walter, B. (1999). Designing transitions from civil war: Demobilization, democratization, and commitments to peace. *International Security, 24,* 127–155.

9

From Social to Political Psychology: The Societal Approach

WILLEM DOISE
CHRISTIAN STAERKLÉ
University of Geneva

The boundaries between social psychology and political psychology are hard to trace in a sharp way. Indeed, a large amount of research in social psychology has been devoted to issues such as racism (Katz & Hass, Kinder & Sears, 1981; 1988; Pettigrew et al., 1998), prejudice (Allport, 1954; Biernat, Vescio, Theno, & Crandall, 1996; Dovidio & Gaertner, 1986), gender (Hoffmann & Hurst, 1990; Lorenzi-Cioldi, 1998), social justice (Bierhoff, Cohen & Greenberg, 1986; Deutsch, 1985), and nationalism (Billig, 1995; Bar-Tal, 1997). All these issues have an important political component. They are present on political agendas and are subject of political debates and decisions.

Even if the relationship between political science and psychology has been termed "a long affair" by McGuire (1993), scholars in social psychology recognize the political dimension of their research topics only to varying degrees. For some, general cognitive processes are at work when people judge, think, and decide about political issues. Typically, they study the way people reason about political phenomena, examine their individual decision-taking strategies, or establish personality- and knowledge-based typologies that explain different political orientations and positionings. Here, the political dimension is largely irrelevant to the extent that general models of information processing and decision making are applied to political issues. Other social psychologists, however, claim that the analysis of individual cognitive processes alone would not suffice for an exhaustive explanation of political processes. Such analyses have to be completed by a more societal perspective that connects explanations on an individual level with analyses of social dynamics such as norms, beliefs, values, and ideologies that guide and give meaning to individual political behavior. In such a perspective, the cognitive processes underlying the relationships individuals establish with their political environment are rather to be considered as manifestations of relational and societal dynamics than as their causes (Sears & Funk, 1991). Hence, in this chapter we use the term *societal psychology* for designating the contributions of a more societal social psychology to political psychology.

In the following pages, we describe examples of such a societal psychology. We adhere to a rather large and integrative conception of societal psychology, one that embraces research that many scholars would probably not consider as part of the political psychology tradition. Our concern is to demonstrate that different research traditions in social psychology are based on analyses of societal dynamics, while trying to account for the intervention of complex societal regulation mechanisms in individuals' cognitions, evaluations, and decisions. Thus, like many others, we extend our perspective clearly beyond a mainly individualistic vision of social psychological analyses, especially when they are applied to the political realm, or, otherwise said, when they become political psychology.

It is also our assumption that social representation theory (see, for instance, Augoustinos & Walker, 1995; Doise, Clémence, & Lorenzi-Cioldi, 1993; Moscovici, 1976) provides the necessary theoretical tools for analyzing the links between individual cognitive functioning and more general analyses of societal factors that direct the way people think, act, and interact in society. As Moscovici (1976, p. 284) wrote ". . . we see two cognitive systems at work, one which operates in terms of associations, inclusions, discriminations, that is to say the cognitive operational system, and the other which controls, verifies and selects in accordance with various logical and other rules; it involves a kind of metasystem which re-works the material produced by the first." At a general level, social representation theory deals with shared knowledge structures about issues debated in society and that orient individual positioning when judging relevant aspects of these social issues. Social representational analyses of normative lay knowledge about social issues debated in the public sphere form a crucial element of a societal psychology. Everyday communication about abstract political issues necessarily presupposes some kind of common understanding between the parties involved in a discussion, otherwise one party would not be able to understand the point of view of the other party. Social representations contribute to the construction of such shared meaning systems that allow individuals to communicate with each other. But social representations concern not only shared and common knowledge. One of the researchers' tasks is to evidence the structure of differences in understanding that typically characterize individual and group positioning toward political issues. Defined a priori or inferred a posteriori, organizing principles of individual and collective positioning, therefore, are central features of a societal psychology.

Unlike research on general psychological processes, societal psychology is concerned with the study of meaning and content in political positioning. It is indeed hard to imagine what politics would be without collective processes of meaning assignment. A democratic functioning of a political community is characterized by antagonistic positionings toward socially relevant topics. One may even conceive of politics as an endless struggle between social categories (such as political parties), aimed at associating specific meanings to abstract concepts (Mouffe, 1993). The meanings of *democracy, human rights, freedom,* or *justice,* to take but a few examples, are not and probably never will be defined in a universally accepted way. Instead, social regulations and complex systems of interaction shape the way people interpret these abstract principles. Furthermore, the focus on differential meaning assignment implies that societal psychology is necessarily embedded in a historical context. Meaning regulation systems are not stable and immutable social knowledge structures, but are transformed as a function of historical events and the political agenda.

It follows that in our view, political psychology should study those social and cognitive processes that take place when individual and social groups position themselves toward issues discussed and debated in a given society. Decision taking in elections and votes is but one example of institutionally organized political processes. Other examples of issues that are embraced by such a societal political psychology concern political involvement, development of attitudes toward legal and political institutions, explanations of political events, as well as judgments of politically relevant social categories. According to a societal approach, all these processes derive from symbolic regulations between social groups, captured in the concept of social representations. In this sense, they are never unproblematic, consensual, and automatic, but rather object of debate and subject to interindividual and temporal variation.

In the following sections, we exemplify our social representational view of societal psychology and discuss different approaches that integrate societal explanations. In all of these, social representations intervene, even if their authors do not explicitly refer to the original theory. They show that shared knowledge on the one hand, and explainable differences in individual and group-based positionings toward these common frames of references on the other hand, provide an appropriate theoretical framework for a societal psychology. The diversity of these research orientations shows the wide range of social–psychological topics, to which societal psychology can be associated. However, the work under review here should by no means be considered as an exhaustive collection of societal psychology.

Before presenting four realms of research, it should be underlined that much of the research presented was not aimed at developing a contribution to political psychology. However, in line with the foregoing ideas, we consider that the reported research trends exemplify a societal approach that is of relevance for political psychology.

THE SOCIETAL FUNCTIONING
OF LOCUS OF CONTROL BELIEFS

Political theories necessarily involve implicit or explicit beliefs about individual psychological functioning. Postulates of political theories bear, for instance, on the nature of basic psychological needs of individuals and on their readiness to commit themselves in social contracts in order to fulfill these needs. Often, however, these beliefs have been studied without framing them in a political perspective, and therefore the role of societal psychology is to highlight the role of such beliefs in political functioning.

The notion of control based on the theory of Rotter (1966) has certainly been successful in describing beliefs about differential individual functioning. In its initial definition, the notion was culturally defined:

> When a reinforcement is perceived by the subject as following some action of his own but not being entirely contingent upon his action, then, in our culture, it is typically perceived as the result of luck, chance, fate, as under the control of powerful others, or as unpredictable because of the great complexity of the forces surrounding him. When the event is interpreted in this way by an individual, we have labeled this a belief in external control. If the person perceives that the event is contingent upon his own behavior or his own relatively permanent characteristics, we have termed this a belief in internal control. (Rotter, 1966, p. 1).

The following postulates were essential in shaping the theory (see Dubois, 1987). Understanding personality is based on an analysis of the interaction between individual and environment. Notions as attitudes, values, expectations are indispensable in such analyses and account for individual consistency in behavior. An important organizing principle of such consistency is the relative importance given by individuals to situational (external) and dispositional (internal) factors in evaluating outcomes of goal-directed actions.

The degree of internality is therefore defined as the likelihood that an expected outcome will result from one's own behavior and/or personal characteristics (traits, skills, attitudes) in specific circumstances. Individuals with high internal control see themselves at the origin of their positive or negative reinforcements; individuals with low internal control look for this origin in external circumstances such as chance, decisions of others, or task difficulty.

Instruments have been developed for measuring the perceived locus of control of individuals. They often consist of questionnaires with forced choice items (see, for instance, Rotter, 1966). Examples of such items with a response choice could be (a) "Most of the accidents that strike people are due to bad luck"; (b) "Misfortunes of individuals are caused by their mistakes" or (a) "In business, most of us are subject to forces beyond our understanding and control"; or (b) "Individuals can control events when participating actively in political and social life." For these two items, (a) choices would indicate an external locus of control whereas (b) choices would indicate an internal one.

In several investigations (for a review, see Dubois, 1987), a high "internal" score has been proven to be a good predictor for academic and professional achievement, and more generally for social adjustment. That it is generally better to believe in one's own internal control than to think that one is externally determined has led developmental psychologists to investigate variations in locus of control over the lifespan.

A first series of research illustrates the general hypothesis that growth in age is accompanied with the acquisition of various skills that make an individual more autonomous and more aware of his or her internal control capacities. Therefore, scores on adapted locus of control scales should increase in internality with age. Such a developmental trend was often verified and acquired almost the status of a consensually accepted fact, and exceptions were considered not to infirm a general rule. Some systematicness was revealed in those exceptions as the drop in internality during initial phases of adolescence (see Crandall, Katkovsky, & Crandall, 1965; Dubois, 1986; Sherman, 1984). Such an exception could easily be explained away as during that phase of development youths are confronted with new challenges and new comparison groups so that they can experience some loss of control during that period of their lives. However, more important is the fact that a review of 20 years of research on the topic led to the conclusion that no systematic trend was observed in about one third of the studies.

Given the variety of instruments and methods used, such a negative finding is not necessarily to be considered as a serious argument against the existence of a developmental trend, but it led researchers to put the question of what exactly is developing with age in the realm of internal versus external control.

An important hint to answer that question is to be found in a research by Bartel (1971) showing that the increase in internal control with age was verified for middle-class children but not for lower class children. More generally, numerous investigations in the United States have found that children of Anglo-Saxon descent were more internal than African or Hispanic Americans, "rich" children more than "poor," and also, but less consistently so, boys more than girls.

These differences could be interpreted in the frame of Rotter's theory: general expectations about efficacy of one's own actions can be affected by the social status of categories one belongs to. A difference could exist in what children of various gender, social, and ethnic categories learn in their environment about the power they can exert in determining their own fate. Yet, a result by Nowicki and Strickland (1973) showed the intervention of stereotypical beliefs about sex differences: children of both genders, when invited to answer the Rotter scale, in a typical masculine or feminine way drastically change their responses, choosing almost no external alternatives for the masculine way and no internal alternatives for the feminine mode. There is, therefore, no doubt left that externality is part of the female stereotype and internality of the masculine one.

Even more generally, one can speak about the existence of a very strong social norm: internality is considered better than externality. Jellison and Green (1981) were among the first to consider that this normative aspect was not just an artifact but an essential ingredient of the locus of control attitude. Main results of their investigations are first, that individuals giving many internal responses are considered more favorably than those with a few such responses, and second, that individuals are aware of the existence of such a difference in valorization. When asked to answer for themselves or as a average student, and when they are invited to embody a positive or negative self-image in their answers, the scores of internality are significantly higher in conditions where a positive self-image is at stake.

Beauvois (1984), Le Poultier (1986), and Dubois (1994) generalized these findings in several settings: school, social work, training sessions. Overall, individuals who express more internal control and more dispositional explanations for their behavior are better considered and more easily accepted, a criterion of success in these different settings being the increase of belief in internal control as a consequence of education, treatment, or training. Results reported by Beauvois and Dubois (1988) show that 11-year-old pupils are aware of the desirability of "internal" responses, even though not in such a strong way as was the case for the students participating in the studies of Jellison and Green (1981).

The explanation for the importance of this internality norm offered by our French colleagues is in terms of social evaluation processes that imply that individuals are considered responsible for their fate. Belief in internal explanations and control of behavior are to be shared by those who evaluate and who are evaluated in socialization processes, although they do not necessarily know very much about what effectively determines and controls human behavior.

Hence, this is a typical example of a societal reinterpretation of a line of research that has mainly focused on consequences of individual differences without taking into account the structural organization of these differences. What was considered to be a psychological characteristic is now also interpreted as a basic belief that assumes an important societal function in contemporary political systems. Thus, a belief according to which one's own behavior leads to the expected outcomes may prevent commitment in collective endeavors. Paradoxically, the belief in individual autonomy and responsibility may lead to a modern, that is, voluntary, form of serfdom (Beauvois, 1994), and therefore potentially lessens people's readiness for active participation in political processes.

RESEARCH ON POLITICAL SOCIALIZATION

An explanatory model almost entirely based on the development of individual cognitive competencies has often been used for analyzing individual appropriation of meaning systems in the realm of politics: The more complex the cognitive instruments a child possesses, the more complex the political judgements he or she is able to make. This is the main conclusion of Connell's (1971) work, *The Child's Construction of Politics*. Such an approach is also exemplified in Inhelder and Piaget's (1958) explanations of adolescents' political activism: The acquisition of formal thinking would enable the construction of alternative views on society. On the other hand, the content of political ideas of youth was often explained by adherence to the political orientation of their parents and of other significant figures such as peers and teachers (see Jennings & Niemi, 1974).

Growth in cognitive complexity and transmission of partisanship are not the only factors that modulate political thought over the lifespan. Political socialization is the construction of a meaning system that involves, of course, cognitive operations and that evolves in a frame of societal regulations in a complex way.

The European value study published by Stoetzel (1983) showed a general trend of change in values across different societies. Such changes cannot be explained without societal analyses. At the level of the individual, they involve complex patterns of interrelationships between attitudes and beliefs that are progressively elaborated and that are emphasized in some cases by partisan choices. Examples are given in a study on tolerance by Vollebergh (1989).

The general change in values does not prevent a fraction of adolescents from manifesting intolerant attitudes usually described as ethnocentrism and sexism. A psychodynamic interpretation was proposed by Adorno and his colleagues (Adorno, Frenkel-Brunswik, Levinson, & Nevitt Sanford,

1950), who attribute to authoritarian educational practices of parents the origin of aggressive drives that exteriorize themselves in detriment of weaker targets. Vollebergh (1989) expresses doubts about such an interpretation and reports data on significant differences between pupils from more or less prestigious educational tracks and also between boys and girls, the former being more often authoritarian, ethnocentric, or sexist than the latter. Furthermore, more consistent patterns of high correlations between these different syndromes appear for pupils from the more prestigious track, but they are rather low for girls of the lower track. All these data are very difficult to explain in terms of a psychodynamic interpretation, and Vollebergh proposed a model of political intolerance of minorities as an organizing principle of the interindividual differences related to these various syndromes. Indeed, her data are intriguing, especially so the absence of significant differences in authoritarianism, ethnocentrism, and racism between boys and girls who still did not develop political party preference and the presence of differences when party preferences do exist, the boys being more authoritarian than the girls. However, a consistent significant difference in sexism and antifeminism exists before as well as after the appearance of party preferences. The process would then be one in two steps: Sexist boys would be attracted by political parties and once they are involved in politics a generalization of their intolerance takes place. For females, the same organizing principle is socially more difficult to be actualized, hence the persistence of their more tolerant attitudes.

Another important factor in shaping political attitudes is the awareness of the existence of social conflicts. Clémence (1994) found that both for youngsters (19 to 20 years) and for their parents, awareness of conflict, even experimentally induced, led to more favorable attitudes toward institutional supports for different categories in need. This finding is to be related to findings reported by Torney-Purta (1983). Awareness of the existence of social conflict is generally related to social origin of children, at least in France (Percheron, 1978): When they are of a lower class origin, they are more aware of the existence of different kinds of political conflicts, especially distrust of the government, than when they are of a higher class origin, but this difference is much more important for children under the age of 14 than for children above 13 years of age. Older children from higher class origins become almost as distrustful as children from lower class origins. More generally, Percheron, Chiche, and Muxel-Douaire (1991), in a study of a representative sample of Parisian youth (16 to 21 years), showed that their opinions toward judiciary institutions are organized on the basis of a twofold principle: trust versus distrust in the judicial system (respectively confidence in the system and belief that rights of the accused are respected, versus absence of such confidence and belief that justice is unfair and does not respect rights of the accused), and contractual versus naturalistic conceptions of justice (laws did not always exist or are no longer adequate, they should be changed versus laws have always existed and remain adequate, they should not be changed).

In a questionnaire study (Doise, Staerklé, Clémence, & Savory, 1998), carried out in Geneva with 849 youths of different ages, school streams, and preprofessional training, we showed that institutionalized definitions of human rights become more salient as a function of progress in age and scholastic experience. Links with advancement in educational level were particularly salient when analyzing individual positioning. With advancement in degree, many more individuals evoked public rights, whereas a more libertarian positioning, and to a lesser extent an egalitarian positioning, decreased with advancement in degree. Progress in degree is significantly linked to an increase of definitions in less concrete and more positive terms, and to a very significant decrease of a reserved attitude toward protest against the establishment.

Finally, a more principled and enlarged human rights definition, as opposed to a more restricted and concrete conception, was furthered by advancement in degree, as well as left-wing and communitarian political orientation, together with doubts about the usefulness of some public organizations for the individual and general attitudes that are less favorable toward family, religion, and sport clubs.

On the whole, these studies on political socialization show the intervention of different societal factors in the development of political concepts. Growth in cognitive complexity is but one explanatory principle, among others, that accounts for the development of political attitudes and it therefore needs to be articulated with analyses of social regulation mechanisms.

HUMAN RIGHTS AND DEMOCRACY STUDIED AS NORMATIVE SOCIAL REPRESENTATIONS

Social representations can be considered as defining the organizing principles of the symbolic relationships between individuals and groups (Doise, Clémence, & Lorenzi-Cioldi, 1993). This assumes that various members of a population under study share common views about a given social issue. A system necessitates common frames of reference for participating individuals and groups. An important phase in each study of social representations is the search for a common map or cognitive organization of the issues at stake. In Moscovici's study (1976), this aspect deals with objectification. However, social representation theory does not imply that individuals sharing common references necessarily hold the same positions. Individuals may differ according to the strength of their adherence to various opinions, attitudes, or stereotypes: we therefore search for the organizing principles of individual differences in a representational field. A further assumption is that such systematic variations are anchored in other collective realities, in social psychological experiences shared to different extents by individuals, and in their beliefs about other aspects of social reality (Doise, 1992–1993).

A working definition of human rights may be based on the idea that mutual interactions and communications between humans generate normative representations. While interacting with each other, individuals know that their fate will be affected by that interaction, at least in certain domains, to a certain extent, at a certain cost. Normative representations exist about what these mutual effects should be. As there are many kinds of interactions, characterized by all sorts of differences in status, purposes, interdependency, and formality (Deutsch, 1985), there exist also various models of acceptable relationships, prototypes of fair and just relationships, and principles of contracts that govern these relationships, and they are part of human cultures. Human rights are such principles. They should, at least by intention, organize our social interactions. For historical (i.e., economical, political, military, religious, and also scientific) reasons, Western societies organized relationships within national and cultural boundaries, but also across them.

Studying human rights in social representations terms first of all implies a search for common reference systems and for their organization. To what extent does the Universal Declaration of Human Rights, or other institutional definitions, offer references that are common to the populations under consideration?

There are two kinds of studies dealing with this in a transcultural setting. The first kind derived from an interdisciplinary interview study about representations of violations. In a questionnaire study (Clémence, Doise, De Rosa, & Gonzalez, 1995), pupils and students aged 13 to 20 years old and living in four countries (Costa Rica, France, Italy, and Switzerland) were invited to answer 21 items presenting various situations involving violations or limitations of individual rights. Some of these situations (for instance, racial discrimination, imprisonment without trial or legal assistance, starvation) can easily be referred to classical definitions contained in the Universal Declaration. Other situations, dealing with the rights of children or with family affairs, are less explicitly related to the Declaration. Some situations dealing with economic inequality or health matters (e.g., prohibition of smoking or hospitalization in case of contagious illness) are not covered by official definitions of rights. The results were very clear: For the various situations, the order of frequencies of relating them to human rights violations is very similar across countries.

The complete text of the Declaration was also presented to students of 35 countries (Doise, Spini, & Clémence, 1999). Subjects were asked to answer questions about personal involvement, agreement, and efficacy, as well as governmental efficacy for each of the 30 Articles of the Declaration. The respondents were university students in psychology, law, science, social work, and various other fields from the five continents. A hierarchical cluster analysis resulted in the division of the articles into two main classes that, in turn, divided into two subclasses. These subclasses showed an almost complete correspondence with the categories described by René Cassin, the chairman of the drafting committee of the Declaration. He classified the 30 articles of the Declaration in six groups, which 50 years later still are relevant.

The first main cluster opposes the whole of the more social rights (classes 5, 4, and 3) and basic individual rights (protection from torture and slavery and right to life) to a cluster of judicial individual rights (class 2), principles (class 1), and the three articles concerning societal order (class 6). In each national group, respondents showed greater adherence to the basic and social rights than to the rest of the rights. These results clearly support the idea of a common organization of responses in various countries.

Social representation theory does not imply that individuals sharing common references hold the same positions. It is therefore important to investigate the differences in individual positions. Modulators of position are beliefs about personal efficacy and the efficacy of institutions (for instance, governments) in respect of human rights. Human rights positions bear a relationship with value choices (Schwartz, 1992). Values are considered general to the extent that they supposedly organize symbolic relationships within a social environment. Other relationships are to be sought in the representations individuals hold concerning the nature of conflicts between social groups and categories.

In studying the articles of the Declaration, we combined an analysis of respondents' human rights positioning, their value choices, and representations of conflict and injustice. We were led to the conclusion that, in general, strong support for the values of universalism and social harmony are systematically related to more favorable human rights attitudes. Intense experience of collective injustice, together with less concern for personal happiness, led to more personal involvement rather than to reliance on governmental efficacy. It was found that skepticism was relatively stronger in Japan and India and personal involvement was more often found in countries with serious rights problems, according to the ratings by Humana (1992), and with human development problems, according to the ratings by the United Nations Development Programme (1996). Stronger reliance on governmental efficacy was characteristic of more developed countries or countries who changed recently to a democratic regime. There are clearly differences within countries (Spini & Doise, 1998), for instance, respondents who strongly favor universalistic values have more favorable human rights positionings independently of national group. But it is also true that in countries where adherence to universalistic values is higher, attitudes to rights are more favorable. The same reasoning holds for the links involving other value choices, and perceptions of injustice and tensions.

We also investigated individual positioning in our four-country study on violations and found that the first two factors were clearly organized by judgments on violations of rights explicitly mentioned in the Declaration. Individual positions were strongly related to the defense of individual rights against political and economic authorities or to a fatalistic world view minimizing individual initiatives but accepting more willingly managerial and state control.

This exemplifies that people's attitudes are embedded in representations of the relationship between individuals and political as well as other types of institutions. Findings of our research on social representations of human rights are another illustration of the heuristic value of the societal psychology approach. Individual positioning in the realm of human rights is not only assessed as an individual attitude varying in strength, but as a societally anchored pattern of beliefs about the respective roles of individuals and governments.

RESEARCH ON JUSTIFICATION OF INEQUALITIES AND NORMATIVE GROUP REPRESENTATIONS

Up to now, we have discussed research dealing with the intervention of societal forms of knowledge in judgments, evaluations, and positionings toward shared representations. The impact of norms and ideologies on individual cognitive functioning was evidenced through examples in the realm of attribution processes, political socialization, and social representations of human rights. In this last section we provide examples of societal psychology at the level of group representations, usually referred to as *stereotypes*. As different kinds of inequalities and status differentials between social categories are at the center of political debate, we focus on representational dynamics associated to dominant high-status and subordinate low-status groups. The analysis of the processes underlying people's representations of their own social status as well the status of relevant outgroups is indeed an important aspect of societal psychology. After all, people's support or opposition to political measures concerning social inequalities can be considered as positionings toward shared representations of inequalities. First, justification mechanisms of inequalities are discussed. We then continue with research illustrating the role of representations of national populations, held by Westerners, in the construction of judgments on the political situation across Western and non-Western countries. This line of research exemplifies representational strategies developed by a high-status group

(Western countries), to account for a relationship with a low-status group (non-Western countries). (See also Jervis, this volume, for a more political approach to nation perception.)

It has been recognized for some time that group representations fulfil social functions. They are seen as social and cognitive devices that help to explain and give meaning to the characteristics of members of a social group. They account for the current situation of the group in a given social setting, and thus justify and legitimize inequalities between social categories (Doise, 1978; Tajfel, 1981). In this perspective, representations associated to high- and low-status groups are socially constructed and allow individuals to perceive favorable and unfavorable social positions as legitimate and "normal."

Justification mechanisms occur at different levels. Jost and Banaji (1994) developed a conceptual distinction between group and system justification in order to account for findings inconsistent with previous theorizing on social justification.

> Group justification refers to those attitudes and behaviors that promote the material and psychological interests of the ingroup at the expense of relevant outgroups, whereas the attitudes and behaviors associated to system justification serve to maintain the integrity of the current social system, even at the expense of the ingroups' interest. (Rabinowitz, 1999, p. 18)

This distinction has an important consequence, as it accounts for different justification strategies adopted by low- and high-status groups in a social setting. For members of high-status groups, the two tendencies of group and system justification are consistent with one another, whereas for individuals belonging to low-status groups, they reflect conflicting interests. In the latter case, devotion to the interests of the oppressed ingroup works against the interests of the present, inequitable social system. This argument is supported by a meta-analyis in Jost and Banaji's work (1994) of studies on the broadly accepted hypothesis that people evaluate members of their own group more positively than they judge members of outgroups (Tajfel, 1982). They found that 85% of low-status groups evaluated outgroups more positively than their own groups.

It is especially the system justification angle that is related to societal psychology. Shared attitudes and behaviors destined to protect the value system that underlies the divisions of the surrounding world can be considered a strong case for the intervention of social representations in individual cognitive processes. System justification is mainly a strategy adopted by dominant high-status groups to secure the social status quo. Several researchers have indeed pointed out that stereotypes of low-status groups, held by members of high-status groups, are surprisingly similar, even if the groups under consideration such as women, children, or the unemployed do not have much in common (Doise, 1973; Condor, 1990; Jost & Banaji, 1994). It is hard to imagine which processes, if not shared representations of what it means to be in a low-status position, can account for this finding. Both of these arguments provide evidence for a system justification mechanism that accounts for findings inconsistent with Tajfel's social identity theory. In what follows, we further elaborate on representations destined to rationalize a social situation opposing a low- and a high-status group.

Although social psychologists share a broad consensus about this social function of stereotypes, relatively little research has been carried out on this specific topic. The studies of Hoffmann and Hurst (1990) are an exception to this lack of empirical support to the justification hypothesis. Developing the work on stereotypes in the social learning tradition (Eagly & Steffen, 1984), they argued that people construe images of gender groups not solely because they perceive women and men in different social roles, but because gender stereotypes allow them to rationalize the division of labor between the two gender groups. Their results showed that participants associate female traits to members of a fictitious "child raiser" group and male traits to members of a "city worker" group. This attribution of stereotypical traits was even stronger for respondents who were requested to find explanations for the division of labor and also for those who were told that the two groups were "different species," rather than "different subgroups of the same culture." Thus, the rationalization process operates by associating intrinsic, "natural," differences between social categories. The perceived attributes of members of dominant and subordinate groups are congruent with their relative position in a social setting and allow individuals, therefore, to explain the status differences between the groups.

The findings reported here provide tentative support to a relatively new concept in social psychology: *essentialism.* According to Rothbart and Taylor (1992), essentialism describes the mechanism through which an arbitrary social category is perceived in much the same way as a natural category. Essentialism refers to the belief that an attribute common to all members of a category organizes the different elements of a group representation. This common "essence" confers to the group that is perceived in an essentialist way a specific ontological status. The group, along with all the attributes that are associated to it, is defined on the basis of this common, and supposedly profound, feature of the group. Group attributes are thus viewed as stable and common to all group members. Therefore, essentialised social groups are viewed as natural, close to biological, categories. The lay belief that a common feature defines group membership is connected to a great explanatory power of the essence that allows people to easily draw inferences on the characteristics of group members. This implies that once people know to which group given individuals belong, they think they know a great deal about the characteristics of those given individuals.

This essentialisation process is likely to occur for groups defined with salient surface characteristics such as the color of the skin, gender or age. On the basis of these visible attributes, people infer deeper characteristics that are linked together by a naive theory. More importantly however, the essentialist images associated to groups reflect specific social settings and are therefore best considered as a consequence of existing relationships. Essentialist representations of groups help to maintain the prevailing social setting and provide tools to justify social inequalities. That is why low-status and minority groups are most likely to be represented in an essentialist manner, distinctively different from other groups and with a high level of perceived homogeneity among their members (Abelson, Dasgupta, Park, & Banaji, 1998; Lorenzi-Cioldi, 1998; Mullen, 1991). Members of high-status groups should therefore be especially likely to adhere to essentialist conceptions about low-status groups. As the study by Hoffmann and Hurst (1990) suggested, an essentialist perception of social categories goes hand in hand with the rationalization of social inequalities, precisely because the immutable character of essentialist attributes supports the idea of social and political status quo. "Members of a given social situation are likely to refer to some intrinsic feature of the parties involved in order to strengthen social stability" (Yzerbyt, Rocher, & Schadron, 1997, p. 40).

Studies that connect essentialist categorization and justification processes are still quite uncommon. We therefore would like to exemplify this point by showing how people living in a Western country, Switzerland, think about the political situation in Western and non-Western countries in general. This allows us to illustrate that representations associated to subordinate low-status groups can be analyzed even at a global level of comparison. At the same time, these studies provide an example of representation and justification processes that do not concern inequalities within a nation, but between nations. Indeed, studies on the perception and explanation of inequalities have mostly focussed on the situation of low- and high-status groups within national contexts. It is therefore important to examine to what extent the same mechanisms, as evidenced in studies at the intra-national level, can be applied to the perception of international relations.

In a series of studies (Staerklé, Clémence, & Doise, 1998), we investigated representational processes associated to countries described as democratic and nondemocratic, a distinction hypothesized as equivalent to representations associated to Western and non-Western countries. We were interested in understanding how people construe their representation of the political situation, measured with perceived respect of a series of human rights, across Western and non-Western national contexts and how they explain the favorable and unfavorable political situation in these national contexts. The first hypothesis stated that people should associate representations of society, operationalized as the inhabitants, to representations of the state, described as the government. We expected that participants would judge these political contexts as if they were following the ancient statement according to which "The inhabitants have the government they deserve." A second prediction concerned the asymmetry between political judgments on Western and non-Western contexts: If people adhere to a normative conception of liberal democracy, they should see national populations, more than governments, as the driving political force in Western countries. When judging non-Western countries however, they should perceive their government as omnipotent and the inhabitants as weak, submissive, and passive. A final prediction stated that people would account for an unfavorable political situation in a country with judgments of a lesser political involvement of its inhabitants.

The basic paradigm of these studies was experimental: participants, Swiss students, read a short description of a country where political decisions are taken either democratically or nondemocratically. Another description referred to a country described with stereotypically positive or negative attributes associated to the national population. Respondents were then asked to list up to three countries that correspond to the formal description.

In a first study, respondents read *either* a description of a democratic or nondemocratic government *or* a description of positively or negatively described national population. Results showed that participants drew similar inferences on the political situation on the basis of a democratic government and a positively described national population on the one hand and on the basis of a nondemocratic government and a negatively described population on the other hand. Thus, people establish links between the government and the national population in order to construe a representation of the political situation in a national context.

In order to determine the respective weight of the positive–negative information and the government–population information, a second study crossed the two descriptions of the government and the inhabitants. Thus, each participant was informed about the political organization and the stereotypical national character of the population. Here, results showed that when a negatively described population is combined with a democratic government, the perceived respect of human rights is very clearly lower than when a democracy is inhabited by a positively described population. In nondemocratic contexts, however, the population information does not have any impact on the unfavorable evaluation of the human rights situation. These results confirmed that the representation of the political situation depends on the character of the inhabitants in a Western country and on the political system in a non-Western country. Furthermore, in both of these two studies, a greater proportion of inhabitants was perceived as being opposed to human rights violations in Western than in non-Western countries.

A third study finally corroborated these findings by showing that in Western countries, inhabitants are seen as more responsible than the government for the favorable political situation. In non-Western contexts, however, the government is clearly more responsible than the inhabitants. This latter result revealed that participants recognize that human rights violations are perpetrated by various governments in non-Western countries, but it implies at the same time that non-Western national populations are viewed as unable to resist the political dysfunctionings of their governments.

On the whole, the results of these studies provide evidence that when people living in a supposedly democratic country (Switzerland) judge other countries, they refer to shared representations concerning the main features of typical Western and non-Western countries. Contrary to the widely shared assumption that perceivers should be familiar with the national contexts they are judging, they demonstrate that a representation of a Western or non-Western country *as such* is sufficient to activate a series of images that are best captured as lay conceptions of the relationships between state and society across Western and non-Western national contexts. These lay conceptions embrace justification processes of inequalities between Western and non-Western countries and show that the rationalization of a given hierarchical social structure may take different forms. In these studies, they operate by way of representations of normative qualities associated to democratic citizens, such as political involvement, which in turn is denied for inhabitants of non-Western countries. Therefore, the general mechanism according to which high-status groups develop representations of the social structure where each group is at its right place, operates in a quite similar manner within countries as well as between countries. Ongoing research indeed confirms that people use stereotypical and counterstereotypical attributes of national populations in order to justify material and other inequalities between Western and non-Western countries.

CONCLUSION

Our contribution was aimed at pointing toward links between social and political psychology. Research in social psychology has many political components, and it is not an easy task to draw clear boundaries between these two research traditions. Therefore, we suggested that the contribution of social psychology to political psychology is to be found in a general approach we termed *societal psychology*. The main objective of this perspective is the investigation of the intervention of societal forms of shared knowledge such as ideologies, norms, and social representations in individual cognitive functioning.

The research traditions we presented as prototypical examples of societal psychology can seem to be very heterogeneous. A first series of research originated in the realm of personality research, a second series dealt with developmental issues, a third was investigating the cross-cultural nature of human rights studied as social representations, and the last series dealt more directly with the traditional social–psychological theme of intergroup perception and discrimination.

However, our putting into perspective of each of these research trends was guided by a common concern. We tried to show that societal functioning intervenes in very different endeavors, such as evaluating oneself or another person, becoming politically socialized, understanding universal judicial norms, or intergroup evaluations.

The societal perspective allows us to understand that internality is first of all a criterion for establishing the degree of congruence with the dominant norm of individual autonomy and responsibility. Political socialization is not just a matter of growth in cognitive complexity, it is also a construction of a meaning system evolving in a frame of societal regulations. Our human rights studies try to investigate the extent to which such regulations reach beyond societal borders and enable institutionalized human rights definitions to function as common reference systems. But if such universalistic, normative representations cross borders, justifications of existing inequalities also extend into the realm of differences between governmental regimes.

REFERENCES

Adorno, T. W., Frenkel-Brunswik, E., Levinson, D. J., & Nevitt Sanford, R. (1950). *The authoritarian personality.* New York: Norton & Company.

Abelson, R. P., Dasgupta, N., Park, J., & Banaji, M. R. (1998). Perceptions of the collective other. *Personality and Social Psychology Review, 2,* 243–250.

Allport, G. W. (1954). *The nature of prejudice.* Cambridge, MA: Addison-Wesley.

Augoustinos, M., & Walker, I. (1995). *Social cognition: An integrated introduction.* London: Sage.

Bar-Tal, D. (1997). Formation and change of ethnic and national stereotypes: An integrative model. *International Journal of Intercultural Relations, 21,* 491–523.

Bartel, N. (1971). Locus of control and achievement in middle and lower-class children. *Child Development, 42,* 1099–1107.

Beauvois, J.-L. (1984). *La psychologie quotidienne* [Everyday psychology]. Paris: Presses Universitaires de France.

Beauvois, J.-L. (1994). *Traité de la servitude libérale. Analyse de la soumission* [Treatise on liberal serfdom: An analysis of submissiveness]. Paris: Dunod.

Beauvois, J.-L., & Dubois, N. (1988). The norm of internality in the explanation of psychological events. *European Journal of Social Psychology, 18,* 299–316.

Bierhoff, H. W., Cohen, R. L., & Greenberg, J. (Eds.). (1986). *Justice in social relations.* New York and London: Plenum.

Biernat, M., Vescio, T. K., Theno, S. A., & Crandall, C. S. (1996). Values and prejudice: Toward understanding the impact of American values on outgroup attitudes. In C. Seligman, J. M. Olson, & M. P. Zanna (Eds.), *The psychology of values: The Ontario symposium, 8* (pp. 153–189). Mahwah, NJ: Lawrence Erlbaum Associates.

Billig, M. (1995). *Banal nationalism.* London: Sage.

Clémence, A. (1994). *Solidarités sociales en Suisse* [Social solidarity in Switzerland]. Lausanne, Switzerland: Réalités Sociales.

Clémence, A., Doise, W., De Rosa, A. S., & Gonzalez, L. (1995). La représentation sociale des droits de l'homme: Une recherche internationale sur l'étendue et les limites de l'universalité. *Journal International de Psychologie, 30,* 181–212.

Condor, S. (1990). Social stereotypes and social identity. In D. Abrams & M. Hogg (Eds.), *Social identity theory: Constructive and critical advances.* Hemel Hempstead: Harvester Wheatsheaf.

Connell, R. W. (1971). *The child's construction of politics.* Carlton: Melbourne University Press.

Crandall, V. C., Katovsky, W., & Crandall, V. J. (1965). Childrens' belief in their own control of reinforcement in intellectual–academic situations. *Child Development, 36,* 91–109.

Deutsch, M. (1985). *Distributive justice.* New Haven, CT: Yale University Press.

Doise, W. (1973). Relations et Représentations Intergroupes [Intergroup relations and representations]. In S. Moscovici (Ed.), *Introduction à la psychologie sociale, Vol. 2.* Paris: Librairie Larousse.

Doise, W. (1978). *Groups and individuals: Explanations in social psychology.* Cambridge, UK: Cambridge University Press.

Doise, W. (1992–1993). L'ancrage dans les études sur les représentations sociales [Anchoring processes in studies on social representations]. *Bulletin de Psychologie, XLV, 405,* 189–195.

Doise, W., Clémence, A., & Lorenzi-Cioldi, F. (1993). *The quantitative analysis of social representations,* Hemel Hempstead: Harvester Wheatsheaf.

Doise, W., Spini, D., & Clémence, A. (1999). Human rights studied as social representations in a cross-national context. *European Journal of Social psychology, 29,* 1–30.

Doise, W., Staerklé, C., Clémence, A., & Savory, F. (1998). Human rights and Genevan youth: A developmental study of social representations. *The Swiss Journal of Psychology, 57*(2), 86–100.

Dovidio, J. F., & Gaertner, S. L. (Eds.). (1986). *Prejudice, discrimination and racism.* New York: Academic Press.

Dubois, N. (1986). Aspects normatifs versus cognitifs de l'évolution de l'enfant vers la norme d'internalité [Normative versus cognitive aspects in the child's development toward the internality norm]. *Psychologie française, 31,* 109–114.

Dubois, N. (1987). *La psychologie du contrôle, les croyances internes et externes* [The psychology of control: Internal and external beliefs]. Grenoble: Presses Universitaires de Grenoble.

Dubois, N. (1994). *La norme d'internalité et le libéralisme* [Internality norm and liberalism]. Grenoble: Presses Universitaires de Grenoble.

Eagly, A., & Steffen, V. (1984). Gender stereotypes stem from the distribution of women and men into social roles. *Journal of Personality and Social Psychology, 46,* 735–754.

Hoffmann, C., & Hurst, N. (1990). Gender stereotypes: Perception or rationalization? *Journal of Personality and Social Psychology, 58*(2), 197–208.

Humana, C. (1992). *World human rights guide* (3rd ed.). New York: Oxford University Press.

Inhelder, B., & Piaget, J. (1958). *The growth of logical thinking from childhood to adolescence.* New York: Basic Books.

Jellison, J. M., & Green, J. (1981). A self-presentation approach to fundamental attribution error: the norm of internality. *Journal of Personality and Social Psychology, 40,* 643–649.

Jennings, M. K., & Niemi, R. G. (1974). *The political character of adolescence: The influence of families and schools.* Princeton, NJ: Princeton University Press.

Jost, J., & Banaji, M. (1994). The role of stereotyping in system-justification and the production of false consciousness. *British Journal of Social Psychology, 33,* 1–27.

Katz, I., & Hass, R. G. (1988). Racial ambivalence and American value conflict: Correlational and priming studies of dual cognitive structures. *Journal of Personality and Social Psychology, 55*, 893–905.

Kinder, D. R., & Sears, D. O. (1981). Prejudice and politics: Symbolic racism versus racial threats to the good life. *Journal of Personality and Social Psychology, 40*, 414–431.

Le Poultier, F. (1986). *Travail social, inadaptation sociale et processus cognitifs* [Social work, social inadaptation, and cognitive processes]. Paris: Presses Universitaires de France.

Lorenzi-Cioldi, F. (1998). Group status and perceptions of homogeneity. In W. Stroebe & M. Hewstone (Eds.), *European Review of Social Psychology, 9* (pp. 31–75). Chichest, UK: John Wiley.

McGuire, W. J. (1993). The poly-psy relationship: Three phases of a long affair. In S. Iyengar & W. J. McGuire (Eds.), *Current approaches to political psychology* (pp. 9–35). Durham, NC: Duke University Press.

Moscovici, S. (1976). *La Psychanalyse, son image, son public* [Psychoanalysis, its image, and its public]. Paris: Presses Universitaires de France.

Mouffe, C. (1993). *The return of the political.* London: Verso.

Mullen, B. (1991). Group composition, salience, and cognitive representations: The phenomenology of being in a group. *Journal of Experimental Social Psychology, 27*, 297–323.

Nowicki, S., & Strickland, B. R. (1973). A locus of control scale for children. *Journal of Consulting and Clinical Psychology, 40*, 148–154.

Percheron, A. (1978). *Les 10–16 ans & la politique* [Youth of age 10 to 16 and politics]. Paris: Presses de la Fondation Nationale des Sciences Politiques.

Percheron, A., Chiche, J., & Muxel-Douaire, A. (1991). *Le droit à 20 ans* [The law at 20 years of age]. Paris: Institut de Formation Continue du Barreau de Paris.

Pettigrew, T. F., Jackson, J. S., Brika, J. B., Lemaine, G., Meertens, R. W., Wagner, U., & Zick, A. (1998). Outgroup prejudice in western Europe. In W. Stroebe & M. Hewstone (Eds.), *European review of social psychology* (Vol. 8, pp. 241–273). Chichester, England: John Wiley & Sons.

Rabinowitz, J. L. (1999). Go with the flow or fight the power? The interactive effects of social dominance orientation and perceived injustice on support for the status quo. *Political Psychology, 20*, 1–24.

Rothbart, M., & Taylor, M. (1992). Category labels and social reality: Do we view social categories as natural kinds? In G. Semin & K. Fiedler (Eds.), *Language, interaction and social cognition* (pp. 11–36). London: Sage.

Rotter, J. B. (1966). Generalized expectancies for internal versus external control of reinforcement. *Psychological Monographs: General and Applied, 80*, No. 609.

Schwartz, S. H. (1992). Universals in the content and structure of values: Theoretical advances and empirical tests in 20 countries. In M. P. Zanna (Ed.), *Advances in experimental social psychology* (Vol. 25, pp. 1–65). New York: Academic Press.

Sears, D. O., & Funk, C. (1991). The role of self-interest in social and political attitudes. In M. Zanna (Ed.), *Advances in experimental social psychology* (Vol. 24, pp. 1–91). Orlando, FL: Academic Press.

Sherman, L. W. (1984). Development of children's perceptions of internal locus of control. *Human development, 25*, 250–281.

Spini, D., & Doise, W. (1998). Organising principles of involvement in human rights and their social anchoring in value priorities. *European Journal of Social Psychology, 28*, 603–622.

Staerklé, C., Clémence, A., & Doise, W. (1998). Representation of human rights across different national contexts: The role of democratic and non-democratic populations and governments. *European Journal of Social Psychology, 28*, 207–226.

Stoetzel, J. (1983). *Les valeurs du temps présent* [Values of present times]. Paris: Presses Universitaires de France.

Tajfel, H. (1981). *Human groups and social categories: Studies in social psychology.* Cambridge: Cambridge University Press.

Tajfel, H. (1982). *Social identity and intergroup relations.* Cambridge: Cambridge University Press; Paris: Maison des Sciences de l'Homme.

Torney-Purta, J. (1983). The development of views about the role of social institutions in redressing inequaltiy and promoting human rights. In R. L. Leahy (Ed.), *The child's construction of social inequality* (pp. 287–310). New York: Academic Press.

United Nations Development Programme (1996). *Human development report.* New York: Author.

Vollebergh, W. (1989). Politisches Interesse and politische Intoleranz bei Heranwachsenden [Political interest and political intolerance among youth]. In B. Claussen (Ed.), *Politische sozialisation jugendlicher in Ost and West* (pp. 238–252). Darmstadt: May & Co.

Yzerbyt, V., Rocher, S., & Schadron, G. (1997). Stereotypes as explanations: A subjective essentialistic view of group perception. In R. Spears, P. Oakes, N. Ellemers, & S. Haslam (Eds.), *The social psychology of stereotyping and group life* (pp. 20–50). Oxford, UK & Cambridge, MA: Blackwell Publishers.

10

The (Social) Psychological Legacy for Political Psychology

DANIEL BAR-TAL
Tel-Aviv University

In providing concepts and theories for the analysis of the political realm, psychology is an inseparable part of political psychology. It is therefore important to examine this psychological foundation and to consider its legacy. This chapter, therefore, first examines the psychological basis of political psychology by defining its nature and describing its scope. Here it is shown that political psychology draws much of its psychological basis from cognitive social psychology. Subsequently, the second part outlines three social psychological derivations that are of importance for political psychology.

PSYCHOLOGICAL BASIS OF POLITICAL PSYCHOLOGY

The political realm does not exist independently of human actors who think politically, activate political systems, and behave politically. People plan and carry out political acts, support or object to political issues, participate in political organizations and systems, vote, engage in violence, make peace, learn different political concepts and attitudes, and lead, or follow, leaders. Although not all of the field covered by political science is directly related to human behavior, any analysis of the political process and its systems must take into account the psychology of the people involved.

Political science is concerned with political processes and political behavior (e.g., political parties, public opinion, voting), political institutions of the state (e.g., legislation, political executives, public administration), nations and their relationships (Finifter, 1993). This wide scope of areas does not require always the knowledge of psychology. For instance, the abstract notions that define democracy or socialism can be analyzed independently of actual human behavior. However, whenever the analysis of political systems or processes involves individuals and/or groups, psychology is needed. Psychology provides the knowledge that enables an understanding of human behavior. This knowledge is necessary to political science because psychological principles guide human behavior in the political context. It is thus not surprising that there have been political scientists who based their analysis on psychological knowledge (see Apter, 1977; Greenstein, 1973; Sprout & Sprout, 1965). The occasional lack of recognition of psychology's contribution to analysis of political behavior can be explained by the wide-spread assumption that psychological principles of behavior are an inseparable part of human knowledge and do not necessarily have to be based on the knowledge accumulated in scientific psychology. Individuals, acting as lay psychologists, spend large portions of their reflection, interactions, or communications with other people on psychological explanations and predictions of human behavior (Kelley, 1992).

Everyone acquires lay psychological knowledge in the course of his or her life. Personal experience, cultural products such as books or films, mass media (i.e., newspapers, magazines, radio, and television), social interaction and communication—all provide information that serves as an input to the individual's repertoire of lay psychological knowledge. The question that can be posed is whether such naive psychological insight is sufficient for the understanding of political behavior. Psychology as a science, through decades of theorizing and empirical investigation, has created a body of systematic knowledge of human behavior that differs from lay psychology (Fletcher, 1984; Kelley, 1992). A similar question can be posed with regard to political issues. Many people discuss politics and come up with different analyses of the issues on the agenda. Does this make such people into political scientists? The unequivocal answer is no—although, as in lay psychological analyses, people can make creative political observations, reach original conclusions, and even make valid predictions.

The Meaning of Political Psychology

What makes political psychology so intriguing and unique is its combination of two disciplines: psychology and political science. *Political psychology* can be defined as a science concerned with the influence of psychological factors, such as perceptions, beliefs, attitudes, values, motives, personality, cognitive styles, dynamic processes, group membership, group characteristics, structure and performance, and ways of social influence, on political beliefs, attitudes, and behaviors of individuals and groups alike, on the one hand, and with the influence of political culture, systems, movements, parties, ideologies, mechanisms of political socialization, and intergroup relations on the human repertoire, on the other (see Hermann, 1986a; Stone & Schaffner, 1988).

Contributions to political psychology take two main forms. The first is purely psychological: Psychologists concerned with psychological issues take political problems as examples or illustrations for their research interest. An example can be the work of a cognitive psychologist interested in decision making, who studies how individuals vote in elections. In this case, the voting decision is only a particular instance of the general cognitive process of decision making that is of interest for the psychologist. Similarly, a developmental psychologist who is interested in social development may study children's understanding of such concepts as government, war, or democracy. For him or her, these concepts are only examples of social concepts. Although this line of research contributes to the understanding of political socialization, it does not turn the psychologist who conducts it into a political psychologist. The psychologist in the first example remains a cognitive psychologist and the psychologist in the second example remains a developmental psychologist. Neither is a political psychologist. Their work can be called "psychology for political science."

The second type of contribution is made by political psychology. Political psychology defines its problems from the point of view of the realm of politics. Political psychology is concerned with those political issues that involve the political functioning of both individuals and groups. Implicit in this approach is an assumption that psychology is not automatically relevant to political behavior. Political psychology focuses on specific aspects of human behavior that are related to political contents—political systems, political processes, or events (see for example, Hermann, 1986b; Knutson, 1973; Long, 1981; Sniderman, Brody, & Tetlock, 1991). Thus, the agenda of a political psychologist consists of political research problems. They may concern public opinion, political influence, leadership, political participation, political decision making, political socialization, voting behavior, political personality and political behavior, political values, attitudes and beliefs, deterrence, intergroup conflicts and their resolutions, violence, and so on. What makes political psychologists unique is their conceptual tools. They always use psychological terms, conceptions, theories, and/or empirically accumulated psychological knowledge in order to analyze political issues. Political psychologists, thus, do not have to be either psychologists or political scientists, but they must be social or behavioral scientists who are interested in political problems and use psychological tools for analysis.

TABLE 10.1

Articles in *Political Psychology* (Vol. 1–19) Classified According to
Their Disciplinary Basis in Psychology (% in parentheses)

	Social Psychology	Personality	Clinical Psychology	Developmental Psychology	Cognitive Psychology	Health Psychology	Organizational Psychology	Other	Total
Political beliefs and attitudes	115	12	5	7	4			1	144 (29.6)
Leaders and leadership	29	27	6	5	2	7			76 (15.6)
Political behavior	46	6	2	1				2	57 (11.7)
Decision making	22	1			11				34 (7.0)
Prejudice	25	3		1					29 (6.0)
Political personality	1	23	4						28 (5.8)
Conflict	15	3	2	2					22 (4.6)
Conflict resolution	14				1				15 (3.1)
Political socialization	4			10					14 (2.9)
Political motivation	5	3	1	1					10 (2.1)
Mass movement	6		2						8 (1.6)
Organizations		2	1				4		7 (1.5)
National character	4	2							6 (1.2)
International relations	2				2			1	5 (1.0)
Mass media	3	2	1		1				7 (1.4)
Alienation	3								3 (0.6)
Other	10	3	6					2	21 (4.3)
	304 (62.6)	87 (17.9)	30 (6.2)	27 (5.6)	21 (4.3)	7 (1.4)	4 (.8)	6 (1.2)	486

The Psychological Scope of Political Psychology

In an effort to examine the psychological basis of political psychology and to illustrate the contributions of different psychological areas in political analysis, I classified articles[1] published in volumes 1 through 19 (i.e., between 1979 and 1998) of *Political Psychology*, the main journal of political psychology and the formal organ of the International Society of Political Psychology, according to their disciplinary basis in psychology. Table 10.1 presents the resulting classification.

Table 10.1 shows that social psychology was the main disciplinary framework for the articles under consideration: about 62.6% derived from social psychology and about 17.9% were oriented toward personality, which is traditionally affiliated with social psychology. (Indeed, major psychological journals and many university training programs combine social psychology and personality.) To lesser extents, clinical psychology (6.2%), developmental psychology (5.6%) and cognitive psychology (4.3%) served as a basis for articles in *Political Psychology*. Health psychology (1.4%) and organizational psychology (0.8%) appeared very infrequently. Single articles, put together in the category "other" were based on educational psychology, physiological psychology, community psychology, cultural psychology, and general psychology.

Developmental psychology serves as a basis for the articles that deal with political socialization. It also underlies all work covering the acquisition of political beliefs and attitudes and the influence of childhood experiences on leaders' behavior. In another direction, clinical psychology provides the basis for the analysis of any pathological element in political behavior, found in discussions of leaders, the political personality, or political beliefs and attitudes. Not surprisingly, cognitive psychology was the framework for articles about political decision making and, to some extent, about political beliefs and attitudes.

Another way to review the contribution of psychology to the understanding of political issues is through psychological theories, especially what are called the *grand theories*. They are major psychological approaches that describe, explain, and predict various aspects of human behavior, as for example, human development, social behavior, personality, and psychopathology.

Table 10.2 presents the classification of the *Political Psychology* articles according to the political themes and grand theories that were used for their analysis, showing that about 84% of the articles use cognitive theory,

---

[1]The classification included only articles based on psychology. Book reviews, notes, commentaries, short topic discussions, and reactions to major articles were not included in the classification.

TABLE 10.2
Articles in *Political Psychology* (Vol. 1–19) Classified According to
Their Theoretical Basis in Psychology (% in parentheses)

	Cognitive Theory	Learning Theory	Psychoanalytic Theory	Humanistic Theory	Genetic Theory	Other	Eclectic	No Theory	Total
Political beliefs and attitudes	79	34	23			3	3	2	144 (29.6)
Leaders and leadership	23	15	15	1	1		1	21	76 (15.6)
Political behavior	22	26	2		1	3		2	57 (11.7)
Decision making	30	3						1	34 (7.0)
Prejudice	8	12	3			1	3	2	29 (6.0)
Political personality	2	10	8	2		1	2	3	28 (5.8)
Conflict	9	5	7			1	—		22 (4.6)
Conflict resolution	10	3				1		1	15 (3.1)
Political socialization	2	12							14 (2.9)
Political motivation	2	5	1	1			1		10 (2.1)
Mass movement		3	4					1	8 (1.6)
Organizations		2	4					1	7 (1.5)
National character	1	2	2					1	6 (1.2)
International relations	3						2		5 (1.0)
Mass media	3	2	1					1	7 (1.4)
Alienation	1	1						1	3 (0.6)
Other	3	5	6			2	3	1	21 (4.3)
	185 (40.8)	140 (28.8)	76 (15.6)	4 (0.9)	2 (0.4)	12 (2.5)	16 (3.3)	38 (7.8)	486

learning theory, or psychoanalytic theory. Other grand theories (e.g., humanistic theory, genetic theory, or biopsychological theory) were used minimally. Among the three most prevalent theories, cognitive theory has by far the strongest presence (41%). Cognitive theory explains human behavior by focusing on mental processes and structures. It assumes that people perceive their environment, evaluate and organize their perceptions and thoughts, impose meaning on the perceived world, form beliefs and attitudes about various topics, people, or events, and act according to these perceptions and interpretations. During the last decades, cognitive theory has had a dominant position in psychological research (Gardner, 1985), and this is reflected in political psychology. Table 10.2 reveals that about 30% of all the classified articles pertain to the strongly cognitive theme of political beliefs and attitudes. Cognitive theory is also used in articles about decision making, leaders' thinking, political behavior as influenced by political beliefs, and so on.

After cognitive theory, learning theory is the next most influential—about 29% of the categorized articles were based on it. This theory posits that human behavior is determined by prior learning, and it focuses on the ways in which the environment influences behavior. Political behavior, much like other types of behavior, is partly determined by learning, which is an important factor in the acquisition of political beliefs, attitudes, and various types of political behavior. Learning theory plays a central role in explaining political socialization.

A third grand theory that considerably influences political psychology is psychoanalytic theory. About 16% of the articles in *Political Psychology* were based on this theory. Psychoanalytic theory, largely shaped by the seminal work of Sigmund Freud, refers to a dynamics of inner forces, both conscious and unconscious, that energize and direct behavior. It focuses on the emotional processes that shape human behavior in the early stages of the individual's life. Political psychologists who base their work on psychoanalytic theory use it to explain issues involving political personality, political beliefs and attitudes, leaders' behavior, or even conflicts. Table 10.2 also shows that about 8% of the articles are not based on any theory: They usually describe a political event and draw some conclusions. About 3% of the articles integrate several grand theories to explain political issues at hand.

This analysis considered the roots of political psychology. It indicates that social psychology, with its dominant cognitive orientation, serves as a major basis for the development of political psychology. The second part of the chapter elaborates on the legacy of social cognitive psychology on political psychology.

THE LEGACY OF SOCIAL PSYCHOLOGY

That political psychology is so strongly derived from social psychology is not surprising in view of the nature and scope of the latter discipline. Social psychology is preoccupied with the understanding of the general category of social behavior of which political behavior is part. Social psychology encompasses the study of thoughts, feelings and behaviors of individuals as they are influenced by the actual, imagined, or implied presence and behaviors of others (i.e., individuals and groups) and their products (Allport, 1985; McGrath, 1964). This general definition of social behavior includes behaviors in various domains, contexts, situations, and settings, including the political. The predominant topics of social psychology are social perception, social cognition, attitudes, social motivation, social self, interpersonal relations, group behavior, intergroup relations, social influence—which are relevant to political psychology, as well.

By providing the basis for the development of political psychology, social psychology stamped political psychology with its own cognitive orientation (Brewer, 1997; Farr, 1996; Jones, 1998). In its line of development, the study of social cognition has become the primary focus of social psychology. Ostrom (1994), in the foreword to the *Handbook of Social Cognition,* suggested "that constructs relevant to cognitive representation and process are fundamental to understanding all human responses, regardless of whether those responses are social or nonsocial in nature" (p. ix).

The focus on perception and cognition, and their relationship to affect, motivation, and behavior is very salient in political psychology, too. This focus has specific implications because the accumulated knowledge of the study of social perception and cognition suggests several general derivations about the nature of social (including political) behavior. I consider these derivations as legacy of social psychology and believe that they should be specified for political psychology. Thus, this part outlines these derivations.

Although relatively much has been written on the derivation that concerns perceptual and cognitive biases and errors (e.g., Cohen, 1979; Eldridge, 1979; Jervis, 1976; Sylvan & Chan, 1984; Vertzberger, 1990; White, 1970; and the chapter by Jervis in this volume), I focus on three other, less discussed derivations. The first deals with subjectivism, the second concerns commonalism (i.e., shared beliefs), and the third focuses on the differentiation between universal and particular observations.

Subjectivism

The subjectivity derivation suggests that reality, as perceived and cognized by the individual, is subjective. A person's unique experiences lead to the formation and accumulation of beliefs (i.e., personal knowledge), which in essence constitute a set of individual representations (i.e., cognitions) of the world (see Jones, 1998). These personal beliefs, in turn, serve as the determinative factor in the further perception, interpretation and evaluation of incoming information (see for example, Fiske & Taylor, 1991; Higgins, 1996; Markus & Zajonc, 1985). As Wyer and Carlston (1994) pointed out, "When people are exposed to information about a social stimulus (a person, object, or event), they often attend to it selectively, focusing on some features while disregarding others. They interpret these features in terms of previously acquired concepts and knowledge" (p. 42).

The other consequence of the personal set of experiences is that individuals act uniquely toward the social world because their behaviors are contingent on their perception of the situation. The subjective basis of beliefs is increased by the influence of affect and motivations on the understanding of the world and information processing (see for example, Clore, Schwarz, & Conway, 1994; Isen, 1984; Kruglanski, 1996; Sorrentino & Higgins, 1986). *Affect* is a generic term that includes personal preferences, evaluations, moods, and emotions (Fiske & Taylor, 1991) and *motivation* refers to internal desires, needs, concerns, and goals (Pittman, 1998). According to that view, each person is a captive of his or her own perspective, a perspective which is not stable. Individuals encounter new experiences and information, and may modify or even drastically change their view of the world. Nevertheless, this does imply that personal subjective beliefs are the sole determinants of human perception and behavior. Clearly, the context in which the individual perceives and behaves constrains and influences inferences made or behaviors exhibited (see Higgins & Stangor, 1988), but these always closely interact with the stored personal beliefs.

Subjectivism assumes that our understanding of an individual's behavior is contingent on knowing his or her beliefs. As Heider noted (1958), "If a person believes that the lines in his palm foretell his future, this belief must be taken into account in explaining certain of his expectations and actions" (p. 5).

Some political psychologists have indeed emphasized the importance of cognition and affect in the study of political behavior. Examples of major notions in political psychology are developed on the cognitive basis of *operational code* developed by George (1969) and of *cognitive map* developed by Axelrod (1976). The notion of *operational code* assumes that general beliefs about human nature and politics underlie tendencies to favor particular interpretations of events and political action. The *cognitive map* posits that representations of events, groups, objects, or acts relate to each other, forming a cognitive map of causes and effects with positive and negative implications that underlie decision making.

The subjectivity derivation implies that neither in the formulation of a theory, nor in the investigation of political behavior, should political psychologists impose "objective" definitions of specific individual beliefs. On the contrary, it must be recognized that belief contents are of unlimited scope and individuals differ, both in terms of beliefs stored and of their accessibility at any given moment. Thus, for example, the relations between political attitude and behavior relations should be assessed by asking respondents what types of behavior they perceive as implied by the relevant attitude. It should not be assumed that a given attitude necessarily implies any specific behavior. Similarly, it cannot be assumed that particular situational variables have the same stable and universal qualities for all individuals, so that all perceive, interpret, and evaluate situations in the same way. For example, research on leadership tends to predict the behavior of followers on the basis of such characteristics as task structure, leader's personality, organizational environment, or power structure (e.g., Hunt & Larson, 1974) out of many possible variables and possible ways of their perception.

The same is true for research on political personality. The assumption behind conceptions of personality characteristics such as dogmatism, authoritarianism, or machiavellianism is that individuals who possess certain personality traits maintain certain types of beliefs in every situation, at all times. Subjectivism suggests that we cannot assume that the same beliefs are available to everyone all the time. Beliefs (i.e., cognitions) are dynamic and may change from time to time and from situation to situation. Any assessment of cognitions to predict particular behavior requires knowledge of the cognitive repertoire in the "phenomenological field" at specific times and in specific situations. This makes it difficult for political psychologists to formulate rules on how an individual will act in specific situations. Even if political psychologists do make observations in one situation, any change in situational features, or even time, may change the observational outcomes.

In sum, the subjectivism derivation stresses the limitations on political psychology in understanding and predicting political attitudes and behaviors. Individuals have their coherent construction of the world, which makes sense from their point of view. Any analysis of an individual's attitudinal structure or behavior that ignores the individual's repertoire of beliefs, affects, and motivations, will look irrational or incoherent. This may happen when political psychologists impose their own perspective on the examined world views of other individuals, in their attempt to understand personal political attitudes or behaviors.

Commonalism

A second derivation from cognitive social psychology is that individuals share beliefs inasmuch as all cognitions (i.e., beliefs) are embedded in historical, cultural, and social–relational contexts as a result of social interaction and communication (Damon, 1991). This implies that individuals' subjective world is partly shared by other individuals, some of whom are group members. Commonalism has been widely studied in the social sciences for decades, but I present it from a narrow, social psychological perspective, that of social cognition.

Commonalism assumes that although individuals form their own unique reality, there also exists a common reality (e.g., Bar-Tal, 1990, 2000; Fraser & Gaskell, 1990; Moscovici, 1984, 1988; Resnick, Levine, & Teasley, 1991). Of special importance for political psychology are group members' shared beliefs related to group life. Individuals who have similar experiences due to being members of the same group and to being exposed to the same channels of communication also form common perceptions and understanding (see Asch, 1952; Bar-Tal, 1990; Levine, Resnick, & Higgins, 1993; Turner, 1987). Groups, however, differ with regard to the degree and nature of their commonality. Although in some groups—for example, closed religious sects—the common cognitive–affective repertoire constitutes a major part and plays a determinative role in the lives of group members, in other more open groups, these commonalities leave a less decisive mark on their members. In all groups and societies, however, shared beliefs have a significant function. Fraser and Gaskell (1990) suggested in this vein that "Shared attitudes and beliefs play an important role in defining groups and groups behaviors, in the formation and maintenance of social identities and more broadly in collective realities" (p. 8).

In addition to social identity, these beliefs and attitudes provide the basis for the development of a sense of unity, solidarity, and interdependence, and they support the coordination of group activity—all necessary conditions for the functioning of social systems. They have an important influence on group behavior. Coordinated behaviors of group members always have an epistemic basis, that is, they never begin automatically or instinctively; rather, they rely on a priori rationale, which often consists of shared beliefs.

Because there is continuous interaction between the shared beliefs and new experiences of the society, new experiences, on one hand, serve as a source for the formation for new group beliefs, whereas on the other hand, the already accumulated shared beliefs serve as a prism through which the new experiences are understood and new beliefs are formed. Group beliefs enable the construction of a firm group reality, even though their contents often concern ambiguous social events, abstract concepts, and information that in most cases is not observed or experienced firsthand.

If groups are characterized by shared beliefs, then voluntary group membership requires holding these beliefs. Sharing group beliefs is one of the conditions for being a group member, as it turns any aggregation of individuals into a group. It is thus necessary that society members adopt shared beliefs, if they want to join the society. It is indeed well established that in defining themselves as group members, people internalize various beliefs that are viewed as central to that group (Bar-Tal, 1998; Levine, Bogart, & Zdaniuk, 1996; Turner, 1987). To achieve this goal, groups use different modes of dissemination to impart and maintain shared beliefs. Processes of dissemination begin with interpersonal influence and end with well-planned, systematic societal indoctrination.

However, group members are not passively stimulated, influenced, or persuaded. They are active human beings who process information, evaluate it, make inferences and judgments, select the knowledge that suits them, argue, oppose, struggle for their ideas, and try to persuade other group members of the rightness of their beliefs. Hence, the formation, dissemination, and maintenance of shared beliefs is a continuous process of negotiation in which shared beliefs are formed and changed (see Burr, 1995; Potter & Wetherell, 1987).

Commonalism has a number of implications for political psychology. First, it suggests that there is a need to systematically study the shared political beliefs of groups and societies in order to comprehend their perceived political reality, the epistemic basis of their political decisions, and actions. It is necessary, however, to note that the earlier discussed implications of subjectivism also apply here. Shared beliefs of one group differ from those of other groups, and each group has its unique set of shared beliefs resulting from its unique experiences. Groups, societies, or nations act differently in the same situation as they perceive and evaluate it differently. Moreover, because it is hard to predict which shared beliefs will be accessible in a particular situation, it also will be hard to predict a group's political behavior in a particular situation. Commonalism, secondly, also encourages political psychologists to study the channels of communication and the institutions that impart shared political knowledge. They determine the ability of group members to negotiate the contents and meaning of shared political beliefs, as well as their ability to change them.

In sum, commonalism is an important political phenomenon. Shared beliefs are often used by leaders to justify their policies and are also frequently used by group members to influence the leaders to adopt a certain course of action.

Universalism Versus Particularism

The third derivation refers to the difference between what can be universally generalized and what can be generalized only to certain cases or be particular. The former type of generalization can be used in a description of human behavior in any place, time, or situation. The latter type is limited to individuals who maintain a similar repertoire of beliefs and therefore may behave similarly in the same situations, or to certain situations that may similarly affect different individuals. Universal generalization does not imply that induction justifies universal statements, inasmuch as there is no method or logic to determine a priori whether or not a generalization is universal. Nevertheless, once a universal principle is proposed, its generalizability should be examined with the available evidence. As long as exceptions are not found, the formulated principle can then be considered as universal.

Often, when political psychologists have attempted to formulate universal generalizations, they in fact often theorized and performed studies that enabled them to derive only particularistic generalizations. Examples of specific conclusions, which are treated as if they were universal, are, for instance: if one side in a conflict takes a small step to reduce tension, the other side will reciprocate; mediation facilitates voluntary agreements through negotiation; low self-esteem leads to striving for power; shared illusion of invulnerability encourages extreme risk taking in a group; perception of threat increases authoritarianism; perception of threat is determined by perception of intention and capability. These so-called laws cannot be universally generalized; at most, they may hold for specific populations in given situations.

How individuals or groups behave in certain situation depends on how they perceive, interpret, and evaluate it. Because cognitive processes are dynamic, the availability of specific cognitions may change in time and according to situation, and for both individuals and groups, it is difficult to predict which cognitions will be accessed to in a given situation. Different individuals or groups have different cognitions, and exhibit different behaviors, in different situations.

In order to further explore the difference between universal and particularistic generalization, I suggest we examine the distinction between content and process distinction. *Contents* refer to cognitions that individuals or groups use to characterize people, behaviors, topics, events, objects, places, or situations (for example, peace, deterrence, nationalism). *Processes* refer to sequences of operations performed by individuals or groups that describe principles of overt and covert behaviors (for example, resolving conflict, evaluating situation). Both contents and processes may have different levels of universality. Certain contents of cognitions may be held by an individual or group in a certain situation and at a certain point in time (for example, viewing the Soviet Union as an evil empire), or even by a large portion of the human population, in many situations, along periods of time (e.g., viewing a conflict in a situation of negating goals). In the same way, it is possible to describe particular processes of specific behaviors that pertain to certain individuals, groups, times, or situations (for example, evaluating that Japan will not attack the United States in 1941), and it is possible to describe a general underlying process of a behavior category that pertains to all the human beings (e.g., making a decision).

Nevertheless, I suggest that it is less feasible to formulate universal laws based on contents than on processes. That is, whereas universal content does not imply that it is always available, and therefore it cannot always be used in explaining and predicting human behavior, a universal process, which underlies a given behavior, can always be used to explain and predict that behavior. This is so because universal processes are not dependent on the contents that may or may not be in an individual's (the naïve person) repertoire. Instead, they may describe sequences of operations in general and abstract terms. Therefore, they do not have to be in every individual's head, but used only by the analyst of human behavior. Moreover, the study of universal processes is more likely to yield causal understanding of political behavior than the study of universal contents.

An example of an universal theory is the lay-epistemic theory proposed by Kruglanski (1989), which tries to elucidate the epistemic process of knowledge acquisition. It describes the sequence of cognitive operations performed by individuals on their way to a given knowledge, irrespective of specific contents. Kruglanski proposed that the process of knowledge acquisition consists of two phases: first, the cognitive generation stage wherein the contents of knowledge come into existence in our mind; second, the cognitive validation stage, which concerns assessment of the degree of confidence that is attributed to the generated contents. This phase is accomplished via deductive logic based on the consistency principle, which assumes that the acceptance of knowledge depends on the consistency of one's conclusion with one's premises.

The study of universal process in political psychology has two functions. First, it provides parsimonious and general explanations of political behavior. These explanations are suitable for any specific behaviors to which the given process gives rise and thus may provide an integration of political-psychological knowledge collected in political psychology. Second, it allows us to make specific predictions when specific, relevant contents of the political behavior are known. The mere knowledge of contents does not enable us to describe people's political behavior.

An important point that should be emphasized is that the present perspective does not preclude the study of contents, but only indicates the limitation of this direction of research. Often political psychology does not require familiarity with all the specific contents related to the prediction, because they are based on the implicit assumption that certain contents are universal and that, therefore, it is not necessary to measure them in each group. Such theories could be said to provide a "stereotypic" approach, an approach that may lead to errors. Predictions, in political psychology as in real life, require knowledge of the specific contents involved. But since, as political psychologists, we want to explain generally and not just specifically predict, we have to find the universal process that underlies the particular behavior.

Political psychology is largely directed to a study of contents, some of which are believed to be universal, as for example patriotism, discrimination, conservatism, authoritarianism, peace, war, or security, and some are specific to a particular individual or group, in particular situations and period of time, such as the intentions of Truman during the Yalta meeting, or the phases of the Israeli–Egyptian peace process, or the perception of Americans during the Vietnam war.

The study of contents, I believe, has three main objectives: performing particularistic descriptions; elucidating and examining universal processes; and enabling intervention. Particularistic research indeed focuses on the study of specific contents in order to characterize certain individuals, groups, or situations. This is the major thrust of political psychology. Particularistic studies, for example, may attempt to map the repertoire of particular political beliefs held by a certain group, in order to describe beliefs triggered in a specific group in a given situation, or to study the relationship between beliefs and behavior of a group in a given situation or to examine beliefs of a specific leader. Universal process is described in abstract terms and is used as a universal principle. Any examination of universal process, however, has to be done within a content-bound framework—that is, specific variables have to be inserted into the abstract concepts if one intends to study process or describe a specific case of an individual or group behavior. Finally, political intervention with groups is impossible without knowing the contents that characterize the target population in the specific situation. Only on the basis of this knowledge is it possible to understand both the antecedents and outcomes of the behavior of a certain group and thus to plan the direction of intervention and its effects.

Content-bound research, thus, does not generate universal laws of behavior, but rather aims to describe the political behavior of specific individuals or groups functioning in a specific time, place, and situation. It is possible, however, that certain contents characterize a number of groups, or even that they are universal. The major effort of political psychology today is directed at particularistic, content-bound theory and research. As long as political psychologists recognize the limitation of such endeavors, their research objectives will remain realistic.

CONCLUSIONS

The classified data of the *Political Psychology* articles indicate that although political psychology draws its basis from different areas of psychology, social psychology plays a major role in providing theoretical and conceptual foundations. This state of the discipline is not surprising in view of the fact that political behavior can be considered as one category of social behavior.

Nevertheless, the roots of understanding political behavior are found in all the areas of psychology.

Indeed, what makes political psychology unique is, first of all, preoccupation with political contents and particular political processes. The general concepts and the underlying universal processes are taken from psychology. Thus, students of political psychology are required to know the basic concepts, theories, and relevant findings of psychology. They cannot rely solely on their lay psychological knowledge. The accumulated knowledge in the science of psychology provides an enlightening perspective for understanding political contents and processes. Some of it is even counter to the human intuition.

Of special importance for the development of political psychology is the finding that social cognitive theoretical basis serves as a major basis for studies in political psychology. This finding is not surprising in view of the dominance of cognitive approach in psychology, as Gardner (1985) noted: ". . . cognitive psychologists have won the battle on their chosen field within psychology. . . . Nearly all researchers accept the need—and the advisability—of positing a level of mental representation" (p. 130). Political psychologists, too, recognize the determinative influence of human perception and cognition on political functioning. This trend is especially salient in view of the fact that political psychology borrows much of its knowledge from social psychology, which is almost entirely cognitive. It is Ostrom (1994), one of the founders of social cognitive psychology, who pointed out that "The social cognition approach is based on the conviction that constructs relevant to cognitive representation and process are fundamental to understanding all human responses, regardless of whether those responses are social or nonsocial in nature" (p. ix).

The social cognitive orientation implies four derivations, three of which —subjectivism, commonalism, and universalism—are discussed at length in this chapter. The fourth derivation concerns perceptual and cognitive biases and errors presented in Jervis' chapter, later in this book.

The three derivations are complementary and should be seen as reinforcing one another in the construction of a psychological framework for political psychology.

This framework focuses on people's political knowledge, which functions as a basis for their political behavior. Political knowledge consists of beliefs about political themes: Human beings actively process information and, on this basis, form their political beliefs. Political knowledge is personal, subjective, and potentially biased; it is not static, but dynamic. Not only does an individual's political knowledge change through the years, but in addition, political beliefs accessible at any given moment vary. Nevertheless, this does not preclude the possibility that individuals, who are members of social groups and share common experiences, also form common political beliefs. These common political beliefs are the basis for the common political behaviors that are so often observed among members of a group.

The framework presented in this chapter outlines the directions that political psychologists can take in studying the universal and the particular. Universal generalizations can be expressed in terms of the processes underlying political behavior, irrespective of the specific contents. The discovery of these processes is a necessary objective if political psychologists desire to explain and predict political behavior. However, their elucidation is only one necessary direction of political psychology, which also must address specific groups or societies, in their specific setting. When following this direction of research, political psychologists should rely on the political contents that are typical of the studied group. However, the acquired political knowledge about a specific group may be only particularistically and not universally generalized.

The distinction between universal and particularistic generalization is crucial for political psychologists. Although focus on specific political contents limits the ability to generate universal knowledge, their study allows explanation and maybe even prediction of particular individuals and groups, in particular situations. The study of universal processes allows a generation of general theory that can be used in analyses of particular cases. Both directions of research are necessary for the further development of political psychology.

ACKNOWLEDGMENT

The author thanks Yoram Bar-Tal for inspirational talks that influenced the contents of the chapter.

REFERENCES

Allport, G. W. (1985). The historical background of social psychology. In G. Lindzey & E. Aronson (Eds.), *Handbook of social psychology* (3rd ed., Vol. 1, pp. 1–46). New York: Random House.

Apter, O. E. (1977). *Introduction to political analysis*. Cambridge, MA: Winthrop.

Asch, S. E. (1952). *Social psychology*. Englewood Cliffs, NJ: Prentice Hall.

Axelrod, R. (Ed.). (1976). *Structure of decision: The cognitve maps of political elites*. Princeton, NJ: Princeton University Press.

Bar-Tal, D. (1990). *Group beliefs: A conception for analyzing group structure, processes, and behavior*. New York: Springer-Verlag.

Bar-Tal, D. (1998). Group beliefs as an expression of social identity. In S. Worchel, J. F. Morales, D. Paez, & J. C. Deschamps (Eds.), *Social identity: International perspective* (pp. 93–113). Thousands Oaks, CA: Sage.

Bar-Tal, D. (2000). *Shared beliefs in a society: Social psychological analysis.* Thousands Oaks, CA: Sage.

Brewer, M. B. (1997). On the social origins of human nature. In C. McGarty & S. A. Haslam (Eds.), *The message of social psychology: Perspectives on mind in society* (pp. 54–62). Cambridge, MA: Blackwell.

Burr, V. (1995). *An introduction to social constructionism.* London: Routledge.

Clore, G. L., Schwarz, N., & Conway, M. (1994). Affective causes and consequences of social information processing. In R. S. Wyer, Jr. & T. K. Srull (Eds.), *Handbook of social cognition* (2nd ed., Vol. 1, pp. 323–417). Hillsdale, NJ: Lawrence Erlbaum Associates.

Cohen, R. (1979). *Threat perception in international crisis.* Madison: University of Wisconsin Press.

Damon, W. (1991). Problems of direction in socially shared cognition. In L. B. Resnick, J. M. Levine, & S. D. Feasley (Eds.), *Perspectives on socially shared cognition* (pp. 384–397). Washington, DC: American Psychological Association.

Eldridge, A. F. (1979). *Images of conflict.* New York: St. Martin's Press.

Farr, P. M. (1996). *The roots of modern social psychology 1982–1954.* Oxford: Blackwell.

Finifter, A. W. (Ed.). (1993). *Political science: The state of the discipline II.* Washington, DC: American Political Science Association.

Fiske, S. T., & Taylor, S. E. (1991). *Social cognition* (2nd ed.). New York: McGraw-Hill.

Fletcher, G. J. (1984). Psychology and common sense. *American Psychologist, 39,* 203–213.

Fraser, C., & Gaskell, G. (Eds.). (1990). *The social psychology of widespread beliefs.* Oxford: Clarendon Press.

Gardner, H. (1985). *The mind's new science: A history of the cognitive revolution.* New York: Basic Books.

George, A. (1969). The operational code: A neglected approach to the study of political leaders and decision making. *International Studies Quarterly, 13,* 190–222.

Greenstein, F. I. (1973). Political psychology: A pluralistic universe. In J. N. Knutson (Ed.), *Handbook of political psychology* (pp. 438–469). San Francisco, CA: Jossey-Bass.

Heider, F. (1958). *The psychology of interpersonal relations.* New York: John Wiley & Sons.

Hermann, M. G. (1986a). What is political psychology? In M. G. Hermann (Ed.), *Political psychology* (pp. 1–10). San Francisco, CA: Jossey-Bass.

Hermann, M. G. (Ed.). (1986b). *Political psychology.* San Francisco, CA: Jossey-Bass.

Higgins, E. T. (1996). Knowledge activation: Accessibility, applicability, and salience. In E. T. Higgins & A. W. Kruglanski (Eds.), *Social psychology: Handbook of basic principles* (pp. 133–168). New York: Guilford Press.

Higgins, E. T., & Stangor, C. (1988). Context-driven social judgment and memory: When "behavior engulfs the field" in reconstructive memory. In D. Bar-Tal & A. W. Kruglanski (Eds.), *The social psychology of knowledge* (pp. 262–298). Cambridge: Cambridge University Press.

Hunt, G. J., & Larson, L. L. (Eds.). (1974). *Contingency approaches to leadership.* Carbondale: Southern Illinois University Press.

Isen, A. M. (1984). Toward understanding the role of affect in cognition. In R. S. Wyer, Jr. & T. K. Srull (Eds.), *Handbook of social cognition* (Vol. 3, pp. 179–236). Hillsdale, NJ: Lawrence Erlbaum Associates.

Jervis, R. (1976). *Perception and misperception in international politics.* Princeton: Princeton University Press.

Jones, E. E. (1998). Major developments in five decades of social psychology. In D. T. Gilbert, S. T. Fiske, & G. Lindsey (Eds.), *The handbook of social psychology* (4th ed., Vol. 1, pp. 3–57). Boston: McGraw-Hill.

Kelley, H. H. (1992). Common-sense psychology and scientific psychology. *Annual Review of Psychology, 43,* 1–23.

Knutson, J. N. (Ed.). (1973). *Handbook of political psychology.* San Francisco, CA: Jossey-Bass.

Kruglanski, A. W. (1989). *Lay epistemics and human knowledge*. New York: Plenum.

Kruglanski, A. W. (1996). Motivated social cognition: Principles of the interface. In E. T. Higgins & A. W. Kruglanski (Eds.), *Social psychology: Handbook of basic principles* (pp. 493–520). New York: Guilford Press.

Levine, J. M., Bogart, L. M., & Zdaniuk, B. (1996). Impact of anticipated group membership on cognition. In R. M. Sorentino & E. T. Higgins (Eds.), *Handbook of motivation and cognition* (Vol. 3, pp. 531–569). New York: Guilford Press.

Levine, J. M., Resnick, L. B., & Higgins, E. T. (1993). Social foundations of cognition. *Annual Review of Psychology, 44,* 585–612.

Long, S. L. (Ed.). (1981). *The handbook of political behavior* (Vol. 1–5). New York: Plenum Press.

Markus, H., & Zajonc, R. B. (1985). The cognitive perspective in social psychology. In G. Lindzey & E. Aronson (Eds.), *Handbook of social psychology* (3rd ed., Vol. 1, pp. 137–230). New York: Random House.

McGrath, J. E. (1964). *Social psychology*. New York: Holt, Rinehart and Winston.

Moscovici, S. (1984). The phenomenon of social representations. In R. M. Farr & S. Moscovici (Eds.), *Social representations* (pp. 3–69). Cambridge: Cambridge University Press.

Moscovici, S. (1988). Notes towards a description of social representations. *European Journal of Social Psychology, 18,* 211–250.

Ostrom, T. M. (1994). Foreword. In R. S. Wyer, Jr., & T. K. Srull (Eds.), *Handbook of social cognition* (2nd ed., Vol. 1, pp. vii–xii). Hillsdale, NJ: Lawrence Erlbaum Associates.

Pittman, T. S. (1998). Motivation. In D. T. Gilbert, S. T. Fiske, & G. Lindzey (Eds.), *The handbook of social psychology* (4th ed., Vol. 1, pp. 549–590). Boston, MA: McGraw-Hill.

Potter, Y., & Wetherell, M. (1987). *Discourse and social psychology: Beyond attitude and behavior.* London: Sage.

Resnick, L. B., Levine, J. M., & Teasley, S. D. (Eds.). (1991). *Perspectives on socially shared cognition*. Washington, DC: American Psychological Association.

Sniderman, P. M., Brody, R. A., & Tetlock, P. E. (1991). *Reasoning and choice: Explorations in political psychology*. Cambridge: Cambridge University Press.

Sorrentino, R. M., & Higgins, E. T. (Eds.). (1986). *Handbook of motivation and cognition: Foundations of social behavior.* New York: Guilford Press.

Sprout, H., & Sprout, M. (1965). *The ecological perspective on human affairs*. Princeton, NJ: Princeton University Press.

Stone, W. F., & Schaffner, P. E. (1988). *The psychology of politics* (2nd ed.). New York: Springer-Verlag.

Sylvan, D. A., & Chan, S. (Eds.). (1984). *Foreign policy and decision making: Perception, cognition and artificial intelligence*. New York: Praeger.

Turner, J. C. (1987). *Rediscovering the social group. A self-categorization theory*. Oxford, Basil Blackwell.

Vertzberger, Y. (1990). *The world in their minds*. Palo Alto, CA: Stanford University.

White, R. K. (1970). *Nobody wanted war: Misperception in Vietnam and other wars*. Garden City, NY: Doubleday.

Wyer, R. S. Jr., & Carlston, D. E. (1994). The cognitive representation of persons and events. In R. S. Wyer, Jr. & T. K. Srull (Eds.), *Handbook of social cognition* (2nd ed., Vol. 1, pp. 41–98). Hillsdale, NJ: Lawrence Erlbaum Associates.

11

Group Psychology
Is the State of Nature

C. FRED ALFORD
University of Maryland

> *Human beings make their own history, but they do not make it just as they please; they do not make it under circumstances chosen by themselves, but under circumstances directly encountered, given and transmitted from the past. The tradition of all the dead generations weighs like a nightmare on the brain of the living.*
>
> —Karl Marx (1852/1978),
> *The Eighteenth Brumaire of Louis Bonaparte*

The contribution of political psychology is immediately evident if we conceive of the past that Marx was talking about not in terms of objective history, but rather as a psychological past, going back to infancy, comprised of layers of experience that Freud compared to an archeological dig. Political psychology studies the influence of this psychological past on the present. In particular, political psychology studies how groups of people come to share a psychological past that they draw on to make a collective world. This world is no less real because we make it out of our hopes, dreams, fears, and desires. However, unless we understand where this world comes from—deep inside the minds of men and women who live in it—we will never be in a position to awaken from the nightmare that is (all too often) human history.

I came to political psychology from the study of the Frankfurt School of Critical Theory, particularly the work of Jürgen Habermas and Herbert Marcuse. The Frankfurt School emerged in the years before and after World

War II. Its great contribution, as I see it, was to bring Freud into contact with Marx, using Freud to explain what happened to the proletariat. Not only did the masses not revolt, but they put up little resistance to the Nazis, more often embracing nationalism, racism, and murder.

I do not claim that this is how political psychology started. Others in this collection have done that piece of history. Rather, this is how political psychology started for me, as an attempt to explain the horrors of World War II and the Holocaust. There are, of course, lots of ways to explain history. What I was so struck with—and remain transfixed by to this day—is the propensity of men and women to persecute and kill each other. There must be a part of each of us, including you and me, that likes these things. What part is this, how does it work, and how can it be tamed? These are the questions that sent me to political psychology.

These are, I believe, the same questions that sent earlier generations of political thinkers to the *state of nature,* as they called it. The state of nature that Hobbes, Locke, and Rousseau wrote about never existed, of course, and they knew it. The state of nature is a hypothesis about human nature: Given the worst propensities of humans, what is the best political regime we can hope for? To know what politics should be, we must know the forces within humans with which it must contend. Plato, Aristotle, Saint Thomas Aquinas, as well as Hobbes, Locke, and Rousseau, were the original political psychologists. It is only recently that political theory has been sundered from political psychology.

Rawls' (1971) *A Theory of Justice* is often cited as the work that revived political theory, as it did. However, it had a negative effect as well, dividing political theory from political psychology. Whatever makes Rawls' work great, it is not his insight into human nature, which in his account is remarkably thin and superficial, exceedingly and excessively rational.

Political psychology is exciting because it promises to connect once more the study of political science with the study of human nature. Political psychology has the potential to take over where state of nature theory left off, combining experiment and theory to study the state of human nature on which all our theorizing depends, even those theories that regard human nature as a reification. To study human nature is not to make it one fixed thing forever; it is to make human nature once again problematic, the leading problematic of the human sciences.

However, if political psychology is intellectually exciting, it is also tremendously sobering. Inner reality, the world of drives, desires, hopes, and fears is even less mutable than external reality. To know this inner world is not necessarily to be able to change it, or even control it. To know this inner world is to know that none of the horrors of the 20th century are alien to human nature. Far from being deviations or perversions, the Holocaust and the mass murders in Kosovo are entirely in accord with everything we know about human nature. They are a result of what I (Alford, 1994) call *humanity's groupishness,* its willingness to do virtually anything to belong to the group, including murdering those who do not.

The Frankfurt School came to an impasse. No historical change that it could imagine would be enough to change the human nature that gets us into so much trouble. Marcuse imagined a world without work as the only solution. Only in such a world would Eros be free to defeat Thanatos, the death instinct. Adorno imagined some sort of ineffable reconciliation with nature as the solution. Needless to say, these are not practical answers.

Does political psychology offer answers? I tell my students that it does not, and by this I mean that it provides no solutions. Then why learn political psychology in the first place? If we cannot change human nature, why bother knowing about it? My answer is in the form of a metaphor. A sailor can do nothing about the weather. If, however, the sailor learns about weather and seamanship, he may keep his ship afloat, working with the sea, not against it. If we imagine that the sea is human nature, then this is a good reason to learn political psychology, so that we can live with the political psychology in ourselves and others, working with it to minimize the damage it can inflict.

So far I have characterized political psychology in terms of its project— what I think political psychology is properly about in the broadest terms: understanding the irrational forces in human nature that manifest themselves in the nightmares of genocide, mass murder, war, racism, hatred, and gross inequality. One response to this project might be to argue that it is misconceived from the beginning. Who says all these terrible things are irrational? All that is rational is not good. War may be quite rational, and so is inequality, especially if one is on top. Although this is undoubtedly true to some degree, one must draw a sharp distinction between rationality and rationalization.

Much of what passes as rationality is actually a rationalization, an after-the-fact account designed to convince the self and others that one is not in the grip of powerful unknown forces. That, said Freud (1953), is one narcissistic injury (an injury to one's pride or self-esteem) that humanity cannot stand. It will, concludes Freud, take men and women as long to come to terms with that truth as with the truth that men and women are not special creatures of God, the pinnacle of creation.

Many political scientists, it seems, would rather contemplate a rational creature bent on conquest and domination than an irrational creature who is the victim of its own fears and desires. Better to imagine man as the wolf than man as a deeply needy and dependent creature. In fact, it is precisely man's needy dependence that sometimes turns him into a wolf, and at other times into a moral creature.

Freud was not a political psychologist. Or was he? It is worthwhile trying to distinguish political psychology from psychology overall. One way to do this is personal. As a political psychologist, I stand at the intersection of disciplines. Not just politics and psychology, but philosophy, history, and sociology are my concerns. On my campus I have some contact with philosophers, some with sociologists, and some with colleagues in English literature, who seem to be interested in everything. I have no professional contact with the psychologists. Nothing they do seems to have much to do with what I do, and it is worth considering why.

Psychologists assume that individual men and women exist. I do not. What can this mean? It means that most academic psychologists, like most contemporary political philosophers (another group to which I belong), assume that individual psychology precedes group psychology. The individual is born a social isolate who must gradually be socialized into the group to which he or she belongs. Most of the disorders and problems of individual psychology stem from the conflict between individual desire and social need.

Some people think this is what Freud said, but it is not. Freud (1959) said group psychology comes first:

> We must conclude that the psychology of groups is the oldest human psychology; what we have isolated as individual psychology, by neglecting all traces of the group, has only since come into prominence out of the old group psychology, by a gradual process which may still, perhaps, be described as incomplete. (p. 55)

Let us consider an implication of this claim for political science, and politics generally, drawing on the work of Hobbes (1968), who inspires not just political theorists, but many who would make of politics a rational science —that is, a science of rationality. Man, said Hobbes, writing at the time of Galileo, is born isolated and alone. Were he left to himself, he would spend all his days fighting with others, terrified that they would kill him before he could kill them. This Hobbes calls the *state of nature*, in which life is famously nasty, brutish, and short. There is no civilization, no commerce, hardly any family life, only attack and defense, which leads the rational man or woman to choose preemptive attack as the preferred strategy for survival.

For this is what men and women want to do most: survive. Conversely, what they most fear is violent death. Eventually they figure out that this interest is best survived by agreeing among themselves to contract with a sovereign, to whom they give all power—not because they want to, but because the alternative is worse, the war of all against all. Frightening and prone to corruption as he may be, an absolute sovereign (whom Hobbes calls a leviathan) can keep order and so allow the emergence of civilization for the first time. The absolute sovereign is the result of rational calculation and bargaining: Better the possible depredations of an absolute sovereign than certain disorder, constant war, and chaos.

Hobbes is read by most students in courses in political theory, but he is not just a political theorist. He is, I have tried to suggest, the first rational modeler, as well as the first individualist. Some have even called him the first liberal, because for Hobbes the individual, not the state, is the source of all value. The state, no matter how extreme, exists to serve the security, prosperity, and happiness of the individual, not vice versa. Contemporary political science (and, I suggest, contemporary academic psychology as well) is built on Hobbes: Man is first of all the fearful individual who wants only to be secure and happy, but hardly ever is.

Not only is Hobbes mistaken, but he has it backwards, or at least those who take him literally do. Think about it. Hobbes' system of order is built on the claim that what men and women fear most of all is their own violent death. What could be more rational and self-interested than that? Except that it is not remotely true. For millennia, men and women have been sacrificing their lives for the group, whether it is called family, tribe, nation, or religion. How many millions have given their lives, sometimes reluctantly, often eagerly, for their king, their prophet, their God, their Führer, the homes and hearths of their own kind? Sometimes, it seems, this what men and women do best—die for their beliefs. That, of course, takes other men and women to kill for theirs.

Civilization as we know it would be impossible if people were not eager to die for their group and their leader. Although we might wish it were true that civilization as we know it (as opposed to civilization as we wish it) were impossible, inasmuch as it is, we should try to figure out why. Explaining the eagerness of men and women to live, die, and kill for each other should be the number one task of political psychology—if, that is, we conceive of political psychology as a foundational discipline—a discipline concerned with what makes society possible (and, sad to say, a peaceful world impossible).

In fact, Hobbes never believed men and women feared violent death above all else. What he believed is that if the recently literate bourgeois public could be convinced of this fact, they could be governed more easily, as they could be threatened with greater precision and effect. They could, in other words, be singled out and threatened with death. Seen from this perspective, it is not the deductive ingenuity of Hobbes' science that is so important, but the function of science as image, metaphor, and rhetoric (Johnston, 1986). It is this same science that serves today to help convince us that men and women are rational, calculating, utility maximizing individuals, whose choices can be modeled with theories drawn from economics. However, unlike Hobbes, we have forgotten that such assumptions are rhetoric. This would be as good a definition of ideology as any: rhetoric that has come to think of itself as reality. From this perspective, too much political science has become ideology.

I believe that the value of political psychology stems from its recognition of the fact that men and women are first of all creatures of attachment, creatures of the group. To be sure, most political psychologists do not go around stating this fact. They go around analyzing political phenomena. Among the things that political psychologists study are the development of political attitudes, the perception of political leaders, the sources of party identification, the attribution of traits to enemies and allies, the relationship between ideology, attitude, and act, social trust, and the attractions of authoritarianism. I take these topics from articles in recent issues of *Political Psychology*, the leading journal in the field.

As diverse as they are, each of these studies is characterized by an assumption, frequently implicit, that the group is in the individual as much as the individual is in the group. Brown (1966) put it this way.

> The existence of the "let's pretend" boundary [between individuals] does not prevent the continuance of the real traffic across it. . . . "There is a continual unconscious wandering of other personalities into ourselves." Every person, then, is many persons; a multitude made into one person. (pp. 146–147)

Brown was a psychoanalytic theorist loosely associated with the Frankfurt School. As such, he put the issue in especially stark and radical terms. Most political psychologists do not, and would not, put it this way, but I believe that this is the working assumption, often tacit, even unconscious, of most political psychologists.

For reasons of analytic neatness, I wish I could say that all political psychologists share this assumption, and that no other discipline does. But this is not true. Some political psychologists, such as those who study political cognition, often do not. Political psychology is a discipline defined by its field of study, not its method or approaches. Conversely, others, such as many sociologists, share the assumption that the group is in the individual as much as the individual is in the group. The difference is that sociologists, while seeing the group in the individual, tend not to consider the way in which the individual struggles to liberate himself from the same group he or she cannot live without. Goffman's (1962) classical sociological study of *Asylums: Essays on the Social Situation of Mental Patients and Other Inmates*, is exemplary. For Goffman, the individual is the role he finds himself in. There are no hidden conflicts because there is nothing hidden; it is all on the surface because there are no depths.

In fact, the individual is often at conflict, not just with the role he has been assigned, but with the very experience of being a group animal. Bion (1961) put it this way: "The individual is a group animal at war, not simply with the group but with himself for being a group animal and with those aspects of his personality that constitute his 'groupishness' " (p. 95). To say that men and women are group animals is not to say that they always follow the group. It is to say that men and women always define themselves in terms of the group, even when they do so in contrast to the group, generally by emphasizing their membership in another group.

A simple example would be studies that show that party affiliation is as much about defining oneself as not belonging to one group, say Republicans, as it is about belonging to another, say Democrats (Greene, 1999). What about independent voters, it might be asked? Whatever else may be said of independents, they are hardly without group membership. Indeed, it has long been held that it is the cross-pressure they experience from belonging to different groups that deters independents from identifying with a major party. These are simple examples, from the mainstream of political psychology, the psychology of voting, but that is the point. One finds the principles of groupishness everywhere.

I suggest that we extrapolate from the most mundane, the topics that the average political psychologist studies (if there is such a creature), to the tacit principles behind these studies. There one finds, I believe, a radical (by which I mean going to the root) view of human nature that contrasts sharply with the individualism that characterizes much of the rest of political science, for whom the rational self-interested individual is king—or rather, for whom the rational self-interested individual exists.

POLITICAL PSYCHOLOGY AS POLITICAL THEORY?

If the view of human nature implicit in political psychology deviates from that held by many political scientists, it remains a view that is reflected in the works of many of the classical political theorists, especially those who have questioned the meaning of individualism. Alexis de Tocqueville's study of humanity's groupishness, including the conflict it generates within the individual, the conflict referred to by Bion, is a good example. For centuries, indeed millennia, said Tocqueville, humanity defined itself in terms of the group. This is what feudalism means, a regime in which every creature has its place in the Great Chain of Being. Tocqueville was, he said, terrified at the breakup of this old system, fearful that men and women were losing the ties that bound them to this order, and hence to the world itself. How would people behave in a regime without such connections? How, in other words, would men and women behave in the new American democracy?

They would, said Tocqueville, believe themselves to be independent and free, while clinging to an imaginary group ever more tightly. They would, in other words, imagine themselves to be rational self-interested individuals, even as they were more dependent on the group than ever before. Men and women would deal with their conflict over their groupishness by pretending to be free of the group's influence, while clinging ever more tightly to its imaginary counterpart.

Tocqueville was fascinated by the way in which individualism and conformity, seemingly so antithetical, go together in American life. Individualism isolates the individual within the solitude of his own heart, cutting him off from traditional sources of support within the community. In his isolation, the individual is likely to turn to others for confirmation of his own judgment—not individual others, but the group.

> The same equality which renders him independent of each of his fellow-citizens taken severally, exposes him alone and unprotected to the influence of the greater number. The public has therefore, among a democratic people, a singular power . . . for it does not persuade to certain opinions, but it enforces them, and infuses them into the intellect by a sort of enormous pressure of the minds of all upon the reason of each. . . . I know of no country in which there is so little independence of mind and real freedom of discussion as in America. (Tocqueville, 1956, pp. 148, 117–118)

One hundred seventy years later, the problem remains. When people do not understand their own groupishness, their own need for community, their own fear of isolation, they are more—not less—likely to mistake selfishness for independence, alienation for freedom. They also are much more likely to conform without knowing it. Everyone may be "Bowling Alone," to use the title of Putnam's (1995) recent and widely read essay on the decline of community in American life, but they are still bowling—that is, doing what everybody else does. They are just doing it side by side, almost as though they were together. Conformity is poor quality togetherness. It is poor quality individuality, too.

One of the most important lessons political psychology has to teach is the intensity of our groupishness, something our culture seems organized to deny, probably because it requires recognizing how dependent we all are on others, and this is not an easy country to be dependent in. Taking their title from a phrase in Tocqueville, *Habits of the Heart*, by Bellah, Madsen, Sullivan, Swidler, and Tipton (1985), is a fine study of this denial. Americans, Bellah and his associates argued, lack the language and cultural resources to express the need to belong that they so intensely feel. The language of rational individualism, they conclude, is deeply impoverished.

I (Alford, 1999) recently completed a research project in one of the most group-oriented countries on earth, South Korea. The project involved extensive interviews with more than 250 South Koreans from all walks of life on issues related to individual and group identity. Korea is the most Confucianized country on earth, and under Confucianism the family group is everything, the individual nothing, or so the story goes. In fact, many Koreans, particularly younger ones, were actually more self-aware than many Americans, precisely because the Koreans understood how much they depended on the group and how much they were willing to sacrifice to belong. Koreans did not always like what they were willing to do to fit in, but they knew they were doing it. The psychological conflict was more intense, but it was also more on the surface, available for inspection and introspection.

Many younger Koreans know they are group animals at war with their own groupishness. One even put it in almost these terms. "My nature is to belong to the group. But sometimes I resist my nature. I think that must be my nature too." The result of such insight (which was widespread, although far from universal) is actually a richer and more nuanced sense of identity. The person who is most dependent on the group is the one who does not know it, who thinks everybody else's thoughts while calling them his own.

This is the leading lesson I seek to teach in my undergraduate courses in political theory and political psychology. Undergraduates generally think they are more individualistic than they are, frequently mistaking signs of relatively superficial nonconformity, such as political cynicism (or perhaps political cynicism is today the leading instance of conformity) for genuine individuality and freedom. Genuine individuality and freedom are based on the ability and willingness to say no to authority, refusing obedience to malevolent authority. Cynical contempt for authority, on the other hand, is entirely compatible with obedience to it. This, I tell my students, is the situation for most of them, or else they would not be in my class; perhaps they would not even be in college.

That is a harsh statement, probably not true. No doubt it is excessively cynical; certainly it is an exaggeration. I say it to make a point. We do not know how groupish we are until we try to defy the group, in this case parents and peers who generally expect young men and women to go to college. Cynical conformism is not defiance; it is going along while pretending we are not, the worst of both worlds. Tocqueville would have understood.

If this is true, what should political psychology be now? What should it be studying? What should it be teaching? Political psychology should not and need not transform itself wholesale. Political psychology should be studying and teaching everything it currently studies and teaches, while becoming more aware of how different its assumptions are from those of most political scientists, for whom the autonomous, rational individual exists.

It seems to me, however, that political psychology has a special contribution to make to the study of the greatest horrors of this century, genocide and mass murder. From a political-psychological perspective, these horrors are not just crimes of obedience, as they have been called (Kelman & Hamilton, 1989). They are crimes of attachment, signs of the lengths to which people will go to belong to the group, even a group of two.

Recall the most dramatic experiment in political psychology ever conducted, Milgram's (1974) famous studies in *Obedience to Authority*.[1] Intending to study the disposition to obedience in postwar Germany, Milgram set up a deceptively simple experiment, placing the naive subject in front of a shock generator, capable of generating (or so the subject was led to believe) dangerous shocks up to 450 volts. After bringing in a mild-mannered "learner with a heart condition" (actually a confederate of the experimenter), Milgram ordered the naive teacher to deliver shocks of up to 450 volts whenever the learner made a mistake in memorizing word pairs. In one variation of the experiment, the learner screamed, shouted, and begged to be released from the experiment, finally saying his heart was failing him before falling silent.

Intending only to conduct preliminary tests in New Haven before moving on to Germany, Milgram never made it across the Atlantic. He did not need to go so far to find shockingly high levels of obedience. Under the conditions just depicted (called voice-proximity), almost 65% of the subjects delivered the full battery of shocks, including three at 450 volts, despite the learner's cries and screams. Anyone who has seen the film from the experiment knows that the "teachers" do not appear to like what they are ordered to do. They just cannot help themselves. They protest, some argue with the experimenter who orders them to go on, but 65% deliver the full battery of shocks, continuing to do so until they are finally ordered to stop.

Milgram interpreted the results of his experiment in terms compatible with the political psychology I have described. It is human nature to obey because ordered hierarchy is the arrangement that best preserves the stability of the group. We are born to obey, because we are born to belong to groups. One is a condition of the other.

This would not be precisely my explanation, although it comes close. I would argue in terms of the psychology of human attachment, the psychology of object relations theory, as it is called, whose leading figures include Fairbairn (1952) and Winnicott (1986) in England, and Kernberg (1985) in the United States.[2] From a perspective that emphasizes the psychology of attachment, it would be more accurate to say that the teachers obeyed the experimenter out of a type of love, identification with the group. Freud (1959) said we give ourselves up to the group out of love, by which he

---

[1] Almost four decades old, the experiment remains the single most influential experiment in the social sciences in this century. *The Journal of Social Issues* (1995) recently devoted an issue to the legacy of the experiment. There will be no more Milgram experiments. For some time now, Human Subject Review Committees have banned its replication.

[2] It is called *object relations theory* primarily in order to maintain a misleading continuity with Freud, who wrote about the object of a drive. It should properly be called *relationship theory*.

means that we substitute for our own ego the ego ideal of the group, "aus ihnen zu liebe"—out of love of the group.

> If an individual gives up his distinctiveness in a group and lets its other members influence him by suggestion, it gives one the impression that he does it because he feels the need of being in harmony with them rather than in opposition to them—so that perhaps after all he does it "ihnen zu liebe." (p. 24)

So strong is this love that men and women will do almost anything for it, including murder innocents. The leader represents the group, and so his influence is strongest, but there is almost nothing that men and women will not do to remain part of the group, as Browning's (1992) study of *Ordinary Men* reveals.

Members of Police Battalion 101 from Hamburg during World War II, the ordinary men about whom Browning wrote were stationed in Poland, where they were ordered to shoot Jewish men, women, and children at close range under grisly conditions. Almost all complied, even though it was remarkably easy to refuse, or just get lost for a couple of hours. Not one member of the Battalion suffered reprisals for failing to participate, yet fewer than 5% opted out. Browning (1992) concluded that it was not fear of retaliation, but fear of not belonging to the group, that led these ordinary men to murder Jews with their bare hands.[3]

Genocide and mass murder are the worst evils our species confronts, and political psychology has a unique insight into the sources of these horrors. Above all, the political psychologist knows how normal and natural they are, as well as how ironic. It is the same attachment to the group that allows us to murder innocents that leads us to give up our lives for the group and to sacrifice ourselves for our highest values, to which we attach ourselves as we attach ourselves to the group. Above all, political psychology is insight into this irony.

Insight does not equal solution, of course, but insight can help us recognize the danger signs, the warning signs along the path by which humans move down the road from groupishness (nationalism and chauvinism) to the devaluation and eventual destruction of outsiders. Staub's (1989) *The Roots of Evil: The Origins of Evil and Other Group Violence* is a fine example of this type of work, a guidebook for sailors on the stormy sea of human nature, to invoke a previous metaphor.

The study of genocide and mass murder from a political psychological perspective is, I have suggested, foundational, revealing the depth of human attachment to the group, as well as the irony of morality that stems from this fact—the attachments that make us moral are the same attachments that

---

[3]Browning called them ordinary men because most were not dedicated Nazis, but older men called up for this "light duty" late in the war.

may make us immoral. Or as Sagan (1988) put it, the problem with the Nazis is not that they had too little superego, but too much. Conscience (what Freud called the superego) is not the little voice that says "be good." It is the little voice that says "do as the group does." Originally this group is mother and father. Eventually it is a society and political regime. Political psychology is the study of the connections between these groups.

Once we know this, many of the issues studied by political scientists are cast in a different light, above all the assumption of the free, rational, and autonomous individual, with which so much political science is still concerned. A particular interest of mine is what used to be called moral psychology, or the moral sense. Instead of deriving morality from principles of reason, as theorists from Kant to Rawls have done, it may be more fruitful to study the sources of morality in attachment, such as the empathy we feel for the suffering of others to whom we feel connected, perhaps simply because they are human like us.

This may seem obvious, but it is not how most moral theory is constructed. Instead, it is derived from first principles, such as the fear of being the least advantaged member of society, as Rawls (1971) would have it in *A Theory of Justice*. Fortunately, a number of political psychologists such as Monroe (1996) have begun to see morality as a subject of empirical study, in which "is" (how people experience the world in moral terms) stands in dialogue with "ought" (how they should).

Seen from this perspective, political psychology is foundational without being abstract. It is concerned with the sources of our most fundamental experiences, such as belonging and morality, while treating these experiences as subject to empirical study. In this regard, political psychology has the potential to be more than an adjunct to political science and more than a subdiscipline. It has the potential to reinvigorate the traditional study of the state of nature, and so become the new political theory.

REFERENCES

Alford, C. F. (1994). *Group psychology and political theory*. New Haven, CT: Yale University Press.

Alford, C. F. (1999). *Think no evil: Korean values in the age of globalization*. Ithaca, NY: Cornell University Press.

Bellah, R., Madsen, R. Sullivan, W., Swidler, A. & Tipton, S. (1985). *Habits of the heart: Individualism and commitment in American life*. Berkeley: University of California Press.

Bion, W. (1961). *Experiences in groups*. New York: Basic Books.

Brown, N. O. (1966). *Love's body*. New York: Vintage Books.

Browning, C. (1992). *Ordinary men: Police Battalion 101 and the final solution in Poland*. New York: Harper Perennial.

Fairbairn, W. R. D. (1952). *Psychoanalytic studies of the personality*. London: Routledge and Kegan Paul.

Freud, S. (1953). The resistances to psycho-analysis. In J. Strachey (Ed.), *The standard edition of the complete psychological works of Sigmund Freud* (Vol. 19, pp. 213–224). London: Hogarth Press.

Freud, S. (1959). *Group psychology and the analysis of the ego*, J. Strachey (Trans.). New York: W. W. Norton.

Goffman, E. (1962). *Asylums: Essays on the social situation of mental patients and other inmates.* Chicago: Aldine.

Greene, S. (1999). Understanding party identification: A social identity approach." *Political Psychology, 20*(2), 393–403.

Hobbes, T. (1968). *Leviathan.* Harmondsworth, England: Penguin Books.

Johnston, D. (1986). *The rhetoric of Leviathan.* Princeton, NJ: Princeton University Press.

Journal of Social Issues (1995). *51* (Fall).

Kelman, H., & Hamilton, L. (1989). *Crimes of obedience: Toward a social psychology of authority and responsibility.* New Haven, CT: Yale University Press.

Kernberg, O. (1985). *Internal world and external reality: Object relations theory applied.* Northvale, NJ: Jason Aronson.

Marx, K. (1978). The Eighteenth Brumaire of Louis Bonaparte. In R. Tucker (Ed.), *The Marx-Engels Reader* (2nd ed.). New York: W. W. Norton. (Original work published 1852)

Milgram, S. (1974). *Obedience to authority: An experimental view.* New York: Harper & Row.

Monroe, K. R. (1996). *The heart of altruism: Perceptions of a common humanity.* Princeton, NJ: Princeton University Press.

Putnam, R. (1995). Bowling alone: America's declining social capital. *Journal of Democracy, 6*(1), 65–79.

Rawls, J. (1971). *A theory of justice.* Cambridge, MA: Belknap Press of Harvard University Press.

Sagan, E. (1988). *Freud, women and morality: The psychology of good and evil.* New York: Basic Books.

Staub, E. (1989). *The roots of evil: The origins of genocide and other group violence.* Cambridge: Cambridge University Press.

Tocqueville, A. de. (1956). *Democracy in America.* New York: New American Library.

Winnicott, D. W. (1986). *Holding and interpretation.* New York: Grove Press.

PART III

Special Areas of Application

12

Institutional Organization of Choice Spaces: A Political Conception of Political Psychology

SIMON JACKMAN
PAUL M. SNIDERMAN
Stanford University

It is uncontroversial that a psychologically oriented study of politics must be politically grounded. Yet it is undeniably controversial whether a politically oriented study of politics can be psychologically grounded. To many students of politics, explanations of political choices that follow from expressly psychological premises, if not strictly a category error, seem reductionist, tone-deaf to what makes politics a distinctive domain of behavior.

Part of the problem is obvious. It is hard to take seriously the claim that psychology should be treated as a foundational science for the study of human behavior when its leading ideas and vocabulary exhibit a rapid fashion cycle. But the problem goes deeper. Real politics involves commitment, values, judgment. Politics is an area of life that can evoke people's deepest emotions: allegiances, identification, the application of their principles to controversial choices, their judgment of the intentions and qualities of allies and opponents—their honesty, trustworthiness, competence, aggressiveness and the like. It would be odd indeed if, to make use of an older language, the study of the passions and the interests had nothing to learn from psychological inquiry.

Accordingly, our objective is constructive, not critical. We begin by outlining, briefly, the principal opposing positions—*internalist* and *externalist*, as we designate them. Then we sketch conceptual machinery to integrate them. "Sketch" is a word we use advisedly. We can describe the shape of the theory we are in the process of developing, not its details, precisely because it is still in the process of development. However, we are far enough down the road to see the outline of the causal story. Political psychology, we suggest, has tried to ground an account of political choice in the psychology of citizens, and for all the variety of ways that psychology itself has been conceived, we think that an account of public opinion should travel in just the opposite direction, from politics to the reasoning of citizens about political choices, not the other way around.

INTERNALIST AND EXTERNALIST PERSPECTIVES

A pair of polar alternatives have dominated the study of political choice—internalism and externalism. These two alternatives are available in more than one version. For the purpose of sketching the logic of each, we have selected a paradigmatic example of each—symbolic politics to epitomize an internalist perspective; rational choice, to illustrate an externalist one. Our aim in juxtaposing the two is not to draw an invidious contrast in favor of one or the other, but rather to suggest a way, through the concept of a choice space, to link each to the other and thereby develop a political conception of political psychology.

A paradigmatic internalist account of political choice is the symbolic political approach. Developed by Sears and his students (e.g., Sears, 1993), it is rooted jointly in the conceptual perspective of Edelman (1964) on the study of symbols and in the empirical approach of Campbell and his colleagues (1960) to the study of voting. The symbolic politics approach rests on a string of propositions: (a) that political choices are rooted in attitudinal or symbolic predispositions, (b) that are normally acquired in early life, (c) remain relatively stable through adult life, and (d) are, at moments of political choice, evoked by particular objects (e) whose evaluative meaning is determined by their symbolic associations, (f) which evoke embedded dispositions on the basis of semantic similarity, (g) through a process that is automatic and affective (Sears, 1993, pp. 121–122).

This string of propositions constitutes the internalist account. Citizens choose as they choose because they have internalized general dispositions —party identification is one example, racial prejudice another. General dispositions operate like an internal gyroscope, leading individuals consistently to respond positively or negatively to a class of political choices. Because symbolic dispositions are highly stable, enduring throughout a citizen's political life even in the face of profound changes in the political world itself or of their own personal experience,[1] the result is a view of political choice neither rational in the sense of maximizing self-interest, nor boundedly rational in the sense of compensating for limited information (Sears, 1993, pp. 135–137), but emotional, reflexive, fixed, indifferent to the substantive clashes over public policy and political leadership that dominate the headlines—above all, internally constrained.

Contrast an externalist account of political choice, the Satz–Ferejohn (1994) formulation of rational choice. Their starting point is a provocative concession. Rational choice theories under any description have enjoyed little explanatory success applied to individual voters.[2] The reason for this lack of success, according to Satz and Ferejohn, is two-fold: individual voters typically face negligible consequences for violations of strict maximization of their interests and, what is not an entirely independent consideration, "There do not seem to be any competitive forces that would act to shape or constrain the kinds of preferences that ordinary citizens hold" (Satz & Ferejohn, 1994, p. 80). Rational choice theories enjoy substantial success by contrast, they argued, applied to political parties because of the clarity of both consequences and competition. From this contrast of the weakness of rational choice theories of voters and their strength as theories of political parties, Satz and Ferejohn derived the claim that rational choice is most successful as an approach to the understanding of political choice when it is in a position to rely on "interests that are determined by features of the agent's environment."[3] The core of an explanation of political choice is thus not internal characteristics of citizens but rather external pressures, or as Satz and Ferejohn (1994) put it, "Rational-choice explanations are most plausible in settings in which individual action is severely constrained, and thus where the theory gets its explanatory power [is] from structure-generated interests and not from actual individual psychology" (p. 72). To their credit, Satz and Ferejohn recognized the irony of their claim—namely, that "the theory of rational choice is most powerful in contexts where choice is limited" (p. 72).

What we believe is distinctive about the approach we propose is that, so far from taking internalist and externalist approaches to be competitive,

---

[1] One mechanism for change is the politics of labelling, which allows issues to evoke different symbolic predispositions depending on media labelling. (See Sears, 1993, pp. 128–129.)

[2] By contrast, Satz and Ferejohn claim that rational choice theories have enjoyed substantial success applied to political parties, and it is the explanation of why rational choice should be instructive at the level of parties but not at that of voters that is the core of their analytic story.

[3] Satz and Ferejohn (1994, p. 81). Or, as they put it in an alternative formulation, "The psychology of the agent in such cases is an entirely imputed one: 'preferences' are derived on the basis of an agent's location in a social structure." (1994, p. 72).

our objective is to integrate them. The concept of a choice space is the vehicle to pull together the two approaches. By a *choice space* we mean the number of alternatives open for consideration by citizens and the arrangement of these alternatives. Consistent with an externalist account, we suggest that political institutions organize citizens' choice spaces, and specifically that the alternatives open for consideration by citizens tend to be coordinated through the logic of party competition so that a large portion of the public can make choices that are approximately rational. On the other hand, consistent with an internalist account, we suggest that citizens characteristically choose between the alternatives open for consideration in the light of their political dispositions, that is, enduring general orientations such as party identification or liberalism–conservatism. The notion of a choice space accordingly provides a mechanism to link the politics of elites with the choices of citizens.

SIMON'S SECOND PUZZLE:
WHERE DO POLITICAL ALTERNATIVES COME FROM?

Simon's first puzzle—we refer, obviously, to Herbert Simon—is how it is possible for decision-makers to make reasonable choices[4] notwithstanding the limit on their informational fund and computational capacities. This puzzle—of how citizens may compensate for informational and computational shortfalls—was at the center of a burgeoning field of research in political psychology in the 1980s. The organizing ideas were straightforward and, for a time, fertile. Citizens spend the largest part of their time and energy, it was agreed on all sides, engaged with concerns about their work, their families, the quality of life in their neighborhoods, the whir of projects and activities of the groups to which they devote so much time, caught up, as it were, in the rhythms of the social life around them. Certainly politics can command their attention, but, as a rule, only under unusual circumstances—for example, scandals at home or crises abroad—and then only for relatively brief periods of time. Accordingly, citizens tend to make political choices with only a limited amount of information. On the assumption that a nontrivial portion of the public nonetheless can make approximately rational choices, the question for research then became "How was this possible?" According to a leading hypothesis, citizens compensate for informational shortfalls by taking advantage of shortcuts in judgment: hence the focus on the role of judgmental heuristics and the notion of "low information rationality."[5]

---

[4]For an explanation of the usage of "reasonable," see Scanlon, 1999.

[5]The notion of "low information rationality" is, from our perspective, an unfortunate one, inasmuch as it suggests a presumption of optimality. When we say that citizens take advantage

The research literature on Simon's first puzzle has, we think, thrown some light on how citizens reason about politics. Elsewhere we have elaborated our criticisms.[6] Citizens are woefully short of useful political knowledge, but a nontrivial fraction of them overcome their informational shortage by taking advantage of judgmental heuristics. But how are they so fortunate as to come by these heuristics? These are, after all, not shortcuts in reasoning that are invoked to explain how they get things wrong, as the heuristics of Kahneman and Tversky (to cite a deservedly celebrated research program in psychology), are invoked to account for errors and biases in judgment (Tversky & Kahneman, 1982). On the contrary, in the literature on political choice, heuristics are mechanisms for making reasonable, even if not necessarily optimal, choices. Isn't it fair to ask, if citizens are so inattentive to politics and so poorly informed about public affairs, why are they so clever at figuring out efficient shortcuts in reasoning about political choices?

The problem here, we suggest, comes from putting the cart before the horse. To understand how citizens make political choices, we must first understand the structure of the political choices that, as citizens, they make. How are political choices organized, and how do they become organized that way and not some other? How many alternatives do citizens characteristically get to choose among—and why that number and not some other? How are the alternatives open for consideration characteristically arranged—and why that arrangement and not some other?

It is this family of questions to which Simon called attention. But he noted that it consisted of not one, but two puzzles. He argued:

> To understand political choices, we need to understand where the frame of reference for the actors' thinking comes from—how it is evoked. An important component of the frame of reference is the set of alternatives that are given consideration in the choice process. We need to understand not only how people reason about alternatives, but where the alternatives come from in the first place. (Simon 1985, p. 302)

The first puzzle is familiar: how citizens "reason about alternatives," notwithstanding their informational shortfalls; but the second puzzle, of "where the alternatives come from in the first place," so far from being familiar, has gone virtually unexplored. An excellent reason that it has gone unexplored is that it seems nearly unsolvable. What would it mean to specify "where the alternatives come from" for a domain of activity like politics

---

of judgmental shortcuts to compensate for informational shortfalls, all that we are suggesting is that they make more reasonable choices than they otherwise would.

[6]See Sniderman (2000).

as seemingly complex, turbulent, conditional, and inescapably open-ended as it is?[7]

We offer a theory of where, from a citizen's frame of reference, the alternatives for political choice come from. Political institutions—above all, political parties—coordinate the alternatives open to citizens for consideration. This coordination of alternatives through political parties characteristically imposes a specific set of properties—bipolarity, stability, and ideological patterning, among them—on the political choices that citizens are asked as citizens to make. On the theory we offer, the solution to both of Simon's puzzles lies in their interdependence. We argue that it is precisely because political institutions, and especially political parties, organize and coordinate citizens' choices that large numbers of citizens are able to take advantage of the judgmental shortcuts and so choose approximately rationally. In short, citizens choose as they do because their choices are organized as they are.

POLITICAL PARTIES AND THE ORGANIZATION OF CHOICE SPACES

We begin with two standard axioms: (a) it is in the interest of candidates to win elections that they contest; (b) an effective strategy for winning elections is for candidates to back proposals for coping with problems of general concern that they believe will appeal to a winning coalition. We refer to this as the standard set-up.

There are two implications of the standard set-up to draw out. The first concerns the role of political parties in large-scale representative democracies. Some electoral offices, particularly at lower levels, are nonpartisan, and rare individuals—Perot, for example—make a run at public office by running against the parties. These exceptions aside, political parties are the channel for electoral office in modern democracies. Political parties, for their part, may have come into being in part to facilitate the efforts of individuals to win public office.[8] Once they are up and running, for an individual to win government office at an election, he must first win the backing of a political party. Parties, in effect, are vote brokers, putting buyers of votes (office-seekers), in touch with sellers of votes (citizens). In this way, parties can be considered as solving a coordination problem.

The second implication concerns the constraints on proposals advanced by candidates for the solution of problems of public concern. Those who

---

[7]Simon offered two pieces of advice, one pointing to Riker's work in political science on heresthetics, the other to recent work in psychology on creativity. We find the former of more use than the latter.

[8]For a summary of arguments along this line, see Aldrich (1995, ch. 2).

win office find themselves having to deal with problems of public concern. The nature of the problem constrains the range of alternatives advanced for consideration, and other things being equal, office-holders should prefer a proposal that they themselves believe will do the job.

These seem to us reasonable premises, roughly consistent with a good deal of actual political experience. Consider, then, three of their implications for the organization of choice spaces for politics. The first concerns the number and arrangement of alternatives for any given issue. Candidates, to be effective, must compete as agents of a political party. Insofar as policy alternatives are identified with political parties, pressures to reduce the number of parties serve to reduce the number of policy alternatives.

In the second place, political choices tend to be framed not merely in terms of dual alternatives, but the alternatives themselves tend to be posed as bipolar. To be in favor of one is to be opposed to the other, and vice versa. This bipolarity constraint, it is worth underlining, is political, not strictly logical, and has its roots in the incentives that political elites have for maintaining unidimensional choice spaces (we return to this issue in a moment). For example, there is no necessity in logic to treat the alternatives of the government doing more to help African Americans, or of African Americans doing more to help to themselves, as contraries.

In the third place, although individual candidates may have an interest in varying policy alternatives, political parties tend to have a longer run interest in preserving them. In political systems like the American, motives —in the form of political ideas—matter, and parties accordingly are organized around them. But since one or the other major party controls entry to public office, individuals must make their way through one of the parties. Insofar as others before them have become active and influential in a party because it is identified with an alternative on policy, individual candidates are under pressure to accommodate their positions to the established views of the party as a whole. Although over the short term, candidate positions may exhibit considerable variation around a long-term party mean, the party-based inertia of policy alternatives lays a basis for the stability of citizens' attachments to parties.

Yet any story of the organization of alternatives for a given issue goes only a short distance analytically. What is crucial is the organization of alternatives across issues. We see political parties as the primary mechanism coordinating alternatives across issues.

First, the logic of party competition ensures that policy alternatives tend to be structured along a left–right continuum, or, equivalently, that choice spaces tend to be unidimensional. It is well known that higher dimensional choice spaces threaten existing party groupings with destabilization, and perhaps even a realignment of the party system itself. When the dimensionality of the choice space exceeds one, partisans who are in reasonable agreement on the dominant left–right ideological dimension could well find themselves in disagreement on issues such as racial tolerance, abortion, gun control, or euthanasia, to name a few. "Coalition management" becomes difficult in the presence of cross-cutting issues, and the threat of partisan realignment increases when such conditions arise. Indeed, in most democracies, elites of the out-party (or out-parties) can be reasonably presumed to be searching for cross-cutting "wedge issues," designed to destabilize the in-party more than they destabilize their own partisans.[9] At the same time, in-parties enjoy considerable agenda-setting power, which they can be reasonably expected to use to maintain the salience of the left–right dimension (that saw them elected in the first place), diminishing the ability of out-parties to pursue wedge issues.

Consider also the nature of the problems for which aspirants for public office must propose solutions. In modern democracies the questions that political candidates and parties have to answer are what governments should do, if indeed it should do anything at all, say, in coping with problems of the economy, or of those who are badly off for a host of reasons, or the character and quality of social life. Furthermore, candidates ultimately have to be effective in dealing problems that they have said they will deal with, if elected. Other things being equal, they will make judgments about what government can do on the basis of their own best guesses about reality—it would be foolish for political leaders to bet against their own best guesses over the long run of a political career. Ideology, so conceived, is a genuine hypothesis—the best guess as to what kind of problem government actually is competent at dealing with and how, supposing it should do something to relieve a public concern, it should go about doing it.

Thinking of ideologies as hypotheses is useful for two reasons. On the one hand, it points to the constraints imposed by reality on political choices. Politicians' interests may be dominated by their self-interest in winning, but self-interest, so far from undercutting ideology, can underpin it. It is necessary to have some ideas to advance, and it is better to be identified with ones that work than with ones that fail. Those who want public office choose the party they will work through for more than one reason, including the chances that their winning a particular office are conditional on joining one rather than another party. But just so far as it is in their interest to be successful if they do win public office, they will choose which party that they

---

[9]Carmines and Stimson (1989) described this process as "issue evolution," whereas Riker (1983, 1984) used the term *heresthetic* to refer to the "art of political strategy" whereby choice spaces are strategically structured so as to lead collective decision-making toward a particular outcome. In addition, scholars such as Sundquist (1983), Poole and Rosenthal (1993), and Inglehart (1977, 1990) all base their accounts of change in American and European party systems around the notion of partisan elites maintaining and organizing coalitions of partisans in ideological spaces.

will work through at least in part on the basis of their own bets on which party's outlook on government, the economy, and society is most likely actually to work. On the other hand, thinking of ideologies as hypotheses points to reality-grounded incentives for political argument. Ideologies are no more than hypotheses or educated guesses, to borrow William Whewell's classic definition (Medawar, 1982). Thus ideologies are inherently contestable both because they are intrinsically uncertain and because they are inescapably incomplete. And just so far as ideologies are inherently contestable, it is not in the power of any side to bring political arguments to an end.

The third factor is a candidate's desire to be persuasive. In any given election, there are different issues about which candidates must develop a persuasive story; some issues are salient for more or less exogenous reasons, whereas other issues have been selected by political leaders for strategic reasons. In either case, candidates require an account of why the particular problem has come about, who or what should be held responsible for it, how it best can be dealt with. Indeed, party ideologies constrain the ways candidates can raise these questions in the first instance. However, imagine if different issues are unconnected, or at least are perceived to be unconnected. Candidates would need to develop different, unconnected stories for each, and the more different and unconnected the stories for each are, the less likely it is that the overall story they want to convey about their being able to deal with problems of public concern is to be comprehensible, let alone persuasive, to the public at large. Other things being equal, it is generally to the advantage of a candidate to appear principled. But insofar as candidates appear to tell quite different stories in response to different issues without being able to appeal to a common core of political principle, they risk appearing to take positions on political issues in a way that is not merely disjointed or capricious but, worse, opportunistic and self-serving. Ideology is a way to coordinate stories across issues by taking advantage of a common store of organizing ideas, rhetorical symbols, and explanatory metaphors. Ideology is a way to connect the dots.

For all these reasons—the logic of party competition, the nature of the public problems that candidates must deal with if elected to public office, their desire to be effective if elected, and to the extent ideological coherence and persuasiveness helps them get elected—political parties in modern democracies characteristically co-ordinate choices across issues on a left-right ideological continuum.

THE STRUCTURE OF CHOICE SPACES
AND THE STRUCTURE OF PUBLIC OPINION

This organization of choice spaces has a number of important implications for the study of public opinion, which we now describe.

The Effectiveness of Heuristics

Our aim is to tie together, through the concept of a choice space, external-ist and internalist accounts of political choice. To this point, we have argued that political parties organize choice spaces, largely via the logic of electoral competition. This organization of choice spaces by political par-ties is the externalist side of our account. Now we wish to turn to the inter-nalist side, and in particular consider the connection between the organi-zation of choice spaces and the effectiveness of judgmental heuristics.

Why do judgmental shortcuts tend work in politics? Why are they effec-tive in compensating for shortfalls in information, helping citizens estimate where the major political actors stand on the issues of the day, and helping citizens locate themselves on those same issues.

It is not, we emphasize, a matter of citizens operating as political theo-rists *manque*, overcoming their shortage of information by devising judg-mental shortcuts to cleverly simplify and organize the political choices before them. It is just the other way around. Citizens can effectively take advantage of judgmental shortcuts just so far as the political choices before them have been simplified and organized. Specifically, it is just so far as pol-icy alternatives tend to be bipolar and coordinated across issues that judg-mental shortcuts like the likability heuristic or party identification work. These heuristics can be thought of as keys to making political choices ap-proximately rationally. Like any key, however, they work only because the locks they fit are have an extremely specialized design. That is, political institutions in mature democracies ensure that the decision problem faced by most citizens is usually no harder that of choosing between two alterna-tives in a low-dimensional (typically unidimensional) space.[10]

In many works expounding the usefulness of heuristics for political psy-chology, reference is made to the "drunkard's search" (e.g., Popkin, 1994, p. 74). A drunken person has lost his or her keys on a dark street. Rather than roam the entire street, the drunkard looks for the keys under a street lamp. Why? Because if the keys are there, they will surely be found! That is, cheap and reliable information on the location of the keys is available under the street lamp. Yet, we question how appropriate this analogy is for mass political behavior. Most of the time, the sorts of political decisions most citizens make are almost trivial compared to the problem of recover-ing lost keys in a dark street.

Replace the drunkard with an "ordinary citizen" who is deciding whom to vote for in a partisan election, or what he or she believes about a given

---

[10]Indeed, many citizens opt out of this decision, abstaining from voting; we think this is less to do with the apparent complexity of the choice they face, and more to do with indifference, ignorance, apathy, or alienation.

political issue. Note immediately that there are just a few places where the keys can be. The search domain is not a darkened street, but more closely resembles a well-lit room, with as few as just two prominently labeled doors. Indeed, it seems a stretch to call our citizen's problem a "search," since it is in reality closer to a binary choice: the ordinary citizen knows that "keys" can be found in either of an extremely limited number of rooms. But one room is close by, its contents familiar (our ordinary citizen has found useful things there before), perhaps even friendly; the other room is further away, relatively unfamiliar, perhaps even threatening. Where, then, do we think our "ordinary citizen" will search? Note that many ostensibly psychological elements are present in this hypothetical example: memory, source attribution, affect, and so on. But what we find compelling is "the nature of the situation," the context of choice, the number and arrangement of alternatives, or, as we term it, the *choice space*.

The Special Role of Party Identification

Our argument stresses that democratic politics is a game played by elites in specific institutional settings; we think this observation ought to guide our conjectures about public opinion and political psychology. We think party identification provides an excellent demonstration of the practical implications of our argument: that the structure of mass political attitudes inexorably follows from the way institutional features structure the choices that elites make.

Consider, for the sake of contrast, the standard conception of party identification. In their classic work, *The American Voter,* Campbell, Converse, Miller, and Stokes (1960) defined party identification as an "affective orientation to an important group object" (p. 121). A trio of properties, on this account, define the political significance of party identification: continuity, both over the life span of individuals and across generations; functionality, allowing citizens to solve information processing and decision problems; and potency, committing voters in the place that counts most politically, the voting booth. So the starting point for the standard story of party identification is socialization by the family, the end point the stability of electoral regimes.

This is a paradigmatic "bottom-up" story, reasoning from the characteristics of citizens to the properties of political systems. Our story of party identification is "top-down," reasoning from the machinery of electoral politics, party systems, to the electoral behavior of citizens. Citizens do not make the political world anew because, save for the most extraordinary of circumstances, they are not required to. The political world is presented to most citizens largely "prefabricated": in mature democracies like the United States, political institutions and actors are well defined, with parties and party leaders figuring prominently. Party identification figures so prominently not because of patterns of childhood socialization, but because political parties are the way that elites have organized competition among themselves for public power.

So viewed, party identification is neither an organic nor a spontaneous development by citizens. Rather, party identification has a substantial top-down component and is not exclusively manufactured by ordinary citizens. Party identification may be an affective orientation to an important group object, but the group object and its importance come from elites and the institutions in which and for which they compete. Just as constitutional arrangements and electoral procedures constrain the number of parties in a given political system (e.g., Riker, 1982), so, too, is the universe of available partisan identities constrained. Party identification is largely determined by elites leading and citizens following: citizens simply cannot identify with parties that do not exist.

We are far from minimizing the contribution, empirical and analytical, of *The American Voter.* We think, on the contrary, that Campbell et al.'s analytic focus is more acute than often appreciated. They did not, it is worth remarking, base their account of American political attitudes and behavior on ideological self-identification, evaluations of candidates, or group membership. Rather, *party* identification occupies center stage in their account. And they demonstrated that party identification could serve as an anchor, holding voters in place over their lives, and act as a prism through which citizens appraise candidates and issue positions, and organize the political world more generally. However, we are persuaded that the parties elites form and the political competition that ensues does most of the hard work for ordinary citizens as they make sense of politics and political conflict.

Recall that our argument is premised on the understanding that elites compete in an ideological or policy space, a choice space, as we have termed it here. The properties of this space follow from the dynamics of party competition. Elites organize into parties and compete ideologically, yet when we analyze citizens' vote choices, we find that most of them parse political competition through the prism of party identification. This dramatically simplifies political competition, reducing what could well be (unstable) high-dimensional ideological conflict at the elite level, to unidimensional conflict or, in the case of a two-party system, bipolar conflict at the level of ordinary citizens. That is, to the extent that ordinary citizens parse elite-level competition through the lens of party identification, then the opportunities for "heresthetic destabilization" (evoking Riker) via the introduction of cross-cutting ideological dimensions are far less than they might be otherwise. Quite simply, partisan identifiers tend not to see a high-dimensional ideological conflict among political elites; they see and participate in a bipolar struggle between "their party" and the "other party" that possibly, although not necessarily, involves a contest between "their ideas" and the other party's ideas.

No less consequentially, via party identification, ordinary citizens wind up interpreting and participating in politics in substantially the same terms that it is conducted at the elite level. Ultimately, political competition is about which group winds up controlling the state; indeed, this is Schatt-schneider's definition of a political party, and bluntly highlights what elites are competing for.[11] In addition, political struggle is ideological at the elite level, but for the most part, each party puts forward a more-or-less agreed upon ensemble of ideas about government. The strategic bundling of these ideas—for example, the selection of issues, and the coordination of stances across issues—a critical component of elite-level politics, is not observed by most citizens. But the results of these processes—the aggregation of political conflict into a choice between a limited number of alternatives—certainly are available to citizens. Party identification is prominent in the political psychology of many citizens precisely because of the way institutions compel elites to conduct politics.

The Dimensionality of Public Opinion

A classic paradox in the study of public opinion is the dimensionality of elite and mass belief systems. The number of dimensions in a political belief system is inversely proportional to the level of political sophistication. Accordingly, among more politically aware and informed citizens, we find fewer distinguishable dimensions in their beliefs about politics; as political information decreases, we tend to find more dimensions.[12]

The robustness of the findings notwithstanding, the result seems puzzling. Isn't complexity a sign of sophistication? Isn't the mark of a person who is genuinely drawn to politics and political ideas a capacity to acknowledge differences, to draw distinctions, to appreciate the plausibility of rival explanations, to recognize the multiplicity of factors at work and the tangled skein of their causal impact in politics and society? How is it that the more attention people pay to public affairs and the better informed they are about them, the simpler the structure of their thinking about politics?

Again, we contend that the answer lies not in the psychology of the ordinary citizen, but in the institutional features of elite politics. Political parties are the gatekeeper organizations for elected office in modern democracies. To get a chance to win the public support necessary to win an elected office, it is first necessary to win the support of a political party. Aspirants

---

[11] In the opening page of the preface to his celebrated *Party Government*, Schattschneider writes, "A political party is an organized attempt to get control of the government" (1977, p. ix).

[12] For example, see Carmines and Stimson (1989, ch. 5).

for elected office need to work within a party to get anywhere. In a word, elites are themselves constrained so far as they must compete for public power through the medium of political parties.

This is not to say that parties are ideologically monolithic or unchanging. Struggles for control of a political party are some of the most important in a democracy: Control of the state is predicated on control of a political party. The contest to control a party is inescapably ideological—a struggle between bearers of competing hypotheses of what makes for good government. On this basis, one might suspect party activists to have complex, multidimensional political ideologies. Yet they do not. And parties tend to cohere and endure more than they dissolve and exit the political stage.

Why? Because after the intraparty competition is said and done, parties are in the business of winning elections, a goal that involves defeating an opposing party. In this sense, party activists are united (perhaps unwillingly) and hence constrained by a larger goal. Internal party struggles can only be tolerated so long before they threaten the party's primary goal, winning elections and control of the state. A party that tolerates prolonged internal ideological struggle is close to conceding electoral defeat, basically handing a wedge to its opponents, and in effect, doing the work of the opponent party on its behalf. Occasionally there are prizes for coming in second in a democracy: Constitutional arrangements may be such that there may be plenty of spoils still available to a party that doesn't win the election.[13] But these exceptions aside, it is still generally the case that more electoral success is better than less, and almost always, electoral success is more likely if the party's internal ideological brawls are put to bed. It follows, then, that in general, the closer citizens get to the elite game of politics—that is, the higher their level of political understanding and political sophistication—the more likely we are to see them understanding politics as elites contest it: unidimensional, or even bipolar in a two-party system.

QUALIFICATIONS AND CONCLUSIONS

Faced with an especially zealous critic, William James once remarked: "I feel as if Mr. Joseph almost pounced on my words singly, without giving the sentences time to get out of my mouth" (Ayer, 1968, p. 175). Throughout

---

[13]For instance, committee chairs are valuable resources in the U.S. Congress, even if the incumbent president is not a fellow partisan. But even obtaining committee chairs requires that one's party obtain a majority of legislative seats. In multiparty systems, ministerial appointments may flow to representatives of minor parties willing to trade their legislative support to a governing coalition, and there may even be incentives in these cases to promote a cross-cutting ideological dimension in these circumstances (e.g., Green parties in European parliaments, and religious parties in the Knesset).

this chapter, we have felt like Joseph rather than James, aware at so many points of incompleteness, vagueness, and potential inconsistencies. If our account is to be genuinely of value, it must be worked out thoroughly, formally. Not only has our argument been presented in embarrassingly skeletal form, its sources have not been properly acknowledged, perhaps the most grievous omissions being those of Schattschneider and Key in political science and Gibson in psychology. To the standard plea of limits of time and space, we add an additional consideration in extenuation: the argument of our chapter in this book has as its principal purpose criticizing the limits of the work of one of us (Sniderman) over the last decade or so. Self-criticism should not require justification, but it does take time, and this project of self-criticism is far from complete.

There is, however, a specific point of self-criticism, not of previous work, but of this very project, that we cannot escape underlining. Our political story centers on the consequences of party competition for the organization of choice spaces—in particular, for the number and arrangement of alternatives open for consideration for any given issue and across issues. Our story line centers on the incentives that candidates for public office, who must work through political parties to compete for public office, have to develop contrasting alternatives for citizens to consider. Sometimes they do not. Sometimes one party, typically the one disadvantaged on a dimension of choice, assimilates rather than contrasts its position to that of the other. More broadly, we have accented one set of institutional incentives favoring ideological divergence between the parties. There are, of course, countervailing incentives owing to the logic of electoral competition that see voters targeting the median voter. Finally, we note that some political choices are not as easy as others. Our running example has been vote choice in a partisan election given a small number of parties. More difficult cases are easily imagined, for example, primary elections in the United States, or multiparty elections in European democracies.

These qualifications noted, we want to underline the principal themes in our argument. A political theory of public choice should begin, not with psychological theories of how citizens go about choosing between alternatives, but rather with the question of where the alternatives come from in the first place. In representative democracies, citizens do not directly choose the alternatives; they choose between the alternatives open to them for consideration. Delimiting and coordinating these alternatives is the work of political institutions, above all, of the party system. To recognize how political parties define the number and arrangement of alternatives open for consideration by citizens is not at all to write off the importance of a theory of how they come to choose between them. It is, however, to insist that how people solve a problem depends on the structure of the problem that they are attempting to solve. It follows that to give a proper account of how citizens go about choosing between political alternatives, it is first necessary to give an account of how political institutions coordinate the number and arrangement of alternatives open for their consideration.

REFERENCES

Aldrich, J. H. (1995). *Why parties?: The origin and transformation of party politics in America.* Chicago: University of Chicago Press.

Ayer, A. J. (1968). *The origins of pragmatism.* San Francisco: Freeman, Cooper.

Campbell, A., Converse, P. E., Miller, W. E., & Stokes, D. E. (1960). *The American voter.* New York: Wiley.

Carmines, E. G., & Stimson, J. A. (1989). *Issue evolution: Race and the transformation of American politics.* Princeton: Princeton University Press.

Edelman, M. (1964). *The symbolic uses of politics.* Urbana: University of Illinois Press.

Inglehart, R. (1977). *The silent revolution.* Ann Arbor: University of Michigan Press.

Inglehart, R. (1990). *Culture shift in advanced industrial society.* Princeton, NJ: Princeton University Press.

Medawar, P. (1982). *Plato's Republic.* New York: Oxford University Press.

Poole, K. T., & Rosenthal, H. (1993). Spatial realignment and the mapping of issues in American history. In W. H. Riker (Ed.), *Agenda formation* (pp. 13–29). Ann Arbor: University of Michigan Press.

Popkin, S. L. (1994). *The reasoning voter* (2nd ed.). Chicago: University of Chicago Press.

Riker, W. H. (1982). The two-party system and Duverger's Law: An essay on the history of political science. *American Political Science Review, 76,* 753–766.

Riker, W. H. (1983). Political theory and the art of heresthetics. In A. W. Finifter (Ed.), *Political science: The state of the discipline* (pp. 47–67). Washington, DC: American Political Science Association.

Riker, W. H. (1984). The heresthetics of constitution-making. *American Political Science Review, 78,* 1–16.

Satz, D., & Ferejohn, J. (1994). Rational choice and social theory. *The Journal of Philosophy, 91*(2), 71–87.

Scanlon, T. (1999). *What we owe to each other.* Cambridge, MA: Harvard University Press.

Schattschneider, E. E. (1977). *Party government.* Westport, CT: Greenwood Press. (Original work published 1942)

Sears, D. O. (1993). Symbolic politics. In S. Iyengar & W. J. McGuire (Eds.), *Explorations in political psychology* (pp. 113–149). Durham, NC: Duke University Press.

Simon, H. A. (1985). Human nature in politics: The dialogue of psychology with political science. *American Political Science Review, 72,* 293–304.

Sniderman, P. M. (2000). Taking sides: A fixed choice theory of political reasoning. In A. Lupia, M. McCubbins, & S. Popkin (Eds.), *Elements of political reason: Understanding and expanding the limits of rationality* (pp. 67–84). New York: Cambridge University Press.

Sundquist, J. L. (1983). *Dynamics of the party system: Alignment and realignment of political parties in the United States* (Rev. ed.). Washington, DC: Brookings Insitution.

Tversky, A., & Kahneman, D. (1982). Judgement under uncertainty: Heuristics and biases. In D. Kahneman, P. Slovic, & A. Tversky (Eds.), *Judgement under uncertainty: Heuristics and biases* (pp. 3–20). Cambridge, UK: Cambridge Universty Press.

13

On-Line Versus Memory-Based Process Models of Political Evaluation

State University of New York at Stony Brook

> *Nothing in science—nothing in life, for that matter—makes sense without theory. It is our nature to put all knowledge into context in order to tell a story and to re-create the world by this means.* —E. O. Wilson, 1998, p. 56

Political psychology, as an interdisciplinary pursuit, applies psychological concepts and methods to test theories about elite and mass political behavior. Traditionally, much of the borrowing has been from the subfields of personality and social psychology, and more recently with the "new look" of the information processing perspective, from the subfield of social cognition (Kinder, 1998a; Lodge, 1995; McGuire, 1993). As the cognitive perspective has been steadily absorbed into the mainstream of political psychology over the last decade, political scientists have become increasingly concerned not only with behavioral outcomes (matters of *what* and *when*) but with the cognitive processes that produce them (matters of *how* and *why*). By appropriating the theoretical frameworks and methodological tools developed by psychologists, political scientists have begun to pry open the black box of cognitive processes that connect the causes and consequences of political behavior (e.g., Huckfeldt, Levine, Morgan, & Sprague, 1999; Lavine, Thomsen, & Gonzales, 1997; Lodge, McGraw, & Stroh, 1989; Zaller, 1992; Zaller & Feldman, 1992). In doing so, political scientists stand to gain a more complete understanding of *how* personality and the political environment, as well as values, beliefs, and attitudes, guide political choices.

Cognitive processes (i.e., mental operations used to make judgments and guide behaviors) have long been accorded a central role in psychological theories of social perception, attitude formation and change, and behavior (e.g., Bartlett, 1932; Heider, 1958; James, 1890; McDougall, 1908). However, because cognitive processes are not directly observable, they cannot be measured directly or easily. What distinguishes contemporary political psychology from traditional studies of political behavior is the relatively more formal way in which such unobservable processes are treated. Traditional research has generally inferred the existence of cognitive processes on the basis of overt behavioral data (e.g., Kelley & Mirer, 1974; for a review within the candidate appraisal domain, see Lodge, Stroh, & Wahlke, 1990). By using outcome data (i.e., behavior) to explore questions of process (i.e., cognitive processing), traditional research has, in effect, employed stimulus–response (S–R) methodologies to test stimulus–organism–response (S–O–R) models of political behavior. In contrast, the thrust of the information processing perspective is to provide more conceptual models of—and consequently more direct and detailed evidence for—the mediating role of cognitive processes.

In this chapter, I review information processing or "process" models of political opinion formation. I begin with the argument that traditional studies of opinion consisted primarily of S–R models concerned with *prediction* and were relatively silent with respect to *explanation*. I then delineate the ingredients required for developing and testing S–O–R models of opinion formation in which the causal chain of psychological events is brought into sharper theoretical and empirical focus. I focus specifically on examples of "memory-based" and "on-line" models of opinion formation, and I consider such factors as respondent dispositions, variation in the types of attitude objects studied (e.g., issues vs. candidates), and the political context, that regulate how political information is encoded and represented in memory, as well as the cognitive processes that operate on these representations to produce opinions. I also suggest new directions for increasing the explanatory power of public opinion models through the specification and measurement of information processing.

The study of opinion formation provides a useful context for contrasting S–R (predictive) and S–O–R (explanatory) models. The traditional S–R question is: "What ingredients underlie the formation of attitudes toward political policies and candidates and form the basis of political behavior?" The seminal studies of voting behavior (e.g., *The People's Choice, The American Voter*) —consisting principally of predictive frameworks organized around sociological, social psychological, or rational-choice themes—have been a resounding success in answering this question (for a review, see Lodge et al., 1990). To wit, these frameworks can account for upwards of 95% of the variance in vote choice (e.g., Enelow & Hinich, 1984; Kelley, 1983; Kelley &

Mirer, 1974; Kinder, 1986). The predominate causal ingredients appear to include partisanship, issue proximity, and judgments of character. However, in distinguishing between content and process in public opinion, Kinder (1998a) recently noted that "Identifying the ingredients that go into public opinion and determining their relative importance is a real accomplishment, but it tells us nothing about how citizens assemble their views, about how they put the various ingredients together" (p. 812). Such S–O–R (*how* rather than *what*) questions have proved more complex at the conceptual level and much more difficult to substantiate at the empirical level. They require a theory about how political information is encoded, cognitively represented in memory, retrieved, and formatted to guide political choices.

Cognitive process models of public opinion can be roughly divided into two theoretical traditions, referred to as *memory-based* and *on-line* models (Hastie & Park, 1986; Kinder, 1998b; Lodge et al., 1989; Lodge & Stroh, 1993). Proponents of the two schools make different assumptions about the manner in which political information is represented in the cognitive system and about the processes that underlie the construction of opinions. All memory-based models make the implicit assumption that citizens' conscious *recollections* of issue and candidate information mediate political judgments. In this way, public opinion is hypothesized to be constrained by *memory*—by citizens' capacity to recall what they like and dislike about political issues and candidates as they enter the voting booth or when they are asked to express an opinion in a survey.[1] In contrast, proponents of on-line models argue that citizens spontaneously extract the evaluative implications of political information as soon as they are exposed to it, integrate these implications into an ongoing summary counter or running tally, and then proceed to forget the nongist descriptive details of the information. Thus, judgments are not constrained by the pros and cons citizens can subsequently recollect; to express an opinion, they need only to retrieve from long-term memory the current value of the summary counter (Lodge, Steenbergen, & Brau, 1995).

In what follows, I review these two divergent process models of public opinion, one of which has been tested largely within the realm of policy attitudes, the other tested in the domain of candidate evaluation. An interesting implication of this analysis is that if, in their pure form, each of these models is to be accepted, citizens would be viewed as utilizing strikingly different information processing strategies in forming opinions about political *policies* on one hand and political *candidates* on the other. After laying

---

[1]It should be noted that although traditional models of vote choice did not explicitly address the cognitive mechanisms involved, they can all be classified as memory-based models in that the mix of pro and con information in memory mediate candidate evaluations.

out the assumptions of each model and the principle data supporting its validity, I present arguments both in favor of and against the likelihood that citizens have evolved qualitatively different approaches for evaluating issues and candidates. I then sketch the outlines of a contingent model of opinion processes in which citizen predispositions (e.g., related to capacity and motivation), situational factors, and qualities of the attitude object regulate whether opinion formation will follow a memory-based, an on-line, or a hybrid process.

ATTITUDES TOWARD POLICY ISSUES

Investigators of public opinion have gained valuable theoretical insights into the nature and functioning of policy attitudes by focusing on how citizens generate survey responses (e.g., Tourangeau & Rasinski, 1988; Zaller & Feldman, 1992). Traditionally, policy attitudes are conceptualized as evaluations that exist in memory in "precomputed" or summary form (e.g., "capital punishment is bad," "affirmative action is good"). That is, once citizens initially form an opinion, "good" or "bad" summary labels or "affective tags" become attached to it, and these affective tags are directly retrieved from long-term memory when survey responses are requested (for reviews, see Feldman, 1995; Lavine, Huff, Wagner, & Sweeney, 1998). Once an initial attitude is formed and the corresponding affective tag is attached to the issue in long-term memory, the future retrieval and use of the opinion does not require a revisiting of the original considerations on which the summary evaluation was based. In fact, the considerations themselves may be forgotten altogether as they are no longer relevant or functional (Lodge et al., 1989; Lodge & Taber, 2000).

Recently, however, this direct retrieval model has been challenged. Specifically, theorists have disputed the notion that most citizens have available in memory precomputed policy opinions with direct retrieval access for the myriad of issues of interest to social scientists and survey researchers (Huckfeldt et al., 1999; Zaller, 1992; Zaller & Feldman, 1992). Given the pessimistic view of the average citizen's capability and motivation in the political realm (e.g., "awash in ignorance," see Kinder, 1998a), the precomputed/direct retrieval model seems highly implausible (Feldman, 1995). The new view is that opinions are episodically constructed on the basis of whatever considerations are momentarily salient.[2] From this *episodic-constructionist* perspective, the survey response process consists of four sequential stages: interpretation of the question, canvassing of memory for relevant consid-

---

[2]Salience is determined by features of the external environment as well as by individual differences in the importance of political issues.

erations and retrieval of the most accessible ones, integration of the beliefs to formulate a coherent—albeit, temporary—opinion, and the editing of a response (Feldman, 1995; Tourangeau & Rasinski, 1988, Wilson & Hodges, 1992; Zaller & Feldman, 1992). In doing so, rather than retrieving a representative sample of considerations, people tend to oversample from whichever considerations are most accessible at the time.[3]

That the accessibility of underlying considerations varies within individuals over time renders the attitude response process probabilistic: the valence of the belief elements retrieved from memory and used to construct an attitude at Time 1 can differ greatly from those used to construct the attitude at Time 2 (for examples, see Feldman & Zaller, 1992). The probabilistic nature of the memory search can explain two noted vagaries in studies of public opinion that the direct retrieval model cannot accommodate: the temporal instability of policy attitudes, and the occurrence of response effects.[4] The former refers to the well-known finding that the stochastic component in statistical estimates of attitude stability is often large (Achen, 1975; Converse, 1964; Erikson, 1979; Feldman, 1989, 1995). The latter refers to the equally well-known finding that variations in question form, order, or content can exert nontrivial effects on responses to subsequently encountered survey items (Bishop, 1990; Krosnick & Schuman, 1988; Schuman & Presser, 1981). Theoretically, each of these effects occurs as a result of variation in the considerations that citizens use in constructing their opinions. For example, attitudes will be unstable over time to the extent that the considerations that are accessible at Time 1 are different in valence from those that are accessible at Time 2. Similarly, response effects are likely to occur when variation in the content of surveys (or variations in exposure to elite discourse on an issue) leads to the activation of different sets of considerations (with different valences) and therefore alters the ingredients used to construct policy opinions (e.g., Kinder & Sanders, 1990; Tourangeau et al., 1989).

By focusing on the cognitive processes that underlie survey responses, political psychologists have fundamentally changed their views of the nature and functioning of public opinion (Feldman, 1995; Zaller, 1992). Perhaps most important, the episodic-constructionist view implies that citizens are

---

[3]Accessibility is based on individual differences in the long-term salience or centrality of particular political beliefs (chronic accessibility; e.g., political ideology) as well as the extent to which the external environment (e.g., the framing effects of elite discourse) activates particular beliefs (temporary accessibility; see Lavine, Sullivan, Borgida, & Thomsen, 1996).

[4]Both the nonattitude (Converse, 1964) and error measurement models (Achen, 1975) also explain temporal instability. However, the error measurement model does not address the question of response effects, and the nonattitude thesis does not consistently predict differential susceptibility to response effects based on attitude strength (Bassili & Krosnick, 2000; Bishop, 1990; Krosnick & Schuman, 1988; Lavine et al., 1998; Tourangeau et al., 1989).

unlikely to possess any one "true" policy attitude; instead, they may be thought to possess a distribution of possible attitudes (based on a distribution of considerations with fluctuating activation levels), depending on the valence and extremity of each available consideration and the likelihood that a given consideration will be used in constructing the opinion. The activation values of the considerations vary over time as a function of the content of elite discourse, media coverage, and salient political events in addition to the chronic accessibility of issue-relevant and more general (e.g., partisanship, ideology) beliefs and predispositions (Zaller, 1992). The episodic-constructionist perspective also implies that political opinions lack the durability traditionally ascribed to them. Within this framework, opinions are constructed to satisfy a specific goal (e.g., to guide the assessment of political candidates, to respond to a survey question, to participate in a political debate), and once that goal is satisfied, they decay in memory. If the opinion becomes relevant to a goal at a future time, it must be recomputed on the basis of available considerations and is subject to the influence of chronic and temporary belief accessibility.

The validity of the episodic-constructionist model of policy opinion formation is bolstered by recent work indicating that the occurrence of context effects in surveys depends on attitude strength. Specifically, when opinions are held with high levels of certainty, importance, and extremity, Lavine et al. (1998) found survey responses on policy issues to be relatively impervious to variations in the content of prior items. It seems reasonable to argue that policy attitudes about which people are certain and that are held with intense affect are influenced not only by context-driven (i.e., temporary) accessibility—based on political events or variation in the content of prior items—but also by the long-term or chronic accessibility of internal inputs. That is, in addition to contextual influences, citizens with strong opinions toward a given issue should reliably draw on a chronically accessible set of core feelings and beliefs in the construction of their attitudes. In contrast, citizens with relatively weak opinions should base their responses to a greater extent on the integration of feelings and beliefs made accessible by contextually (i.e., externally) provided cues. Because chronically accessible beliefs are relatively context independent, individuals with strong opinions should be less likely to succumb to response effects than those with weak opinions.[5]

---

[5]The moderating effects of attitude strength on the susceptibility to response effects have been tested in the past with negative results (e.g., Bishop, 1990; Krosnick & Schuman, 1988). Lavine et al. (1998) argued that the failure of these studies to find strength-moderated effects is due to a variety of methodological considerations, primary among which are measurement issues associated with the reliability and validity of the assessment of attitude strength (although see Bassili & Krosnick, 2000).

The possibility that attitude strength regulates the occurrence and/or magnitude of response effects (see Lavine et al., 1998; Tourangeau et al., 1989) provides the first steps toward a more contingent view of the cognitive processes that underlie the formation and subsequent retrieval/ expression of policy attitudes. Specifically, opinion formation processes may differ qualitatively across levels of attitude strength such that opinion objects with strong affective tags attached to them conform to the traditional view of attitudes as stable constructs stored in memory in summary form with direct retrieval capacity (see Lodge & Taber, 2000). Weak attitudes, in contrast, are likely to conform to the contemporary episodic-constructionist view (Zaller & Feldman, 1992), where the canvassing and integration of considerations is required to compute a temporary attitude. An implication of this dual-process perspective is that the opinion formation process (direct retrieval vs. episodic construction) should differ both across individuals, within individuals over time, and across policy domains. For example, individuals should possess precomputed opinions with relatively easy direct retrieval access for their most cherished opinions. Think of citizens who are behaviorally involved in the abortion debate. Do we suppose that these individuals need to bring to mind a list of pro and con considerations to inform their responses? For other (most?) issues, however, they should find it necessary to engage in the memory canvassing and belief integration stages of the episodic model to *construct* temporary opinions. Moreover, as I develop more fully next, variation in issue salience brought about by attention from political elites and the media may also alter the cognitive processes through which opinions are formed and expressed.

ATTITUDES TOWARD POLITICAL CANDIDATES

I have suggested that the formation of policy attitudes may be mediated by the integration of evaluative information generated from a probabilistic memory search (e.g., Lavine et al., 1998; Zaller & Feldman, 1992). Within this framework, policy attitudes would consist of temporary constructions based on situationally salient recollections. Contemporary process models of candidate evaluation offer a very different theoretical framework for understanding how received information is translated into expressed preferences (for in-depth discussions, see Lodge, 1995; Lodge & Stroh, 1993).

Proponents of on-line models make three distinct information processing assumptions related respectively to the encoding, representation, and retrieval of impression-related information: The important encoding assumption is that when exposed to campaign information, citizens immediately extract and separate the evaluative (i.e., "good" or "bad") implications from the descriptive content within which it is embedded. Once the relevant (i.e., evaluative) aspects of the information are extracted, they are integrated into a running tally that summarizes the voter's current affective response to the candidate. In contrast, the purely descriptive aspects of the information are not given the additional thought necessary to form long-term memory traces as they no longer facilitate the goal of forming an impression (see Higgins, Rholes, & Jones, 1977; Lodge et al., 1989; Wyer & Srull, 1986).

Consistent with the view that the average citizen's store of political information is rather meager (for a recent review, see Kinder, 1998a), the on-line model's memorial assumption consists of little more than the notion of the cumulative affective tally. The selective retention of evaluative implications —with little memory for the raw data—explains why citizens can make reasonably informed voting decisions without knowing (i.e., remembering) much about politics. The cumulative affective tally is then assumed to be directly retrieved from long-term memory and reported as the candidate evaluation (e.g., NES thermometer rating) or used as the principle basis of the vote decision. Laboratory experiments conducted by Lodge and his Stony Brook associates (e.g., Lodge et al., 1989; Lodge et al., 1995; McGraw, Lodge, & Stroh, 1990) demonstrated that affective tallies of the candidates can be predicted reasonably well from the valence of candidate information presented to respondents, who, after a short distraction, are unable to recall or recognize many of the considerations that entered into the evaluation. In particular, when participants are instructed to form an impression (rather than to simply attempt to remember the information), the correlation between memory for candidate information and summary candidate evaluation is vanishingly small. The absence of a strong memory–judgment relation suggests that respondents do not construct on-the-spot candidate evaluations from items of recalled information; rather, it is consistent with the on-line model's assumptions of real-time evaluation and the direct retrieval of the summary counter, followed by the voters' inability to recall the raw data on which it was based.

Although the data from laboratory experiments are supportive of the on-line framework, contemporary research on the structure and function of affect suggests that the representation and retrieval assumptions of the on-line model may be theoretically misspecified. Specifically, the on-line model holds that a unidimensional bipolar summary candidate attitude is constructed during the course of an election campaign. Each salient item of evaluation, whether positive or negative, is integrated into a single overall impression of the candidate. However, there is increasing evidence that individuals maintain *separate* stores of positive and negative affect toward a wide variety of social objects, including political candidates, issues, and groups (see Abelson, Kinder, Peters, & Fiske, 1982; Cacioppo & Gardner, 1999;

Cacioppo, Gardner, & Berntson, 1997; Feldman & Zaller, 1992; Katz & Hass, 1988; Lavine, 2001; Lavine, Thomsen, Zanna, & Borgida, 1998; Meffert, Guge, & Lodge, 2000; Thompson, Zanna, & Griffin, 1995). Thus, affect toward political candidates as well as issues and groups is likely to be represented in bidimensional unipolar terms (i.e., positive *and* negative) rather than in unidimensional bipolar terms (i.e., very negative to very positive).

Beyond the question of structure, evidence for the *functional* separation of positive and negative affect has now been observed at a variety of levels, from studies of asymmetrical cortical processing of positive and negative affect (Davidson, Ekman, Saron, Senulis, & Friesen, 1990) to brain imaging studies in which positive and negative affect produce increased blood flow in distinguishable brain regions (George et al., 1995) to verbal self-reports (Abelson et al., 1982; Cacioppo et al., 1997; Marcus & MacKuen, 1993; Nelson, 1999). Within the candidate appraisal context, both Abelson et al. (1982) and Marcus and MacKuen (1993) found that the positive and negative emotions engendered by presidential candidates constitute separate (and virtually uncorrelated) dimensions of evaluation rather than endpoints of the same candidate affect continuum (for a methodological critique of the bidimensional model, see Green & Citrin, 1994; Green, Goldman, & Salovey, 1993). Similarly, Nelson's (1999) analysis of the structure of attitudes toward social groups revealed substantial independence in ratings of positive and negative affect, even after systematic error variance (which can spuriously create bidimensionality; see Green et al., 1993) is taken into account. Positivity and negativity are thus not simply the obverse of one another (as in the bipolar model), but constitute separate affective responses that can vary independently of one another.

If the bidimensionality assumption is correct—if degrees of liking *and* disliking are represented along separate dimensions of evaluation—the bipolar representational assumption of the on-line model needs to be revised. To reflect bidimensionality, the model would require that voters construct separate tallies of positive and negative affect. Given the strength of the evidence, this would not seem to be too unreasonable a proposition. It does, however, raise two interesting questions: How are the two affect stores integrated (and when)? Do positive and negative affect serve qualitatively different functions in the appraisal of political candidates? The most straightforward answer to the first question is that the positive and negative summary counters are simply averaged together into an overall evaluation (Anderson, 1981). Alternatively, reflecting the finding that negative information exerts a greater influence on judgments than positive information (e.g., Klein, 1996; Lau, 1985), the negative tally may be weighted more heavily in the averaging process. A third possibility is that the weights are determined by their relative accessibility at the time a judgment is rendered. Consistent with the literature on response effects, short-term political events (e.g., the Gulf War) or media coverage (e.g., *Newsweek* magazine's cover story on Carter's failed foreign policy one week before the 1980 election) can heighten the salience of positive or negative affect, thereby altering overall summary judgments. This injects a significant memory-based stage into an otherwise on-line judgment process. Context-based variation in the accessibility of positive and negative affect stores may exert particularly strong effects on the judgments of highly ambivalent voters (i.e., those with strong positive and negative affective tallies). Theoretically, voters with many likes *and* dislikes toward a candidate should fluctuate the most across contexts, thereby reducing the reliability of the candidate evaluation process among these voters (Lavine, in press).

The bidimensional model also allows for the possibility that positive and negative affect serve different cognitive and behavioral functions. According to physiological theories of motivation and personality (e.g., Gray, 1987), negative affect serves to disrupt ongoing behavior and promote attention to potential threat, and is sensitive to signals of punishment and novelty. Negative affect thus regulates aversive motivation (Carver & White, 1994). In contrast, positive affect is involved in the initiation of goal-directed behavior and is sensitive to reward and the escape from punishment. Positive affect thus regulates appetitive motivation. One functional affective distinction in the candidate appraisal realm is based on Marcus and MacKuen's (1993) model of the different roles that anxiety (negative affect) and enthusiasm (positive affect) play in organizing voting behavior. Specifically, anxiety promotes systematic processing of information in order to reduce threat and mediates political learning, whereas enthusiasm promotes political involvement and directly guides vote choice. Their analyses of the 1980 and 1988 presidential elections strongly support the independence of function hypothesis: positive affect strongly predicted candidate preference across three waves of the 1988 election campaign; it also predicted increased involvement over the course of the 1980 campaign. Negative affect, in contrast, was not associated with these variables. However, high negative affect shifted the basis of candidate preference from the general heuristic of partisanship to more specific candidate-centered factors and positively predicted learning about the candidates' issue positions over the course of the campaign. Positive affect, however, was not linked to these processes.

A CONTINGENT MODEL OF PUBLIC OPINION PROCESSES: WHICH PROCESS, WHEN?

Thus far, this review has highlighted two qualitatively different processing routes through which political opinions may be formed. The memory-based (episodic-constructionist) model highlights the reliance on memory and the probabilistic and constructive nature of the attitude response process. It emphasizes the notion that most citizens do not have preformed opinions about most political issues, but instead must retrieve and integrate accessible considerations on the spot. The model provides a strong theoretical account for both response effects in attitude surveys and for the instability of opinions over time (Feldman, 1995; Lavine, 2001). Moreover, its memory-based assumptions are in accord with many theorists' views of the political information processing proclivities of average citizens. The on-line model emphasizes a more goal-directed and efficient political information processor. It assumes that citizens have spontaneous affective responses to political actors and events and that they maintain and update a single summary evaluation toward each candidate as new information becomes available throughout the course of an election campaign. From a normative standpoint, the on-line processing of candidate information is highly efficient. It allows voters to focus on and extract out the most relevant (i.e., evaluative) aspects of the booming buzz of campaign rhetoric. It also minimizes response instability and potential judgment error by eliminating the probabilistic nature of the attitude response process. Finally, the summary counter provides an interpretive framework through which subsequent (often ambiguous) information can be decoded.

A review of the literature on cognitive process models of opinion formation (Kinder, 1998a) provides numerous examples of the putative occurrence of both memory-based and on-line processing. The questions I wish to pursue here are: Under what circumstances are opinions formed through a memory-based process, and under what circumstances are they formed through an on-line process? Moreover, are there contexts within which hybrid processes (i.e., those that combine elements of each of the pure models) occur? Two general determinants of processing mode are likely to be ability and motivation (for similar distinctions in the persuasion and attitude–behavior relations literatures, see Chaiken, Liberman, & Eagly, 1989; Fazio, 1990; Petty & Cacioppo, 1986). On-line processing requires more of both (see McGraw et al., 1990; Rahn, Aldrich, & Borgida, 1994). Directly retrievable summary opinions require that citizens possess both the willingness (and in some cases the ability) to attend to politics and to form evaluative responses toward political objects. Moreover, they require that summary opinions be of sufficient accessibility to guide political choices (Fazio & Williams, 1986). In effect, then, predictions about processing mode are tantamount to identifying the factors that promote the motivation and ability of citizens to form political evaluations in an on-line manner.

What are the major causes of ability and motivation? Fortunately, political psychologists have been exploring this question for some time. Much of the extant research has focused on individual differences. A wealth of research in political cognition points to the fact that substantial individual differences exist in both the ingredients and the processes that citizens use to make sense of the political world (e.g., Fiske, Kinder, & Larter, 1983; Lavine et al., 1997; Luskin, 1987; McGraw et al., 1990; Sniderman, Brody, & Tetlock, 1991). Thus, in developing a contingent model of opinion processes, my first hypothesis is that robust differences exist in the extent to which citizens are both motivated and able to extract out in "real time" the evaluative implications of issue- and candidate-based information and update a summary counter (i.e., engage in on-line processing). Because of their greater interest in politics, sophisticates should be especially motivated to selectively focus on the evaluative implications of political information in order to form impressions of candidates and attitudes toward policy issues (Hastie & Park, 1986; McGraw et al., 1990). Moreover, as a result of their relatively elaborate political knowledge structures and efficient, well-rehearsed information processing capabilities (e.g., Fiske et al., 1983; McGraw & Pinney, 1990), sophisticates should be better equipped than their less sophisticated counterparts to perform the cognitive operations necessary to engage in on-line processing.

Experimental work underscores the sophistication hypothesis. McGraw et al. (1990) found that respondents' on-line summary counter (operationalized in terms of reactions to a fictitious candidate's policy positions) was a much stronger predictor of candidate evaluations among sophisticates than nonsophisticates. Moreover, there was some evidence that nonsophisticates utilized memory-based processing in their candidate evaluations. In contrast to sophisticates (who relied on information presented to them both early and later in the experiment), nonsophisticates relied disproportionately on later-provided information. This "recency" effect suggests that nonsophisticated respondents relied heavily on information that was most accessible in memory in forming a candidate evaluation. That is, nonsophisticates relied on the evaluative implications of whatever subset of information they could recall at the time the judgment was requested.

In addition to individual differences in sophistication, situational factors can also influence processing motivation and ability, and thus determine the processing mode through which opinions are formed. One well-known factor within this category is the processing objective or goal of the individual. Among the most robust findings in the experimental person perception literature is that explicit instructions to form or update an impression of a target person increases the motivation to engage in on-line processing (e.g., Hastie & Park, 1986; Rahn, 1995). Under these circumstances, the memory–judgment relationship is typically severely attenuated, whereas on-line tallies are highly predictive of overall impressions. In contrast, when the processing goal is to merely learn or memorize the information, evaluative extraction and on-line updating are less likely to occur, and judgments are more strongly correlated with the evaluative implications of recalled information (Hastie & Park, 1986; Lodge et al., 1989).

Both the motivation and ability to form summary opinions would seem to be greater within the context of forming opinions toward candidates than toward issues. First, we spontaneously make trait inferences from observed behaviors in everyday impression formation situations (see Wyer & Srull, 1986). The evaluative extraction of person information is thus likely to be a well-rehearsed cognitive process. Second, attitudes toward political candidates serve specific behavioral functions that are typically not relevant (or as relevant) to policy attitudes. Specifically, summary candidate evaluations serve as the primary basis for vote choice (e.g., Rahn, Aldrich, Borgida, & Sullivan, 1990). Given the direct causal connection between candidate attitudes and the most important form of political behavior, it is in the voter's best interests to process political information efficiently— that is, on-line.

Is the candidate versus issue distinction thus a basic one in terms of processing mode? That is, to express a policy attitude, must individuals necessarily retrieve and integrate temporarily accessible items of information from memory, whereas to express a candidate attitude they need merely to retrieve a preformed, updated affective tally? Alternatively, is the distinction confounded with such factors as the behavioral relevance of the opinion? I suspect that although *on average* the candidate opinion formation process may possess more on-line features than the issue opinion formation process, the latter can, under particular conditions, become fully on-line. Attitudes toward political policies should be formed on-line under two conditions: when they are to serve as an important if not the primary basis of political behavior, and when they become the focus of national political debate. The evaluative implications of policy information should be extracted at the moment of encoding and used to form and update a summary counter when a highly publicized and debated referendum is included on the ballot during an election campaign.[6] Within the referendum context, policy attitudes serve the same behavioral function as candidate attitudes do in an election context. Thus, when policy attitudes are attached to a well-specified behavioral goal, on-line processing becomes more normatively functional.

The issue versus candidate distinction could be pitted against the behavioral relevance of the opinion within a 2 (opinion type: issues vs. candidates) × 2 (behavioral relevance: low vs. high) experimental design. Indicators of processing mode (e.g., the memory–judgment correlation, attitude accessibility) would serve as dependent variables. The issue-type hypothesis holds

---

[6]This assumes, of course, that the individual is aware of and sufficiently interested in casting a vote on the referendum.

that the memory–judgment relation should be stronger for issues than for candidates (indicating more memory-based processing for issues than candidates) whereas respondents' evaluation of the presented information should correlate more strongly with attitudes toward candidates than attitudes toward issues (indicating more on-line processing for candidates than issues). By contrast, the behavioral relevance hypothesis holds that on-line versus memory-based variation in opinion processing depends not on whether the attitude object is an issue or a candidate, but on *whether* and *how* that attitude is to be used in a behavioral context. Specifically, the behavioral relevance hypothesis predicts that the memory–judgment relation should be stronger when the behavioral relevance of the attitude is low than when it is high, whereas evaluations of the presented information should correlate more strongly with attitudes when the behavioral relevance of the attitude is high than when it is low. The behavioral relevance perspective reflects the pragmatic Jamesian notion that "thinking is for doing" (see Fiske, 1992).

The formation of policy attitudes is also more likely to occur on-line when a policy domain occupies center stage in the national political debate. Public opinion on an issue should crystallize when it attracts the attention of political elites and the media. For example, Iyengar and Kinder (1987; Krosnick & Kinder, 1990) have shown that increased television news coverage of an issue heightens both its perceived importance on the national agenda and its electoral influence. What is important for the present purposes is the possibility that elite and media attention to an issue increases citizens' motivation to think about and elaborate on the issue, to form an opinion on the issue, and to discuss the issue with others in their social networks. The important mechanism here is that these processes should heighten the frequency of "evaluative repetition," or the number of times that the evaluation of the attitude object is retrieved from memory (Judd & Brauer, 1995). In turn, evaluative repetition has been shown to heighten an attitude's accessibility (see Fazio, Chen, McDonel, & Sherman, 1982; Fazio, Sanbonmatsu, Powell, & Kardes, 1986), thereby promoting both direct retrieval capability and the on-line extraction of the evaluative implications of issue-relevant information. In effect, then, as long as the issue remains situationally salient, it is likely to promote on-line rather than memory-based processing.[7]

Figure 13.1 summarizes the foregoing ideas about how motivation and ability affect the cognitive processes underlying opinion formation. The first set of factors refers to *motivation*. Motivation to process on-line should

---

[7]Information about issues that invoke high levels of self-interest, value-relevance, or social identification—and are thus of high personal important—should also be processed in an on-line manner (Lavine et al., 1996).

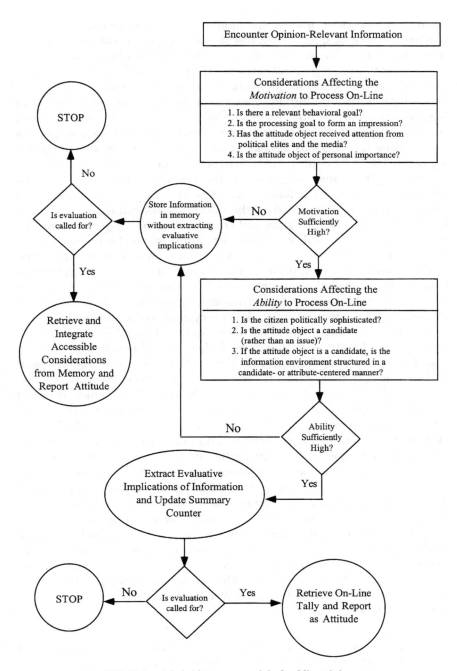

FIG. 13.1. A hybrid process model of public opinion.

be high to the extent that: (a) the opinion-relevant information is related to a behavioral goal (e.g., voting, discussion of an issue), (b) the individual is motivated to form an impression, (c) the attitude object has received recent attention from political elites and the media, and (d) the object is of personal importance to the individual. To the extent that these requirements have not been satisfied, the opinion information will be stored in long-term memory without extraction of the evaluative implications and the forming and updating of a summary counter. Next, the *ability* to process on-line should be high to the extent that: (a) the individual is politically sophisticated, (b) the information is structured in a person-centered manner, and (c) the attitude object is a political candidate rather than a political issue (see Rahn, 1995; Rahn et al., 1994). If both the motivational and ability requirements are satisfied, the individual will extract the evaluative implications of the information and create a summary counter; moreover, the summary counter will be updated as new information becomes available. The on-line tally will be retrieved from long-term memory and be reported as the attitude. However, if either the motivation or ability requirements have not been satisfied, the individual will retrieve and integrate accessible belief considerations from long-term memory when an evaluation is called for and report the temporary summary judgment as the attitude.[8]

Opinion processing may be characterized as "hybrid" in the following developmental stage model: In Stage 1, "piecemeal" processing occurs in that the evaluative implications of beliefs come to mind and are integrated in the typical memory-based fashion. In Stage 2, over time and with repeated evaluative repetition, a summary affective tally becomes linked to the central object node. With continued evaluative repetition, the association between the node and the summary affective tag (i.e., the object–evaluation linkage; see Fazio, 1986) becomes stronger and more accessible, and increasingly comes to dominate the attitudinal response. In Stage 3, the summary affective tag is automatically activated on exposure to the object (i.e., the concept node). An anchoring and adjustment process is then initiated such that the overall evaluative response reflects first and foremost the affective tally (i.e., anchoring), weighted by adjustments— typically insufficient adjustments—on the basis of the evaluative implications of linked beliefs. The adjustment process should be "insufficient" in that it is likely to be motivated or biased such that beliefs that are evaluatively consistent with the summary affective tally are bolstered (i.e., given increased weight) whereas incongruent beliefs are suppressed or rejected (i.e., given decreased weight).

---

[8]In addition to these processes, individuals might—for reasons of motivation, ability, or both—fail to store the opinion information in memory altogether. A "nonattitude" (Converse, 1964) would simply be "made up on the spot" if called for in this situation.

This process of anchoring and adjustment is conceptually similar to Tesser's (1978) work on thought-induced attitude change in that on-line tallies serve as schemas that direct which considerations enter into the construction of the attitude and which are rejected in the service of cognitive consistency goals. Two aspects of this stage model deserve comment. First, the model is doubly hybrid in that it combines automatic (accessibility) and controlled (the deliberate weighting of beliefs in working memory) processing in addition to on-line and memory-based processing. Second, the model makes use of "motivated reasoning" (Lavine, Borgida, & Sullivan, 2000; Lodge & Taber, 2000) in that beliefs are integrated into or rejected from the constructed attitude to the extent that they are consonant with the affective tally. Although the tenets of this developmental hybrid model await empirical test, a simple anchoring and averaging computational model built by Boynton (1995) succeeded in predicting global evaluations by anchoring on the affective tally of the primed concept (which enters working memory first) and adjusting this tally by averaging in the affective tags of its five strongest associations.

CONCLUSION

Theoretical and methodological advances in social cognition over the past two decades have been steadily incorporated into models of political cognition and behavior. Accordingly, the study of political behavior has witnessed a broad shift in emphasis from S–R models of prediction (e.g., "What ingredients account for political behavior?") to S–O–R models of explanation in which the nature of the processes that mediate behavioral phenomena are of primary scientific concern. This evolution from the study of outcomes to the study of processes makes good chronological sense; we need to understand the relevant ingredients of political opinion and behavior before we set our sights on understanding how those ingredients are assembled. However, to truly explain political behavior, we need a grasp on both content and process: "To know both the considerations *and* the rule is to explain the choice" (Kelley, 1983, p. 10, my italics).

In this chapter, I have sought to integrate contemporary theory and research in political psychology on the nature of opinion processes. Classic memory-based and on-line models provide highly divergent views about the nature of these processes. They make radically different assumptions about how opinion information is encoded (the occurrence or nonoccurrence of evaluative extraction), stored (as a summary affective tally or as unintegrated beliefs in long-term memory), and retrieved (direct retrieval of the tally vs. the situational weighting of temporarily accessible beliefs). The appeal of memory-based models lies in their ability to explain the occurrence and magnitude of response effects and temporal instability. The attraction of on-line models is normative; they emphasize the efficiency and consistency in public opinion. My argument is that memory-based and on-line models characterize the opinion processing of different citizens (e.g., nonsophisticates and sophisticates) as well as the same citizens across (a) different regions of their belief systems (central vs. peripheral), (b) divergent political contexts (behavioral vs. nonbehavioral contexts), and (c) different types of political objects (candidates vs. issues). Moreover, I specified circumstances under which hybrid models—in which aspects of both memory-based and on-line processes occur—may come closer to the truth.

The models that I sketched out provide only a few examples of on-line, memory-based, and hybrid accounts of opinion information. Although I believe these to be among the most likely possibilities, others could no doubt be conceived. I close with some general thoughts on theory and method. First, matters of representation and structure necessarily precede those of process; thus, I suggest that future work on opinion processes be situated in well-grounded structural assumptions (e.g., "spreading activation" operates within semantic associative network representations). In this regard, affect needs to be incorporated into working models of attitude structure, perhaps as affective tags or "hot cognitions" (see Lodge & Taber, 2000). Second, the processes underlying the formation of political opinions most likely include both spontaneous and deliberate (i.e., "automatic" and "controlled") elements (see Fazio, 1990). Contexts such as elite frames may influence the accessibility of considerations and thus determine, through automatic processing, which beliefs get moved from long-term memory into working memory; however, not *all* automatically activated considerations must necessarily be included in the construction of an overall opinion. Given sufficient motivation and ability, citizens can use controlled processing to scrutinize the contents of working memory and weight the considerations in terms of their own value priorities (e.g., Nelson, Clawson, & Oxley, 1997). Third, much of the work on opinion processes is perforce conducted in the laboratory, and thus tends to rely on undergraduate research subjects. Although I acknowledge the limits of generalizability in this work, I would argue that *process-oriented* work is probably much more generalizable than work that focuses on content or outcomes. That is, although I would hardly expect college students to mirror the opinions of the public at large, I do believe that the basic cognitive processes—encoding, representation, and retrieval—that underlie opinion formation are substantially similar among undergraduates and adults.

In terms of general method, I believe that survey experiments that integrate representative samples with the experimental control of questions represent the most valuable tool for gaining access to the processes that underlie opinion formation. In particular, I believe that the role of accessibility in explaining both response effects and instability in policy attitudes needs direct empirical scrutiny. Panel designs that include repeated response latencies would be most helpful in this regard. Instability in the importance of issue-related considerations and in more general values should also be investigated as mediators of response effects and temporal instability (Nelson et al., 1997). The accessibility and importance explanations suggest very different mechanisms—automatic vs. controlled types of processing— underlying the structure and functioning of public opinion, and our understanding would be measurably improved by examining their relative contribution.

REFERENCES

Abelson, R. P., Kinder, D. R., Peters, M. D., & Fiske, S. T. (1982). Affective and semantic components in political person perception. *Journal of Personality and Social Psychology, 42,* 619–630.

Achen, C. H. (1975). Mass political attitudes and the survey response. *American Political Science Review, 69,* 1218–1223.

Anderson, N. (1981). *Foundations of information integration theory.* San Diego: CA: Academic Press.

Bartlett, F. A. (1932). *A study in experimental and social psychology.* New York: Cambridge University Press.

Bassili, J. N., & Krosnick, J. A. (2000). Do strength-related attitude properties determine susceptibility to response effects? New evidence from response latency, attitude extremity, and aggregate indices. *Political Psychology, 21,* 107–132.

Bishop, G. F. (1990). Issue involvement and response effects in public opinion surveys. *Public Opinion Quarterly, 54,* 209–218.

Boynton, G. R. (1995). Computational modeling: A computational model of a survey respondent. In M. Lodge & K. M. McGraw (Eds.), *Political judgment: Structure and process* (pp. 229–248). Ann Arbor: University of Michigan Press.

Cacioppo, J. T., & Gardner, W. L. (1999). Emotion. *Annual Review of Psychology, 50,* 191–214.

Cacioppo, J. T., Gardner, W. L., & Berntson, G. G. (1997). Beyond bipolar conceptualizations and measures: The case of attitudes and evaluative space. *Personality and Social Psychology Review, 1,* 3–25.

Carver, C. S., & White, T. L. (1994). Behavioral inhibition, behavioral activation, and affective responses to impending reward and punishment: The BIS/BAS scales. *Journal of Personality and Social Psychology, 67,* 319–333.

Chaiken, S., Liberman, A., & Eagly, A. H. (1989). Heuristic and systematic processing within and beyond the persuasion context. In J. S. Uleman & J. A. Bargh (Eds.), *Unintended thought* (pp. 212–252). New York: Guilford.

Converse, P. E. (1964). The nature of belief systems in mass publics. In D. E. Apter (Ed.), *Ideology and discontent* (pp. 206–261). New York: Free Press.

Davidson, R. J., Ekman, P., Saron, C. D., Senulis, J. A., & Friesen, W. V. (1990). Approach–withdrawal and cerebral asymmetry: Emotional expression and brain physiology. *Journal of Personality and Social Psychology, 58,* 330–341.

Enelow, J. M., & Hinich, M. (1984). *The spatial theory of voting: An introduction.* New York: Cambridge University Press.

Erikson, R. S. (1979). The SRC panel data and mass political attitudes. *British Journal of Political Science, 9,* 89–114.

Fazio, R. H. (1986). How do attitudes guide behavior? In R. M. Sorrentino & E. T. Higgins (Eds.), *Handbook of motivation and cognition: Foundations of social behavior* (pp. 204–243). New York: Guilford Press.

Fazio, R. H. (1990). Multiple processes by which attitudes guide behavior: The MODE model as an integrative framework. In M. P. Zanna (Ed.), *Advances in experimental social psychology* (Vol. 23, pp. 75–109). San Diego: Academic Press.

Fazio, R. H., Chen, J. M., McDonel, E. C., & Sherman, S. J. (1982). Attitude accessibility, attitude-behavior consistency, and the strength of the object-evaluation association. *Journal of Experimental Social Psychology, 18,* 339–357.

Fazio, R. H., Sanbonmatsu, D. M., Powell, M. C., & Kardes, F. R. (1986). On the automatic activation of attitudes. *Journal of Personality and Social Psychology, 50,* 229–238.

Fazio, R. H., & Williams, C. (1986). Attitude accessibility as a moderator of the attitude–perception and attitude–behavior relations: An investigation of the 1984 presidential election. *Journal of Personality and Social Psychology, 51,* 505–514.

Feldman, S. (1989). Measuring issue preferences: The problem of response instability. *Political Analysis, 1,* 25–60.

Feldman, S. (1995). Answering survey questions: The measurement and meaning of public opinion. In M. Lodge & K. McGraw (Eds.), *Political judgment: Structure and process.* Ann Arbor, MI: University of Michigan Press.

Feldman, S., & Zaller, J. R. (1992). The political culture of ambivalence: Ideological responses to the welfare state. *American Journal of Political Science, 36,* 268–307.

Fiske, S. T. (1992). Thinking is for doing: Portraits of social cognition from daguerreotype to laserphoto. *Journal of Personality and Social Psychology, 63,* 877–889.

Fiske, S. T., Kinder, D. R., & Larter, M. (1983). The novice and the expert: Knowledge-based strategies in political cognition. *Journal of Experimental Social Psychology, 19,* 381–400.

George, M. S., Ketter, T. A., Parekh, P. I., Horwitz, B., Herscovitch, P., & Post, R. M. (1995). Brain activity during transient sadness and happiness in healthy women. *American Journal of Psychiatry, 152,* 341–351.

Gray, J. A. (1987). *The psychology of fear and stress.* Cambridge: Cambridge University Press.

Green, D. P., & Citrin, J. (1994). Measurement error and the structure of attitudes: Are positive and negative judgments opposite? *American Journal of Political Science, 38,* 256–281.

Green, D. P., Goldman, S. L., & Salovey, P. (1993). Measurement error masks bipolarity in affect ratings. *Journal of Personality and Social Psychology, 64,* 1029–1041.

Hastie, R., & Park, B. (1986). The relationship between memory and judgment depends on whether the task is memory-based or on-line. *Psychological Review, 93,* 258–268.

Heider, F. (1958). *The psychology of interpersonal relations.* New York: Wiley.

Higgins, E. T., Rholes, W. S., & Jones, C. R. (1977). Category accessibility and impression formation. *Journal of Experimental Social Psychology, 13,* 141–154.

Huckfeldt, R., Levine, J., Morgan, W., & Sprague, J. (1999). Accessibility and the political utility of partisan and ideological orientations. *American Journal of Political Science, 43,* 888–911.

Iyengar, S., & Kinder, D. R. (1987). *News that matters: Television news and American public opinion.* Chicago: University of Chicago Press.

James, W. (1890). *The principles of psychology.* Cambridge, MA: Harvard University Press.

Judd, C. M., & Brauer, M. (1995). Repetition and attitude extremity. In R. E. Petty & J. A. Krosnick (Eds.), *Attitude strength: Antecedents and consequences* (pp. 43–72). Mahwah, NJ: Lawrence Erlbaum Associates.

Katz, I., & Hass, R. G. (1988). Racial ambivalence and American value conflict: Correlational and priming studies of dual cognitive processes. *Journal of Personality and Social Psychology, 55,* 893–905.

Kelley, S. (1983). *Interpreting elections.* Princeton, NJ: Princeton University Press.

Kelley, S., & Mirer, T. W. (1974). The simple act of voting. *American Political Science Review, 68,* 572–591.

Kinder, D. R. (1986). Presidential character revisited. In R. R. Lau & D. O. Sears (Eds.), *Political cognition* (pp. 233–256). Hillsdale, NJ: Lawrence Erlbaum Associates.

Kinder, D. R. (1998a). Opinion and action in the realm of politics. In D. T. Gilbert, S. T. Fiske, & G. Lindzey (Eds.), *Handbook of social psychology* (4th ed., pp. 778–867). NewYork: McGraw-Hill.

Kinder, D. R. (1998b). Communication and opinion. *Annual Review of Political Science, 1,* 167–197.

Kinder, D. R., & Sanders, L. M. (1990). Mimicking political debate with survey questions: The case of white opinion on affirmative action for blacks. *Social Cognition, 8,* 73–103.

Klein, J. G. (1996). Negativity in impressions of presidential candidates revisited: The 1992 election. *Personality and Social Psychology Bulletin, 22,* 288–295.

Krosnick, J. A., & Kinder, D. R. (1990). Altering the foundations of support for the president through priming. *The American Political Science Review, 84,* 497–512.

Krosnick, J. A., & Schuman, H. (1988). Attitude intensity, importance, and certainty and susceptibility to response effects. *Journal of Personality and Social Psychology, 54,* 940–952.

Lau, R. R. (1985). Two explanations for negativity effects in political behavior. *American Journal of Political Science, 29,* 119–138.

Lavine, H. (2001). The electoral consequences of ambivalence toward presidential candidates. *American Journal of Political Science, 45,* 915–929.

Lavine, H., Borgida, E., & Sullivan, J. L (2000). On the origins of attitude accessibility: A cognitive-motivational model of political information processing. *Political Psychology, 21,* 81–106.

Lavine, H., Huff, J. W., Wagner, S. H., & Sweeney, D. (1998). The moderating influence of attitude strength on the susceptibility to context effects in attitude surveys. *Journal of Personality and Social Psychology, 75,* 359–373.

Lavine, H., Sullivan, J. L., Borgida, E., & Thomsen, C. J. (1996). The relationship of national and personal issue salience to attitude accessibility on foreign and domestic policy issues. *Political Psychology, 17,* 293–316.

Lavine, H., Thomsen, C. J., & Gonzales, M. H. (1997). The development of interattitudinal consistency: The shared consequences model. *Journal of Personality and Social Psychology, 72,* 735–749.

Lavine, H., Thomsen, C. J., Zanna, M. P., & Borgida, E (1998). On the primacy of affect in the determination of attitudes and behavior: The moderating influence of affective-cognitive ambivalence. *Journal of Experimental Social Psychology, 34,* 398–421.

Lodge, M. (1995). Toward a procedural model of candidate evaluation. In M. Lodge & K. M. McGraw (Eds.), *Political judgment: Structure and process* (pp. 111–140). Ann Arbor: University of Michigan Press.

Lodge, M., McGraw, K., & Stroh, P. (1989). An impression-driven model of candidate evaluation. *American Political Science Review, 83,* 399–419.

Lodge, M., Steenbergen, M. R., & Brau, S. (1995). The responsive voter: Campaign information and the dynamics of candidate evaluation. *American Political Science Review, 89,* 309–326.

Lodge, M., & Stroh, P. (1993). Inside the mental voting booth: An impression-driven process model of candidate evaluation. In S. Iyengar & W. J. McGuire (Eds.), *Explorations in political psychology* (pp. 225–263). Durham, NC: Duke University Press.

Lodge, M., Stroh, P., & Wahlke, J. (1990). Black-box models of candidate evaluation. *Political Behavior, 12,* 5–18.

Lodge, M., & Taber, C. S. (2000). Three steps toward a theory of motivated political reasoning. In A. Lupia, M. D. McCubbins, & S. L. Popkin (Eds.), *Elements of reason: Understanding and expanding the limits of political rationality* (pp. 183–213). London: Cambridge University Press.

Luskin, R. C. (1987). Measuring political sophistication. *American Journal of Political Science, 31,* 856–899.

Marcus, G. E., & MacKuen, M. B. (1993). Anxiety, enthusiasm, and the vote: The emotional underpinnings of learning and involvement during presidential campaigns. *American Political Science Review, 87,* 672–685.

McDougall, W. (1908). *Social psychology.* Boston: John W. Luce & Co.

McGraw, K. M., Lodge, M., & Stroh, P. (1990). On-line processing in candidate evaluation: The effects of issue order, issue importance, and sophistication. *Political Behavior, 12,* 41–58.

McGraw, K. M., & Pinney, N. (1990). The effects of general and domain-specific expertise on political memory and judgment. *Social Cognition, 8,* 9–30.

McGuire, W. J. (1993). The poly-psy relationship: Three phases of a long affair. In S. Iyengar & W. J. McGuire (Eds.), *Explorations in political psychology.* Durham, NC: Duke University Press.

Meffert, M. F., Guge, M., & Lodge, M. (2000). Good, bad, and ambivalent: The consequences of multidimensional political attitudes. In W. E. Saris & P. Sniderman (Eds.), *The issue of belief: Essays in the intersection of nonattitudes and attitude change* (pp. 67–102). Amsterdam: University of Amsterdam Press.

Nelson, T. E. (1999). Group affect and attribution in social policy opinion. *Journal of Politics, 61,* 331–362.

Nelson, T. E., Clawson, R. A., & Oxley, Z. M. (1997). Media framing of a civil liberties conflict and its effects on tolerance. *American Political Science Review, 91,* 567–583.

Petty, R. E., & Cacioppo, J. T. (1986). The elaboration likelihood model of persuasion. In L. Berkowitz (Ed.), *Advances in experimental social psychology* (Vol. 19, pp. 123–205). San Diego, CA: Academic Press.

Rahn, W. M. (1995). Candidate evaluation in complex information environments: Cognitive organization and comparison process. In M. Lodge & K. M. McGraw (Eds.), *Political judgment: Structure and process* (pp. 43–64). Ann Arbor: University of Michigan Press.

Rahn, W. M., Aldrich, J. H., & Borgida, E. (1994). Individual and contextual variations in political candidate appraisal. *American Political Science Review, 88,* 193–199.

Rahn, W. M., Aldrich, J. H., Borgida, E., & Sullivan, J. L. (1990). A social-cognitive model of candidate appraisal. In J. A. Ferejohn & J. H. Kuklinski (Eds.), *Information and democratic process* (pp. 136–159). Urbana, IL: University of Illinois Press.

Schuman, H., & Presser, S. (1981). *Questions and answers in attitude surveys: experiments on question form, wording, and context.* New York: Academic Press.

Sniderman, P. M., Brody, R. A., & Tetlock, P. E. (1991). *Reasoning and choice: Explorations in political psychology.* Cambridge, England: Cambridge University Press.

Tesser, A. (1978). Self-generated attitude change. In L. Berkowitz (Ed.), *Advances in experimental social psychology* (Vol. 11, pp. 289–338). New York: Academic Press.

Thompson, M. M., Zanna, M. P., & Griffin, D. W. (1995). Let's not be indifferent about (attitudinal) ambivalence. In R. E. Petty & J. A. Krosnick (Eds.), *Attitude strength: Antecedents and consequences* (pp. 361–386). Hillsdale, NJ: Lawrence Erlbaum Associates.

Tourangeau, R., & Rasinski, K. A. (1988). Cognitive processes underlying context effects in attitude measurement. *Psychological Bulletin, 103,* 299–314.

Tourangeau, R., Rasinski, K. A., Bradburn, N., & D'Andrade, R. (1989). Belief accessibility and context effects in attitude measurement. *Journal of Experimental Social Psychology, 25,* 401–421.

Wilson, E. O. (1998). *Consilience: The unity of knowledge.* New York: Knopf.

Wilson, T. D., & Hodges, S. D. (1992). Attitudes as temporary constructions. In A. Tesser & L. Martin (Eds.), *The construction of social judgment* (pp. 37–65). Mahwah, NJ: Lawrence Erlbaum Associates.

Wyer, R. S. Jr., & Srull, T. K. (1986). Human cognition in its social context. *Psychological Review, 93,* 322–359.

Zaller, J. R. (1992). *The nature and origins of mass opinion.* New York: Cambridge University Press.

Zaller, J. R., & Feldman, S. (1992). A simple theory of the survey response: Answering questions versus revealing preferences. *American Journal of Political Science, 36,* 579–616.

14

Long-Term Psychological Consequences of Political Events

David O. Sears
University of California, Los Angeles

Debates about democratic theory are inevitably layered on political psychological assumptions. One point of tension concerns the quality of the ordinary citizens' political thinking. Do they have sufficiently informed, stable, and thoughtful preferences to make rational political choices? Do they process information well enough to have trustworthy judgment? Or are they poorly informed, emotional, easily swayed, and with judgment so poor that it should be kept at some distance from the instruments of political power? Key (1966), perhaps echoing some early Jeffersonian sentiment, is famously quoted as saying that "voters are no fools," while the Federalists were considerably more concerned about the momentary passions that might sway ordinary people, and helped construct a republican political system that diluted the voice of "the people."

A second point of tension concerns the relationship between political life on the one hand, and ordinary daily life on the other. Sometimes it is thought that the psychological dynamics involved in responding to the two are very similar. I think not, for reasons I give in this chapter.

A third point concerns the relationship between elites and the mass public. Do elites typically manipulate the mass public's preferences in their own interests? Or at the other extreme, are elites so dependent on public opinion that they spend their time anxiously taking polls in the hope of finding campaign appeals and policy proposals that will generate public support? In between these two extremes there is obviously considerable room for a variety of more nuanced combinations of the two views, and it is one of those that I develop here.

THREE MODELS OF SHORT-TERM EVENT IMPACT

One criterion for assessing the robustness of a democracy is whether or not the citizenry responds sensibly to ongoing political events. My main goal here is to understand the long-term public response to major political events, but to do so one must first address immediate or short-term responses. My strategy is to let parsimony dominate at the start and so begin with the simplest models possible, adding complications only if needed. There are three standard models in the political behavior literature that I present with some cases for which they seem perfectly adequate. Then we turn to my main purpose, which is to describe some cases in which these standard models seem not to be adequate, and to suggest some other psychological dynamics that need to be taken into consideration.

A common-sensical starting point is a *hedonically rational* model of event impact: namely, that people will like objectively good events and support those responsible for them, and dislike objectively bad events and reject those responsible. The popularity of rational choice models in political science has led to the elevation of theories holding that campaigns and other events lead the public to quite sensible decisions. In the study of mass politics the obvious starting points are Downs' (1957) theory that people choose candidates on the basis of issue proximity, and Kramer's (1971) observation that congressional voting is closely related to macroeconomic trends, at least at the aggregate level.

Among the currently most-fashionable models of political behavior are those drawn from economic theory, especially those embedded in formal models. These typically involve three psychological assumptions: utilitarian motives, such that personal and material utilities drive behavior more than do other incentives; rational processing, such that within the limits of available information, people make reasonable decisions; and elite-driven politics, viewing the mass public as primarily responsive to elite initiatives because elites have much more information and better cognitive processing faculties.

At the level of individual survey data, applications include Key's (1966) view that voters pick the candidate that best deals with the issues they care about, Fiorina's (1981) "retrospective voting" principle that voters respond rationally to incumbents' performance, and Miller and Shanks' (1996) *New American Voter* that builds both issue proximity and performance-based voting into their models. Another recent example is Zaller's (1998) interpretation of the public's slightly increased approval of Bill Clinton during the early stages of the Monica Lewinsky scandal. He argued that the public showed sense in weighing "the bottom line" (peace, prosperity, and ideological moderation) more heavily than possible private sexual misbehavior in evaluating presidential performance. The same point, carried out over more extended time periods, is made by Page and Shapiro's (1992) argument that the "rational public" moves in slow but steady ways on a long-term basis toward the objectively more worthy issue positions.

These are, perhaps, all cases in which the public quite sensibly appraises good or bad outcomes for what they are. Indeed, in politics we have the widespread notion of a "well-run campaign" that succeeds and a "poorly run campaign" that results in failure. However, one man's rationality is another man's deceptive trickery. So another version of the simple hedonic line of thinking emphasizes *demagogic manipulation.* In the 1930s and 1940s, the conventional wisdom was that modern propagandists had developed principles that made them dangerously effective. The Institute for Propaganda Analysis (1939) analyzed the demagogic Catholic priest Father Charles Coughlin's radio speeches in detail as an exemplar of the effective "tricks of the trade" he employed. Later, Edelman (1964) developed a theory of symbolic politics that rested on similar assumptions about the abilities of demagogues and other political elites to arouse a quiescent public by appealing to various political symbols. More recently, this view emerges most vividly in the many books written about the clever tricks of campaign consultants in domestic politics (e.g., Jamieson, 1984; McGuiness, 1969).

A spinoff of this view was the psychodynamic theory embodied in *The Authoritarian Personality* (Adorno, Frenkel-Brunswik, Levinson, & Sanford, 1950). This portrayed individuals as varying in personality dispositions that would provide them with an internal gyroscope for responding to a wide variety of political events in a consistent manner. This placed the situational context in the background, although it did place a premium on political agitators who could arouse authoritarian tendencies in those so predisposed. However, much of contemporary social psychology has constituted a protracted reaction against that dispositionally centered view. A recent summary of this work (Ross & Nisbett, 1991) suggested that "situational factors often prove to be more powerful determinants of behavior than the vast majority of us—scientists and laypeople alike—would have guessed . . . people from different backgrounds, people with different beliefs, even people with apparently different personalities, must understand and react to some situations rather uniformly" (p. 24).

Many other examples mix rationality and demagoguery but still emphasize unidirectional effects. One is "rally round the flag" effects that occur when a president takes a bold international action. Most of the time this leads to a supportive public response, although perhaps not on those relatively rare occasions when the political opposition speaks out (Brody, 1991). Whether the bold president is acting rationally or engaging in manipulation is a judgment call, just as is whether the silent opposition is being responsible or just protecting its political future.

A third alternative is a sociopsychological model that focuses attention on citizens' powerful psychological predispositions, suggesting that those predispositions control their responses to political events. Polarization rather than unidirectional persuasion is a common effect of salient events. This model usually involves several propositions at the individual psychological level: (a) predispositions develop toward specific attitude objects through a process of associative conditioning, (b) the most powerful conditioning occurs relatively early in the life span (most often specified as adolescence and early adulthood), (c) predispositional strength depends on the volume and valence of the information to which the individual is exposed, (d) the strongest predispositions tend to persist through the remainder of the life, and (e) evaluations of incoming political information are strongly influenced by these persisting predispositions.

This sociopsychological theory of predispositions and polarization is one that I and others have promoted under the label of a *symbolic politics theory* (e.g., Citrin, Green, Reingold, & Walters, 1990; Sears, 1983, 1993; Sears, Huddy, & Schaffer, 1986). However, its generic elements are common to a great deal of the theorizing and research on political behavior done over the past half century, so we should make no great claim of originality concerning the larger view it represents. In the area of media studies, this model initially formed a reaction against the demagogic manipulation perspective. The early empirical studies of the mass media emerged with the portrait of an audience that interpreted and accepted mass communications selectively, according to their own predispositions. It emphasized that the ordinary citizen's stable predispositions made such elite-driven manipulation more difficult than initially thought. Communications faced an "obstinate audience" (Bauer, 1964), and were more likely to "reinforce" existing attitudes than to "convert" people (Klapper, 1960). Early voting studies similarly depicted an electorate that responded to the flow of election campaigns more in terms of their own predispositions than in terms of the whims of the campaigners (Campbell, Converse, Miller, & Stokes, 1960; Lazarsfeld, Berelson, & Gaudet, 1948).

The symbolic politics model contains two key assertions of fact. One concerns the long-term stability of basic political predispositions. One test of that involved the Terman longitudinal study of a cohort of gifted children. We tracked them from 1940 to 1977, which for most was approximately from age 30 to retirement age. Their left–right orientation was strikingly stable over time, with stability coefficients of over .80 across each decade, and .65 for the full 37-year span (Sears & Funk, 1999).

The other is that events tend to polarize attitudes around predispositions in the short run. A simple example comes from presidential debates. Following every presidential debate since 1960, viewers have had a strong tendency to see the candidate they initially preferred as having won the debate (e.g., Katz & Feldman, 1962; Lanoue, 1991; Sears & Chaffee, 1979). There is no simple swing to the objectively better or demagogically most effective side. This is a fairly standard response when individuals with strong predispositions are exposed to complex political information.

The current generation of applications of such predispositional theories to media studies suggests that incoming information primes basic predispositions. For example, Mendelberg (1997) showed experimentally that exposure to the George Bush campaign's 1988 racially tinged campaign ads increased the contribution of racial prejudice to the racial policy attitudes of whites. Changing the focus of individuals' attention, or changing the political agenda, can therefore change the bases on which they evaluate political leaders (Iyengar & Kinder, 1987). Moreover, incoming information can be framed in a wide variety of ways, and that framing determines which predisposition is primed. For example, Kinder and Sanders (1990) found that framing affirmative action as "unfair advantages for blacks" evoked anti-black prejudices and other racial attitudes. Framing it as "reverse discrimination against whites" was more likely to evoke feelings of threat to whites.

Political campaigns, then, seek to manipulate the "spin" that is placed on events during the campaign, such as debates or candidate gaffes, in order to insure that the most favorable predispositions are evoked. The early Clinton health initiative became redefined as just more Democratic "big government" politics rather than as a bipartisan public health measure after millions were spent by opponents in effective attack advertising. Elites compete to control the political agenda so that the public will attend most to the issues their own side "owns" and that will most easily bring votes their way (Petrocik, 1996).

These elite-driven agenda-setting, priming, and framing phenomena have dominated the conventional wisdom about media effects in recent years. These have in common the view that the media are strikingly effective in manipulating the public, telling the public "what to think about," how exactly to think about it, and which attitudes and values to bring to bear in reaching a decision. The "myth of massive media impact" is no longer a myth, according to Zaller (1997). Rather, the "minimal effects model" is said to be discredited. Similarly, another increasingly popular piece of conventional wisdom in political science is that macroeconomic conditions dictate election outcomes. National elections are largely foregone conclusions once the economic numbers are in. The voters' responses to the particular candidates, their campaigns, and to the relevant campaign issues are of secondary importance. In understanding mass politics, we should not start with a theory about individual choice but with a top-down approach that focuses primarily on elites' competition and what alternatives they offer to a passively onlooking citizenry.

The symbolic politics view proposed here argues instead for the importance of the public's predispositions. It also argues that they interact with elite-driven stimuli, but in a very specific sort of way. Political events are important among adults, but perhaps only insofar as they evoke symbolic predispositions. Television coverage of Kosovars being herded into cattle cars for deportation to Macedonia is important primarily because it evokes memories of Jews transported to death camps in similar railway cars in World War II. Events may also be important because they help form such predispositions among young people. An election campaign is important because its intense information flow can help form youthful preferences. However, I would acknowledge that a predispositional theory is at least counter-cyclical and possibly contrarian in an era that more often views the public either as cold-bloodedly market-oriented or as passive followers of elite-driven fads.[1]

LONGER-TERM EFFECTS OF POLITICAL EVENTS

Extrapolating from these analyses of short-term impact of political events, one proposition might be that *polarization is also characteristic of responses to longer-term events* such as presidential campaigns (Campbell et al., 1960; Lazarsfeld et al., 1948; Miller & Shanks, 1996) or outbreaks of intergroup conflict, such as riots, when each group tends to see the other as to blame (Sears & McConahay, 1973; Sears, 1994).[2] Polarization resulting from political events can last for many years, of course, far beyond the memory of any alive at the time. Bosnian Serbs justified their attack on Bosnian Muslims as retaliation for a military defeat in 1392, over half a millennium ago. The divisions between royalists and revolutionaries during the French Revolution continued to polarize French school children over symbols of the Revolution as late as the 1960s (Roig & Billon-Grand, 1968). Similarly, white Georgians were strongly polarized in 1994 about whether or not to remove the Confederate battle emblem from the Georgia state flag, along lines harkening back the 133 years since the founding of the Confederacy. Those

---

[1]For example, it would be hard to find much difference between it and Hyman's (1959) treatment of political socialization, Klapper's (1960) theory of media effects, *The American Voter* (Campbell et al., 1960) model of voting behavior, Alwin and colleagues' (1991) treatment of the Bennington study, or Zaller's (1992) discussion of public opinion. In all these areas, of course, there have been modifications with time and sophistication, but the basic propositions I have outlined are, I think, common to all.

[2]For an early application of this principle to viewers of a highly competitive football game, see Hastorf and Cantril (1954).

most resistant to any change had been born in the South, were still loyal to the Confederacy, and held the most racial prejudice (Reingold & Wike, 1998). Presumably they had been socialized by people nostalgically idealizing the Confederacy and resisting racial equality, and the controversy about the state flag generated hot political polarization around those longstanding predispositions more than a century after the end of the Civil War.

Another example is Zaller's (1992, p. 103) analysis of the effects on public opinion of changes in elite communication over the course of the Vietnam War. He makes the case that in its early years, elite communication was largely favorable to American participation in the war, and so greater exposure to political information increased public support for the war. With the growth of antiwar agitation later in the war, elites became polarized, and well-informed liberals and conservatives in the general public became highly polarized as well.

A second proposition is that *political events are central to initial political socialization.* Without political campaigns, scandals, wars, and assassinations, most young people would not be exposed to much political communication. So it is on the occasion of such high-profile events that much political socialization takes place. It might be noted that this proposition is a shift of emphasis from the older literature on political socialization that focused most on routine communication in family and school and other nonpolitical settings. A paradigmatic case of this event-driven political socialization concerns the 1980 presidential campaign (Sears & Valentino, 1997; Valentino & Sears, 1998). Adolescents' partisan attitudes crystallized quite sharply over the course of the election year, from before the primaries to just before Election Day. There was no comparable increase in crystallization in the year following the election, during what was presumably a considerably less information-rich period. The adult parents of these adolescents did not show such gains, presumably because their partisan predispositions were already fairly fully formed. The campaign triggered no comparable increase in the teenagers' attitude crystallization in domains that were peripheral to the campaign. Indeed in such domains their attitudes remained far less crystallized than adults', just because no political event had come along to stimulate strong socialization.[3]

More generally, third, *political events tend to increase attitudinal consistency.* Dennis, Chaffee, & Choe (1979) have shown that exposure to presidential debates increases the consistency of attitudes toward issues, parties, and candidates, a phenomenon they describe as *bonding.* That, of course, is a short-term effect. An example of a longer term effect is what we (Sears &

---

[3]This raises questions about *life cycle effects.* The symbolic politics approach (Sears, 1983) suggests such predispositions tend to be weaker among the young, to strengthen with age, and to be stronger in domains that involve high levels of information flow over the years.

McConahay, 1973, p. 172) described as the development of a "riot ideology" in South-Central Los Angeles in the months following the deadly and
destructive Watts riots in 1965. As the months passed after the conclusion
of the rioting, black respondents increasingly came to believe that the riot
had represented a meaningful political protest against racial discrimination, and that it would in fact have desirable effects. This interpretation of
the riot as a protest and optimism about its effects also became more tightly
correlated with time; we described that package as a "riot ideology."

The critical element for long-term impact may be the long-term and
affectively charged symbolic residues, such as occurred in the attacks on
Fort Sumter, the battleship Maine, the Lusitania, and Pearl Harbor, the
Serb defeat in Kosovo in 1389, or the revolutionary events of 1776 and
1789. Concrete symbolic representations such as museums, memorials,
songs, slogans, or dramatic representations may be most important.

The short-term framing, priming, and agenda-setting effects presented
earlier have parallels in long-term effects as well. Political events also can
frame issues on a longer-term basis, priming crystallized predispositions
and linking them cognitively to the issue at hand. For example, the invasion
of Kuwait by Iraq in August 1990 placed that crisis at the center of the public agenda. It soon absorbed the great majority of network news time, and
by November had risen to the status of the most important problem in the
nation (Iyengar & Simon, 1993). Over time, evaluations of President Bush
increasingly were dependent on evaluations of his response to the Gulf
crisis (Krosnick & Brannon, 1993).

A quasiexperimental test of this proposition comes from two high visibility (and successful) initiative campaigns in California, on issues central
to racial and ethnic minorities (Sears & van Laar, 1999). On the November
1996 ballot, Proposition 209, the California Civil Rights Initiative (CCRI),
called for the abolition of preferential treatment by state and local government on the basis of ethnicity, race, or gender. In principle, it applied to all
racial and ethnic minorities, and to women as well, but the pro-209 campaign itself focused most heavily on blacks. As a result, it primed attitudes
toward blacks more than attitudes toward other groups, so that anti-black
antagonism increasingly influenced preferences about policies explicitly
targeted for Hispanics, such as preferential treatment for them in jobs.

A contrasting case was Proposition 187 on the November 1994 ballot,
which made illegal aliens ineligible for many public services such as public
schools, social services, or nonemergency public health care. The pro-187
campaign focused intensely at the end of the campaign on illegal immigrants, most of who were of Mexican ancestry. The campaign paid virtually
no attention at all to blacks, as essentially irrelevant to any debate about
illegal immigration. As a result, attitudes toward Hispanics should have
been the most strongly primed. Indeed, whites' attitudes about immigration

became more closely connected to anti-Hispanic attitudes and less closely connected to anti-black attitudes. In other words, a campaign about a measure that affected all minorities and women, but that focused primarily on blacks, resulted in intruding anti-black antagonism even into whites' preferences about policies explicitly targeted for other minority groups. However, a campaign focused almost exclusively on Latinos successfully primed antagonisms toward them.

ELITE–MASS INTERACTION

Having said all this, it is important to recognize that political events do not command public response in a mechanical fashion. The top-down analysis misses something vitally important about popular democracy. The effects of political events on the mass public depend very much on what the public brings to the table when they occur. What is required is a more nuanced analysis of the interaction between elite and mass public.

Limits on Top-Down Effects

Perhaps the closest to a textbook case of that interaction is party realignment in the 1960s around racial issues. Carmines and Stimson's (1989) analysis begins with the Democratic surge in the 1958 House elections, producing increased ideological polarization between the two congressional party caucuses. The civil rights movement of the early 1960s, exogenous to partisan politics, forced the parties to take clear policy positions on racial segregation. Finally in 1964, the mass public entered the fray, dividing its loyalties between the now racially liberal Democrats and the now racially conservative Republicans.

But three elements seem to me shortchanged in this classic account, all reflecting the public's influence over the process of change. One is the election of 1958 that triggered the change in Congress. This is interpreted largely as a reflection of the recession of that year. That seems too simple to me, in the sixth year of a presidency held by a party much in the minority. The second is the exogeneity of the civil rights movement. That seems to me to oversimplify a set of events that had great mass participation and support. For example, the Kennedy administration's ultimate decision to support the civil rights side against the strong Southern contingent in the Democratic party had much to do with its own base of support in the mass public, black and white, and with the rapidly growing Northern condemnation of the Southern segregationist system. And third, the power of the Southern white public's racial attitudes is understated. Lyndon Johnson understood it very well when he observed that in signing civil rights legislation, he was signing the death knell of the Southern Democratic party for a generation. The history of civil rights policies ever since has been one of liberal elites' being increasingly constrained by a more conservative general public, reflecting a strengthened Republican party and its conservative Supreme Court appointees (Thernstrom & Thernstrom, 1997).

A second instructive case is the Clinton impeachment. While Republicans strove mightily to frame the issue as a flagrant violation of the law against perjury, and Democrats as a case of a minor sexual indiscretion, public opinion did not budge an iota over the course of a year of some of the most intensive political propaganda in the nation's history. It remained sharply polarized along party lines, strongly tilted toward support for Clinton, despite massively negative elite communication about him.

The lesson is that when the public is informed, elites must tailor their policy proposals to what is acceptable to the public. Cognitive consistency theory long ago taught us that evaluations of a communicator's message and those of the communicator himself have reciprocal influences on each other, leading both to issue-proximity effects on candidate evaluation and communicator-credibility effects on message evaluation. It would go too far to say that elected officials are only interested in being elected and not in influencing public policy, but if they had to choose, would it not most often be to hitch their candidacies to a set of policies preferred by the citizenry?

A More Skeptical Look at Framing Effects

Events can frame an issue effectively and influence quite profoundly which predispositions come into play, then. But mere framing may not have as much muscle when it comes to longer term events as it does in one-shot experiments. One obvious example is the Gulf War. Its beneficial effects on President Bush's popularity were short-lived. By November 1992, it was "the economy, stupid," the Gulf War a fond but irrelevant memory and Bush unemployed.

One classic example of a framing effect was Kinder and Sanders' (1990) demonstration that describing affirmative action as reverse discrimination against whites evoked very different predispositions than framing it as unfair advantage to blacks. In this case overall opposition to affirmative action was unaffected. It is easy to find contrary examples, however, in which substantial changes in the framing of an attitude object affect the *valence* of responses to an object quite substantially, but make very little difference in which predispositions it evokes.

One such example concerns public opinion about government spending. In our study of the California tax revolt, we found that a "smaller government providing fewer services" was preferred by more than a 2 to 1 margin (Sears & Citrin, 1985, p. 46). However, on a different set of questions, about public spending in a variety of specific service areas, respondents overwhelmingly wanted spending to be *increased* rather than cut, across several surveys and regardless of service area. Framing greatly affected aggregate opinion, therefore, but the predictors of attitudes about government and spending were about the same regardless of framing. The most dramatic example was the case of welfare. In every survey a majority wanted "welfare" cut, yet the predictors of attitudes toward welfare were almost exactly the same as they were for service areas like public schools that the majority wanted supported. Framing greatly affected public support, but did not affect which predispositions were evoked.

A similar example concerns school integration. In the 1960s, conflicts over school integration mostly revolved around federal efforts (by both the Supreme Court and the Executive branch) to overcome Southerners' resistance to dismantling their system of officially segregated schools. The relevant question in the National Election Studies was: "Do you think the government in Washington should see to it that white and black children go to the same schools, or stay out of this area, as it is not its business?" Later, in the 1970s, busing began to be mandated as a solution to school segregation; the relevant question concerned "busing children to schools out of their own neighborhoods." This differential framing made a major difference in aggregate white support for school integration; in 1972, federal school intervention was favored by 45%, but busing by only 9% (Sears, Hensler, & Speer, 1979). However, the regression coefficients explaining such policy attitudes were very similar in both cases. Again, framing affected aggregate opinion but not which predispositions predicted opposition.

The same result holds for attitudes about diverse racial policies in the contemporary era. Contemporary racial policy issues differ greatly in the level of support they draw from whites; for example, special preferences for blacks in hiring and promotion draw considerable opposition, whereas federal assistance to blacks and government assurance of equal opportunity draw rather evenly divided reactions (Schuman, Steeh, Bobo, & Krysan, 1997; Sniderman & Carmines, 1997). But the predictors of all three sets of racial policy attitudes are much the same (Sears, Van Laar, Carillo, & Kosterman, 1997). Framing racial policy in different terms affects overall support levels, but not which predispositions they evoke.

In short, experimentally varying framing of political issues can alter the underlying predispositions they evoke in the short run. However, when we turn to issues that have been around for a longer time, we find examples of exactly the opposite: even when differential framing alters the division of public opinion, and even to the extent that majority opinion becomes minority opinion, the predispositions evoked remain almost exactly the same. Why? The symbolic politics theory needs to be elaborated in two ways. One is to accommodate associative networks or schemas that may connect attitude objects with quite different manifest contents. This schematic version of a symbolic politics theory would allow us to know when people will bring the same basic predispositions to bear on an object no matter how it is framed (Sears, 1993; Sears & Huddy, 1992; Sears, Huddy, & Schaffer, 1986). Second, the models would seem to be underspecified by failing to specify the predispositions that differentiate responses to, say, "racial preferences" from "equal opportunity." Perhaps to understand public response to such issues (whether in surveys or on the campaign trail or in Congress) will depend in part on identifying other cognitive elements that have not been well captured to date.

COLLECTIVE MEMORIES: PERSONAL EXPERIENCE OR SYMBOLIC PUBLIC EVENTS?

To understand the long-term effects of political events, we need to look at "collective memories," that is, at the public's memories for political events that happened many years ago. The simple predispositional theory posed here would suggest that some simple index of information flow, especially of elite communication, would be the best predictor of an event's memorability. The lengthy and highly publicized murder trial of a famous football star should be remembered better and by more people than a week-long unpublicized murder trial of an obscure gang member in a drive-by shooting. However, perhaps there are other elements of events that make them especially memorable.

One important general finding is that the events remembered as most important are those that happened when we were young. Good examples come from a 1985 national sample asked to think of "'national or world events or changes' that have occurred over the past 50 years and to name 'one or two . . . that seem to you to have been especially important'" (Schuman & Scott, 1989, p. 362), and later surveys that asked about "a few words and names from the past . . . tell me which ones you have heard of . . . and . . . what they refer to in a few words" (Schuman, Belli, & Bischoping, 1997). World War II was selected most often by the cohort averaging age 20 in 1943, and the Vietnam War by the cohort averaging age 20 in 1968. Memory for the Works Progress Administration (WPA), the New Deal agency that paid the unemployed for engaging in public works, was most vivid in the cohort who averaged 19 years old when it was instituted, in 1938.

The location of collective memories in the cohort around age 20 is politically important, because it gives a generational basis for issue importance, but the reason is unclear. Memory for the WPA was especially great among the less educated, perhaps because they found it a critical source of personal income in the depth of the Depression (Schuman, Belli, & Bischoping, 1997). Similarly, the Depression was cited as the most important event mainly by people old enough to have experienced its devastating effects personally. The Tet offensive of 1968, a major turning point in the Vietnam War, was most memorable to men in the cohort aged 20 then. Perhaps vulnerability to the draft is the main reason that Vietnam stands out so vividly 25 years later to these now middle-aged baby boomers. More generally, it is tempting to assume that *personal experience* makes such events especially memorable.

However, it must be remembered that other research has shown that nonpolitical personal experience is not a strong contributor to political attitudes (Sears & Funk, 1991). Vulnerability to the draft or to combat is not a strong predictor of attitudes about a war (see Lau, Brown, & Sears, 1978; Mueller, 1973). There is more to the experience of war than personal threat or direct personal involvement. Many Americans were killed in Korea, but it is not on the radar screen of collective memories; only 1% mentioned it (Schuman & Scott, 1989). There is more about Vietnam that makes it stick in collective memory than young men's direct experience of it.

EMOTIONALLY EVOCATIVE EVENTS

The three simple models I began with are splendidly parsimonious, depending almost entirely on the content of information flow stimulated by political events. That is the nature of routine democratic life. But on some occasions political events can be quite emotionally evocative. That may not happen often, but when it does, the events may be particularly important to the society. For example, more complex psychodynamic analyses may be needed to supplement analyses of information flow. And we may need other methodologies than standard survey or experimental techniques.

The Assassination of JFK

One case concerns the assassination of President Kennedy. Let us refresh our memory about what an unusual political event that was. It was an extreme outlier in three ways. It exposed people to an extraordinary volume of political communication. For 4 days the average adult spent at least 8 hours a day watching on television or listening on the radio to the assassination-related events, the ceremonies, and remembering the Kennedy administration and Kennedy's life. About a quarter of the public was so completely absorbed that they spent 13 or more hours per day immersed in the media. Moreover, almost all that communication was highly favorable to Kennedy. Beyond that, it was extraordinarily emotionally evocative. Most people (54%) said they could not carry on with their normal activities; only 19%

said they carried on "pretty much as usual." During that period, 53% said they cried and 48% said they had trouble getting to sleep, over twice the normal rate (Sheatsley & Feldman, 1965).

The long-term evaluation of his death as especially important peaks in the cohort whose average age was then 15 (Schuman & Scott, 1989). That is, those most lastingly affected by the Kennedy assassination were mid-adolescents in 1963. To be so memorable, and to have such a lasting effect, perhaps a political event needs to induce a significant emotional experience, even if it is completely at a remote, symbolic level.

The psychoanalyst Martha Wolfenstein (1965) reported two major age-related findings about the reactions of children and adolescence to the assassination: the "*intensity* of reaction seemed to increase from latency to prepuberty to adolescence, with probably a sharp rise between the latter two phases . . . and was maintained from there on into later adolescence and adulthood" (p. 76), and the ". . . *duration* of grief . . . first rises in the same way [as intensity of reaction] as we move from earlier childhood into adolescence, [but] it then declines as we proceed into adulthood. The persisting disbelief of both younger and older adolescents does not, I think, find a counterpart in adults" (pp. 76–77) [emphasis added]. How can we interpret these two trajectories—the intensity of grief rising sharply to asymptote in adolescence, and the duration of grief peaking among adolescents and then dropping off with age?

Younger children evidenced what she described as a "bland reaction," "oblivious or positively jaunty," a "short sadness span," even a jocular response (pp. 65, 68, 74). They naturally had little ability to connect emotionally with objects so remote from their own lives. Nonetheless, she says, on this occasion, "children were exposed to the unaccustomed sight of their parents, teachers, and other adults openly weeping. This emotional breakdown of the grownups was probably quite alarming to the children" (p. 68).

Young adolescents were quite different. She provides quotes from essays they wrote in the schools, expressing deep grief, observing that "with advancing age children could attach more feeling to the President . . . so as we move into adolescence, we find children reacting with such strong emotion to the President's death" (p. 70). An intrinsically emotionally evocative political event naturally will affect adolescents more than it will younger children.

However, she makes two important further points about the strong and enduring emotional reactions of adolescents that involve a phenomenon she calls *mourning at a distance* (p. 74). How it differs from mourning in daily life is crucial to our basic question about the unique quality of remote political events. First, "children of this age tend to show strong inhibitions of affect when someone in their own family has died. Yet they could feel and express outspoken grief for the death of the President" (pp. 65–66).

Why? When the object is distant, adolescents are more able to release their sad feelings, because they are less complicated by ambivalence and guilt than those about a family member. Second, "the feeling of disbelief and . . . its persistence after a considerable time would be more characteristic of this age group than of adults" (p. 75). Adults became more readily reconciled to the loss. Adolescents had more difficulty working through the feeling of loss, because "the work of mourning, the protracted process . . . in which memories are painfully renounced . . . and the lost person is little by little given up . . . becomes possible only after adolescence" (p. 75). "The problem of giving up a loved and admired leader coincided with the basic unresolved task of their time in life, that of giving up their childhood attachment to their parents. It will be of great psychological interest to observe how this national tragedy will eventually be assimilated by these young people" (p. 77).

Did the death of JFK have long-term political effects? Here we can only speculate. The level of hostility felt by the Democratic left toward Lyndon Johnson in the years following Kennedy's death has always seemed to me out of keeping with standard political alliances. The youthful political left directed the chant "Hey hey LBJ, who did you kill today?" at the man who led perhaps the most liberal and egalitarian presidency in American history. Why did it cleave its natural constituency so completely? A common component of adolescent mourning for a parent's loss (by death or divorce) is anger toward any replacement person. When the surviving parent takes on a new partner, that individual often falls short of the idealized lost parent and is seen as a usurper. Hamlet exemplifies this dynamic perhaps as well as any other widely known figure, but his father returned only in dreams and fantasy. Unhappily for LBJ, JFK returned over and over on TV.

Second, the late 1960s witnessed a truly unique politicization of young Americans, especially the college educated. It had a wide variety of manifestations, including the civil rights movement, the antiwar movement, the women's movement, and the striking departure from conventional lifestyles described as "the counterculture." The prior generation, of the 1950s, was not highly politicized, and indeed was widely critiqued for its excessive devotion to privatism and conformity (e.g., Riesman, 1969). Much has also been written about the increasing level of political disengagement of post-1960s cohorts (Putnam, 2000; Miller & Shanks, 1996).

Why was the 1960s generation so politicized? The usual explanations have never satisfied me. The Vietnam war was our most protested war, but scarcely our most immoral. The Watergate scandal was thoroughly redressed through standard legal and political procedures, pretty much to everyone's satisfaction, and with considerable healthy partisan zest. The cohort that was most highly politicized in the late 1960s, of average age 20 at the time of the Tet offensive and Chicago Democratic convention, and

22 at the time of the Cambodian invasion and the Kent State killings, was exactly the adolescent cohort that Wolfenstein described as so aggrieved by the Kennedy assassination, and who many years later continued to find it so important. The subsequent cohort, disengaged by all reports, had been Wolfenstein's "bland and jaunty" children in 1963, perhaps whistling past the graveyard. One wonders whether the bewilderment those children had experienced contributed to their later distancing themselves from a sphere of life that had produced such alarming effects.

Generational Lag: The Incarceration of Japanese Americans

One final example of an apparent generational difference in response to an emotionally evocative political event: About 10 weeks after Pearl Harbor, on February 19, 1942, President Franklin D. Roosevelt issued Executive Order 9066 that called for the rounding up of approximately 40,000 Japanese citizens living in the continental United States and 80,000 American citizens of Japanese ancestry. By August 1942 they had been imprisoned in 10 camps spread across the western United States well away from the coast of the Pacific Ocean. In general, the internees did not engage in active political protest, although the Tule Lake camp in California became a "segregation center" for "renunciants" and "trouble-makers," and some independent Japanese-language schools began to train children to return to Japan after the war (Wollenberg, 1976, p. 78). At the end of the war the camps were closed, and the Japanese Americans attempted to return to what remained of their prewar lives.

During the period of internship, few of the internees, predominantly *Nisei* (second generation in America) engaged in much political protest (although 2,000 of the Tule Lake internees did choose to return to Japan after they were released). Rhea (1997) noted that the internee generation often found the experience personally humiliating and rarely even discussed it with their children in later years. In contrast, in the late 1960s, the *Sansei* (youths from the third generation) began to politicize the memory of the intern experience. Indeed "resistance to the Vietnam War touched off a search for 'a common Asian American identity rooted in a past history of oppression and a present struggle for liberation'" among them (p. 43). They began pilgrimages to the camp sites, and there was a briefly flourishing Asian race pride movement. Rhea quoted one prominent academic leader of that later generation as saying, "To be a Japanese American . . . should mean that the Internment remains at the forefront of our collective memory, and the basis of the most distinct contribution that we can make to society" (p. 64).

Rhea noted that sometimes the events of the past may come to take on even greater significance for later generations than for those who lived through them. "One Nisei internee, joking about the younger revisionist historians, touched on this, saying, 'If anything, they felt it was a greater wrong than we who were there feel it was'" (pp. 64–65). In other words, the incarceration of the earlier Nisei generation did not itself lead to an angry political response. Political events may only become more important in later generations because contemporary personal experience may be too complex and emotionally ambivalent. With some distance, the emotions themselves may become more black and white, and the experience becomes clarified through the development of simplifying political ideologies. In this way, too, distal political events may draw on different psychological processes than proximal daily life.

CONCLUSIONS

I have used the long-term effects of political events as a lever to pry open several points about political psychology. First of all, one can go some distance with a relatively simple generic predispositional theory that involves little more than stable predispositions and an assessment of information flow, with the expectation that the latter will make attitudes more consistent, polarize them around such predispositions if they exist, and help to create them if they do not. Left in this form, one might come away with the impression that elites play the major role in politics, inasmuch as they, by and large, are responsible for the events and play an important role in how they are framed, which in turn clearly influences public response to them.

However, I argue that there are some fairly stringent limits on elites' abilities to manipulate the public. The public does not blindly mimic elite opinion. The Clinton impeachment matter and the Vietnam war are clear evidence of that, both representing rather clear elite consensus that resulted in sharp public polarization and majority opinion contrary to that elite consensus. Moreover, the public, when informed, often tends to see through to the underlying questions regardless of elite framing. Several instances of the limits on framing were presented: in each, public response was consistent with the same set of underlying predispositions regardless of framing, although the valence of public response depended on the unique features of each proposal. Elite-driven political events are also not invariably exogenous to the public's preferences. On the contrary, elites' actions may be quite responsive to them. The placement of a radical property-tax-cutting proposition on the ballot or the effort by a governor to jumpstart his presidential campaign by supporting an immigrant-bashing proposition on the ballot are scarcely exogenous. In these cases, elites make strategic calculations based on their appraisal of public opinion, rather than manipulating it in some top-down fashion. The elite–mass relationship is fundamentally and intrinsically interactive. That provides political psychology with a comparative advantage in studying it, with events at the heart of the matter. Elites are constrained by and must work with such residues. The citizenry is not a tabula rasa. This is not to romanticize either the general public's knowledge and rationality, nor to claim that the public is immune from manipulation, but on issues that the public is informed about and cares about, elites tread carefully.

Institutional movement toward more and more direct democracy seems to have been steady since the founding of the nation, through such institutions as broadened voter registration, popular election of U.S. Senators, "one man one vote" court decisions, widespread use of primary elections to choose delegates to the national presidential conventions, the broadened use of popular referenda as alternatives to representative bodies in making public policy decisions, and the ubiquity of public opinion polling as a guide to elites' campaign and policy decisions. Is that movement irreversible, for better or for worse? I would not be willing to bet against the possibility.

A second point is that the psychological processes behind public response to political events may not always obey the conventional wisdom. It is tempting to see utilitarian motives at work, but that may not often be the case. Remote political events may have some features that draw on different psychological processes than does proximal daily life. The personal may not be so political, after all, and vice versa. Moreover, even the simple symbolic politics model may not be as good a fit when strong emotions are involved. Strong emotions may overwhelm the citizenry and immobilize them, as with the Nisei and the young children exposed to the Kennedy tragedy. A more complex psychological analysis may be required, whether one that involves schemata or deep psychodynamic forces. And that may, in turn, require methodologies other than conventional survey or experimental techniques.

ACKNOWLEDGMENT

An earlier version of this chapter was presented at the annual meeting of the International Society for Political Psychology, Montreal, Canada, July 13, 1998.

REFERENCES

Adorno, T. W., Frenkel-Brunswik, E., Levinson, D. J., & Sanford, R. N. (1950). *The authoritarian personality*. New York: Harper & Row.

Alwin, D. F., Cohen, R. L., & Newcomb, T. M. (1991). *Aging, personality and social change: Attitude persistence and change over the life-span*. Madison: University of Wisconsin Press.

Bauer, R. A. (1964). The obstinate audience: The influence process from the point of view of social communication. *American Psychologist, 19,* 319–328.

Brody, R. A. (1991). *Assessing the president: The media, elite opinion, and public support*. Stanford: Stanford University Press.

Campbell, A., Converse, P. E., Miller, W. E., & Stokes, D. E. (1960). *The American voter.* New York: Wiley.

Carmines, E. G., & Stimson, J. A. (1989). *Issue evolution: Race and the transformation of American politics*. Princeton, NJ: Princeton University Press.

Citrin, J., Green, D. P., Reingold, B., & Walters, E. P. (1990). The "official English" movement and the symbolic politics of language in the United States. *Western Political Quarterly, 43,* 85–108.

Dennis, J., Chaffee, S. H., & Choe, S. Y. (1979). Impact on partisan, image, and issue voting. In S. Kraus (Ed.), *The great debates: Carter vs. Ford 1976* (pp. 314–330). Bloomington: Indiana University Press.

Downs, A. (1957). *An economic theory of democracy*. New York: Harper-Row.

Edelman, M. (1964). *Symbolic uses of politics*. Urbana: University of Illinois Press.

Fiorina, M. P. (1981). *Retrospective voting in American national elections*. New Haven, CT: Yale University Press.

Hastorf, A. H., & Cantril, H. (1954). They saw a game: A case study. *Journal of Abnormal and Social Psychology, 49,* 129–134.

Hyman, H. H. (1959). *Political socialization*. Glencoe, IL: Free Press.

Institute for Propaganda Analysis. (1939). *The fine art of propaganda: A study of Father Coughlin's speeches*. New York: Harcourt and Brace.

Iyengar, S., & Kinder, D. R. (1987). *News that matters: Television and American opinion*. Chicago, IL: University of Chicago Press.

Iyengar, S., & Simon, A. (1993). News coverage of the Gulf Crisis and public opinion: A study of agenda-setting, priming, and framing. *Communication Research, 20,* 365–383.

Jamieson, K. H. (1984). *Packaging the presidency: A history and criticism of presidential campaign advertising*. New York: Oxford University Press.

Katz, E., & Feldman, J. J. (1962). The debates in the light of research: A survey of surveys. In S. Kraus (Ed.), *The great debates* (pp. 173–223). Bloomington: Indiana University Press.

Key, V. O., Jr. (1966). *The responsible electorate*. Cambridge, MA: Harvard University Press.

Kinder, D. R., & Sanders, L. M. (1990). Mimicking political debate with survey questions: The case of white opinion on affirmative action for blacks. *Social Cognition, 8,* 73–103.

Klapper, J. T. (1960). *The effects of mass communications*. Glencoe, IL: Free Press.

Kramer, G. H. (1971). Short-term fluctuations in U.S. voting behavior, 1896–1964. *American Political Science Review, 65,* 131–143.

Krosnick, J. A., & Brannon, L. A. (1993). The media and the foundations of presidential support: George Bush and the Persian Gulf conflict. *Journal of Social Issues, 49,* 167–182.

Lanoue, D. J. (1991). The "turning point": Viewers' reactions to the second 1988 presidential debate. *American Politics Quarterly, 19,* 80–95.

Lau, R. R., Brown, T. A., & Sears, D. O. (1978). Self-interest and civilians' attitudes toward the Vietnam war. *Public Opinion Quarterly, 42,* 464–483.

Lazarsfeld, P. F., Berelson, B., & Gaudet, H. (1948). *The people's choice* (2nd ed). New York: Columbia University Press.

McGuiness, J. (1969). *The selling of the president, 1968*. New York: Trident Press.

Mendelberg, T. (1997). Executing Hortons: Racial crime in the 1988 presidential campaign. *Public Opinion Quarterly, 61,* 134–157.

Miller, W. E., & Shanks, J. M. (1996). *The new American voter.* Cambridge, MA: Harvard University Press.

Mueller, J. E. (1973). *War, presidents, and public opinion.* New York: John Wiley & Sons.

Page, B. I., & Shapiro, R. Y. (1992). *The rational public: Fifty years of trends in Americans' policy preferences.* Chicago, IL: University of Chicago Press.

Petrocik, J. R. (1996). Issue ownership in presidential elections, with a 1980 case study. *American Journal of Political Science, 40*(3), 825–850.

Putnam, R. D. (2000). *Bowling alone: The collapse and revival of American community.* New York: Simon & Schuster.

Reingold, B., & Wike, R. (1998). Confederate symbols, southern identity, and racial attitudes: The case of the Georgia state flag. *Social Science Quarterly, 79,* 568–580.

Rhea, J. T. (1997). *Race pride and the American identity.* Cambridge, MA: Harvard University Press.

Riesman, D. (1969). *The lonely crowd: A study of the changing American character.* New Haven, CT: Yale University Press.

Roig, C., & Billon-Grand, F. (1968). La socialisation politique des enfants [The political socialization of children]. *Cahiers de la Fondation Nationale des Sciences Politique,* No. 163. Paris.

Ross, L., & Nisbett, R. E. (1991). *The person and the situation: Perspectives of social psychology.* New York: McGraw-Hill.

Schuman, H., & Scott, J. (1989). Generations and collective memories. *American Sociological Review, 54,* 359–381.

Schuman, H., Belli, R. F., & Bischoping, K. (1997). The generational basis of historical knowledge. In J. W. Pennebaker, D. Paez, & B. Rime (Eds.), *Collective memory of political events: Social psychological perspectives* (pp. 47–77). Mahwah, NJ: Lawrence Erlbaum Associates.

Schuman, H., Steeh, C., Bobo, L., & Krysan, M. (1997). *Racial attitudes in America: Trends and interpretations.* Revised Edition. Cambridge, MA: Harvard University Press.

Sears, D. O. (1983). The persistence of early political predispositions: The roles of attitude object and life stage. In L. Wheeler & P. Shaver (Eds.), *Review of Personality and Social Psychology* (Vol. 4, pp. 79–116). Beverly Hills: Sage.

Sears, D. O. (1993). Symbolic politics: A socio-psychological theory. In S. Iyengar & W. J. McGuire (Eds.), *Explorations in political psychology* (pp. 113–149). Durham, NC: Duke University Press.

Sears, D. O. (1994). Urban rioting in Los Angeles: A comparison of 1965 with 1992. In M. Baldassare (Ed.), *The Los Angeles riots: Lessons for the urban future* (pp. 237–254). Boulder, CO: Westview Press.

Sears, D. O., & Chaffee, S. H. (1979). Uses and effects of the 1976 debates: An overview of empirical studies. In S. Kraus (Ed.), *The great debates, 1976: Ford vs. Carter* (pp. 223–261). Bloomington: Indiana University Press.

Sears, D. O., & Citrin, J. (1985). *Tax revolt: Something for nothing in California* (Enlarged ed.). Cambridge, MA: Harvard University Press.

Sears, D. O., & Funk, C. L. (1991). The role of self-interest in social and political attitudes. In M. Zanna (Ed.), *Advances in experimental social psychology, 24,* 1–91. Orlando: Academic Press.

Sears, D. O., & Funk, C. L. (1999). Evidence of the long-term persistence of adults' political predispositions. *Journal of Politics, 61,* 1–28.

Sears, D. O., Hensler, C. P., & Speer, L. K. (1979). Whites' opposition to "busing": Self-interest or symbolic politics? *American Political Science Review, 73,* 369–384.

Sears, D. O., & Huddy, L. (1992). The symbolic politics of opposition to bilingual education. In J. Simpson & S. Worchel (Eds.), *Conflict between people and peoples* (pp. 145–169). Chicago: Nelson-Hall.

Sears, D. O., Huddy, L., & Schaffer, L. G. (1986). A schematic variant of symbolic politics theory, as applied to racial and gender equality. In R. R. Lau & D. O. Sears (Eds.), *Political cog-*

nition: The 19th annual Carnegie symposium on cognition (pp. 159–202). Hillsdale, NJ: Lawrence Erlbaum Associates.

Sears, D. O., & McConahay, J. B. (1973). *The politics of violence: The new urban blacks and the Watts riot.* Boston: Houghton-Mifflin. Reprinted by University Press of America, 1981.

Sears, D. O., & Valentino, N. A. (1997). Politics matters: Political events as catalysts for preadult socialization. *American Political Science Review, 91,* 45–65.

Sears, D. O., & van Laar, C. (1999). *Black exceptionalism in a culturally diverse society.* Unpublished manuscript. University of California, Los Angeles.

Sears, D. O., van Laar, C., Carrillo, M., & Kosterman, R. (1997). Is it really racism? The origins of white Americans' opposition to race-targeted policies. *Public Opinion Quarterly, 61,* 16–53.

Sheatsley, P. B., & Feldman, J. J. (1965). A national survey of public reactions and behavior. In B. S. Greenberg & E. B. Parker (Eds.), *The Kennedy assassination and the American public* (pp. 149–177). Stanford, CA: Stanford University Press.

Sniderman, P. M., & Carmines, E. G. (1997). *Reaching beyond race.* Cambridge, MA.: Harvard University Press.

Thernstrom, S., & Thernstrom, A. (1997). *America in black and white: One nation, indivisible.* New York: Simon & Schuster.

Valentino, N. A., & Sears, D. O. (1998). Event-driven political communication and the preadult socialization of partisanship. *Political Behavior, 20,* 127–154.

Wolfenstein, M. (1965). Death of a parent and death of a president: Children's reactions to two kinds of loss. In M. Wolfenstein & G. Kliman (Eds.), *Children and the death of a president* (pp. 62–79). Garden City, NY: Doubleday & Company, Inc.

Wollenberg, C. (1976). *All deliberate speed: Segregation and exclusion in California schools, 1855–1975.* Berkeley: University of California Press.

Zaller, J. (1992). *The nature and origins of mass opinion.* New York: Cambridge University Press.

Zaller, J. (1997). The myth of massive media impact revived: New support for a discredited idea. In D. Mutz, P. M. Sniderman, & R. A. Brody (Eds.), *Political persuasion and attitude change.* Ann Arbor, MI: University of Michigan Press.

Zaller, J. (1998). Monica Lewinsky's contribution to political science. *PS: Political Science and Politics,* June, 182–189.

15

Crossing the Methodological and Disciplinary Divide: Political Stability, Political Change, and Research Method

LEONIE HUDDY
State University of New York at Stony Brook

Political psychology is a diverse blend of intellectual threads from within political science and psychology, as can be gleaned from the titles and content of chapters in this volume. The fertile exchange between political science and psychology may be somewhat one-sided, as argued by Krosnick and McGraw (this volume), with political science providing the problems and psychology proffering the solutions. Nonetheless, topics in this volume reflect the field's interdisciplinary bent and range from the strategic communications of world leaders (Jervis, this volume) to the effects of early political socialization (Sears, this volume).

The intellectual breadth of political psychology is also accompanied by a diverse set of methodological tools. The field enjoys a more diversified analytic tool kit than either discipline alone. Moreover, methodological diversity is on the increase in both major disciplines and certainly within political psychology. Yet in the spirit of constructive criticism shared with many other chapters in this volume, I urge for greater methodological pluralism within political psychology and its respective parent disciplines. There are subfields of political psychology that embrace this pluralism wholeheartedly, with encouraging results. The field of political tolerance is exemplary in this regard (see Chong, 1991; Marcus, Sullivan, Theiss-Morse, & Wood, 1995; Sullivan, Piereson, & Marcus, 1982). Other fields within political psychology demonstrate the benefits of employing at least two different methods. The study of racial attitudes, for example, has routinely employed both experiments and surveys and, at times, experiments embedded within surveys (as an example, see Sniderman & Carmines, 1997).

Other areas of political psychology, however, are characterized by a schism between psychology and political science, with political scientists employing one method and psychology another to arrive at quite different conclusions. Recent research on attitudes and persuasion is perhaps one of the most notable examples. Psychologists working within an experimental tradition have emphasized the pliability and responsiveness of attitudes, whereas political scientists concentrating on survey results have emphasized their relative stability (see Eagly & Chaiken, 1993, for a summary of psychological research and contrast this with Alwin, Cohen, & Newcomb, 1991; Converse & Markus, 1979; Jennings & Markus, 1984; Sears, 1988). Such obvious differences beg for resolution and one is now beginning to emerge from research conducted by both psychologists and political scientists interested in motivated reasoning (Lodge & Taber, 2000). However, more is needed to bridge this methodological and disciplinary divide on a range of topics. Finally, some subfields of political psychology are characterized by methodological singularity both within political science and psychology. The study of ideology and values provides an important example within political science. Almost all of this research is based on survey data.

My goal is to highlight the benefits of methodological pluralism by drawing on findings from within several subfields of political psychology. With these examples, I hope to demonstrate the way in which method can influence research findings and build a case against dependence on a single approach. Methodological diversity helps to alleviate concerns about reliance on a single method by decreasing the likelihood that a particular finding is determined solely by the method used to examine the problem (Campbell & Fiske, 1959).

To counteract possible criticism that I see the glass as half empty when it is, in fact, half full, this critique is written as a celebration of interdisciplinary work. One of the pleasures of working within an interdisciplinary field is the ability to escape the shackles of a well-established research field with its associated (and often rigid) rules of engagement. Indeed, the very attraction of a field such as political psychology is its incredible intellectual freedom. Despite the practical difficulty of becoming conversant with diverse methods, the same spirit of adventure and freedom can also liberate our approach to research problems. Donald Campbell, a committed advocate of methodological diversity, believed that theories and models should be subject to a process akin to natural selection (Richards 1981;

Toulmin 1981). It is only fitting that this competition among social science ideas occur in a multimethod arena.

METHODS USED IN POLITICAL PSYCHOLOGY

Before embarking on a critical appraisal of methods currently employed by political psychologists, a brief review of the political psychology research arsenal is in order.

Experiment

The experiment is growing in popularity among political scientists but remains the primary research tool of social psychologists.[1] Social psychologists rely heavily on the experiment because of its ability to ensure internal validity. The experimental method has been used less commonly in political science, although its use has been increasing (Kinder & Palfrey, 1993; McGraw & Hoekstra, 1994).

Kinder and Palfrey (1993) listed three crucial features of an experiment: A controlled setting; treatment conditions that attempt to isolate a single causal factor; and recorded observations that are not contaminated by outside, nonexperimental causes. The ultimate goal of an experiment is to arrive at the true cause of an attitude or behavior. This is accomplished by the random assignment of participants to treatment conditions and often, although not always, the existence of a control group that is not subject to the key experimental treatment. Areas of political psychology in which political psychology experiments are quite common include the study and impact of the media (e.g., Iyengar & Kinder, 1987), the evaluation of political candidates (e.g., Lodge, McGraw, & Stroh, 1989), and racial attitudes (e.g., Sniderman & Carmines, 1997). The study of both candidate evaluation and racial attitudes benefit from survey data, although the study of racial attitudes may be unique in its frequent incorporation of experiments within surveys (Piazza, Sniderman, & Tetlock, 1989).

Experiments are designed to maximize internal validity, but they are also criticized within political science for their minimization of external validity, a fatal flaw for some political psychologists. To a large extent social psychological and to a somewhat lesser extent nonsurvey political psychology experiments depend on college student subjects (see Marcus et al., 1995,

---

[1]A number of the examples developed here draw from research in social psychology. This fits with Bar-Tal's (this volume) assessment that roughly 80% of articles in the journal *Political Psychology* are based on social or personality psychology. Nonetheless, as Marcus (this volume) points out, social psychology is only one branch of psychology that has influenced political psychology. Others include developmental, clinical, personality, and cognitive psychology.

and Lodge et al., 1989, for notable exceptions). It is obviously difficult to generalize from college students to the broader public, a point that has been made forcefully and in greater detail by Sears (1986). There are additional concerns about experiments (Kinder & Palfrey, 1993). Some political scientists question the meaning and external validity of specific experimental treatments that strike them as overly artificial or unable to capture the complex parameters of political context (McGraw & Krosnick, Jackman & Sniderman, this volume). Experiments are also faulted for their inability to capture the large cultural, historical, and societal forces that can move political attitudes and behavior over time but are not encapsulated within a single experimental situation (see Renshon, this volume).

Nonetheless, experiments remain an important tool for political psychologists, in part because they provide a convincing demonstration of causality. Perhaps even more importantly, they give purchase on contextual effects, including the impact of one's immediate environment. Political psychology has moved progressively away from a sole emphasis on longstanding predispositions as the root cause of political attitudes and behavior to examine more carefully the impact of the immediate environment. This interest emerges in research on the framing of political issues (Kinder & Sanders, 1990; Nelson, Clawson, & Oxley 1997), the effects of threat on intolerance (Feldman & Stenner, 1997; Marcus et al., 1995), the impact of persuasive information on attitude change (Huddy & Gunthorsdottir, 2000; Mutz, 1998), the impact of information on evaluations of political candidates (Lodge et al., 1989; McGraw, Best, & Timpone, 1995), and the effects of the information environment on the expression of racial attitudes (Mendelberg, 1997). Indeed, the findings of such experiments have indelibly altered political psychology by introducing the view from social psychology that situations play a key role in shaping attitudes and behavior. This research has challenged conventional wisdom in political behavior by producing results that often differ from those generated by surveys, a point to which we will return. Finally, experiments have also helped to demonstrate the existence and nature of race and gender stereotypes in a setting less tinged with obvious social desirability than an overt survey question (Huddy & Terkildsen, 1993; Terkildsen, 1993).

Survey

The survey is arguably one of the most common methods employed by political behavior researchers within political science. It thus requires little introduction. Perhaps the survey's two key features are a representative sample and a fixed set of questions, asked or read in a predetermined order. The use of a representative sample (and the absence of an artificial experimental situation) heightens external validity and is one of the major strengths of a survey. High external validity ensures the continued use of the survey to assess political attitudes and behavioral intentions in their "natural" state. In addition to describing public opinion, the survey has been used to analyze the structure of political beliefs and vote intentions, a key set of topics for political behavior researchers.

One of the major drawbacks to surveys is what has been referred to collectively as survey response effects. These include respondents providing different answers to survey questions based on the order of questions, their specific wording, the race and gender of the interviewer, and the order in which response options are presented (Alwin & Krosnick, 1991; Huddy et al., 1997; Schuman & Presser, 1981). Some researchers have further investigated these effects in order to learn more about the dynamics of public opinion and the nature of survey responses (Tourangeau & Rasinski, 1988; Zaller & Feldman, 1992). Detractors of the survey, however, see the variability reflected in response effects as a major flaw in the method.

Nonetheless, the survey remains a crucial tool for political psychologists. It has been combined increasingly with experiments embedded within random population surveys (Fletcher & Chalmers, 1991; Sniderman, Carmines, Layman, & Carter, 1996; Sniderman, Piazza, Tetlock, & Kendrick, 1991). Much of this research has focused on the expression of racial attitudes. Survey experiments have been designed to more accurately assess respondents' stereotypes by describing a scenario in which the protagonist is either Black or White, thus minimizing the social desirability that would accompany an outright question on race. However, experiments embedded within representative surveys have the additional advantage of demonstrating the effects of experimentally manipulated information, designed to parallel the effects of one's immediate context, among a representative group of people (e.g., Lau, Smith, & Fiske 1991; Mutz, 1998). They are thus of particular benefit to political psychologists interested in the contrasting effects of contemporaneous and long-standing influences on political attitudes and behavior.

Other Methods

These are by no means the only methods employed by political psychologists. Some political psychologists have analyzed the content of news stories to better understand the nature of the extant information environment (Danielan & Page, 1994; Huddy, 1997a; Just et al., 1996). Others have used the findings of media content analyses to design experiments that explicitly examine the impact of such natural variation in the news. Kinder and Sanders (1990), for example, designed a set of experiments to examine the framing of arguments against affirmative action as based on either reverse discrimination or unfair advantages, drawing on a content analysis of the news conducted by Gamson and Modigliani (1987).

Focus groups have been used within political psychology to examine the expression of opinions and beliefs in a natural social setting. Delli Carpini and Williams (1994) uncovered evidence from focus groups that people construct rather than retrieve their views on complex issues, by demonstrating the conflicting comments made by the same person on a single issue. Gamson (1992) used focus groups to demonstrate that citizens are not always influenced by the way issues are framed in the news. He found that the influence of media frames is common on remote issues such as the Israeli–Palestinian conflict, but it is less likely to affect views on issues that are closer to home, such as affirmative action. Deliberative polls in which citizens gather for a weekend to become better informed about politics constitute another method by which to examine the development of political beliefs (Fishkin, 1991; 1996; Merkle, 1996).

Qualitative techniques are also used by political psychologists. The interpretive analysis of case studies that formed the core of Freudian psychoanalytic treatment can be seen in the kind of leadership studies performed by Renshon (1996), Robins and Post (1997) or Volkan (Volkan, Itzkowitzk, & Dod, 1997). Although this technique has been criticized by many for its unscientific nature, when applied with care it can yield insights into the character and cognitive framework of decision makers who are either politically protected by their political office (George & George, 1998; Renshon, 1996) or long dead (Dean, 1997). In this volume, Monroe suggests the need to build a new paradigm in social science utilizing the subtle shifts in how actors see themselves in relation to others, and argues that rational choice theory can be replaced by such a paradigm. All of her empirical work supporting this call for theoretical innovation is based on work using the interpretive analysis of in-depth interviews (Monroe, 1996).

Similarly, one might also mention the important work from neuroscience that is yielding insight into our models of human decision making (Damasio, 1994; LeDoux, 1996; see also Marcus, this volume). This work suggests the need to modify the most basic research on political psychology, especially the interplay between cognition and emotion. Although I focus almost exclusively on surveys and experiments, the basic point that choice of method can influence the substantive conclusions of our research holds for these other approaches as well.

POLITICAL TOLERANCE

One of the central divides in political psychology is between the experimental and survey approaches. As noted earlier, surveys are good at getting at people's habitual responses, whereas experiments excel in tapping the influence of contemporary forces. Thus, it is not surprising to find that experiments tend to err on the side of attitude fluidity and change, whereas surveys emphasize stability and continuity. This distinction holds important implications for the study of political behavior and has emerged as a schism in several areas of political psychology. I take three of these areas—the study of tolerance, the investigation of attitude change and persuasion, and stability and change in political identity—to highlight how such discrepancies can enrich theoretical debate and strengthen confidence in empirical findings.

The benefit of using diverse methods is well illustrated by research on political tolerance. The methods used by political tolerance researchers range from surveys to experiments to in-depth interviews (Chong, 1991; Marcus et al., 1995; Sullivan et al., 1982). This multimethod approach has proven quite useful in the study of political tolerance, in part, because researchers have been motivated by a related set of central questions. As I discuss when examining the study of political persuasion, multiple methods have proven less fruitful when researchers working on a similar set of problems are motivated by different questions and tackle the problems from divergent theoretical and methodological perspectives.

There is a major puzzle that emerged early on in the study of political tolerance. From the outset, researchers found that people expressed support in the abstract for general democratic principles such as freedom of speech, but readily withdrew such freedoms for specific groups such as Communists or the Ku Klux Klan (Prothro & Grigg, 1960; McClosky, 1964; McClosky & Brill, 1983). Some of the original factors used to explain intolerance were individual differences such as dogmatism and education (see Marcus et al., 1995, pp. 30–32, for a summary of this research). But such factors are hopelessly inadequate to explain why an individual supports a broad democratic principle but opposes its application to a specific group.

Researchers have tackled the discrepancy between abstract principles and their application from different perspectives with considerable success. Chong (1991) reanalyzed data collected by McClosky and Brill (1983) as part of a small pretest for their larger 1977 survey. Chong examined these in-depth interviews and found the way an issue was framed helped to explain why people held tentative and, at times, contradictory views concerning tolerance. He found that many respondents were quite ambivalent about questions related to tolerance and were strongly affected by the question frame. Thus, some people gave an intolerant answer when asked about the rights of the majority only to change their minds and express a tolerant view when reminded of minority rights. Others thought immediately about the affected group (e.g., Communists) and based their decision on that. Still, these individuals who appeared intolerant by opposing the rights of a negatively regarded group changed their mind when confronted with the abstract principles of freedom of speech. Chong concluded that the divide between principles and their application is one of framing and top-of-the-head considerations. Better educated individuals show greater consistency in this regard because they are more chronically aware of abstract democratic principles, whereas those less educated are more influenced by the nature of the group under consideration. In this instance, the analysis of in-depth interviews lends substantial insight into the contradictions and reasoning processes that underlie deliberations about tolerance.

Marcus and colleagues (1995) tackled the problem from another perspective. They documented the emphasis within tolerance research on long-standing predispositions such as support for democratic principles or personality factors and argue that a crucial contemporary ingredient—the threat posed by a group—is missing from tolerance studies. Not surprisingly, much of the research that documents the influence of long standing predispositions on tolerance judgments is based on cross-sectional survey research, the method that is probably least suited to the study of contemporaneous influences. Marcus and colleagues conducted a series of experiments in which they manipulated the threat posed by a fictitious group in order to assess whether immediate threats can override the tendencies that arise from enduring predispositions. One of their basic findings is that individuals are less tolerant of groups that threaten unrest or violence. This finding gives additional weight to Chong's conclusion that considerations about a specific group can outweigh abstract democratic principles.

Chong provided evidence that specific groups shape tolerance judgments. But Marcus and colleagues isolated more exactly the specific attribute of a group that heightens intolerance. In their basic experimental design, respondents first answer background questions about themselves. Then 2 weeks later they are exposed to lengthier information about a group; their tolerance of the group is assessed immediately after exposure to this information. The group in the experimental manipulation is fictitious but resembles a group that the person dislikes, as assessed in the first phase of the study. Two aspects of the group are varied systematically: their potential for belligerence and the likelihood that they would gain power in the future. Of these two factors, only the group's potential for threatening action leads to intolerance. Marcus et al. concluded that this potential for violence and disorderly conduct triggers a threat reaction that promotes intolerance. But the other manipulated facet of the group—their future power—has no impact on tolerance judgments. The experiment thus helps to isolate a specific group attribute that promotes intolerance.

A second key finding to emerge from Marcus et al.'s (1995) experimental studies is that the meaning of democratic norms shifts with the way in which they are framed. The researchers added information on a bystander's views of the potentially threatening group to the research design just described. In some instances, the bystander expressed positive norms (e.g., free speech, importance of dissent) that would encourage a tolerant response to the group. In other instances, the bystander expressed negative norms (e.g., majority rights, group would abolish free speech) likely to promote intolerance. This manipulation produced greater tolerance among individuals exposed to positive norms but fostered greater intolerance among those exposed to negative norms. This finding adds an important addition to the debate on tolerance. It demonstrates that democratic norms themselves are subject to contemporary framing pressures. Citizens support various and competing principles concerning democracy and when one of those principles is made salient over another, tolerance reactions are affected. These conclusions also reinforce Chong's (1991) finding that interviewees shifted from intolerance when asked about the rights of the majority to tolerance when minority rights are made salient.

All told, the addition of in-depth interviews and experiments has added surprising depth to research on political tolerance. Both approaches help to resolve the dilemma between support for broad principles of tolerance and their checkered application to specific groups by focusing on groups and the threat they pose to the majority. Previous surveys had uncovered evidence that some groups elicited more intolerant responses than others. Both the in-depth interview and experimental approaches help to explain the exact nature of groups that elicit intolerance and the conditions under which this occurs. Both approaches thus demonstrate how tolerance judgments are affected by contemporary information. Chong provided evidence that political decisions unfold dynamically in the course of an in-depth interview. Marcus and colleagues demonstrated that the framing of values and norms affects tolerance decisions, a process that may be analogous to the impact of natural variations in political rhetoric. Simply focusing on education and other long-standing predispositions and beliefs as precursors to political tolerance is insufficient to explain the dynamic nature of tolerance judgments. Diverse research methods help to highlight the complex interplay of long-standing and contemporary forces in shaping tolerance judgments.

ATTITUDE CHANGE AND PERSUASION

Research on tolerance demonstrates considerable consensus across diverse methods, but this is not always the outcome of multimethod research, especially when researchers are separated not only by method but also by theoretical perspective and underlying assumptions. In this case, diverse methods can result in discrepant findings. A clear example is provided by research on attitude change and persuasion, a set of topics central to both social psychology and political psychology.

Social psychologists have always shown a keen interest in attitude change and persuasion, topics that have dominated the field since at least the 1950s, and have often emphasized the dynamism of public opinion by focusing on the factors that create attitude change (Eagly & Chaiken, 1993). This has resulted in a greater emphasis on attitude change than stability, although their relative emphasis has varied over time. The emphasis shifted toward attitude change in the 1980s and mid-1990s, influenced in no small degree by Petty and Cacioppo's (1986a, 1986b) *elaboration likelihood model* (ELM). In the experimental paradigm developed to test this model, Petty and Cacioppo found that someone who is directly affected by an issue, such as the imposition of mandatory exams for graduating seniors, will scrutinize the message more carefully and be most affected by a strong argument contained in the message (Petty & Cacioppo, 1979, 1990). These individuals process the message *centrally*. On the other hand, individuals who are not motivated or who are unable to process a message's intellectual content will be swayed by its visual and other superficial elements. They do not process the intellectual content of the message centrally but rather follow a *peripheral* route to persuasion (Eagly & Chaiken, 1993; Petty & Cacioppo, 1986a, 1986b; Petty, Cacioppo, & Goldman, 1981). In either case, attitude change is the key focus of investigation.

However, this approach fits less well with political behavior research based on surveys and panel studies that demonstrate remarkable stability in political attitudes, especially partisan identification and other long-standing values and group-related attitudes (Alwin et al., 1991; Converse & Markus, 1979; Jennings & Niemi, 1981; Sears, 1983). Zaller (1992), drawing on an earlier model of attitude change developed by McGuire (1985), argued that there are two barriers to attitude change within the general public: first, individuals have to be exposed to a message to be persuaded, and second, they have to accept it. Clearly partisan messages, a commonplace within politics, are rejected by those on the other side of the political divide, minimizing the number of individuals affected by such a message. An emphasis on attitude change is also inconsistent with the bulk of media studies that demonstrate quite meager direct effects of the news on opinions and attitudes, sometimes referred to as the *minimal effects model* of media impact (Kinder & Sears, 1985). How can we reconcile these two bodies of research? Psychologists emphasize attitude change while political scientists tout attitude stability. This difference has tended to minimize the impact of recent work on persuasion within political science, especially the ELM model, until quite recently (Cobb & Kuklinski, 1997; Mutz, 1998; Sniderman, Brody, & Tetlock, 1991).

One possible reason for this interdisciplinary difference in findings is research method. The bulk of political science studies that demonstrate stability are based on surveys, whereas most of the social psychological studies highlighting change rest on the findings of experiments. And as we noted at the outset, the experimental setting is perhaps best suited to the study of volatile contemporary forces, whereas surveys excel in assessing long-standing beliefs and values.

Methodology does account, in part, for the different emphasis within psychology and political science, although the story is somewhat more complex. In addition to methodology, there are also differences between political scientists and psychologists in the kinds of attitudes they study. Perhaps because social psychologists have expressed a keen interest in attitude change, researchers working within the ELM and related models have typically chosen to study relatively obscure issues that elicit few prior thoughts or feelings but have some immediate impact on study participants. Not surprisingly, the intellectual content of a message concerning a little-known issue with direct personal relevance receives careful scrutiny and, in this situation, strong intellectual arguments are more persuasive than weak ones. Johnson and Eagly (1989), however, investigating the impact of issue involvement, demonstrated that the success of a persuasive message depends on the basis of one's involvement in an issue.[2] Among individuals whose involvement rests on the defense of cherished values (value-relevant involvement), there is marked resistance to all arguments against one's position regardless of their strength (Johnson & Eagly, 1989). This is an important finding for political psychologists. It helps to explain why they uncover relative stability while psychologists report considerable attitude change. The difference arises, in part, because of differences in the attitudes investigated; political scientists focus on strongly held beliefs and values; psychologists examine new or weakly held issue positions.

Evidence that value-laden attitudes are most resistant to change led Zuwerink and Devine (1996) to look more closely at why involved individuals are more resistant to persuasive messages. Their answer is relatively straightforward. Individuals in their study who strongly supported gays in the military were more irritated by counterarguments against gay military personnel and generated more negative feelings and thoughts about the message; together, these affective and cognitive reactions resulted in greater resistance to the message. They claimed that "individuals can respond to persuasive messages with both thoughts and feelings and that both types of responses can contribute to resistance" (p. 932). Involved individuals not only generate strong emotions in response to a counterargument, they also respond more emotionally to evidence that fits with their position. Supportive evidence came from a study by Roser and Thompson (1995) in which students involved in environmental issues reacted with greater emotion

---

[2]For further discussion on the varied nature of attitude involvement see also Abelson (1988), Boninger, Krosnick, and Berent (1995), Krosnick and Abelson (1992).

than less involved students to a film on the threat of contamination from a nuclear power plant. Furthermore, this emotional arousal deepened their commitment to action on the issue.

In other words, there is considerable motivation to defend strongly held views. This fact is not unknown to political psychologists. Indeed, models developed by McGuire (1985), Hovland, Harvey, and Sherif (1957), and others emphasized the resistant nature of many social and political attitudes. However, political scientists have had difficulty in applying more recent approaches to attitude change, such as the ELM, because of its emphasis on attitude change. Social psychologists' recent revitalized interest in attitude stability is more in sync with political science evidence and guarantees that this work will have an impact on political psychology. Indeed, political psychologists have been quick to study motivated reasoning and the powerful ways in which individuals argue against new, contrary information (Lodge & Taber, 2000). If social psychologists had been working with survey data through the 1980s and 1990s, they may have emphasized the conditions under which attitudes both change and remain stable, rather than placing an undue emphasis on attitude change. In the case of attitude change and persuasion research, multimethod and cross-disciplinary fertilization would have given greater realism to attitude research within social psychology.

FLUIDITY AND CHANGE IN IDENTITY

A similar problem has emerged in studies of social and political identity. Social psychologists working within a social identity paradigm have emphasized the fluidity of identities, but research in political science based on panel studies highlights the enduring nature of partisan and other political identifications. In this instance, it is probably fair to conclude that social psychologists and political scientists have something to learn from each other and their respective research methods. Political identities appear both malleable and stable.

Within social psychology, social identity theorists have devoted considerable research attention to social identities and their variability across situations. One of the key insights of both social identity theory and its offshoot, self-categorization theory, is that principles governing the categorization of everyday objects can be extended to explain the categorization of people, including oneself, into social groupings (Lakoff, 1987; Neisser, 1987; Tajfel, 1981; Turner, Hogg, Oakes, Reicher, & Wetherell, 1987).[3] From a self-

---

[3]Tajfel documented the astonishing effects of simple social categorization, which are quite well known by now. Blue eyes, a preference for the painter Kadinsky over Klee, calling some

categorization perspective, identities vary, in part, because social categories such as age or gender vary in salience across situations. A group can increase in salience, for example, when group members are in a numerical minority.

Studies of existing social identities illustrate nicely the effects of salience on social identity. McGuire and colleagues reported evidence that children in an ethnic minority in their classroom (and whose ethnicity is therefore more salient) are more likely to describe themselves in terms of their ethnicity and children in families where there are more members of the opposite gender are more likely to mention their gender when describing themselves (McGuire, McGuire, Child, & Fujioka, 1978; McGuire & Padawer-Singer, 1976). But salience is not just a long-standing attribute of family structure or classroom makeup. It also varies with immediate social context. Hogg and Turner (1985) found, for example, that increasing the salience of study participants' gender increased the likelihood that they thought of themselves in gender-stereotypic terms.

Variability in the attributes of typical group members is a second factor that contributes to the development of political identity. Self-categorization theory views social identity as deriving from one's perceived similarity to typical group members, referred to as the group prototype (Hogg, 1996; Hogg, Cooper-Shaw, & Holzworth, 1993; Hogg & Hains, 1996; McGarty, Turner, Hogg, David, & Wetherell, 1992; Turner et al., 1987). From this perspective, it is not only salience but also category content that changes across social settings. This belief is based on the broad principles of categorization in which categories are defined on the basis of both what they are and what they are not (Rosch, 1978). According to these principles, individuals are more likely to think of themselves as members of social groups under conditions in which the use of a group label maximizes the similarities between oneself and other group members, and heightens one's differences with outsiders (Turner et al., 1987). A prototype emerges to capture this commonality among group members and can either be the most typical group member—an actual person—or a fictional member who embodies the most common or most frequent attributes shared among group members (Lakoff, 1987; Neisser, 1987; Rosch, 1978).[4]

---

people dot overestimators and others underestimators, were sufficient to produce a preference for fellow group members and elicit discrimination against outsiders (Allen & Wilder, 1975; Billig & Tajfel, 1973; Brewer & Silver, 1978; Tajfel, Billig, & Bundy, 1971; see Brewer, 1979, for a summary).

[4]The notion of prototypes reflects a shift away from a classical view of categories as defined by a set of clear rules or a set of common features to view categories instead as a fuzzy set with unclear boundaries and a "graded" or probabilistic structure in which some members are rated as more typical or better members of the category than others (Lakoff, 1987; Neisser, 1987; Rosch, 1978). Lakoff (1987) commented on the extensive empirical evidence in support of this conclusion, which he referred to as "prototype theory." Time and again, subjects rate

As noted, Turner and colleagues believe that these group prototypes vary across social settings and thus contribute further to shifts in identity. This view is captured in the following quote from Hogg, Terry, and White (1995, p. 261), who stated that "Social identity is highly dynamic: it is responsive, in both type and content, to intergroup dimensions of immediate social comparative contexts." In this statement, type refers to changes in category salience while content implies a change in the group prototype. From this perspective, a working woman might view herself as a feminist when in a group of homemakers, but may reject this identity when surrounded by women who are actively involved in the feminist movement. This shift is not due to a change in category salience but rather a shift in the meaning of feminist identity. Women who have chosen not to work outside the home highlight the meaning of feminism as involvement in the work force. Feminist activists, on the other hand, bring to light a view of feminists as women actively involved in politics.

There is no question that self-categorization theory has made a major contribution to the study of social identities by underscoring the importance of context in identity formation and change. Yet, the extreme view of identity fluidity put forward by John Turner and colleagues is at odds with the findings of survey-based research that documents considerable identity stability.[5] Indeed, partisan and social identities demonstrate remarkable stability over time when assessed in surveys on social and political topics and are much more stable than a range of other social and political attitudes (Alwin et al., 1991; Converse & Markus, 1979; Ethier & Deaux, 1994; Sears, 1983; Sears & Henry, 1999). This highlights an intriguing contradiction between the findings of experimental social psychologists who document considerable identity shift and the more stable view of identity provided by survey research in the social sciences.

As noted earlier, this discrepancy may arise, in part, from differences in research method. Surveys are likely to overestimate the stability of political identity because they often assess identities at intervals separated by several

---

some objects as better or more typical members of a natural category than others; they take less time to judge that a prototypic member belongs to the category; they are more likely to mention prototypic members when generating a list of category members; less typical examples are rated as more like the prototype than the prototype is like the unusual instance; and information about a prototype is more likely to generalize to an atypical group member than vice versa. From Rosch's (1978) perspective, a prototype "is simply a convenient grammatical fiction;" what is really referred to are judgments of degree of prototypicality.

[5]For example, John Turner and colleagues stated in a paper on Australian stereotypes of Americans that "salient self-categories are . . . intrinsically variable and fluid, not merely being passively 'activated' but actively constructed 'on the spot' to reflect the contemporary properties of self and others" (Haslam, Turner, Oakes, McGarty, & Hayes, 1992; p. 5). Not all social identity researchers confer, however. As noted by Hogg (1996, p. 74) this view can become unmanageable when taken to the extreme in which each new situation produces a fleeting social identity.

years and are unable to detect many of the micro changes that occur over a shorter time period in response to immediate events. It is possible to find evidence of this variability even within survey data. Consider Lau's (1989) finding that individuals whose views could be objectively characterized as liberal or conservative, expressed stronger levels of ideological identification in the 1972 and 1976 National Election Study in areas with a congressional candidate who shared their ideology. This presumably arose because the candidate made the respondent's ideology a more salient feature of the election in these congressional districts.

Huddy's research on the dynamics of feminist identity provided additional evidence that political identities evince both stability and change. In this work, social identity theory is applied to the development of feminist identity, and the ease with which feminist identity changes in response to information about the social and political characteristics of feminists and their opponents is examined (Huddy, 1997b, 1998). The findings provided limited support for a fluid view of identities while also identifying sources of identity stability. In support of a social identity approach, feminist identity depends on feeling similar to the types of women depicted as typical feminists (e.g., NOW members or members of other women's rights groups), independently of their beliefs (Huddy, 1998). In this research, experimental variations in the appearance and apparent gender role of typical feminists are a source of identity change. At the same time, there is considerable stability in feminist identity that is at odds with Turner and other social categorization researchers' view that social identities are highly changeable (Haslam, Turner, Oakes, McGarty, & Hayes, 1992; Hogg et al., 1995). In essence, the studies revealed that it is difficult to reverse cultural definitions of a typical feminist (for example, by depicting feminists as homemakers) and, more importantly, such culturally established group prototypes create a powerful source of identity stability (Huddy, 1997b). Sources of stability and change in political identities suggest that both the survey and experimental approaches shed light on the nature of political identity.

In the end, political identities probably change more than suggested by political scientists and yet are more stable than acknowledged by social psychologists. As noted by Markus and Kunda (1986), the self-concept is "in some respects quite stable" although marked by "significant local variations that arise when the individual responds systematically to events in the social environment" (p. 859). Diverse methods would help to provide a more balanced view of the changeability of political and social identities.

CONCLUSION

Political psychology is an interdisciplinary field, and I have outlined in this chapter why I think its methodological diversity should keep pace with its diverse intellectual origins. One of the key concerns raised in this review is the need to broach the methodological divide between political science and psychology. Psychologists have tended to rely heavily on experiments as their primary research medium, but, as noted, this can reduce external validity to the point where findings seem highly artificial and of little interest to political psychologists. An emphasis on weakly held attitudes within studies of the ELM model provides a compelling example. Although some political psychologists are interested in the formation of new attitudes, political psychologists are more commonly interested in the stability and change of strongly held opinions on issues such as the death penalty or legalized abortion.

Political scientists, on the other hand, usually employ the survey as their major research tool. Here, evidence of stability and consistency can mask short-term changes in political attitudes in response to contemporary forces. Such immediate events are the stuff of political campaigns and the daily news and although they may not always cumulate in long-term attitude change, such everyday changes are missed by a sole reliance on cross-sectional survey data. These short-term changes do matter politically and contribute, for instance, to the dynamics of an electoral campaign. The study of political tolerance provides an obvious example of the way in which experiments can be used to supplement surveys and provide a more fine-grained and situation-specific account of tolerance judgments. Another example arises from the study of political identity. Experimental studies of feminist identity demonstrate that such identities are among the most labile of attitudes in a given experimental situation despite the longer range stability within surveys of other political identities such as partisanship.

As political psychology researchers expand their tool kit to incorporate experiments, surveys, experiments embedded within surveys, and in-depth interviews, they are positioned to lend invaluable insight into the dynamics of public opinion within political science and the study of attitudes within social psychology more generally.

ACKNOWLEDGMENT

I thank Kristen Monroe for her insight and helpful comments on this manuscript.

REFERENCES

Alwin, D. F., & Krosnick, J. A. (1991). The reliability of survey attitude measurement: The influence of question and respondent attributes. *Sociological Methods and Research, 20,* 139–181.

Abelson, R. P. (1988). Conviction. Meeting of the American Psychological Association (1987, New York). *American Psychologist, 43*(4), 267–275.

Alwin, D. F., Cohen, R. L., & Newcomb, T. M. (1991). *Political attitudes over the life span: The Bennington women after fifty years.* Madison, WI: University of Wisconsin Press.

Allen, V. L., & Wilder, D. A. (1975). Categorization, belief similarity, and group discrimination. *Journal of Personality and Social Psychology, 32,* 971–977.

Billig, M., & Tajfel, H. (1973). Social categorization and similarity in inter-group behavior. *European Journal of Social Psychology, 3,* 27–52.

Brewer, M. B. (1979). In-group bias in the minimal inter-group situation: A cognitive motivational analysis. *Psychological Bulletin, 86,* 307–324.

Brewer, M. B., & Silver, M. (1978). In-group bias as a function of task characteristics. *European Journal of Social Psychology, 8,* 393–400.

Boninger, D. S., Krosnick, J. A., & Berent, M. K. (1995). Origins of attitude importance: Self-interest, social identification, and value relevance. *Journal of Personality and Social Psychology, 68*(1), 61–80.

Campbell, D. T., & Fiske, D. W. (1959). Convergent and discriminant validation by the multi-trait-multimethod matrix. *Psychological Bulletin, 56,* 81–105.

Chong, D. (1991). *Collective action and the civil rights movement.* Chicago: University of Chicago Press.

Cobb, M. D., & Kuklinski, J. H. (1997). Changing minds: Political arguments and political persuasion. *American Journal of Political Science, 41*(1), 88–121.

Converse, P. E., & Markus, G. B. (1979). Plus ça change . . . : The new CPS election study panel. *American Political Science Review, 73,* 2–49.

Damasio, A. R. (1994). *Descartes' error: Emotion, reason, and the human brain.* New York: G. P. Putnam.

Danielan, L. H., & Page, B. I. (1994). The heavenly chorus: Interest groups on TV news. *American Journal of Political Science, 38,* 1056–1078.

Dean, E. T., Jr. (1997). *Shook over Hell: Post-traumatic stress, Vietnam, and the civil war.* Cambridge, MA: Harvard University Press.

Delli Carpini, M. X., & Williams, B. (1994). The method is the message: Focus groups as a method of social, psychological, and political inquiry. In M. X. Delli-Carpini, L. Huddy, & R. Y. Shapiro (Eds.), *Research in micropolitics: New directions in political psychology* (Vol. 4). Greenwich, CT: JAI Press.

Eagly, A. H., & Chaiken, S. (1993). *The psychology of attitudes.* Ft Worth, TX: Harcourt Brace Jovanovich College Publishers.

Ethier, K. A., & Deaux, K. (1994). Negotiating social identity when contexts change: Maintaining identification and responding to threat. *Journal of Personality & Social Psychology, 67,* 243–251.

Feldman, S., & Stenner, K. (1997). Perceived threat and authoritarianism. *Political Psychology, 18,* 741–770.

Fishkin, J. S. (1991). *Democracy and deliberation: New directions for democratic reform.* New Haven: Yale University Press.

Fishkin, J. S. (1996). *The voice of the people: Public opinion and democracy.* New Haven: Yale University Press.

Fletcher, J. F., & Chalmers, M. (1991). Counterarguments in survey research: Non-attitudes and issue publics. *Political Behavior, 13*(1), 69–97.

Gamson, W. A. (1992). *Talking politics.* New York and Cambridge: Cambridge University Press.

Gamson, W. A., & Modigliani, A. (1987). The changing culture of affirmative action. *Research in Political Sociology, 3,* 137–77.

George, A. L., & George, J. L. (1998). *Presidential personality and performance.* Boulder, CO: Westview Press.

Haslam, S. A., Turner, J. C., Oakes, P. J., McGarty, C., & Hayes, B. K. (1992). Context-dependent variation in social stereotyping 1: The effects of intergroup relations as mediated by social change and frame of reference. *European Journal of Social Psychology, 22,* 3–20.

Hogg, M. A. (1996). Intragroup processes, group structure, and social identity. In W. P. Robinson (Ed.), *Social groups and identities: Developing the legacy of Henri Tajfel* (pp. 65–93). Oxford: Butterworth-Heinemann.

Hogg, M. A., Cooper-Shaw, L., & Holzworth, D. W. (1993). Group prototypicality and depersonalized attraction in small interactive groups. *Personality and Social Psychology Bulletin, 19,* 452–465.

Hogg, M. A., & Hains, S. C. (1996). Intergroup relations and group solidarity: Effects of group identification and social beliefs on depersonalized attraction. *Journal of Personality and Social Psychology, 70,* 295–309.

Hogg, M. A., Terry, D. J., & White, K. M. (1995). A tale of two theories: A critical comparison of identity theory with social learning theory. *Social Psychology Quarterly, 58,* 255–269.

Hogg, M. A., & Turner, J. C. (1985). Interpersonal attraction, social identification, and psychological group formation. *European Journal of Social Psychology, 15,* 51–66.

Hovland, C. I., Harvey, O. J., & Sherif, M. (1957). Assimilation and contrast effects in reactions to communication and attitude change. *Journal of Abnormal and Social Psychology, 55,* 244–252.

Huddy, L. (1997a). Feminists and feminism in the news. In P. Norris (Ed.), *Women, the media, and politics* (pp. 183–204). New York: Oxford University Press.

Huddy, L. (1997b). *Political identification as social identity.* Paper presented at the annual meeting of the American Political Science Association, Washington, DC.

Huddy, L. (1998). *The social nature of political identity: Feminist image and feminist identity.* Paper presented at the annual meeting of the American Political Science Association, Boston, MA.

Huddy, L., Billig, J., Bracciodieta, J., Hoeffler, L., Moynihan, P., & Pugliani, P. (1997). The effects of interviewer gender on the survey response. *Political Behavior 19,* 197–220.

Huddy, L., & Gunthorsdottir, A. (2000). The persuasive effects of emotive visual imagery: Superficial manipulation or a deepening of conviction? *Political Psychology, 21,* 745–778.

Huddy, L., & Terkildsen, N. (1993). Gender stereotypes and the perception of male and female candidates. *American Journal of Political Science, 37,* 119–147.

Iyengar, S., & Kinder, D. R. (1987). *News that matters: Television and American opinion.* Chicago: University of Chicago Press.

Jennings, M. K., & Markus, G. B. (1984). Partisan orientations over the long haul: Results from the three-wave political socialization panel study. *American Political Science Review, 78,* 1001–1018.

Jennings, M. K., & Niemi, R. G. (1981). *Generations and politics.* Princeton: Princeton University Press.

Johnson, B. T., & Eagly, A. H. (1989). Effects of involvement on persuasion: A meta-analysis. *Psychological Bulletin, 106*(2), 290–314.

Just, M. R., Crigler, A. N., Alger, D. E., Cook, T. E., Kern, M., & West, D. M. (1996). *Crosstalk: Citizens, candidates, and the media in a presidential campaign, American politics and political economy.* Chicago: The University of Chicago Press.

Kinder, D. R., & Palfrey, T. R. (1993). *Experimental foundations of political science, Michigan studies in political analysis.* Ann Arbor: University of Michigan Press.

Kinder, D. R., & Sanders, L. M. (1990). Mimicking political debate with survey questions: The case of white opinion on affirmative action for blacks. *Social Cognition, 8,* 73–103.

Kinder, D. R., & Sears, D. O. (1985). Public opinion and political action. In G. Lindzey & E. Aronson (Eds.), *Handbook of social psychology* (pp. 659–741). New York: Random House.

Krosnick, J. A., and Abelson, R. P. (1992). The case for measuring attitude strength in surveys. In J. M. Tanur (Ed.), *Questions about questions: Inquiries into the cognitive bases of surveys* (pp. 177–203). New York: Russell Sage Foundation.

Lakoff, G. (1987). *Women, fire, and dangerous things: What categories reveal about the mind.* Chicago: University of Chicago Press.

Lau, R. R. (1989). Individual and contextual influences on group identification. *Social Psychology Quarterly, 52,* 220–231.

Lau, R. R., Smith, R. A., & Fiske, S. T. (1991). Political beliefs, policy interpretations, and political persuasion. *Journal of Politics, 53,* 644–675.

LeDoux, J. (1996). *The emotional brain: The mysterious underpinnings of emotional life.* New York: Simon & Schuster.

Lodge, M., McGraw, K. M., & Stroh, P. (1989). An impression-driven model of candidate evaluation. *American Political Science Review, 83,* 399–419.

Lodge, M., & Taber, C. (2000). Three steps toward a theory of motivated political reasoning. In A. Lupia, M. McCubbins, & S. Popkin (Eds.), *Elements of political reasoning: Understanding and expanding the limits of rationality* (pp. 183–213). London: Cambridge University Press.

Marcus, G. E., Sullivan, J. L., Theiss-Morse, E., & Wood, S. L. (1995). *With malice toward some: How people make civil liberties judgments.* Cambridge, MA: Cambridge University Press.

Markus, H., & Kunda, Z. (1986). Stability and malleability of the self-concept. *Journal of Personality and Social Psychology, 51,* 858–866.

McClosky, H. (1964) Consensus and ideology in American politics. *American Political Science Review, 58,* 772–781.

McClosky, H., & Brill, A. (1983). *Dimensions of tolerance.* New York: Sage.

McGarty, C., Turner, J. C., Hogg, M. A., David, B., & Wetherell, M. S. (1992). Group polarization as conformity to the prototypical group member. *British Journal of Social Psychology, 31,* 1–20.

McGraw, K. M., Best, S., & Timpone, R. (1995). What they say or what they do: The impact of elite explanation and policy outcomes on public opinion. *American Journal of Political Science, 39,* 53–74.

McGraw, K. M., & Hoekstra, V. (1994). Experimentation in political science: Historical and future directions. In M. X. Delli-Carpini, L. Huddy, & R. Y. Shapiro (Eds.), *Research in micropolitics: New directions in political psychology* (Vol. 4, pp. 3–29). Greenwich, CT: JAI Press.

McGuire, W. J. (1985). Attitudes and attitude change. In G. Lindzey and E. Aronson (Eds.), *Handbook of social psychology* (pp. 233–246). New York: Random House.

McGuire, W. J., McGuire, C. V., Child, P., & Fujioka, T. (1978). Salience of ethnicity in the spontaneous self-concept as a function of one's ethnic distinctiveness in the social environment. *Journal of Personality & Social Psychology, 36,* 511–520.

McGuire, W. J., & Padawer-Singer, A. (1976). Trait salience in the spontaneous self-concept. *Journal of Personality and Social Psychology, 33,* 743–754.

Mendelberg, T. (1997). Executing Hortons: Racial crime in the 1988 presidential campaign. *Public Opinion Quarterly, 61,* 134–157.

Merkle, D. (1996). The polls—Review: The national issues convention deliberative poll. *Public Opinion Quarterly, 60,* 588–619.

Monroe, K. R. (1996). *The heart of altruism.* Princeton, NJ: Princeton University Press.

Mutz, D. C. (1998). *Impersonal influence: How perceptions of mass collectives affect political attitudes.* Cambridge: Cambridge University Press.

Neisser, U. (1987). From direct perception to conceptual structure. In U. Neisser (Ed.), *Concepts and conceptual development: Ecological and intellectual factors in categorization* (pp. 11–24). Cambridge: Cambridge University Press.

Nelson, T. E., Clawson, R. A., & Oxley, Z. M. (1997). Media framing of a civil liberties conflict and its effect on tolerance. *American Political Science Review, 91,* 567–583.

Petty, R. E., & Cacioppo, J. T. (1979). Issue involvement can increase or decrease persuasion by enhancing message-relevant cognitive responses. *Journal of Personality and Social Psychology, 37,* 1915–1926.

Petty, R. E., & Cacioppo, J. T. (1986a). *Communication and persuasion: Central and peripheral routes to attitude change. Springer series in social psychology.* New York: Springer-Verlag.

Petty, R. E., & Cacioppo, J. T. (1986b). The elaboration likelihood model of persuasion. In L. Berkowitz (Ed.), *Advances in experimental social psychology* (pp. 123–205). San Diego, CA: Academic Press.

Petty, R. E., & Cacioppo, J. T. (1990). Involvement and persuasion: Tradition versus integration. *Psychological Bulletin, 107*(3), 367–374.

Petty, R. E., Cacioppo, J. T., & Goldman, R. (1981). Personal involvement as a determinant of argument-based persuasion. *Journal of Personality and Social Psychology, 41,* 847–855.

Piazza, T., Sniderman, P. M., & Tetlock, P. E. (1989). Analysis of the dynamics of political reasoning: A general computer-assisted methodology. *Political Analysis, 1,* 99–119.

Prothro, J. W., & Grigg, C. W. (1960). Fundamental principles of democracy: Bases of agreement and disagreement. *Journal of Politics, 22,* 276–294.

Renshon, S. (1996). *High hopes: The Clinton presidency and the politics of ambition.* New York: New York University Press.

Richards, R. J. (1981). Natural selection and other models in the historiography of science. In M. B. Brewer & M. E. Collins (Eds.), *Scientific inquiry and the social sciences: A volume in honor of Donald Campbell* (pp. 37–76). San Francisco: Jossey-Bass.

Robins, R. S., & Post, J. M. (1997). *Political paranoia: The psychopolitics of hatred.* New Haven: Yale University Press.

Rosch, E. (1978). Principles of categorization. In E. Rosch & B. B. Lloyd (Eds.), *Cognition and categorization* (pp. 27–48). Hillsdale, NJ: Lawrence Erlbaum Associates.

Roser, C., & Thompson, M. (1995). Fear appeals and the formation of active publics. *Journal of Communication, 45*(1), 103–121.

Schuman, H., & Presser, S. (1981). *Questions and answers in attitude surveys: Experiments in question form, wording, and context.* New York: Academic Press.

Sears, D. O. (1983). The persistence of early political predispositions: The roles of attitude object and life stage. In L. Wheeler & P. Shaver (Eds.), *Review of personality and social psychology* (Vol. 4, pp. 79–116). Beverly Hills, CA: Sage Publications.

Sears, D. O. (1986). College sophomores in the laboratory: Influences of a narrow database on social psychology's view of human nature. *Journal of Personality and Social Psychology, 51,* 515–530.

Sears, D. O. (1988). Symbolic racism. In P. A. Katz & D. A. Taylor (Eds.), *Eliminating racism: Profiles in controversy* (pp. 53–84). New York: Plenum.

Sears, D. O., & Henry, P. J. (1999). Ethnic identity and group threat in American politics. *The Political Psychologist, 4*(2), 12–17.

Sniderman, P. M., Brody, R. A., & Tetlock, P. E. (Eds.). (1991). *Reasoning and choice.* Cambridge: Cambridge University Press.

Sniderman, P. M., & Carmines, E. G. (1997). *Reaching beyond race.* Cambridge, MA: Harvard University Press.

Sniderman, P. M., Carmines, E. G., Layman, G. C., & Carter, M. (1996). Beyond race: Universalistic v. particularistic policies. *American Journal of Political Science, 40,* 33–55.

Sniderman, P. M., Piazza, T., Tetlock, P., & Kendrick, A. (1991). The new racism. *American Journal of Political Science, 35*(2), 423–447.

Sullivan, J. L., Piereson, J., & Marcus, G. E. (1982). *Political tolerance and American democracy.* Chicago: University of Chicago Press.

Tajfel, H. (1981). *Human groups and social categories.* Cambridge: Cambridge University Press.

Tajfel, H. C., Billig, M. G., & Bundy, R. P. (1971). Social categorization and intergroup behavior. *European Journal of Social Psychology, 1,* 149–178.

Terkildsen, N. (1993). When white voters evaluate black candidates: The processing implications of candidate skin color, prejudice, and self-monitoring. *American Journal of Political Science, 37,* 1032–1053.

Toulmin, S. (1981). Evolution, adaptation, and human understanding. In M. B. Brewer & M. E. Collins (Eds.), *Scientific inquiry and the social sciences: A volume in honor of Donald Campbell* (pp. 18–36). San Francisco: Jossey-Bass.

Tourangeau, R., & Rasinski, K. A. (1988). Cognitive processes underlying context effects in attitude measurement. *Psychological Bulletin, 103,* 299–314.

Turner, J. C., Hogg, M. A., Oakes, P. J., Reicher, S. D., & Wetherell, M. S. (1987). *Rediscovering the social group: A self-categorization theory.* Oxford: Basil Blackwell.

Volkan, V. D., Itzkowitz, N., & Dod, A. (1997). *Richard Nixon.* New York: Columbia University Press.

Zaller, J. (1992). *The nature and origins of mass opinion.* Cambridge and New York: Cambridge University Press.

Zaller, J., & Feldman, S. (1992). A simple theory of the survey response: Answering questions versus revealing preferences. *American Journal of Political Science, 36,* 579–616.

Zuwerink, J. R., & Devine, P. G. (1996). Attitude importance and resistance to persuasion: It's not just the thought that counts. *Journal of Personality and Social Psychology, 70,* 931–944.

16

Signaling and Perception: Drawing Inferences and Projecting Images

ROBERT JERVIS
Columbia University

> *Some essential part of the study of mixed-motive games is necessarily empirical. This is not to say just that it is an empirical question how people do actually perform in mixed-motives games, especially games too complicated for intellectual mastery. It is a stronger statement: that the principles relevant to successful play, the strategic principles, the propositions of a normative theory, cannot be derived by purely analytical means from a priori considerations.* —Schelling, 1960, pp. 162–63

> *A marriage commitment is a very personal thing. It shouldn't be used to judge someone's character.* —Barbara Cozzi, manager of a retail store, commenting on the military adultery scandals in the spring of 1997, quoted in Goldberg, 1997

The varied contributions to this volume make clear that political psychology is a *they* rather than an *it:* There are many kinds of political psychology, proceeding from different assumptions and employing different approaches. Nevertheless, most forms share five distinguishing characteristics.

First is the belief that to understand human behavior, we have to understand how people think, interpret their environments, and reach decisions. Simple stimulus–response models rarely will do. To turn to international politics, theories that stress the importance of the state's external environment, although extremely useful for some purposes, leave many central questions unanswered. To understand international behavior, we need

293

to look inside the "black box" of the state, and indeed to study the goals, beliefs, and perceptions of the decision makers.

A related way of putting this is to note that standard notions of rationality are not so much incorrect as insufficient to catch either the objectives toward which people strive or the means by which they try to reach them. This does not mean, however, that the perspectives of political psychology and rational choice theory are antithetical. The form of rational choice that is most appropriate to the study of international politics is *game theory*, which revolves around actors' anticipations of others' behavior and of others' anticipation of their behavior. But game theory cannot put flesh on this skeleton because it cannot speak to how these expectations are formed and what they will be (Kreps, 1990). Political psychology is essential here.

The second component of political psychology is that looking at decision making reveals both common patterns and idiosyncrasies. As I discuss at the end of this chapter, there are important common strands in the way that most political leaders think and perceive. These patterns are consistent with the results of laboratory experiments and studies of how people behave in other spheres of life, and, although not necessarily representing irrationality, neither do they fit well with theories that make simple assumptions about how people reason. But in addition to commonalities, people differ in the ways they process information, draw inferences, and reach decisions. Political leaders are less prone than scholars to homogenize people and so devote serious attention to trying to understand those with whom they are dealing.

Third, behavior is related to the self-images and identities, which are so important to people.[1] Although much remains to be understood, it is clear that the way individuals and groups view others and the way they view themselves are reciprocally related. Thus people sometimes think badly of others in order to think well of themselves, or see another state as aggressive because they think that their own state is peaceful. They often define themselves as different from—and usually better than—others, and, conversely, are prone to find or create differences with those they dislike. Most people also want to see their own behavior as rational and consistent, which can lead to behavior not readily explicable in terms of the situation the person or state is currently facing (Bem, 1972; Larson, 1985). In related ways, actors interpret information about the environment, others, and their own behavior to reinforce their self-conceptions.

Fourth, as the previous discussion implies, people have emotions as well as beliefs; cognition is often "hot." But political scientists rarely talk about affect (exceptions are Crawford, 2000; Mercer, 1996a; also see Jennings,

---

[1] Social constructivists who stress that the world around us is created by human activity and thought have rediscovered these concepts, which are new to those with little knowledge of psychology. A clear general discussion of constructivism is Hacking, 1999; a sympathetic but balanced treatment as applied to international politics is Hopf, 1998.

1999). Anger, longing, love, and humiliation are not part of their language or landscape. Fear is discussed more often, especially in international politics, where scholars talk about one state fearing another or explain an arms race in terms of mutual fear. However, in most cases one could substitute the term *threat perception* without distorting the author's meaning because the emotional connotation of fear is drained from the analysis. Even more strikingly, hatred is rarely mentioned—but who could expect to understand international conflict without creating a space for this impulse, which is so palpable throughout history?

The final essential element of political psychology is the rejection of a priori reasoning and the deep commitment to empirical research. Abstract theorizing is crucial, but we must also examine a great many cases if our understanding is to advance. Such data not only test and modify our theories, but also lead to important ideas. A fine and socially important example is Treiseman's (1985) work on why many Black students do badly in college mathematics classes and, even more importantly, what can be done about it. He started with propositions that seemed almost self-evident—e.g., the high failure rate among Blacks could be explained by lack of high school preparation, motivation, or parental support—but found that none of them were correct. Only after 18 months of following the students around in something like ethnographic field work did he discover that the operating incentive structure differed from what he had assumed from the outside and that the students' beliefs and self-images were crucial. Because these young men and women viewed themselves as strong students, the extra classes could not be touted as remedial and in fact had to include extremely difficult problems; because most of them had succeeded in high school by resisting peer pressure, they had to be brought to the idea that working with their fellow students could be legitimate and mutually beneficial.

I do not mean to suggest that all of us would have done what Treiseman did, although I wish that were the case. But I do think that political psychology leads us to explore the diverse yet patterned ways that people develop and pursue their goals, perceive and act in their environments, and make sense of their lives. While many approaches to the study of politics take for granted the actors' preferences and ideas about how to reach them, these are often the most important parts of the explanation for behavior, and it is doubtful if we can understand them without employing political psychology.

SIGNALING AND PERCEPTION

The utility of political psychology can be illustrated by examining how actors communicate with each other, especially in international politics. Some professional autobiography is relevant here. My dissertation began as a study of how countries form images of others and predict what they will do, but after a bit of thought, I realized that studying perception and mis-perception in isolation would be one-sided. Just as actors need to predict what others will do, so they also want others to make desired predictions about their own behavior; actors not only perceive others, they signal in order to project images that may be either true or false. (Indeed, when they interpret others' behavior, they realize that the others are also trying to project desired images.) At a certain point, however, the understanding that the topics of drawing inferences and projecting images were intimately related became less pressing than the realization that I could not analyze both if I were to finish my dissertation in the foreseeable future. So I split the topics apart, taking what I thought was the more manageable subject of projecting images for my thesis and returning to misperception when it was done. The dissertation turned into *The Logic of Images in International Relations* (Jervis, 1970) and the second study appeared as *Perception and Misperception in International Politics* (Jervis, 1976).

Although the two studies did touch on each other in a few places, as I wrote them they really did not represent two sides of the same coin. What makes this more than a personal anecdote is that the topics of how actors seek to influence others' perceptions of them and how they perceive others have been kept separate by other scholars as well. One impetus for this chapter is my view that much recent work on signaling carried out by econ-omists and those influenced by them is flawed by the failure to see that the two topics should be joined (Banks, 1991; Morrow, 1994). This means, of course, that this chapter should unite them, but after 35 years I can still make only limited steps in that direction.

THE PROBLEM ACTORS FACE

The general problem is easily enough stated. In order to establish their own policies, actors need to estimate what others will do and how they will react to alternative kinds of behavior on the part of the actor.[2] *Logic of Images* and the more recent economistic approaches have the same starting point: the only behaviors that are informative are those that distinguish among actors who will react differently, or, to use the term now often employed, actor "types." If I am to figure out whether another state is bluffing or not, or whether its apparent hostility is rooted in fear or expansionism, or whether a potential ally will come to my assistance if I am attacked, I should look only at behavior that discriminates between the alternative possibilities. Thus I should pay no attention to the things that both a bluffer and a seri-

---

[2]Exceptions to this generalization are not trivial, but are largely put aside here.

ous state would do, to a posture that both a fearful state and an aggressor would assume, or to a promise that both a trustworthy and an untrustworthy ally would make.[3] The inference process is rendered especially difficult because actors who know that they are being observed and want to influence others have powerful incentives to project images that will lead perceivers to draw the desired impression whether or not it is accurate.

PERCEPTIONS CONTROL

The value of various kinds of behaviors for determining how the actor will behave in the future is the linchpin of signaling and perception. The former must depend on the latter because the impression conveyed by any behavior depends on how it is perceived. This is obscured by much of our discourse because we talk about how actors should behave in order to project a given image and the sort of information perceivers should pay attention to. The language is prescriptive because this theorizing is more deductive than empirical. But what if (all? some?) perceivers infer differently? Indeed, if signaling theories are arcane, perceivers who have not read the literature will draw inferences differently, which means that the theory will neither describe the thoughts of perceivers nor prescribe the signalers' behavior. A theory of signaling, then, requires a careful investigation of how signals are perceived.

When I wrote this chapter, two news stories appeared that help explain what I mean. When the chief of the Indonesian armed forces, General Wiranto, travelled to East Timor in the wake of the militia violence that followed the referendum for independence, the capital city of Dili was calm. The Indonesians presumably wanted to show that they could keep the peace. However, the British representative to the UN thought that this "illustrates that you can never know whether these people are going to switch [the violence] on or switch it off" (Mydans, 1999). The second story involved a murder suspect who had freely undergone a prolonged police interrogation. The police chief was suspicious: "How many innocent people do you know who will sit there and answer questions for hours?" (Bennet, 1999) Perception is laden with interpretation and theory. Almost no inferences—perhaps none at all—are self-evident in the sense that all people under all circumstances looking at the information would draw the same

---

[3]Implicit in the discussion so far—and an assumption for everything that follows—is that there are significant differences among actors: that they not only differ in their capabilities, but in their goals, beliefs about how to reach those goals, and willingness to pay costs to do so. This seems self-evident, just as it used to be considered self-evident that individuals had stable personalities that strongly influenced their behavior. However, it can be argued that this assumption is incorrect and that situational variables determine behavior.

conclusion. Thus, knowing how theorists read a signal does not tell us how the perceiver does.

A few more examples may make the problems clearer and flag some questions. The other evening I was walking down Broadway and saw 12 policemen in about as many blocks. Should I have been reassured that so many policemen were there to guarantee my safety, or alarmed that the neighborhood is so dangerous as to require this force? When a university institutes a teaching award, is this a signal that it takes teaching seriously or that it did not take it seriously before? Or is it a signal that it wants others to believe that it takes teaching seriously, and, if so, how and in what direction does this correlate with taking it seriously? If a previous winner of the teaching award was just given tenure, will (should?) other assistant professors think that winning the award will boost their chances, or infer that the university, having ostentatiously rewarded one good instructor, will not feel the need to do so again in the near future? When I see a sign in a restaurant bathroom saying "Employees must wash their hands," am I reassured that the hygiene standards are appropriately high, disturbed that the people handling my food must be reminded to follow the dictates of common sense, or do I fear that they will respond to the insult by not washing?

As these examples show, most communications convey two messages: what the actor is saying and the fact that he needs to say it. For a bank to increase its reserves against possible losses strengthens its position, but the opposite effect may be produced when others learn that it has done so and infer that its solvency is in doubt. For an actor to claim that it is committed to taking a certain action will increase the costs it will pay if it behaves otherwise, and if this were the only effect, this would increase others' estimates of how likely it is to carry out this act. However, the fact that the actor felt the need to commit itself conveys information, and others may infer that only the weak need to try to bolster their resolve. In much the same way, when a state tries to reassure its ally that it will stand by it, the ally's uneasiness may increase as it infers both that the threat is greater than it had believed and that the patron feels that such reassurances are necessary.

My point is that although behavior may reveal something important about the actor, often it is not clear exactly what is being revealed, what is intended to be revealed, and what others will think is being revealed. If a husband leaves his wife and small children for another woman, should the new love infer that he is likely to remain faithful to her because he has made such a sacrifice to be with her, or should she worry that someone who has deserted one family is likely to repeat the offense? What inferences do we expect the Soviets to have drawn from the Western bombing of Dresden at the end of World War II? That, as some Western leaders thought at the time, the willingness to kill a large number of Germans and weaken their Eastern front in order to facilitate Soviet victories showed that they took

Soviet interests into account? Or that the West was brutal and likely to try to coerce the USSR in the postwar world?

It might seem as though consistency provides the key. For example, observers should infer that the actor is "tough" (i.e., has high resolve) if it behaves strongly. In a situation resembling a game of chicken in which high conflict or war is the worst possible outcome for both sides, a strong reaction is one that runs a significant risk of an undesired clash. A belligerent response would therefore unambiguously show resolve. But this is too simple. Observers' interpretations remain crucial as they have to decide what is risky, whether the actor thought the behavior was risky, and whether the behavior is likely to be repeated. Furthermore, to the extent that resolve is inferred from actions that the observer thinks the actor believes have a significant chance of leading to war, we run into a paradox of the kind that deterrence and game theory have made familiar: what is believed to be risky is actually safe and vice versa. If the adversary believes that only a state that was willing to go further would take such a bold step, then the step would be safe because the adversary would back down in the face of such a response. But this, in turn, would mean that a state that was not willing to take much risk of additional escalation, as well as a state that was, would be willing to act in this way, thereby permitting deception and robbing the behavior of much of its meaning (Jervis, 1997, pp. 255–258, pp. 266–271). This twist of the argument would be true only if perceivers believed it, however, which reinforces the point that the impact of behavior depends on the perceiver's beliefs about the links between the other's present and future actions.

It is exactly the meaning of the similarity of behavior and the nature of these links that requires theorizing and so is often subject to dispute. Thus when President Clinton hired the high-powered Washington lawyer Robert Bennett to defend him against the sexual harassment charges by Paula Jones, not only did the *Washington Post* sharply increase its coverage of the story, but, in a very different arena, confidence in the dollar increased. "If Paula Jones has no case, the *Post* editors figured, how come Clinton needs a hired gun like Bennett?" ("Clinton versus Paula Jones," 1997) According to a currency trader, hiring Bennett "was really a boon for the dollar. We were starting to lose faith in him and that helped turn things" (Friedman, 1994). These inferences overlap in seeing Clinton as taking the charges seriously but differed because the perceivers have different substantive interests and the currency traders were looking for a character trait, a willingness to act strongly in the face of adversity rather than becoming paralyzed and indecisive, whereas the *Post* (and others) were estimating whether the charges had merit. What is central, however, is that the inferences will strike many observers as strange and that neither the existence of links nor why some people discerned them is entirely clear.

TYPOLOGIES OF INFORMATIVE BEHAVIOR

Not all behavior is equally informative about what actors will do in the future. The distinction of intuitive appeal is between words and deeds. But, even putting aside what the philosopher J. L. Austin called *performative utterances*—cases in which "in saying what I do, I actually perform that action," such as naming a ship in a christening and saying "I do" in a marriage ceremony (Austin, 1961, pp. 220–39)—words can carry significant evidence of their validity. Indeed, if this were not so, it would be hard to explain why actors who mistrust each other bother to listen—or talk—at all. Many deeds, furthermore, are ambiguous or can be used for deception.

Two alternative distinctions have been proposed; neither is completely satisfactory. In *Logic of Images* I distinguished between indices and Signals (I will use the term Signals with a capital S when talking about this concept and write signals in the lower case for all behavior that the sender or the perceiver believes carries information). Signals (with a capital S) are like a language in that their meanings are established by agreement, implicit if not explicit. Thus words, special forms of communication like diplomatic language, and many actions have meaning because both the signaler and the perceiver agree as to the message that the former is trying to convey. The obvious difficulty for both sides is that Signals can be used to project a false as well as a true image.

Indices, by contrast, are behaviors (either verbal or nonverbal) that the perceiver believes are inextricably linked to a characteristic that helps predict what the actor will do in the future. Observers therefore see them as reliable and not available for deception. Most attention has been focused on actors' intentions or types, but let me give an example of capabilities. Anyone can claim to be strong; being able to lift a heavy weight provides more credible evidence of that characteristic. Similarly, having a screaming fit is an index to being hot-tempered, although people in everyday life and statesmen (e.g., Hitler) have been known to put on acts for the benefit of observers. These indices can be seen as samples of the behavior of interest; others are believed to be correlates—and perhaps causes—of it, as when democracy is used as an index of the propensity to follow a peaceful foreign policy.

For behavior to be taken as an index, the perceiver must believe that the actor cannot manipulate it to project a false image, either because manipulation is impossible or excessively costly or because the actor is unaware that the perceiver is tracking it. But the meaning and indeed the existence of indices depends on the perceiver's theories about the links between the behavior and underlying characteristics. Thus, in many of the cases discussed earlier, behavior was interpreted differently by different observers because some of them saw a certain correlation whereas others either saw none or believed that the correlation was quite different.

Costly Signals and Cheap Talk

Economists, and political scientists who have been influenced by them, have distinguished between "costly signals" and "cheap talk." The basic argument follows from Schelling's intuition that a behavior that costs nothing can be equally well taken by an actor of any type and so provides no information (Schelling, 1966, p. 150). Statements of intent, for example, are cheap in that both a Hitler and a statesman who really was committed to peace could equally well declaim benign goals. It follows that perceivers should focus on behavior that is costly to undertake. Such behavior cannot readily be faked: Only an actor that is willing and able to behave in a certain way can have the ability and incentives to send these costly signals.

Many costly signals fit within my category of indices. As I noted in *Logic of Images*, when states feel the need to impress others with their resolve, they often increase their defense spending irrespective of the increase in capability that will result, and indeed occasionally at the cost of such capability. But the distinction between cheap and costly behavior has a number of difficulties, some of which are shared with my discussion of Signals and indices. To start with, cheap talk is sometimes defined as behavior that does not cost the actor anything to undertake and sometimes as behavior that can be taken equally well by an actor of any type. These definitions overlap, but are not identical. Indeed, behavior often is highly diagnostic if it is cheap for an actor of one type but not for an actor of another kind. Thus if a state is peaceful, giving up offensive weapons will be far less of a sacrifice than if it is an expansionist, which is why such a move carries great credibility.

We must also distinguish between two different kinds of costly signals. One consists of cases in which the cost is incurred as the behavior is undertaken. For example, taking an action in the face of significant domestic opposition can be a costly signal of the decision makers' commitment to the policy. But the term *commitment* shows a second category of costly signals: threats and promises that will be costly to break. This is the function of Signals that the state is committed to following a given policy. Here the cost comes not with the issuing of the Signal, however, but only later if the actor does not live up to it (Schelling, 1960; also see Fearon, 1997).

It might seem that problems of interpretation do not arise with costly signals because costs are objective and will be seen the same way by all participants. But what the actor feels to be a cost, observers may not so categorize, or vice versa, as the example of Br'er Rabbit reminds us. Had the United States engaged in high defense spending in the late 1940s, it would have been felt as costly by American political leaders. But Stalin might not have seen it that way because he believed that insufficient demand was the main danger facing the American economy, which therefore would have benefitted from higher spending. Indeed, throughout the Cold War the Soviets claimed that the periodic increases in the U.S. defense budget reflected the power of arms manufacturers or the needs of the economy, in which case they would not have been taken as indications that the United States was willing to sacrifice blood in a limited war or run high risks during a crisis.

The central role of perceivers' beliefs leads to another difficulty with the notion of costly signals, one that is also brought out by the example just given. In some cases, the cost that is borne is very tightly related to the characteristic being judged, but often it is not. For example, high defense spending may be an index, but exactly what is it an index of? The perceiver must do a great deal of interpretive work to answer this question. For the Soviets, it might be an index of the power of various groups and classes in the United States, and so might yield valuable information about which sectors were dominant. Depending on other beliefs, this could lead to the judgment that the United States was aggressive, or that it would behave cautiously in a crisis because these sectors would not want to risk a conflict that might undermine their positions. Observers, Marxist or not, might also infer that the United States lacked confidence in its military might, that it was seeking to substitute arms for the willingness to shed blood in a war, or that it hoped to impress others, which would save money in the long run. Others with different theories could draw the opposite inference: Only a country that was a "tough" type would be willing to spend a lot on defense. Knowing that the behavior is costly, then, tells us little about what inferences observers will draw; it is probably fruitless to argue about what inferences they should draw.

Changing Types.   Most discussions assume that the actor's type remains constant. Indeed, this assumption underpins the use of signals to predict future policy. Behavior can change as well as reveal an actor's type, however, and this is particularly true for costly measures. For example, fighting in Vietnam undermined America's containment policy because having paid a high price for one limited war, it would not do so again. It was the Soviet appreciation of this change in American domestic opinion, not the fact that the United States would not pay the price necessary to secure victory, that drove the (limited) Soviet perceptions of American weakness in the aftermath of the war (Hopf, 1994). Similarly, psychologically as much as materially, Britain and France were shattered by World War I and so were unwilling to follow the same kind of stiff policy toward Germany in the 1930s that they had adopted in the earlier period. They were no longer the same type of actors as they had been, as most perceivers—most acutely Hitler—realized. I suspect that it is generally true that paying a significant price will set off a variety of political, social, and psychological processes that can alter the actor's goals, views of the world, self-image, and other characteristics that underpin its behavior. Here, too, much depends on how the actor and observers understand the previous policy, most obviously whether they see it as a success and worth the effort (for the literatiure on learning, see Breslauer & Tetlock, 1991; Leng, 1988; Levy, 1994).

Indices

Although the category of costly signals overlaps with the concept of indices, it does not exhaust it. The basic logic is that only an actor of a certain type would behave in this way and that the behavior is a good predictor of what the actor will do in the future. When an index approximates a sample of the behavior that is expected in the future, the belief about its significance is likely to be seen as self-evident. Other indices invoke much more interpretive work, as when states attribute certain foreign policy propensities to states according to their domestic regimes. But the form of the inference is the same: only an actor of type X would undertake action Y, therefore the actor is of type X.

These links may seem clear to an observer, but there is room for dispute and error. Thus after the Soviets shot down the Korean airliner that strayed over their territory in August 1983, Ronald Reagan asked, "What can be the hope of legitimate and moral discourse with a state whose values permit such atrocities?" (quoted in Sherry, 1995, p. 403) and in the summer of 1959, when Khrushchev complained to Nixon about the American placement of missiles in Turkey, he asked: "If you intend to make war on us, I understand; if not, why [do this]?" (quoted in Bernstein, 1992, p. 59). Similarly, in the months preceding the Japanese decision to attack Pearl Harbor, the military argued that if the Americans "do not accede to the conditions we have presented [in the negotiations], we must take the view that they harbor designs to bring Japan to its knees; thus, it is clear that if we make concessions we will soon be put to their poisoned sword" (quoted in Morley, 1994, p. 171). The Poles reacted so strongly to the discovery of the Katyn massacre in 1943 not only because of its intrinsic horror, but also because they saw it as an index of the Soviet rejection of the possibility of a non-Communist Polish government after the war. The Soviet leaders, in turn, took the Polish refusal to accept the Soviet false claim that the officers had been killed by the Nazis as evidence that this regime would not accommodate Soviet interests. None of these inferences were foolish, but all could be debated, either at the time or later. The connections that seemed so clear to the perceivers rested on a set of unarticulated generalizations about politics and classes of actors.

Inasmuch as the interpretation of indices depends on theories, perceivers are likely to go astray when these are incorrect. Furthermore, actors who understand the theories and can manipulate the behavior that is being used as an index can project a desired image even if it is false. Of course, perceivers use indices because they believe that actors cannot manipulate them, but only in some cases is this correct. Even indices that seem to tap the relevant characteristic quite directly and that involve high costs can be controlled by actors who are willing to pay the price, which was the case with the behavior of Jesus Guajardo, who was hired to infiltrate the camp of the Mexican rebel leader Emilano Zapata in order to kill him. So:

> Guajaredo . . . "deserted" to Zapata with his entire unit and asked to be taken into his army. Such a development represented welcome reinforcements for Zapata, who desperately needed soldiers and, above all, arms. Nonetheless, he was skeptical, and he ordered Guajardo to attack a Carranzist garrison to prove his revolutionary commitment. Guajardo provided his "proof." He not only carried out the attack, but even executed the Carranzist soldiers he captured. After that, Zapata felt he could trust Guajardo and agreed to a meeting at the Chinameca hacienda. On 10 April 1919 he proceeded there with several companions. Guajardo received him with an honor guard standing at attention. When Zapata approached, a "salute of honor" was fired and Zapata was killed instantly. (Katz, 1981, p. 533)

Signals and Reputation

Perceivers can use an index to draw inferences even—and especially—when they do not think the actor is trying to communicate anything. By contrast, Signals imply that the actor intends to communicate, and the perceiver's first task is to try to determine what the actor is trying to say. A necessary condition for the effective use of a Signal is that senders and perceivers interpret it in the same way. Thus diplomatic language is often employed because the meanings of words and phrases have come to be precisely understood and, on other occasions, actors take care to see that their Signals are ambiguous and so can be disavowed if need be. Even when ambiguity is not intended, however, Signals frequently fail because the perceiver does not understand what message the actor is trying to communicate.

Understanding does not mean believing, however, because deceivers as well as honest actors can send the same Signals. As noted earlier, Signals are cheap to send, but this does not mean that costs do not enter in. Signals are implicit or explicit statements of how the actor will behave in the future, and costs are incurred if and when the actor does not behave accordingly. This is one of the main reasons why perceivers pay attention to Signals and is usually discussed in terms of the importance to an actor of its reputation.

Putting aside the validity of these claims (Hopf, 1994; Mercer, 1996b), we need to distinguish reputation, which involves general beliefs about the actor's type, from Signaling reputation. The latter is the actor's reputation for living up to its word, for usually doing as it says it will do. Of course, actors may not have Signaling reputations overall, but Signaling reputations in particular areas. Thus I might be believed to be ready to carry out my promises but not my threats; to send valid Signals about my capabilities but not about my intentions; to be willing and able to keep my word in the economic area but not on military issues. Even so, Signaling reputation needs to be distinguished from a more general reputation. For example, most of us know of at least a few colleagues who, while being conscientious and carrying out a large number of duties, regularly promise to do more than they can. This contrasts with others who do much less, but who can be counted on to live up to the few commitments that they make. In a parallel manner, in the spring of 1997 a Cambodia expert said that he was predisposed to accept the Khmer Rouge statements about the split within the group, including the killing of the former second in command and the fall of Pol Pot: "They don't call people traitors who are not traitors. They don't announce they have arrested people who are not arrested. This is not to suggest that they are angels; just to suggest that they operate along a fairly standard, well-known script" (quoted in Mydans, 1997a). In much the same way, referring to himself in the third person, a Cambodian leader declared, "What Hun Sen threatens, Hun Sen dares to do" (quoted in Mydans, 1997b). The truth of this statement says nothing about the range of objectives for which Hun Sen will threaten and act.

Turning to international politics, a state may be known as willing to pay a high price to protect its allies, to be a bully, or to be generally predisposed to cooperate with international organizations irrespective of whether it has previously issued Signals to that effect. Past behavior can be used as an index to the state's characteristics and to how it will behave in the future in a way that does not depend on Signals.[4] For example, fighting in Korea should have given the United States a reputation for defending countries against aggression even though—or perhaps partly because—it had not made a commitment to do so. The other side of this coin is that it is a concern with Signaling reputation rather than general reputation that leads actors to feel

---

[4]I think attribution theory is very useful here and have applied it in *Perception and Misperception*, chapter 2. Elsewhere (Jervis, 1989, pp. 513–514) I have flagged—but not answered—the question of the extent to which reputation attaches to an individual leader, a state, or a category of states (democracies, revolutionary regimes, etc.). It appears that the reason why the Hutu extremists killed the Belgian peacekeepers at the beginning of the Rwandan genocide was that the American withdrawal from Somalia convinced them that other Western democracies would pull their troops out of a peacekeeping mission if they were faced with even a small number of casualties (Jones, personal communication and 1999, p. 133).

that they must live up to a promise or a threat, although if they had known this would prove necessary, they would not have issued it in the first place.

PERCEPTUAL BIASES

Signals affect behavior only as they are perceived and interpreted, and the difficulty with constructing a parsimonious theory is that perceptions and their causes are quite varied. Nevertheless, several main tendencies can be detected. Although I cannot build them into a unified theory of signaling and perception, any such attempt has to center on them.

In their efforts to make sense of their world, people are moved by both motivated (that is, affect-driven) and unmotivated (purely cognitive) biases. The former derive from the need to maintain psychological well-being and a desired self-image, the latter from the need for short-cuts to rationality in an environment characterized by complex and ambiguous information. Motivated and cognitive influences are hard to separate (Kaufmann, 1994; Levi and Tetlock, 1982), and I merely discuss the single most important bias of each type.

The generalization that is most powerful, in the sense of occurring most often and exercising most control over perceptions, is that information is interpreted within the framework established by pre-existing beliefs (Jervis, 1976, chapter 4). Three implications are crucial here. First, images of other states are strongly influenced by the often implicit theories held by statesmen that specify the existence and meaning of indices (e.g., democracies are peaceful; countries experiencing rapid economic growth will demand an increased international role). These can vary from one individual or society to another and often are related to general ideas about how people and politics function. For example, if a new regime in a country suppressed democracy and civil liberties and proclaimed the superiority of the dominant racial group, many observers would predict that it would menace its neighbors. Indeed, it might be seen as a potential Nazi Germany. But it was the Nazi experience itself that made these links between domestic and international politics so salient; one reason for the appeasement policy was that in the 1930s, oppressive regimes were not believed to be especially aggressive. A second consequence of the influence of pre-existing beliefs is that images of individual states, once established, will change only in response to discrepant information that is high in quantity or low in ambiguity. This helps account for the inertia of many policies and the frequency with which states are taken by surprise. Third, and relatedly, observers who believe different theories or hold different images of the state will draw different inferences from its behavior. The same Signals and indices will be read very differently by observers with different beliefs about the actor.

This means that if observers—and actors—are to estimate how signals will be received, they need to understand the theories and cognitive predispositions of the perceivers. If you want to know whether an act will be seen as hostile or not, you should first inquire as to whether the observer already has an image of the actor as malign; to tell whether a promise or a threat will be viewed as credible, it is crucial to discern the perceivers' theories and beliefs about the actor. This is true irrespective of the truthfulness of the signals. The famous "Double-Cross" system that the British used during World War II to control the Nazi spy network in Britain and feed it misleading messages would not have worked had the British not cracked many German codes, thus enabling them to understand what reports the Germans would believe (Masterman, 1972).

This shows the psychological naivete of signaling theories which, although acknowledging the importance of pre-existing beliefs, argue that new information is combined with old as specified by Bayesian updating of prior beliefs on the basis of new information. The model generally used is of a person who has to estimate the proportions of red and blue chips in a paper bag; increasing evidence is provided as one chip after another is drawn at random from the bag. The assumption, appropriate for this example, is that judgments of specific bits of evidence are independent of expectations. That is, whether I think the bag contains mostly red or mostly blue chips does not affect whether I see any particular chip as red or blue; the color of the chip is objective and will be perceived the same way by all people, irrespective of their prior beliefs. But this is a poor model for perceptions of actors' types: how I perceive your signal is strongly influenced by what I already think of you. Even what might seem to be the clearest signals will make no impression if the perceiver's mind is made up or is focused elsewhere. It did not require the impeachment trial of President Clinton to show us that people with different beliefs and interests differ not only in their estimates of how much new evidence should change priors, but also in their evaluations of whether this evidence points in one direction or its opposite.

Cold cognitive processes driven by the requirement to simplify the contradictory and complex informational environment are not the only ones at work. Affective forces or "motivated biases" also influence how signals are perceived. The most important force of this type is an aversion to facing psychologically painful value trade-offs. Although, of course, people choose all the time, when central values are involved and the evidence is ambiguous, we tend to believe that whatever course of action we adopt is better than the alternative on many logically independent value dimensions (Farnham, 1997; Jervis, 1976, pp. 128–142; Neustadt, 1986).

An implication for signaling is that motivated biases often reinforce cognitive inertia. A decision maker who has staked his or her ego and/or domestic fortunes on a line of policy will find it difficult to recognize that it is likely to fail. Perceptions will be systematically distorted in order to shield the person from excessively painful choices. Lebow showed this process at work in defeating the appreciation of indications that the state is heading for an undesired war unless it changes its policy (Jervis, Lebow, & Stein, 1985; Lebow, 1981; the underlying psychology is found in Janis & Mann, 1977). Thus it is to Nehru's political and psychological commitment to his "forward policy" and not to China's lack of adequate signals that we must attribute his failure to see that the PRC would attack in the fall of 1962 if India did not make concessions. Similarly, although German secrecy and deception played a large role, much of the reason why British intelligence misread Germany in the 1930s was that the analysts did not want to draw inferences that contradicted British policy (Wark, 1985).

Motivated biases also help explain faulty signaling. Actors often misunderstand how others will interpret their behavior not only because they fail to grasp others' theories and images of them, but because they view their own behavior in a biased way. Individuals and states generally think well of themselves, believe that they have benevolent motives, and see their actions as reasonable and legitimate. So it is not surprising that in some cases, these views are not only rejected by those with whom they are interacting, but also are at variance with what disinterested observers see (for examples, see Garthoff, 1994a). Self-justification, if not self-righteousness, can lead actors to believe that their acts will be seen as benign when there is good reason for others to draw a very different inference. A state may thus believe that it is signaling firm but nonaggressive intentions by behavior that most reasonable perceivers would take to be hostile and threatening.

CONCLUDING NOTE ON METHODOLOGY

Understanding signaling and perception requires us to study them together. A theory of perception that ignored the fact that perceivers realize that actors have strategic objectives and may be trying to deceive them would be faulty; so would a theory of signaling that neglects how observers perceive and how actors think that observers perceive. What we need, then, are studies that are two-sided in looking at both the actor and perceiver (assuming for the sake of convenience only bilateral rather than multilateral cases). Scholars can then look at the image an actor is trying to project, the behaviors that it adopts to do so, and then, shifting attention to the perceiver, examine what influences the perceiver and what inferences it draws. At the next stage we can see what the perceiver thinks it must do in order to send the desired message in response, what it does to reach this goal, and how the actor in turn judges both the other's behavior and determines how the other perceived its behavior. I suspect that it is rare for actors, especially adversaries, to understand the situation the same way, to be able to discern how the other sees them and their behavior, or even to know what signals are taken to be most important.

Of course, the story will rarely be simple and unambiguous, and there are many obstacles to such investigations: actors may not articulate their objectives, even in internal memoranda; the links between policies adopted and objectives sought are often elusive to later observers, and perhaps to decision makers themselves; it is difficult to track the information that is received and the inferences that are drawn; events often come thick and fast, obscuring the relative impact of each. Nevertheless, a number of studies have proceeded in this way, some more explicitly than others, and they can be both mined for insights and used as models (Garthoff, 1994a, 1994b; Holsti, North, & Brody, 1968; Hosoya, 1968; May, 1959; Neustadt, 1970, 1999; Theis, 1980). Indeed, the end of the Cold War has provided an unusual opportunity to combine interviews and documents from several countries in a way that lends itself to studies of this kind (Allyn, Blight, & Welch, 1992; Blight, Allyn, & Welch, 1993; Blight & Welch, 1989; Gaddis, 1997; Larson, 1997; Wohlforth, 1996).

CONCLUSION

Politics, especially international politics, falls at the intersection of psychology and game theory. The latter is crucial because not only are outcomes the product of the interaction of separate national policies, but each actor needs to anticipate what others will do in light of the fact that they are symmetrically trying to anticipate what the actor will do. (Although in some cases individuals and states ignore strategic interaction and act as though others are on auto-pilot and will not react to what they do, these cases are exceptional, even though they are important because they often lead to disaster.) But if reactions, anticipations, and anticipations of reactions drive politics, the beliefs, perceptions, and images that give life to them cannot be understood by the use of highly simplified assumptions and stylized facts. The way Signals and indices will be read are determined by the perceivers' needs, theories, and expectations. There are powerful generalizations about international interactions, but they rest in part on how people analyze information. Furthermore, our generalizations only take us so far and need to be supplemented by an understanding of how different individuals see the world and how particular conjunctions of circumstances combine to affect perceptions. Inasmuch as signals convey meaning, peoples' interpretations must be at the center of our attention.

REFERENCES

Allyn, B., Blight, J., & Welch, D. (1992). *Back to the brink: Proceedings of the Moscow Conference on the the cuban missile crisis.* Lanham, MD: University Press of America.

Austin, J. L. (1961). *Philosophical papers.* London: Oxford University Press.

Banks, J. (1991). *Signaling games in political science.* New York: Gordon and Breach.

Bem, D. (1972). Self-perception theory. In L. Berkowitz (Ed.), *Advances in experimental social psychology* (pp. 1–62). New York: Academic Press.

Bennet, J. (1999, September 12). His life as a murder suspect. *New York Times Magazine,* pp. 48–53.

Bernstein, B. (1992). Reconsidering the missile crisis. In J. Nathan (Ed.), *The Cuban missile crisis revisited* (pp. 55–129). New York: St. Martin's Press.

Blight, J., Allyn, B., & Welch, D. (1993). *Cuba on the brink: Castro, the missile crisis and the soviet collapse.* New York: Pantheon.

Blight, J., & Welch, D. (1989). *On the brink: Americans and Soviets reexamine the Cuban missile crisis.* New York: Hill and Wang.

Breslauer, G., & Tetlock, P. (Eds.). (1991). *Learning in US and Soviet foreign policy.* Boulder, CO: Westview.

Clinton versus Paula Jones. (1997, January 13). *Newsweek,* p. 31.

Crawford, N. (2000). The passion of world politics: Propositions on emotion and emotional relationships. *International Security, 24,* 116–156.

Farnham, B. (1997). *Roosevelt and the Munich Crisis.* Princeton, NJ: Princeton University Press.

Fearon, J. (1997). Signaling foreign policy interests: Tying hands versus sinking costs. *Journal of Conflict Resolution, 41,* 68–80.

Friedman, T. (1994, May 8). It's a mad, mad, mad, world money market. *New York Times,* p. E1.

Gaddis, J. (1997). *We now know: Rethinking cold war history.* New York: Oxford University Press.

Garthoff, R. (1994a). *Détente and confrontation: American-Soviet relations from Nixon to Reagan* (Rev. ed.). Washington, DC: Brookings Institution.

Garthoff, R. (1994b). *The great transition.* Washington, DC: Brookings Institution.

Goldberg, C. (1997, June 9). On adultery issue, many aren't ready to cast first stone. *New York Times,* p. 18.

Hacking, I. (1999). *The social constructivism of what?* Cambridge, MA: Harvard University Press.

Holsti, O., North, R., & Brody, R. (1968). Perception and action in the 1914 crisis. In J. D. Singer (Ed.), *Quantitative international politics* (pp. 123–158). New York: Free Press.

Hopf, T. (1994). *Peripheral visions: Deterrence theory and American foreign policy in the Third World, 1965–1990.* Ann Arbor, MI: University of Michigan Press.

Hopf, T. (1998). The promise of constructivism in international relations theory. *International Security, 23,* 171–200.

Hosoya, C. (1968). Miscalculations in deterrence policy: Japanese–US Relations, 1938–41. *Journal of Peace Research, 2,* 97–115.

Janis, I., & Mann, L. (1977). *Decision making.* New York: Free Press.

Jennings, M. K. (1999). Political response to pain and loss. *American Political Science Review, 93,* 1–14.

Jervis, R. (1970). *The logic of images in international relations.* Princeton, NJ: Princeton University Press; 2d ed., New York: Columbia University Press, 1989.

Jervis, R. (1976). *Perception and misperception in international politics.* Princeton, NJ: Princeton University Press.

Jervis, R. (1989). Additional thoughts on political psychology and rational choice. *Political Psychology, 10,* 511–515.

Jervis, R. (1997). *System effects: Complexity in social and political life.* Princeton, NJ: Princeton University Press.

Jervis, R., Lebow, R. N., & Stein, J. G. (1985). *Psychology and deterrence.* Baltimore, MD: Johns Hopkins University Press.

Jones, B. (1999) Military intervention in Rwanda's two wars: Partisanship and indifference. In B. Walter & J. Snyder (Eds.), *Civil wars, insecurity, and intervention* (pp. 116–145). New York: Columbia University Press.

Katz, F. (1981). *The secret war in Mexico: Europe, the United States, and the Mexican Revolution.* Chicago, IL: University of Chicago Press.

Kaufmann, C. (1994). Out of the lab and into the archives: A method for testing psychological explanations of political decision making. *International Studies Quarterly, 38,* 557–86.

Kreps, D. (1990). *Game theory and economic modelling.* New York: Oxford University Press.

Larson, D. (1985). *The origins of containment: A psychological explanation.* Princeton, NJ: Princeton University Press.

Larson, D. (1997). *Anatomy of mistrust: US–Soviet relations during the Cold War.* Ithaca, NY: Cornell University Press.

Lebow, R. N. (1981). *Between peace and war.* Baltimore, MD: John Hopkins University Press.

Leng, R. (1988). Crisis learning games. *American Political Science Review, 82,* 179–194.

Levi, A., & Tetlock, P. (1982). Attribution bias: On the inconclusiveness of the cognition–motivation debate. *Journal of Experimental Psychology, 18,* 68–88.

Levy, J. (1994). Learning and foreign policy. *International Organization, 48,* 279–312.

Masterman, J. C. (1972). *The double-cross system in the War of 1939 to 1945.* New Haven, CT: Yale University Press.

May, E. (1959). *The World War and American isolation, 1914–1917.* Cambridge, MA: Harvard University Press.

Mercer, J. (1996a, April). *Approaching emotions in international politics.* Paper delivered at meeting of the International Studies Association, San Diego, CA.

Mercer, J. (1996b). *Reputation and international politics.* Ithaca, NY: Cornell University Press.

Morley, J. (Ed.). (1994). *The final confrontation: Japan's negotiations with the United States, 1941. Japan's Road to the Pacific War, 5,* New York: Columbia University Press.

Morrow, J. (1994). *Game theory for political scientists.* Princeton, NJ: Princeton University Press.

Mydans, S. (1997a, June 22). Cambodian rivals say they will bring Pol Pot to justice. *New York Times,* p. 8.

Mydans, S. (1997b, July 11). Hun Sen says he's enjoying being Cambodia's sole ruler. *New York Times,* p. A12.

Mydans, S. (1999, September 12). Jakarta concedes a loss of control over Timor forces. *New York Times,* p. 8.

Neustadt, R. (1970). *Alliance politics.* New York: Columbia University Press.

Neustadt, R. (1986, May 13). *Presidents, politics and analysis.* Brewster Denny Lecture Series, Institute of Public Management, Graduate School of Public Affairs. Seattle: University of Washington.

Neustadt, R. (1999). *Report to JFK: The skybolt crisis in perspective.* Ithaca, NY: Cornell University Press.

Schelling, T. (1960). *The strategy of conflict.* Cambridge, MA: Harvard University Press.

Schelling, T. (1966). *Arms and influence.* New Haven, CT: Yale University Press.

Sherry, M. (1995). *In the shadow of war: The US since the late 1930s.* New Haven, CT: Yale University Press.

Theis, W. (1980). *When governments collide: Coercion and diplomacy in the Vietman conflict, 1964–1968.* New Haven, CT: Yale University Press.

Treiseman, P. (1985). *A study of the mathematics performance of black students at the University of California, Berkeley.* Unpublished dissertation, University of California, Berkeley.

Wark, W. (1985). *The ultimate enemy: British intelligence and Nazi Germany, 1933–1939*. Ithaca, NY: Cornell University Press.

Wohlforth, W. (Ed.). (1996). *Witnesses to the end of the cold war.* Baltimore, MD: Johns Hopkins University Press.

PART IV

Focus on the Future

17

Postmodernism, Identity Politics, and Other Political Influences in Political Psychology

PETER SUEDFELD
University of British Columbia

POLITICAL PSYCHOLOGY AND THE CULTURE WARS

Traditionally, social scientists were taught that good research is not only rigorous but is also designed, conducted, and reported in an objective way. The "value-free" ideal incorporated the value of unbiased scholarship (see Proctor, 1991). Most people knew that this was indeed an ideal, and that human beings could not completely suspend their likes and dislikes, loyalties and ideologies when they put on their "researcher" hat. However, when so behatted they were expected to—and, I think, almost all tried to—follow procedures that would at least minimize bias.

In the last couple of decades, humanists and to some extent social scientists have experienced increasing pressure from colleagues who, under the label of *postmodernism,* have rejected the possibility that objective truths can be discovered, or even that such truths exist, in the domains of these disciplines. Instead, they argue that all truth is "construction," a function of historical, cultural, and geographical context interacting with demographic categories such as sex, class, ethnicity, and so on. One hallmark of this view is the use of derogatory quotation marks around the word "truth" wherever it appears.

Each of these demographic groups supposedly has different "truths," and should insist that only their own members can understand (and, a fortiori, teach or write about) any aspect of the group ("particularism"). Regressing to earlier racist and sexist assumptions, they argue that members of different groups have mutually incompatible ways of learning, thinking, and behavior. Therefore, they need special and often separate courses, readings, professors, students, advisors, dormitories, campus centers, et cetera, whose primary task is to advance their group's recognition and agenda through political as well as intellectual means ("identity politics"). Identity politics is an offshoot of postmodernism in its denial of universal, objective truths (and of the position that finding such truths is the goal of scholarship), but many researchers have accepted the implications of constructivism without knowingly subscribing to it as a general philosophy of science.

Paradoxically, practitioners of postmodernism and identity politics criticize the adherents of traditional scientific objectivity for not having lived up to their ideals, and simultaneously argue that objectivity is inherently impossible to attain and, anyway, morally wrong. They have suggested that the primary purpose of research and teaching should be to reshape society for the benefit of particular groups (Gross & Levitt, 1994; Searle, 1993–1994), and that research that might hamper such social change should (a) not be conducted, (b) if conducted, not be published, and (c) in any case, certainly not taught.[1]

The emergence of postmodernism, constructivism, and identity politics has led to a situation that académe has not seen since the time when most universities were religious establishments. The clash between the old and new epistemologies, fraught with ad hominem arguments, character assassination, demonization of opponents, motive mongering, and guilt by association, reaches a level of acerbity and hostility that comes close to deserving the metaphorical label of *culture wars* (Hunter, 1991).

THE POSITIONS OF PSYCHOLOGY AND OF POLITICAL PSYCHOLOGY

On the whole, psychology has been less susceptible to postmodern trends than many other humanities and social sciences. This may be because psychology is closer to the biological sciences; it is difficult to argue that the

---

[1]I refer here only to true believers in this ideology. Many more professors are afraid to teach these materials for fear of harassment (by students, colleagues, administrators, or the media), poor student ratings, and adverse career consequences. Perhaps the most salient such taboo in North America is against studies indicating that the undeniable difference in average IQ scores between American Whites and Blacks is substantially due to genetic factors (Glazer, 1995). By the same token, it is considered laudable to do research, such as the current work on "stereotype threat" (Steele & Aronson, 1995), that offers alternative explanations for the IQ gap.

truth of how the cerebral cortex functions is merely a culturally accepted convention based on the power of White middle-class men.

The softer end of the discipline's spectrum, social psychology and related subdisciplines, has been somewhat less impervious. One lingering consequence of the "crisis of social psychology" in the 1960s and 1970s (e.g., McGuire, 1973) has been a shaking of confidence in the scientific validity of social psychological theories and data. As a result, there was some favorable response to postmodernism as it was applied to social psychology by Harré and Secord (1972), followed by Gergen (1973), who argued that social psychology is a historical discipline rather than a universalistic science. This argument has made a positive contribution in enhancing our recognition that scientific questions and answers are influenced by the personality, experiences, and attitudes of the researcher, and that cultural and temporal factors are among the important independent and mediating variables in social and/or political psychology. However, paying more attention to such variables is not the same as believing that their impact invalidates the scientific basis of the field (cf. Renshon & Duckitt, 1997). That belief is contradicted by the area's substantial array of reliable and valid knowledge, which has been generated by traditional scientific methodologies.

Identity politics has been more influential than postmodernism in general (Sampson, 1993), with the proliferation of courses and organizations focusing on the psychology of women, Black psychology, "indigenous" psychology, et cetera. Major professional organizations have endorsed discriminatory practices in faculty hiring and student admissions. Much of this, of course, is dictated by outside forces, although in my view our colleagues have numbered too many collaborators and passive bystanders and too few resistors.

A small number of psychologists have openly slanted their research on political grounds. Practitioners of self-labeled "critical" psychology (as of "critical legal studies" and the like; Kleinfeld, 1993–1994) interpret the adjective as being equivalent to "critical of American society" and the Western tradition in general, and have called on psychology to be ever more radical in focusing on changing, not just studying and teaching about, aspects of those societies (Fox, 1999). More subtly, unspoken political biases are influencing both researchers and "gatekeepers" such as journal editors and reviewers. Numerically, the weight is toward a liberal slant as currently defined within American politics. Most defenders of postmodernism, identity politics, and politicized research are to the left of center politically—as are most North American academics, particularly those in the humanities and social sciences.

Political psychology is, to a great extent, an offshoot of social psychology and the study of personality. It is also derived from political science (especially the subfields of international relations, political leadership, and public opinion), history, and sociology (Davies, 1973). Thus, its roots are in the "soft" areas of social science and the humanities. It is, therefore, relatively susceptible to the ideological pressures described earlier. The postmodernist distortions detract from the very real scientific accomplishments of political psychology. The area has added considerably to knowledge in many relevant fields, including the study of leader and follower personality, political attitudes and values, rhetoric, voting behavior, decision making, conflict resolution, cultural differences and similarities in the political process, and so on.

SOME INTERESTING CHALLENGES AND RESPONSES

Here, I discuss a few topics where political psychology has made significant advances in knowledge and also has been engaged in controversy, the latter apparently correlated with political differences among colleagues. Although in some of these controversies the researchers' attitudes toward identity politics play a part, the "hard" version of postmodern constructivism is difficult to find. Political psychologists (or, perhaps, journal editors) are willing to posit that social context affects perceptions, beliefs, and behavior, but they explicitly adhere to traditional epistemologies. They do not agree to the proposition that the truth about a scholarly issue is inherently unidentifiable or nonexistent.

The positive contribution of disagreement is variable across domains. Next, I discuss five topics within political psychology where constructivism, identity politics, and political biases have influenced research, theory, and dialogue. In some (e.g., authoritarianism/cognitive styles and complex decision making), the controversy has fueled further innovation and improvement in research and theory. In other cases (e.g., voter behavior and assessment at a distance), the field progresses, but politically based disagreements have added little if anything to its development. In still others (e.g., modern racism/sexism theory), one viewpoint is so consonant with the *Zeitgeist* that its critics are seldom even noted in, for example, textbooks. The ship sails serenely on, ignoring the critical icebergs looming nearby.[2]

Authoritarianism, Right and Left

Question: Are people to the right of center on the political spectrum likely to become Fascists, and/or do they generally think in different ways from everyone else?

From the very beginning of the research, there has been recognition that the originators of the authoritarian personality construct (Adorno,

---

[2]The judgments that follow are my own, and therefore perhaps idiosyncratic. The references are primarily for illustrative purposes; this is not a literature review.

Frenkel-Brunswik, Levinson, & Sanford, 1950) equated it with extreme right-wing political ideology. There has been a prolonged argument as to whether authoritarian styles of thinking—rigid adherence to norms promulgated by accepted authorities, closed-mindedness, submissiveness to superiors, domineering over subordinates, prejudice against outgroups, and so on—can also be found on the extreme left (Rokeach, 1960; Stone, 1980). Those who prefer to ascribe these undesirable traits only to conservatives have on occasion redefined both "right wing" and "authoritarian" to explain away findings that the extreme right (the adherents of Hitler and Mussolini) and the extreme left (the followers of Stalin and Mao) actually share certain cognitive characteristics (e.g., Altemeyer, 1988).

Leaving this interminable argument behind, some theorists have attempted to disaggregate cognitive style from cognitive content: that is, to look at *how* people think rather than at *what* they think (Suedfeld, 2000). Research on variables such as need for cognition, need for closure, tolerance of ambiguity, cognitive complexity, and open-mindedness has succeeded in making the structure–content separation to a considerable degree (Suedfeld & Tetlock, 2001). It appears that although there are cognitive style differences across the ideological continuum, they are strongly influenced by mediating factors such as underlying values and political power. Other things being equal, adherents to both the right- and left-wing extremes tend to show similar patterns of what could conveniently be summarized as closed-mindedness (Eysenck & Coulter, 1972).

It may suffice to say that the original definition, assessment, and explanation of the authoritarian personality may have been adequate for its purpose—an attempt at the scientific study of the Fascism-prone personality of the midcentury—and that we should not try to generalize the work beyond that (Meloen, 1997). Such a circumscription is warranted, inter alia, by the obsolescence of the authoritarianism theory and methodology. For example, the sine qua non of the original authoritarian personality pattern was anti-Semitism (see, e.g., Smith, 1997), yet there now seems to be only a small, inconsistent, and marginal relationship between the two constructs (Raden, 1999). Future theorizing and research could move beyond the fruitless arguments about inferences drawn from Adorno et al. and concentrate on the personality and cognitive correlates of present-day political (and nonpolitical) ideologies, including attitudes about such issues as environmentalism, abortion, animal rights, et cetera.

Traditional Versus Modern "Isms"

Question: Are the White and male citizens of the United States (North America, the West) irredeemably prejudiced against non-White ethnic groups and women, no matter what they claim to think or feel about these groups?

American social psychologists began systematically to trace popular attitudes toward minority ethnic groups as far back as the 1930s. Although at first the research concentrated on a variety of (mostly European) immigrant ethnic groups and American Blacks, the focus has widened with the increase in immigration from Latin America and Asia and the rise of the women's movement. Successive studies on this issue have found a pattern of decreasing negative stereotyping,[3] decreasing preferences for social distance, and increasing acceptance of civil rights and equal opportunities for employment, education, and the like (Bobo, in press; Dovidio & Gaertner, 1996; Karlins, Coffman, & Walters, 1969; Pettigrew, 1979; Sniderman & Carmines, 1997; Swim, Aikin, Hall, & Hunter, 1995; Taylor, Sheatsley, & Greeley, 1978). Another interpretation of racial preference (Wood, 1994) noted that what some theorists interpret as White animosity toward Blacks may in fact be White identity-formation through the process of in-group solidarity, a process much studied by social psychologists. Presumably, the converse is also true (since in-group solidarity is a universal tendency).

However, some political psychologists argue that these trends only reflect increasing wariness about openly expressing one's prejudices, and that derogatory feelings toward women and minorities (per se) are in reality at least as strong as before. They are merely disguised, or expressed more subtly, with traditional American values being used as camouflage for opposition to policies that are designed to overcome historical disadvantages and move toward true equality. This "symbolic" or "modern" racism and sexism must be measured by subtle means (e.g., by measuring attitudes toward legalized racial preferences or school busing), because respondents know better than to voice their racist or sexist biases in a straightforward manner (Kinder, 1986; Sears, 1988; Swim et al., 1995).

Critics of this position (e.g., Sniderman & Tetlock, 1986) have maintained that the new measures in fact inextricably confound two factors: principled conservatism (adherence to long-established American values such as individualism, limited government, and the merit principle) and traditional, old-fashioned prejudice. They do not deny the existence or impact of racism and sexism, but question whether a new form of these attitudes has emerged and, if it has, whether it is well defined or measured by the "symbolic ism" models. Going even further, it is possible that a scale of symbolic or modern prejudice defines as sexist a position based on conservative principles, whereas scores labeled as showing a lack of bias actually

---

[3]Incidentally, very little scientific attention has been paid to the stereotypes and prejudices that minority groups hold toward each other and toward the majority, which are often at least as negative and injurious as those held by the majority.

indicate "reverse sexism"—that is, support for discrimination against men (Trapnell, Paulhus, & Suedfeld, 1999).[4]

It seems to me that "symbolic ism" models are conceptually and therefore methodologically confused (see also Weigel & Howes, 1985), and that authors sometimes engage in convoluted and empirically untested reasoning to "find" evidence supporting them (e.g., Harvie, Marshall-McCaskey, & Johnston, 1998). This does not necessarily mean that symbolic racism and sexism do not exist, only that their reality and consequences have not yet been convincingly established.

Voter (Mis)behavior

Question: Are the citizens of democracies so politically apathetic, ignorant, and/or confused that they have no clear sense of the issues and therefore no rational bases for choices?

Political scientists and political psychologists have been engaged for a long time in measuring the ideas and attitudes of the citizenry concerning political parties, platforms, candidates, policies, and ideologies. Related issues include voter participation (the decision to vote or not to vote is obviously just as political as choosing for whom to vote), the individual's position for or against various policies and party platform planks, and the electoral choice. Whether they collect their own data or use the results of national surveys, many social scientists have concluded that voters are incapable and/or unwilling to view these issues in a broad context (Zaller, 1992), that they do not have coherent political cognitive maps (Converse, 1975), and that their electoral preferences invoke irrelevant factors such as the candidate's appearance and verbal facility, advertising, the operation of cognitive and emotional heuristics, and the like (Bennett, 1995).

Dissenters (e.g., Page & Shapiro, 1992) counterargue that the measures on which such conclusions are based are inadequate. When, for example, the public is asked focused questions about the positions of different parties and candidates, it exhibits considerably more knowledge than is inferred from questions about general party ideologies. In choosing between foreign policy alternatives, citizens consider both pervasive political values and situation-specific information (Herrmann, Tetlock, & Visser, 1999). It is also possible that a political position seems nonrational to observers because respondents are not able or willing to explain to a pollster the reasons on which they based their choice (Tetlock, 1998).

---

[4]Although the "reverse sexism" (or racism) label is widely used, what it refers to is not "reverse" anything. Discrimination against men is sexist, and against Whites, racist, just as discrimination against women and Blacks is sexist and racist. The real reverse of discrimination is nondiscrimination.

The critical (not to say condescending) view of some social scientists toward their fellow citizens may reflect the fact that the average voter is less verbally skilled than the average social scientist and may therefore not be able to express political ideas as clearly. It may also be influenced by the fact that the U.S. electorate is generally more conservative than social scientists, thereby earning the disapproval of the latter. In any case, more careful and sensitive methods of enquiry, clarifying bonds among individual attitude systems, specific issues and options, and overarching ideologies, may help to elucidate the behavior of the "ordinary" voter (for an example, see Chittick, Billingsley, & Travis, 1990).

Leader Assessment at a Distance

Question: Is it possible to understand why political leaders do the things they do by somehow analyzing their publicly available writings and sayings? If so, what kind of analysis is valid?

Starting long before the notorious psychiatrists' poll about Senator Goldwater during the 1964 presidential election (see Rogow, 1970) and up through an equally presumptuous remote-control psychiatric diagnosis of the Canadian politician Lucien Bouchard over 30 years later ("The Bouchard File," 1997), leader assessment at a distance has been misused for political purposes. Such efforts have earned considerable and well-deserved opprobrium. Even aside from such infamous examples as the two just cited, many analyses of this sort clearly reflect political biases in various stages of the research (Cocks, 1986). Psychohistorians and other qualitative researchers have drawn conclusions from minimal known facts about the early life of their subject, selected episodes and materials unsystematically to support their hypotheses, and used tautological reasoning to denigrate leaders whom they found uncongenial while exalting those they admired (Stannard, 1980). The researcher's own political position seems to be a highly salient confound in this area of research.

However, assessment at a distance has also been used less invidiously. The study of leaders has engaged research methods, including thematic content analyses (Smith, 1992) and Q-sorts (Kowert, 1996), that use objective and quantified criteria to measure aspects of emotion, cognition, motivation, and personality. Such studies have shed light on nonobvious aspects of leadership, and to some extent have been successful in predicting how a leader would act under definable circumstances (Hermann, 1977; Post, 2001). Coupled with such techniques, qualitative and other subjective approaches—especially if they make their criteria and procedures explicit (e.g., Lyons, 1997)—can present new insights, point to promising further investigations, and give more quantitative studies a useful component of immediacy and impact.

Cognitive Vigilance and Complexity

Question: Is complex thinking likely to lead to more successful and/or more ethically acceptable solutions than simple thinking?

There is a marked bias among academics in favor of judgment and decision making that does not involve heuristics, precedents, emotions, moral codes, and other "shortcuts." Good judgment is considered to be the outcome of complex information processing based on an extensive information search, an understanding of probabilities and the rules of logic, an exhaustive consideration and reconsideration of alternative choices, flexibility, open-mindedness, an ability to understand and appreciate other viewpoints, resistance to conformity and obedience pressures, and so on. Much of political decision making, especially under stress, does not meet these criteria; consequently, social scientists have strongly criticized the behavior of policymakers and executives (a view that I call the *cognitive klutz* model). Some have taken this to the point where a low level of complexity is characterized as a moral defect (see Suedfeld, 1992).

Studies have reliably shown that simple strategies, employing a variety of shortcuts, are quite appropriate for the solution of many problems, even complex ones. In fact, through various cognitive mechanisms, excessive complexity may lead to an increased probability of error. It also exacts a cost in time, energy, attentional focusing, and resources that may be out of proportion with the importance of a particular problem within the context of that time and situation. Not only is high complexity not always the most effective strategy, it may sometimes be less morally valid as well: flexibility and compromise in dealing with some issues can mean an erosion of commitment to higher ideals (Suedfeld & Tetlock, 2001).

The political bias in this area is intriguing. There is considerable evidence that—with many exceptions based on the specific situation or topic—political liberals tend to think in more complex ways than conservatives (e.g., Tetlock, 1986). Given prevailing views in the social sciences, we would expect, therefore, that people in our disciplines would both practice and value complex thinking. It would be interesting to test whether more conservative researchers have relatively nuanced views of the pervasive desirability of complex cognition, and whether there is a complexity difference in the writings of the scholars themselves. Aside from those provocative thoughts, I believe that the optimal course of future research is to identify and test conditions under which different kinds of strategies are optimal and cognitive characteristics that affect people's likelihood of using optimal strategies under those conditions.

Some Possible Resolutions

How should we handle the role of political bias in our research and theorizing? The traditional answer is to try to recognize our prejudices and minimize their effect by conscious effort. Such efforts can be enhanced by the application of corrective techniques such as separating questions of fact from recommendations about policy or running thought experiments in which the poles of a dimension are reversed—for example, Tetlock's "symbolic Marxism" study (Tetlock, 1994). However, given that such tactics are unlikely to eliminate bias convincingly, here are some other possibilities:

Generalized Tolerance.   One possible orientation toward the roles of objective versus "critical" research, universal versus contextualized science, qualitative versus quantitative methods, and the like, is to pursue all of these philosophies and strategies in parallel. This, to some extent, is the current policy of the International Society of Political Psychology and its journal, *Political Psychology:* All of these points of view are accepted for presentation or publication, if the work passes the criteria appropriate to its outlook. These criteria are based on merit, but merit is defined differently depending on the nature of the work. Thus, readers of the journal will find a wide range, from highly mathematical analyses of large databases to the personal reflections and value judgments of an individual colleague. Except for the latter category, there are very few papers that ignore or deny the need for empirical evidence regarding testable hypotheses or assertions.

Mutual Criticism.   Another strategy is to encourage more critical evaluation of other people's work. Both the conferences and the journal might, for example, include an occasional focus paper with invited critiques. It would obviously be interesting to have the focus papers represent different positions on the continua identified here, giving every side a chance to present its views and to find flaws in those of the other side. This kind of approach has occurred in the past, for example with Tetlock's article on "politicized psychology" and responses from his targets as well as defenders (Tetlock, 1994). An airing of the arguments on both sides can be informative for third parties, even if the contenders end up "Agreeing to disagree" (as Tetlock titled his answer to White). Ideally, there may also be scope for self-criticism, where adherents of a particular school of thought could publicly identify its shortcomings as well as its strengths; but this may require more objectivity than most of us can muster.

Conjoint, Converging, and Integrated Research.   With the increasing sanctification of multi-, inter-, and transdisciplinary research being trumpeted by university administrations and funding agencies, it may be opportune to apply the same idea to political psychology. After all, the field is multidisciplinary by definition. Colleagues who give their allegiance to different and even opposing philosophies and methodologies may conduct research together or in parallel on a particular topic, question, hypothesis, or issue, and may find that the approach of each can enrich and validate the work as a whole. Thesis, antithesis, synthesis may be one structure for such research, but finding a consensually satisfying synthesis is not necessary: the collaborators may finally disagree. At least they, and their audience, would get a more rounded picture of the relevant factors and the multiple ways of asking and answering questions (see, e.g., Mellers, Hertwig, & Kahneman, 2001).

CONCLUSION

In the foregoing, I outlined what I see as some of the more interesting issues affected by the political viewpoints of researchers themselves and how I think such influences can become productive rather than destructive factors in our discipline. The strong pressures of postmodernism and identity politics reinforce the temptation to direct research and its interpretations to serve political ends. To the extent that colleagues compromise their belief in the existence and attainability of truth, or subordinate the search for truth to the advancement of their own sociopolitical agendas, political psychology becomes a scientifically useless propaganda exercise. Regrettably, there have been instances and movements that have not been able (or did not want) to resist this temptation. Perhaps increased awareness of the erosion of our knowledge base and our credibility will alert those who have unthinkingly followed the trends of postmodernism to take a second look.

REFERENCES

Adorno, T. W., Frenkel-Brunswik, E., Levinson, D. J., & Sanford, N. (1950). *The authoritarian personality.* New York: Harper.

Altemeyer, B. (1988). *Enemies of freedom: Understanding right-wing authoritarianism.* San Francisco: Jossey-Bass.

Bennett, W. L. (1995). The cueless public: Bill Clinton meets the new American voter in Campaign '92. In S. A. Renshon (Ed.), *The Clinton presidency: Campaigning, governing, and the psychology of leadership* (pp. 91–112). Boulder, CO: Westview.

Bobo, L. (in press). Racial attitudes and relations at the close of the twentieth century. In N. Smelser & W. J. Wilson (Eds.), *Racial trends in America.* Washington, DC: National Academy of Sciences Press.

Chittick, W. O., Billingsley, K. R., & Travis, R. (1990). Persistence and change in elite and mass attitudes toward U.S. foreign policy. *Political Psychology, 11,* 385–401.

Cocks, G. (1986). Contributions of psychohistory to understanding politics. In M. G. Hermann (Gen. Ed.), *Political psychology* (pp. 139–166). San Francisco: Jossey-Bass.

Converse, P. E. (1975). Public opinion and voting behavior. In F. Greenstein & N. Polsby (Eds.), *Handbook of political science* (Vol. 4, Ch. 2). Reading, MA: Addison-Wesley.

Davies, J. C. (1973). Where from and where to? In J. N. Knutson (Gen. Ed.), *Handbook of political psychology* (pp. 1–27). San Francisco: Jossey-Bass.

Dovidio, J. F., & Gaertner, S. L. (1996). Affirmative action, unintentional racial biases, and intergroup relations. *Journal of Social Issues, 52,* 51–75.

Eysenck, H. J., & Coulter, T. T. (1972). The personality and attitudes of working class British communists and fascists. *Journal of Social Psychology, 87,* 59–73.

Fox, D. (1999). The Critical Psychology Project: Transforming society and transforming psychology. In T. Sloan (Ed.), *Voices for critical psychology.* Manuscript submitted for publication.

Glazer, N. (1995). Scientific truth and the American dilemma. In S. Fraser (Ed.), *The Bell Curve wars: Race, intelligence, and the future of America* (pp. 139–148). New York: Basic Books.

Gross, P. R., & Levitt, N. (1994). *Higher superstition: The academic Left and its quarrels with science.* Baltimore: Johns Hopkins.

Gergen, K. J. (1973). Social psychology as history. *Journal of Personality and Social Psychology, 26,* 309–320.

Harré, R., & Secord, P. F. (1972). *The explanation of social behavior.* Oxford, UK: Blackwell.

Harvie, K., Marshall-McCaskey, J., & Johnston, L. (1998). Gender-based biases in occupational hiring decisions. *Journal of Applied Social Psychology, 28,* 1698–1711.

Hermann, M. G. (Ed., with T. W. Milburn). (1977). *A psychological examination of political leaders.* New York: Free Press.

Herrmann, R. K., Tetlock, P. E., & Visser, P. S. (1999). *Mass public decisions on going to war: A cognitive-interactionist framework.* Unpublished manuscript, Ohio State University.

Hunter, J. D. (1991). *Culture wars.* New York: Basic Books.

Karlins, M., Coffman, T. L., & Walters, G. (1969). On the fading of social stereotypes: Studies in three generations of college students. *Journal of Personality and Social Psychology, 13,* 1–16.

Kinder, D. R. (1986). The continuing American dilemma: White resistance to racial change 40 years after Myrdal. *Journal of Social Issues, 42,* 151–171.

Kleinfeld, A. (1993–1994, Winter). Politicization: From the law schools to the courts. *Academic Questions, 7*(1), 9–19.

Kowert, P. A. (1996). Where does the buck stop? Assessing the impact of presidential personality. *Political Psychology, 17,* 421–452.

Lyons, M. (1997). Presidential character revisited. *Political Psychology, 18,* 791–811.

McGuire, W. J. (1973). The yin and yang of progress in social psychology: Seven koan. *Journal of Personality and Social Psychology, 26,* 446–456.

Mellers, B., Hertwig, R., & Kahneman, D. (2001). Do frequency representations eliminate conjunction effects? An exercise in adversarial collaboration. *Psychological Science, 12,* 269–275.

Meloen, J. (1997). The humdrum of rhetorics: A reply to Durrheim's "Theoretical conundrum." *Political Psychology, 18,* 649–656.

Page, B. I., & Shapiro, R. Y. (1992). *The rational public: Fifty years of trends in Americans' policy preferences.* Chicago: University of Chicago Press.

Pettigrew, T. F. (1979). Racial changes and racial policy. *Annals of the American Academy of Political Science and Sociology, 441,* 114–131.

Post, J. (Ed.) (2001). *The psychological evaluation of political leaders: Method and application.* Manuscript submitted for publication.

Proctor, R. N. (1991). *Value-free science? Purity and power in modern knowledge.* Cambridge, MA: Harvard University Press.

Raden, D. (1999). Is anti-Semitism currently part of an authoritarian attitude syndrome? *Political Psychology, 20,* 323–343.

Renshon, S., & Duckitt, J. (1997). Cultural and cross-cultural political psychology: Toward the development of a new subfield. In J. Duckitt & S. Renshon (Eds.), Special issue on cultural and cross-cultural dimensions of political psychology, *Political Psychology, 18,* 233–240.

Rogow, A. (1970). *The psychiatrists.* New York: Putnam.

Rokeach, M. (1960). *The open and closed mind.* New York: Basic Books.

Sampson, E. E. (1993). Identity politics: Challenges to psychology's understanding. *American Psychologist, 48,* 1219–1230.

Searle, J. R. (1993–1994, Winter). The mission of the university: Intellectual discovery or social transformation? *Academic Questions, 7*(1), 80–85.

Sears, D. O. (1988). Symbolic racism. In P. A. Katz & D. A Taylor (Eds.), *Eliminating racism: Profiles in controversy* (pp. 53–84). New York: Plenum.

Smith, C. P. (Ed.). (1992). *Handbook of thematic analysis.* New York: Cambridge University Press.

Smith, M. B. (1997). *The Authoritarian Personality:* A re-review 46 years later. *Political Psychology, 18,* 159–164.

Sniderman, P. M., & Carmines, E. G. (1997). *Reaching beyond race.* Cambridge, MA: Harvard University Press.

Sniderman, P. M., & Tetlock, P. E. (1986). Symbolic racism: Problems of motive attribution in political analysis. *Journal of Social Issues, 42,* 129–150.

Stannard, D. E. (1980). *Shrinking history: On Freud and the failure of psychohistory.* New York: Oxford University Press.

Steele, C. M., & Aronson, J. (1995). Stereotype threat and the intellectual test performance of African Americans. *Journal of Personality and Social Psychology, 69,* 797–811.

Stone, W. F. (1980). The myth of left-wing authoritarianism. *Political Psychology, 2,* 3–19.

Suedfeld, P. (1992). Cognitive managers and their critics. *Political Psychology, 13,* 435–453.

Suedfeld, P. (2000). Cognitive styles: Personality. In A. E. Kazdin (Ed. in Chief), *Encyclopedia of psychology* (Vol. 2, pp. 166–169). New York and Washington: Oxford University Press and American Psychological Association.

Suedfeld, P., & Tetlock, P. E. (2001). Individual differences in information processing. In A. Tesser & N. Schwartz (Eds.), *The Blackwell handbook of social psychology, Vol. 1: Intraindividual processes* (pp. 284–304). London: Blackwell.

Swim, J. K., Aikin, K. J., Hall, W. S., & Hunter, B. A. (1995). Sexism and racism: Old-fashioned and modern prejudices. *Journal of Personality and Social Psychology, 68,* 199–214.

Taylor, D. G., Sheatsley, P. B., & Greeley, A. M. (1978). Attitudes toward racial integration. *Scientific American, 238,* 42–49.

Tetlock, P. E. (1986). A value pluralism model of ideological reasoning. *Journal of Personality and Social Psychology, 50,* 819–827.

Tetlock, P. E. (1994). Political psychology or politicized psychology: Is the road to scientific hell paved with good moral intentions? With commentary by L. Etheredge, P. Sniderman, D. Sears, V. Sapiro, & B. Kroeger. Special symposium on Political psychology and politicized psychology, *Political Psychology, 15,* 509–577; continued in Letters to the Editor by R. K. White & P. E. Tetlock (1995), *Political Psychology, 16,* 663–675.

Tetlock, P. E. (1998, Fall). The ever-shifting psychological foundations of democratic theory: Do citizens have the right stuff? *Critical Review, 12*(4), 1–17.

"The Bouchard file." (1997, Sept. 1). *Mclean's,* p. 12.

Trapnell, P., Paulhus, D., & Suedfeld, P. (1999). *Prejudice, politics, and the Modern Sexism Scale.* Unpublished manuscript, University of British Columbia.

Weigel, R. H., & Howes, P. W. (1985). Conceptions of racial prejudice: Symbolic racism reconsidered. *Journal of Social Issues, 41,* 117–138.

Wood, J. (1994). Is "symbolic racism" racism? A review informed by intergroup behavior. *Political Psychology, 15,* 673–686.

Zaller, J. R. (1992). *The nature and origins of mass opinion.* New York: Cambridge University Press.

18

Reconstructing Political Psychology: Current Obstacles and New Direction

SHAWN ROSENBERG
University of California, Irvine

Political psychology, along with the rest of the social sciences, is at something of a crossroads. In part, this is an internal matter—the result of the exhaustion of existing paradigms. The product of psychological or sociological theorizing of the early and mid-20th century, these research paradigms have oriented political psychological research for most of the last 50 years. They did so because they were heuristically valuable and because they yielded considerable insight into the nature of political thought and behavior. Now, however, there is an increasing awareness that most of what can be done within these frameworks has indeed been accomplished. In response, there is a call for new direction emerging from within political psychology. The contributions in this volume by Robert Lane, David Winter, and Kristen Monroe are good examples of this.

At the same time, political psychology is being challenged from without. This is coming from two sources. Most direct is the challenge of contemporary social theory. Beginning with the poststructuralism of Foucault (1979, 1980) and continuing perhaps more radically with the postmodernism of the 1980s and 1990s (e.g., Derrida, 1978; Lyotard, 1984), theorists have challenged some of the foundational assumptions on which the social sciences in general and political psychology in particular have been built. They argue that our notions of what is true and real are less a result of some direct (or even mediated) experience of the world and are more a matter of culture. No longer anchored in an objective reality, free-floating truth is a social construction, one that is consistent with the aims and structure of particular groups or societies. What is believed to be true is thus viewed as an exercise not of science, but of power. In this light, most current political psychology is regarded as suspect. One concern is that the choice of research focus is politically motivated. More fundamental, the research methods themselves are no longer viewed as neutral or necessary. Instead, they are regarded as an expression of the power of dominant cultural groups or narratives in Western society. A few social and political psychologists have responded to these concerns by either rejecting the criticism or attempting to modify their practice (e.g., Gergen, 1973; Sampson, 1993). In this volume, Peter Suedfeld rejects the postmodernist critique.

Understanding this academic objection to the current conduct of political psychology leads to the recognition of another, perhaps more basic, challenge. Whereas some may regard postmodern and poststructural theories to be specious, a critique that fails to offer workable alternatives, the tremendous growth in popularity these theories have enjoyed over the last 15 years cannot be denied. The question is why. Undoubtedly, postmodern theorizing is a reflection of our times—a period where largely shared (or at least dominant) ways of understanding the world are being called into question.[1] Filling the vacuum are a plethora of understandings of the world, some of which are anchored in old or new religions and others that are cultural manifestations of the recently empowered ethnic and racial minorities. In the resulting welter of competing definitions and values, people are either forced to retreat to the shelter of some form of cultural chauvinism or they are left with an amorphous, postmodern world where all value and knowledge is relative. The implicit challenge for political psychology is to offer understanding and normative direction that both fully recognizes and transcends this current state of affairs.

These, then, are the challenges that a reconstructed political psychology must meet: It must generate a new analytical foundation to guide further conceptualization and research, and it must clarify the relationship of that foundation to a normative position. The latter includes the twin tasks of addressing the more trenchant criticisms of the postmodernists and of providing cultural and political direction for an increasingly multicultural world. In the following, I sketch the direction that I believe political psychology should follow in order to meet these challenges.

---

[1] For interesting analyses of the social structural bases of postmodernist thought, see Harvey (1989) and Jameson (1991).

NEW ANALYTICAL DIRECTION:
TOWARD AN INTEGRATIVE POLITICAL PSYCHOLOGY

Historically, political psychology has been something of an intellectual sideshow. The center stage was occupied by a social psychology struggling against the already entrenched disciplines of psychology and sociology. Whereas the battle to construct an interdisciplinary approach was thus fought by others, the issues raised and the obstacles encountered clearly speak to the central concerns of a political psychology. During the late 19th century, the interdisciplinary battle for determining how to best make sense of social life had begun in earnest. In *The Grundrisse* and *Capital*, Marx (1967, 1971) constructed a strongly sociological conception of human affairs in which social life was structured by collective forces. Individual's beliefs and desires were understood to be derivative, a more or less direct product of socially structured circumstances. The relegation of individual-level or microsociological concerns to a secondary status was made more explicit in later sociological theory. A classic example of this is Durkheim's *Rules of Sociological Method* (1982). At approximately the same time, the psychological alternative was emerging. For example, in Sigmund Freud's psychoanalysis, the largely unconscious affective life of individuals is regarded as the central driving force in human affairs. In such works as *Civilization and its Discontents* (1930), Freud made quite clear how cultural forms and social organization are best understood not as the causes of individual behavior, but as its outcomes.

By the early 20th century, these two positions were incorporated as university departments in the United States and the disciplines (an ironically appropriate choice of words) of sociology and psychology were created. It was in this context that an attempt was made to establish a social psychology. For many social scientists, the hegemonic position of either sociology or psychology was regarded as clearly inadequate. The early psychological work on personality, cognition, and cognitive development provided strong indications that significant aspects of human behavior could not be explained as the simple product of social forces. It was clear that a sociology that viewed people as derivative or irrelevant could not address these matters. In a world that was fraught with failed revolutionary attempts and yet was clearly in the throes of change, it was also apparent that such a sociology could not consider how individuals might contribute to the definition of social life, either by resisting dominant cultural definitions or by providing the impetus and possibly even the direction for social transformation. At the same time, it was equally clear that a psychology that seemed to presume that mind and affect were either self-constituting or biologically determined was also inadequate. There were indications that human nature was affected by the social and historical conditions of their lives. This seemed to penetrate not only the content of their expressed values and beliefs, but also the very structure and processes whereby their understandings and affect where constructed.

Between the two world wars, this dissatisfaction gave rise to lively debate regarding the possibility and nature of a truly interdisciplinary or, more appropriately, an integrative discipline of social psychology. Some, like Allport (1924), argued that social psychology was properly just an extension of psychology as it was applied to social thought and behavior. Others argued the need for an integrative social psychology that transcended the limits of the two earlier social scientific perspectives. Perhaps most prominent among them was Mead (1924–1925, 1934). With his social behaviorism and his focus on social interaction, he tried to carve out a middle ground that highlighted the interplay between mind and society in both constructing a social self and establishing social control. In a manner relevant to our concerns here, Mead's social psychology had direct implications for political psychology and the analysis of democracy (e.g., Dewey, 1916; Mead, 1934).

Difficulty to Overcome—Reductionism

The effort to establish an integrative social psychology never fully succeeded. In part this is evidenced by the fact that today, there is, to the best of my knowledge, only one department of social psychology in the English-speaking world.[2] Apart from this exception, social psychologists have been absorbed into departments of psychology and, to a lesser degree, sociology. Their tendency has been to comply with the disciplinary imperatives (theoretical and methodological) of their home department and to apply them to the study of social cognition and behavior. Thus there are social psychologists in sociology departments who focus on socialization processes and rely primarily on survey techniques and social psychologists in psychology departments who apply the basic work on cognition or affect and rely primarily on experimental methods. In this context, the work of social psychologists has been regarded as secondary or peripheral.

Perhaps more important than this inability to achieve separate institutional status, social psychologists have failed to generate the requisite theoretical framework with which an integrative social psychology could be constructed. Whereas several attempts have been made, the integration they have achieved typically has been at the cost of reducing either collective

---

[2]Reference here is to the department at the London School of Economics and Political Science. Like the school where it is located, the department has a history of unusually progressive leadership.

considerations to individual ones or individual considerations to collective ones. A good example of a psychologically reductionist integration (certainly one that has been highly influential in political science) is offered by neoclassical economics. Certain basic assumptions are made about the perception, rationality, and choice of individuals, and these are then utilized to analyze the collective results of individuals interacting in this way.[3] The psychological reductionism of this approach is evident in two ways. First, it explains collective phenomena with reference to individual level phenomena, in this case, individual choices. Second, although it suggests that extra-individual circumstances affect the substance of the choices individuals make, there is no suggestion that basic psychological processes such as perception, cognition, or rational decision making are significantly affected by culture or sociohistorical conditions.

This tendency toward psychological reductionism is also exemplified by several of the contributions in this volume.[4] For example, although Monroe offers an interesting and much needed antidote to rational actor theory, her alternative, perspective theory, is essentially psychological. The focus is on individuals and their perceptions, their representations, and their construction of self. Although the substance of these perceptions and representations are partly socially determined and the salience of any one is socially cued, how a person perceives and how she represents her experience are understood as essentially psychological processes whose basic functioning is largely unaffected by social circumstance. Another case in point is Lane's effort to define a new agenda for political psychology. Although he makes the very interesting move of suggesting a focus on the ends rather than the means of action, his orientation remains psychological. The ends to be examined are solely individual ends—subjective well-being and personal development. He certainly recognizes that the criteria whereby these are defined are culturally relative, but his core contribution, the definition of ends, focuses only at the individual level. There is no consideration of essentially collective ends such as cultural coherence, systems maintenance, or societal development.

Complementing this tendency toward psychological reductionism is a sociological equivalent. Where there is clear consideration of psychological phenomena such as cognition or personality, the tendency is to make sense of these in largely sociological terms. A good example, one that has oriented the majority of mainstream American political science, is the seminal work of Parsons (1964; Parsons & Bales, 1955). Parsons shows a serious

---

[3]For classic examples of this approach in political science, see Downs (1957), Olson (1965), and Riker and Ordeshook (1973). For a more contemporary statement directed to political psychology, see Riker (1995).

[4]For an early prominent example, see Lasswell's *Psychopathology and Politics* (1960).

interest in the structure of personality; however, he conceives of this structure as isomorphic with and ultimately a product of the larger social structure of which the individual is a part. Even so, Parsons' work is unusual. More commonly, a sociologically reductionist social or political psychology has a less holistic concept of the individual. Rather than considering the individual as an integrated whole, she is conceived as a collage of socially determined aspects. In this vein, there is a focus on such socially determined attributes of the individual as the roles they perform, the discourses they participate in, or the identities they assume. Insofar as there is an interest in processes, the key concern is how socialization (generally regarded as successful) occurs. Within political psychology, the latter was a dominant focus of research from the late 1950s through the 1970s.[5]

Finally, let me briefly mention attempts that have been made to essentially preserve the integrity of each of the mother disciplines while at the same time going beyond the limits of each pursued on its own. Lacking any integrative framework for preceding, this involves advocating a kind of intellectual pluralism. Recognizing that no single discipline adequately captures the complexity of social action, the suggestion is to let all flowers bloom in the hope that more of the phenomena will be illuminated. A good example of this is offered by David Winter's recommendation that political psychology (in the present volume) should draw on both psychology, with its substantive and methodological insights, and political science, with its attention to contextual and institutional influences. His catholic attitude extends to the inclusion of literary and historical studies for the special contributions they can offer.

An eclectic strategy of this type does indeed succeed in going beyond the limits of single discipline analysis; however, it poses the problem of an integrative social or political psychology rather than solves it. Following Winter's strategy can at best yield a collage of interesting hypotheses and a variety of different types of evidence. The question then becomes, how do these various disparate pieces of the puzzle fit together. Despite the avowed eclecticism of the approach, such an integrative or supradisciplinary concern is unavoidable. There may be a number of possible partial explanations and a variety of causes and consequences, but the fact remains that social interaction and discourse are singular phenomena. There may be multiple forces that operate, but they combine, integrate, or interact to produce a singular effect, concrete interaction, and discourse. Moreover, this singular effect then becomes a cause that may generate multiple effects. Consequently, there is a need to understand the interrelationship among the various disci-

---

[5]This focus on socialization was evident in both the study of adults (e.g., the seminal work of Campbell, Philip, MIller, & Stokes, 1960; followed by Nie, Verba, & Petrocik, 1976) and in the study of children (e.g., Easton & Dennis, 1969; Greenstein, 1965; Jennings & Niemi, 1974).

plinary perspectives adopted and among the social or psychological causes and effects each identifies as its proprietary object of inquiry.

Toward a Truly Integrative Social/Political Psychology

As suggested earlier, most attempts to go beyond the limits of the separate disciplines of sociology and psychology have led either to a more catholic call for a combined approach that draws on both disciplines or, where a true integration is sought, to the reduction of the concerns of one discipline to the terms of the other. This raises the following question: Why have most attempts to integrate sociological and psychological considerations ended in one or another form of reductionism? *In my view, the key obstacle is the orienting presumption guiding these efforts, that there is a single locus or immanent source of meaning and value in human affairs.* For psychology, this is to be found in the cognitive and/or emotional life of the individual. Consequently, all the concerns of social science including social interaction, discourse, and political institutions as well as subjective thought and personal action must ultimately be interpreted (or described) and, in the last instance, explained with reference to the individual's cognition and affect. For sociology, the source of meaning and value in social life is to be found in culture (alternatively conceived as a system of meaning, a language, or a discourse) or in social structure. Thus subjectivity and personal action as well as social interaction and political institutions, must be interpreted and explained in these terms. Given this epistemological foundation, the social theorist lacks the basic theoretical framework that would enable her to do any more than explicate social life in the singular and hence reductionist terms of either a sociology (where meaning and value is collective) or a psychology (where meaning and value is personal).

The foregoing argument suggests that in order to move beyond the limits of contemporary social and political psychological approaches, a fundamentally new theoretical orientation is required. Such an orientation must recognize that social life is dually structured, by both thinking, feeling individuals and by socially structured, discursively constituted groups and that both individuals and groups are at least quasi-independent sources of meaning and value. Furthermore, a nonreductionist social or political psychology must also recognize that these two sources may operate in significantly different ways. In other words, the theorizing must be predicated on the recognition that the meaning and value of social exchange may, at any given moment, be constituted in two different ways.[6]

---

[6]This reference to social life as dually structured should not be confused with the analysis of the agency-structure relationship offered by Giddens (1984). Although Giddens is critical of the sociological reduction of agents to "structural dopes," he does little more than suggest that agents do have some kind of creative input into social life. In his theory, however, there is

To illustrate this dual structuration, let us consider our experience of teaching a university seminar. Here it is not unusual to find that students who are becoming conversant in a new theory are quite capable of engaging in meaningful discussion of aspects of the theory or the political issues it illuminates. Indeed, their discussion may flow in a quite coherent fashion. Yet at the same time, matters change substantially if one interrupts and asks one or another student to explain specifically what she meant by a statement or claim she had just made. At this point, the student often flounders and is unable to offer a clear, coherent response. Sometimes the student will simply admit, with some evident bewilderment, that she does not understand what she has said.

From either a psychological focus on subjective understanding or a sociological focus on discourse, this result is confusing. For the psychologist, the presumption would be that the students' capacity to participate in a conversation about a theory would ultimately be constrained by their own cognitive capacities or subjectively understanding. How they engage one another should reflect the power and limits of their underlying ability to reason. For the sociologist, the presumption would be that the kinds of discourse in which people can participate would constitute their personal understandings. Thus they would engage one another and respond to questions in a discursively meaningful fashion. In either case, the disjuncture between the quality of a socially constructed discourse and the quality of the subjective understandings of the individual participants, such that individuals are at a level beyond what they understand, is not easily explained. At best, an attempt can be made to minimize the importance of such a circumstance by claiming that it is unusual, temporary, or more apparent than real. However, I argue that such a disjunction is a common, enduring, and real feature of social life. I further suggest that this disjunction need not induce confusion, but in fact can be readily understood if one begins with the epistemological assumption that meaning and action are dually structured.

The preceding example focuses on the limited context of the classroom. To complement it, we may also examine the broader context of contemporary Western, particularly American, society. To an increasing degree over the last several decades, academics and social commentators have spoken of the "crisis of postmodernity" (sometimes referred to as late or hypermodernity). The basic argument is that with the advent of late capitalism, rapid technological change, multiculturalism, and globalization, more tra-

---

little room to explicate the nature of this input or the manner of its genesis. Structure (and hence the organization of action) remains a collective phenomenon, while agents are amorphous entities that are, in the end, reduced to being the mere conduits whereby this structure is realized. Relative to Giddens' conception, the approach I advocate would suggest the need to begin by elaborating a more structural concept of agency, but one that is not reduced to the social structural terms of analysis Giddens does offer.

ditional, authoritative, stable, and culturally homogeneous forms of life have broken down. Faced with the ensuing heterogeneity, complexity, and fluidity of contemporary life, people are being asked to actively and self-consciously participate with other people in the definition (and likely reconstruction) of their own and others' identities and in the construction of the rules and values whereby their interaction will be regulated. The crisis is that individuals seem to lack the cognitive and emotional resources to respond in the way required. They do not seem to fully understand what is required of them and how to proceed. The result is often discomfort, withdrawal, or various minor forms of psychopathology. At the collective level, this is reflected in a range of phenomena from the recent popularity of self-help groups to the rapid growth of "regressive social movements" that, in their racism, nationalism, or neotraditionalism, actively reject the trends of postmodern life.[7]

In the present context, the interesting feature of this crisis is the difficulty with which it is explained. Adopting a sociological perspective, one assumes that meaning and value are a social construction. Considering the postmodern period, the sociologist would try to characterize the distinctive way in which meaning and value are being constructed at this time and to explain this with reference to changes in social structure or forms of discourse. In so doing, she may offer a coherent account of what is happening at the collective level, but this does not leave the theoretical space to consider the full nature of the current crisis. The problem here is that the crisis of postmodernity (as I have characterized it) is not essentially a matter of the internal contradiction among collective forces (the kind of crisis suggested by Marx or Foucault). Rather, at its core, it embodies the contradiction between collective organization and cultural definitions on the one hand and personal affective orientations and subjective understandings on the other. The sociologist typically assumes that the thoughts and values of individuals are products of socialization and thus are collectively determined. The difficulty here is that the crisis of postmodernity is one in which socialization seems to have failed and individuals' thoughts and values are constructed in a way that resists social determination. As such, the very nature of the crisis seems to deny basic assumptions of sociology and therefore cannot readily be comprehended in its terms.

The psychological perspective does not fare much better than its sociological complement. Like the sociologist, the psychologist is ultimately limited to one level of analysis. Social life is explicated with reference to the subjectively constructed thoughts and values of individuals and their personally directed action. In this light, crisis is understood as individual crisis

---

[7]For various examples of this diagnosis of the crisis of postmodernity, see Giddens (1990), Lasch (1984), Lyotard (1984), and Riesman (1950).

or psychopathology, a breakdown in the coherence or the maintenance of the individual self. This then provides a basis for understanding how individuals might behave in maladaptive and ultimately self-destructive ways. The problem with this approach when applied to the crisis of postmodernity is that the crisis in question is evidently not one of psychopathology. It does not involve the incoherence of the self or manifest self-destruction. Rather, it stems from the individual's battle to maintain her self in the face of a way of postmodern life that threatens the coherence in terms of which that self is constituted. The underlying problem here is not one of the disintegration of the self, but the disjuncture between an integrated self and a dominant social structure or cultural discourse. Given the methodological individualism of their approach and the assumed derivative quality of social life, psychologists cannot address this disjuncture. To the contrary, when addressing the nature and genesis of social life, the tendency is to assume that collective life is an aggregation of individual causes and thus reflects or parallels individual understandings and needs. This is evident in Freudian analysis of social constraint or in the more recent analyses of culture as national character.[8]

As in the earlier example of the classroom, the crisis of postmodernity is more easily approached from the more social psychological perspective of dual structuration. From this point of view, the possible disjuncture between collective and individual constructions of meaning or organizations of action is assumed at the outset. Consequently, the basic contours of the crisis of postmodernity are readily understood. There is no need to explain the possibility of such a disjunction. Rather, analysis begins with an effort to characterize the present disjunction by describing the quality of the constructions at each level and the nature of the differences or incompatibilities between them. This then opens the door to an attempt to understand

---

[8]In some more psychological approaches (e.g., that of neoclassical economics) there is a clear recognition that the aggregation of individual initiatives may produce unintended consequences. This may create an incompatibility between an individual's desires and the value of the collective outcomes that the pursuit of those desires produces. According to my view, there are two limits to this analysis of the disjuncture between individuals and the collectivity. First, the disjuncture defined in neoclassical economic theory is a substantive one, a matter of differing evaluations of specific outcomes. The kind of disjuncture I am suggesting, one of meaning and the systemic organization of action, is a much more general phenomenon. Second, and related to the first, the substantive disjuncture between individual desires and collective outcomes is likely to be self-correcting. Individuals understand the unsatisfactory nature of the collective outcome and respond with choices to better realize their interests. The kind of disjuncture I am referring to implies a general uncoupling of individual and collective phenomena such that constructions at one level are generally opaque to constructions at the other level. Thus I assume individuals typically will not properly perceive or understand the collective or institutional conditions of their action and therefore they will not be able to respond effectively to them.

when the disjunction is likely to be more or less evident, more or less pro-
nounced, and more or less consequential either for individuals or for the
social organizations and cultural discourses in which they participate. In the
end, a much more fruitful consideration of the present crisis may be offered.

Although important, the assumption of dual structuration is not sufficient unto itself for the development of an integrated social psychology.
The presumption of the distinctiveness of collective and individual constructions of meaning and value must be supplemented by the recognition
that these constructions are necessarily intertwined. Although they are distinct, collective and individual constructions are necessarily realized on the
common ground of what people do and say to one another. As a result,
each construction impacts the other.

To illustrate, let us take a specific example of the postmodern condition,
a marriage. In a traditionally defined marriage, the roles and subsequent
behaviors of husband and wife are authoritatively defined. Recast in postmodern terms, marriage is understood as a relationship between two self-
defining, self-directing entities, each of which may have quite unique
strengths and needs. In this context, marriage no longer defines the individuals related nor can it dictate the specific ways they will interact. Instead,
it is a relationship that must be constructed (and potentially reconstructed)
by the participants in a way that is consistent with each of their individual
natures. Now let us imagine a woman who marries but can only conceive
of relationships in the more concrete and rigid terms characteristic of
more traditional definitions. The result is a disjuncture between the understandings and orientations of the individual and of the socially structured
relationship in which she finds herself. She will engage her spouse in a
manner consistent with her more concrete and rigid understandings and
expect her spouse to respond accordingly. At the same time, the quality of
the interaction between the two individuals will reflect social structural
regulations and cultural definitions. These demand that individuals self-
consciously participate in constructing a relationship that is potentially
unique and fluid. The net result is that despite her intentions and expectations, the individual's relationship with her spouse will often prove more
complex and changeable than she expects. At the same time, the interaction between the partners may often be less reflexive and constructive
than is socially required. In more abstract terms, the intended regulation
of interaction and discourse constructed by one source of structuration
(individual or collective) is always subject to potential reconstruction by the
other source because both are realized on the common ground of what
people specifically do and say to one another.

*In my view, a truly integrative social or political psychology must take this complex
relationship between the individual structuring of meaning and action on the one
hand and the collective structuring of meaning and action on the other as its point of*

departure. This relationship is likely to be a force unto itself, one that has a reverberating impact on both the personal and collective structuring of action. To begin, the relationship is likely to delimit the forms the personal and the collective may take. Because the individual and collective structures provide the context for each other's realization, each constrains the possibilities of the other. Clearly the opportunities and demands that the social environment places on the individual's interaction with others delimits the kinds of understandings she can construct and the kinds of action strategies she can initiate. This raises important concerns regarding the political and cultural dimensions of cognition and affect. In complementary fashion, the capacity of individuals to make cognitive connections and respond to demands for action delimits the kinds of institutions or discourses that can be constructed to regulate their interaction. This last aspect of the relationship opens the door for social and political psychologists to address interesting questions regarding the social psychological dimensions of institution-building and effective policymaking.

The relationship between the individual and collective structuring of social life also has the potential to be transforming. In addition to limiting the possibilities for their institutional or cultural regulation, individuals may also create pressure for the transformation of that collective regulation. Insofar as their capacities to cognize and direct action exceed the capacity of social institutions to define and organize action, individuals will regard social rules and definitions as arbitrary and readily manipulated. The result is a likely breakdown in effective social regulation that will in turn contribute to pressures and possibilities for qualitative change in the structure of collective life. As individuals may create pressure for social change from below, so the institutions and discourses of social life may create pressure for individual change from above. Insofar as the individual is confronted with tasks to perform and discourse to participate in that she does not understand and cannot effectively manage, the adequacy of her own construction of meaning and value is likely to be called into question. Given the appropriate circumstances, this is likely to foster a qualitative change in reasoning and action.[9] This transformative dimension of the relationship between the individual and the collective opens the door for an interesting analysis of the conditions and limits of both psychological and social change.

What is offered here is a direction for a future social and political psychological inquiry. Returning to the issues that first gave rise to social psychology, this is a call for a truly integrative approach. The goal is not an

---

[9]Dewey (1916) analyzes the effect of social and political institutions in these terms. His analysis of both the political institutions of democracy and the social institutions of education are cast accordingly.

interdisciplinary effort in which the theory or methods of one or the other "mother" discipline is drawn upon to inform empirical research in the substantive domain of the other. Nor is it an interdisciplinary call to eclectically combine the disparate insights of psychology, sociology, and political science. Rather, the aim is to construct a supradisciplinary understanding of the collective and individual aspects of social and political life. The assumption is that the insights and methods of the separate disciplines of sociology, psychology, and political science will have to be reconceived in this light.

As suggested at the outset, the development of such a truly integrative social or political psychology requires an epistemological position that can facilitate theorizing about the practical interdependence of subjectivity and culture and the nature of a social life that is dually structured. Existing epistemologies can not readily do this. Consequently, the attempt to reconstruct political psychology must include the development of an appropriate epistemological foundation. On this basis, clearer guidelines for theorizing and empirical research can be established. As a step in this direction, let us first consider issues of truth, value, and power as they relate to political psychological theory and research.

TRUTH AND VALUE IN POLITICAL PSYCHOLOGY

Here we turn to the challenges to political psychology being issued from without. One is the postmodernist challenge that political psychology, despite its assertions to the contrary, is not and cannot be a neutral social science. In this view, the analytical concepts and empirical methods of political psychology are not so much a matter of neutral inquiry into the nature of objective facts as they are a manifestation of the dominant discourses in society. Thus political psychology, like the social sciences more generally, is not about truth, but about the assertion of value by the powerful.[10] The other challenge—a quite different one, posed by contemporary social life—is that even if political psychology is not a source of value, it should be. American society is clearly in transition. Once workable cultural definitions and norms are being questioned and rejected as inadequate. New more adequate ones are yet to be satisfactorily formulated. Caught in a past being superceded and a future still not attained, there are demands at the level of both individuals and entire communities for new moral and political direction.

For the most part, contemporary political psychologists have ignored or rejected both challenges. The prevailing assumption is that their theories

---

[10]Within this theoretical discourse, the forces that are deemed powerful are not particular people or even institutions. Rather, reference here is to dominant discourses or discourse communities.

and certainly their research methods are value neutral. On this basis, claims of value bias or requests for value direction are typically rejected as beyond the proper purview of political psychological research.[11] Whereas such a rather flippant response may have sufficed in the past, I do not think it does so now. The truth/value or science/ideology question is being raised with sufficient strength by sufficient numbers of colleagues (in the social sciences as well as the humanities) that a more considered response is necessary. In addition, the times in which we now live are uncertain. Globalization, multiculturalism, and rapid social change have undermined old definitions and values. New ones are needed in order to decide such questions as what form democracy should take, what lessons our schools should be teaching our children, and what values should guide the conduct of our own personal lives. In this environment, a simple refusal to engage criticisms and challenges seriously is politically irresponsible.

Apart from the intellectual and practical politics of the matter, I think a good deal can be learned from taking these challenges seriously. Like the issue of interdisciplinary integration, the issue of value in political research provides impetus and direction for a reconstruction of political psychology. Indeed, our consideration of the first issue helps illuminate a way of addressing the second. Here I approach the truth/value issue in two ways. To begin, I address the more substantive ways in which truth and value have regularly been intertwined in both psychological and political analysis. The key claim here is that the resulting stipulations of the normal and the good are improved by truly political psychological considerations. Following this, I consider the more difficult issue of the formal or logical relationship between analytical and normative social inquiry. Here there is an attempt to draw on the foundation laid in the preceding section on the relationships between sociological and psychological inquiry to address the value concerns of both mainstream social scientists and their postmodernist critics. The aim is not only to better understand the parameters of the debate, but also to use the debate to determine the normative dimensions of an integrative political psychology.

Psychological and Political Judgments of the Good

Despite frequent claims of value neutrality made by both psychologists and political scientists, it is clear that the analytical and empirical efforts of each discipline influences its normative claims and these normative claims ori-

---

[11]Of course, a great deal of political psychological research operates in the service of valued ends, but these ends are assumed to be external to the theories and methods guiding the research. Thus in different instances, the same research strategies can be deployed to foster the realization of different or even opposite values.

ent analytical and empirical research. In psychology, a good example is offered by the study of cognitive development. On the one hand, the empirical research on cognition from childhood to late adolescence has charted the evolution of thinking from an operational activity that is relatively fragmented, concrete, and simple to one that is more coherent, abstract, and complex. This empirical work has served to define normative standards of appropriate development at each stage in a person's first 15 to 17 years of life. These standards guide the clinical evaluation of children and can lead to remedial or therapeutic intervention in cases where a child does not meet the prescribed norms for her age group. The net result is a clear inference from "is" to "ought."[12] On the other hand, empirical research is oriented by normative definitions of good cognitive functioning. A priori conceptions of what thinking essentially is and thus should be guide subsequent investigation. An example of this is Piaget's early use of Kant's philosophical definition of the dimensions of adult thought to guide his choice of what aspects of children's thought to empirically investigate (Piaget, 1970, 1973). Another example is Kohlberg's use of a liberal, rights-oriented conception of justice to orient his study of the development of moral reasoning (Kohlberg, 1984).

The strategy of using a priori normative conceptions to guide empirical research is also evident in most studies of adult cognition. Here the research focuses on what are posited to be the central or the most important elements of good thinking. Examples include capacities for sustained focus, complexity, abstraction, and rationality. Aspects of thinking that are deemed unimportant or undesirable, such as the quality of the humor, the capacity to think a little about a number of things simultaneously, or the sensitivity to the coloration or intensity of experience, receive little or no attention. These are all instances of how a conception of the "ought" orients the analysis of the "is."

This interrelationship between the analysis of the facts and the determination of what is valuable is also apparent in the characterization of personality. Here normative claims and empirical research are interwoven in the determination of standards of the "normal" or "healthy" personality. Very often the nature of a healthy personality is simply stipulated. In this vein, it is often assumed to consist of such dimensions as stability over time, adaptability to prevalent social demands, and the capacity for independence and self-direction. Research then focuses on the correlates and causes of these various aspects of health. In this light, empirical observation can lead to normative judgments of health or pathology of society's existing

---

[12]For a good, but rare example, of a psychologist directly addressing the is–ought problem, see Lawrence Kohlberg's 1971 essay, "From is to ought: How to commit the naturalist fallacy and get away with it." (reprinted, Kohlberg, 1984).

social regulations and normal patterns of behavior.[13] A similar mixing of normative and empirical considerations is evident in personality research that relies on criterion groups to orient the development of clinical assessment instruments. Here the empirical strategy is to choose criterion groups, that is, collections of individuals who exhibit what are assumed to be either desirable or undesirable (dysfunctional) qualities. The behavioral, attitudinal, and emotional characteristics of these people are then examined to discover what are the correlates of healthy behavior. In a metaphorical way, the interdependence of evaluation and analysis in personality research is manifest in the dual meanings of the central term, "normal," as both an empirical commonplace and a desired standard.

The interdependence of analysis and evaluation is also evident in political science. In political theory, there is a long tradition of drawing on inferences of what is true to determine what is good. This is apparent in the approach of Hobbes (1958) and Locke (1924, 1952). Here analysis begins with observations of human nature. This leads to inferences regarding the problems that arise when individuals are placed in social relationships with one another. To address these problems, deductions are made and empirical research is conducted regarding the best ways to organize and govern people. In this manner, empirical analysis yields normative direction. Such an empiricist strategy is quite explicit in the otherwise quite different approach of Emile Durkheim. Eschewing the individualism of Hobbes and Locke, Durkheim suggested that social goods are inherently collective. These can only be known by examining the qualities of functioning societies, not the qualities of individuals. By observing what is common to them all, one can make inferences about what types of values, beliefs, or behaviors are functionally necessary and therefore are normal or good. Durkheim offered trenchant examples of this in his analysis of what are typically presumed to be undesirable behaviors such as crime (1982) and suicide (1951). In traditional Marxist analysis, the relationship between the true and the desirable is taken a step further. In the utopian aspect of his vision, the true not only guides the analysis of the valuable, but through proletarian revolution, that truth also inexorably leads to the realization of value.

Of course, the relationship of truth and value in political science is not simply a matter of the determination of what is true providing a basis for inferring what is good. The relationship can also be reversed. This reversal in the direction of influence is insightfully elaborated in the Marxist analysis of ideology. In this view, both the substance of what is assumed to be true and the methods that are deemed appropriate for the investigation of the

---

[13] Good examples of analysis that suggests that the normal behavior of individuals in a society is pathological or abnormal include Fromm's *Escape from Freedom* (1941) and Lasch's *The Minimal Self* (1984).

truth are regarded as expressions of hegemonic power relations and related cultural values. An example of this might be the dominant notions of knowledge associated with the hegemony of the Catholic Church in medieval Europe. This hegemony was expressed in its determination that the reality to be known was an essentially spiritual reality and the method of "knowing" this reality was a matter of insight and faith. Other foci or other methods of inquiry (e.g., those of a materialist and empirical science) were regarded first as evil and secondarily as incorrect. In a Marxist view, this conception of the nature of knowledge and the means of knowing are consistent with maintaining the authority and power of the Church.

A more contemporary example would be the very political research that presents itself as value neutral. This work claims to restrict itself to explanation and description that are bereft of critique and it accepts methods oriented exclusively by standards of reliable observation. In this light, normative analysis is seen to be arbitrary and a matter of endless debate. Any empirical methods associated with it (e.g., observation that entails critical interpretation or includes participation and intervention) are regarded as suspect. Thus it is legitimate to analyze processes of democratization, but illegitimate or at least beyond the scope of empirical research to critique the desirability of democracy or democratic institutions themselves. Similarly, it is legitimate to analyze why people vote, but it is illegitimate for empirical research to include either a critique of voting as a limited form of participation or an attempt to change the attitudes of the voters studied. In a Marxist analysis, this purportedly value-neutral social and political science is a perfect expression of knowledge formation processes oriented to maintaining existing power relations in a technologically oriented, class-based society.

Cross-Disciplinary Critiques.   In the foregoing, I illustrated the interdependence of truth and value (or of analysis and evaluation) in psychology and political science. It is clear that in each case, the search for truth is oriented by normative claims and the normative evaluations are oriented by claims of fact. Viewed from an integrative social and political psychological perspective, it is apparent that the normatively oriented analysis of each of these disciplinary inquiries suffers when it is pursued in isolation. This becomes evident once the concerns of the one discipline are introduced into the considerations of the other. Although not fully integrative, such a cross-disciplinary effort does set the stage for a more truly interdisciplinary one.

Consider first how the introduction of typical political science concerns into psychological research lays bare the cultural and political biases inherent in the latter research. In the case of developmental psychology, this is clear in both Piaget's and Kohlberg's research on cognition. In Piaget's case, the definition of formal operations, with their emphasis on abstraction and integration as the end-goal of development, may be viewed as reflection (and reification) of the view of cognition fostered in male dominated, Western industrial societies. A similar critique may be offered of Kohlberg's work. Thus his characterization of morality with reference to justice and the integrity of individuals has been characterized as a reification of specifically masculine (Gilligan, 1982) and liberal conceptions of morality (Emler, Renwick, & Malone, 1983). This political critique also applies to the concepts that orient cognitive psychology. Here it is noted that the focus on complexity, abstraction, and problem solving addresses precisely those aspects of thinking that are critical to meeting the demands of effective participation in the highly organized world of modern international business and dense urban coexistence dominated by men. Forms of cognition that are more consistent with traditional, conservative, feminine, or spiritual conceptions of the world are typically ignored or devalued.

The previously discussed research on personality also can and has been critiqued on similar grounds. Laing (1960) critiqued clinical psychological conceptions of health as inherently oppressive. In this vein, he argued against the designation of certain personality orders such as schizophrenia, defending them as free and unsocialized thought. In a similar vein, Szasz (1961) accused psychiatrists of being nothing more than defenders of the social order, a kind of "culture police." Adopting a less anarchistic view, one can consider the social and cultural conditions of the identification of new personality disorders. Thus one may note that the initial identification of and significant interest in disorders of enmeshment (when one person becomes too emotionally dependent on another) have emerged in the highly individualistic societies of the United States and Germany. Not surprisingly, there is far less interest and indeed some skepticism regarding this disorder in more communitarian societies such as Greece, Poland, or Japan. Similarly, it seems the case that the recent identification of attention deficit disorder may be associated with the overcrowding that is now common in urban American public schools. One could argue that difficulty of coping with larger class size requires removing children that are less conforming, in one way or another, to the increasingly restrictive requirements of classroom organization. Overall, the suggestion here is that what psychologists identify as healthy or dysfunctional is at least in part a product of particular social, cultural, and political demands. Because of the constraining perspective of their discipline, psychologists typically do not give sufficient attention to the cultural bases and political consequences of their determinations of what are the central, normal, or desirable features of cognition and human nature.

Of course, political science is equally vulnerable to this cross-disciplinary critique. An example of this is the approach advocated by Lane in this volume and in his earlier work on market society (Lane, 2000). Essentially,

Lane is suggesting that political values be subject to empirical psychological validation and potential critique. Thus he recognizes that the values of democracy, equality, and freedom are quite dominant in contemporary Western political culture. They also are consistent with the organizational requirements of contemporary social and economic life in modern industrial (and especially postindustrial) societies. Part of the valuation of these forms of life—that is, the democratic, the equal, and the free—is to stipulate that they are also good for individuals. They are the realization of a natural, if sometimes politically distorted or oppressed, human nature. It is here that Lane's psychological consideration of politics is engaged. He argues that it is not necessarily the case that these political values are, in fact, good for individuals. At the very least, psychological investigation is required determined to see if people who are free, equal, or democratic are better off as individuals than people who are not.[14]

This essentially psychological approach to political issues may also be extended to postmodernist claims about the nature of meaning and value. Complementing the view that meaning and value are discursively constructed and culturally variable is the psychological claim that individuals' cognition and affect are derivative. More typically, the suggestion here is that an individual's thought and self are piecemeal constructions. Each is a collection of culturally defined fragments whose substance and interrelationships are socially constructed.[15] A psychologist can challenge this conception by giving evidence of the independent structure of cognition or personality. Typically, this is done by offering an empirical demonstration of how social definitions are reconstructed according to the quality of an individual's reasoning or the nature of his or her personality and thereby come to have a distinct, psychologically determined meaning.[16] Evidence of this kind provides the basis for a challenge to a long tradition of social theory that ignores psychology from Durkheim at the beginning of the 20th century to Lyotard and Baudrillard at the century's end.

In sum, a cross-disciplinary pollination between political science and psychology is useful in providing some perspective on the assumptions that orient the analyses and evaluations of each discipline. The foregoing cross-

---

[14]Another example of this is offered by Suedfeld in this volume. He invokes psychological research to argue against left wing political thought and research. Thus he suggests that authoritarianism is as prevalent on the left as the right and that racism is in fact declining in the United States.

[15]Again, there are examples where those adopting a more sociopolitical perspective assume cognition or personality does have a structure. Still, this structure is seen a simple product of social structural organization. An example of this is the work of Parsons discussed earlier. Postmodernists do however, not take such a view.

[16]Examples of this kind of structural psychological research include Freudian analysis of unconscious mentation (e.g., S. Freud, 1955; A. Freud, 1966) and cognitive developmental analysis of the structure of consicous thought (e.g., Piaget, 1973; Kohlberg, 1984).

disciplinary consideration of the limits of the evaluative orientation of psychology on the one hand and political science on the other illustrates the consequences of reductionism of one form or the other. However, it should be noted that this cross-disciplinary review does not constitute an integration of political science and psychology, but rather a simple reversal of the direction of reduction. Thus assumptions orienting psychology were first subjected to more macrolevel political considerations and then assumptions orienting political science were subjected to more microlevel psychological considerations. If one desired, this reduction could be reversed again, providing another iteration of cross-disciplinary critique. In the end, all this offers is another illustration of the inescapable interdependence of these two academic disciplines that typically regarded themselves as self-contained fields of inquiry.

In this light, it is clear that cross-disciplinary analysis in which the central concerns of one discipline are reconsidered from the vantage point of the other is illuminating, but ultimately inadequate. This type of analysis demonstrates that the perspective of each discipline simultaneously depends upon and can critically illuminate the assumptions of the other. Taken through two or three iterations, this analysis also suggests that rather than jumping back and forth from one perspective to the other, it might be better to consider both perspectives simultaneously. This requires abandoning cross-disciplinary approaches in favor of an integrative political psychological approach of the kind suggested earlier. In such a political psychology, evaluation and analysis would be oriented by the assumption that both subjective and intersubjective constructions of meaning and value are operative and that each is operative in a manner that is related to, but also independent of the other. This would demand a shift in evaluative strategy away from making assumptions about either basic human nature or the inherent demands of social (or political) organization to a strategy that is premised on an understanding of the relationship between the these two sources of meaning and value. *In a political psychological approach it is not subjectivity or intersubjectivity, but the relationship between the two that is fundamental and determining.*

This relational orientation shifts the focus of evaluation and analysis. To begin, it suggests the need to consider how the demands or requirements of one type limit possible formations of value and meaning of the other. This could extend to an analysis of how structural changes at one level (that of personality and cognitive structure on the one hand or of social structure and culture on the other) may be resisted or undermined by the structure of operation at the other level. The crisis of postmodernity discussed earlier could fruitfully be reconsidered in this light. This focus on mutual limitation and resistance should be complemented by a consideration of the potentially transforming effect that personal and collective constructions of value may have on one another. Such a consideration would yield both explanations of current changes and prescriptions for future ones. It thus could illuminate what individuals are and should be and what society now is and ought to be. Cast in these terms, an integrated political psychology not only constitutes a conceptual advance beyond the separate efforts of psychology and political science, but it also provides a foundation for responding to current demands for personal and political direction.

Formal Considerations:
The Modernist Versus Postmodernist Debate

In the preceding section, I examined the substantive ways in which considerations of truth and value were intertwined in both political science and psychology and concluded that neither political science nor psychology was a value-neutral science. I also illustrated how the evaluative and analytical efforts of each discipline depend on the substantive assumptions of the other and therefore argued that an integrative political psychology would offer a better basis for both political and psychological judgment. In this section, I continue with the more formal concerns posed by the postmodern critique of modernist political science and psychology. Of course, the issues raised are complex and varied. Here I only wish to consider how the concerns raised in this debate dovetail with the concerns relevant to the construction of a political psychology. This forces a direct consideration of the possible epistemological foundations of political psychology. Implicit in this argument is the claim that the construction of a truly integrative political psychology requires the appropriate metatheoretical structure to support such an effort.

Cast in the context of current academic debates, modernists are distinguished by the set of epistemological assumptions they adopt. A key assumption is that thought is an attribute of individuals, a reflection of their subjective activity. For the most part, thought is viewed as having two aspects. On the one hand, it is representational. Thought mirrors and thereby is connected to an external objective reality to which the individual is exposed. On the other hand, thought is associative or combinatorial. It establishes relations between the elements of reality by juxtaposing them to one another. This may involve active reflection or imagination, or a more passive representation of how elements are observed to be associated with one another in reality. Modernist social inquiry is oriented accordingly. It focuses on individuals and views collective entities as aggregative and therefore largely transparent to observation. Empirical efforts are consequently devoted to the reliable and unprejudiced collection of factual data on individuals. Normative efforts focus on elucidating the essential nature of the individual as an abstract (particularly as abstracted from a particular social or cultural context) entity. The requisites of this abstract nature then define universal human values.

The postmodernists attack the epistemological basis of modernist empirical and normative inquiry. Thus they reject modernist assertions that thought is subjective, that it is linked to a distinct objective reality, and that it is associative or combinatorial. Instead, postmodernists suggest that thought is an intersubjective, self-referential, and creative exercise. In their view, thought (or meaning, the more appropriate term in this context) is discursively constructed. Consequently, meaning is less a function of its connection to an objective reality and more a product of intersubjective negotiation or cultural determination. Disconnected from an external reality, the narratives of socially constructed meaning create their own intersubjectively constituted reality (complete with intersubjectively constituted means for exploring that reality) in its place. Oriented by these epistemological assumptions, postmodernist theorizing abandons a vocabulary of representation, truth, and absolute knowledge in favor of a language of construction, meaning, and relative understanding.

In this frame of reference, empirical research becomes less a systematic effort to observe and order data and more an attempt to interpret the culturally or discursively relative meaning of what is observed. The relationship between observation and theory construction posited by the modernist is reversed. Observation is no longer anchored in the experience of reality and thus a potential basis for rejecting old knowledge or building new knowledge. Rather, it is viewed as a manifestation of existing discursively constructed meanings and as a vehicle for defining a reality the participants in the discourse will share. In this light, the theories, empirical methods, and normative orientations of the social sciences are regarded as expressions of dominant discourses and therefore as socially and historically relative. Where these theories and methods are brought to bear on other weaker discourses or groups, the result is not enlightenment or productive debate, but rather the mere assertion of power of one discourse or cultural ethos over another.[17]

---

[17]In this manner, postmodernism goes beyond and ultimately rejects Marxism. Although recognizing the force of ideology, Marxism sustains the distinction between truth and value. This is ultimately the task of science (as Marx defines it). A critical, politically aware, and interpretative inquiry that focuses on praxis (action), scientific inquiry can penetrate the value-distorted vision produced by ideology and offer a true understanding of social relations. In the postmodernist view, this last refuge of the distinction between truth and value disintegrates. With its focus on discourse and language, the link between the construction of meaning and any reality outside of a discursively constructed one is eliminated. A reality external to cultural constructions or ideologies is thus lost and with it the point of departure for any kind of neutral or objective science. In this free-floating world of intersubjectively constructed and competing meanings, truth and value collapse onto one another, as both become parallel expressions of the same dominant discourse.

Viewed from the perspective of a political psychologist, both sides of the present debate offer important insight. The modernist view has the advantage of recognizing the importance of the link between thought or meaning and something outside of itself. The postmodernist tendency to obliterate this link runs into all the difficulties and conundrums of early idealist philosophizing. A number of contrapuntal considerations may be raised. For example, there is the somewhat obvious suggestion that even if we agree we can walk through walls, we will probably find that we cannot. A more subtle and perhaps more intractable move would be to ask how discourses (as internally differentiated and self-referential entities) are ever learned. Within a postmodernist frame of reference, to explain how a language might constitute the understandings of a speaker is a fairly straightforward exercise. However, to figure out how someone who does not understand the language can ever come to use it appropriately is more difficult. Nor should this latter situation be regarded as peripheral or unusual. We should not forget that all competent participants in discourses began (as children) not understanding any language. The latter circumstance suggests that a common feature of all language, its capacity to reach individuals whose understandings are not yet discursively or linguistically mediated, implies the existence of a link or common ground between language and something external to it. Given the circumstance of this discourse-less, language-less learner, it is clear that this link must incorporate elements that can only be termed subjective and/or objective in nature.

The modernist view also has the advantage of recognizing that people do think and do construct meanings and understandings. By suggesting that individuals are not significant contributors to the construction of meaning, postmodernists are put in the untenable position of assuming that people understand what they say in a manner that parallels the discursive or intersubjective definition of they are saying. I suggest that any person who has engaged in an extended conversation about a personally significant topic will quickly come to the recognition that to claim that the only meanings are discursively constituted ones is manifestly incorrect. A rejoinder to this might be an acknowledgment that discursive meanings may be subjectively distorted, but this is of no social consequence. Again, I suggest common experience dictates otherwise. Present misunderstandings/distortions typically have consequences for subsequent moves in conversation or later action.

For its part, postmodernism offers important insight into the constructive and pragmatic aspects of thought. Modernist claims that thought is simply associative or combinatorial implies that although the substance of thinking may vary from person to person, its basic qualities do not. For anyone who has taught in a college classroom, this is evidently not the case. Not only does what students know vary, but so does the quality of how they know it. Some are clearly capable of thinking about information in abstract, integrative, or critical ways. Given the same information, other students, despite comparable exposure and effort, process the information in a rather concrete, fragmented, and largely uncritical fashion. If thinking were merely an act of representation complemented by associative combination, this would be very hard to understand. It becomes more sensible if thinking is a constructive activity that produces the kinds of representations and associations that can be established. This pragmatic view of thinking as constructive activity establishes a more complex view of the relationship between subject and object, one in which both contribute to the definition of the quality of the relationships and the elements that distinguish a particular mode of thinking.

With its emphasis on the social construction of meaning, the postmodernist critique also corrects the overly subjectivist conception of modernism. Assuming that thought is only subjective, the modernist is left to conclude that any variation in the quality of thinking is evidence of neurophysiological detriment or disorder. Accounting for difference is a biological question. Deviating from the early pragmatists (e.g., Charles Sanders Peirce and William James), postmodernists stipulate that key pragmatic relationship is an intersubjective and discursively mediated one. If we adopt this postmodernist concern with discourse but do not (as postmodernists do) eliminate subjectivity, it is clear that the quality of subjectivity—that is, the quality of an individual's thinking—is significantly determined by the quality of the discursive exchanges in which he or she participates. This suggests that differences in thinking across individuals may be accounted for with reference to sociocultural and linguistic determinants. This in turn requires a focus on collective phenomena and an analysis of differences in forms of discourse and in the quality of cultural meanings and judgments that are associated with them.

The postmodernist concern with the collective production of meaning leads us well beyond the focus on differences in the substance of shared cultural values and beliefs that is characteristic of modernist attempts to address cultural variation. This is true in two respects. First, these values and beliefs are understood to be embedded in narratives and thus are pragmatically defined. They cannot, therefore be described in isolation from one another. Rather, they must be interpreted in light of the broader discourse in which they are articulated.[18] Second, the modernist perspective

---

[18]Compare examples of modernist (e.g., Almond & Verba, 1963; Inglehart, 1990) and poststructuralist (e.g., Foucault's histories of the asylum or punishment, 1965, 1979) characterization of differences among cultures. For an interesting attempt to incorporate some of the constructivist, pragmatic, and culturally relativist critiques of modernism while still retaining core modernist aspirations, see Habermas (1987). His attempt to characterize forms of discourse is particularly relevant here.

assumes that cultural values and beliefs cohere and are broadly shared by the society. The postmodern view denies this coherence and commonality. With late modernist structuralism as its target, postmodernism emphasizes the conflict among meaning-producing discourses and examines the relations of power that exist between them.

In this context, we can also address the implications of these epistemological claims for an understanding of value. For the modernist, an epistemological individualism forces an ethical individualism. Like knowledge, value reflects the relationship between the individual and reality. Here, however, the relationship is reversed. In the value relationship, it is the qualities of the individual, as she is related to reality, that are determining. Thus it is her basic requirements or needs that are conceived as real or true values. Because they are characteristics of the individual qua individual, these values are regarded as universal and cultural formations are judged with reference to them. The postmodernist rejects this individualism, suggesting that value, like meaning, is not linked to a reality (psychological or objective), but rather is discursively mediated. Thus value is a cultural construction, a collective (if contested) outcome that shapes the individual's personal sense of what her true needs are.

Our preceding consideration of modern and postmodern epistemologies suggests that both these ethical stances stand as partial correctives to one another. The postmodern contribution is its greater sensitivity to cultural and historical variation in the definition of values than is possible with a modernist universal ethic. This forces a greater self-awareness of the source of the values the social analyst is espousing and a greater recognition of the politics involved in the conflict between discursive communities. On the other hand, the modernist anchoring of value in relation to reality (either that of the universal individual or that of the archetypal social structure) provides a basis for ethical critique. In a postmodern conception, where value is wholly artificial and relative, ethical discourse can only be an arena for the assertion of power of one discourse community over another. Nothing transcends this. In this light, even contemporary multiculturalist assertions of the ethical value of allowing each discursive community its voice is only another masked attempt on the part of some (in this case, temporarily allied minorities) to assert power over others. Retaining a link to personal or collective realities, modernism offers a foundation, albeit a relatively complex one, for an ethical discourse that may be more than an exercise in power.

In sum, both sides of the modernist–postmodernist debate offer significant insight and each side corrects evident deficiencies of the other. The key epistemological contributions on the modernist side are: (a) its attention to the quality of subjectivity, (b) its emphasis on the coherence of subjective constructions (or the tendency toward coherence), and (c) its recognition of the link between subjective constructions (or cultural ones) on the one hand and a concrete reality on the other. These also provide the ground for meaningful and critical ethical discourse. The key epistemological contributions on the postmodernist side are: (a) its emphasis on intersubjectivity and discourse, (b) its attention to the conflict among discourses, and (c) its recognition that meaning is self-referential and discursively determined. These provide the basis for recognizing fundamental differences among ethical claims and the political dimension of the conflict between them.

Recognizing both sets of contributions, it seems appropriate to resist taking the modernist–postmodernist debate on its own terms, thereby avoiding the unsatisfactory choice of opting for one side the other. A more fruitful approach would be to regard the debate as a point of departure for the construction of a more adequate epistemology and ethics, ones more suited to the needs of social and political analysis. Adopting this approach, it is clear that an effort must be made to incorporate the insights of both positions. However, care should be taken to remember that these positions are antithetical to one another and their insights cannot simply be combined. Rather a third, alternative position must be developed. Effectively, this would provide a basis for reconstituting the insights of modernism and postmodernism in different terms and thus facilitate the incorporation of their otherwise opposed claims. Finally, when conducting this epistemological exercise, we should not lose sight of what was learned from our earlier, more substantive consideration of the relationship between psychological and political scientific inquiry.

STRUCTURAL PRAGMATICS: AN EPISTEMOLOGICAL FOUNDATION FOR POLITICAL PSYCHOLOGY[19]

In this last section, I build on the preceding discussion of the modernist–postmodernist debate in order to flesh out the epistemological foundations of the integrative political psychology discussed in the first part of this chapter. To begin, the concept of structuration as the means for constructing meaning is presented. As discussed here, meaning is both internally elaborated (as in postmodernist arguments) and referential (as in modernist arguments). With this elemental concept in place, I then reintroduce the previously discussed notion of the duality of structuration. This sets the stage for the further consideration of the pivotal concern, the relationship between sources of structuration. I conclude by drawing out the theoretical, methodological, and normative implications of this foundation for the conduct of political psychology.

---

[19]For a more elaborated explication of structural pragmatics, see my discussion in chapter 2 of *The Not So Common Sense* (Rosenberg, 2001).

Structuration

As already noted, postmodernism suggests that meaning is constructed and internally elaborated. In this sense, it is a system of interrelations unto itself. This epistemological insight is both substantiated and extended by psychological and political scientific theory and research discussed earlier. Visions that are sociological in nature suggest that the meanings that constitute a culture may differ from one community to the next in qualitative ways. More strongly psychological visions indicate that subjectively constructed meanings may differ from one individual to the next in similarly qualitative ways. The integrative vision suggested here augments these claims by adding that cultural meaning may differ qualitatively from the meaning constructed by individuals.

Together, the foregoing claims suggest first that meaning is constructed. Whether the constructing entity is a discourse community or an individual, the construction process itself consists of the active engagement of one person by another. The result is a characteristic way of acting (or at the collective level, interacting), be it a more physical act or a speech act,[20] and a way of conceiving the actions and reactions of others. This way of acting or conceiving action is manifest in particular concrete instances of engagement as a way of placing aspects or moments of an action (or interaction) in a practical or pragmatic relationship to one another. These elements or moments are thereby rendered meaningful. Over time, the number of these relationships increase and the connections between them are elaborated. The result is a structure of interrelated statements and actions that constitute the meaning or understanding of a given discourse community or individual.[21]

It is important to note that this constructed structure of meaning does not simply constitute a particular arrangement of objectively constituted elements. The nature of the active engagement not only determines the constitution of the relationships that can be constructed, it also determines the elemental acts that can thus be related. If one can only engage the environment through immediate, concrete, and personal action, the elements of one's constructed definition of reality will be constituted accordingly.

---

[20] By the term *speech act*, I refer to the use of the concept in the pragmatic philosophy of language of the later Wittgenstein (1953) and Searle (1971).

[21] Note that in this view of structuration, I am reversing the typical relationship between the ideas of structure and structuration. In most structuralist thought, structures are pre-existing, virtual entities that construct and thus define the manifest reality on which they operate. As such, they cannot be significantly affected by the reality upon which they operate—constructive influence operates in only one direction. Following a notion of structure more similar to Piaget (1970), I suggest that structures are a product of structuration processes. This opens a conceptual door to consider the influence that manifest reality has on virtual structures as well as vice versa.

They will consist of what is observable now (present concrete experience). If one can engage the environment through directed reflection and abstraction, the constitutive elements of the one's concept of reality will extend to include what was present and now is absent (past experience), what never has been present but could be (hypothetical experience), and what never has been and never could be present (abstraction). As these examples indicate, the construction of meaning is very much a creative act.

There are several important implications of this view of construction. A first is that there are different forms of construction or structuration. Insofar as the mode of engagement or operation of one construction process differs from another, the quality of the action that can be initiated and thus the kinds of connections that can be forged among acts and statements will differ. As a result, there will be general qualitative or formal differences between the structures of understanding that each mode of engagement yields. For example, when constructive engagement consists of focusing on a single act and then initiating or defining other acts relative to it, the resulting conceptual relationships will tend to forge linear associations between concretely experienced elements. Such a mode of construction is likely to yield an understanding that is concrete in substance, embedded in past experience, and fragmentary in structure. Another form of constructive engagement may entail focusing on these linear relationships among actions and then juxtaposing them relative to one another. In this juxtaposition of relationships, meaningful connection is anchored in the juxtaposition itself rather than in one or another of the linear relationships observed. These juxtapositions can themselves be juxtaposed, allowing for the self-conscious construction of a weave of relationships (a system of meaning unto itself) at several levels of generality. The resulting structure of understanding is likely to be self-consciously interpretative, abstract, hypothetical, and integrative. The point here is that, as the mode of construction varies, so will the quality of the understandings constructed. Oriented by this epistemological claim, we can better understand the differences among cultures, among individuals, and between a culture and the individual participants in it.

A second related implication is that meaning has a formal structure. The process of constructing meaning begins with an existing, general way in which the environment and other people are engaged with one another. This implies that what is being engaged varies with specific circumstances, but how that engagement is conducted does not. As a result, the various particular relationships constructed in the course of actively engaging different specific circumstances will certainly vary in substance (that is, with regard to the specific elements related), but they will share the same basic quality or form. Returning to our consideration of communities and individuals, this suggests that, for a given culture or discourse community, the quality of the various discursive exchanges and the meanings constructed will share a common form. Similarly, for a given individual, the quality of the various claims she makes or the purposes she pursues will also share the same basic form. This in turn suggests that for any individual or discourse community, there will be a formal or structural identity between the construction of relationships that constitute an understanding and the construction of relationships that constitute a judgment or evaluation. Oriented by this epistemological claim of structure, we can complement our understanding about what is different from one culture or person to the next with an appreciation of the internal similarities among the various manifestations of a single culture or personal way of constructing meaning.

A third implication reflects a retention of the modernist insight that meaning has an objective dimension to it. The suggestion here is that, even if meaning is actively constructed, structured, and internally elaborated, it is at the same time anchored in a reality external to it. A structure, although it may operate to organize and define action, is a virtual entity. It is only realized in the concrete specificity of what actually occurs, a specificity that it attempts to shape but also must reflect. As a result, the structuration of meaning and action not only determines, but is also determined by, the manifest ways in which statements and actions are interconnected. In the latter regard, a structure is always potentially vulnerable to the recursive effects of the outcome of its own concrete realization.[22] This suggests that the discursive or subjective structuration of meaning is always subject to the actual ways in which conversations and interactions unfold.

Duality of Structuration. In elaborating the epistemological concept of the structuration of meaning, we have considered both discourse communities and individuals, but we have considered them in isolation from one another. Now it is necessary to develop this concept further in light of my earlier claim that these two sources of structuration, an integrating community (or discourse) and a thinking subject, are interrelated. The key point of departure here is that structures are both virtual and operational. They define manifest reality by operating on it, that is, by regulating the specific, concrete ways in which statements and actions actually connect

---

[22]Giddens (1984) also uses the concept "duality of structuration." His view is rather different from the one presented here. Like the view being expressed here, Giddens refers to the recursive relationship between a virtual structure and its specific realization in particular action that is being discussed here. The limit of his conception, from my perspective, is the characterization of the realization of structure as simple, concrete, and specific. Lacking any formal or structural quality, deviant realization can be disruptive, but cannot be creative or directing. This renders the transformation of structures, that is, social or psychological change, impossible to understand. As in Giddens' work on intimacy (1992), such a transformation can be observed, but cannot be readily explained or anticipated.

with one another. Extrapolating to the case of individuals and communities as structuring forces, their interrelationship can be understood as one in which both operating structures are attempting to regulate the same concrete ground of interaction. At the same time that a culture or community is attempting to regulate how specific conversations and interactions may unfold, the individuals involved are attempting to direct what they say and do and how others will respond or react. Thus, as an individual is deconstructing and reconstructing social exchange in her own terms, the culture and community are deconstructing and reconstructing her initiatives and responses in its terms. As virtual structures that not only define and regulate interactions but also reflect how they actually transpire, cultures and subjects are each vulnerable to the restructuring effects of the other. Thus, although distinct from one another, these two sources of structuration are practically (or pragmatically) and inextricably intertwined. This illuminates the nature of the mutual constraint and potentially transformative effect individuals and communities exercise on one another.

Here it is important to note that sociological and psychological observations complicate this epistemological conception. Thus far, this social psychological duality implies a relationship between forces that, although different from one another, are internally homogeneous. The postmodernist vision alerts us to the danger of this. The community is clearly a diverse entity comprised of multiple enterprises, groups, and sites of interaction. Each of these may constitute a discursive community that varies not only in its substance but also in its structure. As the postmodernist suggests, how these operate on one another is very much a matter of power. Now, we may supplement this claim with a recognition that whereas discourses may be isolated from and opposed to one another in a society, they are subject to the forms of integration that may be practically imposed by individuals who deploy them in a subjectively determined way. This adds a strongly psychological, and heretofore largely ignored, component to the analysis of culture.

In complementary fashion, psychological research and everyday experience suggests that although individual subjects may reason in a singularly structured fashion, there are conditions that may evoke qualitatively different kinds of reasoning from the same individual. An example is clinical psychological insight into how childhood experience is structured differently from adult experience. Although adults typically operate at their mature level of cognition, specific experience, especially emotionally loaded experience, may cue more child-like or earlier ways of thinking. The net result is a complex view of the subject as a source of structuration. In the present context, this psychological view of the dynamics of subjective structuration may be supplemented by a recognition that, in the course of their daily lives, subjects participate in and are thus regulated by a number of potentially quite different discourse communities. This may also cue different forms of subjective engagement in a way that has largely been ignored by clinical or especially cognitive developmental psychologists.

Implications for the Conduct of Political Psychology

In the preceding discussion, I offered a sketch of an epistemology that I believe can profitably orient further work in political psychology. To conclude, I briefly consider the theoretical, methodological, and normative implications of this position.

Theory. The foregoing structural pragmatic epistemology provides clear direction for theory development in political psychology. To begin, it suggests the need to clearly specify the various structural forms that do or can operate in the ordering of social and political life. There are clearly psychological and sociological dimensions to this task. On the psychological side, there is a need to explicate the forms that subjectively constructed understandings and evaluations may take. This requires delineating the forms of coherence that underlie the manifest diversity of a given individual's cognitive and emotional activity.[23] At the same time, this general search for coherence must be tempered by a sensitivity to possible alternative sources of structuration that may operate in the case of a particular individual. This requires a consideration of how the individual subject retains the residue of a personal history that allows her to draw on more than one form of subjectively directed engagement, and how the individual's structuration of meaning can be affected by the socially structured conditions of interaction.[24] This suggests a need to theorize not only about the modes of engagement and subjectively constructed structures of meaning, but also to make clear how and when either personal history or social forces may elicit different modes of engagement than that which an individual typically employs.

On the sociological side of this investigation of structure, there is a need to explicate the structural forms that collectively or intersubjectively structured cultures and social (or political) organizations may take. This requires discovering the type of coherence that is characteristic of a community's

---

[23]For examples of such an attempt, see Piaget's work on stages of cognitive development (e.g., Inhelder & Piaget, 1958), Kegan's work on stages of emotional development (Kegan, 1982, 1994) and my own work on types of social and political thinking (e.g., Rosenberg, 1988, chapter 4; 2001, chapters 3–7).

[24]For an interesting example of early theory about the social structuration of types of cognition, see the Russian research on development by Vygotsky (1962, 1978) and Luria (1976). For a interesting extension of this, see Wertsch (1991).

discourses or its patterns of social interaction.[25] Again, this search for a dominant or typical structuration of meaning and action must be complemented by a consideration of both how that community is internally differentiated and thus may consist of a number of structurally different and competing sources of social structuration, and how the social structuring of meaning can be affected by the subjective reconstruction of that meaning by the individuals involved. Thus the analysis of social structuration must include theory that addresses how and when either alternative discourses within a society or the subjective contributions of its individual members may lead to different modes of social regulation than is typical of dominant social and political institutions.

As I have suggested, the theoretical explication of sociopolitical or psychological structures must address the relationship between the two. This would include an explanation of how these two levels of structuration delimit each other's operation and thus the quality of the structure each constructs. These rather general concerns would probably have to be elaborated through more specific consideration of how different forms of either social or psychological structuration impinge on one another. It is not clear that all forms would necessarily have the same deconstructive/reconstructive effect. This consideration of the relationship between subjective and intersubjective structures in turn requires a reconsideration of the quality of the structures themselves. Each source of structuration would have to be reconceived in light of its penetration by the other. For example, a social organization would have to be conceived as an internally differentiated structure that can accommodate existing differences in the capacities of its individual members to respond to that organization and interact with one another. Similarly, an individual's thought would have to be conceived as an internally differentiated structure that can accommodate existing differences in the types of social organizations and cultural discourses in which that individual participates.

A final and quite central concern raised by the relationship between individual and sociopolitical structurations of meaning revolves around problems of social change. One goal is to offer theory that indicates how and under what conditions structuration of one kind is likely to undermine structural transformations at the other level. An example would be to explicate how and if individuals may resist and perhaps undermine the current cultural and social structural transformations characteristic of the transition to a postmodern society. A second complementary goal is to theorize about the conditions under which one source of structuration may force a transformation in the structure of the other. This raises questions regard-

---

[25]For a good example of this, see Habermas' analysis of forms of discourse (Habermas, 1987).

ing the direction of such transformation and the possible need to distinguish between regressive and progressive transformations. Whereas all these issues may be addressed in a quite general way, it is clear that the resulting theory will have to be elaborated by considering how these interactive dynamics may be worked out differently in the case of different forms of sociopolitical or psychological structuration. What effectively produces resistance or transformation under one set of structurally delimited conditions, may not do so under conditions that are constituted differently.

Method.   Clearly, the specific hypotheses that orient political psychological research will be dictated by the substance of the particular theory developed. These will include questions about the validity of claims about what typical or dominant form of structuration is characteristic of a given community or an individual. The formulation of research hypotheses will also reflect a need to validate whatever typology forms of sociopolitical or subjective structuration is offered. Finally, claims regarding how particular sociopolitical and subjective forms of structuration constrain and transform one another will have to be examined.

The empirical methods employed to investigate these questions will have to be crafted in light of the epistemological claims guiding the research. The claim that meaning is structured suggests the corollary caveat that the substance and meaning of statements or action can only be determined with reference to the dually structured context in which it occurs. The latter suggests that any empirical investigation of statements and action cannot assume in advance that the nature of these objects of inquiry is known. To the contrary, methods must be crafted that allow for an interpretation of the quality and meaning of those statements. This requires data collection techniques that allow for an observation of the apparent way in which a number of statements and actions are interrelated in the unfolding of a given person's expression or purposive action or a given community's discourse or social interaction. Once collected, a bootstrapping effort is required in which successive attempts are made (a) to infer the structure underlying the observed relationships, (b) then to check the fit between the inferred structure and existing or additional observations of how actions do lead to one another, and (c) to adjust the initial understanding of the structure accordingly. A good example of such an empirical method is provided by the so-called "clinical experiments" conducted by cognitive developmental psychologists and their efforts to offer an interpretative account of the underlying structure of the reasoning they have observed.

One further methodological caveat must also be considered in conjunction with this emphasis on interpretation. In more conventional, interpretative research such as the psychological research of cognitive developmentalists or psychoanalysts or the sociological research of structural Marxists and poststructuralists, the researcher's act of interpretation is regarded as a typically personal, reflective enterprise. Viewed from a structural pragmatic perspective, this is clearly an important dimension of interpretative activity. However, it is not its sole component. Adequate interpretation requires a dialogical component. This may require a direct discourse among reflective researchers to guide the interpretation. Indeed, it may even require a collaborative discourse between researchers and the people they are studying.

This emphasis on interpretation does not preclude more standard survey and experimental research. Rather, it suggests that such research cannot be used at the outset. The problem is that evidence of correlation discovered in a survey or causal relation discovered in an experiment does not allow for an interpretation of the quality of the correlative or causal relationship observed. Instead, the meaning or quality of the relationship is assumed to be transparent and each discovered relationship is considered on its own terms. The epistemology guiding the proposed political psychological research suggests that this approach and its underlying assumption are incorrect. Whether the correlation or causal relationship is intrapersonal or interpersonal, a structural pragmatic epistemology suggests that the quality of that relationship is structurally determined. It is necessarily dictated both by the structuring force of the cultural context and the subjective contributions of the individuals involved. Insofar as either of these structuring forces is ignored, it is likely that the "discovered" relationship will be misunderstood, that is its own nature and connection to other related phenomena will not be correctly apprehended. As a result, any attempt to predict the conditions under which the observed relationship will hold (or change) is likely to fail. That said, once the dually structured conditions of an observed situation or set of situations are understood, the particular relationships may be explored using traditional survey and experimental methods.

Normative Considerations.   A structural pragmatic epistemology also offers direction for deciding the ends and means of normative or ethical inquiry. In both instances, considerations are conditioned by the claim that values and judgments are sociohistorically and subjectively relative constructions.

In the case of the determination of the ends of normative inquiry, this structural pragmatic understanding shifts analysis from a focus on values and judgments themselves to the processes whereby they are constructed. This in turn leads to several levels of ethical consideration. To begin, there is a consideration of the compatibility of the values advocated and the quality of the structuring forces that are operative. Thus if individuals are thinking in concretely experientially guided terms and society consists of specific and ritualistic regulations of interaction, the values of freedom and choice make little cultural or subjective sense. Indeed, to the degree that these values can be practically introduced, the general effect would be a negative one of personal and cultural disintegration. At another level, there would be an assessment of the relative input of individuals and communities into the value determination process. Clearly, the comprehensibility and practicality of values or evaluative practices is relative to the structures of meaning and action into which they are incorporated. Insofar as the construction of value tends to be dominated either by individuals or by their community, the meanings and needs of the weaker structuring force may be (within certain limits that need to be understood) ignored. This may prove destructive for either the individual selves or for their community thus subordinated. In this manner, the ethical worth of particular value claims or evaluative practices may be judged from this expressly social psychological point of view.

The epistemology suggested here also has methodological implications. These implications for ethical inquiry parallel those for empirical research discussed earlier. Thus normative inquiry requires the interpretative analysis of the quality or meaning of the values and evaluative practices observed or considered. This in turn implies that ethical inquiry must be conducted in a manner that is sensitive to the sociocultural and psychological relativity of the normative standards to be inferred. In addition, structural pragmatics suggests that normative inquiry cannot be the isolated enterprise of the philosopher or political theorist. Although such subjective aspects of the inquiry are important, the inquiry must also be discursive. In the latter regard, it must also engage those whose values are being judged, and it must do so in full recognition of the potential for irresolvable disagreement that may follow.

CONCLUSION

As I stated at the beginning of this chapter, political psychology is at a crossroads. New theoretical direction is being demanded from within and a greater epistemological sophistication and ethical relevance is being demanded from without. In this context, I have suggested the need for a reconstructed, truly integrative political psychology that can meet these various demands. I have also outlined the epistemological foundations and the basic theoretical framework that such a political psychology requires. Of course, the reader may well disagree with the particular solution I have offered. That said, I firmly believe that the demands confronting political psychology are real and pivotal. They constitute a challenge and an opportunity. A more adequate political psychology must be responsive to them.

REFERENCES

Almond, G. A., & Verba, S. (1963). *The civic culture: Political attitudes and democracy in five nations.* Princeton, NJ: Princeton University Press.

Allport, F. H. (1924). *Social Psychology.* Boston: Houghton Mifflin.

Campbell, A., Converse, P. E., Miller, W. E., & Stokes, D. E. (1960). *The American voter.* New York: John Wiley.

Dewey, J. (1916). *Democracy and education: An introduction to the philosophy of education.* New York: Macmillan.

Derrida, J. (1978). *Writing and difference.* Chicago: University of Chicago Press.

Downs, A. (1957). *An economic theory of democracy.* New York: Harper & Row.

Durkheim, É. (1951). *Suicide, a study in sociology.* Glencoe, IL: Free Press.

Durkheim, E. (1982). *The rules of sociological method, and selected texts on sociology and its method.* London: Macmillan.

Easton, D., & Dennis, J. (1969). *Children in the political system: Origins of political legitimacy.* New York: McGraw-Hill.

Emler, N. R., Renwick, S., & Malone, B. (1983). The relationship between moral reasoning and political orientation. *Journal of Personality and Social Psychology, 45*(5), 1073–1080.

Foucault, M. (1965). *Madness and civilization: A history of insanity in the age of reason.* New York: Pantheon.

Foucault, M. (1979). *Discipline and punish: The birth of the prison.* New York: Vintage.

Foucault, M. (1980). *Power/knowledge: Selected interviews and other writings, 1972–1977.* New York: Pantheon.

Freud, A. (1966). *The ego and the mechanisms of defense* (Rev. ed.). New York: International Universities Press.

Freud, S. (1930). *Civilization and its discontents.* London: Hogarth Press.

Freud, S. (1955). *The interpretation of dreams.* New York: Basic Books.

Fromm, E. (1941). *Escape from freedom.* New York: Farrar & Rinehart.

Giddens, A. (1984). *The constitution of society.* Berkeley: University of California Press.

Giddens, A. (1990). *The consequences of modernity.* Stanford, CA: Stanford University Press.

Giddens, A. (1992). *The transformation of intimacy: Sexuality, love, and eroticism in modern societies.* Cambridge, UK: Polity Press.

Gergen, K. J. (1973). Social psychology as history. *Journal of Personality and Social Psychology, 26,* 309–320.

Gilligan, C. (1982). *In a different voice: Psychological theory and women's development.* Cambridge, MA: Harvard University Press.

Greenstein, F. I. (1965). *Children and politics.* New Haven, CT: Yale University Press.

Habermas, J. (1984). *The theory of communicative action* (Vol. 1). Boston: Beacon.

Habermas, J. (1987). *The theory of communicative action* (Vol. 2). Boston: Beacon Press.

Harvey, D. (1989). *The condition of postmodernity.* Oxford, UK: Basil Blackwell.

Hobbes, T. (1958). *Leviathan.* Oxford, UK: Clarendon Press.

Inglehart, R. (1990). *Culture shift in advanced industrial society.* Princeton, NJ: Princeton University Press.

Inhelder, B., & Piaget, J. (1958). *The growth of logical thinking from childhood to adolescence: An essay on the construction of formal operational structures.* New York: Basic Books.

Jameson, F. (1991). *Postmodernism, or, the cultural logic of late capitalism.* Durham, NC: Duke University Press.

Jennings, M. K., & Niemi, R. G. (1974). *The political character of adolescence: The influence of families and schools.* Princeton, NJ: Princeton University Press.

Kegan, R. (1982). *The evolving self: Problem and process in human development.* Cambridge, MA: Harvard University Press.

Kegan, R. (1994). *In over our heads: The mental demands of modern life.* Cambridge, MA: Harvard University Press.

Kohlberg, L. (1984). *Essays on moral development* (Vol. 2). New York: Harper and Row.

Laing, R. D. (1960). *The divided self: A study of sanity and madness.* Chicago: Quadrangle Books.

Lane, R. D. (2000). *The loss of happiness in market societies.* New Haven, CT: Yale University Press.

Lasch, C. (1984). *The minimal self.* New York: W. W. Norton.

Lasswell, H. (1960). *Psychopathology and politics.* New York: Viking.

Locke, J. (1924). *An essay concerning human understanding.* Oxford, UK: Clarendon Press.

Locke, J. (1952). *The second treatise of government.* New York: Bobbs-Merrill.

Luria, A. R (1976). *Cognitive development: Its cultural and social foundations.* Cambridge, MA: Harvard University Press.

Lyotard, J. F. (1984). *The postmodern condition: A report on knowledge.* Minneapolis: University of Minnesota Press.

Marx, K. (1967). *Capital.* New York: International Publishers.

Marx, K. (1971). *The Grundrisse.* New York: Harper & Row.

Mead, G. H. (1924–1925). The genesis of the self and social control. *International Journal of Ethics, 35,* 251–277.

Mead, G. H. (1934). *Mind, self & society from the standpoint of a social behaviorist.* Chicago: University of Chicago Press.

Nie, N. H., Verba, S., & Petrocik, J. R. (1976). *The changing American voter.* Cambridge, MA: Harvard University Press.

Olson, M. (1965). *The logic of collective action.* Cambridge, MA: Harvard University Press.

Parsons, T. (1964). *Social structure and personality.* New York: Free Press of Glencoe.

Parsons, T., & Bales, R. F. (1955). *Family, socialization and interaction process.* Glencoe, IL: Free Press.

Piaget, J. (1970). *Structuralism.* New York: Basic Books.

Piaget, J. (1973). *The psychology of intelligence.* Totowa, NJ: Littlefield, Adams.

Riesman, D. (1950). *The lonely crowd: A study of the changing American character.* New Haven, CT: Yale University Press.

Riker, W. (1995). The political psychology of rational choice. *Political Psychology, 14,* 23–44.

Riker, W., & Ordeshook, P. C. (1973). *An introduction to positive political theory.* Englewood Cliffs, NJ: Prentice-Hall.

Rosenberg, S. W. (1988). *Reason, ideology and politics.* Princeton, NJ: Princeton University Press.

Rosenberg, S. W. (2001). *The not so common sense: Differences in how people judge social and political life.* New Haven, CT: Yale University Press.

Sampson, E. E. (1993). Identity politics: Challenges to psychology's undertanding. *American Psychologist, 48,* 1219–1230.

Searle, J. R. (1971). *The philosophy of language.* New York: Oxford University Press.

Szasz, T. (1961). *The myth of mental illness.* New York: Hoeber.

Vygotsky, L. S. (1962). *Thought and language.* New York: Wiley.

Vygotsky, L. S. (1978). *Mind in society: The development of higher psychological processes.* Cambridge, MA: Harvard University Press.

Wertsch, J. V. (1991). *Voices of the mind: A sociocultural approach to mediated action.* Cambridge, MA: Harvard University Press.

Wittgenstein, L. (1953). *Philosophical investigations.* Oxford, UK: Basil Blackwell.

19

Turning Political Psychology Upside Down

ROBERT E. LANE
Yale University

What would happen if, in addition to using psychological research and theory to explain political outcomes, we also used political psychological theory and research to explain psychological outcomes? Political scientists might say that thereby they forsook their mission, but I do not think this is true. Some psychological outcomes, in fact, represent the specification of what, as political scientists, we have always been interested in. In my opinion, indeed, turning political psychology upside down has the benefit of dealing with what can be called the true ends of our inquiries, instead of the means that traditionally served as the subject of our research. This chapter is an inquiry into the risks and benefits of devoting some of our talents in political psychology to a study of two such psychological outcomes, subjective well-being (SWB) and human development.

USING PSYCHOLOGY TO EXPLAIN POLITICAL OUTCOMES

What makes political psychology different from other kinds of political science, or, indeed, from most sociology, economics, and anthropology, is its explicit recognition of what the discipline of psychology has to offer. This is not an extension of political science but an essential feature of it. I do not believe it is possible to account for the decisions and behavior of presidents,

367

parliaments, judges, electorates, or the relation among nations without understanding motivation, learning, attribution, aggression, and so forth. Whereas some explanations find adequate accounts in situational variables, political psychology never finds these external accounts sufficient. A long history of controversy over the adequacy of situational variables compared to dispositional variables has, I think, been resolved by the assumption that it is *interaction* among these factors of an accounting system that offers the greatest capacity to explain outcomes. Consequently, we are all "psychologists," some drawing on a developed body of research and some still amateur.

We have come a long way from the early pioneers, Wallas (1909), McDougall (1920), and Lasswell (1951). Inevitably, the journey has often been guided by the historical agenda of the times: the psychology of Nazism, fascism, and the authoritarian personality; the appeals of Communism; the influence of personality on presidential and judicial behavior; the causes of terrorism; and the way mass communications work their influences. It is an honorable history of self-correction, as where "the benevolent leader" (Eisenhower) yielded to children's less benign images of political leaders (Nixon), and where the theory of adolescent fixation of political orientations was softened to open up space for continual changes in adulthood. In the absence of axioms (as in economics—see Schumpeter's [1954] claim for economic psychology),[1] hypotheses were continuously tested and revised.

Thus, in proposing to turn political psychology upside down, I do not at all reject what we have done, but rather propose an extension, one that meets what I see as a need to explain something beyond the political agenda of political psychology as currently understood. The inverted version of political psychology has three characteristics: (a) it identifies ends more universal than those specified by political scientists (whose ends are actually only means) and thereby promises to change political theory itself; (b) it unites political theory and psychology in a common interpretative exercise; and (c) it moves political psychology to the center of the political science discipline, where it should be. It is upside down in the sense that what is to be explained and what we use for explaining are partially reversed.

THE ENDS OF POLITICAL PSYCHOLOGY

Start with a simple, pregnant finding from quality of life research. Across 23 countries, Veenhoven (1993) analyzed the contribution to (self-reported)

---

[1]For Schumpeter (1954), the concept of declining marginal utility is a logical "axiom," invulnerable to empirical examination. Thus, he says, "Economists have never allowed their analysis to be influenced by the professional psychologists of their times, but have always framed for themselves such assumptions about psychological processes as they thought it desirable to make" (p. 28).

happiness and life satisfaction of democratic government, operationalized as regularity of elections, the presence of functioning opposition parties and parliaments, and the absence of military coups. The zero order correlation was substantial: .54 ($p = .01$), but when level of per capita income was controlled, the relationship disappeared (−.02). Across nations, it was level of income, not democracy, that increased subjective well-being (SWB). True, in Europe SWB is strongly associated with a longer history of democracy (Inglehart, 1990), but the history of democracy is not quite the same as the presence of democracy. Furthermore, the advanced economies of Europe show much weaker relations of per capita income to SWB than does a more global accounting. That is, income controls affect the relationships of democracy to well-being much less in Europe than elsewhere. If there is a relation between democracy and SWB, it applies only to developed countries.

I cite these data prematurely because they raise the questions I address here: Are the criteria employed to assess political outcomes and functioning really ends in any meaningful sense, or are they merely means to the ends that, finally, concern us? On what grounds do we base our faith that democracy is a necessary or at least beneficial condition for the well-being and welfare of mankind? There are two steps to this argument: What are the costs of the assumed benefits of democracy and of implementing democratic values? And what are the ultimate goods toward which these benefits contribute? Two "primary goods"—to use Rawls' (1971) phrase—stand out: freedom and equality, both, in my opinion, means to more important ends.

Freedom

Following Berlin (1969), we may think of negative freedom as the absence of constraints and of positive freedom as the ability to control one's own fate by effective action. In both senses freedom means expanded choices. It is a measure of our reliance on slogans (and our market-driven conceptualization) that few scholars question the benefits of more freedom and expanded choices (although in particular cases, as in the use of referenda and the long ballot, scholars do draw back). In this thicket of democratic clichés, consider two lines of inquiry showing first a defensive posture toward existing choice and second a cost in welfare of expanded choices. The first is found in the study of what Brehm (1972) called *reactance,* the tendency to protect one's familiar choices from encroachment. The gist of this research shows that if one originally prefers A to B to C and is told one cannot have C, one then prefers C to A and B—a confirmation of our resistance to constraints, to encroachments on negative freedom. Similarly, children told that they cannot play with a certain toy then, compared to controls, are more likely to choose that forbidden toy in preference to others (Wilson & Lassiter, 1982). However, there is little evidence of a demand for choices or freedoms not previously experienced. The publicized *Wish to be Free* (Weinstein & Platt, 1969) is historically constrained by experience with existing freedoms.

A suggestive study on the costs of increased choices comes from marketing studies. Offering 4 or 8 or 12 brands of laundry detergent, Jacoby, Speller, and Kohn (1974) found that although buyers liked the increased number of choices, by the standards they established in advance for their preferred detergent, more options led to poorer choices. Candidates and referenda are not detergents, but the pathologies of overload are similar — and constitute a form of stress that takes a dramatic physiological toll on modern man (Sapolsky, 1999; Selye, 1979). In spite of Rawls's (1971) assignment to freedom of a lexicographic priority, more freedom may be costly in human welfare. It is a paradox: In some cases the more freedoms we have, the less well do we choose among the options offered and the less successfully do we pursue our life goals! Proposals to extend freedom are not democratic imperatives but empirical hypotheses about how to extend our well-being and welfare.

Equality

Equality has an epistemological standing different from that of freedom, for, like Hare (1981), we might say that it is logical for like things to be treated in like manner, or we might provide a theological justification for treating God's creatures with identical concern, or, like Kant (1949), we might say that because human dignity is not to be bartered, it has no exchange rate, or like Rawls (1971), that, because justice itself is defined by equal treatment, any departure from equality needs to be justified. Like all science, psychology is speechless in the face of such defenses. However, once a consequential argument is entered, then we are in empirical territory and cannot use the a priori justifications of ethics but rather must follow causal chains to achieve a cost–benefit analysis for any policy. Does, for example, equality of circumstances contribute to subjective well-being? Again let us glance at some evidence. Veenhoven's (1993) analysis of the relation between income equality and well-being across 23 nations found no such relation, although measures of dispersion of income are related to the dispersion of well-being and indicators of sexual equality are, indeed, related to average level of well-being. There are conflicting data (Diener, Diener, & Diener, 1995), to be sure, but the relation, if there is one, is apparently not sufficiently strong to rest the case for equality on any effects it may have on SWB. The introduction of the known positive hedonic effect of downward comparisons may also inhibit equality from maximizing SWB in any given population (Brickman & Campbell, 1971). Stripped of their a priori standing, arguments for equality must then confront its effects on striving and motivation, the possible rise of envy over small differences as equality becomes the standard, and whether or not people want income equality. (I have found that income equality frightened working class people who did not care about the higher income of elites but greatly resented the idea that the underclass people down the street would have as much income as they did [Lane, 1959].)

The point is that the values that seem to justify making such democratic goals as freedom and equality the standards by which we judge our institutions and practices are not ultimate goods but rather means to the ultimate goods that we have not yet explored.

THE SEARCH FOR ULTIMATE ENDS

MacIntyre (1981) once said that the content of ethics is what ethicists and other philosophers have talked about over the ages. In that spirit one might say that the ultimate ends of human endeavor are those things philosophers have identified as ultimate ends in the long history of their discourse. Here is a sample: wisdom (Plato and Aristotle), virtue as excellence in lifesmanship (Aristotle) or as moral living (Spinoza), an appropriate relation to the infinite or at least to the all-powerful gods (salvation, in Western versions—Augustine, Aquinas), harmony with man and nature (Stoics), beauty (G. E. Moore), fellowship (also Moore and the Stoics), performance of duty and benevolence (Kant), truth as valid knowledge (David Ross, with qualifications), justice (Rawls), autonomy as a condition for dignity (Kant and Mill), love (Christian theology), and happiness, as contentment (Stoics) or only if merited (Ross, Rescher) or when coupled with equality (utilitarians). In the final analysis, these are assertions, as they must be, whose strength lies in their supporting arguments. For scientists, the idea that the ends of life are to be found by argument and concluded by assertion must seem unsatisfactory, but I think there is no other way. As Popper (1963) pointed out, whereas means are subject to rational inference and empirical investigation, ends are not.

In a prescient statement about ultimate ends, Ross (1930) asked us to imagine a world without mind, and in that world, he said, "You will fail to find anything in it that you can call good in itself . . . [although] the existence of a material universe may . . . be a necessary condition for the existence of many things that are good in themselves" (p. 140). The statement is incomplete, for not everything about the mind is good in itself, and by itself the mind is only part of the human response system that we care about, a system that also includes the capacity to respond with such emotions as empathy and kindness. (The limbic system, amygdala, and hypothalamus are as important to our humanity as is the cortex.) So I take Ross's statement to mean that something about our humanity is the subject of the ultimate ends toward which we should strive and that our institutions should be constructed to promote as best they can. But it must be selective, for human nature itself is as much a product of our genes (neither good nor bad in themselves) as of a culture, guided, as Wilson (1998) said, by epigenetic rules that help us select among ends.

Bereft of certainty, appealing to argument and the history of argument, I suggest that political psychology accept two ends that embrace much of the philosophical argument and that are at least congruent with and, I think, are supported by the philosophical implications (or do I mean premises?) of empirical psychology. These two ends are *subjective well-being* (the "happiness" of philosophers) and *human development*. The addition of human development is designed partly to overcome the anemic versions of people employed by utilitarians, and partly to embrace the ethical goals of other kinds of philosophy. But by posing at least two forms of the good as coordinate maximands, the scheme encounters at the outset the question of balancing two goods without a specified common criterion to resolve the conflicts. Inasmuch as this is the common state of affairs in everyday choices where criteria vary from day to day, we must live, as we always have, with the lack of a single common standard to reconcile conflicts of values. We must optimize rather than maximize.

SUBJECTIVE WELL-BEING

Among the 300 people at the 1997 First Annual Meeting of the International Society for Quality-of-Life Studies (ISQOLS), I found no political scientists or psychologists identified with political psychology. Can it be that political psychologists are more interested in, say, voting behavior, communications and influence, or terrorism than in explicating and explaining the quality of the lives lived by those who are subject to these processes and threats? If so, I think we are too close to our data, institutions, and practices to ask what the general purpose of better institutions and practices may be. In dealing with the concept "quality of life," we are on loose terrain for which there are no standard maps (see Cummins, 1998), but that is an opportunity, not a handicap. Among the central meanings of quality of life is subjective well-being, first identified as a mood, happiness, than as an appraisal, satisfaction with one's life, and now, because positive and negative affect are found to be not only separately appraised but also, as mentioned, derived from different parts of the brain and hormonal system, extended to mean "affect balance." Most studies include all three components, summarized as SWB. The latest development is to extend these concepts to include enjoyment and suffering, especially their physical sources and manifestations (Kahneman, Diener, & Schwarz, 1999)—a good example of Wilson's proposal to extend the social sciences "downward" to include human and animal biology.

With the empirical investigation of SWB, a great veil of mystery and obfuscation is lifted and the concept suddenly emerges from the tautologies of "utility," and the early speculations of Bentham and the later speculations of modern day utilitarians—even the best of them like Hardin (1988) and Rescher (1966). But before we celebrate the final arrival of what Ross (1930) might call "valid knowledge" about happiness, note that the measures of happiness are excessively "soft," subject to day-to-day variations caused by weather or the victory of one's favorite team. Evaluations of one's satisfaction with life are more cognitive and less effervescent, but they, too, are influenced by temporary events. Both are social judgments with all the defects that Nisbett and Ross (1980) once characterized as "shortcomings" in our judgmental processes. In spite of these defects, however, the best and often the most critical scholars in this area have concluded that the weight of the evidence suggests that people keep a kind of running account of their positive and negative feelings, strike a balance, and report results that, by objective criteria, make sense (Kahneman, 1999). Although there is a large genetic component to SWB, in order to account for the changes in mood when, say, a person gets married or loses a job, it is necessary to leave room for the independent and variable assessment of the person enjoying or suffering these events.

Quite prudently, Diener and Suh (1999) suggested that the measures of SWB are not yet ready to be the sole guide for policy but rather that they should serve as supplementary criteria for policies with other, more objective, goals.[2] What is supplementary and what is primary can easily be reversed, but multiple benefits are always desirable. In any event, from many national and cross-national studies, we know enough to suggest what the main sources of SWB are and to address these priorities in public policy. A main point, now familiar to students of quality-of-life and SWB, is the low contribution, beyond the poverty level in advanced economies, of greater income to SWB (Lane, 2000a). In the common phrase, money does not buy happiness, let alone "utility," whether as preference satisfaction or something more substantive. Furthermore, as Scitovsky (1977) pointed out almost 25 years ago, work is not a disutility, for there is more pleasure in intrinsic work satisfaction (and sense of achievement) than in any commodities people can buy. The economist's paradigm has it wrong, and when the government borrows from

---

[2] "If policy makers are to use SWB indicators effectively, they will be best served by a variety of indicators. . . . Furthermore, global indicators are unlikely to be sufficient for for the policy makers' needs because so many different factors influence global SWB" (Diener & Suh, 1999, p. 484).

economists, it gets its priorities wrong, as well. (The de-economization of our public policy is a worthy goal for political psychologists.)

If money is not the currency of SWB, what is? It is good family relations and companionship whose satisfaction contributes more to SWB, at least in the West, than anything else. It is our relations with people, not money, that make us happy and sad (Lane, 2000a), as even economists often realize when they reflect on their families, colleagues, friends—and salaries. Cross-culturally, it is not quite that simple. Across the globe, collectivist (interdependent) societies emphasize social harmony and family connections with, in some cases, sacrifices to careers and economic prosperity. In contrast to the individualistic West, for the poorer of these societies, increased income contributes more to SWB than do these human relations. Thus, the best formulation, in my opinion (Lane, 2000a), is that both material welfare and good social relations make a contribution to SWB in proportion to what is scarcer in that society. In the economistic society of the West, companionship is the scarcer good and carries the main freight of SWB, but in the collectivist societies of the East, that is not the case and, if the societies are poor, money carries the freight. If, however, the society is rich, as are Japan, Taiwan, Singapore, and Hong Kong, a fearful conflict takes place between the two goods, with some damage to each of them as their societies seek to reconcile their values. In Japan in the early 1990s and in the others in 1997, the unyielding imperatives of the market have eroded their companionable ideals while the ancient ideals, reflected in nepotism and cronyism, inhibit their economies (Lane, 2000a).

The displacement of companionship by economic pursuits in the United States and to a lesser extent in Asia and Europe, is reflected in the postwar rise of unhappiness in the United States and the rise of major depression in most advanced economies including, although to lesser degree, Taiwan and South Korea (Cross-National Collaborative Group, 1992). Something has gone wrong. Avoiding cultural universals, we may say that in the United States and other advanced economies, the balance between material welfare and social well-being has been distorted with the consequence that we suffer loss of SWB from companionship deprivation.

Because markets have no way of providing companionship or, as it happens, intrinsic work satisfaction, both of which are generally unpriced, SWB is a market externality. In spite of the democratic promise to facilitate the pursuit of happiness, SWB may also be an externality for democracies. Democratic theory has more or less ignored the question. Turning political psychology upside down, we ask how democracy can contribute to SWB, how political institutions and practices can address the basically psychological problems of subjective well-being. But there are more limits to SWB as the sole and ultimate end than those imposed by its companion–competitor, human development.

LIMITS TO SWB AS THE SOLE END

Making SWB the only good would risk the perils of an unrelieved utilitarianism; we jeopardize values that we cherish, including such instrumental values as freedom and human rights. There are four principal counts against pure utilitarian arguments (Lane, 2000b; for a rebuttal see Singer, 1993; Smart & Williams, 1973).

The first count is the infirm ethics of a strict SWB standard: "the greatest happiness of the greatest number" leaves open the exploitation of a minority by a majority (Bentham, 1780/1969, said that the doctrine of rights was "nonsense on stilts.") Thus, the utilities (including life itself) of individuals and minorities may be sacrificed to majorities because the slight preferences of the larger number outweigh the intense preferences of the minorities. In democracies these minorities are protected by rights, and "rights-based considerations . . . go against utilitarianism" (Sen & Williams, 1982).

On the second count, the utilitarian image of humanity, two eminent contemporary philosophers (one of whom is also an economist) characterize this image in the following terms: "Essentially, utilitarianism sees persons as locations of their respective utilities—as the sites at which such activities as desiring and having pleasure and pain take place. Once note has been taken of the person's utility, utilitarianism has no further direct interest in any information about them. . . . [Utilitarianism especially shows] the neglect of a person's *autonomy*" and "lack of interest in a person's integrity" (Sen & Williams, 1982, pp. 5–6). That is why human development is an additional good.

The third count is the utilitarians' threat to freedom. For example, most Americans consider atheism to be an amoral and repulsive doctrine (Theodore Roosevelt called Thomas Paine "a dirty little atheist."). To silence this offensive doctrine would, I think, marginally increase the happiness of the American people, unless, as in the case of "Bolsheviks," there is more pleasure in hating them than pain in tolerating them. In a subtle analysis, Sen (1979) showed the way utilitarian thinking can justify the torture by a sadist of an innocent person and the denial by "Prude" of "Lewd's" decision to read *Lady Chatterly's Lover.*

Finally, pleasures are not equal and require an additional criterion. "It is better to be a human being dissatisfied," said Mill (1910b), "than a pig satisfied; better to be Socrates dissatisfied than a fool satisfied. And if the fool, or the pig, are of different opinion, it is because they only know their own side of the question. The other party to the comparison [Socrates or someone who has experienced both "higher" and "lower" pleasures] knows both sides" (p. 32).

There is a second fork to this argument against sole reliance on SWB as an end: One cannot pursue happiness in the abstract, but, as Mill (1969) said, only *en passant* while pursuing some other goal. If we were interested only in happiness, we would say that the best other goal is the one that yields the most happiness, but that defeats the purpose of pursuing a second goal. Bentham (1954, pp. 437–438) thought that money is "the most accurate measure of the quantity of pain or pleasure a man can be made to receive" but we now know that is not the case and, indeed, the "materialists" who believe it are markedly less happy than others (Kasser & Ryan, 1993). It would be convenient to find (with Aristotle and Spinoza) that pursuing ethical goals is the best route to happiness, but there is no evidence for that (except for the finding that happy people engage in prosocial behavior more than others, a pursuit that, if met with approval, does make them happier [Eisenberg, 2000]). I suggest that human development is the best candidate for the companion goal for SWB, but I pause here simply to note that the logic of happiness requires a supplementary goal—and to add one other argument.

Does happiness cloy? Elsewhere, I (Lane, 2000b) have pointed to the person who reports himself or herself to be very happy but, in moments of candor, asks if there is not something further to life? For that person, I suggest, there is a declining marginal utility to happiness itself. That is not a paradox. Whether "utility" is used as preference satisfaction in the economists' sense, or simply as a mood, in Bentham's sense, it is quite plausible to believe that such a person might have in mind something that has value but is not in itself a source of happiness, such as self-knowledge (rarely a source of hedonic gain) or self-development. And relying on the plural meanings of SWB, we may note that there are satisfactions not encompassed by moods.

HUMAN DEVELOPMENT

If the one thing that gives intrinsic value to life is humanity, we would want not only well-being for that precious humanity but also the fullest expression of its potential. This is not a necessary inference, but it is a plausible one, resting in part on one of the ideas of value itself. The magnitude of value, said Baier (1969, p. 39), is "the extent to which a thing, if entered in a certain sort of competition, would satisfy the desiderata" of that kind of thing. X is a valuable X if it does X-things well or better than other things in that category. This is pure Aristotle as it applies to the living of lives. More than that, by making human development an ultimate value, we incorporate much else from this philosophical discourse, such as ethical sensitivity, appreciation of beauty, wisdom, honesty, capacity for fellowship, and so forth. We also embrace Sen's (1993) emphasis on what people can do for themselves and others. Over the past 20 years, Sen has created and argued for an approach to national and international development based on people's *capabilities*. In a statement with Drèze, Sen (1989, p. 12) claimed "the object of public action can be seen to be the enhancement of the capability of people to undertake valuable and valued 'doings and beings.'" The philosopher Nussbaum (1992), who has collaborated with Sen, took a similar position. In response to "an evaluative inquiry into what is deepest and most indispensable in our lives," Nussbaum (1992, p. 222) developed a concept of "essentialist functioning" for evaluating well-being (confabulating, I think, two separate goals). She derived her list of the qualities of persons necessary, first, for a life to be considered fully human and, second, for a *high* quality of life, that is, from an interpretative evaluation of life itself. Others, like Braybrooke (1987), have arrived at a similar concept of what qualities are essential to "be fully human." Scientists will be uncomfortable with this style of argument, but they will be partly reassured by Rescher's (1969) exposition of the empirical foundation of values, at least insofar as they imply consequences (which they usually do).

Among others, Aristotle (*Politics,* 1280b), Durkheim (in Lukes, 1973), and Mill (1910) have made the quality of people in a political system the criterion for assessing the quality of its government, but the understandings of the production functions of various human qualities by these authors has been weak. Nor has political psychology drawn its talents from those psychologists who specialize in human development, a failing that turning political psychology upside down might remedy. At the moment, most of the beliefs about how government influences the character of its citizens is based on simple isomorphism of social structure and personality (e.g., Norton, 1991): If the polity is more inclusive, fewer people will have the low self-esteem of the excluded; if people are given voting rights, they will gain new feelings of empowerment; if tax policies are more progressive, people will feel more equal (and treat each other more equally); if the safety net of welfare and disability insurance are more generous, the ensuing sense of security will alleviate despair and promote enterprise; and if people participate in self-government in industry, they will be more politically participant. In each case, there is research falsifying these common sense assumptions — and other research supporting them. We do not have a science or much of a theory of how governments can make more self-confident, psychologically secure, humane, empathic, responsible citizens — if, indeed, it is in the power of governments to do these things.

The enterprise is more inviting if there are glimpses of promising research to point to. Although I tried to show how markets influence personality traits in *The Market Experience* (Lane, 1991), I am not a good guide to the human development literature. With many apologies, here are some promising samples. *Malignant obedience*, substituting for one's own conscience the orders of an authority figure—as in Milgram's (1974) experiments and My Lai (Kelman & Hamilton, 1989) —is inhibited both by internal attribution and experience in questioning authority. Democracies can encourage such questioning. The narrow cognitive style called *field dependence* seems to be encouraged by living in authoritarian regimes, whereas *field independence* is more often found in democratic settings (Witkin, Dyk, Faterson, Goodenough, & Karp, 1974). Belief that one is effective in influencing the circumstances of one's life, *internality,* is taught by actual experience in acting and perceiving the intended changes in one's environment (contingent reinforcement), something not visible in national elections but sometimes perceptible in smaller settings where the link between individual acts and policy changes are more readily apparent (Frey & Stutzer, 2000). *Moral development* is a function of both education and praxis, actually doing moral acts, the latter generally outside the sphere of political competence. But moral codes are also learned by imitation and absorbed through publicly encouraged social norms. I am not at all certain that lax public morals (corruption, fiscal irresponsibility) have much influence on individual citizens, but I do know that members of the public often use their understandings of publicly approved behaviors as templates for their own behavior (Lane, 1962). What is generalized from public to private domains depends on how people categorize and analogize events, a matter for empirical inquiry. In the light of frequent failures to teach morality (Wooster, 1990), modeling seems to offer a more effective approach (Bandura, 1977)[3]—if, in the atmosphere of 1998–1999, the idea that public officials can serve as models for moral development is not laughed out of court. (The morality I have in mind is compassion toward the disadvantaged, not "sexual morality," a private matter.)

CAN AND SHOULD GOVERNMENT PROMOTE SWB AND HUMAN DEVELOPMENT?

If political psychologists are to promote the ends we have discussed, happiness and human development, they must understand the limits of what governments can do without trespassing on other values. The two ends have different degrees of acceptability. There will be less concern over governmental promotion of the pursuit of happiness, already endorsed by Jefferson and Madison, than of governmental responsibility for human development, but the bogey of paternalism haunts both.

---

[3] "One can get people to behave altruistically, to volunteer their services, to delay or seek gratification, to show affection, to behave punitively, to prefer certain foods and apparel, to converse on particular topics, to be inquisitive or passive, and to engage in most any course of action by having such conduct exemplified" (Bandura, 1977, p. 88).

Facilitating the Pursuit of Happiness

Some simple heuristics launch the inquiry. First, governments can more easily frame the circumstances of people's lives than direct the course of lives: the key concepts are Levinson's (1978) idea of a "life structure," or, better still, Vygotsky's *scaffolding,* the support structures within which lives are led (see Fischer & Silvern, 1985). In this structuring of how lives are led, the most emancipating idea is an understanding of the *economistic fallacy* that says that beyond the poverty level in advanced economies increased income is irrelevant to SWB (Lane, 1991). More concretely, governments can do more to promote SWB by relieving poverty, which has a demonstrable effect on SWB, than by promoting equality, which does not. Further, because in advanced economies companionship and good family relations contribute more to SWB than does income, governments can subsidize firms to give maternity and paternity leave for employees with new family responsibilities—as the Swedes do—even at the cost of some loss of productivity. Companionships are disrupted by firm relocation; governments can retard (as they have promoted) firm relocations. Above the poverty level, income insecurity is a greater drain on SWB than is failure to increase income (Lane, 2000a); therefore some "sand in the gears" to slow down the engines that maximize economic efficiency at the cost of job security might be worthwhile. Enlarging property rights in a job is another device available to governments. These are random examples; they are not a program guided by a theory of governmental facilitation of the pursuit of happiness and, more important, the discouragement of unhappiness and depression.

Human Development

Disruptive arguments over the meaning of happiness and unhappiness are trivial compared to arguments over the content of human development. In addition to the frightening record of 16th-century Puritan regimes in England and 17th-century New England, two accounts of recent government efforts to improve the qualities of its citizens are instructive. What might be called the Mackinnon Error illustrates one caveat: Eager to discourage the sexual exploitation of women, Katherine Mackinnon successfully promoted its criminalization. In the resulting legislation, the police chiefs found the legislative instrument they were looking for to criminalize homosexuality. Those unfamiliar with research on human development will read the lesson: Governments have no business defining better and worse kinds of human personality. Philosophically, that is paternalism (and invasion of privacy) of the most egregious kind (Mead, 1997; VanDeVeer, 1986).

The other caveat is from an attempt by the state of California (and some schools in the East) to increase self-esteem directly by telling people how worthy they were and, especially, by indiscriminately awarding pupils honors for qualities that were simply the conditions of being there. Unearned awards quickly lost their power to increase a person's sense of worthiness and the programs were dropped. You can fool some of the people some of the time . . . and so forth.

However, let us return to the idea of scaffolding, creating the conditions within which it is easier, rather than harder, for a person to develop into a thinking, emotionally mature, moral person.

Cognitive Development. In a large and flourishing field of research, three examples from home, work, and the public domain must suffice. Cognitive development is greatly increased by stimulation in the first 2 years of life, something inhibited by poverty and by too many children at home, and encouraged by well-run government subsidized crèches (Cornia & Danziger, 1997). Partly for this reason, Schultz (1981) once said that the most important contribution to economic development is investment in the education of women. Because the dogma of minimal government has not infected France as it has the United States, French governments protect their children much better than do U.S. governments (Bergman, 1998).

In a 10-year longitudinal study, Kohn and Schooler (1983) showed that relative autonomy at work and the complexity of the work one does actually increases a worker's cognitive flexibility. Even at the sacrifice of some productivity (material, not human, productivity), governments might encourage the circumstances where work is cognitively stimulating, protecting and teaching the least well educated along the way. Finally, in the public domain, Piaget (1965) showed how children and youth developed a knowledge of rules, first by using them and then by understanding their purposes so that they can modify them to suit their legitimate purposes. Can governments convey, along with the content of law, an understanding of the purposes of law to help people go beyond the "law and order" mentality of not quite mature moral reasoning (Kohlberg, 1964)? There are border areas where cognitive development is captive of ideology, but much of it is consensual, at least in the individualist West.

Emotional Maturity. Cognitive development might be ranked on, say, a Guttman scale such that any given "score" tells us just exactly what a person can and cannot do (although IQ is not of that character and, in any event, tells us about only one of at least three important dimensions of intelligence [Sternberg, 1997]). However, emotional development is likely to prove even less linear. Without implying any particular preference for one emotional constellation over another (love, empathy, fear), I believe that there are developmental criteria that meet quite general acceptance. In this rich field, again I can only illustrate. People are better off and use their "emotional intelligence" (Goleman, 1995) to their own advantage when they can identify their own emotions and respond accordingly, something that varies greatly among individuals in the West and between Eastern and Western cultures (Suh, Diener, Oishi, & Triandis, 1998). People thrive when they know how to handle and schedule their emotions. Thus, in New Haven (and other) schools, children are taught "how to handle their grief and anger, how to negotiate rather than fight, and how to cooperate in the classroom." The consequence in New Haven was a 34% drop in suspensions from school "and an increase in children's ability to think before they act, and to pay attention and learn" (Goleman, 1994, p. C1). Finally, recognizing that cognitive judgments and emotional judgments are separate—facts are stored in the brain separately from feelings (LeDoux, 1996)—and that emotional judgments usually precede cognitive judgments and are more trusted (Zajonc, 1980), the capacity to synthesize these two sources of evaluations and decisions is an essential part of emotional maturity.

A humanistically inadequate but culturally persuasive feature of emotional maturity of these kinds is that it promotes both individual and firm productivity. Goleman (1995) studied more than 500 organizations worldwide and found that "emotional intelligence matters twice as much as technical and analytic skill combined for star performances. And the higher people move up in the company, the more crucial emotional intelligence becomes" (Murray, 1998). Moreover, in individualist, but not collectivist (Chinese), cultures, emotional conflicts are closely and negatively related (−.37) to SWB (Suh et al., 1998), suggesting that relief of these conflicts by self-knowledge is important for well-being in the West.

Government can use schools, to a lesser extent workplaces, and perhaps even public services to encourage emotional maturity. Police, teachers, public health workers can be (and sometimes are) trained to this end. (Gorer [1955] once said that the British public went from a bear-baiting savagery to a politely queuing civility because of the models of the bobby for the working class and the civil servant for the middle class.) But politicians thrive on emotional arousal in sound-bite morsels. Without evidence (because political psychologists have been looking in another direction), one cannot claim that democratic politics is an appropriate domain for developing either cognitive complexity or emotional maturity. Cross-cultural studies of emotion show great variation in responses to a variety of stimuli (Scherer, Wallbott, & Summerfield, 1981), but evidence of variation by political system is weak. One study, however, showed that three politically relevant emotions (control, responsibility, and anticipated effort) varied among Japanese, Chinese, and U.S. respondents (Mauro, Sato, & Tucker, 1992), and Inglehart (1997) demonstrated the power of political culture, as well as economic development, to shape values. Political culture is very much alive and only waiting to be interpreted and extended.

Can democracy facilitate cognitive development and emotional maturity? It is a subject worth pursuing.

REFERENCES

Aristotle. 1908. *Politics*. Jowett translation. Oxford: Clarendon Press.

Baier, K. (1969). What is value? The analysis of a concept. In K. Baier & N. Rescher (Eds.), *Values and the future* (pp. 33–67). New York: Free Press.

Bandura, A. (1977). *Social learning theory*. Englewood Cliffs, NJ: Prentice-Hall.

Bentham, J. (1954). The rationale of punishment. In *Works* (Vol. 1, pp. 468–469). Republished in W. Stark (Ed.), *Jeremy Bentham's economic writings* (Vol. 3, pp. 437–438). Royal Economic Society by George Allen & Unwin. (Original work published 1830)

Bentham, J. (1969). *An introduction to the principles of morals and legislation*. In M. P. Mack (Ed.), *A Bentham reader* (pp. 73–144). New York: Pegasus. (Original work begun in 1778, first published 1780, rev. 1789)

Bergman, B. (1998). *Saving our children from poverty: What the United States can learn from France*. New York: Russell Sage Foundation.

Berlin, I. (1969). Two concepts of liberty. In his *Four Essays on Liberty*. London: Oxford University Press.

Braybrooke, D. (1987). *Meeting needs*. Princeton, NJ: Princeton University Press.

Brehm, J. W. (1972). *Responses to the loss of freedom: A theory of psychological reactance*. Morristown, NJ: General Learning Press.

Brickman, P., & Campbell, D. T. (1971). Hedonic relativism and planning the good society. In M. H. Appley (Ed.), *Adaptation-level theory: A symposium* (pp. 287–302). New York: Academic Press.

Cornia, G. A., & Danziger, S. (Eds.). (1997). *Child poverty and deprivation in the industrialized countries*. New York: Clarendon Press.

Cross-National Collaborative Group. (1992, December 2). The changing rate of depression: Cross-national comparisons. *Journal of the American Medical Association, 268*, 3098–3105.

Cummins, R. A. (Ed.). (1998). *Quality of life: Definitions and terminology*. Blacksburg, VA: International Society for Quality of Life Studies.

Diener, E., Diener, M., & Diener, C. (1995). Factors predicting the subjective well-being of nations. *Journal of Personality and Social Psychology, 69*, 851–864.

Diener, E., & Suh, E. M. (1999). National differences in subjective well-being. In D. Kahneman, E. Diener, & N. Schwarz (Eds.), *Well-being, the foundations of hedonic psychology* (pp. 434–450). New York: Russell Sage Foundation.

Eisenberg, N. (2000). Emotion, regulation, and moral development. *Annual Review of Psychology, 51*, 665–697.

Fischer, K. W., & Silvern, L. (1985). Stages and individual differences in cognitive development. *Annual Review of Psychology, 36*, 613–648.

Frey, B. S., & Stutzer, A. (2000). Measuring preferences by subjective well-being. *Journal of Institutional and Theoretical Economics, 155*, 755–778.

Goleman, D. (1994, March 10). To 3R's some schools add emotional skills. *New York Times*, p. C1.

Goleman, D. (1995). *Emotional intelligence: Why it matters more than IQ*. New York: Bantam.

Gorer, G. (1955). *Exploring English character*. London: Cresset Press.

Hardin, R. (1988). *Morality within limits of reason*. Chicago: University of Chicago Press.

Hare, R. M. (1981). *Moral thinking: Its levels, method, and point*. Oxford: Clarendon Press.

Inglehart, R. (1997). *Modernization and postmodernization: Cultural, economic, and political change in 43 societies*. Princeton, NJ: Princeton University Press.

Inglehart, R. (1990). *Culture shift in advanced industrial societies.* Princeton: Princeton University Press.

Jacoby, J. Speller, D. E., & Kohn, C. A. (1974). Brand choice behavior as a function of information load. *Journal of Marketing Research, 11,* 63–69

Kahneman, D. (1999). Objective happiness. In D. Kahneman, E. Diener, & N. Schwarz (Eds.), *Well-being: The foundations of hedonic psychology* (pp. 3–25). New York: Russell Sage Foundation.

Kahneman, D., Diener, E., & Schwarz, N. (Eds.). (1999). *Well-being: Foundations of hedonic psychology.* New York: Russell Sage Foundation.

Kant, I. (1949). *Fundamental principles of the metaphysic of morals* (T. K. Abbott, Tran.). Indianapolis: Bobbs-Merrill.

Kasser, T., & Ryan, R. M. (1993). A dark side of the American dream: Correlates of financial success as a central life aspiration. *Journal of Personality and Social Psychology, 65,* 410–422.

Kelman, H. C., & Hamilton, V. L. (1989). *Crimes of obedience: Toward a social psychology of authority and responsibility.* New Haven: Yale University Press.

Kohlberg, L. (1964). Development of moral character and ideology. In M. L. Hoffman & L. W. Hoffman (Eds.), *Review of child development* (Vol. 1, pp. 383–431). New York: Russell Sage Foundation.

Kohn, M., & Schooler, C. (1983). *Work and personality: An inquiry into the impact of social stratification.* Norwood, NJ: Ablex.

Lane, R. E. (1959). The fear of equality. *American Political Science Review, 53,* 35–51.

Lane, R. E. (1962). *Political ideology: Why the American common man believes what he does.* New York: Free Press.

Lane, R. E. (1991). *The market experience.* New York: Cambridge University Press.

Lane, R. E. (2000a). *Loss of happiness in market democracies.* New Haven: Yale University Press.

Lane, R. E. (2000b). Diminishing returns to income, companionship,—and happiness. *Journal of happiness studies, 1,* 103–119.

Lasswell, H. D. (1951). *Psychopathology and politics.* Chicago: University of Chicago Press, reprinted in *The Political Writings of Harold Lasswell.* Glencoe, IL: Free Press. (Original work published 1930)

LeDoux, J. (1996). *The emotional brain.* New York: Simon & Schuster.

Levinson, D. J. (1978). *The seasons in a man's life.* New York: Knopf.

Lukes, S. (1973). *Emile Durkheim: His life and work* (quoting from *Formes et essence du socialisme*). London: Allen Lane/Penguin.

MacIntyre, A. (1981). *After virtue: A study in moral theory.* Notre Dame, IN: Notre Dame University Press.

Mauro, R. Sato, K., & Tucker, J. (1992). The role of appraisal in human emotions: A cross-cultural study. *Journal of Personality and Social Psychology, 62,* 301–317.

McDougall, W. (1920). *The group mind.* Cambridge: Cambridge University Press.

Mead, L. M. (Ed.) (1997). *The new paternalism: Supervisory approaches to poverty.* Washington, DC: Brookings.

Milgram, S. (1974). *Obedience to authority: An experimental view.* New York: Harper & Row.

Mill, J. S. (1910a). *Representative government.* Reprinted in *Utilitarianism, liberty, and representative government* (pp. 173–393). London: Dent.

Mill, J. S. (1910b). *Utilitarianism* [1861]. Reprinted in *Utilitarianism, liberty and representative government* (pp. 1–60). London: Dent.

Mill, J. S. (1969). *Autobiography.* Oxford: Oxford University Press.

Murray, B. (1998). Does "emotional intelligence" matter in the workplace? *APA Monitor, 29,* 21.

Nisbett, R., & Ross, L. (1980). *Human inference: Strategies and shortcomings of social judgment.* Englewood Cliffs, NJ: Prentice-Hall.

Norton, D. L. (1991). *Democracy and moral development: A politics of virtue.* Berkeley, CA: University of California Press.

Nussbaum, M. (1992). Human functioning and social justice. *Political Theory, 20,* 202–246.

Piaget, J. (1965). *The moral judgment of the child* (M. Gabin, Trans.). New York: Free Press. (Original work published 1932)

Popper, K. (1963). *Conjectures and refutations: The growth of scientific knowledge.* London: Routledge & Kegan Paul.

Rawls, J. (1971). *A theory of justice.* Cambridge, MA: Harvard University Press.

Rescher, N. (1966). *Distributive justice: A constructive critique of the utilitarian theory of distribution.* Indianapolis: Bobbs-Merrill.

Rescher, N. (1969). *Introduction to value theory.* Englewood Cliffs, NJ: Prentice-Hall.

Ross, W. D. (1930). *The right and the good.* Oxford: Clarendon Press.

Sapolsky, R. M. (1999). The physiology and pathophysiology of unhappiness. In D. Kahneman, E. Diener, & N. Schwarz (Eds.). *Well-being: The foundations of hedonic psychology* (pp. 453–469). New York: Russell Sage Foundation.

Scherer, K. R., Wallbott, H. G., & Summerfield, A. B. (Eds.). (1981). *Experiencing emotion: A cross cultural study.* Cambridge: Cambridge University Press.

Schultz, T. W. (1981). *Investing in people: The economics of population quality.* Berkeley, CA: University of California Press.

Schumpeter, J. A. (1954). *History of economic analysis.* Edited from manuscript by E. B. Schumpeter. New York: Oxford University Press.

Scitovsky, T. (1977). *The joyless economy.* New York: Oxford University Press.

Selye, H. (1975). *Stress without distress.* New York: New American Library.

Sen, A. (1979). Utilitarianism and welfarism. *Journal of Philosophy, 76,* 463–488.

Sen, A. (1993). Capability and well-being. In M. Nussbaum & A. Sen (Eds.), *The quality of life* (pp. 30–53). Oxford: Clarendon Press.

Sen, A., & Drèze, J. (1989). *Hunger and public action.* Oxford: Clarendon.

Sen, A., & Williams, B. (1982). Introduction. In A. Sen & B. Williams (Eds.), *Utilitarianism and beyond* (pp. 3–7). Cambridge: Cambridge University Press.

Singer, P. (1993). *Practical ethics* (2nd ed.). Cambridge: Cambridge University Press.

Smart, J. J. C., & Williams, B. (Eds.). (1973). *Utilitarianism, for and against.* Cambridge: Cambridge University Press, especially Introduction by Smart.

Sternberg, R. J. (1997). The concept of intelligence and its role in lifelong learning and success. *American Psychologist, 52,* 1030–1037.

Suh, E., Diener, E., Oishi, S., & Triandis, H. C. (1998). The shifting basis of life satisfaction judgments across cultures: Emotions versus norms. *Journal of Personality and Social Psychology, 74,* 482–493.

VanDeVeer, D. (1986). *Paternalistic intervention: The moral bounds of benevolence.* Princeton, NJ: Princeton University Press.

Veenhoven, R. (1993). *Happiness in nations.* Rotterdam: Erasmus University.

Wallas, G. (1909). *Human nature in politics.* Boston: Houghton Mifflin.

Weinstein, F., & Platt, G. M. (1969). *The wish to be free.* Berkeley, CA: University of California Press.

Wilson, E. O. (1998). *Consilience: The unity of knowledge.* Boston & London: Little, Brown.

Wilson, T. D., & Lassiter, G. D. (1982). Increasing intrinsic interest with superfluous extrinsic constraints. *Journal of Personality and Social Psychology, 42,* 811–819.

Witkin, H. A., Dyk, R. B., Faterson, H. F., Goodenough, D. R., & Karp, S. A. (1974). *Psychological differentiation.* New York: Wiley/Erlbaum.

Wooster, M. M. (1990). Can character be taught? *The American Enterprise, 1,* 50–55.

Zajonc, R. B. (1980). Feeling and thinking: Preferences need no inferences. *American Psychologist, 35,* 151–175.

20

An Intellectual Agenda
for Political Psychology

DAVID G. WINTER
University of Michigan

In my 1999 presidential address to the International Society of Political Psychology (Winter, 1999b), I suggested that some of the most characteristic features of the 20th century (things that our forebears back in 1899 probably did not expect of the new century) involve the themes of power, sex, and violence—both by themselves and also in various unholy combinations with each other. Each of these themes can be approached from the perspectives of many disciplines, but most notably the disciplines of psychology and politics. Inasmuch as political psychology is an interdisciplinary field focused on the complex and reciprocal relationships between these two disciplines, I believe that political psychology is uniquely poised to understand such a confluence of power, sex, and violence. Indeed, I believe that understanding the psychological, social structural, and cultural dynamics of these three themes must become an urgent intellectual agenda for political psychology, if we all are to survive the next century.

In this chapter, I am more detailed about such an agenda. More specifically, I suggest that three broad topics deserve special theoretical and empirical attention from political psychologists: Understanding the striving for power that, especially in the context of perceived "difference," often leads to violence; understanding the construction of difference itself, with gender being perhaps the original prototype or template for all other differences;[1] and exploring whether it is possible for people and societies to

---

[1] Cf. MacKinnon (1984) on "Difference and dominance."

live "beyond" power and difference. For each topic, I suggest some questions that political psychology could ask and some contributions we could make.

UNDERSTANDING THE STRIVING FOR POWER

Diagnosis: What is the Striving for Power Really About?

First, power and the striving for power. Many researchers (e.g., Winter, 1999a) suggest that there may be two fundamentally different kinds of power-striving. One is said to be "offensive;" that is, it originates in the sense of omnipotence and entitlement. Such *direct power-striving* in adults is said to grow out of early childhood experiences of positive reinforcement for assertive and aggressive behavior (e.g., McClelland & Pilon, 1983). The other, "defensive," power-striving is said to be rooted in a sense of weakness and inferiority. This is *power as compensation* (George, 1968): Adults who strive for power are "really" only trying to overcome feelings of weakness or low self-esteem rooted in early experiences of powerlessness and being the target of others' power. The notion that power drives are (only) compensatory is especially popular among optimistic people who do not like power (Americans especially, perhaps), because it offers an explanation of how people who are inherently "good" can, nevertheless, can come to pursue "bad" power.

The important question for political psychologists is whether there are really two fundamentally different kinds of power-striving, or is one a mask for the other? And if there are two, then what is the relationship between them? Do they have different sources? Should we use different tactics in responding to each?

Here we may find a useful analogy in Jervis's (1976, pp. 58–113) distinction between "deterrence" and "spiral" crises in international relations. Defensive, compensatory power might be engaged by a spiraling arms race (as in 1914). The fear or sense of weakness that is at the root of this kind of power drive can perhaps be appeased. In contrast, however, other kinds of aggression are only made worse by appeasement (as in Europe, before World War II); they can only be deterred. The motivational basis of this kind of aggression may be offensive power. As Jervis argued, it is essential to get the diagnosis right, because a policy that is appropriate for one type of crisis (i.e., for one kind of power) will almost certainly lead to disaster if applied to the other type. So how do we decide whether there are one or two kinds of power, and how do we distinguish between them? Answers to these questions would clearly draw on personality, developmental, and social psychologies, as well as systematic and comparative studies of international relations.

Tempering Power

If the striving for power is always present in human affairs, and sometimes even useful, then how can we tame or temper power so that we can live with it in peace? At the individual level, many mechanisms of control have been suggested. For example, Freud believed that our destructive power instinct could be restrained by bringing "Eros, its antagonist, into play against it" (1933/1964, p. 212), as well as by the "soft" voice of human intellect (1927/1961, p. 53). Other psychologists have suggested a wide variety of mechanisms. For example, one cluster of variables that might restrain power and aggressive motives involves concepts such as *self-regulation* (Carver, 1998; Heckhausen & Dweck, 1998; Shoda, Mischel, & Peake, 1990), *emotional intelligence* (Salovey, Hsee, & Mayer, 1993), *inhibition* (Kagan, Snidman, & Arcus, 1993), *activity inhibition* (McClelland & Boyatzis, 1982), *ego control* (Block & Block, 1980), *responsibility* (Winter & Barenbaum, 1985), and *maturity* (McClelland, 1975). Alternatively, this cluster could be described in terms of its opposite pole as being low in *impulsivity* (Eysenck, 1987; Gray, 1987; Revelle, 1987) or *sensation-seeking* (Zuckerman, 1994).

In recent years, psychologists have shown increased interest in understanding a variety of cognitive mechanisms by which people regulate and control their emotions, both deliberately and implicitly (see, for example, Gross, 1998; Nolen-Hoeksema, 1998; Rusting & Nolen-Hoeksema, 1998). A recent study by Zurbriggen (2000) showed how men's power motivation, in combination with certain cognitive structures linking concepts of power and sexuality, increases the likelihood that they will engage in sexual aggression against women. Zurbriggen's findings might suggest that cognitive associations between power and sex can be modified by a kind of "metaphor retraining." Although these research findings typically involve laboratory studies and have been focused on mostly on depression and other matters of clinical concern, political psychologists have both the training and the perspective to adapt and apply them to the study of controlling power and aggression in real-world political contexts, taking account of the operation of institutional structures and cultural contexts.

Understanding how power might be controlled can come from many fields. For example, the control of power and other "appetites" is a central question in philosophy and theology. Thus for centuries, Christian theologians have argued that the "Christian virtues" of patience and temperance, among others (Mitchell, 1958, p. 165) can restrain the "works of the flesh" (although there seems little evidence that Christian political leaders have been conspicuously successful at practicing Christian virtues and thereby controlling their power drives).

Tempering or controlling power can also be done at the social or institutional level. This is, of course, a staple topic in political science, but it is also a favorite theme in literature, especially in Renaissance and Eliza-bethan times. For example, in *Troilus and Cressida* (Act I, scene iii, lines 109–111), Shakespeare argued that power could only be restrained by "degree," which in his time seems to have meant "station" or "position in the scale of dignity," in other words, a stable structure of power.

The suggestion that the world would be better if only all people would stick to their place or station is, however, not likely to work in the modern world. In an age focused on liberty and mobility, people may prefer Montes-quieu's (1748/1949) prescription for the social control of power: Because "experience shows us that every man invested with power is apt to abuse it," it is therefore necessary that "power should be a check to power" (p. 150 [XI, 4]). This is the philosophical basis of the separation-of-powers doctrine that guided the framers of the United States Constitution (see especially *The Federalist Papers,* nos. 47 and 51). From this "institutional" perspective, the task for political psychologists would be to determine which structural arrangements are most successful at containing or checking the excessive power strivings of individuals and collectivities.

Dealing with the Effects of Power

Power changes people. Being the target of others' power can certainly have traumatic effects; indeed, it may be the most consistent proximal cause of what we now call post-traumatic stress disorder (PTSD). How can these "power injuries" be understood, and then repaired? This is an urgent task for political psychologists involved in the practical applications of their dis-cipline: in negotiation and mediation (both official and "track 2"), in work with refugee populations that inhabit so many regions of today's world, and even in the practice of individual and group therapy.

Those who wield power may all too easily become desensitized to its effects and consequently dehumanized in their practice (Kipnis, 1976). Or they may suffer from "power burnout" (Golembiewski, 1996), thus jeopardiz-ing the beneficial effects of their leadership. Might such power burnout be a *reflexive* form of PTSD—in the words of Canetti (1962), a "sting" of power? How can these "metamorphic effects" of power (Kipnis, 1976) be avoided?

I suggest that political psychologists are strategically poised—with one foot in social science and the other in the real world of power relation-ships—to study both of these problems. We should remember, however, to be both reflexive and reflective about the processes of teaching, consulting, helping, and even healing, for they, too, are exercises of power, with all the inherent risks that such exercise entails.[2]

---

[2]As Lakoff and Coyne (1993) pointed out, Dora (Freud's first major psychoanalytic case) was a victim of power: both the power of the adults who deceived her, and the power of Freud who, in insisting on his own interpretations, thereby colluded with that deception (see also Maddi, 1974).

UNDERSTANDING THE CONSTRUCTION
OF DIFFERENCE

In selecting power targets, people construct, magnify, and then act on differences among themselves. In the political realm, these constructed differences constitute the basis of *nationalism*—another phenomenon whose re-emergence in the late 20th century surprised both academics and policymakers (see, for example, Moynihan, 1993). Perhaps the most important feature of these constructed differences is that they are just that— *constructions*. Although there may be some evolutionary basis to a general tendency for human beings to categorize other humans (see, e.g., Lakoff, 1987; Sidanius, 1999; Sidanius & Pratto, 1993), *where* the actual category lines are drawn, and how permeable and modifiable these boundaries are in practice vary widely among different societies and different people. Difference can be based on language, religion, skin color, biological sex, or sexual orientation. Very often similarity is constructed on the highly abstract sense of shared history (or even literature) as a shared "imagined community" (Anderson, 1983; see also Hall, 1989). And the salience of particular boundaries can change with context: People who might not speak to each other in their "home" social setting may interact like close friends in a distant country (cf. Mead, 1942).

Sometimes, for all their potential differences, heterogeneous populations become, to some extent, successfully alloyed with the passage of time (for example, the 13 British colonies in America, the Jewish population of Israel, or the nation of Brazil). Alternatively, populations that appear quite homogeneous may nevertheless see themselves as having significant differences. Thus the Dutch—to many outsiders viewed as homogeneous and among the most international-minded nations in Europe—sometimes distinguish themselves from the Frisians (who live in the northern Netherlands province of Friesland and speak Frisian, a language different from Dutch). And the rivalry between Amsterdam and Rotterdam is certainly fueled by what Freud (1930/1961, p. 114) called the "narcissism of minor differences."

Constructions of difference change. In the last decades of the 20th century, for example, we saw the shaky ethnopolitical identity category of "Yugoslav" shred itself into many different components. On the other hand, after centuries of enmity, the people who call themselves "deutsch" and "français" have finally started to call themselves "allemand" and "franzözisch," as well as "European."

What psychological mechanisms lead us to draw more and tighter lines of difference on the basis of dimensions such as gender, sexual orientation, ethnicity, race, language, religion, social class, or region? The current concepts of right-wing authoritarianism (Altemeyer, 1996) and social dominance orientation (Sidanius, 1999; see also Pratto, Sidanius, Stall-worth, & Malle, 1994) offer promising leads. At the same time, I suggest that it is important to study mechanisms that work in the opposite direc-tion—that is, "mechanisms of inclusion" that bind together differences into larger wholes. Examples might include empathy, curiosity, cognitive complexity, and a sense of cosmopolitan identity. Such mechanisms are likely increased by exposure to varied experience, at least under certain conditions such as liberal-arts higher education (see Feldman & Newcomb, 1969, ch. 2). In the face of novelty, uncertainty, and possible threat, these mechanisms would lead people toward approach, investigation, and explo-ration—rather than immediately drawing lines in the sand.

What activates right-wing authoritarianism and social dominance ori-entation, instead of the mechanisms of inclusion? Altemeyer's research (1988) suggested that perceptions of external threat and convictions of self-righteousness (often based on certain religious beliefs) are key antecedents of the "differencing" and its frequent sequel, prejudice.[3] The underlying process can be seen as an example of Tajfel's (1957, 1981) principle of social categorization, that *value* or *emotional relevance* (in this case, threat and the sense of self-righteousness) lead us to exaggerate or "stretch" the scales we use to evaluate dimensions of difference that are relevant to the value or emotion. (Tajfel used the example of an "elastic ruler" to charac-terize this process.)

OUR HUMAN HERITAGE

Power-striving and differencing, then, may be two key psychological mech-anisms that underlie the power–sex–violence triad that was so characteristic of the 20th century. Both laboratory and survey evidence (e.g., Winter, 1973, p. 94) suggests that variables reflecting these two mechanisms (power motivation and authoritarianism) are uncorrelated, although both appear to be activated by perceived threat (among other conditions). Here I want to present yet another speculative "just so" story about possible evolution-ary roots of these two mechanisms in our early prehistory as a species. The capacity to construct differences may help people (indeed, all organisms) to distinguish "prey" from "peer" and "predator." Such a categorization, with its concomitant amplification and exaggeration of "threat" or "oppor-tunity," would then facilitate selection of the appropriate response—fight, flight, and fright. All these responses are energized by the sympathetic nervous system, which is linked (McClelland, 1982) to the psychological

---

[3]Perhaps these two perceptions come together in an implicit sense of "protection" that self-righteousness offers to the faithful, against the "threat" of a religious Armageddon.

mechanism of the power motive. These two mechanisms may have ensured our survival and flourishing as a species, but now—linked with technology (Lorenz, 1966)—the combination of differencing, threat amplification, and power striving can be deadly to humanity (see Peterson, Doty, & Winter, 1994, for a cognitive-motivational "model" of how these mechanisms, acting in concert, facilitate aggression).

LIVING BEYOND POWER AND DIFFERENCE

Beyond Power

Do people ever give up power? As addictive as power can often be,[4] it is still possible that some people, sometimes, can move beyond their power concerns. A vivid literary example is Shakespeare's character Prospero in his play *The Tempest*. Throughout the play, Prospero uses his magical power to establish control of an island, enslave the original inhabitant Caliban, create a storm that wrecks his enemies' ship, and overprotect his daughter Miranda. At the end of Act IV, he exults, "At this hour lie at my mercy all mine enemies." Then, a few lines later, he suddenly orders the release of his enemies with the announcement that "My charms I'll break," "this rough magic I here abjure," "I'll break my staff," and "I'll drown my book" (the symbols of his power).

What happened? Why the sudden change? Prospero's words give us no clue. However, in a 1999 Stratford (Ontario) Festival production, actor William Hutt played this scene in an unforgettable way. After delivering the line about "at my mercy all mine enemies," he was silent—for what seemed an eternity, his head slowly sank down to his chest, and his exultant smile slowly faded, giving way first to a vacant expression of emptiness and then to an expression of despair. Hutt's changing posture and facial expression seemed to suggest that the pleasures of power are an illusion, that *once attained, power is not enjoyed*. This same point has been made by authors as diverse as Freud (1940/1964, p. 11n), in his discussion of the death (or aggressive) instincts, and Camus (1944/1965), in his play about the Roman emperor Caligula (see also Winter, 1996).

Further clues to Prospero's renunciation of power can be found by examining the lines immediately preceding the renunciation scene. For example, his spirit-servant Ariel reports the great emotional distress of Prospero's confined enemies: they are "brimful of sorrow and dismay," with

---

[4]Hobbes (1651/1950) vividly captured the addictive, ever-increasing aspect of power drives with these words: "the nature of power . . . is like the motion of heavy bodies, which the further they go, make still more haste" (p. 69).

"tears run down his beard like winter's drops." "If you now beheld them," Ariel asserts, "your affections would become tender." Prospero marvels that if Ariel, "which art but air," can feel their afflictions, then he himself—who is "one of their kind"—should feel even stronger compassion for their plight. Feeling a sense of *empathy*, in other words, may be one antecedent to renouncing power. Against his own "fury," Prospero also mobilizes his "nobler reason," realizing that virtue is "the rarer action" than vengeance. His enemies have expressed penitence; this mental transformation, and not their further suffering, has accomplished "the sole drift of my purpose."

There may be more distal antecedents, too. In the immediately preceding scenes, Prospero's daughter becomes partnered with Ferdinand ("I have given you here a third of mine own life."). In celebration, Prospero enacts a visionary pageant, featuring the goddesses Iris, Ceres, and Juno, to celebrate both a "marriage blessing" and "earth's increase." At the conclusion of the pageant, he proclaims that:

> And, like the baseless fabric of this vision,
> The cloud-capped towers, the gorgeous palaces,
> The solemn temples, the great globe itself,
> Yea, all which it inherit, shall dissolve,
> And, like this insubstantial pageant faded,
> Leave not a rack behind.

Finally, he confesses that "our little life is rounded with a sleep," and that "my old brain is troubled."

Thus we see that Prospero, shortly before he renounces his power, has accomplished the most important task of any living creature: He has reared the next generation and seen it launched on the eternal life cycle of bonding and procreation. Simple age, or stage of life, may be a key factor in the capacity to renounce power. I suggest that Shakespeare's play contains many clues for political psychologists interested in understanding how people can live "beyond power."

Beyond Difference

In addition to moving beyond or tempering our power drives, we can also try to tear down our constructions of difference. Despite its potential for abuse and oppression, the advent of a cosmopolitan, globalized economy might actually help in some ways: Looking at the "other's" global pop CDs (Taylor, 1997), Toyota automobiles, and Windows logo, we may be less inclined to apply the label *other.* One should not exaggerate, however: Friedman's dictum that "no two countries that both had a McDonald's have ever fought a war against each other" (Friedman, 1996; see also 1999, pp. 195–204) has been, sadly, disproved by the 1999 war between NATO and Serbia.

Over the course of human history, cosmopolitanism has at least sometimes been a more powerful force than nationalism and difference. Thus in the time of the Roman Empire, the phrase "Civis Romanus Sum" [I am a citizen of Rome] was a claim that many provincials from the periphery of the empire were proud to make. Even St. Paul, a zealous Jew who helped to create and propagate a new religion, did not hesitate to assert his Roman citizenship and make an appeal to Caesar when he was imprisoned (Acts 22:25, 25:11). And even as local nationalisms were beginning to tear apart the multinational Hapsburg Empire, *some* provincial citizens were proud to be imperial civil servants in Vienna, "at the center of the world" (Michener, 1983, p. 277). More recently, one of the sharpest renunciations of Québec nationalism in favor of a more worldly and cosmopolitan identity, entitled *Québec is Killing Me,* was written by Helene Jutras, a young francophone professional woman who had grown up in the very heartland of Québec separatism (Jutras, 1995). She lamented that "those things which I value— knowledge, intellectual development, are not found here" and concluded that "Québec does not fulfil me" (pp. 10, 14). From the political psychology perspective, the task is to identify those psychological, social, and political structural factors that work against differencing—that foster a sense of inclusive cosmopolitanism rather than narrow nationalism.

FOSTERING AN INTERDISCIPLINARY DISCIPLINE

In my view, the urgent intellectual agenda of political psychology is to increase our understanding of power, sex, and violence as they come together in the political arena. How should political psychologists go about accomplishing such an ambitious goal? How can they best be trained and prepared for the task? Let us examine the unique capabilities and opportunities offered by each of the two main component disciplines of our interdisciplinary field, psychology and political science.

What Psychology Can Provide

Apart from specific research techniques (experiments, surveys, personality assessment, statistical procedures), psychology offers a broad concern with issues of method. Psychologists are usually well-trained in the development of systematic measures. In political psychology, this can result in the development of innovative ways of measuring complex abstract processes (see Simonton, 1990). Also, psychologists tend to think in *operational terms*— that is, the realization that any "variable" is only really defined by the particular operations, in particular contexts, that are used to measure it. Further, these actual operations may be either more than what the researcher thinks they are (e.g., extraneous features, of which the researcher is not aware, that were inadvertently introduced into the measurement procedure) or less than the researcher imagines (e.g., surplus meaning attributed by the researcher but not reflected in any distinctive operations). In other words (to take an example from archival research), "a document is only a document; everything else is an inference." Psychologists often practice a rather ruthless scrutiny of the validity of their own (and other peoples') measures; this training can be a useful contribution to political psychology research.

What Political Science Can Provide

Psychology by itself, however, is not enough, for psychologists are trained to understand social and political phenomena mostly at the individual level, or in terms of universal processes operating at the individual level. Because political scientists are trained to think in terms of *structure* and *complexity,* they are in a position to correct excessive "psychologizing." Structures generate their own dynamics and their own psychological forces, as well as shaping and constraining the expression of individual psychologies. Moreover, political scientists tend to grasp the difference between illustrating a relationship (e.g., that certain psychological variables increase or decrease before conflict escalation) and explaining an event (e.g., the complex of factors that, leading up to World War I, along the way produced certain distinctive psychological variables in the relevant documents).

Beyond Psychology and Political Science

However, I believe that a truly healthy and intellectually vibrant political psychology will not consist only of these two component disciplines. There is—or ought to be—room for many other disciplines to make a contribution. For example, historians are positioned to call attention to factors that may slip through the nets of operational definitions. Thus the historian Joll (1968) emphasized the role of "unspoken assumptions"—beliefs, values, heuristics, and working assumptions that are so "obvious" that they do not need to be articulated and, therefore, may not appear in official documents or published discursive records.

Taking a historical perspective may protect both psychology and political science against assuming a false "causal uniqueness," because in fact many other, alternative causal paths would have led to the same result. That is, certain events and outcomes may be robust with respect to actions, participants, psychological forces, and even structures. For example, in 1945 U.S. President Harry Truman decided to drop the atomic bomb. No doubt his decision reflected certain psychological factors—Truman's decisiveness, his toughness (high power motivation), his tenuous grip on the presidency after Roosevelt's death, his confidence in the military, and so forth. *But,* another president might have made the same decision, for other reasons, because other aspects of their personalities, the decision, and the bomb itself would have been relevant. And if nuclear weapons had not been used by the United States in 1945, *for that very reason* they might well have been used later, by other countries, in other conflicts and contexts. That is, without any prior experience or knowledge of the terrible destructive power of atomic bombs (knowledge that may have restrained American and Soviet leaders during the Cuban Missile Crisis of 1962; see Blight, 1990), political leaders might well have used them in any number of Cold War crises: Korea, Vietnam, or the many conflicts between India and Pakistan or Israel and the Arab states. Thus although Truman's *particular* decision was undoubtedly affected by aspects of his psychology, the use of nuclear weapons —somewhere, sometime—might have had any number of different causal paths.

Finally, I believe that the humanities can make an important contribution to political psychology. (This is probably obvious from my use of Shakespeare and other literary examples in this chapter.) Good writers are like good clinicians: Although they may lack (or eschew) experimental techniques, operational definitions, and statistical pyrotechnics, their intuitions and insights into human nature, their understanding of power, sex, and violence, their insights into the reciprocal relationships of individuals and polities, may often surpass what we can achieve by more systematic means.

Thus I imagine political psychology as a vast interdisciplinary field, far broader than what is implied by the names of its two major constituent disciplines. Our best work is likely to be our broadest work, at least in source and inspiration. As a concluding corollary, it follows that our best scholars and practitioners are likely to be those with the broadest intellectual background and human experience.

ACKNOWLEDGMENT

This chapter draws on material presented in the author's presidential address given at the 22nd Annual Scientific Meeting of the International Society of Political Psychology, Amsterdam, July 19, 1999 (Winter, 1999b).

REFERENCES

Altemeyer, R. (1988). *Enemies of freedom: Understanding right-wing authoritarianism.* San Francisco: Jossey-Bass.
Altemeyer, R. (1996). *The authoritarian specter.* Cambridge, MA: Harvard University Press.

Anderson, B. R. O'G. (1983). *Imagined communities: Reflections on the origin and spread of nationalism*. London: Verso.

Blight, J. G. (1990). *The shattered crystal ball: Fear and learning in the Cuban Missile Crisis*. Savage, MD: Rowman & Littlefield.

Block, J. H., & Block, J. (1980). The role of ego-control and ego-resiliency in the organization of behavior. In W. A. Collins (Ed.), *Minnesota Symposia on Child Psychology* (Vol. 13, pp. 39–101). Hillsdale, NJ: Lawrence Erlbaum Associates.

Camus, A. (1965). *Caligula and cross purpose*. Harmondsworth, Mddx.: Penguin Books. (Original work published 1944)

Canetti, E. (1962). *Crowds and power.* New York: Viking.

Carver, C. S. (1998). *On the self-regulation of behavior.* Cambridge, UK: Cambridge University Press.

Eysenck, H. J. (1987). The place of anxiety and impulsivity in a dimensional framework. *Journal of Research in Personality, 21,* 489–492.

Feldman, K. A., & Newcomb, T. M. (1969). *The impact of college on students*. San Francisco: Jossey-Bass.

Freud, S. (1961). Future of an illusion. In J. Strachey (Ed. & Trans.), *The standard edition of the complete psychological works of Sigmund Freud* (Vol. 21, pp. 1–56). London: Hogarth Press. (Original work published 1927)

Freud, S. (1961). Civilization and its discontents. In J. Strachey (Ed. & Trans.), *The standard edition of the complete psychological works of Sigmund Freud* (Vol. 21, pp. 57–145). London: Hogarth Press. (Original work published 1930)

Freud, S. (1964). Outline of psycho-analysis. In J. Strachey (Ed. & Trans.), *The standard edition of the complete psychological works of Sigmund Freud* (Vol. 23, pp. 144–207). London: Hogarth Press. (Original work published 1940)

Freud, S. (1964). Why war? In J. Strachey (Ed. & Trans.), *The standard edition of the complete psychological works of Sigmund Freud* (Vol. 22, pp. 197–215). London: Hogarth Press. (Original work published 1933)

Friedman, T. L. (1996, December 8). Big Mac I. *The New York Times,* p. IV 15.

Friedman, T. L. (1999). *The Lexus and the olive tree*. New York: Farrar Straus Giroux.

George, A. L. (1968). Power as a compensatory value for political leaders. *Journal of Social Issues, 24*(3), 38–43.

Golembiewski, R. T. (1996). *Global burnout: A worldwide pandemic explored by the phase model*. Greenwich, CT: JAI Press.

Gray, J. A. (1987). Perspectives on anxiety and impulsivity: A commentary. *Journal of Research in Personality, 21,* 493–509.

Gross, J. J. (1998). The emerging field of emotion regulation: An integrative review. *Review of General Psychology: Special Issue: New directions in research on emotion, 2,* 271–299.

Hall, E. (1989). *Inventing the barbarian: Greek self-definition through tragedy*. Oxford: Oxford University Press.

Heckhausen, J., & Dweck, C. S. (Eds.). (1998). *Motivation and self-regulation across the life span*. New York: Cambridge University Press.

Hobbes, T. (1950). *Leviathan*. New York: Dutton. (Original work published 1651)

Jervis, R. (1976). *Perception and misperception in international politics*. Princeton, NJ: Princeton University Press.

Joll, J. (1968). *1914: The unspoken assumptions*. London: Weidenfeld and Nicolson.

Jutras, H. (1995). *Québec is killing me*. Ottawa: Golden Dog Press.

Kagan, J., Snidman, N., & Arcus, D. (1993). On the temperamental categories of inhibited and uninhibited children. In K. H. Rubin (Ed.), *Social withdrawal, inhibition, and shyness in childhood* (pp. 19–28). Hillsdale, NJ: Lawrence Erlbaum Associates.

Kipnis, D. (1976). *The powerholders*. Chicago: University of Chicago Press.

Lakoff, G. (1987). *Women, fire, and dangerous things: What categories reveal about the mind.* Chicago: University of Chicago Press.

Lakoff, R. T., & Coyne, J. C. (1993). *Father knows best: The use and abuse of power in Freud's case of Dora.* New York: Teachers College Press.

Lorenz, K. (1966). *On aggression.* New York: Harcourt, Brace & World.

MacKinnon, C. A. (1984). Difference and dominance. In *Feminism unmodified: Discourses on life and law* (pp. 32–45). Cambridge, MA: Harvard University Press.

Maddi, S. R. (1974, September). The victimization of Dora. *Psychology Today, 8*(4), 90–94.

McClelland, D. C. (1975). *Power: The inner experience.* New York: Irvington.

McClelland, D. C. (1982). The need for power, sympathetic activation, and illness. *Motivation and Emotion, 6,* 31–41.

McClelland, D. C., & Boyatzis, R. E. (1982). The leadership motive pattern and long-term success in management. *Journal of Applied Psychology, 67,* 737–743.

McClelland, D. C., & Pilon, D. A. (1983). Sources of adult motives in patterns of parent behavior in early childhood. *Journal of Personality and Social Psychology, 44,* 564–574.

Mead, M. (1942). *And keep your powder dry: An anthropologist looks at America.* New York: Morrow.

Michener, J. A. (1983). *Poland.* New York: Random House.

Mitchell, B. (1958). The grace of God. In B. Mitchell (Ed.), *Faith and logic* (pp. 149–175). London: Allen & Unwin.

Montesquieu, B. de (1949). *The spirit of the laws.* New York: Hafner. (Original work published 1748)

Moynihan, D. P. (1993). *Pandæmonium: Ethnicity in international politics.* New York: Oxford University Press.

Nolen-Hoeksema, S. (1998). Ruminative coping with depression. In J. Heckhausen & C. S. Dweck (Eds.), *Motivation and self-regulation across the life span* (pp. 237–256). New York: Cambridge University Press.

Peterson, B. E., Doty, R. M., & Winter, D. G. (1994). Laboratory tests of a motivational-perceptual model of conflict escalation. *Journal of Conflict Resolution, 38,* 719–748.

Pratto, F., Sidanius, J., Stallworth, L. M., & Malle, B. F. (1994). Social dominance orientation: A personality variable predicting social and political attitudes. *Journal of Personality and Social Psychology, 67,* 741–763.

Revelle, W. (1987). Personality and motivation: Sources of inefficiency in cognitive performance. *Journal of Research in Personality, 21,* 436–452.

Rusting, C. L., & Nolen-Hoeksema, S. (1998). Regulating responses to anger: Effects of rumination and distraction on angry mood. *Journal of Personality and Social Psychology, 74,* 790–803.

Salovey, P., Hsee, C. K., & Mayer, J. D. (1993). Emotional intelligence and the self-regulation of affect. In D. M. Wegner (Ed.), *Handbook of mental control* (pp. 258–277). Englewood Cliffs, NJ: Prentice-Hall.

Shoda, Y., Mischel, W., & Peake, P. K. (1990). Predicting adolescent cognitive and self-regulatory competencies from preschool delay of gratification: Identifying diagnostic conditions. *Developmental Psychology, 26,* 978–986.

Sidanius, J. (1999). *Social dominance: An intergroup theory of social hierarchy and oppression.* New York: Cambridge University Press.

Sidanius, J., & Pratto, F. (1993). The inevitability of oppression and the dynamics of social dominance. In P. M. Sniderman (Ed.), *Prejudice, politics, and the American dilemma* (pp. 173–211). Stanford, CA: Stanford University Press.

Simonton, D. K. (1990). *Psychology, science, and history: An introduction to historiometry.* New Haven, CT: Yale University Press.

Tajfel, H. (1957). Value and the perceptual judgment of magnitude. *Psychological Review, 64,* 192–204.

Tajfel, H. (1981). *Human groups and social categories.* Cambridge: Cambridge University Press.

Taylor, T. D. (1997). *Global pop: World music, world markets.* New York: Routledge.

Winter, D. G. (1973). *The power motive.* New York: Free Press.

Winter, D. G. (1996, June). *What does power "do" for you and to you, and what can we do to power?* Paper presented at the annual meeting of the Society for the Psychological Study of Social Issues, Ann Arbor, MI.

Winter, D. G. (1999a, August). *Origins of power motivation in males: Data from a longitudinal study.* Paper presented at the annual meeting of the American Psychological Association, Boston.

Winter, D. G. (1999b, July). *Power, sex, and violence: A psychological reconstruction of the twentieth century and an intellectual agenda for political psychology.* Presidential address at the annual scientific meeting of the International Society of Political Psychology, Amsterdam.

Winter, D. G., & Barenbaum, N. B. (1985). Responsibility and the power motive in women and men. *Journal of Personality, 53,* 335–355.

Zuckerman, M. (1994). *Behavioral expressions and biosocial bases of sensation seeking.* New York: Cambridge University Press.

Zurbriggen, E. L. (2000). Social motives and cognitive power/sex associations: Predictors of aggressive and affiliative sexual behavior. *Journal of Personality and Social Psychology, 78,* 559–581.

21

A Paradigm for Political Psychology

KRISTEN R. MONROE
University of California at Irvine

The richness of political psychology is amply illustrated in the previous chapters of this volume. Yet, as one contributor commented, there is no one basic theory associated with political psychology, no underlying paradigm that gives unity and coherence to political psychology as a field.[1] As I assess the field as a whole, I would argue that it is not the lack of theory but rather the overabundance of insightful theories that blinds us to an underlying paradigm in political psychology. Such a paradigm does exist, however, and can be discerned if we review the major theories in political psychology with an eye for the common element. Doing so suggests that many important theories in political psychology rest on implicit assumptions concerning perceptions of the self and others. In this chapter I weave these tacit assumptions together into a simple paradigm for political psychology, and argue that it is the cognitive component of perspective that provides the basic underlying paradigm for political psychology.

I begin this final chapter by describing what I mean by perspective and what I define as its core assumptions. I next suggest how perspective draws on several bodies of literature in political psychology, from framing theory to social cognition theory. I then demonstrate how perspective provides a more encompassing paradigm than rational choice theory, arguably the dominant paradigm existing in social science today and one that essentially is a theory about the human psychology. I argue that if political psychology can refine perspective in the years to come it not only will solidify its own

---

[1] Private conversation with David Sears, the War Tribunals in Holland, Summer, 1999.

intellectual foundation as a discipline but also will provide all of social science with a paradigm that more accurately reflects how the human mind works.

PERSPECTIVE: THE UNIFYING FRAMEWORK

There is, indeed, an underlying theoretical structure that provides a unifying foundation for political psychology as a field. I call this a theory of perspective on self and others and can capture the essential of perspective simply. Our perceptions of ourselves in relation to others effectively delineate and set the domain of options we find available, not just morally but empirically. This effectively makes choice a function of identity and, more particularly, of our self-perceptions, our view of reality, and our perspective on ourselves in relation to that reality, including those around us. Perspective draws on the psychological by emphasizing perceptions, the ideas about reality that exist in the human psyche of every individual agent. This emphasis on human cognition, affect, and emotions thus encompasses what Stein (chapter 6, this volume) makes central in her definition of political psychology: the "patterns of political thinking, feeling, and identity, the interaction of these patterns, and their impact on political choice and other forms of political behavior." Stein is correct in further arguing that "all political psychologists . . . share the assumption that human cognition and emotion mediate the impact of the environment on political action." The emphasis on the actor's perceptions, rather than an objective reality, allows for what the postmoderns have quite properly suggested is wrong with much of contemporary social science's insistence on rational processing of objective facts: People do perceive reality differentially, and there is a heavy subjective element in our decision-making calculus. But the postmoderns go too far in insisting that all is relative and that the analyst can never be objective. Political psychology, as both Rosenberg and Suedfeld suggest, offers a more felicitous and productive response to this problem by emphasizing the role of human cognition and emotion in filtering and mediating the external world. Most works in political psychology attempt to do this in some way. Their emphasis on the actor's thought process and the feelings as the impetus for political behavior reflects the kind of concern that perspective is designed to capture as a paradigm.

By emphasizing the actor's sense of self, perspective draws on identity, also a critical variable for political psychologists, as is evident from the Stein definition and as can be seen in the chapters in this volume by Jervis and Marcus *inter alia*. It is not only the actor's sense of self that is critical for perspective, however; it is the actor's perceptions of self *in relation to others* that is central. It is this that locates the political at the heart of perspective and this that gives perspective the firm foundation on which political psychology as a discipline can build, for it is the interaction of one with another that is the essence of the political. This interaction may take different forms. It may be an interaction of one person with another person, one person with a group of people, or one person with a formal State institution embodied in a policeman, the county clerk, or an IRS bill. The individual actors may be individual people or a formal or de facto institution representing others, in the form of a political party, the State, or any other body that authoritatively allocates values. This conceptualization of the political captures the traditional concept of politics as power and influence (Machiavelli, 1965; Morganthau, 1960). It also allows for the broader conceptualization of politics found in normative political theory, in which the realm of the political is extended beyond formal or de facto institutional structures to include all of our relations with others (Mill, 1963, or contemporary feminist theory à la Pateman, 1969).[2] It also allows for those definitions of the political (Easton, 1997; Eckstein, 1992) that conceptualize politics as the authoritative allocation of values. By basing perspective on the central component of politics, the paradigm of perspective solves the difficulty to which Krosnick and McGraw alert us, a problem that has plagued political psychologists concerned with the basic conceptualization since the discipline's inception: Is political psychology merely a branch of political science or of psychology, and can we construct basic theories of political psychology? By resting on perspective as a paradigm, political psychology has a firm foundation of its own, and we can speak of it as a discipline that can construct basic theories and that intersects with many other fields but that retains its own distinct identity.

PERSPECTIVE AND POLITICAL PSYCHOLOGY

We find glimpses of perspective in many works of political psychology—including my own—even though it has never before been offered explicitly as the underlying paradigm for the field. Indeed, we find glimmers of perspective in some of the many early precursors of contemporary social science that attempt to describe how the human psyche influences behavior, such as Kant (see Brennan, 1998). This is no surprise, since both psychology

---

[2]In this I am differing from the definition of politics offered by my dear friend and colleague, David Easton, who argues that the essence of the political is the authoritative allocation of values. I prefer an earlier definition of politics that encompasses any form of power and influence, even when there is no authoritative aspect there. This conceptualization is a broader one and encompasses the kind of situations feminist theory has alerted us to, in which there are political aspects to most interactions, such as those between members of the same family or between friends.

and political science can trace their origins to ancient philosophy and its concern with our psyche and our relations with others. The process through which these theories were blended so they evolved into a separate discipline of political psychology is ably traced in the chapters in Part 1, as well as in chapters by Alford and Renshon, and I need not replicate the discussion here.

I want to look backwards a bit, however, and to do so, I adopt the metaphor of new parents sitting in their living room, musing about their new child. Much as parents of a new child might ask what traits little Barbara might have inherited from Grandpa Jim or Grandma Trudi, so can we, as intellectual parents of a new discipline, survey our intellectual ancestors, if you will, to speculate about the critical gifts that have been endowed to political psychology as an intellectual field. As with a new baby, a trait from one ancestor may have a quite different interaction when placed in conjunction with other traits and in a different environment. Grandpa Jim's absent-mindedness was accompanied with an intellectual brilliance that might be lacking in the new baby; Grandpa Trudi's love of order might become excessive compulsion if it is channeled differently in the new child. So it is with political psychology, a field in its infancy. Indeed, Hartz (1964) noted a similar phenomenon with countries when he advanced his fragment theory, in which a piece of the Old World effectively sailed away to a new land in which it did not have the same "predators" that had kept it in check in the Old World. In Hartz's example, the strong Tudor monarchy left behind by the Puritans developed quite differently in England, where an established aristocracy existed to check its growth and turn it into the constitutional monarchy under which the British now live. But in the New World, with no established aristocracy to check it, the concept of a strong monarchy, based on the notion of the Tudor kings and queen, developed into the strong executive known as the American Presidency. So it is with political psychology. We may identify certain traits inherited from different branches of psychology and political science, but these traits may grow into quite different shapes in the new discipline. How the trait develops will depend on the intellectual stimuli it encounters in the future.

Psychoanalytic theories alerted us to the importance of the unconscious and preconscious forces that drive behavior.[3] Developmental psychology taught us more about the acquisition of political beliefs and the importance of both genetics and early childhood experiences in shaping our sense of who we are and how we see the world.[4] Cognitive psychology focused attention on our mental processes, including how we first interpret the myriad bits of information that bombard us and then weave these strands together

---

[3]Freud (1973).
[4]Winnicott (1986).

into a narrative that allows us to make sense of reality.[5] It pointed us in the direction of asking how we form beliefs and attitudes and how these perceptions and interpretations about people and events feed back into our interpretation of others' actions.[6] This process in turn affects our actions, political and otherwise. Work on cognitive maps suggested that representations of objects, acts, events, or other actors relate to each other, forming an organizing framework of causes and effects, with positive and negative implications for decision-making, much as a road map gives us an organizing framework for our geographic movements.[7] Social psychology greatly increased our understanding of how the social environment, especially the behavior of others, influences our behavior, often through perceptions.[8] Recent work on social perceptions and social cognition underlined the importance of social influences on our behavior.[9] The importance of constructs and construals of reality, as cognitive representations and processes basic to all our human responses, provided a scientifically based method for understanding the subjective aspects of political actions. Learning theory increased our understanding of how our present behavior is influenced by prior learning. This process works through political socialization as well as through the kind of Bayesian processes that economists posit.

Consider just one example: perspective's heritage in social psychology. We can detect the underlying paradigm of perspective quite clearly in social psychological theories that pertain to politics. (Indeed, if we can define social psychology as a field that attempts the scientific study of the manner in which people's thoughts, feelings, and behaviors are influenced by the real and the imagined presence of other people, then we might also make the argument that the entire field of social psychology rests on perspective. I am not a social psychologist, however, so I restrict my remarks to the field of political psychology.) Social cognition theory can be defined as the study of how people think about themselves and the social and political world. This includes how they select, interpret, and use social information to make judgments and decisions. Their perspectives on themselves, and how they see themselves in relation to others, lies at the heart of such selection, interpretation, and acting on information.

I would argue that work in all of these fields has helped focus political psychology on the importance of perception for the complex interrelationships between political choice, political action, and thinking and feeling about politics. The importance of perceptions is also evident through a phenomenon that may not be immediately obvious: social science's recent

---

[5] Fiske and Taylor (1991).
[6] Aronson, Wilson, and Akert (1999); Stein, chapter 6, this volume.
[7] Axelrod (1976).
[8] Taylor, Peplau, and Sears (2000).
[9] Fiske and Taylor (1991).

flirtation with postmodernism. Although postmodernism may be a natural response to the knowledge that reality is perceived differentially, it also carries serious negatives. It does not, in the long run, offer a fruitful solution for social scientists concerned with this legitimate problem of differential interpretation of a shared reality. Political psychology offers a more productive response, one in which the scientific method is applied to test ideas empirically and in which the existence of an external reality, even though differentially perceived, is not denied.[10]

Let me note just one theoretical illustration suggesting how political psychology, as based on an underlying paradigm of perspective, can reveal the extent to which there are systematic processes by which reality is perceived differentially. Social representations theory (Moscovici, 1988) argues that a person's unique experiences lead to a set of individual representations of the world and that these representations, in turn, influence the perception, interpretation and evaluation of incoming information. Work by Bar-Tal (chapter 10 in this volume), Jervis (1976 and chapter 16 this volume) and George (1969) suggests that behavior is highly dependent on the perception of the situation and is influenced by both affect and motivation. Perspective allows for this process in a way that analysts can hope to ultimately discern and understand. It can provide clues about how cultural factors, for example, may shape social representations in consistent and predictable ways for certain groups of people, or perhaps tell us if there are certain ways in which all people perceive reality.[11] It is this kind of consideration that I have tried to incorporate into my initial formulation of perspective, and on which I hope others will build as the theory is tested and refined by others.

RATIONAL CHOICE AND PERSPECTIVE

Rational choice theory is arguably the dominant theory in contemporary social science.[12] I believe there are several ways in which perspective actually incorporates rational choice theory into a broader framework. This claim can be made best by contrasting the two theories in terms of differences in assumptions and methodologies. Two caveats are in order here. First, although I conclude that rational actor theory can be treated as a limiting case of perspective because perspective allows for a more fully variegated sense of self, both theories have certain weaknesses that must be recognized by the analyst. What is critical for future analysts, I suspect, will be delineating the domain of action for which each theory is best suited, and throughout my discussion, I shall suggest questions I believe will facili-

---

[10]I was particularly happy to read the Suedfeld and the Rosenberg chapters on this topic.
[11]The fundamental attribution error may exemplify this phenomenon.
[12]See Green and Shapiro (1994) or Monroe (1991).

tate this delineation. Second, the heart of economic man is self-interest. But a study of political psychology teaches us that self-interest is only one of the innate aspects of our human nature, and that we need to move beyond self-interest in constructing our most basic theories. I thus concentrate much of my discussion on the different views of the self offered by perspective and rational choice theory. I nonetheless believe the other ways in which perspective differs from rational choice theory may be just as important, even though they are mentioned but briefly here.

Contrasts With Rational Actor Theory

1. Conceptualization of the Self. Self-interest clearly explains much of human behavior. Political psychologists should not discard this construct as part of our theory of perspective. But we need to recognize that rational choice theory's limits are exceeded when it is applied to situations in which individual self-interest is not the dominant force behind behavior and that many significant political acts, in particular, fall into this domain. Although self-interest can remain a basic part of our political theories, it should be balanced by human needs for sociability, defined as a feeling of belonging to a group or collectivity.[13]

To understand when and why we pursue self-interested behavior and when we exhibit more public-spirited behavior—surely a question of some concern to political psychologists who study phenomena as diverse as voting, cooperation, terrorism, altruism, and genocide—we must understand the complex linkages between the actor's attempts to further his or her self-interest and an actor's perception of himself or herself in relation to others. Why is individual self-interest sometimes pursued and group interest pursued at other times? The answer may depend on which of the actor's identities is made most salient by external conditions. Political psychology suggests that one way to solve this problem is through an emphasis on framing and social contexts. Such an accentuation responds positively to both the cultural and the cognitive critiques of rational actor theory.

Another more basic response, however, is simply to focus on the self as the central pillar of a theory of political behavior. For this reason, I pass over other psychological theories that might profitably be applied to politics and focus on identity theory, particularly the literature on the self in relation to others. I do so because I believe the assumption of self-interest is the heart of economic man.[14] Attempts to shift the emphasis of the theory to goal-directed behavior reduce the theory to a tautology in which behavior emanates from preferences that are, in turn, revealed through behavior.[15]

---

[13]This reflects the Aristotelian concept of man as a social being.

[14]Hirschman (1977), Myers (1983).

[15]Ironically, Downs himself acknowledges this point in *An Economic Theory of Democracy* (1957, pp. 6–7).

The theory of perspective is based on the complexity of the personality and the external factors that draw one particular part of this complex identity into political salience. Perspective assumes that the self is highly complex and variegated, far more so than the simple actor assumed in rational choice theory. Perspective assumes that actors have multiple identities, whose importance varies in response to cultural and situational contexts.[16] The key to understanding political behavior would then lie in delineating the actor's constant shift between these identities and the manner in which the actor's perception of his or her identity in relation to others defines the domain of relevant options. To determine when an actor pursues strategies to further individual self-interest and when an agent acts to further interests as a member of a group, we must understand how the perception of a critical identity affects action.

Traditional political economists concerned with collective action have argued that individuals join groups because the group mediates resources for that individual or provides side benefits. But political psychology teaches us that other forces also determine group memberships, for example, parental–offspring bonds or socialization. The logic of social and political (as well as economic) competition is often mediated by a group, and the group to which you give allegiance at a particular moment may be determined by the problems you confront at the time and the way you view yourself in relation to others in the group.

Parsing out the relevant part of the process by which actors shift from individual to group identity necessarily involves understanding the cognitive frameworks of different actors. This allows for both internal stability and changing conditions. It again allows for cultural variations, especially in that most critical variable: the actor's view of the relationship between the individual and society.[17] I hope that future political psychologists will develop theories suggesting how best to allow for the complex ties among individuals, groups, and society in general. There is no one magical methodological solution to this problem, but the focus on identity perception seems the right route to pursue, not the least because it will reduce the individualistic bias of rational actor theory, and will allow us to focus on the polity's role in shaping both public and private identities.

---

[16]See Elster (1986) or the vast literature on the self reviewed in Monroe, Hankin, and Van-Vechten (2000).

[17]Both traditional and bounded concepts of rationality reflect a post-Enlightenment framework that separates the individual from the collectivity. Interests are not identified this way in many non-Western societies, however; and even in Western society, individuals have conceptualized their relationships with society quite differently in other historical eras. This strict differentiation of the individual from society or critical groups may explain why so many Western decision models, based on individualistic assumptions, often fail to predict behavior outside the Western market system.

We thus need to allow for a conceptualization of the self that allows not only for the times when the actor responds as a self-interested individual but also for those times when the actor conceives of him or herself as part of a collective or even as an altruist. Doing so will focus us on the individual, rather than on the individual's preferences, and will encourage analysts to seek to understand how external stimuli shift our perceptions of ourselves in relation to others.

2. The Importance of Others. Perspective posits the self as a central conceptual pillar but not as the *only* pillar supporting the theory. Perspective does not assume the lone actor of social contract theory, an actor that dominates rational choice theory because of its origin in classical economics. Perspective conceptualizes the individual as the basic actor, but conceptualizes this actor as an individual existing in a social world populated by others whose behavior has direct and profound consequences on the actor's behavior, including the actor's sense of self. This broader conceptualization allows us to introduce both psychoanalytic and sociological influences, including culture. It draws on social psychological work that seeks to emphasize the affective aspect of the cognitive processes of individuals.

It also suggests the important interactive effect of human behavior. Scholars critical of rational actor theory[18] have noted this omission, and rational actor theorists have responded by trying—mostly unsuccessfully—to incorporate these interactive effects into the basic theory.[19] Such effects clearly exist, and need to be allowed for in a myriad of ways. Jervis demonstrated one aspect of this in his work on signaling at the international level. Jervis argued persuasively that actors need to pay attention to the cognitive predispositions of the people to whom they are sending signals. If the United States wants to know whether one of its acts will be interpreted as hostile by Russia, the United States needs to know how Russia views it. Does Russia have an image of the United States as a country that means well? Or does Russia view the United States as a hostile actor? Jervis argued:

> Whether a promise or a threat will be viewed as credible, it is crucial to understand the perceivers' theories and beliefs about the actor. This shows the psychological naiveté of economics-based signaling theories which, although acknowledging the importance of pre-existing beliefs, argue that new information is combined with old as specified by Bayesian updating of prior beliefs on the basis of new information. (Jervis, chapter 16, this volume)

Jervis pointed out that we all do this. We perceive events in light of how we perceive the sender of the signal. "Even what might seem to be the clearest

---

[18]I would classify Jervis's (1976) research as work in this mode.
[19]I would classify Axelrod's (1984, 1986) work on the evolution of cooperation as work in this mode.

signals will make no impression if the perceiver's mind is made up or his focus is elsewhere" (Jervis, chapter 16, this volume).

This phenomenon occurs at the most intimate level of personal relationships—such as the trust we place in others because of their past behavior—as well as in politics at both the domestic and the international levels.[20] We need to ask more about how the behavior of others affects us. Such interactive effects are critical parts of our own perceptions of our self in relation to others. They affect both how we interpret others' behavior, and how we construct our own responses toward others.

There is yet a further important aspect of the intermingled relationship of self to others. How do our acts, designed to influence others, in turn affect us, even if we know these acts are designed only to deceive or manipulate others and thus can be said to be "false" to our sense of who we truly are? Our attempts to influence the behavior of others may end by changing us, as Kurt Vonnegut suggested in *Mother Night* or as is depicted in the movie, *Donnie Brassco*. In both these fictional instances, the main character pretends to be something he is not. Vonnegut's Howard W. Campbell, Jr. is an American spy, posing as a radio propagandist for the Nazis while secretly sending coded messages to the Allies. Donnie Brassco is an FBI agent working undercover with mobsters. In both instances, however, the character ends by becoming what he has pretended to be. Campbell becomes the Nazis' most valued propagandist and Brassco ends by committing the horrendous deeds of the mobsters he has been sent to infiltrate.

Although I would argue that the self should be the cornerstone of our theory of perspective, it is important to emphasize the self in relation to others, for all the reasons previously mentioned. This is immediately evident when we consider one of the most famous experiments in political psychology, the Milgram (1974) experiments on authority. Under the guise of an experiment on learning, these experiments asked subjects to administer electric shocks when the respondent gave the wrong answers to a quiz. Motivated by the post-WWII belief that the Germans were more susceptible to cruelty because of their authoritarian upbringing, the tests actually suggested it is the rare individual who is not susceptible to situational or contextual appeals to authority. The political psychological implications of this study are striking. When we underestimate the power of social influence,

---

[20]We can easily modify Jervis's work to illustrate this phenomenon at the level of domestic politics. Assume that Clinton wants to encourage other politicians to engage in behavior that is in Clinton's interests. Perceptions are also critical in this kind of strategic game. Clinton is effectively engaged in signaling designed to further his own interests. But what is revealed? How will others interpret the signals Clinton sends out? How does Clinton know that Gore, for example, has interpreted Clinton's act as Clinton intended it? Signals can portray a false or a true message/image, in electoral politics as at a college mixer or during tense international negotiations.

it gives us a feeling of false security. If the Germans were more authoritarian than other nationalities, then we in the United States would not ever have to worry about committing genocide. But if Milgram's studies are correct, and situational factors can indeed influence most people to obey authority, even when human decency says they should not, then we must fall back on some other protection against such evils. Furthermore, by failing to fully appreciate the power of the situation, we tend to oversimplify complex situations.

These experiments illustrate an important theoretical point. Oversimplification decreases our understanding of the causes of a great deal of human behavior. Among other things, this oversimplification can lead us to blame the victim in situations where the individual was overpowered by social forces too difficult for most of us to resist. By emphasizing the individual set firmly within a social context, and by attempting to determine how that context shapes the individual and his or her action, perspective hopes to avoid such errors.

3. Construals and Perception.

Rational choice theorists would argue that we need only specify the objective properties of the situation, such as how rewarding a particular choice is to people, and then document the behaviors that follow from these objective properties.[21] Rational choice models thus avoid dealing with issues like cognition and feeling, concepts that are vague, mentalistic, and not sufficiently anchored to observable behavior. But years of work in psychology reminds us that cognition and feeling are, indeed, critical to the human social experience; we thus must allow for them in our theories and models, no matter how challenging their detection turns out to be empirically.

Doing so responds to the trenchant criticisms of the rational choice approach by scholars like Kahneman, Slovic, and Tversky (1982) who suggested the importance of heuristics and shortcuts in the basic decision-making process. Other scholars (Nisbett & Ross, 1980) argued that we need to look at the situation from the viewpoint of the people in it, to understand how they construe the world around them. This emphasis on what social psychologists call *construals* has its roots in *Gestalt* psychology. This school originally stressed the importance of studying the subjective way in which an object appears in people's minds, rather than the objective, physical attributes of the object.[22] Lewin (1935) shifted the application of *Gestalt*

---

[21] This is not peculiar to rational choice theorists. Behaviorists followed the same tack. For example, Watson (1930) and Skinner (1938) suggested all behavior could be understood by examining the rewards and punishments in the organism's environment and that there was no need to study such subjective states as thinking and feeling.

[22] See work by Kurt Koffka, Wolfgang Kohler, Max Wertheimer, all *Gestalt* theorists, or work by Kurt Lewin, the founding father of modern experimental social psychology.

principles, moving it beyond the perception of physical objects and toward social perception, to ask how people perceive other people and their motives, intentions, and behaviors. Lewin was one of the first scientists to advocate detecting the perspective of the people in any social situation to understand how they construe—that is, perceive, interpret, and distort—their social environment. Social psychologists now routinely focus on the importance of considering subjective situations—how situations are construed by people. Indeed, social psychology is less concerned with social situations in any objective sense than with how people are influenced by their interpretation or construal of this social environment.

Political psychologists need to follow this lead, and ask how people perceive, comprehend, and interpret the sociopolitical world. Doing so may be more important than understanding the objective properties of the social world itself (Aronson, Wilson, & Akert, 1999, p. 7). Perspective suggests we pay a great deal of attention to the origin of people's interpretations of the social world and try to discover whether there are certain recurring patterns in construals for all people, or if there exist particular patterns among certain groups, according to ethnicity, religion, gender, et cetera.[23] This is one important area I hope will be pursued in the years ahead.

4. Methodology. Perspective places less emphasis on quantitative data than does rational choice theory. This is because perspective seeks to understand how the actor views reality, and the actor's conceptual framework may differ significantly from that of the analyst. The obvious question, of course, is how best to discover how different people construe reality. Direct questions posed via survey questionnaires are probably not the best research methodology since people are not always aware of the origins of their own responses (Nisbett & Wilson, 1977) and thus have a limited understanding of their own motives. Instead, the stories people tell that help them organize and make sense of reality and other's behavior—their narratives—may be a better tool for revealing the tacit assumptions underlying people's behavior when the subjects may be unaware of their motives at a conscious level.[24]

If perspective wants to bring in the importance of our view of others, how do we do this? How do we measure the social situation? We can turn here to social cognition research, which has developed elaborate techniques to suggest how people think about themselves, about the social world, and,

[23]For example, when construing their environment, are most people concerned with making an interpretation that places them in the most positive light, as the fundamental attribution error in psychology suggests?

[24]See Hirschman (1977) for a description of how worldview had to shift before capitalism could come into being. See Patterson and Monroe (1998) on narrative as a general research methodology, including its drawbacks and limitations.

more specifically, how people select, interpret, remember, and use social information.[25] Constructing more systematic measurements of these phenomena will prove exciting new ground for the inquisitive scholar, and I look forward to much innovative methodological research in this area.

5. Reconceptualization of Choice. A serious limitation of rational actor theory results from its overemphasis on conscious choice. We need to reconceptualize the concept of choice, redefining it so it also includes the following different concepts of choice, in addition to the kind of choice as a reflection of the rank ordering of preferences that rational choice theory now makes central.

(a) *Choice as a reflection of self.* Choice can be viewed as a reflection of our entire life experiences, a natural outgrowth of who we are. Scholars studying altruism (Monroe, 1991, 1996; Oliner & Oliner, 1988) found that rescuers of Jews during Nazi Europe had no choice in their actions because of the kind of people they were. A simple analogy of an Olympic figure skater, deciding whether or not to take the third twirl of her jump, reflects this kind of choice at a more mundane level. There is indeed an alternative to be made: whether or not to go for the third twirl or stop at only two. But the actual choice reflects both the years of practice and the skater's instinctive sense of how much momentum she has and whether or not this momentum will carry her through a successful third jump. At a more normative level, this conceptualization builds on the idea in virtue ethics, that to understand moral choice we must understand the entirety of a person's life.[26]

(b) *Conflicts of core values.* Choice enters at the normative level as well whenever we consider an agonistic choice experienced when an actor is confronted with conflicts of core values. A consideration of such agonistic choices drives much of the discussions in moral theory. Do I sacrifice my son in a war to protect my country? Or the fictional choice Styron describes in *Sophie's Choice,* where a woman is forced to choose between her two children by a sadistic Nazi. This choice strikes so deeply at her core that Sophie eventually kills herself because she cannot live with having been forced to choose. This kind of choice touches on our most basic sense of who we are. When they reflect unresolved conflicts over the different parts of our identities, they are particularly wrenching. As with choices that are a reflection of our selves, these agonistic choices also reflect back onto our sense of self, as in Frost's (1915) "two roads diverged in the wood, and I—I took the one less traveled by, and that has made all the difference."

---

[25]Fiske and Taylor (1991) or Nisbett and Ross (1980).

[26]For discussion of virtue ethics, see Crisp and Slote (1997), Hursthouse (1999), or Statman (1997).

(c) *Choice versus strategy.* Another option may be to de-emphasize choice entirely. Explicit choices may well be less important than strategies that lead to successful outcomes. Furthermore, choices need not be conscious. A successful strategy can originate in unconscious choices, emotions, or chance. The conscious element may enter when the success of a strategy is recognized or learned. Even learning does not always require consciousness, however, although in many cases (perhaps even most), consciousness will exist *ex post facto* in recognition of the strategy's successful outcome. Although this recognition may be conscious, it need not be; it must be conscious only insofar as it is reproducible in the future, either by the same actor or by another. This posits a close relationship between outcomes and strategies and emphasizes these instead of individual choice. Such a treatment would allow for nonconscious forces in behavior (such as emotions and intuition), factors that now have to be introduced exogenously in both traditional and bounded rational models. Broadening our analysis beyond traditional conceptualizations of choice, to include nonconscious strategies, would provide perspective with a vitality that rational choice lost when it de-emphasized the emotionally rich passions in preference for the more sterile, albeit quantifiable, preferences after the Marginalist revolution in economics (Whitehead, 1991).

If we design a theory of perspective to include learned strategies that further particular outcomes, rather than just focusing on the process of choice, we also allow a role for culture in replicating the strategy that led to optimization. The critical variables would then not be the actual decisions and choices taken by an actor but would instead be the outcomes, intended or fortuitous. The critical component of rational behavior thus would be the process of evolving toward some stationary optimal point, not an actual decision itself. In this process, critical distinctions should be made between the long term and the short term. Strategies need not be the best (optimal) at any one particular moment, but they must be good enough to allow the individuals following them to survive. Behavior thus need not maximize in the short term, although over the long term it must optimize and do better than all other existing possibilities in order to survive. Optimal strategies, not individual choices, would thus be key. An analysis of political behavior that emphasizes strategies in addition to traditional conceptualizations of choices would enable perspective to allow for strategies that lead through adaptation to survival. Such an approach would incorporate the "muddling through" policy analysts know so well and would introduce some of the evolutionary considerations that scholars such as Axelrod (1984) have introduced in their discussions. This resembles Simon's (1982) satisficing rather than maximizing behavior, but an emphasis on constant movement and local adaptation would set a theory of perspective apart from bounded rationality's emphasis on the internal process of choice instead of the outcome of a process and the forces that induce action.

CONCLUSION

I believe that political psychology does have an underlying theoretical framework on which we can build in the years ahead. More importantly, political psychology's underlying framework may provide a more useful foundation for social science analysis than the paradigm that currently dominates social science, rational choice theory. Certainly, we need to move on, beyond self-interest as the critical driving force behind our political theories, and embrace a richer conceptualization of the self in constructing our political theories. Political psychology will have played a critical role if it can move scholarship from this intellectual rut.

In arguing this, my goal is ambitious. I wish to effect a paradigm shift within social science, away from rational choice theory, arguably the dominant approach since the 1950s, and toward a theory in which we understand political actions as a product of how we see ourselves in relation to others. I call this theoretical framework a theory of perspective, and have argued that rational choice is effectively a limiting case of the broader theory, much as Newtonian physics is a limiting case of Einstein's theoretical world. Just as Newtonian physics works well under certain conditions, and as Einstein's physics allows for and specifies the nature of those conditions, so rational choice works well under certain conditions. But it does not work under all conditions, and our attention should now be on understanding and specifying the conditions under which the limiting case will apply and distinguishing them from situations and conditions under which they will not apply.

Recognizing this will correct an imbalance in intellectual life that has existed since Hobbes argued—too persuasively—that there was a nature of man and that this nature was inherently self-interested. The power of Hobbes's argument was stunning, and led to economics becoming the dominant discipline in the social science that developed over the next 500 years. But Hobbes was wrong. Man's nature is not *just* inherently self-interested. Even the early economists—Adam Smith, for one—argued that human nature revolves around the twin poles of self-interest and sociability, and that our basic economic theories of human nature need to allow for this dual nature if they wished to achieve a realistic model of economic life. Adam Smith was right. When we construct our theories of political life, however, we need to go even farther than Smith suggested.

A successor to rational choice has to be a theory about the human psychology if it wants to accurately predict behavior. Here is where political psychology is particularly useful. Because the heart of rational actor theory is Hobbes's assumption of self-interest, the power of the model comes from the accuracy of Hobbes's understanding of the human psyche, and from the psyche's need to protect itself. What has been omitted, however, is the role of others as affirming and validating the self, and validating it in a manner that provides ontological security. Thus the self in relation to others should play a critical part in constructing theories of human behavior. It is this critical factor—noted by Aristotle when he defined man as a social being—that reduces rational choice theory to a limiting case of a broader theory of the theory of self. Rational choice theory captures only one aspect of this self, the aspect in which we see ourselves in a self-interested mode, and respond accordingly.

Political psychologists allow not just for a dual nature of humankind. Political psychologists know that our basic identities are far more complex and multifaceted, and that what is critical for the analyst seeking to understand political action is to understand which aspects of our identities in relation to others come into play and in response to what outside stimuli. Only by understanding how people see themselves in relation to others can we begin to build a science of politics that allows for these human needs to both protect and further our self-interest *and* to respond to our needs for human sociability.

Social science is a field looking for a new paradigm, a field ready for a new paradigm. Political psychology and identity provide that paradigm through a theory of perspective on self in relation to others.

ACKNOWLEDGMENT

I am grateful to the *International Political Science Review* for allowing me to reprint those parts of this chapter that originally appeared in their journal.

REFERENCES

Aronson, E., Wilson, T, & Akert, R. (1999). *Social psychology* (3rd ed.). New York: Addison Wesley Longman.

Axelrod, R. (1976). *Structure of decision*. Princeton, NJ: Princeton University Press.

Axelrod, R. (1984). *The evolution of cooperation*. New York: Basic Books.

Axelrod, R. (1986). An evolutionary approach to norms. *American Political Science Review, 80*, 1095–1111.

Brennan, J. F. (1998). *History and systems of psychology* (5th ed.). Upper Saddle River, NJ: Prentice-Hall.

Crisp, R., & Slote, M. (Eds.). (1997). *Virtue ethics*. Oxford Univeristy Press.

Downs, A. (1957). *An economic theory of democracy*. New York: Harper and Row.

Easton, D. (1997). The future of the post-behavioral phase in political science. In K. R. Monroe (Ed.), *Contemporary empirical political theory* (pp. 13–46). Berkeley: University of California Press.

Eckstein, H. (Ed.). (1992). *Regarding politics*. Berkeley: University of California Press.

Elster, J. (1986). *The multiple self*. New York: Cambridge University Press.

Fiske, S. T., & Taylor, S. E. (1991). *Social cognition* (2nd ed.). New York: McGraw-Hill.

Freud, S. (1973). *Abstracts of the standard edition of the complete psychological works of Sigmund Freud* (C. Rothbeg, Ed.). New York: International Libraries.

Frost, R. (1915). *The road not taken.* New York: Holt.

George, A. (1969). The operational code: A neglected approach to the study of political leaders and decision-making. *International Studies Quarterly, 13,* 190–222.

Green, D., & Shapiro, I. (1994). *Pathologies of rational choice.* New Haven: Yale University Press.

Hartz, L. (1964). *The founding of new societies.* New York: Harcourt, Brace and World.

Hirschman, A. O. (1977). *The passions and the interests: Political arguments for capitalism before its triumph.* Princeton: Princeton University Press.

Hursthouse, R. (1999). *On virtue ethics.* New York: Oxford University Press.

Jervis, R. (1976). *Perception and misperception in international politics.* Princeton, NJ: Princeton University Press.

Kahneman, D., Slovic, P., & Tversky, A. (1982). *Judgment under uncertainty: Heuristics and biases.* New York: Cambridge University Press.

Lewin, K. (1935). *A dynamic theory of personality.* New York: McGraw Hill.

Machiavelli, N. (1965). *Chief works, and others.* Allan Gilbert (Trans.). Durham, NC: Duke University Press.

Milgram, S. (1974). *Obedience to authority: An experimental view.* New York: Harper and Row.

Mill, J. S. (1963). *Essays on politics and culture.* Garden City, New York: Doubleday.

Monroe, K. R. (1991). *The economic approach to politics: A critical reassessment of the theory of rational action.* New York: HarperCollins.

Monroe, K. R. (1996). *The heart of altruism: Perceptions of a common humanity.* Princeton: Princeton University Press.

Monroe, K. R., Hankin, J., & VanVechten, R. (2000). The psychological foundations of identity politics. *Annual Review of Political Science, 3,* 419–447.

Morganthau, H. (1960). *Politics among nations* (3rd ed.). New York: Knopf.

Moscovici, S. (1988). Notes towards a description of Social Representations. *European Journal of Social Psychology, 18,* 211–250.

Myers, M. (1983). *The soul of economic man.* Chicago: University of Chicago Press.

Nisbett, R. E., & Ross, L. (1980). *Human inference: Strategies and shortcomings of social judgement.* Englewood Cliffs, NJ: Prentice-Hall.

Nisbett, R. E., & Wilson, T. D. (1977). Telling more than we can know: Verbal reports on mental processes. *Psychological Review, 84,* 231–259.

Oliner, S., & Oliner, P. (1988). *The altruistic personality.* New York: Free Press.

Pateman, C. (1969). *The disorder of women.* Cambridge: Polity.

Patterson, M., & Monroe, K. R. (1998). Narrative. In N. Polsby, (Ed.), *Annual Review of Political Science, 1,* 315–331.

Simon, H. (1982). *Models of bounded rationality* (Vols. 1 and 2). Cambridge, MA: MIT Press.

Statman, D. (Ed.). (1997). *Virtue ethics.* New York: Oxford University Press.

Skinner, B. F. (1938). *The behavior of organisms.* New York: Appleton-Century Crofts.

Taylor, S., Peplau, L., & Sears, D. (2000). *Social psychology* (10th ed.). Upper Saddle River, NJ: Prentice-Hall.

Watson, J. (1930). *Behaviorism.* New York: Norton.

Whitehead, J. (1991). The forgotten limits: Reason and regulation in economic theory. In K. R. Monroe (Ed.), *The economic approach to politics* (pp. 53–73). New York: HarperCollins.

Winnicott, D. (1986). *Home is where we start from: Essays by a psychoanalyst.* New York: Penguin Books.

Contributors

C. FRED ALFORD is Professor of Government and Distinguished Scholar–Teacher at the University of Maryland, College Park. He coedits the Psychoanalysis and Society Series at Cornell University Press and has served on the Governing Council of the International Society for Political Psychology. Author of ten books on moral psychology, Alford's most recent works compare Western and Eastern concepts of evil: *What Evil Means to Us* and *Think No Evil: Korean Values in the Age of Globalization*. Alford has just completed a study of the ethics of whistleblowers, *Whistleblowers' Lives: Broken Narratives and Total Organizations*.

DANIEL BAR-TAL is Professor of Psychology at the School of Education, Tel Aviv University. He served as the president of the International Society of Political Psychology (1999–2000). His research interest is in political and social psychology, studying societal beliefs regarding conflict, delegitimization, security, patriotism, and siege mentality. He authored *Group Beliefs* and *Shared Beliefs of a Society,* and coedited *Social Psychology of Intergroup Relations, Stereotyping and Prejudice, Patriotism in the Lives of Individuals and Nations,* and *Concerned with Security: How Children Understand War and Peace.*

MARTHA CRENSHAW is John E. Andrus Professor of Government at Wesleyan University, in Middletown, Connecticut. She is a member of the Executive Board of Women in International Security and past president of both the Political Psychology section of the American Political Science Association and the International Society of Political Psychology. Her research centers on the problem of political terrorism. For example, she is the editor of *Terrorism in Context* and the author of an article on terrorism for the forthcoming *Encyclopedia of Psychology,* published jointly by the American Psychological Association and Oxford University Press.

MORTON DEUTSCH is Professor Emeritus and Director Emeritus of the International Center for Cooperation and Conflict Resolution at Teachers

College, Columbia University. He studied with Kurt Lewin at MIT's Research Center for Group Dynamics, where he obtained his PhD in 1948. He has published extensively and is well known for his pioneering studies in intergroup relations, cooperation–competition, conflict resolution, social conformity, and the social psychology of justice. His books include *Interracial Housing; Research Methods in Social Relations; Preventing World War III: Some Proposals; Theories in Social Psychology; The Resolution of Conflict; Applying Social Psychology; Distributive Justice;* and *The Handbook of Conflict Resolution: Theory and Practice.* Deutsch's work has been widely honored by such awards as the Kurt Lewin Memorial Award, the G. W. Allport Prize, the Carl Hovland Memorial Award, the American Association for the Advancement of Science Socio-psychological Prize, the Samuel Flowerman Award, American Psychological Association's Distinguished Scientific Contribution Award, Society of Experimental Social Psychology Distinguished Research Scientist Award, ISPP's Nevitt Sanford Award, and he is a William James Fellow of APS. He has also received several lifetime achievement awards from various professional associations for his work on conflict management, cooperative learning, peace psychology, and the applications for psychology to social issues. In addition, he has received the Teachers College Medal for his contributions to education, the Helsinki University Medal for his contributions to psychology, and the Doctorate of Human Letters from the City University of New York. Deutsch has been president of the Society for the Psychological Study of Social Issues, the International Society of Political Psychology, the Eastern Psychological Association, and the New York State Psychological Association, as well as several divisions of the American Psychological Association.

WILLEM DOISE was born in Flanders, Belgium, and received his doctorate (supervised by Otto Klineberg) in social psychology at the Sorbonne, Paris, in 1967. He was a researcher at the Centre National de la Recherche Scientifique in Paris between 1967 and 1972 and has been Professor of Experimental Social Psychology at the University of Geneva since 1972. His first French publication appeared in 1968, his first in English in 1969. He was a member of the executive committee of the European Association of Experimental Social Psychology from 1975 to 1981 and president of that association from 1978 to 1981. He has been a visiting professor at the Universities of Brussels, Auckland, Tilburg, Bologna, Rome, Leuven, Belgrano, Otago, Liège, Savoie, and Provence. His main research interests are in intergroup relations, social identity, sociocognitive development, social representations, and explanations in social psychology.

LEONIE HUDDY is an Associate Professor of Political Science at the State University of New York at Stony Brook. Her general field of interest is the psychological origins and dynamics of public opinion. She has written and published numerous articles and book chapters on the application of psychological theories concerning racial and gender stereotypes to political beliefs and attitudes. Her current research focuses on the development of political identity, specifically feminist identity, which she examines from the perspective of social identity theory, examining the origins of political identity in information about the kinds of people who are typically associated with a political ideology.

SIMON JACKMAN obtained his doctorate from the University of Rochester and has held faculty appointments at the University of Chicago and the Australian National University. He is Assistant Professor and Victoria Schuck Faculty Scholar in the Department of Political Science, Stanford University. Jackman has published numerous articles on electoral systems, political participation, public opinion, and political methodology. His recent research has focused on the links between political sophistication and voter turnout in the United States and Australia. With Paul Sniderman, Jackman is completing a major study of French public opinion.

ROBERT JERVIS is Adlai E. Stevenson Professor of International Politics at Columbia University and was President of the American Political Science Association (2000–2001). He has written extensively on signaling and perception and his latest book is *System Effects: Complexity in Political and Social Life*, which won the 1998 Best Book Award from the American Political Science Association Section in Political Psychology.

CATARINA KINNVALL received her doctorate from the London School of Economics and currently teaches at the University of Lund in Sweden. A member of the Governing Council of the International Society of Political Psychology, Kinnvall's recent book is on the politics of ethnic identity in India. She is currently at work on the role of social identity in influencing politics in the states of the former Soviet Union.

JON A. KROSNICK received his PhD in Psychology from the University of Michigan in 1986. He is Professor of Political Science and Psychology at The Ohio State University. His research is broadly concerned with public opinion and mass political behavior; he is particularly interested in the impact of the mass media on public opinion via agenda setting and priming, as well as on the dynamics of issue publics in the American electorate. He is the recipient of the 1995 Erik Erikson Award for Distinguished Early Career Contributions to Political Psychology from the International Society of Political Psychology.

ROBERT E. LANE, Eugene Meyer Professor Emeritus of Political Science at Yale University, is a past president of the American Political Science Association (1970–1971) and of the International Society of Political Psychology (1978–1979). He is a Foreign Fellow of the British Academy. Among his published works are *Political Ideology, The Market Experience,* and *The Loss of Happiness in Market Democracies.*

HOWARD LAVINE is Assistant Professor of Political Science and Psychology at the State University of New York at Stony Brook. His research focuses on the origins, nature, and consequences of consistency and ambivalence in political belief systems, the psychological motivations that underlie political persuasion, and the origins and functions of authoritarianism.

GEORGE E. MARCUS is Professor of Political Science at Williams College. He received his BA from Columbia University. His MA and PhD are from Northwestern University. He is the author, with John L. Sullivan and James E. Piereson, of *Political Tolerance and American Democracy,* and, with John L. Sullivan, Elizabeth Theiss-Morse, and Sandra L. Wood, of *With Malice Toward Some: How People Make Civil Liberties Judgments,* which received the Best Book Award given by the Political Psychology section of the American Political Science Association. His current research continues on political tolerance in the United States and the role of emotion in democratic politics. Marcus was coeditor, with Russ Hanson, of *Reconsidering the Democratic Public,* as well as the contributor to a number of other edited volumes. He was cofounder and coeditor of *Political Methodology* and executive director of the International Society of Political Psychology from 1992 to 1996. He currently serves as vice chairman on the board of directors of the Roper Center, on the editorial board of *Political Psychology,* on the governing council of the APSA, and was vice president of the International Society of Political Psychology.

KATHLEEN M. MCGRAW received her PhD in Psychology from Northwestern University in 1985. She is Professor of Political Science, Psychology, Journalism, and Communication at The Ohio State University. She has broad research interests in political psychology and public opinion, in particularly the dynamics of individual and institutional accountability and cognitive processes in political judgments. She is the recipient of the 1994 Erik Erikson Award for Distinguished Early Career Contributions to Political Psychology from the International Society of Political Psychology.

KRISTEN RENWICK MONROE is Professor of Philosophy and Political Science and Associate Director of the Program in Political Psychology at the University of California at Irvine. She has taught at Princeton, New York University, The State University of New York at Stony Brook, and the University of British Columbia. Monroe's most recent book is *The Heart of Altruism*, awarded the 1997 Best Book Award by the American Political Science Association Section in Political Psychology. She is the editor of several books, including *Contemporary Empirical Political Theory* and *The Economic Approach to Politics: A Critical Reassessment of the Theory of Rational Action*. Monroe has served as a member of the Council of the American Political Science Association, the Governing Council for the International Society of Political Psychology, and the Midwest Political Science Association, of which she also was Vice President. She currently serves on the editorial boards of *Political Psychology*, the *Journal of Theoretical Politics*, and *Political Research Quarterly*.

STANLEY RENSHON is Professor of Political Science and Coordinator of the Interdisciplinary Program in the Psychology of Political Behavior at the City University of New York Graduate Center. He is a certified psychoanalyst and President of the International Society of Political Psychology. He is the author of numerous articles and books, including *Psychological Needs and Political Behavior, The Handbook of Political Socialization, The Political Psychology of the Gulf War, The Clinton Presidency: Campaigning, Governing and the Psychology of Leadership*, and the forthcoming *Political Psychology: Cultural and Cross Cultural Foundations*. Renshon's book on the Clinton presidency, *High Hopes*, won the 1997 American Political Science Association's Richard E. Neustadt Award and the 1998 National Association for the Advancement of Psychoanalysis' Gradiva Award for the best published work that advances psychoanalysis in the category of biography. He served at Harvard University as a Research Fellow at the John F. Kennedy School in the 2000–2001 academic year.

SHAWN ROSENBERG is Professor of Political Science and Psychology and Director of the Graduate Political Psychology Program at the University of California at Irvine. In addition to his general interest in political psychology, Rosenberg has done research on political ideology, cognition, and development. His books include *Reason, Ideology and Politics, Political Reasoning and Cognition* with Dana Ward and Stephen Chilton, and *The Not So Common Sense: Differences in How People Judge Social and Political Events*.

DAVID O. SEARS teaches at the University of California at Los Angeles, where he is Professor of Psychology and Political Science, Director of the Institute for Social Science Research, and Chair of the Program in Political Psychology. Sears is the former Dean of Social Sciences at UCLA, and past president of both the Society for the Advancement of Socio-Economics and the International Society of Political Psychology. He has been a Brookings and a Guggenheim Fellow, and a Fellow of the Center for Advanced Studies in the Behavioral Sciences. His early research focused on experimental studies of communication and attitude change but as a result of the Watts riots in 1965, Sears turned to survey research on ghetto violence, resulting in *The Politics of Violence: The New Urban Blacks and the Watts Riot* with John B. McConahay. Sears has conducted much research on the role of white racism in American politics, especially on the concept of "symbolic racism." His work on a more general theory of symbolic politics generated *Tax Revolt: Something for Nothing in California,* written with Jack Citrin. Sears is coauthor of the best-selling *Social Psychology, Public Opinion,* and coeditor of *Political Cognition* (1986). He has conducted considerable research on selective exposure in communication, political socialization, the gender gap, the use of college students as experimental subjects, the persistence of political attitudes through the life span, and the person positivity bias. His current work focuses on racism in American politics and on public opinion about multiculturalism.

PAUL M. SNIDERMAN is Professor of Political Science at Stanford University and has served as Vice President of the American Political Science Association. He is the author, among other books, of *Reasoning and Choice,* which won the Woodrow Wilson Foundation Award, and of *Reaching Beyond Race,* which won the Gladys Kammerer Award. In 1999, Sniderman was awarded the Harold D. Lasswell Award for distinguished research contribution to the field of political psychology.

CHRISTIAN STAERKLÉ was born in the German-speaking part of Switzerland. He was promoted at the University of Geneva with a doctoral thesis reporting seven experimental investigations on the lay conceptions of Swiss youth about the relationship between state and society across Western and non-Western national contexts. Currently he is lecturer at the University of Geneva. His research interests include social representations of citizenship and democracy as well as essentialism in intergroup relations and stereotyping.

JANICE GROSS STEIN is the Harrowston Professor of Conflict Management and Negotiation at the University of Toronto and is a Fellow of the Royal Society of Canada. She has coauthored *Rational Decision-Making, Psychology and Deterrence,* and *We All Lost the Cold War,* and coedited *Getting to the Table: Processes of International Prenegotiation* and *Choosing to Cooperate: How States Avoid Loss.* She recently completed *Mean Times: Humanitarian Action in Complex Political Emergencies—Stark Choices, Cruel Dilemmas.* Stein is Chair of the Board of *International Organization* and a member of the editorial boards of *International Negotiation* and *Political Psychology* and currently chairs the Research Advisory Board to the Foreign Minister of Canada. Her special area of interest is conflict management and conflict resolution.

PETER SUEDFELD is Professor of Psychology at the University of British Columbia, where he has served as a Department Head and Dean. His research analyzes how people cope with and behave in challenging environments, in situations ranging from persecution during the Holocaust and policy-making in political and military positions to isolation in polar stations, and stimulus-reduction laboratories. Suedfeld has published some 200 articles and book chapters. He is a former chairman of the Canadian Antarctic Research Program and Past President of the Canadian Psychological Association (CPA). He has received the CPA's Donald O. Hebb Award for distinguished contributions to psychology as a science, and the U.S. Antarctica Service Medal. A Fellow of the Royal Society of Canada and various other Canadian and U.S. scientific associations, in 1998 Suedfeld was elected Vice President of the International Society of Political Psychology.

DANA WARD is Executive Director of the International Society of Political Psychology and Professor of Political Studies at Pitzer College, a member of the Claremont Colleges. He has taught political psychology in China at the Johns Hopkins–Nanjing University Center for Chinese and American Studies and in Turkey as a Fulbright Lecturer at Ankara University. He is a coauthor of *Political Reasoning and Cognition: A Piagetian View,* and has published articles and reviews in *Political Psychology.*

DAVID G. WINTER is a past president of the International Society of Political Psychology and Professor of Psychology at the University of Michigan, where he teaches courses on the psychology of personality and political psychology. Winter was educated at Harvard and Oxford and taught at Wesleyan University for many years. His psychological research interests involve the interactive relationships of motives, traits, cognitions, and social context in human personality. His political psychology interests focus on the psychological aspects of conflict escalation, leadership, and the nature of power and power strivings. Winter is the author of *Personality: Analysis and Interpretation of Lives, The Power Motive, A New Case for the Liberal Arts,* and numerous journal articles.

Author Index

Locators annotated with *n* indicate footnotes.

Subject Index

Locators annotated with *f* indicate figures.
Locators annotated with *t* indicate tables.